When the Wind Changed

The Life and Death of Tony Hancock

Cliff Goodwin was born in London in 1950. He was educated in Slough, Berkshire, and joined the town's weekly newspaper as a trainee journalist in 1968. For the next two and a half decades he worked as a reporter, feature writer and sub-editor for numerous newspapers and magazines. His coverage of the 1988 Lockerbie air crash earned him a regional press award. An habitual freelance writer – he has published features in more than 200 newspapers and magazines worldwide – Cliff Goodwin has also worked as a producer and head of news in local radio and in public relations.

In 1993 Cliff Goodwin decided it was time to end his 25 years as a journalist and concentrate on full-time writing. His books include the bestselling biography of Catherine Cookson, *To Be A Lady*, and the first ever biography of cult comedy actor Sid James.

D0185236

Also by Cliff Goodwin

To Be A Lady: Biography of Catherine Cookson
Sid James

WHEN THE
WIND CHANGED

The Life and Death
of Tony Hancock

Cliff Goodwin

ARROW

Published by Arrow Books in 2000

3 5 7 9 10 8 6 4 2

Copyright © Cliff Goodwin 1999

Cliff Goodwin has asserted his right under the Copyright,
Designs and Patents Act, 1988, to be identified as the author of this work

First published in the United Kingdom in 1999 by Century

Arrow Books Limited
The Random House Group Limited
20 Vauxhall Bridge Road, London SW1V 2SA

Random House Australia (Pty) Limited
20 Alfred Street, Milsons Point, Sydney,
New South Wales 2061, Australia

Random House New Zealand Limited
18 Poland Road, Glenfield
Auckland 10, New Zealand

Random House South Africa (Pty) Limited
Endulini, 5A Jubilee Road,
Parktown 2193, South Africa

Random House UK Limited Reg. No. 954009

www.randomhouse.co.uk

A CIP catalogue record for this book
is available from the British Library

Papers used by Random House UK Limited are natural,
recyclable products made from wood grown in sustainable forests.
The manufacturing processes conform to the environmental
regulations of the country of origin.

ISBN 0 09 960941 X

Typeset by Deltatype Ltd, Birkenhead, Merseyside
Printed and bound in Great Britain by
Bookmarque Ltd, Croydon, Surrey

For
Sarah

CONTENTS

INTRODUCTION

TONY HANCOCK WAS the first victim of television comedy. He was, arguably, the first typecast victim of the post-war age. He received such enormous fame from the character he created he was – both professionally and personally – doomed.

In 1956, when Hancock transferred from radio to television, watching television was still an exciting event. Public houses and cinemas were half empty because people did not want to miss a particular show. One of those programmes was *Hancock's Half Hour*. Men and women in the street adopted Hancock as their own working-class hero, battered by life and bamboozled by his friends.

His common touch. His ability to be all things to all men. His acceptance as the bloke next door. You would laugh at his East Cheam cohorts – Sid James and Bill Kerr and Kenneth Williams – but you could only love Hancock. And love is not too strong a word. This was a unique television era which locked in its stars and, in many cases, refused to set them free. For Hancock his Homburg hat and astrakhan-collared coat became the bars to a prison.

The huge fame which Hancock enjoyed – and abhorred – was as short-lived as his own success. After seven years on radio and television there was nowhere left for him to go. A form of megalomania took over. Like Buster Keaton and Charlie Chaplin, he believed he could stand alone, that he could do it all himself, professionally forcing himself to go back to where he started in a deliberate and destructive circle.

One of the great sadnesses of Hancock's life was that he could not enjoy the ups and downs of show business. The name of the game is rejection for most of us in this profession. So to be accepted, and to be loved, and give such happiness to people and still repeatedly turn the dagger on himself was a real tragedy.

For me, Hancock's work is still at its greatest when heard rather than seen. Some of his radio performances are electrifying.

I first saw Hancock when he was appearing with Jimmy Edwards in the 1952 production of *London Laughs*. A few years later, when I was a student at the Royal Academy of Dramatic Art, we would religiously listen to two radio programmes. One was *The Goon Show*. The other was *Hancock's Half Hour*.

I then became really crazy about Hancock. If ever I was down or depressed or rejected – sometimes literally – I needed a Hancock 'fix' to bring me out of it. I was also friendly with another Hancock nutter. He was almost always broke and recorded the radio shows to sell. Once a fortnight a tape of two shows would arrive for which I paid a quid.

My family were not immune from Hancock. Each year during the 1960s and early seventies I would take them on holiday to Cornwall. With us would go eight, maybe ten, *Half Hour* tapes which would be played over and over again.

For me, as a young actor, Hancock was one of the great timers. He could instinctively change rhythm in the middle of a line. He also possessed a musical ear which made him one of the best phrasers of lines I had ever heard, but his real genius was his ability to control pauses. He would pause during a radio show, and hold that pause, and not make a sound, and you would still laugh.

From the start Hancock set himself such high standards that he handicapped and flagellated himself. On many occasions he could not bear the sight or sound of himself. His drinking was, in many ways, part of this self-flight. Alcohol became both the cause and the fuel of his manic depression.

People often say of Hancock that he wasted his talent, that he destroyed himself. But the majority of people, who never drink excessively in their lives, are quite incapable of giving the population such joy and happiness and laughter. The fact he had this conflict between the creative and destructive processes may very well have made him that much funnier.

At his peak Tony Hancock was certainly one of the greatest comedians this country has ever produced.

RICHARD BRIERS

FOREWORD

TONY HANCOCK WAS dead. His remains had been cremated in Sydney and his ashes entrusted to the comedian and raconteur Willie Rushton to return to England.

Rushton carried the urn through Australian customs unhindered and up the steps of the British Overseas Airways Boeing 707. Sitting in an economy-class window seat he placed the casket on the seat beside him. Other passengers were still boarding. A few minutes later a stewardess informed Rushton the adjoining seat was required for another passenger.

Rushton waved the stewardess closer and quietly explained his predicament.

'In that case,' she said, picking up the urn, 'Mr Hancock should travel first class.'

When the plane landed at Heathrow Airport, Rushton went forward to collect the urn from the first-class seat on which it had been placed, just behind the flight deck. Beside the casket was a single red rose and an anonymous note – 'Thank you for making us laugh.'

Author's Note

Tony Hancock has the distinction of being known simply by his surname – Hancock. I have, therefore, where age and circumstance allow, chosen to call him Hancock throughout this biography.

Tony Hancock
1924 to 1968

1924

CERTIFIED COPY of an   **ENTRY OF BIRTH**
Pursuant to the Births and   Deaths Registration Act 1953

CK 947105

B. Cert.
S.R.

			Registration District		Kings Norton				
1924.	Birth in the Sub-district of		Acochs Green		in the	County of	Birmingham CB.		
Columns:—	1	2	3	4	5	6	7	8	9	10*
No.	When and where born	Name, if any	Sex	Name and surname of father	Name, surname and maiden surname of mother	Occupation of father	Signature, description, and residence of informant	When registered	Signature of registrar	Name entered after registration
414	Twelfth May 1924 41 Southan Road Hall Green UD	Anthony John	Boy	John HANCOCK	Lucia Lilian HANCOCK formerly THOMAS	Steamship Owners Branch Manager	John Hancock Father 41 Southan Road Hall Green Birmingham	Twenty third June 1924	F.Co. Thompson Registrar.	

Certified to be a true copy of an entry in a register in my custody.

*See note overleaf.

CAUTION:—It is an offence to falsify a certificate or to make or knowingly use a false certificate or a copy of a false certificate intending it to be accepted as genuine to the prejudice of any person, or to possess a certificate knowing it to be false without lawful authority.

_____ Superintendent Registrar

2/2/1999 Date

WARNING: THIS CERTIFICATE IS NOT EVIDENCE OF THE IDENTITY OF THE PERSON PRESENTING IT.

WITH THIS ENTRY at Kings Norton register office Tony Hancock entered the world of documentation. Forty-four years later he died alone in a foreign city; twice divorced, without children, and with few close friends.

From the early 1950s until his suicide in 1968, Hancock was the best-known living comedian in Britain and what remained of the British Commonwealth. His professional life had lasted little more than eighteen years. Yet Hancock had an extravagant effect on those who knew and worked with him, leaving them – very often in quick succession – beguiled, besotted, bruised or bitter. To most he was an unforgettable man with an extraordinary talent.

His private life had also become public property and the hero of his radio and television shows – wounded and yet somehow never defeated – appeared to embody thinly disguised facets of his own character. Above all he was an enigma.

Anthony John Hancock was the second son of Jack and Lily Hancock, a self-confessed 'lower middle class' family living in one of the greener suburbs of 1920s Birmingham. Jack Hancock was a shipping office manager, earning enough to employ two domestic servants. His wife, a small determined woman, was enjoying their slow but steady ascent of the social ladder. The arrival of another child – unplanned but never unloved – would have no discernible effect on the Hancocks' day-to-day life.

John Hancock and Lucie Lilian Thomas had been married at St Oswald's Church, Bordesley, Birmingham, on 22 August, 1914. It was a curious but uncomplicated union of two socially diverse dynasties; a merger of art and artisan between a proud, hard-working family and a self-made, self-respecting businessman. The afternoon was hot and airless and had a strange urgency about it. Britain had been at war with Germany for eighteen days.

Dressed uncomfortably in ill-fitting suits, several of the groom's Irish relatives had endured the Dublin to Liverpool crossing to attend the ceremony. Other Hancocks had left Ireland almost a century earlier and, as peripatetic navvies, were employed first to enlarge the north of England canals and then the Victorian rail network. By the early 1870s a blustery and bewhiskered William Hancock had arrived in Birmingham and accepted a permanent job with a local building firm. Within a matter of months he had talked himself into the post of foreman.

The Hancock family home at 616 Coventry Road, Birmingham, was cramped but never uncomfortable: short of money but never short of love. William Hancock, a conscientious, powerfully-built man who expected his offspring to work hard and better themselves, fathered three sons. The two elder boys – Cuthbert William and Frederick George – remained in the building trade. Cuthbert, inheriting his father's purpose, eventually rose to manage his own company.

The youngest and favourite of William Hancock's sons was born during the summer of 1888, less than a year before William's death in a site accident. The frail baby grew into a sickly boy prone to attacks of bronchitis and tonsillitis. At one time it was feared John Hancock – called Jack by his father – might be suffering from tuberculosis. Despite his prolonged classroom absences Jack proved a quick learner and when he left school in 1900 he had already received several prizes for arithmetic and handwriting, both excellent qualifications for a future in an office and away from the dirt and hazards of a building site. Even as a teenager Jack Hancock was obsessed with his appearance. A character trait which, although annoying to his immediate family, soon endeared him to the management of Houlder Brothers, a cargo shipping line with a small office in the centre of Birmingham. In his fourteen years with Houlder's, Jack worked his way up from office messenger to representative.

At the time of his wedding, Jack Hancock was a tall and slender 26-year-old with pale, watery blue eyes. His bride was two years younger. Lucie Lilian Thomas was born on 4 September, 1890, the only child of Harry and Clara Thomas.

Harry Samuel Thomas had married Clara Hannah Williams, in November, 1889, after an engagement said, by family legend, to have lasted almost five years. At fourteen he was apprenticed to a Birmingham drawing office where he qualified as a draughtsman. It was a natural career for a neat and logical teenager whose artistic skills far outshone those of his classmates.

By the age of twenty Thomas had grown into a short, stocky, round-shouldered man with a quick-silver temper and a burning desire to improve his lot in life. Within a year he found employment as a lithographic artist and, not long after his daughter's birth, started his own printing company. As trade and his social status increased he moved his family out of their Cooksey Road home to a detached property at 243 Charles Road, Birmingham. He was an enthusiastic soccer fan, and his business provided profits for Thomas to invest in Birmingham City Football Club. In 1906 he secured himself a seat on the board and remained a director for twenty-one years, travelling considerable distances to support the 'Blues'.

Much to his father-in-law's annoyance, Jack Hancock had taken to calling his wife 'Billy'. It was a personal nickname derived from 'Lily', the name adopted by family and friends. 'Almost as soon as I could talk I announced I wanted to be known as Lily,' she explained. 'I hated the name Lucie.'

Within weeks of Jack and Lily's marriage the couple rented a modest, but suitably impressive house in the rural but rapidly developing suburb of Hall Green, four miles to the south-east of Birmingham. Their new home was a late-Victorian property called Tyneholme, situated on Stratford Road. For some reason the house name fascinated Jack Hancock. He would repeat it again and again using a variety of high- and low-brow accents. When a particular inflection tickled Lily, her husband would physically and verbally chase her from room to room until she collapsed in a fit of giggles.

In February, 1916, military conscription was introduced in Britain. Younger men employed in Houlder's various offices around the country and who had somehow escaped Kitchener's jingoism were this time quick to volunteer. The second winter of war saw one hundred and fifteen of the company's shore staff serving in the 2nd (City of London) Fusiliers under Lieutenant Colonel A. G. Houlder. By the late spring half that number were dead or seriously injured. Jack Hancock did not wait for his call-up papers. One evening after work he called at a barrack recruiting centre around the corner from the shipping line office. Lily's nightmare threatened to become reality, but she need not have worried. Her husband's weakly physique and lingering chestiness – one reason for the couple's move out of the city – rendered him unfit for military service. Jack returned to Houlder Brothers. That summer, with staff numbers ever dwindling, he was promoted to office manager and spent the rest of the war behind a desk, helping to keep the Army supplied with bully-beef, plum jam and cigarettes. Life at Houlder Brothers once again settled into a numbing routine.

On Holy Thursday – 28 March – 1918, Lily Hancock gave birth to her first child. Colin Hancock was born two weeks early in Tyneholme's master bedroom. It was a long and painful confinement which left the usually stoic Lily exhausted. Her doctor ordered bed-rest. Jack, unable to take time off work, enlisted the help of friends and relatives, but eventually had to give in to Harry Thomas's suggestion that he should hire a full-time nanny to look after the robust and increasingly noisy child.

As it happened Thomas could recommend a young, but experienced, girl seeking a new position, and by August seventeen-year-old Elsie Sparkes had worked out her notice and moved into Tyneholme. She soon discovered it was a 'happy home full of laughter'. With a baby and live-in nanny the house seemed more cramped than ever. The Hancocks needed a new home with enough space for a growing family and enough respectability to please both Jack's employers and Lily's prestige-minded father. They found it less than half-a-mile away at 41 Southam Road.

Fiercely middle-class, Southam Road boasted the biggest homes and the neatest gardens. Number 41 was a four-bedroomed, semi-detached property built on the apex of a wide curve. Constructed at a cost of £400, its first owners were Jack and Lily Hancock. Within months Jack's brother and sister-in-law, Cuthbert and Caroline Hancock, had rented Number 59 Southam Road, eight doors away.

One of the greatest attractions between Jack and Lily had been their shared sense of the absurd. Sombre and stiff-backed family gatherings were frequently disrupted as a giggling Lily watched Jack pull faces and mimic his relatives. Ever eager to provide a turn at parties, Jack, already a Freemason, was soon accepting bookings for masonic socials and smoking-room concerts throughout the Midlands.

*

'It was a pretty chaotic existence,' recalled Tony Hancock many years later. 'The real love of my father's life was undoubtedly show business. He enjoyed nothing better than making people laugh. My mother, who used to play the piano for him, was the best audience he ever had – even if the act was flopping. She would frequently end up crying with laughter because she was the only one to understand a joke.'

By the early 1920s Jack was beginning to find the demands of his employers less and less fulfilling. As manager he rarely left his second-floor office overlooking the Birmingham and Fazeley Canal, and he missed the personal contact he had enjoyed as a travelling representative. Out of hours Jack was confident, and busy enough, to describe himself as a semi-professional entertainer. His thirty-fifth birthday was approaching and he was desperate for a change. Jack had all but made up his mind to resign and concentrate on developing his show-business career when Lily announced she was pregnant for the second time. The baby, she informed her husband, was due in the late spring of 1924. Jack reluctantly decided to reconsider his avocation.

In keeping with the social order of their occupants, the houses of Southam Road were among the first whose front rooms and parlours boasted a wireless. When the British Broadcasting Company began transmissions in 1922 there were just 35,000 radio sets in Britain. Three years later, with its embodiment as a corporation, the figure soared to more than two million. During the intervening years the readers of the *Radio Times* were invited to invest in an Abbiphone crystal set for a guinea or spend 18s 6d on a pair of Fellows lightweight headphones. Those with greater incomes were offered a Tingey 'Superfive' wireless in a lockable oak cabinet for £56 5s 0d, the greater part of a year's living wage for most manual workers.

The BBC was incorporated by three hundred wireless manufacturers and shareholders at a meeting on 18 October, 1922, and formulated to broadcast short, regular 'sponsored' programmes to the 8,000 people who had paid fifteen shillings each for a constructor's licence. The company received its broadcast licence from the Postmaster General on 18 January the following year, despite having commenced daily broadcasts the previous November when Arthur Burrows read the 6pm news. Early programmes were little more than a series of back-to-back theatre or concert hall performances, complete with scene changes and mishaps. Wireless owners often found themselves listening to performers and engineers making unbroadcastable comments or periods of crackling silence as the studio piano was moved.

Within a year all but the most outlying areas were being served by a network of seven regional studios. One – Station 5IT – was based in Birmingham. Between the national news and simultaneous broadcasts from London, each local station produced and transmitted its own programmes.

The possibilities of wireless were not wasted on Jack Hancock. Radio was cheap and accessible and friendly. Above all it was good, clean family entertainment. It did not, however, deliver much in the way of comedy. One reason was that music-hall owners refused to allow their stars to perform on radio: a situation which evidently suited John Reith, the BBC's managing director, who ruled that 'common and vulgar' comedians should be kept off the air in favour of respectable, middle-class entertainers. The new medium had not yet learned to laugh with the nation. Charles Penrose's 'Laughing Policeman' was still a year away. Slowly, very slowly, the recitals by brass bands and string quartets were punctuated by 'sketches of humorists'. One of the first was Jack Hancock.

In October, 1923, Jack wrote to the Birmingham station manager offering his services. A BBC assistant was dispatched to watch one of his evening performances, and on Friday, 23 November, Jack Hancock made his radio debut. Between 9.15 and the 10.30pm close-down, Station 5IT broadcast a selection of orchestral requests and 'Jack Hancock (Humorist)' filled the fifteen-minute interlude with 'items from his repertoire'. The Wednesday before Christmas – this time listed in the fledgling *Radio Times* as an 'entertainer' – Jack made a second broadcast.

*

Colin Hancock was a bright and lively boy. For six years he had dominated his parents' attention and enjoyed the indulgences of his grandfather, Harry Thomas. He was not looking forward to sharing his life with a baby brother or sister. Lily Hancock, however, was convinced her second child would be a boy – 'there was no doubt in my mind.' Thanks to her nanny she had even chosen a name. Elsie Sparkes was continually talking about the little boy she had left to join the Hancocks. His name was Anthony. Even though she occasionally saw her first charge, she still missed him. 'Mrs Hancock promised me that when her baby was born she would call him Anthony just to keep me happy,' Sparkes recalled many years later.

In the early morning of 23 April, 1924, Harry Thomas's car drew up outside the neat hedge and garden of the Hancocks' house. The car was loaded with Jack and young Colin and a heavily pregnant Lily, and the chauffeur headed south down the A34 for the 105-mile journey to London and the first day of the British Empire Exhibition. At Wembley, Harry Thomas insisted on paying the one-and-sixpenny admission charges before the little group separated. By now well into his mid-sixties, Thomas insisted on walking every inch of the fifteen miles of exhibition avenues and malls. Jack Hancock, however, had other plans. He and Lily would sit through all six of the concerts staged in pavilions around the massive site. His only concession to his equally enthusiastic, but rapidly flagging, wife was that they could use the bus service provided for the two hundred thousand visitors.

Twenty days later – on 12 May, 1924 – Lily Hancock gave birth to a boy in the bay-windowed, front bedroom of the Southam Road house. Despite a warning of complications the delivery was less tiring and more comfortable than her first. Jack was overjoyed. As was customary, he announced the arrival in the *Birmingham Mail*. Two days later the newspaper's births column carried a two-line announcement:

HANCOCK – On the 12th last, to Mr and Mrs Jack Hancock, of 41 Southam Road, Hall Green, a son.

Once again, Jack was less than diligent with the formalities of parenthood. He had waited thirty-five days before registering Colin's birth. On 23 June, 1924 – forty-two days after his second son's arrival – Jack Hancock called at Kings Norton register office. It was the final day allowed by law to record the child's birth.

The baby's name, he informed the registrar, was Anthony John Hancock.

1926

THE HANCOCKS' TWO-year-old son was proving to be an obstinate child. Despite the constant attention of Elsie Sparkes, the boy had so far failed to master even the simplest sentence. As if by some concentration of childhood will, he stubbornly refused to mimic the sound of even the simplest words. Instead he would break the words into syllables in a kind of sing-song chant. The absurdity of the world around him had already begun to fascinate the youngest Hancock. 'El-le ... El-le ... El-le ...' he called Elsie. She would invert a wood and glass utensil and the boy would watch the magic trickle of sand in puzzled silence: 'The plain fact is that my first memory is of an egg-timer,' Hancock admitted. 'Don't ask me why. My memories just happen to contain it.'

The kitchen of the Southam Road house was well lit and well equipped and always smelt delicious. Unlike Colin, who was by now almost eight, Hancock ate his meals in the kitchen with his nanny and the cook – 'a painfully thin woman who, no matter how much food she consumed, never put on a single pound'.

Although she was living as a member of the family, Sparkes was obliged to obey certain domestic, and class, rules. She was not allowed to use the front door, nor roam about the house nor sit in the front room – but there was one exception. Each week the 24-year-old nanny was invited into the lounge, Jack Hancock switched on the huge, veneered sun-burst radio and, as the music grew louder, the family grew silent. The five-minute programme was barely audible. Broadcast live from London, *That Child* captured the imagination of thousands of listeners. Radio comedy – albeit an apprentice attempt – had arrived.

Jack, however, made little effort to upgrade or improve his act. Lily, who accompanied her husband on the piano, still laughed at every joke as if she was hearing or seeing it for the first time. His stage appearances always ended with a monologue about a lonely old man and his dog, and each night Lily would rock with laughter as the tears streamed down her face. Years later, reciting the snippets she remembered, it produced the same effect from her son Tony.

Jack Hancock was visibly losing weight. The hacking cough which dogged him through the autumn and winter of 1926 was beginning to concern his doctor. So, too, was the patient's cavalier attitude to his health. If his physician could do nothing to persuade Jack to give up his forty cigarettes a day he could at least confront him with reality – either Jack moved away from Birmingham or he would die. Somewhere on the south coast of England would be ideal. By chance, one of the doctor's favourite resorts was Bournemouth.

1927

JACK AND LILY Hancock and their nine-year-old son Colin emerged from Bournemouth railway station into the Easter sunshine. After Birmingham the air was crisp and salty, tainted only by the smell of fermenting hops from a nearby brewery. Following a little way behind were the family nanny and her two-year-old charge.

It was a short drive in one of the resort's Austin cabs to Westbourne, a seafront district at the western end of the town where Jack had booked a two-week stay in one of the endless rows of flat-fronted bed and breakfast hotels. From the family's arrival the youngest Hancock – only a month away from his third birthday – was quiet and subdued, a mood he undoubtedly caught from Elsie Sparkes. She recalled: 'Like me, Tony wasn't too happy with his first impressions of Bournemouth. He couldn't understand the accent and the sea frightened him.'

Jack benefited from his brief south-coast holiday. The sea air eased his chest and cough and give him back his appetite. At first the move seemed impractical. However, the ever-forceful Lily saw it not only as a way of saving her husband's life, but also allowing her two sons to escape the pollution of industrial Birmingham. Also, she received some surprising news and support from her father, Harry Thomas, by now a widower and at last resigned to retirement. He had already announced his intention of relinquishing his twenty-year directorship of Birmingham City Football Club. In addition to financing the family migration and lending his son-in-law enough money to buy a small business, he intended moving to Bournemouth with the Hancock family.

During their stay Jack and Lily looked over several possible investments. Nothing appeared suitable until, with their final week fast running out, they were informed of a laundry for sale in a northern suburb of Bournemouth.

The Mayo Hygienic Laundry occupied double-fronted premises on the south side of Wynyard Road, Winton. Its proprietress was a Mrs E. Osbaldestone who lived in the flat above the main shop at Number 37. The adjoining property – Number 39 – was a single-storey building which housed the washroom and laundry. To the rear was a large grassed and fenced garden. The majority of houses in Wynyard Road reflected their owners' attempts to cling to the fast-receding Hampshire countryside, but by the mid-1920s the Braewoods, Heatherbanks and Rosekeens were punctuated by a rambling builder's yard and a noisy boot repair factory.

Jack and, more importantly, Lily were convinced they could revive the ailing business. The couple put in their offer for the Winton laundry and returned to Hall Green. By the second week of June the contracts had been exchanged. All that remained was the disposal of their Southam Road home. On 15 June the property column of the *Birmingham Mail* announced:

> HALL GREEN, Southam Rd; Modern, large rooms, imposing hall, gas fired, electric, Triplex, four bedrooms, verandah [*sic*] £1,350.

Jack Hancock had already resigned his post at Houlder Brothers. He occupied his time with still more concert bookings – sometimes as many as five or six a week – and attempting unsuccessfully to revive his brief wireless career. The status and professionalism of radio was changing fast. On 1 January, the British Broadcasting Corporation was constituted by Royal Charter. Its motto was and remains: 'Nation Shall Speak Peace Unto Nation'. Superseding the British Broadcasting Company, the new corporation was granted a ten-year licence to 'carry on a broadcasting service as a public utility service'. Birmingham's one-time Station 5IT was no longer looking for local, part-time entertainers to fill its concert intervals.

Suddenly the Southam Road house was full of strangers who insisted on examining every room and looking into every cupboard. Even the youngest Hancock's favourite bolt-hole under the kitchen table no longer provided the security it once offered. As a distraction Elsie Sparkes would take her three-year-old, and increasingly boisterous charge, to the park. 'If ever there were any boys around Tony would run off and bring their caps back to you,' she remembered.

Sometime during the early summer the family's possessions were packed and crated and the contents of their home transported south in a large pantechnicon. The family followed in Harry Thomas's car. The journey remained a 'vivid event' in Hancock's memory. 'What a brave band we were,' he said thirty-five years later. 'Every hamlet, every village, every town we passed through accorded us a truly remarkable lack of attention, exceeded only by the complete anonymity of our arrival.'

Jack and Lily, bolstered by the £900 profit they had made from the sale of their Hall Green home, set about taking over and rebuilding the laundry business. Nine-year-old Colin, as befitting the son of a businessman with prospects, was informed that from September he would be sent away to board at Durlston Court Preparatory School, Swanage, in the neighbouring county of Dorset.

For some unrecorded reason, Bournemouth Town Council announced it was amalgamating Wynyard Road with an adjoining street. From New Year's Day, 1928, the Mayo Laundry would be renumbered and re-addressed as 144 and 146 Strouden Road, Winton. Whatever the address, the youngest Hancock hated his new surroundings with a determination and logic only a three-year-old boy can display. He hated his parents for taking him away from his friends. He hated his cramped new home. Above all he hated the smell of bleach and coarse laundry soap which clung to his parents' clothes.

The move had somehow smothered the boy's confidence. 'For a while Tony became very unsure of himself,' said Sparkes. 'At a time when he should have been enjoying life he began to withdraw into himself. He disliked meeting anyone new. Trying anything new.' Under the watchful eye of his nanny, Hancock reluctantly explored the country lanes and fields to the west of Winton: 'He couldn't wait to get home. In fact, the only place he was really happy and relaxed was in the small, fenced-in back garden.'

With her £1 10s a week wages Sparkes bought herself a Box Brownie camera. One of the first photographs she took was of Hancock in the garden of his Wynyard Road home: round-cheeked and healthy he is wearing a shirt and shorts and white, knee-length socks and his sandalled feet are splayed in a pose characteristic of the adult Hancock.

Jack and Lily's hopes that their second son would slowly come to terms with the move were short lived. Despite the distraction of Christmas the youngest Hancock was again showing signs of moodiness. During the day he was tearful and miserable and would complain of feeling tired. Each bedtime he became harder to settle. By the middle of December Elsie Sparkes noticed a swelling around Hancock's wrists and leg joints. A doctor was called. During the examination the boy appeared unable to stand upright; his shoulders remained hunched and stiff; his bones were 'hurting'. The doctor took Lily Hancock aside. Her son, he informed her, was suffering from rickets.

A bone disorder found mainly in children living in towns and cities blanketed by smog and overcast skies, rickets is caused by a deficiency of Vitamin D. It was initially assumed a lack of sunlight was to blame. Vitamin D is produced by the skin after exposure to the sun. Although Hancock was born fairly close to the industrial heart of Birmingham, he was allowed to run free in the garden of his Hall Green home, so it is safe to assume he received adequate sunshine. Why he should fail to eat sufficient foods rich in Vitamin D – milk, eggs, liver and fish – is harder to understand. There is no evidence to suggest he was a finicky eater. Elsie Sparkes remembered him as 'always a lovely chubby little chap'.

One outcome of Hancock's childhood disease is beyond doubt – its ultimate effect on the course of British humour. As the disease takes hold a child's bones soften and malform. Without Vitamin D insufficient calcium salts are deposited in the bone and permanent damage is inevitable. The illness left him with a flat, almost concave, chest and a tendency to hang his neck forward, producing the distinctive Hancock slouch.

1928

SOMETIME BEFORE HANCOCK's fourth birthday his father's application to be a licensee was accepted by Strong and Co., a Romsey-based brewery company.

The Strouden Road laundry – which Jack soon found 'stuffy and claustrophobic' – was sold to a Mrs Deekin, who Lily remembered as 'very round and very enthusiastic'. The move was deliberate, prompted not so much by Jack's desire to join the ranks of the town's victuallers as an ambition to rub shoulders with some of its more prestigious clients.

Holdenhurst Road ran in a dog-leg south-west from Little Down Common almost to the seafront. Number 119 – halfway between the fire station and the Territorial Army drill hall – was the Railway Hotel. Built by Bournemouth Brewery, whose plant and offices were situated behind the pub, the premises originally opened as the Cock and Hen. The late-Victorian, black-tiled façade was designed to attract the eye of the railway traveller. Inside, the buffet bar boasted the finest mahogany fittings in the county and the marble pillars reflected the fine woodwork and plaster friezes. It was renamed the Railway Hotel after a post-war merger with Strong's.

Jack Hancock eagerly accepted the offer to run one of the resort's best-known public houses. Less than a year after their departure from Birmingham the Hancock family was on the move once again, this time to an angular, low-ceilinged flat on the topmost floor of the Railway Hotel. From the kitchen and living-room windows they could look down on to the junction of Holdenhurst Road and St Paul's Road. At the rear the bedrooms overlooked the brewery. To the four-year-old Hancock it seemed as though his parents had maliciously swapped the smell of cheap soap for hops. The stench from the brewhouse rose through each room in turn until it became trapped beneath the eaves of the Railway Hotel.

If Jack took his responsibilities as mine host seriously it was Lily, with her inherited business sense, who realised the true potential of their new position. Situated less than a hundred yards from Bournemouth station the Railway Hotel weathered the town's seasonal troughs better than most. While other establishments survived the winter months on local trade and the weekly outings of a growing number of retired residents, the hotel was frequently the first – and last – stop for business visitors. In spring, when the first summer-season entertainers arrived, its smoky, wood-panelled bars once again filled with big-name stars and down-bill artistes.

'You never saw Jack Hancock working behind the bar,' recalled

Peter Harding who, as a reporter on the *Bournemouth Graphic*, found the Railway Hotel fertile ground for show-business gossip. 'Jack had his regular place at one end of the bar and there he held court. He would occasionally leave it to greet someone he knew, but he would always bring them back to his corner. By the end of the night he would be surrounded by a group of laughing men and women and always with a household name among them.'

There are few surviving photographs of Jack Hancock, but one shows a dapper and bow-tied Jack standing in the entrance of the Railway Hotel with Bournemouth band leader, Percy Pearce. Between them is an elderly Charles Coburn, one of the few men who literally broke the bank at Monte Carlo.

With his older brother away at school and the nights drawing in, the youngest Hancock needed a new diversion. He found it in his imagination and the nooks and crannies of his father's public house. He would become a western hero; but not just any cowboy. The family's Railway Hotel attic flat became Toenail City and young Hancock its swaggering, gun-toting lawman.

As his second Bournemouth Christmas approached Hancock dragged his mother into every toy shop in Bournemouth. There was only one thing he demanded from the Beales department store Father Christmas, a sheriff's outfit.

Six-gun in hand 'Wyatt Earp' Hancock took his law-keeping duties seriously. He patrolled Toenail City dressed in his cowboy hat and waistcoat, silver star, bandanna and chaps. Through Christmas Day he rounded up errant family guests and ambushed his brother Colin. That evening the four-year-old Hancock complained about pains in his legs – Lily discovered her son had strained his muscles after walking in character, bowlegged for hours.

1929

EVERYONE, JACK HANCOCK reasoned, enjoyed the absurdity of a slightly-drunk, slightly-caddish, upper-crust buffoon. He was, as his son later recalled, a 'dude entertainer'.

It was a character ideally suited to his slender physique and aristocratically lined face. His Birmingham accent was soon replaced by a 'squeaky, excited, upper-crust' stage voice. Dressed in a top hat and tails and squinting at his audience through a monocle, Jack looked – and sounded – the part. He would walk on stage carrying a folded copy of *The Times*. Looking back into the wings he would call: 'Put the rolls in the garage, George. I'll butter them later.' From the newspaper he would 'read' humorous stories and anecdotes. It was a contemporary and barbed satirical act, frequently written in the wings only minutes before.

Like most five-year-old sons, Hancock dutifully announced he wanted to follow his father into show business. According to one childhood friend, it was not his only option. Hancock, he recalled, was also dabbling with the idea of becoming an engine driver. 'We would walk across the road from his father's pub to Bournemouth station,' remembered the friend. 'There we would stand in the steam next to the polished and very hot engines and gabble away about the top speed of a particular machine. We were never train spotters. We just dreamed of what it would be like to control all that power.'

Several hours later, smelling of oil and coal dust and red around the eyes, Hancock would return to the Railway Hotel where he was pounced upon by his mother or the nanny. 'They were very keen on baths,' he said. 'I was always so clean I felt I was about to meet someone very important.'

1931

In February the builders moved into the Railway Hotel. Strong and Co. was cashing in on Jack Hancock's growing reputation as a part-time entertainer and full-time personality.

Jack, immaculately dressed in a three-piece suit and apparently oblivious to the showers of dust and debris, would stand amid the rubble chatting and joking with the workmen. Lily Hancock – who sometime before Christmas had informed her husband she was expecting for the third time – suffered the noise and disruption as best she could.

By early March the hotel's palm lounge had been stripped and refurbished. To announce its opening the brewery placed a notice in the *Bournemouth Graphic*. Wedged between an advertisement for the Bournemouth Steam Laundry – 'Prompt! Efficient! Reliable!' – and the Belgian Lace and Lingerie Shop – 'for every six articles you buy you will receive one free of charge' – the town's residents and early-season tourists were invited to 'visit the Railway Hotel's New Palm Lounge and meet Jack Hancock'.

The plush new bar was, the advertisement claimed:

The Ideal Rendezvous for Ladies and Gentlemen, and the latest and most up-to-date Retreat in Central Bournemouth.

Jack, who composed the copy, added the punch-line:

It is said that Trams Stop by Request – others by Desire!

The brewery board was not disappointed. The Railway Hotel was becoming the place for entertainers to be seen. By Easter and the start of the resort's holiday season Jack was holding court in the new lounge and attracting national attention. The gossip column of the *London Evening News* commented:

... news travels fast among thespians and theatricals. In the Hampshire town of Bournemouth they are gathering in The Railway Hotel, an establishment owned [*sic*] by local comedian Jack Hancock ...

*

On 9 June, Lily Hancock gave birth to her third child. Roger Thomas Hancock was born in his parents' Railway Hotel attic bedroom. Jack and Lily lavished the infant Hancock with love and, it seemed to their second son, an undeserved amount of time and gifts. The arrival of a new sibling produced in the seven-year-old Hancock an unfamiliar and frightening sense of loss. For the first time the boy – the middle child in a family of three sons spanning thirteen years – felt himself surrounded by inattention; being, yet no longer belonging. It was a position which left Hancock isolated and insecure and spiritually marooned for the rest of his life.

Colin Hancock, by now a teenager, returned for his second year at St Andrew's College, a rambling and remote establishment near the Berkshire village of Bradfield, west of Reading. Like his older brother before him Tony would attend Durlston Court Preparatory School. The boy's name had been added to the entry register soon after his fifth birthday. Now, his departure for Swanage was only weeks away. Lily Hancock, recovered from her confinement and back behind the bar at the Railway Hotel, decided the department stores and outfitters of Bournemouth were far too parochial to equip her son for life at one of the south of England's best preparatory schools. Mother and son departed for a day's shopping in London.

Late in the afternoon and laden with an assortment of brown paper parcels the pair found themselves in Shaftesbury Avenue. Looking down a side street Lily announced: 'Here's a theatre that's open all day, Anthony. Let's go in ...' Hancock was too exhausted to notice its name. 'This'll do for an hour,' she said, failing to appreciate the strange look from the young woman in the box office.

Inside, Lily and her son settled themselves into their seats. The curtain opened and Lily gasped in horror. The stage was filled with a tableau of half-naked women attempting to portray a scene from history. 'She kept trying to push me under the seat,' Hancock recalled many years later. 'Every time I struggled free and popped my head up she would shove me down again.' As they fled the theatre Hancock looked back over his shoulder. He would never forget its name – The Windmill.

August, 1931, was the hottest for almost a decade. Even with the doors and windows of the Railway Hotel wedged open, the atmosphere in the hotel was close and muggy. In the top-floor flat baby Roger – not yet three months – voiced his disapproval. His older brother, in search of cool air and cheap amusement, took to roaming Undercliff Drive, a beach promenade linking Bournemouth and Boscombe piers.

Sitting on the beach with his chin resting on his knees, the boy watched as the Sand Artist modelled figures and historic scenes from the damp sand. One popular sculpture with the holiday makers and weekend day-trippers was Jesus embracing two small children. Carved in the sand and edged with pebbles were the words: 'Suffer little children to come unto me'. Another showed a dying Nelson surrounded by his fellow officers. Beside his exhibits the Sand Artist had pitched a khaki ridge tent. He sat in the doorway eating sandwiches and brewing tea on a primus stove. When enough people had gathered to examine his handiwork the sculptor would abandon his refuge to deliver a short lecture and pass around the hat.

A little further along the beach a cluster of children would gather in front of a red-and-white striped tent to await the hourly Punch and Judy performances. Standing tight-faced and defiant amid a sea of exuberant children the seven-year-old Hancock was instantly haunted by the masochistic cruelty of Mr Punch. It was a bizarre premonition of his own marriages and relationships. Hancock the child was witnessing Hancock the man. Years later he convinced himself that any kind of puppet – and the malevolent presence of the evil Mr Punch in particular – possessed a malign control over his life. It was, he would come to believe, the cause of his personal guilt and responsible for his professional downfall.

*

George Fairweather, who had joined the Post Office as a telegraph boy at fourteen, was a second-generation semi-professional entertainer. At four each morning he would walk the short distance from his Bournemouth home to the town's sorting office in Old Christchurch Road. His nine-hour shift ended at 1pm. Snatching a few hours' sleep he would be up by teatime and preparing for a night on stage with his parents' Magpies concert party. A natural baritone, their son made his first appearance with The Magpies while still at school, taking over as manager when his mother and father retired.

One Friday evening in late October, the twenty-year-old Fairweather discovered he was booked on the same bill as a 'tall, handsome man with a strange accent' who arrived dressed in top hat and tails and sporting a white silk scarf and silver-topped cane. Fairweather eyed the gent with amusement, thinking, 'he was over-dressed even for a formal night out'.

Although they worked the same circuit of clubs and concert halls, and toured the same network of Hampshire Army bases, Fairweather had never met Jack Hancock. Watching from the wings of the social-club stage the postman-cum-impressionist was overwhelmed by his fellow performer's act and wondered why he had never turned professional. To Fairweather, Jack was a natural comedian. 'Within minutes the audience identified with him,' he remembers. 'Jack may have been dressed as a toff, but there were no class barriers in his routine. He joked about the same things and poked fun at the same people.'

The next day it rained for the first time in weeks. Fairweather slipped his coat over his dark blue post office uniform and walked back along Holdenhurst Road to the Railway Hotel. Jack Hancock greeted Fairweather as if he were a long-lost brother returning from a round-the-world voyage. While the pair chatted a small boy emerged from behind the bar and took his father's hand. Jack bent down, whispered something in his son's ear, and watched the boy skip away.

It was George Fairweather's first, brief sight of Tony Hancock.

1932

WHEN HANCOCK WAS in his first year at Durlston Court Preparatory School one of the boys in his house asked who was the handsome and debonair man who came to visit. It was Jack Hancock. At that moment the eight-year-old boy realised his father possessed a rather special power. For the first time Hancock enjoyed being his father's son.

Jack Hancock was a self-confident and energetic man who, throughout his adult life, attracted the friendship and loyalty of men half his age. Few heard him argue and still less heard him raise his voice. Life was there to be charmed not chastised. In his own fastidious way he took life as it came and twisted it to suit his own standards and sense of fun.

A dapper man who opened his gold cigarette case with a flourish and insisted on chain-smoking his Du Maurier from a holder to stop the nicotine staining his hands, Jack bordered on the obsessional with his personal appearance. He would scrub his hands ten, sometimes twelve, times a day. Each morning he insisted on a freshly starched shirt and collar; the slightest stain or mark would force a change of clothes.

During the Easter holiday the Hancocks took their three sons to the French Riviera. It was the first break the family had had since their arrival in Bournemouth and to ease the discomfort of a twenty-two-hour journey with a ten-month-old baby Jack insisted they travel first class. While Jack relaxed on the hotel veranda or wandered through the promenade palms, Lily and the boys collected shells from the beach and rock pools. On their first night in France their waiter served a whole fish, complete with head, tail and white opaque eyes. The Hancocks' second son curled his nose in horror and announced: 'I'll stick to good old bread and fromage, thank you.' He ate nothing else for the rest of the holiday.

Staying at the same hotel was Sydney Howard, the Yorkshire-born comedian. Jack had first met Howard when the character actor was touring with his West End hit *Ladies Night*. After opening in Leeds, the show moved south to Bournemouth where he was introduced to the publican by a theatre manager. A staunch Methodist and tee-totaller, Howard – who would drink nothing stronger than ginger beer – resolutely refused Jack's invitation to visit the Railway Hotel. Howard, who, like Hancock, would come to treat France as a refuge and retreat, was with his wife, recuperating after making his first film *Up For The Cup*.

Jack considered the Durlston Court uniform his son wore as smart and dignified. Eager to please and despite the Mediterranean heat, Hancock insisted on wearing his black pinstripe school trousers, black jacket and stiff Eton collar. Howard was at first fascinated and then concerned by the daily appearance of the youngest Hancock suited and sweltering in the summer sun – 'he had seen many things in his touring life, but nothing like me.' If Hancock's jacket was dirty Mrs Howard was commanded to brush it. Creased trousers or a dirty collar elicited 'tuts' of disapproval. One morning Howard spotted a small strand of white cotton on the lapel of the boy's school uniform and tried to pinch it away. 'Mustn't go out looking a wreck,' he said.

The cotton kept coming and coming – with the other end attached to the reel in Hancock's pocket. 'You'll go far, sonny,' chuckled the 46-year-old Howard.

When the family returned to England, Jack was surprised to discover the brewery resented his two-week holiday. Throughout the winter Jack's engagements – and his growing popularity – had forced him to spend ever more evenings away from the Railway Hotel. During his holiday, takings fell and the Strong's board unfairly blamed Jack's sanctioned, but resented, absence. As the summer approached the landlord's relationship with his employers deteriorated. Jack complained to his father-in-law Harry Thomas and, for the second time in five years, the elderly businessman offered to finance a new venture.

The Swanmore Hotel and Lodge was a neglected private establishment halfway down Gervis Road East and a short walk from Bournemouth's clifftop promenade. Built as a rambling two-storey hotel, it was surrounded by extensive grounds. To increase the number of bedrooms Jack and Lily intended to replace the sloping roof with a flat-roofed third floor and give it an already outdated art deco facelift. It would be a lengthy and costly job. For the time being they would stay on at the Railway Hotel.

1933

HANCOCK FOUND HE was enjoying life at Durlston Court Preparatory School. In the social hierarchy of public schools his family background kept him firmly in the lower order – 'Even hotel owners were seen as tradesmen.' However, Jack Hancock's stage career – and the show-business stories he told his son – endowed Hancock with a certain dormitory kudos.

To the teaching staff Hancock remained unremarkable. He was a boy who followed his passions and little else. 'He was just an ordinary, very likeable schoolboy,' recalled Mrs Patrick Cox, the headmaster's wife. 'I remember he was very good at games.'

One lifelong passion was cricket. An exceptionally accurate fast bowler, he would practise his action at every opportunity, whether walking along the street or in the confined corridors of the Railway Hotel. Although he was one of the best cricketers the school possessed, a Hampshire schoolboys' trial failed to win him a place in the county team.

Towards the end of each academic year all the Durlston Court pupils were invited to join in a school production of a Gilbert and Sullivan operetta. This year it would be *The Gondoliers*. It was a popular diversion. Between net practice for the school cricket team and rehearsals, Latin and matriculation and history lessons were squeezed to a bare minimum. The nine-year-old Hancock was already sniffing at a stage career and his enthusiasm impressed the music master enough to land him a part; not altogether surprising considering the size of the company required to stage the majority of Gilbert and Sullivan productions.

Hancock often boasted that he had been offered the leading role of the Duke of Plaza Toro in *The Gondoliers* – an unlikely piece of casting considering his obvious discomfort when asked to read aloud in class and his lack of singing experience. He did, however, find himself with an impressive entrance at the head of an entourage of nobles, and with a single line of speech: 'My Lords, the Duke!'

All went well until the dress rehearsal. 'Trembling with excitement, I waited in the wings with my company shuffling and fidgeting behind,' Hancock enjoyed recalling. 'Then came the cue. With a slow, measured tread I led my nobles on to the stage. With dignity we halted in the middle. My hand came up in an impressive gesture of introduction. My mouth opened. It closed and opened again. But the only thing that came out was a strangled gargle.'

The master ordered Hancock and his retinue to make their entrance again. 'Disconsolately the train trooped back to the wings. With much shoving and barging we took up our positions. Once more the slow measured tread . . . the flowing gesture and this time . . . a mouse-like squeak. My jaws were working but my voice wasn't.'

'All right, Hancock,' bellowed the teacher. 'You've had your moment of clowning . . . Off.'

Much to Jack and Lily Hancock's amusement their son was relegated to a fifteen-second, non-speaking walk-on part. It did not stop Jack using his influence to get his son a test at a film studio near London. The audition, like Hancock's stage debut, was a disaster.

The following year Hancock found himself in the chorus of *The Pirates of Penzance*, with little more success. During early rehearsals his voice began to break. 'I sounded like a cross between Paul Robeson and Lily Pons.'

The music master led his failed singer aside. Bending down he whispered in the boy's ear: 'What I really want is a good stage manager.'

Hancock stood his ground; he had been accepted for the chorus and he wanted – he demanded – to be seen on stage. Compromise, his teacher quickly realised, was the only way out. Hancock could stand among the chorus line and open and close his mouth in time to the music, he could even slap his thigh with the rest – as long as he promised not to sing.

1934

FOR A TEN-YEAR-OLD boy the Railway Hotel buzzed with a magnetic and magical attraction. Each week, as one pantomime or summer show ended and another prepared to open, the Holdenhurst Road pub sparkled with exotic and flamboyant characters. 'I had a little spot behind the bar where I could watch some of the famous artistes of the day enjoying a pint,' Hancock would later recall. Some the boy recognised from posters and street corner fliers: the 'Always Merry and Bright' Billy Danvers, whose Lancastrian accent rumbled around the bar like a dropped kettle drum; Clapham and Dwyer; the Housten Sisters; Elsie and Doris Waters and the elegant comic-pianist Norman Long, whose *A Song, a Smile and a Piano* radio broadcasts were among Jack Hancock's favourites.

The hotel's show-business guests were 'different from any other kind of people I had ever met in my young life', said Hancock. 'They seemed to get so much more out of life simply by being alive. They fascinated me. Those old pro's were so much more extrovert than people in the business today. It seemed as though they would go into an act at the drop of a hat. Through them I came to know a lot about life back stage in a theatre – my school cap was almost as familiar a sight in the wings of the Pavilion Theatre as the stage manager's pullover.'

One regular visitor developed a particular friendship with Jack. For many years this Sheffield-born entertainer had scratched a living as a semi-pro comedian using his two Christian names, Arthur Clifford. Like the owner of the Railway Hotel, Clifford had provided light-hearted interludes for his local BBC radio relay station. The 32-year-old comedian's 'punctuated patter' fascinated young Hancock. 'We're a great race comma the British semi-colon all shoulders to the wheel comma all comrades exclamation mark.' It was, Hancock later admitted, the first time he realised the importance of deft timing in raising a rather banal script above the ridiculous. He was even more intrigued by Clifford's stage costume. As an amateur he had seen a suit of armour in a Sheffield shop and got the local firm of Firth Vickers to make him a stainless steel waistcoat. Within months he was wearing a steel hat band, waistcoat buttons that lit up and a revolving luminous bow tie. By 1936 Arthur Clifford had changed his name to Stainless Stephen.

It was during one of his theatre visits that Jack decided to try his hand at producing. More and more social and charity venues were refusing to book individual acts, preferring to hire a complete evening's entertainment. Within days he had recruited Pete Reid, another resort publican, George Fairweather and beach impresario Willie Cave.

One day all four were returning from an Army retirement party at Warrington camp, north of Bournemouth. It was three in the morning when their car pulled in to Bournemouth Square. 'Driver,' announced Jack, 'straight back to the Railway Hotel for a sandwich and warm-up.'

'Not me,' said Fairweather. 'I'm on duty at four.'

When Cave was told Fairweather earned just £1 17s 6d a week as a postman, he was horrified. 'With your talent you must be mad. I'll give you £4 pound a week to come and work for me.'

All four had been drinking and Fairweather was justifiably sceptical: 'Do you really mean it?'

'Of course I do,' said Cave. 'If you come and work for me you'll earn more in a summer than you do in a year as a postman.' An hour later Fairweather was handing in his notice. The next weekend, the Whitsun Holiday, he was on stage as a member of Willie Cave's Rebels.

*

By early summer Jack's position as licensee of the Railway Hotel had become untenable. His impending departure for his own rival establishment had first irritated and then antagonised his brewery bosses. Now, producing his own concert parties had left him with precious little time for his duties as a pub and hotel manager. On 1 July, after the latest in a series of boardroom reprimands, Jack gave a month's notice.

Work on the Swanmore Hotel and Lodge would not be completed until the beginning of September. The white stucco walls of the clifftop hotel had been painted. The garden on either side of the drive had been turned over and replanted. The private apartments and the majority of the bedrooms had been decorated. There was precious little time to complete the bar and dining room and the ground-floor lounges if Lily Hancock was to attract enough retired gentlefolk to see them through the winter until Jack could persuade his theatrical friends to desert the Railway Hotel at the start of the 1935 summer season.

After the excitement of the move, the school holiday dragged into loneliness and neglect. When everybody was too busy to talk to him, Hancock resorted to the simple solution of dipping into the hotel petty cash and taking himself off to the cinema. 'I saw so many pictures during those years. It didn't matter what was on. Provided it moved I was there,' said Hancock. 'And if I particularly liked a film, then I would go to see it time and time again. You might say I was discriminating. Or a very early example of what is now described as a committed audience.'

Another distraction was the boxing tournaments his father refereed. Sometime during his tenancy at the Railway Hotel, Jack volunteered his services as a club official. He was an imposing figure. Two or three inches taller than the majority of contestants, and nimbler on his feet than most, Jack maintained a straight-backed, ever-smiling dignity that defied anyone to challenge his decision. All, that is, except his sons. 'We were the worst audience he ever had,' said Hancock. 'My brother Colin and I trotted along to his fights, sat ourselves in the free ring-side seats, and promptly stood up and booed every decision he gave.'

The late-summer boredom was only relieved by the arrival of the first paying guests. Lily Hancock had steadfastly refused to advertise in the local Hampshire newspapers, preferring, instead, to attract the attention of *Country Life* and *Tatler* readers contemplating a south-coast retirement.

Lily attempted to divert her son by putting him in charge of hotel menus. It was a task ideally suited to Hancock's neat and even handwriting – he never lost the right-hand slant, nor his geographic sense of humour; place names would pole-axe him for the rest of his life. Between the kitchen and the dining-room Hancock would transform the daily soup into something of promise. Each morning he would give it a new and exotic name. On Mondays it might be 'Consommé Italienne' or 'Potage Luxembourg' followed, the next day, by any other European location which took his fancy. To the confused guests it would always remain Brown Windsor.

Both the elder Hancock boys were about to enter their final year at their present schools. Colin Hancock was a tall, elegant young man who looked and sounded like his father. He shared Jack's eyes, broad forehead, and instant smile. At sixteen he was already an inch or two taller than his mother. Although Lily insisted her eldest son took piano lessons, Colin lacked his father's fascination with the stage. He had, however, inherited more from his maternal grandfather, the ambitious and hard-nosed Harry Thomas. For Colin, each new variety star who booked in to the hotel brought with them an entourage of associates and hangers-on. And all spent money in the hotel bar. He was, admitted his younger brother, a 'born businessman'. Jack and Lily Hancock had already decided that when the time came their son Colin should take over the family business.

For the ten-year-old Tony, school stretched ahead like a straight and featureless road. He was never home-sick. He never pined. Yet on the rare occasions when the Durlston Court boys were allowed out of school he would walk to the end of Swanage's Peveril Point and look across Poole Bay to where Bournemouth shimmered in the sea haze. Next year Hancock would follow his older brother to St Andrew's College, Bradfield.

During the third week in September, as the boys were packing for their departure, Jack Hancock announced he was renaming the recently reopened Swanmore Hotel after his sons' preparatory school – from now on it would be known as Durlston Court.

1935

'NONE OF US, my brothers, mother or my father, enjoyed a family life as it is customarily understood,' Hancock once confessed. 'It is quite impossible when you are involved in running a hotel.'

Hancock was adrift in his parents' world. Whenever he threaded his way through the crowded Durlston Court bar to stand beside his father he would be shooed away and out of sight. However, there were moments of family laughter. 'My father was a very funny man,' remembered the adult Hancock. 'At home he had us all in fits of laughter. Even mum had to laugh. She could never stay cross with dad for long. He would pull a funny face, or use a silly voice, and that was that.'

On the rare occasions the Hancock family gathered in their Durlston Court apartment Jack would regale his wife and three sons with anecdotes and observations and try out new jokes for his act. Even as an amateur entertainer Jack knew how to work an audience. He fed out his stories line by line, leaving his family helpless with laughter and gasping for breath. Colin, the eldest, would fall on to his hands and knees, banging his fists on the floor; four-year-old Roger pretended to climb the walls, and Tony, infected by his mother's giggling, would roll on to his back and kick his legs in the air.

The skylarking extended to family photographs. One, taken in the car-park of the four-storey hotel, shows a behatted and fur-wrapped Lily with her three sons. Young Roger is still too self-conscious to relax; Colin is indulgently mimicking his father; only eleven-year-old Tony is confident and mischievous enough to pull a funny face.

From his father, the extrovert and compulsive showman, young Hancock was already catching the urge to perform. It was a contradictory and confusing inheritance, especially for a youth whose maternal bequest had been the ability – the desire – to remain unnoticed while listening to and absorbing the world around him. 'Tony had a natural gift,' said Hancock's future lover, Joan le Mesurier. 'He was a wonderful listener. It helped to make him a star. He had a genuine curiosity about people from all walks of life and knew how to ask the right questions and how to draw them out without being patronising.'

Jack Hancock, whose high-energy, high-society act and giddy enthusiasm soon burned off excess fat, began to lose weight. His cheeks sank in and his chest and throat rasped with a persistent cough, far worse than before the move from Birmingham. During the last Christmas holiday Jack had insisted on keeping his promise to compère a Midnight Matinée at the Regent Theatre for the mayor of Bournemouth's Hospital and Eventide Homes Appeal. His performance left him exhausted and, for most of the next day, he remained in bed. On New Year's Day the family doctor broke the news he had long suspected: Jack was suffering from lung cancer and could not expect to live more than six months.

The Hancocks were glad their two older boys were away at school and spared the sight of their father's spirited but inevitable decline. On 17 February Jack wrote and signed his last will and testament, leaving everything to his wife Lucie Lilian Hancock 'for her unstitable and loving kindnesses' (sic). It was witnessed by his 'greatest friends' Percy Denson, a drug importer who lived in London's Forest Hill district, and his wife Mary.

In a perverse way Jack Hancock's illness had ensured the success of Durlston Court as Bournemouth's newest and plushest theatrical hotel and show-business watering hole. Less than seven months after it was reopened and renamed, the Gervis Road East hotel had accepted bookings from the stars and management of all three summer shows and the majority of touring companies playing the resort that summer.

However, drinkers and Durlston Court guests soon began to see a dramatic change in Jack Hancock's appearance. Always a lean, muscular man 'with a strong outdoor complexion', his angular cheekbones were now almost visible through his skin which, on his face and the backs of his hands, was the pale yellow of beeswax. As he grew weaker he swapped his favourite barstool for an easy chair, but he never deserted his role as landlord and bon viveur. One night, prior to his usual entrance, Jack stripped down to his shorts and vest. His arms and legs looked painfully emaciated. Wrapping a sheet around himself he hobbled into the bar to spend the rest of the evening holding court as Gandhi, the Indian mystic and statesman who in 1931 had visited the Lancashire cotton mills dressed in a loincloth and shawl.

It was over the Easter weekend that Lily first noticed her husband had developed a tender mass in the right side of his abdomen. Despite his emaciated appearance his stomach appeared bloated and swollen. Over the next few days Jack would lapse into a low fever, his skin and the whites of his eyes turning a distinct yellow against the cotton sheets of his bed. The cancer in Jack's right lung had spread to his liver.

Lily could no longer cope with running a busy hotel and nursing a dying husband. Late in June an ambulance arrived to take Jack to a private nursing home. Each step jarring his body, and refusing an oxygen mask, he insisted on walking from his bedroom to the waiting vehicle. A few days later, when his condition worsened still further, he was transferred to the Royal Victoria Hospital, Boscombe.

It was the height of the summer season and Colin and Tony were on holiday. Roger was still too young for school. The boys, shocked by the sight of their faded and morphine-clouded father, paid only occasional visits to the hospital. When Lily arrived late on Saturday, 10 August, Jack was barely conscious. Suddenly he became very alert and lucid and Lily told him the entire cast of the Derickson and Brown Road Show, led by two of America's biggest radio stars, had arrived at

Durlston Court for its week at Boscombe Hippodrome. After a few minutes Jack drifted back to sleep.

Jack Hancock never regained consciousness. He was just forty-seven years old and alone when he died early the next morning.

Monday's *Bournemouth Echo* reported:

> The death occurred in a Bournemouth nursing home [*sic*] yesterday morning of Mr Jack Hancock, a well-known local hotel proprietor, sportsman and entertainer. He had been ill for nearly a year and was 48 [*sic*] years of age.
>
> He had been proprietor of the Durlston Court Hotel, Gervis Road East, since August 1933, and the establishment was only recently reopened after being rebuilt.
>
> Mr Hancock came to Bournemouth from Birmingham about seven years ago, having been manager of the Birmingham office of Messrs Houlder Brothers, shipping agents. During his first five years here he was manager of the Railway Hotel, Holdenhurst Road.
>
> As a licensed boxing referee Mr Hancock had officiated at tournaments in the Winter Gardens, the Stokewood Road Baths, and elsewhere locally. He was also a popular entertainer, and broadcast from the Birmingham studio in the early days of wireless. In Bournemouth he appeared frequently in aid of charities, and one of his last efforts was at the Midnight Matinée in the Regent Theatre for the Mayor of Bournemouth's Hospital and Eventide Homes Appeal.

Jack Hancock was buried at Wimborne Road Cemetery the following Wednesday. Lily Hancock was escorted by her seventeen-year-old son Colin, but both his brothers were considered too young to attend their father's funeral. Tony, bewildered and tearful, and Roger, just sixty days beyond his fourth birthday, were cared for by staff at Durlston Court. The sole family representative from Birmingham was Jack's niece Mabel.

*

At forty-five, Lily had long-since reconciled herself to widowhood. A highly sexual woman, Lily was also an accomplished and gifted flirt. By the end of September, and with the older boys back at school, she had plunged into a passionate affair with a man twelve years her junior. Part of Lily's appeal was undoubtedly the £13,961 Jack Hancock had left in his will.

At thirty-three Robert Gorden Walker was a handsome and athletic man who cherished his reputation as a local hero. The son of a Bournemouth tailor, Walker excelled at schoolboy football and, for ten years, had played as a Boscombe semi-professional. He was now a successful electrical contractor whose company had carried out part of the refurbishment of Durlston Court. He spoke with a loud, high-pitched, self-confident voice and enjoyed telling suggestive jokes. For her part, Lily's jokes, which almost always involved theatrical anecdotes, invariably contained one or two obscenities. One of her favourites involved two elderly comics who toured the music halls with the same tired old act. They would wear the same moth-eaten fur coats and deliver the same lines. During one hot afternoon there were only twenty people in the audience. Their jokes received little enthusiasm and no applause. One comic marched to the front of the stage and announced: 'Ladies and gentlemen, my partner and I wish to thank you for your overwhelming ovation. If you will kindly remain seated we will pass among you and beat the shit out of you with a cricket bat.' Years later Hancock would repeat the same joke almost word for word.

Lily's increasingly open affair disgusted many of Jack's loyal friends; some remained convinced the relationship started during her husband's dying months. When the personal columns of the *Bournemouth Graphic* carried the announcement of the couple's engagement, George Fairweather refused to return to Durlston Court.

On New Year's Day, 1936 – one hundred and forty-two days after Jack's death – Lily married Robert Walker at Bournemouth Register Office. Within six months her new husband had sold his electrical business and taken over as a joint director of Durlston Court.

1939

BRITAIN WAS SLIDING inexorably towards war. On 27 April, 1939 – little more than two weeks before Hancock's fifteenth birthday – the Government announced the military call-up of all men aged twenty and twenty-one. For Colin Hancock it would be only a matter of months before he received his conscription papers. His public-school education would qualify him for a commission, but his interest in aircraft and his regular visits to Hurn, a small airfield north of Bournemouth, predestined him for the Royal Air Force.

In the dormitories and corridors of St Andrew's College the talk was of little else but the European crisis. The older pupils made bravado plans to follow fathers and brothers and uncles into the armed forces. Hancock, too, decided it was time for action. He announced, first to the dean, and then by letter to his mother, that this would be his last summer term at school. 'I knew it was time I did something, I just wasn't sure what,' he admitted many years later.

Desperate to change his mind Lily Walker travelled to Berkshire to discuss her son's future with the college dean. John Hills was an austere but well-liked First World War Lieutenant-Colonel awarded a Military Cross for bravery in Flanders. His reports on Hancock's mediocre progress had failed to blunt Lily's ambition for a university place, followed, she hoped, by an academic career. The head, less convinced of his pupil's future, praised Hancock's prowess as a cricketer, but saw no reason why he should attempt to change the teenager's mind. In class Hancock was doing just enough academically to get by. On the sports field he was enjoying himself immensely. During the winter months he opted for soccer and, by his own admission, was a 'deadly centre-forward, provided I stayed within the penalty area'. Each summer he proved equally deadly as a seam bowler.

The meeting over, Lily enquired where she might find her son. He would be leaving the main building, she was informed, with his classmates.

'How will I recognise him in the crowd?' Lily asked.

'That's simple,' replied the dean. 'He'll be the only one with his mortar board stuffed under his arm and his gown trailing on the ground.'

Homework or prep sessions were often spent writing one- and two-act comedies. In his dormitory before lights out – and frequently after by torchlight – Hancock would act out the sketches to the muffled laughter of his classmates. When the illicit performances were discovered, Hancock was invited to stage his work under the critical eye of the masters and senior boys. Somehow they never seemed as funny.

By July, Hancock was back in Bournemouth and the common-room jingoism had lost its urgency. 'I had a real compulsion to get away and get on the stage,' he explained. 'I still didn't have any idea just what I wanted to do.' He toyed with the notion of joining a repertory company and training as an actor; another fancy saw him as a dramatist, even a scriptwriter. Comedy was still an option, although never a compulsion.

He needed a start and there was only one person Hancock knew who could give him a job. Since the early 1930s Willie Cave's Rebels had provided the summer season entertainment on Bournemouth beach. Between April and September, Cave's pierrot company danced and sang and juggled its way through three shows daily; four on Saturday. The Rebels' beach theatre was constructed of girders and canvas and on a good day could seat five hundred people. The show never stopped. In stormy weather parts of the structure were frequently ripped off by the wind or the sea and hastily rebuilt, the musicians and singers competing with the backstage sawing and hammering.

As a local impresario and performer Willie Cave had been a regular at Durlston Court before Jack Hancock's death. He was also the man who had given George Fairweather his first show-business break. For days that August, and late into each evening, the teenage Hancock haunted the promenade overlooking the makeshift theatre, hoping to spot the seafront producer. He finally cornered the showman and introduced himself. Yes, he remembered Jack's son. No, he would not give the boy a spot in the show. 'You're far too young and inexperienced,' Cave said curtly.

On Sunday, 3 September, 1939, Britain declared war on Germany. The next morning Hancock attended his first lesson in 'commercial skills' at Bournemouth Municipal College, five minutes' walk from his Gervis Road East home. Oddly, Hancock enjoyed the secretarial classes – 'I was the only boy in a class full of girls.' Each morning the tutor would choose a selection of classical records and play them in turn on an old gramophone while his students kept time by tapping out the home keys A-S-D-F-;-L-K-J on their heavy, black Remington typewriters. Hancock's favourite practice pieces were from Bach's *Brandenburg Concertos.*

One former classmate, who admits to having a 'crush on this slim, solitary and very handsome' boy, recalls how Hancock, struck by the robotic absurdity of the scene, would 'frequently and unexpectedly' be overcome by a fit of giggles: 'You could see his shoulders start to shake and then his body would begin to roll from side to side and then, above the clack-clack-clack of the typewriters, you would hear this strangled, painful snigger,' recalled Maureen Woodford. 'Nobody had said anything funny, we weren't allowed to talk. It was just that inside Tony's head the situation had taken on ridiculous proportions. He thought we were all quite mad.'

That autumn Hancock finally made up his mind. During an afternoon break he announced his intention of becoming a comic. 'Tony had always talked about following his father on to the stage,' adds Woodford, 'but he never knew exactly how. One day it was going to be variety, the next films. Out of the blue he announced he "wanted to make people laugh". He was going to be a comedian. We already knew how funny Tony could be, but this somehow made it official. Tony Hancock was going to be a comic – and we never doubted him.'

Her son's decision came as no surprise to Lily Walker. 'It wasn't the way he told jokes,' she said. 'It was the way Tony saw the world. The way he never forgot anything.' The child, the adolescent, was instinctively the adult comedian. It would be more than a decade before Hancock, the stage and radio star, would exploit his hangdog look and put-upon character. Yet Hancock, the teenager, had already acquired his droll distortion of life. People, incidents, even family pets, would enter his memory to crystallise years later as some of his most popular routines and sketches. Lily kept a deep-chested rather cocky budgerigar which strutted defiantly up and down its perch. When life became too much for the manic bird it would hide under its bell, peeking out occasionally to see if the coast was clear. 'Look at that stupid bird,' Hancock told his mother. 'One day I'll do an act about that budgie.'

Early in October, while Hancock was still attending his college classes, his elder brother received his call-up papers. As a director of Durlston Court Hotel, Colin was now effectively its manager. He was also engaged to be married. Lily suggested the wedding should be brought forward to allow the couple at least a few days together before her son's departure for the Royal Air Force.

The ceremony was hurriedly arranged for 4 November at St Peter's Church, Bournemouth. Colin Hancock was twenty-one when he married Pauline Mansfield. His bride was three years older and the daughter of George Mansfield, a local mechanical engineer. Both gave their address as Durlston Court, Gervis Road East.

By the time Colin Hancock arrived in Blackpool during the second week of November the Lancastrian resort was effectively the biggest RAF camp in Britain. To accommodate the 60,000 airmen and women passing through the town at any one time, the RAF took over 5,000 hotels and boarding houses; the managers or landladies were paid £1 a week for each recruit crammed into back-bedrooms and attics. More than forty shops, offices, public buildings and assorted seafront structures had been commandeered by the Air Ministry as stores and training units. One was Blackpool's famous Winter Gardens. On a sky-blue notice board outside the entrance to the venue's Olympia building was the mysterious message:

    -- -- --- ---   -•- •••   •   - •- •••

    --• •••- - ••• ••• • •--• •

The first lesson for each would-be wireless operator was to translate the sign he would pass eight times a day for the next six weeks. It read: 'Morse taught here.'

Colin Hancock was a natural and gifted telegrapher. One flight-sergeant instructor remembers him as 'someone who took to Morse instinctively, almost as a second language'. He would irritate his fellow airmen and impress his NCOs by tapping out whole sentences with a pencil during NAAFI conversations.

Tony's education ended permanently just before Christmas. He never lost the instincts of touch-typing, nor the basics of Pitman shorthand. Years later he would irritate countless secretaries – usually someone else's – by leaning over their shoulders and informing them they had put down a wrong outline.

Lily, always intolerant of idleness, found her son odd jobs around the hotel. 'It was the kind of place which attracted old ladies,' Hancock observed. 'They used to set out for the dining-room at 11.30 and get there just in time for the gong at one o'clock.' The residents were dominated by several dowagers who swept through the hotel lounge and dining-room like galleons under full sail, their frigates of female companions bouncing nervously along in their wake. Here were the people – 'this splendid crew' – Hancock would later distil into his East Cheam 'Ancock. Hidden among the real and pseudo-gentility was the raw spirit with which Hancock imbued the Lad Himself: the 'pretentious, gullible, bombastic, occasionally kindly, superstitious, avaricious, petulant, over-imaginative, semi-educated, gourmandising, incompetent, cunning, obstinate, self-opinionated, impolite, pompous, lecherous, lonely and likeable' character of Roger Wilmut's *Tony Hancock: Artiste*.

Lily Walker took her new duties as chaperon to the lower gentry seriously. She organised tours to local sights, hired conjurors and entertainers, organised parties and refereed games; anything to keep her guests amused. Hancock, who classed her efforts as mild insanity, was in his element. He survived for years on his mother's attempts to entertain her guests:

> One game we had to drop was the Woolworth's Tea. The idea was that everybody came to tea wearing something they had got from Woolworth's which, in those days, meant it had cost not more than 6d. Then your partner had to find out what it was. Fine, until somebody nominated a lady's priceless family heirloom – end of Woolworth's Tea.
>
> Then there was the man who came to the Christmas fancy head-dress party as a Christmas pudding ... he wore the plate round his neck and on his shoulders like a ruff and encased around his head was a papier mâché pudding complete with sprigs of holly on the top. He refused to take it off. He sat through dinner feeding himself through a visorish trap door in the front. We tapped on the side between courses to make sure he was all right.

1940

ANTHONY HANCOCK – TAILOR to the gentry – was available for sartorial advice. Dressed in a newly acquired double-breasted, pin-striped suit, Hancock arrived at the Bournemouth branch of Hector Powe, a nationwide tailoring chain with an up-market reputation. Instead of a tape measure he was handed a teapot. His next piece of equipment was a broom. When the youngest addition to the shop's staff was ordered to clean out a junk-filled cupboard he walked out. Hancock's career as a bespoke tailor had lasted exactly four hours.

Lily Walker was not impressed. Neither was the woman behind the counter at Bournemouth Labour Exchange. She shuffled her way through a box file, comparing Hancock with each job description. 'Ah, yes,' she said at last, 'the Civil Service.' It was Hancock's turn to be unimpressed.

With the onset of war the Board of Trade had moved out of central London and commandeered the resort's Carlton Hotel. For his interview Hancock re-pressed his suit and bought himself an umbrella. He was confronted by a taut-skinned official who appeared undeterred by the applicant's lack of academic qualifications. When Hancock enquired about career prospects the man looked startled.

'Surely, Mr Hancock,' he said, 'it is not necessary for me to outline prospects. This is the Civil Service.' Years later Hancock would use the same voice on radio and television for a variety of pompous officials. The man studied his papers for a few seconds to regain his composure before looking up. 'Very well, I think you'll fit our requirements,' he sniffed. 'We can arrange for you to start in about a week.'

Hancock was not giving in that easily. 'I won't decide right away,' he informed his startled interviewer. 'There are several other irons in the fire, you know. I'll drop you a line in a day or so.' As Hancock later recalled: 'Nothing like this had happened to the Civil Service since tea went on ration.'

A week after his interview – the 'irons' evidently blown away by his mother's anger – Hancock wrote to say he was ready to join the Civil Service as a 'temporary unestablished assistant clerk – grade three'. His job, as he would soon discover, involved endorsing endless letters and forms with rubber stamps. His not unwelcome wage would be £2 10s for a six-day week.

The teenager made one last effort to escape the clutches of the Civil Service. Returning to the Midlands for the first time since his 1927 departure Hancock spent a weekend with his uncle Cuthbert and aunt Caroline, still living in Southam Road. On the Saturday morning he marched into the offices of Birmingham's evening newspaper and confidently offered his services. 'I had two ambitions at that time,' Hancock confessed. 'One was to be a newspaperman. The other was to go on the stage. I saw myself first as the *Birmingham Evening Mail*'s chief reporter and then, a fortnight later, as one of the leading lights of Fleet Street.' He was politely asked to leave the building.

George Fairweather had not seen Lily Walker since the autumn of 1935. As with most of Jack Hancock's friends, his widow's affair and hurried marriage to Robert Walker had left a sour taste in Fairweather's mouth. It was a busy time for the former postman. Since turning professional Fairweather had earned a good living as an impressionist and variety artist. In 1935 he joined Phil Lester's Good Companions for the company's annual summer season on Boscombe pier and that winter made his first panto appearance as Idle Jack in *Dick Whittington*. Soon after the outbreak of war, Fairweather began singing with the Blue Orpheans, the orchestra engaged to entertain the tea-sipping customers at Beales department store. His nights and weekends were busy producing semi-professional shows for the thousands of civilian evacuees and troops stationed in and around Bournemouth.

Late one afternoon, as Fairweather was completing his final Beales performance of the day, he thought he recognised a woman sitting alone at a table near the restaurant dais. Lily Walker waited until the orchestra was about to leave the stage before waving Fairweather over. 'I don't want to hold a pistol to your head,' Lily told him, 'but Jack was very good to you wasn't he?' Fairweather had to agree, he was genuinely grateful to Jack Hancock. 'Tony seems to have inherited his father's talent. He is dying to have a go.'

Lily confessed she had no idea how good her son was – or could be – only that he was 'crackers' about the stage and had 'set his heart' on becoming a stand-up comic. Hancock knew nothing of his mother's approach: she simply wanted Fairweather to give her son a chance. For the second time in less than five minutes he was forced to agree.

Not only was Hancock already 'having a go', he was working hard at poaching an act. The regulation uniform for any young comic of the day was a trilby hat turned up at the front. Hancock went one better. 'In one respect, at least, I was the equal to one of the top comedians. My brown and white shoes, which cost a week's Civil Service pay, were exactly like Max Miller's,' he recalled. 'And all my spare time I spent studying the popular comedians of the day. I decided to work out an act combining the technique and material of all of them – according to my calculations this would be something really new.' He also carried a pencil and paper. 'Whenever a few people would start with, "I say, have you heard this one?", I would speedily get off another riotous gag to add to my collection.'

Just after Easter, the teenager had landed his first professional engagement. He would appear as supporting act at a smoking concert at Bournemouth's Avon Road Labour Hall. The fee, for two spots, was 10s 6d. 'Make 'em laugh or else,' he was warned. A poster advertising the evening announced: 'Anthony Hancock ... the man who put the "blue" in blue pencil.'

Hancock was a shy, spindly youth, one week away from his sixteenth birthday. He strolled on stage, tripped, and fell flat on his face. The audience roared, which is more than his jokes achieved. 'I gave them the lot,' Hancock admitted, 'but beer was being served throughout the act and the noise of the drinkers and the clinking of glasses, plus the fact that nobody paid any attention, made it all rather difficult.' Just as he reached the crucial point of each joke a voice would shout, 'House order, please ... give the lad a chance,' and drown out the punch line.

The Theatre Royal had opened on 7 December, 1882, built at a cost of £10,000. Its opulent design and plush interior quickly earned it a reputation as the 'prettiest and most comfortable theatre in the South of England'. Despite attracting full houses – all 800 seats were sold for an Oscar Wilde lecture – the Royal closed less than five years later and by 1887 the Albert Road building had been converted to Bournemouth Town Hall. When, in the 1920s, it reopened as a theatre, it immediately regained its place as one of the country's premier venues. With the

outbreak of war, and the end of touring productions, the Theatre
Royal took on a new role as the headquarters of Bournemouth War
Services Organisation. It had also become George Fairweather's
unofficial home.

Most evenings he auditioned and rehearsed amateur and semi-
professional performers for his Fairweather Follies. Two or three times
a week the concert party would stage shows at the Theatre Royal or
travel out to Army camps at Wareham, Dorchester and Blandford.
Because the personnel at the bases, which housed the Army Post
Office and Pay Corps, remained fairly constant the shows were
rewritten weekly to include new artistes.

One summer evening in 1940 Fairweather sat in the third row of the
Royal stalls and watched silently as Tony Hancock – whom he had last
seen as a twelve-year-old – delivered his act.

Hancock fixed his eyes on a spot at the back of the auditorium and
attempted to ignore the distracting buzz of activity from the wings. A
large part of his act consisted of odd odes, a form of humorous poem
invented by the comedian Cyril Fletcher. Hancock had written his
own, spiced up by the addition of off-colour material he considered
obligatory for service audiences. One surviving first verse began:

> He came from the mud flats at Putney,
> His tongue hanging out like a tie,
> From the tip of his toes to the top of his head,
> He must have been fifteen stone high.

Another, which ran for twenty-six verses, ended:

> The force of the bang was horrific,
> Every man was blown out of his shoes,
> And a block of tall flats by the side of the road,
> Caught the blast and were turned into mews.

Each ode was punctuated by two or three smutty schoolboy jokes.

'It wasn't good,' Fairweather still remembers. 'In fact it was bloody awful.'

The 29-year-old Fairweather took Hancock aside and attempted to explain where the teenager was going wrong. 'But people laugh at my jokes,' Hancock protested huffily, explaining that since his Labour Hall debut he had become almost a regular on the ten-bob concert circuit as 'Anthony Hancock . . . The Confidential Comic'.

Fairweather remained unimpressed with the teenager's attempts to copy Tommy Trinder, a stage and radio comic who whispered each joke as if sharing a smutty secret with a friend in the audience. 'You can walk on to a stage in front of a theatre full of troops and shout "arseholes" and they'd laugh,' he said. 'But that wouldn't make you a comedian.'

Despite Hancock's obvious antipathy towards advice, an arrogance Fairweather half admired, he agreed to give the sixteen-year-old a try-out – on condition he tone down his material. Hancock reluctantly agreed. He was still mistakenly convinced that jokes which got the biggest and loudest response were automatically the best. His first appearance at the Royal went well, although not as well as Hancock would have wished, so he decided to slip in one or two dubious one-liners. By his third and fourth performances he was getting more laughs, but losing the sympathy of the audience. They had started to laugh *at* him instead of *with* him.

Fairweather took his protégé aside once more. Of course certain audiences would laugh, but their gut reaction told them the youthful comic could not possibly have 'experienced' his own jokes. Hancock, who remained unconvinced, was only using the raw jokes because he still did not have enough confidence in either himself as a performer or his material. 'I warned you to cut out the blue stuff and you wouldn't,' Fairweather told him. 'You'll have to find out the hard way.'

Lily Walker, although not a Catholic, sometimes attended social events at the Sacred Heart Church in Richmond Hill, not far from the Strouden Road laundry she had once owned with her first husband. Through Lily's friendship with the priest, her son secured a booking in a church hall benefit concert for local servicemen. Tea would be served by Sunday-school teachers and other church members would officiate. The 'Confidential Comic' was booked for two appearances during the evening.

The applause which greeted Hancock as he shuffled on stage was the last anyone would hear that evening. His opening jokes produced a ripple of shock and disapproval from the females. The soldiers were too embarrassed to laugh. Hancock ploughed on. Suddenly there was the scuffing sound of chairs being pushed aside as the audience fled. His final – and bluest – gag was delivered to an empty hall. By the time the bewildered teenager reached the wings the priest was waiting. 'Hancock,' he said, 'I know your parents well, and I'm sure that if they had been here they would have been as disgusted as I am.' He was handed his 12s 6d fee and asked to leave.

Protest was useless. Hancock was transfixed by a large woman bearing down on him. 'We shan't require you again,' she bellowed. 'We want to fumigate the hall.'

According to Hancock's own frequently repeated anecdote the evening went slightly differently. In a newspaper feature almost twenty years later he recalled:

> I strolled on to the stage, leaned over the footlights, and whispered the one about the commercial traveller and the blonde. Three old ladies at the back got up and left to catch an early bus. So I gave them the one about the sergeant and the ATS officer. It should have got something. It did. SILENCE.
>
> The land girl and the farm labourer might have gone down better, if people could have heard it. But too many people with other buses to catch were making too much noise.
>
> Then I threw the bishop and the actress at them in sheer desperation. As the story progressed, the shuffling of feet and the scraping of chairs died away. At last I had them. I

looked round to see the vicar waiting to pay me. Everyone else had gone.

Early next day Hancock sought out George Fairweather but before he was halfway through reading his act he was in tears. 'Tony was in shock,' believes Fairweather. 'He was crying with fear and frustration. He never forgot that experience.' No matter how crude or obscene Hancock's language would become in later years – especially towards women – he swore he would never again crack a dirty joke on stage. It was a promise he made and kept for the rest of his life.

Hancock had, at last, found a theatrical mentor. Encouraged by Fairweather, he dropped his odd odes and replaced them with monologues, delivered this time in the style of Billy Bennett. Most came from his own imagination. One that survives is entitled, 'The Sheriff of Toenail City'. The same Toenail City Hancock patrolled as a toddler sheriff.

> In the township of Toenail City
> Lived the sheriff, a man of good class.
> But he drank like a fish, did the sheriff,
> 'Til his breath burned a hole in the glass.
> But the pride of his life was his moustache –
> It was as famous as Niagara Falls
> And his missus when washing on Fridays
> Used the moustache to hang out the smalls.
> His moustache was so long and whippy
> People spoke of it under their breath –
> And the old-timers said that the sheriff once sneezed
> And it practically flogged him to death.
> But whenever the sheriff was shaving,
> You could see him all covered in gore –
> His whiskers just blunted the razor,
> So he hammered them back in his jaw.

In quieter moments Hancock would question Fairweather about his father. 'What was dad like? . . . What was his act like? . . . Tell me what you thought of him.' For the boy it was a way of visualising the hero and the human in his father. Hancock never stopped asking. Years later – triggered by a familiar phrase or situation – he would continue to probe Fairweather's memory, sometimes by telephone at odd hours of the day or night. 'Tony wanted to know everything,' said Fairweather. 'It was as if going over things again and again somehow brought Jack back to life. He never really got over his father's death.'

1941

HANCOCK DECIDED TO change his job: 'As a Civil Service pen-pusher I was not a success,' he conceded.

Pete Reid, another Bournemouth hotelier and publican who had performed with Jack Hancock during the early 1930s, still owned the resort's Pembroke Hotel. For the second time in a year Lily called in a favour from an old friend. 'I'll fix him up,' said Reid loyally. 'We need a new pot man.'

Lily was doubtful. 'I don't think Tony will be very keen to be a pot man,' she said.

The publican thought for a moment. 'In that case I'll change the title of the job,' he said. 'He'll never know the difference.' The next day Hancock joined the Pembroke's staff as the pub's new domestic manager.

Beneath the clifftop premises were several vast cellars. Part of Hancock's job involved sorting and recrating empty beer and spirit bottles and he found he could disappear for hours among the barrels and crates without Reid noticing. It was also the ideal place to rehearse. The stone walls and ceilings reverberated as the teenager wrote and added lines to his latest monologue.

'One day I gave Tony a job decanting port and sorting the empty bottles,' said Reid. 'I had to go out and completely forgot about him.' To alleviate the boredom Hancock began reciting Shakespeare – 'The potent poison quite o'ercrows my spirit'. For dramatic effect he took a dreg of port.

When the landlord returned there was no sign of his pot man. 'I heard some very weird noises, but no Tony,' said Reid. After a lot of searching he found Hancock slumped behind some empty crates in a haze of port fumes and Hamlet – 'Exeunt, bearing off the dead bodies.'

A few weeks later Hancock came down with a chill. Lily scribbled a hurried telegram and handed it to one of the Durlston Court maids to take to the post office. When it arrived at the Pembroke, Pete Reid was informed: 'Tony has child [sic] – stop – many thanks for all your help.'

Clothes rationing was introduced in Britain on 2 June. Four days later Hancock found himself on a train to Bristol and his first professional radio broadcast. 'My mother always claimed there was a connection,' he commented. 'I never quite worked out what.'

Leslie Bridgmont was a producer on the BBC's Forces Programme who had joined the corporation in the early 1930s. Posted to the West Region, he oversaw a series of dance band broadcasts before moving into studio programmes. In 1940 he devised and produced a satirical revue called *Howdy Folks*. It starred Douglas Young, Nan Kenway, Eric Barker and one of Hancock's future producers, Jacques Brown.

Bridgmont had a reputation as one of the BBC's generic 'eccentrics'. A future head of light entertainment, Edward Taylor, described him as: 'Almost a Dickensian character – his starting points were obscured in the mists of memory although he himself produced extraordinary statements like, "When I was duelling with Baron von Richthofen in the First World War ..." He'd been in the Royal Flying Corps, and he'd presumably been on those dawn patrols, so it's conceivable. At other times he said he trained as a medical student and only the chicanery of the British Medical Council, who couldn't face competition of his calibre, kept him from the top of the profession. If ever we met a friend who had cancer or something like that he'd say, "If only they'd listened to me. I could have put paid to cancer in 1938." His cancer cure was all rather involved but, as he explained it, it all seemed rather clever.'

As a radio producer Bridgmont's biggest success would come in 1944 with *Mediterranean Merry Go Round*, but in 1941 he was still based in Bristol and producing *À La Carte – A Mixed Menu of Light Fare*. It featured 'newcomers', the majority with broadcasting experience. Bridgmont toured the country organising auditions and booking suitable acts, and George Fairweather, a slight acquaintance of the producer, urged Hancock to take part. Together they wrote and polished a monologue entitled, *The Night the Opera Caught Fire*. The BBC man was suitably impressed. A contract, he informed Hancock, would arrive within a few days.

It was the first BBC performance contract – the first contract of any kind – the seventeen-year-old Hancock had seen. He read it, showed it to Fairweather, and then reread the single sheet of paper paragraph by paragraph. One clause stipulated that a copy of an artist's script must be lodged with the producer at least three days before a broadcast. Hancock typed out his script and delivered it to a local printer. By the time it reached Bridgmont it had been set in heavy Gothic type and printed on expensive, stiff paper.

'A typewritten copy would have done,' Bridgmont informed his performer before the broadcast.

'I wish I had known,' Hancock commented. 'Ninety per cent of my fee paid for that script.'

Eighteen years after his father had made his radio debut as 'Jack Hancock (Humorist)' the *Radio Times* billed his son even more succinctly as 'Tony J. Hancock'. Also taking part in the live 11am *À La Carte* broadcast were Compton Evans and Ray Monelle, 'Hubert' and Al Durrant's Swing Quintet.

Meanwhile, Hancock had gained enough experience to join George Fairweather's Black Dominoes concert party. His confidence still needed work. Hancock's debut as a war services performer came at Boscombe Hippodrome where he was billed as compère. As the evening opened Hancock – dressed in a top hat, check tie and his brown and white co-respondent shoes – walked to the centre of the stage, only to be greeted by abject silence. Not a single clap. He retreated to the side curtain and refused to come out, making all his announcements unseen from the wings.

His next appearance was in a concert at an Army base fifteen miles north of Bournemouth and produced quite the opposite effect. Most War Services performances were given from makeshift stages hastily erected in camp canteens and drill halls. The audiences could be anything up to five hundred strong and were always seated in strict rank order, the front row reserved for the commanding officer and his staff and every additional row signifying a corresponding drop in military hierarchy.

Hancock was still insisting on using his 'confidential comic' routine. This time he strutted briskly and cheerily on to the stage. As he leant over the footlights they collapsed, somersaulting him into the CO's lap. Finding himself nose-to-nose with the ruffled colonel, Hancock raised his hat. The hysterical laughter from the audience failed to improve the situation. Clambering back on to the stage the seventeen-year-old suddenly remembered it was an Army concert; turned, saluted, and slipped – this time landing in the officer's wife's lap.

Hancock had long abandoned his collection of risqué pub jokes. He was witnessing and, subconsciously, recording a subtler form of humour. Once again his inspiration was George Fairweather. One act involved Hancock – wearing a raincoat and flat cap and carrying an umbrella – hiding in the audience as a stooge until Fairweather called for a volunteer. When his card trick ended in chaos and confusion Fairweather would turn to the audience and, very slowly and deliberately, comment: 'Isn't it marvellous, three thousand people and I have to pick this one.' It was sheer defeated, put-upon, East Cheam Hancock.

The former postman was also developing his own act, concentrating on impressions of Jimmy Durante, Robb Wilton and Maurice Chevalier. His favourite was the snub-nosed and flat-lipped comedy actor George Arliss. When Fairweather wasn't performing he would be in the back row of a cinema memorising mannerisms and affectations or perfecting each voice under his breath.

Like all performers Fairweather suffered from stage nerves. 'My right leg would twitch whenever I started my act,' he explained. 'To hide it I would lean on my leg to stop it shaking.' Hancock's problem was a little more difficult to solve. With Colin serving in the RAF he had the pick of his older brother's wardrobe. He would invariably choose a suit or jacket that was two sizes too big. While delivering his patter Hancock would unconsciously and continually fidget with the lapel, rubbing the cloth between his thumb and forefinger like a child seeking comfort from a blanket. 'Take that bloody hand away from your collar,' Fairweather would hiss from the wings.

'Tell me what I'm doing wrong,' Hancock would demand after the show.

'You don't know what the hell to do with your hands,' said Fairweather. 'The audience will always watch your hands instead of your face.' He was still reluctant to give advice on the teenager's delivery, believing a performer should always find his own way of working.

'But what do I do with them?' Hancock asked.

Fairweather suggested he keep them thrust into his pockets.

Hancock walked on stage. He gave the audience the confidential wink. Before he could open his mouth they dissolved in laughter. Every joke was a winner. They didn't even wait for the punch line. Amazed at the transformation, Fairweather crept out front to watch his star's next performance. Hancock had followed his advice – only this time his hand was moving suggestively up and down inside his trouser pocket.

Late in 1941, George Fairweather received his call-up papers. He volunteered for the Army and Hancock volunteered to take over as head of Bournemouth War Services Organisation. All went well until his twenty performers emerged into the rain after a Dorset concert party. Two hours later the coach to take them home had still not arrived. Hancock had forgotten to order it. 'Everyone was terribly kind,' he said. 'The next day they asked me to resign.'

1942

PAULINE HANCOCK WAS convinced she would never see her husband again. The sporadic, and usually unannounced, weekend leaves had ended with his overseas posting. Colin Hancock wrote almost daily. Sometimes his letters would arrive five or six at a time; sometimes there would be a week with no letters at all. When Pauline could no longer hide her loneliness Lily Walker was always there with an encouraging word. 'Colin is a sensible lad,' she would tell her daughter-in-law. 'He wouldn't do anything silly.'

When her husband joined the Royal Air Force Pauline had taken over as manager at Durlston Court. Despite the war there was a constant stream of weekend guests, and the influx of relocated civil servants and other government bodies kept the bar and dining-room busy, but, however hard she tried, Pauline couldn't shake herself free from the chilling conviction that she would never celebrate her third wedding anniversary.

At a little after 11.30pm on 1 September, 1942, 24-year-old Pilot Officer Colin Hancock climbed aboard Hudson V-9160 – call-sign V-Victor – and settled himself at his wireless desk in the cabin between the aircraft's wings. Before the routine preflight checks he congratulated the pilot, newly promoted Ian Prescott. Earlier that day Prescott had received confirmation of his promotion from flight-sergeant to pilot officer. Prescott joked that having two on the same aircraft was bad luck. At precisely ten minutes to midnight V-Victor accelerated down the Kaldadarnes runway in Iceland and rose into the cloudless sky. The aircraft, carrying a full pay-load of bombs and depth charges, flew out over the Atlantic. It was never seen again.

The last contact with V-Victor came ninety minutes into the flight. Colin Hancock tapped out a brief Morse-coded weather report as Prescott was swinging his Hudson in a wide curve to port. V-Victor's squadron record card – completed the day of the Hudson's disappearance – carries a single line of explanation: 'Aircraft missing. Cause obscure. No WT indication of trouble.'

It is unlikely Colin Hancock's aircraft was shot down. There were no Luftwaffe patrols operating that far out over the Atlantic. Any contact with a German warship or U-boat would have prompted a pre-attack radio report. The control room at Kaldadarnes heard nothing. No bodies or wreckage were ever found. The only possible solution is a sudden and catastrophic mechanical failure or explosion.*

The Air Ministry telegram was addressed to Mrs Pauline Hancock and had arrived soon after breakfast. Pauline handed it unopened to Lily Walker. As she read the words Lily's face appeared to solidify in a calm acceptance. There was no sign of tears. As she later told a friend, 'Someone had to be strong.' Lily shook her head and handed the telegram back to Pauline. In three lines it told her what she had feared for so long. Pilot Officer Colin Hancock was 'missing presumed dead'.

By some cruel conspiracy of fate, less than a week after the family received news that Colin's aircraft had disappeared over the North Atlantic, Tony's call-up papers were delivered to Durlston Court. By November, three years since Colin's enlistment, Hancock was deemed fit for military service. He, too, volunteered for the Royal Air Force, although his poor eye-sight disqualified him from aircrew training.

A few days later, Hancock's travel warrant arrived. Waiting for his train at Bournemouth station he found himself chatting to another recruit. Slim Miller's conscription papers had arrived on the same day as Hancock's and he had also opted for the RAF Regiment. Like Hancock, he had been posted to RAF Locking, near Weston-super-Mare. To complete the string of coincidences, both men wanted to be professional comedians. 'By the time we reached Romsey, just beyond

---

* Pilot Officer Colin William Hancock has no known grave. He is commemorated by name on Panel 69 of the Royal Air Force Runnymede Memorial, Egham, Surrey.

Southampton, we'd written half a show,' Miller recalled, and was soon to become Hancock's first stage partner.

The prime role of the RAF Regiment is to defend airfields and air bases from enemy attack. New arrivals to its Somerset depot were put through a fourteen-week basic training course designed to produce soldiers rather than airmen. Hancock, who had seen the inside of too many camp and barrack messes in the past two years to be intimidated by snarling NCOs, shared none of his fellow recruits' fear of military discipline.

On the first morning after his arrival, Aircraftman Second Class Anthony John Hancock was ordered to parade. The flight-sergeant walked up and down the ranks, minutely examining every recruit.

'Hancock, stick your chest out,' bawled the sergeant, an inch from the teenager's face.

'I can't,' Hancock shouted back. 'I haven't got a chest.' The threat of a charge was lifted only after a visit to the medical officer confirmed his childhood bout of rickets had left Hancock with a concave chest.

The next day Hancock and Slim Miller were introduced to the joys of bayonet practice. Each recruit was issued with a bayonet attached to a Lee Enfield .303 rifle and ordered to spear straw-filled sacks hanging from a wooden scaffold. Hancock indulged the flight-sergeant with two blood-curdling charges before throwing his rifle to the ground. 'I'm not doing this,' he informed the open-mouthed NCO. 'This is bloody barbaric.'

It was while he was attempting to talk his way out of a charge that Hancock persuaded Locking's commanding officer that his real value to the RAF lay as an entertainer and not a 'soldier'. Hancock was immediately attached to the camp concert party, but too late to escape his first route march.

Wednesday was route march day. Every week the march was lengthened by one mile and, by the end of basic training, each flight of recruits was expected to complete a fifteen-mile trek in full battle order and carrying a rifle and ammunition. 'I did the first mile and realised this was not for me,' said Hancock. The day after his first ordeal the commanding officer's order arrived confirming AC2 Hancock was to have every future Wednesday off for concert party duties. Soon after breakfast Hancock would disappear into nearby Weston-super-Mare on the pretext of collecting props or ordering more make-up, and each afternoon, when the march was over, he and Slim Miller would write and rehearse their double act.

Miller remembers how the pair proved a big attraction in the NAAFI and officers' mess. For some reason the sergeants' mess refused to allow them in. 'We put on revues and were very successful both on camp and in local talent shows,' said Miller. 'We went on as double and single acts and teamed up to write each other's material and share the winnings.'

On the day of the fourteen-mile route march Hancock presented his well-worn and creased chit to the flight-sergeant. For some obscure reason the NCO was grinning mischievously. Unknown to Hancock the concert parties had been abandoned. He was ordered to kit up for the march. 'By this time, the rest of the squad were toughened to it,' recalled Hancock. 'I wasn't. I really don't remember the last few miles. They were agonising. My feet were aflame and I had to be helped in by a couple of friends.'

Hancock smothered his grief for his dead brother by distraction and distance. For Lily Walker there were constant reminders of her dead son; his presence seemed to fill the rooms and corridors of Durlston Court as if all it would take was a supreme act of faith to reunite them.

On a cold and blustery evening just before Christmas, Lily walked up Holdenhurst Road, passing the Railway Hotel and the station until she turned right into Northcote Road. Through the black-out she could see the glimmer of other Woolworth sixpenny torches coming towards her along Windham Road. Inside the house, it smelt of coal dust and damp fires and the entire structure vibrated with each passing train. As each person arrived they were ushered up the wooden stairs to a bare front room. A single, large chair had been placed at one end, and facing it was an ill-matched collection of chairs and stools.

Lily Walker remembered few details of the seance. She received no personal message or contact through the medium. She had come, she later admitted to a friend, 'because of some kind of inner conviction, some feeling that the decision had already been made for her'.

Within a year Lily Walker was convinced that through spiritualism she not only could – but did – communicate with her first husband, Jack Hancock, and her son Colin. She regularly attended meetings in Bournemouth and Portsmouth, where she became friends with Helen Duncan, a twenty-stone mother of six who, it was claimed, had materialised a dead sailor three months before the news of the loss of his ship was released by the Admiralty. Lily, like most of Duncan's followers, was unaware that the Scots-born spiritualist was under Special Branch surveillance. In 1944, Duncan was arrested and charged under the 1735 Witchcraft Act. After a seven-day Old Bailey trial she was sentenced to nine months in Holloway. Her campaigners, including Lily Walker, claimed the charges were nothing more than a crude attempt to gag Duncan in the run-up to the D-Day landings.

1943

BASIC TRAINING WAS over. An officer was calling out a list of postings. Standing side by side in the second row of the parade, Hancock and Slim Miller glanced at each other in disbelief. The pair had been attached to a Canadian Air Force unit and ordered to remuster – in Bournemouth.

The Royal Canadian Air Force had a small photographic interpretation unit stationed in the south-coast resort. As RAF Regiment 'soldiers', part of Hancock and Miller's duties was to guard the detachment's offices and laboratories. To their amazement the pair found themselves billeted at the Metropole, one of Bournemouth's plushest hotels.

Hancock was determined to hang on to the posting for as long as possible. Off duty he could eat at Durlston Court and drink with George Fairweather, by now invalided out of the Army and back in charge of the War Services Organisation – 'Nothing was going to go wrong.' Disaster nearly struck at the first roll-call:

'Sikersky?'

'Check, Lootenant.'

'McLaren?'

'Yeah, Red.'

'Anderson?'

'Here, Buster.'

'Hancock?'

'Present and correct, sir.'

The flight-sergeant gasped in disbelief and then exploded: 'We've got a damn limey who's trying to be funny...'

George Fairweather's latest, and most adventurous, production was a twenty-one-week summer season at the town's Pavilion Theatre, and Hancock was desperate to do an impromptu turn. 'He kept appearing in the wings and pestering me to let him go on,' recalled Fairweather. 'It was a professional show and I had not seen him perform for months.'

Hancock was not only inexperienced he was also short of an act. 'You're always taking the mickey out of my act,' Fairweather told the teenager. 'Why not do my impressions the way an amateur would, you know, make them poor but funny?' It was ham-mimicry at its funniest and provided the backbone of Hancock's stage act until he died. To George Arliss and Robert Newton and Maurice Chevalier he added Ronnie Burrel, a popular animal impressionist – 'and as we go through the farmyard gate we meet Rover ... woof-woof, woof-woof.'

The Bournemouth posting lasted less than two months. Hancock, still with Miller in tow, was ordered to report to a transit office in

Blackpool. A week after their departure the Metropole was destroyed in a bombing raid.

Stranraer was as different from Bournemouth as it was distant in miles. Hancock took one look at the town and dubbed it the 'Paris of west Scotland'. Years later he enlarged on his first impression: 'It's a smash. You can't see a sign of life after five o'clock in the afternoon. Chuck a caber, have a quick dance over the swords, cut your feet to ribbons, and away you go. A marvellous Scottish evening out.'

Hancock's original posting had been to RAF Wig Bay, five miles north of Stranraer on the banks of Loch Ryan. As he was about to clamber down from the lorry which collected him from Stranraer railway station, he was informed his journey was not over. A mile further on, near the village of Kirkcolm, he was delivered alone and confused to the Marine Craft Section.

The camp was little more than a collection of assorted huts and workshops clustered around a tarmac parade ground. Casting a permanent shadow over the choppy water from the far side of the loch entrance were hills with remote names like Mid Morie and Cairnscarrow. It was so cold everyone slept with their boots on. Dressing and washing took seconds. 'All you did when you got up was adjust your tie, and you were dressed,' remembered Hancock. 'Everyone shaved fully dressed. You stood in the ablutions at seven-thirty in the morning singing *The Whiffenpoof Song* in the boots you had been wearing in bed.'

Competing with the biting and incessant wind was the drone of Sunderland and Catalina flying boats landing and taking off from Loch Ryan. It was the job of the Marine Craft Section to provide and service boats to tow the aircraft to their moorings and ferry crews back and forth to the shore.

Hancock's new job was only slightly more interesting than the scenery. The section's latest intake was put in charge of an exclusive one-man unit responsible for camp comfort and staff morale. It also carried a title. On the far side of the parade ground was the boiler house. Next to it was a small hut in which Hancock lived and slept and on the door a white stencilled sign. As 'Fuel Controller' Hancock was responsible for shovelling coke into the boiler and keeping every stove on the camp lit and supplied with coal.

'A whole lot of time, effort and materials could have been saved if only the brass at Whitehall had taken note of my fire-lighting efforts,' Hancock later explained. 'There was none of that fuss and bother with wood and paper and getting the right draught. All you needed was a bit of rag well soaked in paraffin and having selected your fire – leaving the door well open behind you – you tossed it among the coal, threw a lighted match after it, and got out quick. They used to go like a bomb. The only thing was the black stains on the ceilings – that seemed to bother them a bit.'

When he wasn't shovelling coal he was shovelling gravel. One day, soon after Hancock's arrival, he was resurfacing a path outside the administration block with barrowloads of stones. From the corner of his eye he saw the commanding officer watching him from his office. A minute or two later the 'Big Man' arrived.

'Oh, no, no, no, no. That's not the way to do it at all,' he said.

'Oh, really,' said Hancock, tugging at his cap. 'I'm sorry, sir, I thought it was.'

'Oh, no. Look. This is how it should be done,' added the CO, grabbing the shovel and demonstrating the correct technique.

'There you are. Now do you see what I mean, Hancock?'

'Well, I think so, sir, but I wonder whether you would mind just showing me that wrist-flick bit again?'

The CO removed his jacket, loosened his tie and the gravel started to fly once more. 'I still don't quite see it, sir. Sorry if I seem a bit dim.'

To keep the CO's jacket crease-free Hancock – according to his favourite war memoir – had draped it around his shoulders. While the station's senior officer finished the new path Hancock took salutes in his place.

Hancock wasn't the only one leaving Bournemouth. Durlston Court had been requisitioned by the Army Pay Corps and Lily and Robert Walker thought it was time to find a small public house somewhere away from Bournemouth. Hoping this would provide the income she needed to support her youngest son's final years at school and the extravagances of her husband, Lily, now fifty-three, decided to return to the Midlands.

There was a second, and far more pressing reason, for leaving Bournemouth. Since their marriage in 1936, Robert Walker had made little attempt to hide his succession of affairs. At first his status as a local football hero and prominent hotelier had allowed him access to a selection of lofty, yet willing, lovers. As the war progressed his affairs became briefer and more blatant, frequently with female members of staff less than half his age.

Agnes Fairweather – no relation to George Fairweather – was employed briefly as a chambermaid at Durlston Court. She remembers Robert Walker as a 'confident almost cocky man' who still retained the clear skin and healthy appearance of an athlete and looked as though he kept himself fit. His clothes, always well cut, never seemed quite to fit him. 'Almost as soon as I joined the staff I was warned never to be caught in a room alone with Robert Walker,' she recalls. 'He could be a very kind and considerate man, which made him even more attractive to women – and he knew it.'

Lily and Robert Walker took over the tenancy of the Green Dragon public house in the village of Sambourne, five miles south of Redditch. In 1943 Sambourne was little more than a cluster of houses at the confluence of five country lanes. It was also less than fifteen miles from Hall Green where some of Jack Hancock's family still lived.

During leaves Tony would stay at the Green Dragon with his RAF friends and run errands for his mother to the village store and post office. Roger Hancock would also spend his school holidays at Sambourne. 'They were some of the happiest times of the war,' he recalled. To clear their bar slates the local farmers traded vegetables and joints of fresh-killed beef and pork. 'We had never eaten so well,' added Roger.

On a base as isolated as Wig Bay and its Marine Section anyone who remotely called themselves entertainers was in demand for the 'corporal's choir', a band of out-of-tune but eager NAAFI performers.

There was no audition. If you were any good you were in. Hancock adapted his Odd Odes and monologues to service life and became an instant hit.

By December the icy Atlantic winds were sweeping down Loch Ryan. As 'deputy fuel controller' Hancock was always busy. His days were filled with shovelling coal and wheel-barrowing it around the camp to keep the cast-iron stoves blazing. Behind the airfield was a range of mountains. In a slack moment, he joked, I would see if any of the sheep had moved. Anything had to be better than this.

One escape route was a transfer to the Entertainments National Services Association. Hancock applied for leave to attend a London audition and filled his time daydreaming about his release from the RAF and the extra money he would get. Each member of ENSA was paid £10 a week, far more than a lowly aircraftman second class. Just before Christmas his pass and travel warrant arrived. Hancock was on his way to the capital and freedom.

The train south was crammed with off-duty servicemen. For most of the twelve-hour journey Hancock was forced to stand in the corridor or doze wedged upright. At Euston station the magnitude of what he was about to do hit him. His mouth was dry and his stomach was churning.

ENSA had its offices and rehearsal rooms in the Drury Lane Theatre. Hancock, dressed in his RAF battledress, shuffled to the centre of the stage. 'Ladies and gentlemen ...' Fear had clamped his throat. His act – and career – were over. Travelling back to Stranraer he worked himself 'into a terrible rage'. Two days later a postcard arrived informing him ENSA had liked his act and would let him know if they needed him.

Back in his bunkhouse-cum-office Hancock grew 'angry and frustrated and even more determined to escape'. He applied for a second ENSA audition. 'This time, just so the official wouldn't be prejudiced, I entered under the name of Fred Brown.'

'Ladies and ...' Hancock caught the next train back to Scotland.

1944

KEEPING THE ROYAL Air Force entertained was big business. By 1944 there were thirteen all-male variety shows, plus two drawn exclusively from the ranks of the Women's Auxiliary Air Force. The tours, for both men and women, could be long and exhausting. One self-contained company performed in Algiers, Italy and the Middle East before playing to every RAF station in India. It was then flown into the besieged Burmese town of Imphal.

To mastermind its world-wide entertainment operation the Air Ministry drafted in Ralph Reader, a talented theatrical producer. Squadron Leader Reader quickly renamed his unit the RAF Gang Show – after his pre-war scout extravaganzas – and each touring gang show was numbered as it was formed. Situated in London's Houghton Street, the Gang Show headquarters contained a small theatre and it was here that Reader auditioned hundreds of volunteer airmen and women from almost every branch in the Air Force. One was a 'very slight, very thin, very small', nineteen-year-old airman called Tony Hancock.

'I asked him if he had any comedy material,' said Reader. 'He rolled off about a dozen jokes. Apart from one, I hadn't heard any of them before. They were not real jokes, but mostly service situations. This was fine because we wanted all-rounders who could play in sketches.'

Reader had not only produced the pre-war scout shows, he had written the scripts and composed the songs. All the productions re-lied heavily on the squadron leader's *Ging Gang Gooly* brand of chirpiness. Each show opened with the same routine; the entire cast would bounce on to the stage wearing red scarves, grey shirts and trousers and singing *We're Riding Along on the Crest of a Wave*. It was obligatory for every entry and exit to be executed at the double and with a wave.

Hancock was posted to No. 9 Gang Show based at Abingdon in Oxfordshire. Its producer and road manager was a perfectionist flight-sergeant called Fred Stone. 'No matter what he felt personally about anything,' recalled Hancock, 'nothing could interfere with a performance.' Stone would later make his name in the stage version of *The Boy Friend*.

On his twentieth birthday, 12 May, Hancock was ordered to pack his kit-bag. Canteen gossip of an imminent allied landing in France took a nasty turn when rumours began to circulate that his unit had been selected to be the first entertainers to perform in liberated mainland Europe. To unanimous consternation No. 9 Gang Show was loaded on board a troopship. 'It suddenly occurred to us we might be going somewhere where the Germans didn't particularly want us,' said Hancock. As the ship left Portsmouth the gang show members began to unpack. One, Robert Moreton, produced a white dinner jacket – 'in case there was a dance on board'. A week later they were still at sea and, to everyone's relief, heading for North Africa.

Hancock had seen all the films. Any wartime airman worthy of the name smoked a pipe. He decided to abandon his Capstan Full Strength cigarettes and bought himself a cherry-bowl pipe from the ship's NAAFI. It was the perfect night to be an RAF hero, the stars were out and the moon was bright and hopeful. Leaning over the rail Hancock carefully filled his new pipe and took his first manly puff. Suddenly the bowl fell off and into the sea. Hancock stood with the stem clenched in his teeth, hoping no one had noticed.

Once ashore at Algiers the unit attempted to catch up with another invasion force. In January the allies had landed at Anzio in Italy so No. 9 Gang Show bounced and unpacked and performed its way across North Africa. By August, it too had landed in Italy.

Each eleven-man Gang Show was self-contained and self-reliant. Its wicker baskets and trunks were crammed with costumes, make-up and props, its Bedford and Hillman trucks with everything to build and equip a small theatre. For some reason the inventory included metal beds; many years later Hancock still remembered his: 'It got rather bent and lying on it was rather like being stretched out on a rack. Your feet and head were on one level and your middle was about a foot higher.'

Reader, who made a point of visiting each of his units, no matter where they were or how heavy the fighting, caught up with No. 9 Gang Show three miles behind the Italian front line. 'Tony loved what he was doing and was a joy to work with,' Reader recalled many years later. 'He was eager to learn and it showed, you didn't have to tell him twice. In those days Tony didn't worry about anything, he seemed to take everything in his stride.'

No. 9's veteran was a circus clown and variety artist called Jack Fossett and, as the only 'professional', he was frequently asked for advice. One day, as they waited in the wings for their cue, Hancock turned to Fossett: 'I'd love to come into the business after the war.'

'Forget it,' the older man replied. 'Go home and work for your mother.' Undeterred, Hancock then asked Fossett how he could improve his stand-up routine. Fossett's verdict was equally succinct. 'I don't think you could get a living with it.'

1945

VE-DAY WAS still a week away when the No. 9 Gang Show returned to Britain. The next day Hancock was given fourteen days' leave and hitched a lift on an American Air Force lorry the hundred miles from his Oxfordshire depot to his mother's Sambourne public house.

The Green Dragon Inn had become a local attraction for the thousands of US servicemen stationed in the bases south of Birmingham. Not only was Lily Walker a natural and affable publican, she also made a point of employing the prettiest barmaids the area could supply.

Geoff Turner was an engineer whose mother owned and ran the

village store. 'You always knew when Tony was on leave because you could hear him coughing as he made his way across the green,' recalled Turner. 'He would come into the shop every morning to buy a packet of Capstan Full Strength.' The pair soon became friends. Turner found Hancock only too willing to exploit his show-business connections to attract women, and 'like all servicemen he had a fondness for beer. He would always be at the bar in the company of a good-looking young lady – usually a different one every time I saw him.'

While Hancock was enjoying his final days' leave another RAF performer was receiving his new orders. Graham Stark had served with No. 4 Gang Show in North Africa and the Middle and Far East. To his surprise he was called to the Gang Show's Houghton Street headquarters, promoted to sergeant and given his own concert party. With the majority of married airmen awaiting demobilisation, Ralph Reader had been ordered to cut back the shows. Each eleven-man unit would be slimmed down to eight. Stark was ordered to make his way to RAF Abingdon and merge the remnants of No. 9 and his own No. 4 Gang Shows.

Hancock had already returned to camp where his reunited unit was staging nightly shows. Stark watched the performance without announcing his arrival. His attention was immediately drawn to 'this strange shuffling airman' with what seemed to be extraordinary feet. 'He was like a penguin,' Stark remembers. 'One foot pointed to one wing and the other to the opposite wing. He was a bit portly. And he had bizarre hair that was apparently stuck to the top of his head – but Christ he was funny.'

The next morning the show's newly appointed sergeant-cum-producer called a meeting to introduce himself. Act by act he reviewed and reformed the show. Not surprisingly Hancock featured in the majority of sketches, a fact not unnoticed by fellow No. 9 Gang Show performer Robert Moreton who fixed the NCO with a twisted grin and, glancing accusingly back and forth at Stark and Hancock, asked: 'Have you two met before?'

'I've never set eyes on him,' Stark answered.

Moreton sniffed disparagingly. 'Then why is he getting all the material?'

'Because,' Stark informed him, 'he's funny.'

The amalgamated Gang Show set off on one final tour, this time by air. Crammed and strapped into an ageing and war-worn Halifax bomber, the unit landed in Gibraltar and was shown to its overnight billet. The only accommodation available was in a cluster of corrugated-iron huts at the end of the headland's main runway. The night was long and noisy. Every few minutes the group was rattled awake as an aircraft took off inches above their heads.

The stage of Gibraltar's garrison theatre was at the far end of a giant rock cavern. Facing the performers, and disappearing back towards the entrance, were row upon row of seats. The acoustics were almost too perfect: each act was greeted by a rolling wave of cheers and applause as the low, impervious ceiling deflected every sound. For Hancock and Stark it was a memorable experience.

One sketch was called *The Old Officers*. 'We were on stage together and were suddenly hit by this phenomenal wall of noise and laughter,' recalled Stark. The pair 'scented victory and from that moment we gave it everything we could and paralysed the audience. It was a magic night.'

For Flying Officer Frank Ball – better known to post-war audiences as the comedy actor Frank Thornton – there were only two budding stars among the entire Gang Show 'squadron' of three hundred men and women. When his flying operations ended, Ball was put under Ralph Reader's command and based at Houghton Street. One of his first duties was a tour of the surviving Gang Shows.

In Germany, Ball watched No. 10 Gang Show. One member of the unit created an immediate impression. 'I watched this brilliant impersonator who then went on to play the drums. He was quite dazzling,' Ball said. The performer's name was Corporal Peter Sellers.

Another member of the audience who remembered Sellers' performance was Marjorie Smith. 'It was a very slick revue, with female impersonations, sketches and a band that brought the place alive ...

the drummer was a gawky young man with dark wavy hair ... this particular young man obviously had a bit extra. His female impersonations were hilarious and his self-assurance and style ... were nothing short of pure professionalism.'

While in Italy the previous year Ball had watched as another young aircraftman with 'hang-dog pomposity' shuffled on stage. Halfway through his act Hancock stopped and announced, 'That's it, I've had it,' and ambled dejectedly away. 'It brought the house down,' says Ball. 'I remember thinking, "Yes, there is something very, very special there."'

Hancock and Sellers had never met. Their first encounter would come in late 1945 and give Hancock the inspiration for one of his most enduring impressions.

The Gang Show philosophy had changed dramatically. With an end to hostilities it was deemed the troops occupying liberated Europe would no longer be satisfied with traditional all-male concert parties. Squadron Leader Reader was ordered to disband his remaining Gang Show units and audition and produce all-female shows drawn from the Women's Auxiliary Air Force. Hancock – like the props and other paraphernalia – found himself transferred to Light Entertainment based at RAF Uxbridge and was informed he would be working in the wardrobe with another one-time Gang Show corporal.

Hancock reported for duty. From the back of the vast store room he heard first a strangled, dribbling growl and then shrieks of fear. Pushing his way through racks of every conceivable costume he found two young WAAFs cowering on a wicker basket as Peter Sellers dragged himself around in a contorted Jekyll and Hyde impression. 'This was no play acting,' Hancock recalled, 'those girls were terrified. Peter's Mr Hyde was really awful ... the clawed hand, the twisted mouth, the snarling voice. It was very good, but very real.' Within a year Hancock was using the same impression, this time as the *Hunchback of Notre Dame*.

It was a relaxed and informal existence and Hancock and Sellers awaited their demobilisation in a comic air of fantasy. They were allowed to wear civilian clothes. Individual squadrons and air bases were now staging their own improvised concerts and troop shows and allowed to borrow costumes and props from the Light Entertainment central store. As the young airmen and WAAFs arrived to collect the gear they were treated to the limp-wristed banter and outlandish experiences of 'Mr de Sellers' and 'Mr le Hancock'.

In little more than eighteen months Hancock had toured fifteen countries and played to thousands of airmen. He had performed on the backs of lorries, under blown-out buildings, in caves and on rooftops. At twenty-one, Hancock thought he was at last ready for a real crack at show business.

1946

HANCOCK RE-ENTERED CIVILIAN life on 6 November, 1946 – four years to the day after he was called up. 'I went through that demob centre like a typhoon,' he said. 'Suit, hat, shirt, it didn't matter whether they fitted or not. The first things I could get hold of went straight into the cardboard suitcase along with my free bag of sweets. I got out of there as fast as I could.'

Hancock was twenty-two years old. His future consisted of a £60 gratuity, a travel warrant to his home town and a chalk-striped demob suit he dubbed the 'railings'. Waiting for his connection at Waterloo, Hancock began to look around the platform. Standing less than ten yards away and about to board the same Bournemouth train was Slim Miller. They had not seen each other since Blackpool three years earlier.

Lily and Robert Walker had returned to Bournemouth from the Midlands a few months earlier. Hancock informed his mother he wanted to go back to London to try his luck as a professional entertainer. 'For some extraordinary reason my mother thought it would work, she gave me immense support,' Hancock recalled. 'She was clearly very successful at hiding her doubts.' Two days later he was on his way back to the capital with the promise of an allowance until he was earning enough to support himself.

As his train crawled and rocked its way through Clapham Junction and into Waterloo station Hancock looked out across the Albert Embankment and the Thames and, for the first time since his childhood summers at Durlston Court, felt truly alone. There was also a feeling of guilt. Hancock had purposely avoided calling on George Fairweather. 'I wanted to prove I could make it in the business on my own,' he admitted. 'I didn't even tell him I was back.'

His first London home was a room at the British Lion Club in Ebury Street, behind what remained of Victoria Coach Station, and to his delight he discovered Graham Stark had already booked in. Hancock's entire wardrobe consisted of his demob suit, two shirts and a change of underwear. To save money he wore celluloid collars: they were stiff and uncomfortable but had the advantage of looking smart and could be scrubbed clean with soap and cold water.

After two weeks Hancock moved to a cramped room in the Union Jack Club opposite Waterloo Station. He later recalled: 'It was like a cell with a very hard bed. But it meant you had a place for the first time in years where you didn't have to be with other people if you didn't want to. It was luxury unimagined. The only visitors were the police who popped in from time to time to see if you were a deserter.'

The room was so small there wasn't enough space for a wardrobe. To press his 'railings' trousers Hancock would fold them carefully and place them under his mattress. He slept in late and went to bed early, partly because he had nowhere to go, but also to avoid the club's other residents, most of whom were rowdy Royal Navy ratings with a rabid hatred for RAF 'Brylcreem boys'.

During the day Hancock would cross the river and walk with Stark, also intent on a career in show business, to the Nuffield Forces Leave Centre in Adelaide Street, just off the Strand. There they would sit in the lounge drinking and eating the free coffee and sandwiches and making a great show of completing the *Daily Telegraph* crossword.

'Ah yes, here's one,' Hancock would announce licking his pencil. 'C blank T, four-legged animal, feline ... It's not easy, is it?'

When Stark landed a part in repertory Hancock decided it was time he moved out of the Union Jack Club and into a bed-sitter in Baron's Court. 'I set up residence and worked out a plan of campaign, I was going to call on every agent in London.'

Each morning Hancock awoke full of confidence. He would shave and dress and attempt to transform himself into his own image of a successful young comedian. If all the agents in London had their offices within walking distance of Baron's Court, Hancock would have been unstoppable. Unfortunately, but far more logically, most were located in the West End, within walking distance of the theatres and venues they supplied. To get there Hancock was forced to endure a fifteen-minute ride on the Piccadilly Line. 'The boisterous confidence got lost somewhere along the way. The thought of calling on agents, and running through an act, didn't actually terrify me ... it gave me a sort of creeping paralysis.'

As he crossed Leicester Square the cold December air would evaporate what was left of the morning's resolution. 'First I'd need a coffee,' Hancock recalled. 'Then a look at the papers, just to keep in touch. By then it was lunchtime and after that I usually found myself going to the pictures.'

One morning he did muster enough courage to climb a long and gloomy flight of stairs to an agent's office. Hancock could feel his heart thumping and his eyes glaze over with fear. He turned the handle, put his weight on the door and burst in. 'I'm Anthony Hancock, comedian,' he announced. 'I wonder if you've got anything?' The small, stocky man seated behind the desk looked impressed. He rose to greet the young man who, hand outstretched, marched towards him and on to a rug. The rug skidded forward and shot Hancock backwards and out through the open door. The agent returned to his seat and Hancock went to the pictures. Twenty years later, Hancock would be one of Bernard Delfont's biggest stars.

Occasionally Lily Walker would come up to town and treat her son to tea at the Regent Palace Hotel. When no one was looking she would slip a fiver into his hand beneath the table. The next day he would return to his survival diet of baked beans and a very cheap and very heavy sausage which, he was to recall, 'tasted like hell, but if you had a couple of glasses of water each day for about three days following, you were all right. You felt full.'

Hundreds of young men and women had turned their backs on pre-war office and factory jobs. The forces had given them a chance to live out their fantasies and lunacies on makeshift stages across the world, and there was no way they were returning to the mundanities of civilian life. Most had never performed professionally before, and all would need an agent – any agent – to represent them.

Phyllis Rounce graduated from a secretarial school in the late 1930s. Her first job was with the BBC where she was hired as secretary to the chief engineer, with an office in St George's Hall. It was a task she found 'excruciatingly boring'. By the time war had broken out Rounce was working in the corporation's Æolian Hall variety department.

The Blitz made it impossible and unsafe to continue live broadcasting from London. The variety department was transferred to Bristol, where its producers soon discovered there was little suitable studio space, so bombed out and partly-gutted public buildings and churches were turned into makeshift studios and offices. One day the music library received a direct hit. 'It took five of us girls to hold the fire hose,' remembers Rounce. 'The pressure of the water was so strong we kept being flung about.' On another occasion the house next door to her office was hit and she spent two days trapped in the basement before being rescued.

As the Luftwaffe increased its bombing of Bristol Docks and the surrounding warehouses, it became obvious the department would have to move a second time. One stray bomb had already destroyed Rounce's lodgings on the outskirts of the city. This time the BBC sought refuge in Llandudno, with Rounce cycling the twenty miles to work from her digs in Anglesey. Then, in 1940 she volunteered for the Auxiliary Territorial Service and was promptly posted back to the War Office in London.

Because of her experience in entertainment she was ordered to produce a touring variety show to raise cash for the Army Welfare Fund, and began auditions and rehearsals. Most volunteers were soldiers who had been wounded, not badly enough to be invalided out of the service yet too badly to return to the front. A few weeks later she was asked to send half the company to sing at a London church service. One of her male officers wanted to change duties and Rounce agreed. During the service the church was hit by a stick of bombs and everyone inside was killed.

With the company reformed Rounce eventually started the tour of Britain, playing at any theatre still standing. She got as far as Darlington. 'We were performing in front of a lot of po-faced miners,' she said. 'They didn't understand what was happening on the stage and didn't want us there anyway. It was a waste of time.'

That night she telephoned an old friend in the War Office. 'Darling,' Rounce told him, 'I'm cheesed off with this, can I leave the show with my male officer to carry on? I'll come back to London.' She was told they could find nothing for her to do. 'Well, you bloody well better do,' Rounce snarled down the phone. 'I'm coming.' She caught the midnight train south and was waiting on the War Office doorstep when her friend arrived for work the next morning.

Rounce's new boss at the War Office was Colonel Bill Alexander. A First World War artillery officer, 'the Colonel', as he was affectionately known, had spent the 1920s and thirties touring the variety circuit as a stand-up comic. He was recalled in 1940 to help organise troop entertainments, and from a small office overlooking Whitehall the pair auditioned and produced concerts for the thousands of wounded servicemen recuperating in camps and hospitals across Britain. With the war in Europe running down, Rounce made use of the talented, but inexperienced, entertainers who had served in the three services and were now awaiting demob.

Early in 1946, however, Rounce and the Colonel also found themselves unemployed. Central London had been blown apart, first by the Blitz and then, when peace appeared in sight, by German buzz-bombs and V2 rockets. Office space was at a premium. The pair eventually found a first-floor office in what remained of a brothel off Leicester Square. The windows of the Irving Street building had been blown out and shattered floorboards allowed rubble to drop through the floors to the basement. 'We had a fireplace, a few boards on the floor, and walls, and that was it,' recalls Rounce. Their only piece of equipment was a typewriter she had acquired and which had 'Not to be removed from the War Office' stamped on the back. At nine o'clock on 30 January the telephone was reconnected, it was freezing cold and Rounce was sitting on the floor. 'What are we going to do now?' she asked.

'I'm buggered if I know,' replied the Colonel. International Artistes – telephone Whitehall 3046 – was in business. It is still in existence and is one of London's oldest surviving theatrical and variety agencies.

Their first task was to make contact with and sign up demobilised entertainers and talented newcomers. Because of their connections, War Office staff would happily pass on International Artistes' address to returning service personnel and it was not long before the agency had recruited a performing company of its own. Rounce and the Colonel would write, produce and direct variety shows and send them off on showcase tours. When an influenza epidemic decimated the cast Rounce found herself in the chorus line. During her first show she slipped off the stage and into the orchestra pit, landing on top of the drummer and hurling his cymbals into the audience.

From her Irving Street office Phyllis Rounce also called in favours from her days at the BBC. Within four years the agency would acquire an impressive client list and some, with the advent of television, were destined for household stardom. They included Dick Emery, who was to have his own TV show; Miriam Karlin, who starred in *The Rag Trade*; Bill Kerr, Hancock's future antagonist, and Dilys Laye, the future *Carry On* regular.

Another was a straight-backed and immaculately turned-out Army sergeant by the name of Thomas Terry Hoar-Stevens. One of his habits was to wear his beret pulled into a peak at the front which, from a distance, resembled an officer's cap. Hoar-Stevens completed his impersonation by sporting a clipped moustache and speaking in a pinched, upper-crust voice. His 'officer' disguise guaranteed prompt service in restaurants and a ready supply of theatre seats. Fellow NCOs who failed to salute were bawled out and given a dressing-down. Rounce persuaded Hoar-Stevens that if he was going to launch his acting career he would need a snappier, easier to remember name. She suggested Terry-Thomas. The hyphen was her creation. 'I thought of it after looking at the gap between his two front teeth,' she admits.

The days were getting shorter. Hancock's survival fund was getting smaller and, after six weeks, he had failed to find himself an agent, let alone a booking. He dragged himself back to Bournemouth for Christmas. This time he made a point of calling on his pre-war mentor. George Fairweather was shocked by Hancock's physical appearance and waxy, grey pallor: 'He looked ghastly. As a teenager Tony had always been thin, but now he looked half-starved.'

As Hancock sat down for his lunch on Christmas Day, 1946, a passenger-cargo ship was being nudged into its berth at London's Tilbury Dock. It was the end of a storm-battered voyage from South Africa. Leaning on the ship's railing to watch the operation was a craggy-faced actor and his pregnant wife. The man – born thirty-three years earlier in Hancock Street, Johannesburg – was Sid James.

1947

THE SECOND WINTER of peace proved to be one of the coldest for decades. By late January, after a mild, frostless Christmas, the temperature plunged and snow began to fall. For the next two months London, and most of Britain, was paralysed. Hancock – still without work – attempted to keep warm and survive on his mother's allowance, but for another out-of-work actor it was an exhilarating experience.

Bill Kerr was a lanky 23-year-old Australian with a deliberately thick outback accent. He had come to England to launch his acting career and needed an agent. Someone had suggested Phyllis Rounce, so he had telephoned to make an appointment. He was now more than half-an-hour late. For some reason Rounce looked out of the window of her office. It was snowing heavily, and on the pavement opposite a man was lying flat on the white carpet, scooping up handfuls of snow and rubbing it in his face. It was Kerr. He had never seen snow before.

Kerr had arrived in England within days of Sid James and, like James with his wide-boy Cockney image, built his career on an acting falsehood. He grew up in a small New South Wales town called Wagga Wagga – pronounced Wooga Wooga – but, like James, was originally from South Africa. He was the son of show-business parents and was born as they toured the colony in 1924. His theatrical debut came at the age of ten weeks when he appeared on stage with his mother, Olive Roberts.

She relaunched her son's career seven years later when she dressed him in a sailor suit, spats and a silver-mounted cane and had cards printed announcing the arrival of 'Wee Willie Kerr – the Jackie Coogan of Australian vaudeville'. The pair rode into Melbourne in a commercial traveller's car and, after several auditions, 'Wee Willie' opened the next weekend at the Bijou on the same bill as George Wallace. A year later she dyed his dark hair with peroxide of ammonia and stood him in the bright sunshine for two hours to secure his first film part.

Graduating from vaudeville road shows, Kerr became a star performer touring with the Young Australian League, as well as taking part in children's radio shows for the Australian Broadcasting Corporation. When his voice broke, he got a job as a bell-boy at the Mayfair Hotel in Melbourne's Kings Cross.

With the outbreak of war he joined the Air Force reserve and then the Army, touring as a comic to entertain the troops throughout the South Pacific. Once demobbed, there was more vaudeville until he worked his way to England on a cattle boat, arriving with just £5 in his pocket. 'I was just about to pawn my suit,' he recalls, 'when I literally bumped into Joy Nichols who had been instrumental in getting me into *The Youth Show* back home. I auditioned for a show she was in called *Navy Mixture* which got me started.'

A naturally cheerful man, Kerr somehow gave the impression of being a miserable and depressed Aussie, a persona exploited from his first appearance on *Variety Bandbox* when he announced, 'I've only got four minutes.' This was a catch phrase he had first used at the Melbourne Tivoli when forced on stage for four minutes to cover for a failed scenery change.

Hancock had been a civilian for almost five months and had still not earned a penny as a professional entertainer. Then, in February, word spread through the NAAFI Club that Ralph Reader, his Gang Show commanding officer, was recruiting ex-RAF men and women for a variety tour, and thousands trudged through the frozen snow to audition at RAF Uxbridge. Hancock arrived still wearing his chalk-striped demob suit. To his surprise he was promised a place on the *Wings over Homeland* tour, more, he later admitted, through his wartime association with Reader than for any obvious talent.

Reader had complained to the Air Ministry that, despite numerous initiatives to ease former RAF personnel back into civilian employment, nothing was being done for those who had come from show business, or intended making it their career. Senior staff officers of the Air Council, many of whom knew first-hand the benefits of wartime entertainment units, agreed to finance the eighteen-week tour and cover any losses. Variety, particularly ex-service shows, was enjoying an energetic but brief revival. One of the most successful was *Stars in Battledress*, whose cast included Harry Secombe and a one-time Royal Artillery gunner named Spike Milligan on guitar.

The inspiration for Reader's tour was a United States Army show called *This is the Army*. Already famous for his spectacular stage numbers, he had grander motives and vision than a simple variety tour. He wanted to tell the story of the Royal Air Force in twenty-six scenes; from the Wright brothers' first 1903 flight, through the First World War and into the second, to include the Battle of Britain, North Africa and D-Day.

To produce the show he formed his own company, Ralph Reader Ltd, and to write the script he recruited another ex-squadron leader. John Pudsey was a poet and journalist whose verses on 'Johnny' were featured in the 1945 film, *Way to the Stars*. To allow Reader's company to make use of RAF facilities it was officially adopted as the Theatre Pageant Unit.

Overseeing the Air Council's interests and to act as the *Wings* commanding officer the RAF chose Squadron Leader R. A. Hamlin. A lively yet outspoken officer, Hamlin was a genuine Battle of Britain hero credited with shooting down five German aircraft on a single day, a fact Hancock never ceased to mention whenever relatives or friends attended a performance. The CO's attitude did not always meet with Reader's approval. The latter, like his cast, was now a civilian, and the pair clashed over one press interview in which Hamlin is said to have claimed: 'We weeded out the scroungers at the start of the show. They thought they were on a sweet thing, but touring with *Wings* is a seven-days-a-week job.'

Hamlin's forte was logistics, not publicity. Part of his responsibility was to manage the huge operation of shuttling the three-hundred-strong unit, its scenery and equipment around the country in a fleet of RAF coaches and lorries. Each night of the tour the company would sleep at the nearest air base or camp.

One problem was the lack of suitable dressing rooms for the seventy ex-WAAFs in the company. Hamlin arranged for seven of the coaches to be parked as close to the stage doors as possible, so that the female cast members could rush from the stage and out of the theatre to change in their mobile dressing rooms before dashing back for their next scene. To keep the way clear, Hamlin enlisted a dozen RAF policemen and ordered them to arrest anyone who got in the way.

The three hundred ex-RAF men and women – including twenty veteran and experienced performers – descended on Blackpool's Opera

House just as the last winter snows were disappearing. Among them was a 22-year-old Tony Hancock.

Ralph Reader saw his decision to open at the Opera House as a debt repaid, not only for the 770,000 RAF personnel who passed through the resort during the war, but also for the venue's previous fundraising efforts. In 1941 several stars, including Anna Neagle, Frank Randle and The Crazy Gang, performed free during a week-long charity production. The show raised £40,000 for the RAF Benevolent Fund and the theatre's owners, the Tower Company, donated an extra £5,000.

As Lily and Robert Walker settled into the red velvet seats of the Opera House, Lily flicked through the *Wings* programme for her son's name; she had travelled to Blackpool without telling him. Tony Hancock was listed as appearing in three scenes. The first, just before the interval, was a depiction of Blackpool sands, a hard expanse of foreshore used by the RAF as a parade ground and open-air gymnasium. Hancock would play a raw recruit.

'The curtain fell and still no Tony,' Lily recalled. 'Then it went up and he came on singing – which was an even bigger thrill because I didn't know he could.' Tears trickled down her face as she listened to her son proclaim, *I'm A Hero To My Mum*.

> I'm just a nuisance to the Sergeant,
> I don't get any break at all,
> I'm just the feller what peels the spuds,
> I'm at everybody's beck and call.
> I'm just the guy who takes the can back,
> They all think I'm dumb.
> But I don't care tuppence,
> For I know darn well
> I'm a Hero to my mum.

In another scene Hancock, the eternal 'sprog', shuffles across the stage in an outsize and ill-fitting uniform. He is halted by the rasping voice of a warrant officer: 'Where do you think you are?' demands the

NCO. 'Look at your jacket. Look at your trousers. You're a disgrace to the service. How long have you been in the Air Force?'

Hancock pauses: 'All bloody day.'

It was a show which survived largely on patriotism and loyalty. The audience – the majority of which still shared memories of wartime troop shows – forgave its rough edges and blatant jingoism. The national critics, who travelled to Lancashire to watch the opening night with members of the Air Staff, were less tolerant. The *Daily Herald* reported:

> The trumpets sound. Six silver trumpets, their call soaring into the vast Opera House, stirring the blood with half-forgotten memories . . .
>
> That opening, and the last scene of the first half of the three-hour show, were the highlights of the evening. The finale of the first half consisted merely of 250 boys and girls of the RAF, gaily attired, singing a rollicking chorus.
>
> Just that, but with what verve and spirit they sang! What a glorious tribute to the spirit and vitality of young Britain. This was the keynote of the show, and it was grand.
>
> The rest? It is a hotchpotch of very good, not-so-good, and frankly poor. The very good is very good indeed – the scene on Blackpool sands for instance.
>
> The not-so-good are the sketches, a little long and a little futile, although the audience mostly liked them.
>
> The tiresome scene on the troopship, with some risky 'jokes' at which the young people were supposed to laugh and applaud, was out of tune and could well be cut. There is no excuse for questionable 'humour' in a show as good as this.

As the first night ended the entire cast was ordered to muster back stage. The Chief of Air Staff, Marshal of the Royal Air Force Lord Tedder, informed them he 'loved the spirit' in which they had performed: 'One can see that all of you, boys and girls alike, are doing everything you can to put this show across.'

Hancock celebrated his twenty-third birthday on tour. That night the show opened at the New Theatre, Hull. The following week, in Sheffield, he received his first newspaper credit as a professional; the fact he was the last – and thirteenth – performer listed did not go unnoticed by the already superstitious Hancock. Six weeks later the *Manchester Evening News* singled out Hancock and baritone Tony Vaughan as 'two valuable types in this hearty parade' and Ernest Lewis, in the *Guardian*, 'liked the "sprog" of Tony Hancock'.

From Sheffield Hancock telephoned his friend Mary Hobley to see if he could stay with her when the *Wings* company moved first to the Theatre Royal, Birmingham, and then for a second week to the nearby Coventry Hippodrome. Hobley, almost thirty, had first met Hancock before the war in Bournemouth, and during one visit to Durlston Court Lily had given the teenager a present of some jewellery she had made from shells collected during a French holiday.

It was a depressing time. Food, including bread, was still rationed and there were rumours of the weekly allowance being cut still further. Starvation and unemployment filled the newspapers. Each day Hancock would return to Hobley's Coventry home, drained and defeated. 'He was very serious and morose at times,' she recalled; meals would go by without a word between them. One day Hobley asked him why he was looking so sad. 'Because life is sad, isn't it?' Hancock replied.

The *Wings* tour was scheduled to end at the 2,200-seat theatre adjoining Morecambe Winter Gardens early in September, 1947. A week later the company reassembled in London for a Sunday night performance at the Royal Albert Hall, this time billed as the *Royal Air Force Association Festival of Reunion*. Like the rest of the cast, Hancock – who earned £10 a week on tour – donated his fee to the RAFA.

The tour's three August bookings had been at the Palace, Plymouth, the New Theatre, Oxford, and Dudley Hippodrome. It was while at Oxford that Hancock was offered his first 'civilian' booking. Frank

Shelley was directing the Christmas panto at the city's Playhouse Theatre and was already recruiting for *Cinderella*; he was also short of an Ugly Sister. Before the *Wings* tour moved on, Hancock had been offered the part. The panto would begin with a children's matinée on Christmas Day and run until 24 January.

Hancock arrived in Oxford on Christmas Eve and found he could afford to feed himself, but not pay for lodgings. In a newsagent's window opposite the theatre he spotted a neatly written postcard headed: 'Accommodation to let'. The address was a farm a little way out of the university city, and when the farmer offered to show him the room, Hancock discovered it was a caravan in the middle of a field – 'a paint-peeled relic which looked as if it had been abandoned by gypsies'. It was mid-winter and he was homeless; the £1-a-week rent was all Hancock could afford.

The first night he fell into a sound sleep. Around four in the morning – Christmas morning – he awoke with a start. The caravan was swaying and rocking as if it was afloat. Wriggling into a sweater he grabbed a torch and flung open the door – to find himself nose-to-nose with a herd of cows. The buffeting continued for more than an hour. When the farmer and his wife arrived to wish their actor lodger 'Happy Christmas', Hancock complained about his early morning alarm call. 'Them cows allus go round that there van first thing in the morning,' said the farmer. 'Allus have done. They sharpens their 'orns on it.'

Over the next three years Hancock endured a variety of horrors at the hands of theatrical landladies. Ever happy telling a joke, he would repeat his experiences to anyone who would listen. All his stories were delivered in an arms-folded, high-pitched, 'Mrs Cravette' voice: 'I've got some nice bread and margarine and some black pudding and ham and some boiled hake and a nice cup of tea with some more nice bread and marg – and that's just for breakfast.'

On one occasion his landlady presented him with a bill for £4 12s. Hancock produced a post-war white five-pound note. 'Take it out of this,' he said handing it to the woman. She looked at it, handed it back and said: 'We don't take cheques.' In another town he was given a fresh-killed chicken. Returning to his digs Hancock offered it to the landlady and demanded: 'Would you cut this up, mince it and boil it for four hours?'

'Yes,' she said.

'I thought you bloody well would,' said Hancock.

John Moffatt, a fellow ex-serviceman, had been cast as Hancock's ugly sibling. The pair became instant and lasting friends. Moffatt remembers Hancock as 'easy going and a great pleasure to work with' with great good taste: 'He couldn't bear any kind of vulgarity or double-entendre on stage. I played the haughty, pretentious sister and he played the draggle-tail who was always letting me down. So he had great opportunities to be vulgar, but never was.'

In one scene Hancock had to sit on Moffatt's shoulders and together they would lurch down a flight of stairs on to the stage. One night, between Christmas and the New Year, Hancock had the idea of throwing his skirt over Moffatt's head: 'It will look much funnier,' he said reassuringly. Unable to see a thing, Moffatt staggered across the stage, wavered for a few seconds above the footlights and, with Hancock still on his shoulders, plunged into the orchestra pit.

Once again, Hancock's performance earned him critical acclaim. The theatre critic of the *Oxford Mail* commented:

> The superb clowning of the Ugly Sisters is the slapstick of a very high order. They [Tony Hancock and John Moffatt] 'had a bash' at almost everything and if Cinderella isn't black and blue already it is surprising.

Hancock would later irreverently recall his Playhouse season: 'It was a very intellectual panto, three minutes of Latin in the wood scene – which had to go – and people chatting about Nietzsche during the ballroom scene. Lots of philosophical chat. Extremely successful for Oxford.'

One panto tradition was for gifts to be handed over the footlights to the female cast members. Endless bouquets appeared, but nothing for the men. Suddenly two young boys leapt on to the stage and presented Hancock and Moffatt with bouquets made from carrots, onions, cabbages and bottles of Guinness. One of those boys later earned his own reputation in comedy – as Ronnie Barker.

The four months between the end of the *Wings* tour and the Oxford pantomime had been long and empty and desperate. Hancock survived with his mother's help, bolstering his ambition by scraping together enough cash for nights out at the theatre, and on one such trip he found a new comic hero. Sid Field was one of the last and greatest comics to have his roots in the music hall. He was born in Edgbaston, Birmingham – little more than five miles from Hancock's Hall Green birthplace – on April Fool's Day, 1904. At the age of twelve he became one of the 'Fourteen Royal Kino Juveniles' and made his first stage appearance at the Bristol Empire in July, 1916. His fiercely ambitious mother taught him that the quickest way to overcome his stage fright was to take a large swig of whisky so, by the time he was thirteen, and long before he had become addicted to applause, Field was dependent on alcohol.

He had waited almost three decades to be discovered. In 1943, after years of provincial touring, he made his West End debut in *Strike a New Note* at the Prince of Wales Theatre. He was thirty-nine years old.

Although hailed by the press as 'London's new comedy star' Field's *New Note* material was the same as he had used in variety for more than a decade. Presented in rather a camp style it was years ahead of its time and his character studies of the Cockney spiv 'Slasher Green', the 'Cinema Organist', the 'Society Photographer' and the 'Golfing Rabbit' established him as one of the greatest comedians since Dan Leno. *Strike a New Note* was followed by *Strike it Again*, then in 1946 he returned to the Prince of Wales to star in one of the first post-war musical successes, *Piccadilly Hayride*. This was also the year he joined the select band of entertainers invited to take part in the Royal Variety Performance two years in succession.

Hancock and Graham Stark had two reasons for catching one of the final performances of *Piccadilly Hayride*. One was Sid Field's ever-growing reputation. The second was to see a musician they had met while waiting to be demobbed from the RAF, Derek Scott. Within days of leaving the Air Force Scott had secured a job in *Hayride*, appearing with Terry-Thomas, the show's second comedian. Thomas had created his own show hit with his 'Technical Hitch' routine in which he was a disc jockey who, when the studio gramophone fails, does impressions of the records he should be playing. He is frantically accompanied on the piano by Scott.

In another sketch Sid Field appeared as King Richard. Terry-Thomas clanked on to the stage in a suit of armour, the legs of which were perfectly round. As Thomas knelt before the king, Field said: 'You want to get a fourteen-pound hammer and put a crease in those.'

When Hancock had finished laughing he turned to Stark and announced: 'That's the one ... He's the model for me.'

1948

LONDON WAS AWASH with would-be variety artistes: singers, dancers, musicians, ventriloquists, magicians, impressionists and stand-up comics. For more than a year the BBC had fulfilled its promise of giving a hearing to any ex-serviceman or woman who wrote in. The response was overwhelming. To cope the corporation opened its rehearsal rooms from ten in the morning until ten at night, five days a week. In one six-month period just over 6,000 auditions were held. The task of vetting and rating the demob hopefuls was given to a 23-year-old assistant producer – and unofficial head of auditioning – called Dennis Main Wilson. 'The quality was not good,' he recalls. 'Most were no better than village hall turns. You were as kind as you could be and told them to go home.'

*

Dennis Wilson[1] was fifteen when the Second World War broke out. He was born on 1 May, 1924 – eleven days before Tony Hancock – at Dulwich in south London, the son of an engineer. His schoolboy German soon secured him a job with the BBC and in 1941, shortly after his seventeenth birthday, he joined the corporation's European Service. Within a year Wilson was transferred to a unit making satirical propaganda programmes, including a comedy series in German, located in Bavaria. 'That was real alternative comedy,' he later admitted. 'Unlike today's comedy where the only enemy is our own society.'

Wilson's two-year career with the BBC ended when he was conscripted into the Army. After a short course at Sandhurst he was commissioned into the Royal Armoured Corps and, in 1944, took part in the D-Day landings. His war ended in Berlin where his broadcasting experience was enough to earn him a secondment to the Control Commission's propaganda service. Within weeks of his twenty-first birthday, Wilson was appointed head of light entertainment for Nordwestdeutscher Rundfunk in Hamburg where he indulged his talent for off-beat comedy and, surprisingly, broadcast without any form of official censorship.

By 1947 Wilson was back in London and civilian clothes. Bitten by the comedy bug he rejoined the BBC and promptly requested a job with the overworked but highly respected variety department. First, however, he had to find a new name.

Throughout the war the BBC had employed a veteran musician and composer, also named Dennis Wilson and to avoid confusion it was 'suggested' the 23-year-old assistant producer should be the one to change his name. With his tongue firmly in his cheek Wilson inserted the word 'main' between his Christian name and surname and signed in for his first day back at Broadcasting House as Dennis Main Wilson.

His unfailing – and unnerving – gift for spotting promising newcomers attracted as much disapproval from the old-school echelons at the BBC as his enthusiasm and dress code. Small and slim, Main Wilson had a penchant for herringbone waistcoats and his bright blue eyes beamed mischief through his huge spectacles. In Main Wilson's hands, raw and nervous young comics were instilled with endless confidence and bolstered with support. 'We felt that whatever strange noises were coming from the top floor of Broadcasting House, for whatever rule you had broken, Dennis would be there to defend you,' remembered Frankie Howerd.

For Hancock things were getting desperate. It was six weeks since his return from Oxford and 1948 stretched out ahead of him like a black, empty night.

One day late in February, Frank Shelley, the Oxford Playhouse director, was crossing London's Charing Cross Road. The theatre boss watched as a familiar figure appeared to be searching the pavement for stray coins. When Hancock pounced on a penny, almost knocking over a City gent, Shelley decided it was time to intervene. 'If you are as hard up as all that,' he told the obviously starving comedian, 'I can use you in this large-cast play we're doing.' Hancock appeared embarrassed, but wanted to know more. The play, Shelley explained, was Noël Coward's *Peace In Our Time*. For a week at the end of April, Hancock was back at the Oxford Playhouse performing three straight walk-on parts. It was too soon to swap comedy for drama and the audience obviously preferred him as an ugly sister.

For one role Hancock borrowed a pair of rimless bifocal spectacles. As a brutal Nazi officer he had to pick up a glass with a menacing gesture, with Frank Shelley's instruction ringing in his ears – 'This is a most unsympathetic role.' The only problem was that the glasses were as thick as the one he was trying to lift. It took him five attempts to locate the beer glass on the bar.

In another scene he played a drunken German soldier. 'What will you have?' the pub landlord asks him.

'Bitte?' Hancock replies.

'Sorry, bitter's off,' says the landlord, 'you'll have to have mild.' This time it was Hancock who fought back the giggles.

His favourite line, which he never quite managed to deliver with Shakespearean gravity, was: 'Good night, Mrs Shattock.'

By early June, with the last of his Playhouse wages gone, Hancock was out of work and destitute and Derek Scott also found himself on the bread line. After the relative security of *Piccadilly Hayride*, Scott had been forced to give up his flat and move back to his mother's house at 83 Natal Road, New Southgate. Hancock took up residence in the front room.

One night the pair went to a friend's party. Scott played the piano while Hancock went through an improvised sketch and it was a great success. The next day, Scott suggested they should polish the party routine and try it as a double act. Each evening for more than a month the pair would rehearse at Scott's home. Hancock admitted though that he was more interested in the suppers his new partner's mother cooked for them – if the work wasn't there at least they weren't starving.

Soon after his return from Oxford, Hancock had persuaded an agent to take him on. The association had so far proved profitless for both sides. When Hancock and Scott were ready, they performed their act, 'Derek Scott and Hank', for Vivienne Black. It consisted of a series of piano-punctuated sketches in the fashion of a pre-war end-of-the-pier concert party. Black told them it needed more work and sent them away to polish it up. It then took almost two weeks for the agent to find anyone willing to sit through an audition.

The *Revudeville* concept was invented by the owner of the Windmill Theatre, Laura Henderson, and perfected by its manager, Vivian Van Damme. Each numbered production was effectively a non-stop variety show, built around a common theme and featuring sketches, song-and-dance routines and nude tableaux. It was little more than an up-market peep show. Under the Lord Chamberlain's regulations 'theatrical' nudity was allowed – provided the cast remained static, posed 'artistically' in subdued lighting and took up or left their positions unseen by the audience.

Van Damme numbered his *Revudeville* shows sequentially. Each show ran back-to-back six times a day, six days a week. It was a format which gobbled up comics and entertainers and provided a valuable filter bed for stamina and endurance – Peter Sellers had already

completed a six-week stint at the Windmill in *Revudeville No. 211* –
but, as Hancock and Scott already knew, there was no shortage of
takers.

Wednesday morning was traditionally audition day at the Windmill.
When the pair arrived Van Damme – or 'VD' as he was more
commonly known – was watching a jittery young comic called Terry
Scott. 'We sat in the wings watching Terry and knowing he was going
to be booked,' Hancock recalled. 'He was so nervous he went berserk.
That only made him funnier.' However, when Van Damme offered
him a part in *Revudeville No. 214*, opening on 12 July, Scott found he
was already booked for another production. The comedy slot was still
vacant.

There was, however, another young comedy duo waiting to be
auditioned. They were called Johnnie Bartholomew and Ernie Wiseman, and Hancock was horrified to find they were equally funny. Van
Damme booked them and 'we knew our luck was out,' said Hancock.

Derek Scott and Hank went through their routine. When they
finished the theatre's manager called them over. 'Look,' said Van
Damme, 'I'll take you on as well as Bartholomew and Wiseman.
Whichever pair lasts the week I'll book permanently for the rest of the
show.'

The day before *No. 214* was due to open, a Sunday, the impresario
ordered a full dress rehearsal. 'We were awful,' recalled Hancock,
'simply awful.' Van Damme had the disconcerting habit of issuing all
his comments and instructions over the house Tannoy system. 'If you
can't do better than that, you'd better not come back,' he bellowed at
them through the loudspeakers. It was the release Hancock needed.
After working through the night to improve the act the pair returned
the next day, 'feeling we were fired anyway'. From that moment,
things began to get better.

The curtain went up on the first show at 12.15pm. The last ended
just before midnight. By Thursday it was Johnnie Bartholomew and
Ernie Wiseman who began flagging under the strain. At the end of the
week they were out. Not long after, Morecambe-born Johnnie

Bartholomew used his birthplace as a stage-name and Ernie Wiseman shortened his name to Wise.

Morecambe and Wise were not the only ones to lose a Windmill date. One Wednesday morning in August a good-looking, wavy-haired teenager arrived for an audition. The eighteen-year-old's gags and punch lines were far too sophisticated for the Windmill's average audience. 'You're a bit young for such adult patter,' Van Damme told him. 'Wait until the end of the rehearsal and I'll see what I can do with you.' The young comic took a seat to watch the other acts. The next comedian was a shy but waspish man Hancock had first known as a member of his RAF Gang Show. Robert Moreton's act involved reading hilarious stories from his 'bumper fun book'. Laughing loudest was the teenage comic with the grown-up jokes. Van Damme beckoned him over. 'If you find him as funny as that,' he said, 'I'll book him instead of you.' Bob Monkhouse had lost his chance of a Windmill booking.*

The non-stop shows allowed Hancock and Scott to change their style and material almost daily. One gag involved Scott stamping on his partner's toe. By the third day Hancock's foot was bruised and painful, but it was the only routine which regularly raised a laugh. Hancock insisted the gag stay in – no matter how swollen his foot became. By the second week the pair had also fine-tuned their day's work. Each afternoon they arrived at the Windmill at exactly 12.15pm. They were on stage four minutes later.

Hancock was still wearing his one and only demob 'railings' suit – 'I wanted to appear casual' – and when he announced he wanted to buy a second stage suit one of the Windmill's female performers suggested he visit her brother, a spiv tailor with a first-floor fitting room in Greek Street. Despite his protests Hancock was persuaded every off-the-peg suit was made for him. 'Aren't the shoulders too padded?' he protested.

---

* Others who failed a Windmill audition were Roy Castle, Benny Hill, Spike Milligan and the drama critic Kenneth Tynan.

'Oh no, sir,' he was assured. 'You've just got too used to wearing battledress.'

On stage Hancock's new outfit was getting more laughs than the pair's routine. Too embarrassed to wear it, he offered the ill-fitting two-piece to other members of the cast and it was eventually sold – at a loss – to a ventriloquist called Harry Worth.

In 1957, Hancock recounted his Windmill exploits for the *Sunday Dispatch*. He was, by then, a household name and expected to make people laugh. Two stories – which may or may not be true – are worth recording. The first has Hancock helping to repel an armed gang:

> So there was 'Ancock, just winding his way down the backstage stairs when there was a scream and the shattering of glass. A gang of thugs were breaking into the theatre.
>
> The girls clustered in their négligés near the stage door, screamed and ran. Razors flashed in the dim light. I hit out wildly, seeing blood all over the doorman's face, and soon the sound of police whistles was added to the general clamour.
>
> We overpowered the gangsters and drove them out just in time for the cops to round them up into a waiting black Maria. It was like a crazy soap opera.
>
> But do you know the funniest thing of all? The thugs didn't know it was the Windmill and what lovely treasures were almost within their grasp! They were East End louts who didn't know the West End, and they wanted to raid a nearby dance club. Hearing the music at the stage door, they made a tragic mistake.

In the second, Hancock claims to have made the stone-faced Windmill audience laugh. A feat in itself:

> I thought I'd posh myself up for the West End, so I went to a hair stylist and had the full treatment, the full Marcel stuff.

After a bit I looked at myself in the mirror and got a fright.

'Please not too much,' I said. But the barber gave me the freeze and just said: 'Do you mind?'

I came out a shorn lamb. And went straight on the Windmill stage to do my burlesque of the *Hunchback of Notre Dame*. In this act, while Derek played the bells, I had to stagger about the stage, tugging at my hair shouting: 'I can't see ... Where are they ... ?'

With my hair cut I had nothing to tug! The audience could see what had gone wrong and were in fits of laughter. My pianist Derek was in hysterics. They were all laughing except me.

Like most agents and producers Phyllis Rounce always took time to visit the Windmill Theatre: 'There was nowhere else to view the emerging talent. The Windmill played a major part in the rebirth of variety after the war.' She was usually the only woman in the audience. During the summer of 1948 London was hosting the Olympic Games and scores of male foreign athletes would descend on the theatre – 'Night after night the place was packed with Mongolian discus throwers.' Most did not speak English and none understood Hancock's act. Whenever a seat near the stage was vacated the men would fight their way to the front to fill it.

The regular customers, Hancock observed, kept to a blinkered routine and steadfastly ignored the comics: 'If you can survive the Windmill you can survive anything. At twelve fifteen the rows of men in front of you are all reading the racing papers, and don't want to know about you. Go back on stage at two o'clock and it's the same mob. And so they stay there all through the day with their flasks of coffee, sandwiches and magazines. Some of them looking like U-boat commanders with their binoculars around their necks.' Hancock would carry on regardless. After one set Rounce went backstage to introduce herself. 'I had to meet someone who was willing to face a blank wall of disinterested silence day after day and still go back for more,' she told Hancock.

'Well, that lot only came to see Gladys starkers,' he said. 'It's the hardest job in the world getting a laugh out of tired men who've been queuing in the rain since ten-thirty.'

Rounce said she understood, which was true. 'That's why I wanted to talk to you about a contract.'

Hancock and Scott explained they were already signed to Vivienne Black but the agent – whom Hancock remembered as a 'charming thing' – assured him she was willing to wait. She would represent Hancock whenever he felt ready. 'Only then did I discover I had been discovered and that I was talking to the representative of International Artistes,' he recalled. 'The big agents.'

Van Damme had originally offered £25 a week for 'Derek Scott and Hank'. Scott did some rapid calculations. For six shows a day, six days a week, they would be getting seven shillings a performance each. The pair haggled and finally forced Van Damme up to £30. That worked out to 8s 3d a performance. 'I had scraped past the bread line,' said Hancock.

In the late 1940s work was a luxury. Like Milligan, Bentine and Sellers and the other comics who inhabited the Grafton Arms or Daddy Alan's Club behind the Windmill Theatre, this luxury was something you were willing to share. 'After the war there was a very special atmosphere among the young comics and actors,' Hancock explained. 'We all seemed to know each other. Anyone who was working helped the others, even paid for their laundry.' During Hancock and Scott's final week in *Revudeville No. 214* another ex-service comic dropped in to the Windmill in search of possible work. Dick Emery[2] had also served in a Ralph Reader Gang Show and he waited in the steamy and cramped backstage corridor for the pair to come off stage. Hancock was appalled at how awful he looked. When Emery explained he had not eaten for a couple of days, Hancock pressured him into taking a pound note.

The next Wednesday, Emery attended Van Damme's open audition. He was hired on the spot and was on stage by 1pm the same day. Born into a show-business family – his parents had a double act called Callan and Emery – he was so successful he remained at the Windmill for thirty-six weeks, one of the theatre's longest-running comedians.

A few weeks later, Emery was walking down Lisle Street, near Leicester Square, when he spotted Hancock with a brown paper parcel under his arm. He was wearing a long overcoat, but no shirt. Emery asked his friend where he was going.

'I'm going to try and get five shillings for my laundry,' Hancock replied.

Emery, who was earning £12 a week at the Windmill, insisted on repaying Hancock the pound, plus another three pounds to buy food.

In September Derek Scott and Hank played two dates at Churchill's, a cabaret club in London's New Bond Street, and the following month there were one-night bookings at the Brixton Empress and theatres in Chelsea and East Ham. They also made a brief BBC appearance on *Radio Olympia*. 'People were beginning to take notice,' said Scott.

Despite the approach by Phyllis Rounce the pair were still not ready to change agents. It was, after all, Black who had ultimately secured the Windmill booking. A week before they were due to end their slot in *Revudeville No. 214* a letter addressed to Tony Hancock arrived at Black's Conduit Street office. It was from the television booking manager at the BBC who, for some reason, had forgotten to sign it. The letter invited Hancock to a 'preliminary audition' at the Star Sound Studios in Rodmarton Mews, on the corner of Blandford and Baker Streets, at 11.15am on 14 September. It went on:

> This audition will not be held under full television studio conditions, but costume and make-up are obviously desirable though not essential. Dressing room accommodation will be available, and artists who intend to change and/or make up should arrive not less than thirty minutes earlier than the time stated above.
>
> Your performance should not exceed ten minutes in length.
>
> In the event of your performance being considered of

prospective interest to our television programmes, you will be informed in due course of any engagement we are able to offer, or may be asked to attend a further audition, under normal television conditions, at Alexandra Palace.

We wish to make it clear that the BBC does not accept liability for travelling or other expenses which you may incur in connection with any audition(s).

Hancock's nerves went into immediate overdrive. His delight at the approach was tempered by Vivienne Black's advice that he should politely decline the invitation. She even hinted – unaware of Phyllis Rounce's interest in her client – that Hancock should seek alternative representation if he intended establishing a career in television. It was a view not uncommon among the majority of London agents, who distrusted the recently revived medium.

On 1 September, 1939 – during a Mickey Mouse cartoon – the screens of the 5,000 or so television sets receiving BBC programmes in the London area had suddenly gone blank. The Government had feared the transmissions from the Alexandra Palace mast could be used as a homing device by German bombers. Seven years later, on 7 June, 1946, the same Walt Disney cartoon reopened the service and announcer Leslie Mitchell quipped: 'As I was saying before we were so rudely interrupted . . .'

Sales of television sets were now booming, although it wasn't until 1949 that viewers in the Midlands were first able to watch BBC programmes. A year earlier television was seen as solely a London entertainment and thus as a threat to the capital's traditional venues. Most variety agents blacklisted any artist who appeared on television, and the Stoll Theatre banned Ivy Benson and her all-girl band from a BBC television booking.

The BBC letter also informed Hancock that an accompanist would be available, although he was at liberty to bring his own pianist. Hancock, naturally, wanted Derek Scott.

Vivienne Black, by now convinced her clients' future lay in variety and stage work, had secured a week's booking at the Grand Hotel,

Grange-over-Sands, a select establishment overlooking Morecambe Bay. Hancock fretted over the television audition but would not commit himself. By 7 September, however, he could delay the inevitable no longer. With just seven days to go, and badgered by Scott, he was forced to write to the BBC, apologising for the delay in accepting the invitation. Hancock claimed an earlier confirmation, written while he was at the Windmill, had not been posted.

The pair arrived at the Star Sound Studios to find themselves part of a long line of television hopefuls. One was a thin-faced young woman with a high-pitched voice called Pat Coombs, later to appear several times in *Hancock's Half Hour*. 'Both of us were troubled by stage fright and commiserated with each other,' recalls Coombs. Hancock excused himself and went to the toilet to be sick. 'When he came back we wondered why we punished ourselves so much.' Coombs performed her monologue and then stayed to watch Hancock and Scott – 'They were very funny.'

Before the end of September the pair attended a second test, this time at Alexandra Palace, and 'under normal television studio conditions'. Within three weeks Hancock decided he needed a new 'more adventurous' agent and on 18 October signed a five-year contract with International Artistes. He shared Phyllis Rounce's faith in television. Unlike his first agent, she saw an invitation to appear on a thirty-minute television programme called *New to You* as a beginning and not an end. The show was transmitted at three in the afternoon on 1 November, and its producer, Richard Afton, reported the broadcast went well, but made no specific comment on the young comic or his pianist. For their first television engagement Derek Scott and Hank received fourteen guineas.

Elsewhere, two teenagers viewed their futures with an equal mixture of uncertainty and determination. Ray Galton was nineteen and working for the Transport and General Workers Union. He was born and still living in Brixton, south of the Thames. Alan Simpson was a year older and working as a shipping clerk. He, too, was living not far from his Paddington birthplace. Both had contracted tuberculosis, a legacy of the crowded and insanitary living conditions which still existed in many British cities three years after the end of the war, and were not expected to survive. 'In those days TB was a ringing-the-bell job, like the plague,' recalled Galton. Treatment could take as long as three years and patients were invariably admitted to an isolation hospital. Galton and Simpson found themselves in adjacent beds at Milford Sanatorium, a rambling hospital in the Surrey countryside south-west of London.

Another patient was to have an immediate effect on their lives – and ultimately on British comedy for the next two decades. Tony Wallis was a 'radio buff' and a skilled electrician. With the blind-eye approval of the doctors and nurses, and strictly against the rules, he had turned his two-bed cubicle into an engineering workshop, complete with power drills and lathes. One wall was covered by rows and rows of spare parts and tools.

Wearing only his pyjamas and chequered dressing gown Wallis would slide under beds and over the hospital rooftops. When he had finished, every patient had the choice of three radio stations, the BBC's Home Service and Light Programme and the sanatorium's own network. 'Broadcast' from a broom-cupboard studio – yet another Wallis enterprise – the network programmes consisted mainly of records provided by hospital charities interspersed with requests, messages and competitions. A radio committee was formed to try and improve things and Ray Galton and Alan Simpson volunteered. Ambitious new programmes were produced with mixed results. *Saturday Grandstand* provided live reports on inter-staff tennis matches while in *A Seat at the Cinema*, the soundtracks of popular films were given a commentary on the action – 'and Humphrey Bogart has now opened the door and walked across the room . . .'

Surviving the numbing routine of long-term hospital treatment requires an element of obsession bordering on lunacy. For Wallis it was the problems of valves and diodes and how to solve them. Others read – four, five, six books a week. Galton and Simpson lost themselves in comedy. 'We used to listen to everything,' Galton recalled. 'Every comedy programme that was broadcast by the BBC. Then, after lights out, we would switch to another illicit network we had rigged up.' One source of future inspiration came from American half-hour situation comedies like *The Phill Harris Show* and *The Jack Benny Show*. It was a format so far untried by the BBC. Other more obscure listening included *Duffy's Tavern*, *Ozzie and Harriet* and *The Great Gildersleeve*. The source for these after-dark gems was a clumsy ex-RAF 1155 radio screwed to the wall near Wallis's bed. Listening to AFM Munich at two in the morning had its own problem for the teenagers – keeping Wallis awake long enough to switch off the set.

At one radio committee meeting Galton and Simpson agreed to write and broadcast some comedy scripts. 'We undertook to do a series of programmes satirising hospital life,' explained Simpson. 'We agreed to do six, but we dried up after four shows.' As well as experience, the pair desperately needed encouragement; more important they needed advice.

By late 1948 one innovative radio comedy had become a favourite with millions of British listeners. Called *Take It From Here*, and starring Jimmy Edwards and Dick Bentley, it was scripted by Frank Muir and Denis Norden. Their letter, in reply to Galton and Simpson's plea for help, was succinct and accurate: 'Thank you very much for your kind comments, the best thing to do is to send any material you've got to the script editor of the BBC who is Gale Pedrick and is always on the lookout for new writers.'

Phyllis Rounce had yet to earn Hancock a penny in wages. The panto booking season was in full swing and a day or so after his television appearance the agent telephoned her new client to break the news that Hancock would be spending Christmas on the south coast, once again as an ugly sister. Other members of the *Cinderella* cast at Brighton's Dolphin Theatre included the future BBC news reader, Richard Baker and comedian and writer Barry Took.

1949

THE HONEYMOON WAS over. Britain's post-war economy was in decline. As the fourth full year of peace began it was evident British industry had failed to recover from the destruction of war and recession seemed a real possibility.

As wages dropped and inflation rose the British public sought a new kind of escapism. Variety and revue audiences plummeted. For less than sixpence you could be entertained by two films, one inevitably American, be informed by a Pathé newsreel and seduced by Pearl and Dean advertisements. By the end of 1948 more than four million people each week had turned the cinema into a habit. Television, too, was breaking free of its image as an exclusively London entertainment. The network was spreading and sales of television sets – for those who could afford them – were rocketing.

The directors of International Artistes were determined to keep their clients in work. Phyllis Rounce and Bill Alexander intensified the daily round of auditions and calls to producers and impresarios. Hancock, however, was proving a problem. His experience had somehow lost touch with demand. His stage act was at last beginning to improve, but not fast enough to attract the attention of big-money booking agents. Hancock, like so many promising performers, was in a classic *Catch 22* situation. Rounce remembers how, 'We were trying everywhere to get Tony a job and nobody wanted to know.'

'Come back when he is on £600 a week and we'll book him,' was the standard reply.

'Okay, but how do we get him to £600 a week if you won't book him now?'

'Well, that's your worry isn't it?' The telephone would go down or the door would shut.

Bridging the gap between stage and radio was more than a question of experience and exposure. 'His voices were wonderful, magic,' said Rounce. 'He was a natural radio talent, but Tony hated audiences, even the three or four people you get at an audition. To him it was the same as performing in front of a full hall.'

In December, 1948, Rounce had accompanied Hancock to a BBC radio audition. Brian Sears was booking unknown and untried acts for *Variety Bandbox*. 'Tony was awful,' Rounce admits, 'truly awful.' Sears reprimanded the agent for wasting his time, but she refused to give up and pestered the producer into giving her client 'one final try'. Just like his second Windmill audition the previous year Hancock talked himself into believing it was all over and that he had nothing to lose. 'He was still bad,' adds Rounce, 'but I talked Brian into giving him a chance.'

Variety Bandbox was the most successful radio show of its kind. Soon after the war, with cinemas closed on Sundays and no television, it was required listening. When the red studio light went on at 6pm agents and would-be performers joined the show's multi-million audience to hear established stars and destined newcomers.

By 1949 the hour-long show had moved to its new nine o'clock slot. Despite misgivings, Sears gave Hancock his first try-out early in January. The show was broadcast live from the Cambridge Theatre and for everyone involved, and particularly Hancock, it was a disaster. He had written his script himself – 'an awful mistake' – and included his *Hunchback of Notre Dame* impression, poached from Peter Sellers three years earlier. It was hardly suitable material for radio. Worse still, a severe attack of nerves reduced Hancock's delivery to a high-pitched mumble.

George Fairweather was already a *Variety Bandbox* regular. The day before the broadcast Hancock telephoned his Bournemouth friend and asked Fairweather to listen to his act. 'I'm trying out something different,' he said, 'and I want your opinion on it.'

On the Monday, Hancock rang back. Fairweather, who could sense he was bitterly disappointed, decided to be honest. 'I can't make up my mind,' he said. 'I just couldn't see any laughs in it.'

In the autumn of 1940, at the height of the Blitz, the War Office had requisitioned the bombed-out shell of the Café de Paris in Coventry Street. The Nuffield Trust for the Forces of the Crown* financed its reconstruction and the building reopened as the Nuffield Forces Leave Centre, a service club for 'other ranks'. Early in 1943 the centre had moved to Getty's Restaurant, a former cabaret restaurant in Adelaide Street, just off the Strand.

After three years of peace its grubby but still luxurious surroundings continued to provide cheap food and free entertainment for the thousands of troops passing through London. It also provided useful experience for the hundreds of ex-servicemen attempting to break into show business. Much like the BBC, any ex-serviceman or woman was promised an 'audition'. Every Tuesday and Friday night hundreds of men and women sat cross-legged on the vast dance floor watching rough and unpolished acts. Each performance was played on and off by a young pianist called Steve Race, who went on to compère several musical quiz shows for BBC radio. The public verdict could be instant and brutal.

Since 1943, the woman in charge of the twice-weekly shows was Mary Cook. In his book, *Laughter in the Air*, Barry Took – himself a veteran of the Nuffield Centre – recalls: 'Mary Cook had a specially soft spot for these unknowns, helping them through bouts of stage fright and gently advising them on how to improve their material. She didn't think that all her geese were swans, but if she saw someone she believed to be outstanding she would contact the BBC and make sure the newcomer was seen and heard by producers. Michael Bentine, Alfred Marks, Frankie Howerd, Peter Sellers, Harry Secombe and Jimmy Edwards all owe their start in some measure to Mary Cook.'

Aware how tight things could be, living on hope and severance pay, Cook made sure anyone who had the courage to audition was at least well fed. 'For many of us this was the best meal of the day, for some, like myself, it was the only one,' recalled Michael Bentine. 'We were

* 1st Viscount Nuffield; William Richard Morris (1877–1963). English motor magnate and philanthropist. The first British manufacturer to develop the mass production of cheap cars. He used part of his fortune to benefit hospitals, charities and Oxford University.

never paid for our efforts, but there was always coffee and tea and a large pile of sandwiches backstage.'

Hancock, who first made use of the Nuffield with Graham Stark, was reluctant to perform. Cook remembered him as a 'thin, very thin, young man'. Phyllis Rounce and Cook, herself a talented professional pianist, were old friends. Between them they finally persuaded Hancock to overcome his shyness. Rounce would also make sure he was noticed. On 22 February she wrote to Phil Ward at Alexandra Palace:

> Some time ago a comic of ours, Tony Hancock, did a television date for Richard Afton in *New to You*. He worked as a double act with Derek Scott at the piano but he is now working a single act and will be appearing at the Nuffield Centre on the Friday of this week, the 25th. He comes on sometime after 9.30pm.
>
> It is an ideal intimate act for Television as there is a lot of excellent facial expression and miming and the comedy is strong. I do hope you will be able to see him.

As a television producer Ward was already aware of Hancock's potential and forwarded a copy of Rounce's letter to Dennis Main Wilson, radio's unofficial head of auditioning.

At the rear of the one-time restaurant was a balcony; the anonymity of the near-darkness attracted producers, impresarios and agents in search of new talent, and Main Wilson was a regular visitor. It was here the BBC producer first saw performances by Michael Bentine, Harry Secombe and Benny Hill. After watching a run of unimpressive Friday-night acts he was about to leave when the compère announced a thin, awkward young man called Tony Hancock.

'He did a one-man, end of the pier, concert party show,' recalled Main Wilson, much the same act Hancock had peddled with Derek Scott. 'He did the stand-up comedian, the juvenile lead in a ham play, the tenor, the impressionist . . . he did all of them not very well, but he stood out. You sensed there was a tremendous latent talent there.' He noted the young comedian's name but made no attempt to talk to him. Hancock's promise, reasoned the producer, lay in what he lacked as a performer: 'He had no body language from the shoulders down. He would slouch on stage. His entire comedy was from his face and his facial expressions.' It was a unique genius which Main Wilson knew would be hard to place on radio.

Thankfully, there was still the occasional variety booking. In April, Hancock travelled to Blackpool for a week at Feldman's, a small theatre which still specialised in nude tableaux and, like its London counterpart, had remained open throughout the war. When he got there he discovered Harry Secombe was also on the bill. The weather was blustery and grey and the audience promised to be as out of season as the resort.

On the opening night – Monday, 11 April – Secombe was called to the manager's office and informed his wife, Myra, had given birth to their first child. He waited in the wings until Hancock had finished his Gaumont British News impressions, and when he excitedly announced he was the father of a baby girl, Hancock demanded they celebrate. By the time the two comedians emerged from the theatre, however, the other half of Blackpool had closed. The only thing they could find open was a fish and chip shop and, with just twelve shillings between them, all they could afford were two portions of rock salmon and chips and two bottles of Tizer. 'Later,' Secombe remembered, 'we wandered down to the seafront and argued about what we would do with the world now we had fought to save it, leaning over the iron bars of the promenade, looking into the dark sea and seeing only brightness.' It was a period, Secombe recalls in his book *Strawberries and Cheam*, when Hancock was 'pristine and shining with ambition and at the threshold of his career'.

Phyllis Rounce first met Larry Stephens at the Nuffield Club. Stephens was a tall, wavy-haired, healthy-cheeked ex-Royal Marine commando major, with a large dimple in the centre of his chin. Before enlisting he had trained as an accountant, although his first love was comedy. The agent, who saw 'something special in Stephens' mind', suggested he try writing material for Hancock.

The pair were introduced in Rounce's Irving Street office and became instant and close friends. For Hancock the relationship was also founded on admiration. While he was barrowing coal around a Scottish air base, Stephens had been taking part in some of the bloodiest and most vicious Pacific commando raids of the war. He was also a gifted pianist and artist. Above all, Hancock and Stephens shared the same slanted sense of humour; his scripts were invariably illustrated with cartoon characters and illuminated one-liners.

Stephens thought and spoke like a prototype Goon, for whose shows he would later collaborate with Spike Milligan. Both men possessed a distorted and very personal view of humanity. Jimmy Grafton once remarked that: 'Spike looked at the world and decided it was peopled with idiots and therefore he'd create his own parallel world of idiots.' It was a description that equally fitted Stephens.[3] Asked about his ancestry, Stephens would describe his family's stately home: 'In 1883 they built a west wing, the following year they added an east wing and the year after . . . it flew away.'

'Larry and Tony were like brothers,' remembers Milligan. 'They seemed to come from nowhere. They both liked to laugh at the human race and they'd have hysterical laughing bouts. Sometimes they didn't go to bed all night and I'd come in the morning, maybe I was writing something with Larry, and there would be this hysterical laughter and it was hurting their heads to laugh.'

Through the winter of 1949 Hancock and Stephens shared a variety of dog-eared and dingy flats. The pair set up home in a derelict book and magazine warehouse in St Martin's Court, at the bottom of Leicester Square. To reach their room you would go down a narrow corridor, still creaking with war damage, and enter through a trap door. Phyllis Rounce was never allowed beyond this door. To converse with Hancock or Stephens she would sit beside it, the flap would lift an inch or so, and Rounce would get down on her hands and knees and talk through the crack. 'Goodness knows what they got up to inside there,' adds Rounce. 'I couldn't see inside and Tony would only talk to me through the trap – it was almost something Larry would have written.'

A regular visitor who progressed beyond the trap door was Dick Emery. He would take up an invitation for breakfast, usually arriving at the St Martin's Court flat before Hancock or Stephens were out of bed. 'There was never any furniture and Hancock never paid the rent,' remembered Emery.

'What would you like for breakfast?' Hancock would grandly enquire, adding as an afterthought, 'We've only got eggs.' His guest would accept. 'I'm afraid we don't have any bread,' Hancock would add again. 'Never mind we'll boil them hard.' The flat's meagre furnishings did not run to egg cups; they would eat the eggs from folded sheets of newspaper.

Hancock and Stephens changed flats almost on a monthly basis. Between them they would dream up get-rich-quick schemes which invariably went wrong, forcing a midnight change of address. Most of the ideas tottered between legality and imprisonment. One Hancock idea was to start a bookmaking business. His plan was to make enough profit to keep them in alcohol and food until they were earning sufficient as full-time comedian and writer. 'They had to change their address very quickly and very quietly,' recalled Milligan.

Stephens tickled Hancock's funny bone, no matter what he said – or what he did. At one time the pair were living in a flat in Craven Hill Gardens, less than half a mile from Paddington railway station. The telephone rang. It was Milligan. 'It's Larry,' he told Hancock, 'he's been in a car crash and hurt his leg. He had to go to hospital.' There was a muffled thud as Hancock hit the floor, followed by shrieks of hysterical laughter.

'It's serious,' Milligan bellowed down the phone. 'He might have broken his leg.'

When Milligan arrived at the Craven Hill flat Hancock asked what had happened. 'We were just on our way to see you in his car and we had a crash and Larry is in hospital.'

A wide smirk broke across Hancock's face.

'He was reading the *Daily Express* at the time.'

Hancock's knees gave way and he giggled his way to the floor. 'He was laughing so much I thought he was going to die,' remembers Milligan.

B. C. Hilliam – B.C. to his friends and associates – was the 'Flotsam' of a singing and comedy pre-war double act called Flotsam and Jetsam. He was partnered by Australian-born Malcolm McEachern. When, in 1945, his partner died Hilliam – always the creative side of the duo – relaunched his solo career on the radio with *Flotsam's Follies*, a 'weekly musical, lyrical and topical half-hour'.

Hilliam was also cashing in on his success by producing the annual summer show at the Esplanade Concert Hall, Bognor Regis, a popular holiday resort on the Sussex coast. Rounce, who had known Hilliam since her time at the BBC, begged the showman to give Hancock a chance. 'We believe in this fellow,' she said. He eventually gave in and gave Hancock a job at £27 10s a week.

Flotsam's Follies would open a fifteen-week season on 13 June and run until the end of September. Hancock was told to report to the Esplanade Concert Hall early in June with five acts. He was, by his own admission, shackled by a conviction that his comedy had to be 'visual', requiring an inordinate number of props. Of his early years he joked: 'I always found that to get an act on stage with me needed about fifteen flying ballet dancers, seventy-eight trumpeting elephants and anything else a scrounging stage manager could lay his hands on.' For days he and the Colonel worked on devising and rehearsing the new material but, even with Alexander's help, he could only manage four acts. When Hancock arrived in Bognor, Hilliam watched the four acts in silence and excused him the fifth. Also in the cast was Pat Coombs, the young comedienne Hancock had first met and commiserated with at the television audition a year earlier.

By the end of the summer Hancock was left with four polished but unimpressive acts – 'four collections of rubbish really' – so from each he extracted what he considered the best and welded them into a single performance. He then left Sussex for London and unemployment. The best Phyllis Rounce could offer was a Saturday night stand-up engagement at the Victoria Hotel, Sidmouth, but it would, Hancock reasoned, be the first airing for his new routine.

Sidmouth is a Devon holiday resort at the western end of Lyme Bay. To make the all-day journey, Hancock needed to catch a train from Waterloo and change to the Sidmouth branch line at Honiton. The return fare was £2. He borrowed the money from his agent, packed his bag and set off for Devon. This, he told himself, was his big break. To mark the occasion he took a taxi from the station to the seafront hotel.

On the wall beside the reception desk was a large poster, on which was listed the week's cabaret acts, culminating in that Saturday night's attraction. Hancock searched the list of acts in vain. By some disastrous error his name had been omitted. He stood back in disbelief.

'Yes, sir,' said the receptionist. 'Can I help you?'

Silently, Hancock pulled out the letter confirming his booking and handed it to the woman. The receptionist read it, smiled and handed it back. When she pointed to the date, Hancock realised he had arrived one week early.

He dragged himself back to the station. To return to London he would have to change trains at Micheldever, north of Southampton. It would be a long, slow journey. The only money he had left was small change: tuppence ha' penny. By the time he got to Micheldever and his two-hour wait he was ravenous. A porter directed him to a café opposite the station. Chalked on a blackboard was the menu. The only thing he could afford was 'Tea – $2\frac{1}{2}$d'.

London seemed bleaker than ever. Even the prospect of a third winter's work in pantomime failed to ignite Hancock's enthusiasm. This time he was to play Buttons at the Royal Artillery Theatre in the centre of London's Woolwich Garrison. When he was sent a copy of the script his heart sank still further. As Buttons his part involved leading the singing of 'Chick-Chick-Chick-Chick-Chicken ... Lay a little egg for me'. Hancock hated singing – especially to children.

On the first night he bounded onto the stage of the beautiful Georgian theatre to the cheers and jeers of his friends. Dennis Main

Wilson had organised a party to help Hancock with his sing-along. The group included the stand-up comedian Leslie Randall and the actress Miriam Karlin. As Hancock clucked into song his supporters drowned out the audience of mothers and children. Sitting at the end of the row, Main Wilson was tapped on the shoulder by a manager in evening dress and before Hancock had finished the number the entire front row had been ejected for being too rowdy.

1950

ONE NIGHT WHILE Hancock was singing 'Chick-Chick-Chick-Chick-Chicken' at the Royal Artillery Theatre in Woolwich for £35 a week his comic hero was dying.

Since the 1946 opening of *Piccadilly Hayride* Sid Field had made two films, starred in a summer season at Blackpool and appeared in two sell-out shows. However, his alcoholism was taking its toll and 'ill health' forced Field to pull out of one West End production.

His screen debut had come as Wesley Ruggles in the film version of *London Town*. This was followed by Walter Forde's film, *The Cardboard Cavalier*, in which Field played a seventeenth-century equivalent of his 'Slasher Green' character, then in January, 1948, the comedian postponed a third film project to replace Mickey Rooney as top of the bill at the London Palladium.

Field also proved he could be a talented straight actor. On New Year's Day, 1949, he once again opened at the Prince of Wales Theatre, this time as Elwood P. Dowd in Mary Chase's Pulitzer Prize-winning comedy *Harvey*. Field was drinking heavily and by August was so 'exhausted' he had to leave the cast to recuperate on a South African cruise. He returned on Boxing Day. Forty days later, on 3 February,

1950, Sid Field collapsed and died. It was, remembers Hancock's agent Phyllis Rounce, 'the only time I saw Tony in tears'.

By the end of the month – 23 February – Britons were voting in the second General Election since the war. For the first time BBC television broadcast the results live from key constituencies and offered instant analysis from its election studio. It was, Hancock claimed, the night he became an inveterate Labour supporter.

Claridges, one of London's top hotels, was holding an election night ball and Hancock and Derek Scott were asked to provide part of the cabaret. There was no fee. It was, Phyllis Rounce assured her client, a 'prestige event' and worth the 'good exposure'. The guests were in full evening dress and looked as though they were expecting royalty to arrive at any moment. Sometime after midnight Hancock made his entrance – and found himself in direct competition with the toast-master.

As Hancock approached the microphone the red-coated and bemedalled master of ceremonies held up his hand. 'My Lords, Your Excellencies, Ladies and Gentlemen, pray silence for ... Mr Hitch-cock.'

Hancock began with his *Hunchback of Notre Dame* impression. It was met by the incessant chink of champagne glasses and a low, disinterested chatter. Nobody seemed to notice he was there. Bent double and with his shoulder deformed, Hancock was about to drag himself around the stage. 'Nobody loves me ...' The toastmaster's white glove was raised a second time. Hancock froze obediently as four or five results were announced. The white glove waved him on. '... Sanctuary, sanctuary.' The process was repeated each time a seat was declared.

Workers' Playtime was a twice-weekly morale-boosting variety programme transmitted live from a works canteen or social club. Its aim was to take the stars and the shows direct to the people and, although launched during the war, it continued well into the 1960s. Phyllis Rounce had for weeks pestered the show's producer to give her client a chance. When Hancock arrived at the audition, a day or two into the New Year, he was surprised to find Cyril Fletcher sitting in on the session.

Fletcher was famous during the 1930s and forties for his 'odd odes', humorous monologues on a variety of subjects. Hancock had lifted the style – if not the material – for his early comedy routines. Fletcher remembered watching the young comedian and thinking how well his audition had gone: 'It was obvious to me he would one day be a great star.' As Hancock was about to leave Fletcher called him over and reassuringly informed the comic he thought he would 'rarely be out of work'. For his first *Workers' Playtime* appearance Hancock travelled to Coventry to entertain the staff of Messrs Sterling Metals.

Hancock had signed with International Artistes partly because Phyllis Rounce had convinced him his ultimate future lay in television. His first appearance, albeit arranged while he was still contracted to Vivienne Black, had provided useful experience and little else. No sooner had Hancock arrived back from the Midlands than Rounce announced he was about to make the second television broadcast of his career. Hancock, however, still needed convincing of his television potential. 'I was never really satisfied with myself,' he confessed. 'I was never quite sure what was coming over on the screen.'

It was 20 February, 1950, and a bitterly cold morning. Hancock arrived at Alexandra Palace to find one of his fellow performers was another International Artistes client. Dilys Laye was a pretty, thirteen-year-old soubrette who had played the child Trottie in the 1949 film *Trottie True*. Both had been booked to take part in a television show called *Flotsam's Follies*, a television transfer of B. C. Hilliam's successful radio programme of the 1940s. Rehearsals for the six-minutes-and-ten-seconds 'Conjuror' sketch went on intermittently all day. The show itself would be broadcast live that night between nine and ten o'clock. Laye, already an experienced actress, was amazed to find how nervous Hancock was. 'Even during the rehearsals he never stopped shaking,' she said, 'he was so frightened, but I still thought he was wonderful.'

Part of the sketch involved Laye passing Hancock a lollipop.

Desperate to be noticed by this 'very slim and very beautiful' man, Laye waited until they were on air before frantically licking the lolly to make it sticky. 'When I gave it to him it stuck to his hand. He was so nervous he didn't even notice,' she added.

Hancock and Larry Stephens had more or less taken up permanent residence in a flat just round the corner from Covent Garden fruit and vegetable market. The early-morning banter and haggling from the stall holders failed to disturb their irregular hours and even more irregular sleep. By now Stephens had a girlfriend: she was a 21-year-old model called Diana Forster who appeared to forgive the squalor in which her boyfriend lived and the scruffy and manic company he kept – at least enough to agree to marry him.

Early in April, Stephens invited his flat mate to a party. His fiancée's friend, also a model, was celebrating her twentieth birthday with an ice-skating party at a Bayswater rink. Hancock accepted and thought nothing more of it. However, the day after the party he ambled into his agent's office, grinning broadly, and confessed: 'I've just met the woman I want to marry.'

Cicely Romanis, the daughter of a Harley Street surgeon, was a high-cheeked, auburn-haired young woman with a fierce determination to win. 'Even as a child,' recalled a family friend, 'she would set her mind to something and no one, not even her parents, could budge her.' In her mid-teens, and with the war only just won, Cicely had announced she wanted to become a model. Her father thought it a 'shame and a waste', yet within four years his daughter was in constant demand as a fashion and photographic model. She was also the first English model to work for Lanvin in Paris.

Away from the cat walk or studio Cicely was relaxed and sophisticated, but, despite her slim figure, she was physically and mentally strong. Once, to protect herself from the unwanted attention models frequently attract, she took a course in judo. She spoke confidently on a variety of subjects from fast cars to Cordon Bleu cooking, but above all she laughed at almost everything Hancock said. Within days of their first meeting Hancock was introduced to Cicely's parents. Somehow, recalled William Romanis, his daughter's new boyfriend gave the impression he had served in the RAF as an aircrew wireless operator – his dead brother's posting – before transferring to Ralph Reader's Gang Show.

Clacton's pier was unique. It was the only freehold, privately owned pier in the country and watched over by an indomitable elderly woman called Mrs Kingsman. The structure's two theatres were leased each summer season to the theatrical agent and impresario Richard Stone who staged *Ocean Revue*, the resort's summer variety. By 1950 he was producing the pier entertainment and also putting shows into Butlin's holiday camps at Clacton, Pwllheli and Skegness, each of which had to carry four complete changes of programme. The man with the daunting task of auditioning and directing all four productions was a young actor called Ian Carmichael. Hancock, by now growing in confidence, evidently impressed Carmichael and was booked as the *Ocean Revue*'s lead comic.

The revue opened in June at the Jolly Roger Theatre, at the seaward extremity of Mrs Kingsman's domain. It was more of a floral hall without the flora. Each day the structure's matriarch, leaning heavily on her walking stick, would hobble up and down the pier smiling benignly at the holiday makers and scowling at the theatrical intruders. 'It was practically impossible to move, sit down or go to the loo, on Mrs Kingsman's pier without spending money,' Carmichael recalls.

As the season progressed Stone transferred the show to the Ocean Theatre at the pier's entrance. For the performers it was modern and better equipped and less open to the cutting sea breezes. Its disadvantage, as Hancock was soon to discover, was that it adjoined a large open-air swimming pool and a vast figure-of-eight roller-coaster called Steel Stella. The only chance the audience got to hear Hancock's routine was between the rattling swoops of the crowded cars and a lull in the screams and laughter from the swimming pool.

Hancock was working seven days a week. The only chance he had of seeing Cicely was when her modelling schedule allowed her to drive up from London. It was during the early summer, among Clacton's candy floss and whelk stalls and jostling Cockney holiday makers, that Hancock proposed. Cicely immediately agreed because, she later admitted, 'I had faith in him – I knew he was going to be a big star.'

They were so much in love that Cicely agreed to move to Clacton and set up home with Hancock. Within a week he had moved out of his theatrical digs and rented a one-bedroom flat within sound, if not sight, of the seafront. 'For the first few months we didn't have much time for each other,' Hancock recalled, 'about half-an-hour in the morning and the same at night. Cicely kept up her London job and living at our first home, in Clacton, meant rising early. When she arrived back at night I was off to the theatre.'

It was a brave decision which shocked, but did not surprise, Mr Romanis. His daughter's apparent infatuation with a precarious comedian worried him less than her willingness to turn her back on the respectable conventions of the time. Cicely refused to move back to London. There were arguments and threats and guarded reconciliations. Hancock, meanwhile, was beginning to enjoy 'married' life.

Late at night, after he had returned from the Ocean Theatre, or on Sunday mornings when Cicely did not have to leave for town, they sat in bed reading to each other. It was a pleasure they continued for many years. Hancock would close his eyes and lie back on his hands listening to passages from his favourite book, the eternal child romping through the eternal summer of A. A. Milne's *Winnie-the-Pooh*. He would hiss and boo Christopher Robin's arrival; Pooh he regarded as a friend, Eeyore, the slow philosophical donkey, as a hero. One particular story appealed to Hancock – five years hence it might well have been conceived by Galton and Simpson. Eeyore is saving some thistles for a birthday treat but Tigger arrives and eats them. 'He's just come,' says Piglet introducing Tigger to the donkey. Eeyore thinks for a while, then asks, 'When's he going?'

Hancock completed his last performance at the Ocean Theatre on 16 September. It was a Saturday night. The next morning he and Cicely caught an early train back to London. At the station they kissed and parted. Cicely would be staying overnight at her parents' Cornwall

Gardens home while Hancock made his way to Larry Stephens' flat in Cranley Gardens, just off the Brompton Road.

On Monday morning Hancock dressed with only a little more care than usual. He had two engagements that day. One was with his agent. The second was his wedding.

Sometimes, when he had nothing better to do, Hancock would climb the stairs to his agent's office and walk in unannounced. Plonking himself in the armchair opposite her desk he would pull his 'bear coat' over his head and sit motionless in a silent heap of grey wool. 'Tony, what about the scripts?' Rounce would ask after half-an-hour without a word. Hancock grunted. An hour later, sometimes two, she would ask: 'What about some lunch?' Another grunt. Rounce would go out to eat and bring back a snack for her client. A hand would appear to retrieve the offering and she would listen to Hancock chomping his way through his food. Quite suddenly, and for no evident reason, he would pull back his coat, brush himself down, and very shyly and politely say: 'Well, I suppose I had better be going.'

On the rare occasions Hancock arrived at Rounce's office in a talkative mood he would collapse into the armchair like a heavy but playful seal. Their conversations would be bright and animated, with Hancock frequently getting up to talk and walk about the room. Words – the sound of a word – had a magic and infectious effect on Hancock. One was 'Cheam'.

Rounce's mother lived at Cheam, a suburb south-west of London. Whenever it was mentioned Hancock would be overcome by a rising tide of giggles. In Rounce's imagination the floppy playful seal had become a fluffy, white, cartoon rabbit. Hancock, clutching his sides, would slide off the chair or collapse on to his knees. 'Come on Tony, I've got to get to Cheam,' the agent would say. Her client was, by now, on his back kicking his feet in the air. 'What's so funny about Cheam?' It had the same effect as tickling his black and imaginary pads with a giant feather. Hancock spluttered laughter and begged her to stop.

Today, however, Hancock was not in a talkative mood. He lowered himself into the armchair and sank into his overcoat until the collar just hid the top of his head. Beneath his coat he was wearing the trousers from one suit and the jacket from another. As usual he settled down into a comfortable and secure silence. There was no expectation or excitement. Rounce was horrified. Hancock was still wearing his unpolished and comfortable black shoes. Leaping up from her desk she began to drag her client out of the office: 'Tony, we've got to buy you some new shoes. You can't get married in those awful things.'

Hancock protested all the way to the nearest branch of Moss Bros in the Charing Cross Road. Rounce, who had not been invited to the wedding, selected and paid for a pair of shoes while her client hobbled and muttered his way up and down the store. 'I later learnt Tony took his other shoes with him and, before he arrived at the church, put on his old pair and threw the new ones away,' said Rounce. 'So he got married to this gorgeous and beautiful woman, wearing an odd suit and with his old shoes on.'

Hancock arrived at Christ Church, Kensington, in a black London cab. His best man, Larry Stephens, was waiting for him. So, too, were his mother and step-father, Lily and Robert Walker. A few minutes later Cicely stepped out of her father's Rolls-Royce. Later, in the vestry twenty-year-old Cicely Janet Elizabeth Romanis completed the register. She gave her address as 3 Cornwall Gardens, SW7, but made no mention of her profession as a model. Hancock, six years older than his bride, described himself as an 'actor' living at 4 Exeter Grange, Bournemouth. It was his mother's address. A photograph of the couple taken in the church grounds shows an unusually confident Hancock wearing a wide-lapelled, double-breasted dark jacket with a matching close-spotted tie and breast-pocket handkerchief. Looking less at ease, Cicely is wearing a pale suit and broad-brimmed hat and, arm in arm with her husband, is clutching an elbow-length glove.

There was no honeymoon. Cicely was in constant demand and earning considerably more than her husband. That afternoon, less than four hours after her wedding, she was modelling clothes for a West End fashion house. Hancock, once again unemployed, returned alone to their Clacton flat. When his bride stepped off the 6.45pm train he was at the station to meet her. The next morning, while Hancock was still in bed, Cicely left for another London fashion show.

On Wednesday – two days after their own wedding – Mr and Mrs Anthony Hancock returned to London to attend the wedding of his best friend Larry Stephens to Diana Forster. Stephens, by now a full-time comedy scriptwriter, gave his occupation on the Kensington register office licence as 'commercial accountant'. Hancock and Cicely acted as witnesses.

Hancock was away for most of October. Cicely either spent nights at her parents' London home or in her own flat in Clacton while her husband of thirteen days set off for Birmingham, Liverpool, Newcastle and then Scotland. At the end of the month the tour arrived in Glasgow and Hancock eyed Sauchiehall Street's mausoleum-like theatre with trepidation. The Glasgow Empire's reputation as a comedians' graveyard was legendary.

The 'comic-bashing' tradition had originally targeted only Cockney funny-men. As true Cockney comedians became rarer, however, it widened to include any Sassenach with enough courage to try and make the Glaswegians laugh. Stan Jarvis was manager at the Empire Theatre for seven years. Its reputation, he claimed, was no myth. 'Most English comics died there,' said Jarvis. 'Everything you ever heard about the place was justified, and the customers took a great pride in their reputation. It was a brave comic who faced them. We didn't say, "Will we get trouble tonight?" We said: "Where in the house will it be?"'

Hancock received the same treatment as Frankie Howerd had four years earlier. The audience could smell blood and when Hancock's confidence – and jokes – began to flag, the 'screwtaps' started to fly. Being hit with an accurately aimed screw top from a beer bottle was painful and demoralising and he took refuge in the wings as the police moved in to clear a near-riot. At the end of the week, Hancock retreated south to Cicely and out-of-season Clacton.

On Sunday, 12 November, Hancock made his seventh appearance on *Variety Bandbox*. It was his ninth broadcast of the year, his fee throughout being twelve guineas. Four days later Phyllis Rounce wrote to the BBC's variety booking manager, Pat Newman, explaining that working for the corporation was 'not an economic proposition'. Her client, she said, had made his last broadcast at a loss: Larry Stephens had been paid ten guineas for the *Bandbox* script – 'and that was by special arrangement with the writer who usually charges far more' – and Derek Scott four guineas for band parts. Rounce suggested a future fee of at least eighteen guineas.

In reply Newman complained the request was, in effect, a fifty per cent increase. 'But, from the facts that you put forward,' he added, 'I imagine you will feel that anything less is not of much value.' From 1 January, 1951 – two days after Hancock's appearance on Bebe Daniels and Ben Lyon's *Radio Parade* – Newman agreed Hancock should be paid a minimum of eighteen guineas.

Whatever money Hancock had in his pocket he was always willing to share, and one recipient of his generosity was Spike Milligan. Always living on the edge of his nerves, Milligan had recently returned from treatment in a psychiatric hospital. Hancock contacted him, complaining that good comedy scripts had all but dried up and asking the future Goon if he could help. 'I wrote what I thought was a very funny script about Father Christmas,' said Milligan. 'Tony gave me £5 for it. Later I asked him if he ever used it. He said, "No, it was nonsense."'

1951

WILLIAM ROMANIS HAD wanted a respectable and uncomplicated marriage for his headstrong daughter. Now he feared her promising and all too short modelling career was over as Cicely announced she wanted to be with her husband during his three-month pantomime booking. It was not a happy experience.

Little Red Riding Hood opened at Nottingham's Theatre Royal on 23 December, 1950, and ran until the middle of March. The panto's principal girl was a fifteen-year-old by the name of Julie Andrews.

'I was the most miserable bloke in the Midlands,' Hancock recalled. Monday to Friday – and twice on Saturdays – he brooded and moped his way through his part as Jolly Jenkins. 'Every night I felt like walking up to the footlights and having it out with them: "You don't like it and neither do I, believe me. It's too long, anyway. Why don't we call it off and all go home?"'

It was an irksome role which demanded Hancock appear soon after curtain-up to imitate a machine while singing a 'factory' number. Then there would be a gap of ninety minutes before Jolly Jenkins reappeared to lead the audience for a 'mind-numbing' 'pig' song. For this Hancock would take a swig of rum in the wings, followed by five minutes of mutual dislike.

For the first time in their four-month marriage Cicely encountered her husband's moody silences and deep, violent temper. After one particularly frustrating pantomime performance Hancock arrived back at their Nottingham digs, frustrated and itching for an argument. The landlady tolerated the raised voices but when her precious possessions began to fly she was forced to step in.

The monotony was relieved only by a steady stream of *Variety Bandbox* bookings; four during the panto run. Each Sunday Cicely would drive Hancock south, first to Clacton and then on to London for rehearsals and the live evening broadcast. They would drive back to Nottingham, after a night at their Essex flat, in time for the first panto performance of the week.

On 3 May, King George VI officially opened the Festival of Britain. The BBC television contribution – which had commenced a month earlier – included Jack Warner in *Music Hall*, coverage of a cricket match played on a ballroom floor, and a discussion of George Bernard Shaw's new alphabet by I. J. Pitman of the Simplified Spelling Society.

Changes were also made to *Kaleidoscope*, a long-running variety programme, and early in April Hancock replaced the resident comedian Walter Ellis. As *Television Weekly* correctly reported, Hancock had, so far, made only two TV appearances. Less accurately it described him as the 'son of an actor and concert singer'. The show included an on-going comedy sketch, written by Godfrey Harrison, entitled *Fools Rush In*. Hancock played George Knight, a 'sympathetic little character always anxious to do right, but invariably doing the reverse'. It was Hancock's first taste of situation comedy.

In 1951, the BBC employed around three hundred producers in its radio drama, feature and variety departments. So far Hancock had worked with less than a dozen, but one producer was about to change Hancock's career for ever.

Roy Speer's office within the BBC variety department's headquarters was situated in the Æolian Hall, across Chandos Street from Broadcasting House. Hancock arrived clutching the note Phyllis Rounce had typed for him and was shown to Speer's cramped office. The room was made even more claustrophobic by the dance band thumping rhythmically overhead. Between constant interruptions and telephone calls Speer, a short, round-faced man, explained he wanted Hancock to appear in not one, but two, of his forthcoming series. Both were to start within a day of each other that August.

To his fellow variety department producers – and to Dennis Main Wilson in particular – Speer embodied 'the perfect English gentleman' who appeared to thrive on the setbacks and disarray of radio production. Less to his liking were the incomprehensible decisions taken by his superiors. The day before Hancock's meeting, Speer had featured in a newspaper interview explaining his task at the BBC. It is worth reproducing, in part, to explain the behind-the-scenes preparation of an early-1950s radio show:

> Putting a show on the air is rather like doing a complicated jigsaw puzzle, using artistes, writers, musicians, effects people, engineers and studios.
>
> In the case of a major series you will be working months ahead, but for an ordinary weekly spot you will have some six weeks in which to get it ready.

First problem? Your budget. Each producer is given a certain amount to spend on everything for his show. That naturally governs quite a number of things.

If your star comedian, for example, is a top-liner commanding a big fee, you will have to think deeply about the rest of your cast and do some 'shopping'.

At the same time, you are trying to find your ideal script-writers. Then there's the music side. Do you hire a special orchestra, which can be expensive, or use one of the BBC resident bands?

Next problem? Get yourself a studio, both for rehearsals and your show when it goes on the air. The BBC have studios all over London, but there are never enough for all demands.

For several weeks all is confusion, a sort of calm, orderly confusion in which there is much telephoning, 'conferencing', writing of letters and memos.

Most producers have a deadly calm about them at this stage of the proceedings and the most they can manage is a wintry smile or a slight gleam of the eye at something that will no doubt convulse the listening audience on the night.

All these details settled, the show moves into the studio for rehearsal.

By this time most of the tough work is – or should be – done. Though there may be horrible last-minute and unforeseen snags, such as an artiste falling sick or something.

We have a read-through to get people accustomed to their parts, then a run-through on the microphone. That run-through is timed. Then the cutting starts. We may be two or three minutes over.

Again you have to use a certain amount of diplomacy in making your cuts. Artistes naturally don't like their best lines taken out. Then you have to make allowances for the audience reaction: how long they will laugh at the jokes and how often. An average time allowed for audience reaction on a half-hour show is four-and-a-half minutes.

With the script cut and the musical numbers rehearsed and timed while the rest of the cast takes a breather, there comes the final rehearsal, corresponding to the dress rehearsal of the theatre.

For this the producer goes into his producer's 'box', the glass-partitioned cubicle which houses the control panel.

Contrary to some people's belief, the producer is not the man who sits at the control panel during the broadcast. That is a technical job done by a programme engineer. The producer usually sits alongside him. But by that time things are almost out of the producer's hands. All he can do is wait for the steady red light from the control room and the green flash of the cue light into the studio. Then he is on the air – and in your hands!

The BBC variety department was responsible for filling 240 spaces each week across the BBC's various services. A date had already been set for one of Speer's new programmes. It would start on Thursday, 2 August, and be called *Happy-Go-Lucky*. Speer did not like the title and said so but he was overruled. The BBC management was seemingly unaware of a superstition among its production staff that any programme with 'happy' in its title was doomed to failure. For Dennis Main Wilson, who would eventually take over the show from Speer, there was another reason. 'It was a BBC top-floor idea,' he explained, 'and there was a rule that anything that came down from above was doomed. It was far better if ideas came from the floor up.' However, for Ray Galton and Alan Simpson – and to some extent for Hancock – the show did contain an element of luck.

Since their discharge from the Milford Sanatorium, Galton and Simpson had done little serious writing. Alan Simpson returned to office work on a part-time basis and Ray Galton was still too frail to consider employment. For about a year they met socially. 'We'd seen each other all that time, but hadn't thought any more about writing,' recalls Simpson. However, when he was asked to write material for an amateur church concert party Simpson recruited his friend to help. The evening sessions inventing snappy, topical sketches established a working relationship which never changed. Ideas would be 'thrown backwards and forwards'. Only when a line was agreed was it committed to paper. It was – and has always remained – Alan Simpson's job to do the actual writing.

One hand-written sketch – they could not afford a typewriter – was fifteen pages of dialogue inspired by *Take It From Here*. Traditionally the show ended with a satirical skit of a current film. The Galton and Simpson version featured the *African Queen*'s Henry Morgan and was created for Joy Nichols, Dick Bentley and Jimmy Edwards. It was, the pair considered, the best they had done. It was also more than a year since they had received Muir and Norden's advice and it was time to submit something to Gale Pedrick at the BBC.

Alan Simpson remembers the day Pedrick's reply arrived: 'He said they found it very amusing and would we go up and have a chat with him. I came home from work and read this letter and immediately hopped on a bus and rushed over to Ray's, waving the letter. All our friends read the letter. That night we got drunk.'

'It was the most exciting thing that had ever happened to us,' adds Ray Galton. 'We had actually got a letter from the BBC, nothing else, just a letter.'

The would-be scriptwriters arrived at Broadcasting House and found Pedrick 'very kind and helpful'. Although he could not give them any immediate commissions he offered to circulate the sketch to other producers who might want 'odd bits and pieces of material'. One of those producers was Roy Speer.

Derek Roy, another performer who had cut his teeth at the Nuffield Centre, called at Speer's office to discuss the final details for *Happy-Go-Lucky* and saw a copy of Galton and Simpson's *African Queen* sketch on the producer's desk. Before Roy had finished reading the first page he asked Speer to call the young writers in for a meeting.

One manifestation of the 'happy' curse was that Speer had been unable to find suitable writers for the programme. Although he agreed with his star's admiration of Galton and Simpson's material, he felt they were too young and inexperienced to be given a fifty-minute show. Roy suggested the pair write jokes for his solo spot. Each week they could submit a list of jokes and one-liners and he would pay five shillings for each one he used. 'We went home and thought of jokes: my wife jokes, fat jokes, thin jokes, anything jokes,' said Simpson. 'On a good week we would split all of thirty-five shillings – 17s 6d each. Enough to buy a couple of pints, two packets of fish and chips, two tickets for the back row at the pictures and the bus fare home.'

Speer was forced to hire a succession of writers for his thirteen-week series. Two were part-timers whose 'day job' was working on the *Scottish Daily Express*. Another was Laurie Wyman, who later went on to create and write *The Navy Lark*, the BBC's longest-running radio comedy.

Graham Stark was living in a Holland Park basement flat, a situation which, after three years, horrified Hancock. Determined to extricate his friend from his chocolate-brown cellar, Hancock had contacted Roy Speer and persuaded the producer that Stark would make an ideal addition to the *Happy-Go-Lucky* cast. It was Stark's first radio engagement. 'The Gang Show brotherhood continued to look after its own,' he recalled.

The idea for *Happy-Go-Lucky* was conceived by Jim Davidson, assistant head of variety at the BBC. During the war Davidson had been a colonel in charge of the Australian equivalent of ENSA. Although the show was basically a vehicle for Derek Roy – who had never had his own programme before – it also included several self-contained comedy sketches. One of these was *The Eager Beavers* in which Hancock would play Mr Ponsonby the scoutmaster in charge of a troop of unruly scouts, performed by Graham Stark, Bill Kerr and Peter Butterworth.

Stark remembers the show as 'so-so'. The verdict is generous considering the friction among the performers; stand-up studio rows were not uncommon. The cast was constantly at war with the members of the Augmented BBC Orchestra, who found themselves at odds with the programme's singers. Hancock, like everyone else, was unimpressed by the original writers. 'For various reasons the show was getting worse and worse. Actually, for an hour's duration, it was ill-conceived,' recalls Ray Galton, who remains convinced he has 'never come across a show more prone to disaster'.

The first edition of *Happy-Go-Lucky* was broadcast at 9pm on Thursday, 2 August. The next evening Hancock was on air once again, this time in *Educating Archie*, the second of Roy Speer's programmes. For eight weeks Hancock found himself in a rather unique position, not only was he appearing in two programmes on consecutive nights, but the quality of each was very different. As one rose the other sank.

Speer was under sustained and increasing pressure. He was accused of neglecting the new series and lavishing his attention on *Educating Archie*, an established and second-series favourite. It was even suggested he was allowing *Happy-Go-Lucky* to founder as a perverse lesson to management. In reality neither was true. Speer was a conscientious old-school producer who simply found himself stretched too far. At the same time he was falsely accused of taking bribes from agents and found himself at the centre of a corruption inquiry. By the end of October the strain proved too much and Speer collapsed with a nervous breakdown.

By coincidence – and possibly in desperation – Speer decided to use some of Ray Galton and Alan Simpson's material in the tenth and final programme in which he was involved. As newly commissioned 'staff' writers Galton and Simpson were in the studio the following week when the head of light entertainment arrived to deliver a 'stiff upper lip' speech and announce Speer's ill-health departure. 'Okay kids,' he said. 'You've got a turkey on your hands. But you are all troupers and you're going to go out there and knock them dead.' Secretly, the BBC management had already decided to axe the series. The man ordered to keep *Happy-Go-Lucky* afloat, at least for the next three weeks, was Dennis Main Wilson.

Hancock's involvement in the series was also diminishing. He did not appear in two of the later programmes and, although he took part in rehearsals for the penultimate programme, Main Wilson found the *Eager Beaver* sketch so dire it was dropped from the show. The sketch was about being sea-sick – 'Aren't you feeling well?' . . . 'I'm throwing it as far as anyone else aren't I?' The standard of jokes was little better than schoolboy humour. Main Wilson was appalled at what he had inherited: 'Basically it was a load of crap. It couldn't get any worse.' He threw out the final three shows and asked the script editor, Gail Edwards, if she knew of any young writers who deserved a break. Edwards suggested Galton and Simpson.

'Do you think you could write the three remaining shows? The whole thing, except for the scoutmaster sketch,' Main Wilson asked Galton and Simpson.

'We swallowed and said "yes",' recalls Ray Galton. 'We didn't really think we could, but the fee was forty guineas a show, which meant about a hundred and twenty quid and we couldn't turn that down. We went home and worried like mad, but somehow finished the scripts.' On the day their first cheque arrived Alan Simpson resigned his office job and bought a typewriter.

After their initial work for Derek Roy, Galton and Simpson never wrote one-liners. What they produced for Main Wilson was a series of one- and two-minute sketches, each a miniature situation comedy. In one Graham Stark asks Hancock if he can ride a motorcycle. The answer is yes. Stark then persuades a reluctant Hancock to attempt the wall of death, 'dead easy'. The machine roars into life and Stark has a last piece of advice for Hancock – 'Don't look behind you, the lion doesn't like it.'

The final *Happy-Go-Lucky* hour was recorded at the Playhouse Theatre in Lower Regent Street. As the cast and crew were dispersing the writers were standing in the stalls, and walking towards them, intent on leaving the theatre as quickly as possible, was Tony Hancock. The trio had never before exchanged a word, but the show had contained a Galton and Simpson sketch about a children's party and as Hancock passed, he said: 'Did you write that sketch?'

Galton and Simpson nodded.

'Very funny,' Hancock said turning away. 'Very funny.'

A few weeks later, Hancock telephoned and asked Galton and Simpson if they would write single, five-minute sketches he could use on stage and in future variety broadcasts. It was, recalled Ray Galton, 'a thrill to write for him in those days because he was up and coming and we could see he would be an interesting guy to work with'.

Galton and Simpson were at last attracting attention. As script-writers – and still with other professions to fall back on – they were only just managing to keep afloat. On a good week they would earn around £5 each. 'How much do you charge?' asked Hancock. The pair admitted they didn't know. 'I'll tell you what,' he said. 'I'll give you half of my fee.' Hancock's next performance earned him £50.

More importantly the writers had impressed the BBC. Having proved they could produce scripts on demand, they were placed on the corporation's list of staff writers. No new series was forthcoming, so for six months Galton and Simpson wrote five- and ten-minute routines for solo comedians like Dick Emery, Peter Butterworth and Bill Kerr and sketches for various shows, including *Workers' Playtime*.

Educating Archie, the second of Speer's programmes, was a surpris-ingly popular comedy-based variety show starring a wooden ventrilo-quist's doll. In 1930 the BBC had made history when Corum with his doll Jerry became the first ventriloquist to 'appear' on radio. It took another five years before the Columbia Broadcasting System demon-strated that a talking doll could capture equal ratings with CBS's human stars. At one time, the *Edgar Bergen and Charlie McCarthy Show* was America's favourite light entertainment programme. It also had the dubious distinction of being the show during which millions of listeners routinely reached for their dials to avoid the regular singing spot. On 30 October, 1938, they stumbled on Orson Welles' notorious dramatisation of *War of the Worlds* – and panicked.

Inspired by *Charlie McCarthy*, which British listeners had heard during the war, the BBC gave Archie Andrews – the eternal schoolboy – a shot at stardom. Within weeks of its launch in 1950 *Educating Archie* proved one of the most popular and endearing shows on radio and it eventually lasted ten years. The combination of a mischievous, blazer-clad, wooden dummy – unseen by millions yet taking an active part in every broadcast – and Peter Brough's larynx proved irresistible. Archie's falsetto voice was unmistakable. Part of his attraction was that everyone was left to create their own image of the naughty schoolboy. Speer's was of a 'boy in his middle teens, naughty but lovable, rather too grown-up for his years, especially where the ladies are concerned, and distinctly cheeky'. The show's theme song added:

> We'll be *Educating Archie*,
> What a job for anyone.
> He's no good at spelling,
> He hasn't a clue,
> He thinks that three sevens
> Make twenty-two.
> What a problem child is he,
> *Educating Archie*.

Peter Brough was both an astute entertainer and businessman. The son of a music-hall ventriloquist, he owned and ran several woollen mills. By his own admission he was never as good a vent as his father. One *Educating Archie* myth has Brough taking an early tutor – possibly Hancock – aside and asking the actor whether he could see the ventriloquist's lips move. 'Only when Archie's speaking,' he was politely informed.

In the second series, Hancock was to take over as Archie's tutor from his No. 9 Gang Show associate, Robert Moreton, and also double whenever another character was needed. The cast also included Julie Andrews – with whom Hancock had appeared in that winter's panto – Hattie Jacques and Max Bygraves. The writers were Eric Sykes and Sid Colin. It was a prize-winning combination and at the conclusion of the 1950 series the show won an instant National Radio Award.

In his book, *Educating Archie*, Peter Brough reflected: 'We were well aware that our surprise victory had not been too well received in certain quarters. There were those who felt and murmured that the prize should have gone to one of the longer-running comedy shows, and there was acute jealousy that a team of youngsters in age and radio experience should have triumphed. This meant that in our second year the knockers and the critics were ready to pounce at any sign of falling off, either in script or performance, and we had to tread with care.'

The morning Hancock arrived at the studio he was introduced to Brough who invited him to 'come and meet Archie'. The ventriloquist ushered Hancock into his dressing room where he picked up the doll.

'It's good to meet you,' Archie said. 'I want to welcome you to the show. I hope you'll be happy working with us.'

Taken aback by Brough's – and Archie's – apparent conviction, Hancock dutifully shook hands with the dummy and replied: 'Thank you. I hope we all have a successful series.'

'Now,' interrupted Brough, 'I'll take you to meet the rest of the cast.'

Hancock, ever looking for maleficent forces, would be haunted by the three-foot dummy. Between rehearsals and the show Brough would hang Archie from a coat hook on the back of his dressing-room door. Dressed as a schoolboy with its head slumped to one side and its wooden mouth open, the spectacle horrified Hancock and he refused to enter the room alone, claiming Archie 'watched him accusingly, his eyes following him around the room'. At night the sight of the limp dummy coming to life turned his dreams into nightmares. Hancock would wake screaming and drenched in sweat.

Archie's only 'appearance' was in front of the studio audience, for rehearsals the dummy was confined to a suitcase, but Hancock insisted Archie 'attend' every script reading and rehearsal. When the ventriloquist protested Hancock told him: 'I can't make the words live unless he's here.' For Brough it was agony. 'Standing there with my leg up like a stork used to give me gyp,' he explained. 'At that time I had a lot of trouble with varicose veins, but no matter what I said Tony always used to insist. "I can't make it work unless I work to him," he would say. "Now come on, let's do it properly."'

One reason for the radio show's enduring success was Peter Brough's insistence on a continuous injection of new names and voices. Although unique, it was a demand based more on self-preservation than altruism. It did, however, turn gifted but relatively unknown beginners into stars. Future credits would include Harry Secombe, Ronald Shiner, Bernard Miles, James Robertson Justice and Bruce Forsyth. Beryl Reid, recruited by Brough to join a future series as Archie's girlfriend Monica, regarded the ventriloquist as a 'genius'. And added: 'When Peter saw new talent his eyes registered pound signs. Everyone he spotted and had on the show became successful in their own right.'

Hancock had already left *Educating Archie* before Reid's arrival and they never worked together, only meeting briefly in studios or at social functions. When Hancock was not concentrating on looking smart, a state he did not enjoy, he frequently gave the impression of being a distracted intellectual. 'Tony always seemed to be having one of his off days,' Reid remembered, 'with his overcoat buttons done up wrongly or part of his collar or shirt hanging out. He always seemed to be troubled, with his mind on something far more important than what he was supposed to be doing.'

It was while working on *Archie* that Hancock first met Hattie Jacques, who played the over-amorous Agatha Dinglebody. In 1959 she would make the first of her fourteen *Carry On* appearances. A year later she began one of television's most endearing and enduring partnerships when she teamed up with *Educating Archie*-writer Eric Sykes to begin a nineteen-year run in *Sykes*. Jacques – who first came to the listeners' attention as Sophie Tuckshop in Tommy Handley's *ITMA* – was living with fellow actor John le Mesurier. The pair occupied most of the rooms in a rambling Victorian house in Eardley Crescent, Earls Court. 'It was the sort of place that attracted poppers-in,' le Mesurier recalled, 'not least those who felt the need for a little motherly comfort.'

In Jacques' partner, Hancock found a listener and a friend. Le Mesurier was twelve years older than Hancock, had spent most of the war in India and, six years after his return to England, still looked gaunt and tanned. As the autumn wore on Hancock took to arriving alone and unannounced. He came not to see Jacques, but to confide in le Mesurier. 'John was the kind of person you knew would one day be your best friend, perhaps not right away, but one day when you needed him,' confessed Hancock. For Hancock that 'friendship' would include stealing his best friend's wife.

Hancock's apparent success as Archie's tutor was as immediate as it was irritating. Le Mesurier later said: 'It was not a role Tony enjoyed. He had little chance to be funny in his own right and he more and more despised the agent of his humiliation, feeling the dummy was somehow exercising a personal spite.' In his first *Archie* show Sykes and Colin had given the hassled Hancock the throwaway line 'flippin' kids'. The response was enormous. 'Flippin' kids' became a national catch phrase. Even the press took it up.

> Tony ('Flippin' Kids') Hancock shoots to star billing in his
> first outing with the *Archie* team. This man is funny. A slick
> script and smooth production mark this a winter winner as
> usual ... Verdict: Flippin' fine.

By January the following year, BBC research indicated most listeners considered Hancock the show's real star. The *Daily Mail* even nominated him the natural successor to his own hero, Sid Field. While appreciating the attention, Hancock hated the catch phrase. When the *Archie* cast were obliged to meet members of the show's fan club Hancock refused to use it, even though he knew it would get him an instant ovation. 'He loathed it,' recalled one colleague. 'He thought they were crutches that failing comedians used. If you were talented you did not need a crutch.'

If Hancock's most successful comedy character – his East Cheam character – can be traced to a single genesis it is to Sykes's early *Educating Archie* scripts. Sykes was the first writer to exploit Hancock's inner self, his inner psyche. From Sykes's writing emerged the raw material on which Hancock was almost compelled to hone his talent. As Ray Galton explained it, 'Eric's biggest gift was giving Tony an attitude to performing.' For Sykes it was a matter of 'only writing for people you really understand', a philosophy he was rapidly coming to apply to Hancock. 'You have to get to know the man as a friend, it can never be just a business arrangement. Then you start to study them technically, by watching them perform, until you know exactly what they can do and what they can't say. It's the little things you have to pick up – whether they get a laugh best with a line or with just a look.'

Sykes knew exactly how he wanted his lines delivered and, to Hancock's delight, often used fantasy word-pictures to explain. One show included the sound of soldiers marching. The next line was Hancock's: 'All from Russia.'

'How would you like me to say it?' he asked Sykes.

'As if you are tapping the ash off a cigarette,' the writer replied.

Radio relied on the listener unravelling his imagination to produce a mental picture. It was the mirror image of Sykes's creative process. 'I write with a camera in my head. I create comic situations. I don't do jokes,' he explained. The result was both believable and ridiculous. One product of Sykes's imagination has his star stranded on Crewe railway station with a couple of elephants. One escapes to a cinema and sits there blocking the view of the row behind until it is ejected by the manager.

Sykes had been earning £3 in post-war repertory and supplementing his income with stand-up comedy when he wrote to Frankie Howerd offering his services as a scriptwriter. When they met, Howerd was immediately impressed by his approach to humour. 'Most people understand jokes about mothers-in-law, kitchens, sex and lavatories,' Sykes explained. 'But nothing makes people laugh like everyday difficulties.'

With the exception of one or two visits to London, Hancock and Cicely had spent the first two-and-a-half months of the year away from their Clacton home. Then, only six months into their marriage, Hancock announced he would be spending every week from July to December on tour with a variety show.

Getting Hancock the booking had been frustratingly hard work because the usually meticulous Phyllis Rounce had failed to take into account her client's feet.

The booker for the big variety tours of the early 1950s was a formidable woman called Cissy Williams – 'In those days they were tough,' recalled Rounce. 'She wouldn't put up with any messing about' – and Williams insisted that all artistes attending an audition should arrive punctually and in full stage dress.

Rounce and her client reported for the try-out at a theatre not far from Sloane Square. Hancock shambled on stage in a pressed but ill-fitting suit and a pair of down-at-heel, black lace-up shoes: the same shoes he had been married in. Williams made a few notes and listened in silence. When Hancock had finished she turned to Rounce and said: 'If he dresses in those shoes he will not be allowed on stage.'

Hancock was in. His favourite shoes were out. Rounce delayed explaining the unusual condition to his contract until the day before rehearsals: 'Tony couldn't understand the need for all the rules and regulations, and getting him to the shop to buy some new shoes was bloody murder.'

Back at his agent's Irving Street office Hancock tried on his new black leather shoes. They were, he claimed, too tight; they were uncomfortable; they made his feet look too big. He refused to wear the shoes until they were broken in. With less than twenty-four hours before the start of the rehearsals Rounce spent most of the afternoon and evening bending the shoes back and forward in a vain attempt to soften the new leather.

Hancock arrived at the theatre a truculent and sulky schoolboy. He dressed for his 'first day at school', defiantly wearing his old shoes. Rounce pushed him into a chair, pulled off the offending footwear and fitted and tied his new shoes. She kissed him on the cheek and pushed him out the door. She had just taken her seat in the auditorium when Hancock shuffled on stage – wearing his old shoes. 'Miss Rounce,' bellowed Cissy Williams. 'Get him off.'

When Rounce reached the wings Hancock looked miserable. She grabbed him by the ear and physically dragged him back to the dressing room. The new shoes were missing. Hancock claimed he had 'lost' them. 'I can't find them,' he protested. 'I don't know what's happened to them.' The shoes were eventually found on the ledge outside the window. This time Rounce escorted him back to the wings to await his cue.

At the risk of neglecting her other clients, Rounce decided to sit through every rehearsal. Each time Hancock made his entrance he was greeted by a blast from Williams: 'Mr Hancock, will you please go off and put your proper shoes on.' Once Hancock even hid his new shoes in the toilet cistern. Rounce attempted to persuade Williams that 'the new shoes are destroying Tony's marvellous shambling walk'. By Thursday, and with time running out, Williams gave in. Hancock could wear his favourite shoes – as long as he polished them.

For Hancock his old and pliable and down-at-heel shoes had become a security blanket, a childish and childlike talisman. As long as he was allowed to wear them – and forget about his feet – he was capable of concentrating on his performance. 'If I had put him in a proper pair of shoes he would not have had an act,' explained Rounce. 'He couldn't wear ordinary shoes like anybody else. He had to have his terrible old shoes and then he was magic. Without those shoes he was a dead duck. He fumbled and mumbled and nearly blew the whole thing – it was quite extraordinary.'

The tour opened with a week at the Shepherd's Bush Empire. In the audience was the actor Frank Thornton who, as Flying Officer Frank Ball, had spotted Hancock's RAF Gang Show potential. Hancock was dressed in a white dinner jacket and performing an act written by Larry Stephens. Watching the comedian after a gap of six years Thornton was saddened to discover that 'something wasn't quite right'. Hancock, he thought, had 'somehow taken a wrong turning'.

Two weeks later the show moved to the County Theatre, Reading. After one evening performance Hancock arranged to have Cicely waiting in their car outside the stage door with the engine running. She drove at break-neck speed down the A4, back to London in time to attend a midnight Palladium benefit for Sid Field. The Duchess of Kent was escorted by Noël Coward and the star-studded bill was brought to a close by the 81-year-old George Robey singing, *If You Were the*

Only Girl in the World. The show raised £17,000 for Field's widow, Connie, and their children.

The tour was scheduled for three days at the Winter Gardens in Bournemouth in September. Lily and Robert Walker were now the owners of the Talbot Hotel, a little way along the coast at Barton-on-Sea, and to Lily's delight the *Bournemouth Echo* carried a four-inch story on her son's arrival:

> Tony Hancock, here this week in *Music For The Millions*, is a Bournemouth boy.
>
> His father, Mr Jack Hancock – well known in boxing circles – kept the Railway Hotel and later Durlston Court, at Swanage [*sic*], and his stepfather and mother, Mr and Mrs Walker, the Talbot Hotel.
>
> Tony made his first stage appearance in one of Jimmy Richardson's troop shows at the Theatre Royal. His first broadcast was with Jack Leonardi on June 6, 1941, from Bristol – and his next visit to Bristol was on June 6, 1951, for another broadcast.
>
> During the war he was stationed with the RAF at the Metropole Hotel, Bournemouth, just before it was bombed.
>
> Tony is now well on the way up. He is in the radio show *Educating Archie* and in Derek Roy's show *Happy-Go-Lucky*.
>
> Flotsam (B. C. Hilliam), who was also in Bournemouth this week, gave him his professional start in *Flotsam's Follies*.

*

Cicely remembered 1951 as a 'year when Tony was always travelling'. It was a feature of her husband's professional life which appears to have left her unmoved and unconcerned. She was equally resigned to her husband's cavalier attitude towards their marriage and her own welfare. By coincidence the Bournemouth booking also spanned the couple's first wedding anniversary on 18 September, a fact Hancock had obviously overlooked. On the Wednesday night before his departure Cicely hinted she was free to go down to the south coast with him. Hancock agreed, but obviously did not know why. By the next morning the arrangements had evaporated. Hancock – 'his mind and fears focused on the coming performance' – kissed his wife goodbye. 'See you on Sunday,' he said.

Hancock had not seen George Fairweather for almost two years. Fairweather, who was now running a gentlemen's hairdressers opposite the Winter Gardens, received a letter from his protégé informing him of the Bournemouth tour date and, almost as an aside, Hancock added he was now married. The pair arranged to meet for tea on Thursday afternoon before the evening performance.

At three o'clock the telephone rang in the Bournemouth salon. The woman's voice was soft and well-spoken. 'I'm Cicely,' the caller informed Fairweather. 'I haven't met you, but I'm looking forward to it.'

'Tony didn't say you were coming down,' said Fairweather.

'No, he doesn't know,' Cicely explained. 'He went off this morning without leaving me any money. I had just enough to get down to Bournemouth.' When Cicely arrived at the salon fifteen minutes later she claimed she had just two pennies left in her purse. Fairweather, expecting a display of emotional fireworks, took her to meet her husband. Hancock glanced at his wife and casually asked: 'What are you doing here, Kid?'

By late autumn Hancock, as Archie's tutor, was attracting the attention of the first of two producers. Both would lead him into the West End.

The impresario Val Parnell appreciated the pulling power of a hit radio show and a national catch phrase and in December Hancock joined the entire *Educating Archie* cast on stage at the Prince of Wales Theatre. Each day the first show was at 11am and the second at 2.30pm. Every seat for every show was sold. In the evenings Hancock returned as headline comic in the twice-nightly adult *Peep Show* revue.

Peter Brough, meanwhile, had been asked to arrange a special Christmas cabaret at Windsor Castle. 'Max Bygraves was also in the show and Tony had the hard task of following him,' Brough later recalled. 'Tony did very well indeed, and towards the end of his act he was getting a lot of laughs. He wanted to back off the stage and take his bow. Round the little stage was a great big bank of flowers. In the excitement of the moment, Tony stepped back too far and right into the middle of all these flowers, sending them flying. Quick as a flash he turned round, looked at the Queen, and said "Don't worry, Ma'am – I'll pay for them."' The entire royal audience dissolved in laughter.

1952

During February Hancock had returned to London for a special engagement he had helped organise; Eric Sykes, the co-writer of the *Archie* scripts, was getting married. Whenever the tour dates allowed, Hancock and Sykes would meet socially. They were close enough friends for the comedian to persuade the engaged couple to hold their wedding reception at Cicely's parents' house in Cornwall Gardens. The date for the wedding was 6 February. Unknown to Sykes, who had a passion for brass bands, Hancock had arranged for the entire brass section of the BBC Variety Orchestra to serenade the couple aboard their honeymoon flight to Jersey, but the plan had to be abandoned when King George VI died earlier the same day.

Jack Hylton was a maverick and philanderer who enjoyed surviving as a loner. He had started his musical career playing the piano in a concert party and soon formed The Dance Band, one of the world's greatest show bands. By December, 1929, his record sales totalled more than six million and his European tours earned him awards from every government on the Continent, including the Légion d'honneur. The only country in which he failed to receive any form of official recognition was his own, an omission Hylton himself claimed was largely due to his well-publicised affairs.

Six years later the Bolton-born musician had attracted the backing of a syndicate of northern businessmen and turned producer. His formula was simple. On the premise that people would pay to see the faces behind their favourite radio voices, Hylton began buying the stage rights of BBC shows, including *Bandwagon*, *Garrison Theatre* and *ITMA*.

He also had a nose for raw talent. During the 1930s he took on a £1-a-week 'prop boy' called Dickie Henderson junior. Another recruit to the Hylton stable was a thirteen-year-old boy from Barnsley. During the second West End week of *Bandwagon* – in which Arthur Askey made his successful transfer from radio – the teenager made his first appearance. Dressed in morning suit, striped trousers, top hat, white gloves, spats and clogs he first sang a popular song and then clog-danced his way off the stage. His name was Ernest Wiseman.

Jack Hylton's business reputation was as sharp as his dress sense. He was a short, round, ginger-haired man and his wardrobe consisted exclusively of Hawes and Curtis suits, Sulka shirts and shoes by Walkers of Albemarle Street. Phyllis Rounce had already heard a rumour that the bandleader-turned-impresario was willing to pay any price to secure Hancock for his new show so, when he telephoned her Irving Street office to discuss terms, Rounce suggested £500. 'I knew Tony was worth it, I just wasn't sure Hylton was willing to pay that much,' she confesses.

There was a pause. 'All right,' said Hylton and replaced the receiver.

Hylton's latest production – *London Laughs* – was originally based on the entire *Take It From Here* team of Jimmy Edwards, Dick Bentley and Joy Nichols. It was an idea which had foundered even before the show opened. Nichols announced she was leaving to have a baby and was replaced by Vera Lynn, and Bentley returned to Australia after a row with his co-star, Jimmy Edwards, over billing. Asked if he could suggest someone to fill Bentley's shoes, Edwards proposed Hancock.

All that remained was for Hylton to extricate Hancock – who was between radio series – from a nationwide variety tour starring Nat King Cole and the Archie Andrews cast. After three Sunday performances around London the show had opened its series of week-long runs at the Empire Theatre in Sunderland.* At the Hippodrome in Hancock's home city of Birmingham he had been applauded and cheered off stage. In Glasgow he had once again been booed and hissed. And on Sunday, 2 March – the day before the variety show was due to open in Leeds – Hancock rejoined the *Educating Archie* team in London to attend the National Radio Awards.

Negotiations to release Hancock from the variety tour took less than a week. Rehearsals for *London Laughs* started at the Adelphi Theatre in the Strand and Hancock was introduced to his co-stars. He shook hands limply with Vera Lynn – he was never really comfortable in the singer's presence – and then through the stage door, recalled Hancock, came a 'portly, beaming gent called Jimmy Edwards'.

Bewhiskered 'Professor' James Keith O'Neill Edwards was a genuine war hero, awarded the Distinguished Flying Cross after being shot down while dropping supplies into Arnhem in 1944. Edwards reeked of the boisterous, bellowing RAF pilots and aircrew Hancock imagined his brother to have become. To the general public at large Edwards was a 'bustling, larger-than-life comedian, with an engaging informal style on stage; never suggesting an actor, but rather a certain type of schoolmaster one used to know'.

Edwards, like Hancock, made his post-war debut at the Windmill, with a trombone-blowing comedy act. His fruity but educated voice was first heard on the BBC's 1946 ex-service series, *They're Out*. Cashing in on his genuine Master of Arts degree, Edwards adopted the title 'Professor' to deliver a light-hearted *Navy Mixture* lecture series called *You May Take Notes*, but it was the 1948 launch of *Take It From Here*, and his collaboration with Joy Nichols and Dick Bentley, which made Edwards a household name.

---

* Twenty-four years later, in 1976, Sid James would suffer a fatal heart attack while on stage at the Sunderland Empire.

When *London Laughs* opened in mid-April Hancock was still addressing Edwards as 'Sir' and waiting patiently to be admitted after knocking on his door. 'We never had a professional quarrel,' said Hancock, 'but we disagreed about almost everything else … from food and drink to cars and politics.' Edwards's dressing room became a sort of dumping ground for Hancock's moods. Like the majority of depressives he needed an audience to witness his agonies. Between the matinée and evening performances Hancock would plunge into an antsy appraisal of his performance. He would sit in the corner of the dressing room in a 'total, deep, black despair', ignoring the constant flow of visitors and Edwards's bullying attempts to cheer him up.

Immediately before each performance Hancock's nerves became overpowering and all-demanding. Edwards and Vera Lynn would retreat to their dressing rooms to relax and await their cue but Hancock took refuge in the wings, within sight of the stage and touching distance of the audience. Head bowed he would pace up and down, muttering his lines over and over, his hands clenched and shaking and the perspiration soaking his collar and cuffs. Sometimes – and for no discernible reason – he failed to make it to the wings. From the corridor outside his dressing room he could be heard vomiting. It was an affliction which never left him. Each new challenge brought with it a set of new fears. Years later Hancock was amused to discover it was a lifelong ordeal he shared with Harold Macmillan, the Conservative MP and future Prime Minister. Major speeches, both in and out of the House of Commons, terrified Macmillan so much that he was physically sick.

Each night Phyllis Rounce would call at the Adelphi to calm and distract her client. She soon discovered it was a copy-cat experience of the previous year's tour audition. Once again Rounce bought her client a new pair of shoes – each night she would place the shoes on his feet and lace them up – by the time she walked from the wings to the front of house, Hancock had changed into his scuffed and badly polished old ones. Within minutes the Adelphi manager had located the agent: 'Miss Rounce, he's not going on tomorrow night with those shoes on. It's new shoes or nothing.'

'Well you blooming well try and get him to wear them then,' the agent would snap back.

For Jimmy Edwards, whose dressing room was frequently the repository for Hancock's new shoes as well as his dejection, it simply added to the fun. He nicknamed his co-star 'Kipper Hancock' and joined in by thinking up new places to hide the footwear.

Cicely, usually an enthusiastic driver, was beginning to find the late-night drive into London to collect her husband demanding and tedious, but on the days Hancock took the train into London she found the Clacton flat isolated and lonely. Hancock agreed they could now afford to move back to London, but showed no inclination to help with the move. For days Cicely made appointments – few of which Hancock kept – and tramped around apartments until she found what she was looking for. Their new home was in an imposing Victorian block in Queen's Gate Terrace, Knightsbridge, a few hundred yards from the Royal Albert Hall and the Natural History Museum and less than half-a-mile from her parents' house in Cornwall Gardens. Once again, Hancock refused to take time off to look over and approve the new flat.

Cicely moved her collection of cook books into the kitchen of the top-floor apartment and set about educating her husband's conservative palate. 'It was the beginning of the end for Tony's waistline,' a friend recalled. 'He was on and off diets for the rest of his life. First he fell in love with Cicely and then he fell in love with food, and French food in particular.' As well as finding his well-worn and favourite clothes no longer fitted quite so well, Hancock also found himself stopping for breath on the five-floor climb to his flat.

With his finances apparently secure, Hancock developed a perverse disinterest in money and rarely carried cash about with him. When they went out Cicely frequently settled the dinner bill because her husband's wallet was empty, and when he needed a few pounds to buy drinks there was always someone offering a loan. After two appearances on *Henry Hall's Guest Night – Highlights of the Show World*, Phyllis Rounce was forced to write to the BBC accounts department admitting 'our client, Tony Hancock, has mislaid his cheque for £35 15s' and asking for a replacement.

Money – other people's money – caused him more anguish than his own. Hancock railed at the amount Rounce could now demand for his services. 'It's the money that worries me,' he would say. 'Look at the vast sums they're paying me and think what that bus driver gets.' When it did arrive, and it was arriving in ever-increasing amounts, Hancock found no pressing reason to part with it. The telephone was frequently disconnected, on one occasion they returned home to find the electricity had been cut off, and it was left to Cicely to pay off the overdue rent on their flat.

Hancock was not drinking excessively, just regularly. The daily intake of alcohol and the combination of restaurant dinners and Cicely's rich food caused him to put on weight and his skin to erupt in spots. When Lily Walker brought Mary Hobley, his *Wings* 'landlady', backstage to see him, she was appalled at how bloated and irritable Hancock had become. Friends would call at his dressing room to find him wearing only his underpants, his back and arms covered in angry sores. He would walk around the room or continue making up, apparently unconcerned by his nakedness or his condition.

One welcome visitor to his Adelphi dressing room was George Fairweather. He was with his protégé shortly before an evening performance when a letter arrived. It was an invitation for Hancock to perform at the 1952 Royal Variety Performance. After excitedly reading the note several times Hancock sat very still. Tears trickled down his face. 'If only Dad could have been here,' he said.

'He will be,' Fairweather assured him.

Hancock thought for a moment. 'I wish I could be as sure as you,' he said, before making his friend promise to attend the royal show in his father's place.

The next day Hancock invited his friend and golfing partner, Clive Dunn, to celebrate and they arranged to meet at Rules restaurant near the Adelphi. 'By the time I arrived he had already ruined a bottle of Champagne and we finished the second one together,' recalls Dunn.

Hancock, whom Dunn regarded as the 'great white hope of British comedy', was good at golf, but never a serious or dedicated player. The pair usually played at Richmond, and Dunn, in his ignorance, frequently broke the rules and naïvely transgressed golfing etiquette. To his dismay, and that of other golfers waiting to play through, Hancock would chortle himself into collapse, rolling about the fairway or green, helpless with laughter at his partner's ignorance.

Hopes were high for the first Royal Variety Performance of Queen Elizabeth II's reign. Hancock's Adelphi cohort, Jimmy Edwards, was making his second command appearance, and joining Hancock among a clutch of up-and-coming stars were the Beverley Sisters, singer Ian Wallace and a zany comedian called Norman Wisdom. Established names included Gracie Fields, Bud Flanagan and the last-minute addition of Maurice Chevalier.

Hancock had persuaded Larry Stephens to write his Palladium script which consisted of three monologues in various styles. The one which appeared to amuse the royal party most was the upper-class commentary of submarine skipper Lieutenant Commander Pumfret-Pumfret, RN. 'The Duke of Edinburgh,' claimed one critic, 'was particularly amused by Tony Hancock's fantastic story, accompanied by mimicry, of the commander who had to swim for it when his submarine submerged.'

By coincidence Stephens had another friend appearing before the royal gathering. Gerry Brereton was a fellow commando, blinded during a raid in which Stephens had taken part. Having memorised his place on stage during rehearsal, Brereton was able to find his 'spot' unaided to sing *Here in my Heart*. Hancock, however, hardly noticed the ex-soldier's contribution over the backstage Tannoy. He was sharing a dressing room with several other comedians, including Norman Wisdom, Ted Ray and Jerry Desmonde. As the others chatted and joked, Hancock sat in silence. On his dressing table was a bottle of brandy. Every few minutes he would pour and drink another glass. The bottle was almost empty before Wisdom dared interrupt and suggested Hancock had had enough. 'I asked how the hell he was going to perform if he had any more to drink,' Wisdom recalls.

Hancock informed him gruffly he was all right and promptly poured himself another glass of brandy.

When his call came Hancock slowly rose, switched off the loudspeaker and left. As soon as the door was closed the trio of fellow comedians switched the Tannoy back on and listened anxiously for the drunken Hancock's inevitable disaster. To their surprise 'his delivery and timing were superb,' recalls Wisdom and Hancock left the stage to thunderous applause. He arrived back in the dressing room drenched in sweat and apparently unmoved by his colleagues' jubilation. 'Thank you,' Hancock said flatly. Walking to his dressing table he downed the last of the brandy, put on his coat and slipped unnoticed out of the stage door. He spent the rest of the evening in a nearby pub until he was needed for the grand finale.

The entire show had been recorded by the BBC so that highlights could be broadcast on the Light Programme a few days later. Hancock's act – itself based on a James Fitzpatrick travelogue – was edited down to six minutes. He was third on the radio bill and the first solo performer. The royal show was broadcast only once and for more than forty years it was assumed the recording had been lost, but in the mid-1990s it was discovered in the corporation archive. With the exception of one episode of *Educating Archie*, from the same year, the tape is the earliest example of Hancock at work. It is certainly the earliest recording of Hancock on stage. Hawaiian music is playing and Hancock speaks in a drawling mid-Atlantic voice:

Margate, lovely, lovely Margate, city of love and laughter . . . as far as the cyc can see stretches the ay-zure blue of the sky, as the sea slowly laps over the great jagged rocks that form the beach. Sitting on the beach are the natives, wearing the national headgear of a white handkerchief knotted in each corner . . . Let us pause for a moment and listen to the merry chatter of the natives on the beaches . . .

(*Hancock shouting*) Edie! . . . Edie! . . . put that shark down, you don't know where it's been . . .

On we go through the leafy lanes of England when we hear a

familiar sound ... (*Hancock whistles shrilly twice*) ... and we ask ourselves, what is Ronnie Ronalde doing up that tree?

But we couldn't leave England without a visit to the British Navy. So let's look out to sea, where the British Navy are on manoeuvres. Down below the surface is a British submarine commanded by Lieutenant Commander Pumfret-Pumfret, RN. He speaks to his men in his rough, sailor-like fashion.

(*Upper class voice*) Careful there Johnson, don't bang yourself on that torpedo now ... Come away Jones. Jones come away, you'll get your hands covered in grease. Up periscope ... Put me down Hathaway ... no grog for you. Well, it's half past four, I think we'll pull up for tea. Put the kettle on Harmsworth ... what's that ... oh, you've put the kettle on ... yes I see you have ... I think it suits you too. All right men, prepare to dive. (*Hancock imitates klaxon*) Submerge! ... Well let me get in ... Fools.

But back to the show where we find the natives of England enjoying their favourite recreation ... watching workmen digging up the road. We pause again. Outside the ropes the people are watching. Inside the ropes the workmen are working. The last brick is laid. The last of the mortar scraped off. The foreman steps forward, takes off his cap and says ... Well, ladies and gentlemen, on be'arf of the entire company I'd like to thank you for the support you have given us this week ... if you've enjoyed watching us as much as we've enjoyed working for you then it's all been worthwhile. Next week we shall be appearing at the corner of Corporation Road and High Street with a little thing calling Digging the Drains Up. We shall be featuring 'Arry Trubshawe on the steamroller (*band cheers*). We shall also be featuring a special solo on pneumatic drill by Charlie Perkins (*another cheer from band*). I think we can persuade Mr Perkins (*more cheers from band*) to put his drill down for a few moments. He'll be good enough to say a few words.

(*Hancock stutters*) W ... w ... well th ... th ... thank you, l ... l ... ladies a ... a ... and gentlemen ...

And so it is with great regret, as the sun pulls away from the shore and our ship sinks slowly in the west, we say farewell to England, lovely, lovely England.

Hancock's sudden release from the regional tour that spring proved doubly providential. The BBC had launched *Calling All Forces* in 1950. A programme aimed primarily at servicemen and women stationed around Britain and in Germany, it quickly attracted a devoted civilian following. More than thirty million listeners tuned in each week. In March, 1952, the programme's regular compère and comedian Ted Ray announced he wanted to concentrate on his own show, *Ray's a Laugh*, so the BBC began searching for a replacement. In a bid to revamp the increasingly predictable format, the corporation announced the show's two new resident stars would be Tony Hancock and Charlie Chester.[4]

At thirty-eight Chester was already a veteran performer and comic. Born Cecil Victor Manser, at Eastbourne in 1914, he turned professional soon after his thirteenth birthday. At seventeen he had formed his own accordion band. Then, having worked for a time as Duke Daly, he settled on Charlie (because he thought it sounded 'friendly') and the surname Chester (after the railway station). Two years later he was being professionally managed and booked for West End dates: 'I died on my feet nightly.' By the late 1930s he was doing well, both in cabaret and as a supporting act to Norman Wayne. Early in his career Chester was compared to Max Miller, who turned up at one of his shows accompanied by a lawyer to see if his material was being stolen. 'Miller used his power to keep me off the Moss Empires' circuit for nine years,' complained Chester.

When the Second World War broke out, he joined ENSA and was entertaining British troops in France just before the Dunkirk retreat. Soon after, he joined the Army and became a sergeant in the Irish Fusiliers. He helped stage regimental shows and form *Stars in Battledress*. 'We've shown Charlie Chester we can laugh,' said Dwight D. Eisenhower, 'now we'll show the Hun, we can fight.' When the

BBC decided an Army show was needed to balance the Navy's *Waterlogged Spa* and the RAF's *Much Binding in the Marsh*, Chester was asked to create it. The result was the *Stand Easy* comedy series which he wrote and fronted. The line-up included Arthur Haynes and the pair created a memorable act as two spivs, Tish and Tosh, with Chester speaking so fast the audience could hardly catch the jokes.

After the war Chester quickly became a popular star of programmes like *Come to Charlie* and hosted the BBC's first television game show, *Take Pot Luck* – the first prize was an electric iron and the second prize was a bunch of coat-hangers.

Hancock, meanwhile, had already made a solo 'star' appearance on *Calling All Forces* in February. On Easter Monday, 1952, he teamed up with Charlie Chester to present the first of sixteen programmes. Chester, the unquenchable optimist, found Hancock aloof and solitary. 'I have never met a man or a woman in this life that I didn't want to like,' claimed Chester. 'Mind you, some wouldn't let you.'

The partnership, as far as Hancock was concerned, was one-sided. He complained to his agent Phyllis Rounce, who dutifully complained to the BBC, that his recent success with *Educating Archie* should have given him enough kudos to allow him alone to replace Ted Ray. To apply still more pressure, the *London Laughs* management reproached the corporation over Hancock's lack of microphone credits. The BBC had, so far, refused to acknowledge Hancock as a West End performer. It was, Hancock pompously moaned, 'a slight on my reputation'. A letter from George Black, the show's producer, put it more tactfully:

> May we appeal to you to give this further consideration. The reason for asking is that we have a credit for Jimmy Edwards, and Vera Lynn will be having a credit too. It would keep everyone happy if the third star of the Adelphi show, *London Laughs*, had a similar credit and Tony Hancock, in particular, feels rather badly about this. In the profession it is generally believed that the microphone credit is governed by salary and, in this case, the implication is that Tony Hancock is in a lower

wage bracket than the other two stars who are billed equally with him.

The BBC reluctantly gave in. Less than four weeks into the run Hancock returned to Rounce's Irving Street office petulant and fretful and threatening to walk out of the radio show. This time he had developed a growing dislike for Jacques Brown, the *Calling All Forces* producer. Among Hancock's complaints were that Brown was autocratic and that he refused to listen to script suggestions or allow any kind of group discussion on material. Charlie Chester remembers it differently. 'I had the feeling he was a very unhappy person,' he recalled.

The first ten scripts were written by Bob Monkhouse and Denis Goodwin and rarely pleased Hancock. After the initial read-through he would invariably slide into a doleful silence and count each joke and punch line. Chester, he moaned, always got more laughs. He also complained the scriptwriters did not appreciate his 'character' as Eric Sykes did. 'Tony was a very insular and unhappy man,' Chester added.

Phyllis Rounce wrote to the producer requesting a meeting with the joint compères and the scriptwriters. The suggestion had come from Hancock. 'The object of the meeting was an endeavour to improve the programme,' Rounce explained. To Hancock's surprise he was ordered to attend a private meeting with Jacques Brown and the BBC's head of variety, Pat Hillyard. It sounded, Hancock claimed, 'like a ten-year-old schoolboy being hauled before the headmaster for a dressing down'.

Rounce refused to let Hancock attend the meeting, saying 'any attendance by him alone might prejudice the good relations he enjoys with Charles [Chester]'. It was left to Rounce to express her client's feelings tactfully:

Tony wishes me to emphasise the question of his relationship with the producer. He has no personal feelings whatsoever, and his only anxiety is to lend his full weight to the success of the production which under present circumstances he doesn't consider possible.

He feels that, generally speaking, his participation in the programme has been under-written, more especially in the last two programmes, and would like to express himself (and know that others have the opportunity to do likewise) before all concerned in the hope that some mutual benefit can be established. He emphasises that his present position in the West End places him under an obligation to his management who have already commented on his position in the programme, as have listeners.

Sometime in early May, Jacques Brown contacted Ray Galton and Alan Simpson, by now established on the BBC list of scriptwriters. He explained the regular *Calling All Forces* writers, Bob Monkhouse and Denis Goodwin, 'were getting rather tired and wanted a holiday' and asked if they could write the last six shows in the series. 'We hadn't been in the forces and we thought, "God, is it possible for us to write a comedy for service men and women?"' recalls Galton. 'Again we said "yes". We needed the money.' It was their big break. It was also the first time they would create a script especially for Tony Hancock.

As with the previous ten programmes, each hour-long show included established stars as well as promising newcomers. Galton and Simpson had to write a sketch between Charlie Chester and Hancock, then a sketch for both compères and the guest musician. This would be followed in turn by sketches introducing the guest singer and comic. The longest, and final, sketch was traditionally a take-off of a current film or play – similar material to the *African Queen* skit Galton and Simpson had submitted two years earlier – and always with Hancock as the hero.

For the new writers it was a question more of developing Hancock's character rather than establishing a new one. He had taken to using what one BBC producer called a 'strangulated Cockney' voice, painfully high pitched. 'Ancock was already dropping his aitches.

The first *Hancock's Half Hour* was still more than two years away. Although the quartet – Hancock, Main Wilson, Galton and Simpson –

who launched and developed the series are often credited with its origination it was, in fact, Larry Stephens who first persuaded Hancock to explore the possibilities of creating a unique style of situation comedy. Long after their flat-sharing days were over, Hancock and Stephens would sit through nights, and even entire weekends, dreaming up script and programme ideas and during one session Stephens had suggested a new radio role for his friend. The idea hovered in limbo until the summer of 1952.

On 29 June Hancock appeared in a Saturday morning children's programme called *Hullo There*. Although it was broadcast live, his own contribution had been recorded more than a week earlier. The studio session so impressed the programme's producer, Lionel Gamlin, he commented to Hancock, almost as an aside, that the comedian 'should do very well in silent studio comedy', that is, in a show recorded without the presence of an audience. It was a concept which had not previously occurred to Hancock, whose talent had, so far, relied entirely on short sketches and audience feedback.

Hancock mentioned the notion to Stephens who immediately resurrected the situation comedy idea and together they approached Peter Eton, a drama producer at the BBC. On Tuesday, 8 July, Eton dictated a memo to the head of variety. In four typed paragraphs he was to outline a comedy concept that was to make Hancock famous.

Tony Hancock plays the part of an estate-agent-cum-bachelor-town counsellor, who lives with his old aunt in one of those frightful semi-detached villas in a small south-coast town. Our hero is an unimaginative, unenterprising, charming idiot who has a lot of trouble with his eccentric aunt because of her ambition for him to marry into the county 'set'. Tony, on the other hand, prefers the local girls and is, of course, considered an eligible and reliable bachelor by their mothers. The villain of the piece is a local garage proprietor, a loud-mouthed, witless, back-slapping oaf, always ready with a clumsy, unfunny leg pull and a raucous laugh.

Apart from the fact that each of the six or more half-hour programmes would consist of a complete story about Tony's pompous, yet likeable, blundering, there would be no set formula.

No audience – no orchestra – and no singers would be required. Recorded music would be used for opening, closing and links.

Scribbled beneath in Eton's hand is the question: 'Shall I encourage them to go further?' Before passing the memo to his deputy, the head of variety had added his own hand-written comment: 'Here is an interesting suggestion – any good?'

Exactly a week later the outline was back on Eton's desk with a note encouraging him to run with the idea. Across the top right-hand corner is written: 'Yes please. See what you can develop. We could pay, say, fifteen guineas for a script treatment.'

A few days later Eton took Hancock and Stephens on a day trip to Seaford on the Sussex coast. A favourite with the BBC producer, it was exactly the kind of 'location' he imagined for the series. That afternoon they settled on a title for the comedy. They would called it, *Welcome to Whelkham*. Stephens went to work and produced a pilot script, but it foundered, more through interdepartmental rivalry at Broadcasting House than any lack of potential. Eton was officially informed that, as part of the drama department, he would not be allowed to produce a comedy series which, strictly speaking, was the domain of variety. *Welcome to Whelkham* was shelved.

1953

THE FIRST OF May was Labour Day. It was also Dennis Main Wilson's twenty-ninth birthday. More importantly, it was the day he filed the definitive patent on a new comedy art form – situation comedy.*

Main Wilson had unofficially promised Hancock his own show as long ago as 1951. 'I wanted to abandon the formula of first sketch . . . singer . . . second sketch . . . band number . . .' explained the producer. With Ray Galton and Alan Simpson as writers the time was right, he felt, to break away from traditional, domestic-based, cosy comedy. So, later that day his memo landed on the desk of the BBC's head of variety. It was an outline for a shift to a new kind of radio comedy in which the cast were played by comedians and there would be no catch phrases or funny voices or long-running jokes. Neither would there be a musical interlude. 'I believe,' Main Wilson wrote, 'we can entertain most of the people, most of the time, without having to drop our sights – either intellectually or in terms of entertainment.'

His thirty-minute situation comedy would follow the misadventures of a central character and his associates – 'based on reality and truth, as opposed to jokes, merry quips and wheezes' – a concept surprisingly similar to Larry Stephens's *Welcome to Whelkham* outline.

Weeks of discussion followed, and Main Wilson began to lobby other influential executives at the BBC. Most doubted the viability of a programme so far removed from the comedy norm. In a second memo to the assistant head of variety the producer explained the format in greater detail:

His show would not be tied down to any set number of comedy spots each week – indeed, the construction of the show will have as loose a formula as possible – some weeks three different spots

---

* In 1926 the BBC had broadcast *That Child*, a series of five-minute 'domestic' comedies. It is generally assumed the world's first situation comedy was *Myrtle and Bertie*, transmitted by Radio Luxembourg in 1935. It starred Claude Hulbert and Enid Trevor.

on three different subjects – some weeks a complete *half hour* storyline – occasionally running a serial story over into the next week if the situation presents itself . . . The comedy style will be purely situation in which we shall try to build Tony as a real-life character in real-life surroundings. There will be no 'Goon' or contrived comedy approaches at all.

The formula was the antithesis of *The Goons*, an earlier Main Wilson success, and of most radio comedy since the war. Ted Kavanagh, the *ITMA* writer, had summed up the accepted philosophy in using sound 'for all it was worth, the sound of different voices and accents, the use of catch phrases, the impact of funny sounds in words, of grotesque effects to give atmosphere – every device to create the illusion of rather crazy or inverted reality'.

However, the 'reality' of everyday life was exactly what Main Wilson wanted to portray, and putting reality under the microscope was the best way of examining and exploiting its absurdities. To convince any remaining doubters within the corporation – 'and to give you some idea of the eventual approach' – Main Wilson and the two writers had decided to experiment with a 'semi-domestic Hancock' whenever a variety programme allowed.

Meanwhile, the new formula for *Forces All-Star Bill* was obviously not working. For fifteen months the BBC shuffled both the format and the title, and the task of reviving the series had been given, in the summer of 1951, to Main Wilson with whom Hancock had first worked on *Happy-Go-Lucky*. The producer immediately changed the title and the scriptwriters and Spike Milligan and Larry Stephens were commissioned to write the hour-long scripts. Hancock was contracted to compère only one show. Main Wilson was still not satisfied and, after just eight broadcasts, he changed the name yet again, this time to the shortened *All-Star Bill*. He also hired Galton and Simpson as scriptwriters. Again, Hancock made a single appearance as compère.

By January, 1953, the BBC attempted a more drastic overhaul. The show was moved to Tuesday nights and relegated to a fortnightly slot, alternating with *The Forces Show* starring Richard Murdoch, Kenneth Horne and Sam Costa.

Dennis Main Wilson, who had already earned a reputation as the most innovative light entertainment producer at the BBC, would go to extraordinary technical lengths to perfect a broadcast, and he wanted to record the *Forces All-Star Bill* programmes at the Paris Cinema, an underground auditorium first leased to the BBC in the early months of the war, to allow it to continue producing programmes during the Blitz. The studio was booked each Sunday night for *Take It From Here*, so Peter Sellers suggested Main Wilson contact his uncle Bertie Ray, at that time managing the Jack Buchanan-owned Garrick Theatre.

For several years the BBC had deemed the optimum size for a studio audience was two hundred. Larger audiences, it ruled, would 'slow down' a recording session. The Garrick could seat almost eight hundred, a number which Main Wilson found added greater depth to recorded audience reaction. However, there were more practical problems to overcome. Unlike the Paris, which had long since ended its role as a cinema, the Garrick was still a working theatre. Each Saturday night, after the evening performance, the staff struck the set and cleared the stage, and then, during the early hours of Sunday morning, the BBC engineers would install and test the cumbersome OBA/8 portable broadcasting equipment, a war relic with a cantankerous reputation. The only room suitable for a control cubicle was the saloon bar, behind the stalls.

There would be no regular compère. Main Wilson wanted to keep each show as fluid as possible, but show by show Hancock's verbal mannerisms were already beginning to form. Although far less subtly than in their future scripts, Galton and Simpson were already writing 'exclusively' for Hancock; and Hancock, albeit subconsciously, had begun to adopt the gullible character created for him. When a journalist suggested Hancock was the only star in *Forces All-Star Bill* he reacted by claiming: 'There is no star ... the show is the star' – a curious statement in the light of his growing preoccupation with fame.

The first *Forces All-Star Bill* of 1953 went out on 6 January. It was compèred by Ted Ray and starred Hancock, Joan Heal, Graham Stark and a variety of musicians. In it, Hancock has fallen in love with Heal and attempts to explain his infatuation to Ted Ray. With a little imagination one can see that the exchange would work equally well with Sid James – Hancock's *Half Hour* foil – reading Ray's part.

> Hancock: Well, Edward, it's happened. After twenty-eight years of bachelorhood, brisk walks, PT and cold showers, Hancock the impervious has had his armour pierced by a member of the opposite mob.

> Ray: Tony, you don't mean a woman?

> Hancock: Can you think of anything more opposite?

> Ray: Why, Tony, that's wonderful. Does she reciprocate?

> Hancock: (*shocked*) Ted, please, I've only just met her.

> Ray: Tony, don't look now but your brain just stuck a white flag out of the top of your head. Who is this girl, anyway?

> Hancock: My fiancée, Joan Heal.

> Ray: Joan Heal! She's a lovely piece of crackling. Your first girl friend? Shouldn't you have got something for a beginner? Where did you meet her?

> Hancock: Last week, at Broadcasting House. She was waiting for one lift and I was waiting for the other. Then she opened her gates, stepped in and went up, and I opened my gates, stepped in, and . . .

> Ray: You went up.

> Hancock: No, I went down – the lift wasn't there. And as I was lying there, Ted, my mind began to

wander.

Ray: You can't blame it, there's a lot of space in
          there.

Hancock: (*ignores him*) I started thinking to myself
          'Hancock, my boy, this girl is just your type.'

Ray: How do you mean?

Hancock: She was breathing.

*

The announcement that Dennis Main Wilson was leaving *Forces All-Star Bill* both stunned and disorientated Hancock. Within days, speculation about his possible successor began to circulate. The hot favourite for the remaining five shows, Hancock was assured, was Jacques Brown, the 'autocratic' *Calling All Forces* producer he had clashed with the year before. Once again, Phyllis Rounce at International Artistes found herself 'aground' with one of Hancock's 'endless problems'. This time Hancock flatly refused to be part of the next show, scheduled for 31 March.

Rounce wrote to Pat Hillyard at the BBC; the 'official' news of Brown's appointment had, as Rounce envisaged, 'put the cat among the pigeons'. She informed the head of variety:

Tony has given the matter an awful lot of thought and has
expressed himself to me most sincerely, and whilst he admires
Jacques' work and likes him as a person, this is a case where the
two personalities simply do not 'jell'. It is no use blinding
ourselves to this, and so strongly does Tony feel, that he has
asked me to approach you (to use his own words 'in the nicest
possible way') to ask you to release him from his contract to
appear in the series *Forces All-Star Bill*.

You see Pat, he is confident that he and Jacques cannot work
together and this was clearly proved as you will remember in the
case of *Calling All Forces* where they both tried and tried again,
but failed hopelessly.

The next day Rounce received a telephone call from Hillyard. The pair, who were old friends, chatted amicably. Across the top of her confidential letter Hillyard scribbled the '... producer in question not to handle this production in any case'. The crisis – if indeed there had been a crisis – was purely of Hancock's making. 'Tony needed equilibrium,' Rounce recalls. 'The slightest problem – or threat of a problem – could throw him off balance.' The remaining shows had been given, as Hillyard had intended all along, to Alistair Scott-Johnston, and Hancock, who had worked with Scott-Johnston the previous year on two editions of *Henry Hall's Guest Night*, was delighted.

Dennis Main Wilson did more to extend the boundaries of post-war comedy than any other BBC producer. Sharing not only a sense of humour, but a sense of anarchy, he acted as a conduit for the new generation of comedians desperate to hone their talent. 'It seemed ridiculous,' he argued, 'for us to have the pick of the light entertainment talent and then fail to match it with the best production facilities and equipment.' Each of his shows broke new and fertile ground for those which followed, whether it was the reflective humour of Eric Barker or the surreal and timeless lunacy of the *Goons*. By the 1960s his list of credits would include such classics as *The Rag Trade*, *The Dick Emery Show* and *Till Death Us Do Part*.

The problem was that – however innovative the performers and their writers – Main Wilson still found himself bound by the corporation's legendary 'Blue Book'. To avoid offending its worldwide audience – and its board of governors – Michael Standing, the director of variety, compiled, wrote and issued a set of guidelines for writers and producers 'to set out the BBC's general policy toward this type of material, to list the principal "taboos", to indicate traps for the unwary or inexperienced, and to summarise the main guidance so far issued of more than a short-term application'.

These guidelines became known as the 'Blue Book', although in reality the 'private and confidential' volume issued to producers had a green cover. The rules it contained were frequently contradictory. 'Niggers' was banned. 'Nigger Minstrels' was not.

The final decision on whether material transgressed the variety department's policy ultimately rested with individual producers. Underscoring any material was the maxim 'when in doubt, take it out'. Hancock's new series, however ground-breaking, would be governed by the same 'Blue Book' rules:

VULGARITY

Programmes must at all cost be kept free of crudities, coarseness and innuendo. Humour must be clean and untainted directly or by association with vulgarity and suggestiveness. Music hall, stage, and to a lesser degree, screen standards, are not suitable to broadcasting. Producers, artists and writers must recognise this fact and the strictest watch must be kept. There can be no compromise with doubtful material. It must be cut.

General. Well known vulgar jokes (e.g. the Brass Monkey) 'cleaned up', are not normally admissible since the humour in such cases is almost invariably evident only if the vulgar version is known.

There is an absolute ban upon the following:

Jokes about –
　　Lavatories
　　Effeminacy in men
　　Immorality of any kind

Suggestive references to –
　　Honeymoon couples
　　Chambermaids
　　Fig leaves
　　Prostitution
　　Ladies' underwear, e.g. winter draws on
　　Animals' habits, e.g. rabbits
　　Lodgers

Extreme care should be taken in dealing with references to or jokes about –
Pre-natal influences (e.g. 'His mother was frightened by a donkey')
Marital infidelity

Good taste and decency are the obvious governing considerations. The vulgar use of such words as 'basket' must also be avoided.

BIBLICAL REFERENCES

Sayings of Christ or descriptions of Him are, of course, inadmissible for light entertainment programmes.

Jokes built around the Bible stories, e.g. Adam and Eve, Cain and Abel, David and Goliath, must also be avoided or any sort of parody of them. References to a few biblical characters, e.g. Noah, are sometimes permissible but, since there is seldom anything to be gained by them and since they can engender much resentment they are best avoided altogether.

RELIGIOUS REFERENCES

Reference to and jokes about different religions or religious denominations are banned. The following are also inadmissible –
Jokes about A.D or B.C. (e.g. before Crosby)
Jokes or comic songs about spiritualism, christenings, religious ceremonies of any description (e.g. weddings, funerals)
Parodies of Christmas carols
Offensive references to Jews (or any other religious sect)

PHYSICAL AND MENTAL INFIRMITIES

Very great distress can be caused to invalids and their relatives by thoughtless jokes about any kind of physical disability.
The following are therefore barred –
Jocular references to all forms of physical infirmity or disease,

e.g. blindness, deafness, loss of limbs, paralysis, cancer, consumption, smallpox.

Jokes about war injuries of any description.

Jokes about more embarrassing disabilities, e.g. bow-legs, cross-eyes, stammering (this is the most common 'gag' subject of this kind).

Jokes about any form of mental deficiency.

DRINK

References to and jokes about drink are allowed in strict moderation so long as they can really be justified on entertainment grounds. Long 'drunk' stories or scenes should, however, be avoided and the number of references in any one programme carefully watched. There is no objection to the use of well-known drinking songs, e.g. 'Another Little Drink', 'Little Brown Jug', in their proper contexts. Trade slogans, e.g. 'Beer is Best', are barred. Remarks such as 'one for the road' are also inadmissible on road safety grounds.

EXPLETIVES

Generally speaking the use of expletives and forceful language on the air can only be justified in a serious dramatic setting where the action of the play demands them. They have no place at all in light entertainment and all such words as God, Good God, My God, Blast, Hell, Damn, Bloody, Gorblimey, Ruddy, etc., etc., should be deleted from scripts and innocuous expressions substituted.

IMPERSONATIONS

All impersonations need the permission of the people being impersonated and producers must reassure themselves that this has been given before allowing any to be broadcast.

Certain artists have notified the Corporation that no unauthorised impersonations may be broadcast. The present list is given below but should be checked from time to time with the Variety Booking Manager.

Gracie Fields
Ethel Revnell (with or without Gracie West)
Renee Houston
Nat Mills and Bobbie
Vera Lynn
Jeanne de Casalis (Mrs. Feather)
Harry Hemsley

MISCELLANEOUS POINTS

Avoid derogatory references to –
    Professions, trades and 'classes', e.g. solicitors, commercial travellers, miners, 'the working class'
    Coloured races
Avoid any jokes or references that might be taken to encourage –
Strikes or industrial disputes
    The Black Market
    Spivs and drones
Avoid any reference to 'The MacGillicuddy of the Reeks' or jokes about his name.
    Do not refer to Negroes as 'Niggers' ('Nigger Minstrels' is allowed).
    'Warming up' sequences with studio before broadcasts should conform to the same standards as the programmes themselves. Sample recordings should be the subject of the same vigilance as transmission.

*

Meanwhile, in the summer of 1953, Hancock made his first film, *Orders are Orders*. It was a reworking of a breezy British farce – a skit on film-making – first filmed twenty years earlier under the title *Orders is Orders*, and Hancock did not enjoy working on it.

The picture's campaign brochure, circulated to cinema managers by distributors British Lion, promised 'one long laugh from beginning to end' with 'word-of-mouth publicity paying great dividends at the box office'. The plot outline made only slightly more sense than the film itself:

> The story – as if it matters, with such a load of talent – is about a film unit entering an Army barracks for the purpose of shooting scenes for a picture about invaders from Mars. Unfortunately, they arrive without permission from the colonel in charge. He is won over, however, and even consents to make a film test himself.
>
> The barracks is soon in a chaotic state with glamorous lovelies dashing here, there and everywhere, the producer issuing orders to everyone, and soldiers hastening to help. Into the midst of all this chaos comes a visit of inspection from the General Commanding the Division.
>
> The impact of his sudden and unexpected arrival has to be seen to be fully enjoyed.

Made at Beaconsfield Studios, *Orders are Orders* redeemed itself only by the number of established and up-and-coming stars among the credits. Sid James is cast as Waggermeyer, the barking, rasping American film director; Peter Sellers plays Private Goffin, a bored and bloated steward in the officers' mess at Bilchester Barracks, and Eric Sykes – curiously credited with additional dialogue but with no cast entry – is bandsman Private Waterhouse. The film's official new celebrity is Tony Hancock, 'introduced' to cinema audiences as the despairing bandmaster, Lieutenant Cartroad. Its true star is Sellers who, unwittingly, follows Sid James's maxim and underplays to perfection his role as barman to the officers of the 1st Battalion, Royal Loyals. 'What other performer would have used such a tiny role as an opportunity to stretch himself?' asks Roger Lewis in his book *The Life and Death of Peter Sellers*. 'Hancock certainly didn't. He's in *Orders are Orders*, fat, slouched and liverish ... A little of his round shouldered grimacing, when the musicians hit duff notes, goes a long way.'

Panned by the critics, the film was dubbed by Sid James a 'bit of a stinker'. Hancock would tell, soon after the film's 1954 release, how he had sneaked into the cinema where it was showing and asked if there were any empty seats in the circle. 'A seat?' the box office girl replied. 'You can have the first fifteen rows.'

One significant development to come from Hancock's appearance in *Orders are Orders* was his decision to turn his back on International Artistes and Phyllis Rounce. Although he saw himself primarily as a radio comedian, with hopes of his own series still very much alive, Hancock thought his ultimate future – and fortune – lay in films. His meetings with Sid James on the *Orders* set were sporadic and brief, and talking to the South African-born actor, Hancock deluded himself by falsely comparing his own career with that of James. *Orders are Orders* was James's thirty-seventh production since his arrival in Britain on Christmas Day, 1946, and his eighth so far that year. Film offers were arriving at the rate of four or five a month. Hancock was suddenly aware of what he was missing – and blamed his agent.

Phyllis Rounce considered her client 'emotionally unsuitable' to face the rigours and disappointments of film auditions. More practically, 'Tony was too inexperienced an actor. It was the wrong time in his career.' When Rounce attempted to explain this to Hancock they argued and he stormed out of her office.

The next day Hancock telephoned Sid James and they arranged to meet at the offices of James's agent, Archie Parnell & Co, in Golden Square, just behind Regent Street. Here Hancock was introduced to Phyllis Parnell. The agency client list was impressive and Parnell had personally managed James since the late 1940s. Other artists included Jack Warner, Morecambe and Wise and Terry-Thomas, who Phyllis Rounce had discovered and named. More importantly to Hancock, Parnell had also handled Sid Field until his death in 1950.

Having decided to quit International Artistes, Hancock now faced the dilemma of informing Rounce. It was a confrontation he was not looking forward to and could not face. He got as far as the front door of his agent's office before losing his nerve and bolting. He spent the afternoon two doors away at the Irving, a tiny seventy-five-seat theatre above an Indian restaurant. The all-male revue was managed by Ted Gatty, who spent each Christmas season in the provinces as a panto dame. Hancock just had time to catch the first early-evening sets before the fifteen-minute walk back to the Adelphi. Top of the bill was Danny Carroll, a female impersonator who would soon change his name to Danny La Rue.

London Laughs was still playing at the Adelphi Theatre. Each night for more than a year Rounce would arrive half-an-hour before curtain up and search the nearby pubs until she had located Hancock, then walk him back to his dressing room. It was a ritual as much for the agent as it was for her client, but on Tuesday, 13 October, she could not find him. 'I thought for once in his life he had gone straight to the Adelphi,' said Rounce. 'He had.'

As she walked past the keeper's lodge on her way to Hancock's basement dressing room 'Toothless Fred', the Adelphi stage door keeper, called her back. He looked apologetic. 'I'm sorry, Miss,' he said. 'I've been given instructions not to allow you down to Mr Hancock's dressing room.' When Rounce asked who had banned her from seeing her client, the door keeper shook his head and walked away.

'I was sad, very sad,' remembers Rounce. 'We had been, and still were, very close and Tony had given me no indication something was wrong.' Not long before they had laid plans for Hancock's long-term career and his eventual move to television. As she waited for a taxi to take her home, the full implication hit her. Rounce walked to her Irving Street office and extracted Hancock's contract from the file: it was dated 13 October, 1948. Hancock's five-year agreement with International Artistes expired at midnight.

The next day and 'terribly upset', Rounce dictated letters informing the various BBC heads of department that 'Tony Hancock is no longer represented by this office'. To Tim Holland Bennett at BBC Television she joked:

I shall miss the friendly wrangle I expected I might have with you over the fee for the possible TV series in the spring! However, maybe I'll find someone else to wrangle over with you instead!

And to Ronald Waldman she advised:

With regard to the discussions which were in course for the possible TV series in the spring, I think the best thing will be for you to contact him [Hancock] direct at his home, telephone number Western 7966.

That night Rounce returned to the Adelphi and insisted on seeing Hancock. It was, she said, an extraordinary encounter: 'I was asking for an explanation and he just sat there like a great woolly bear and said nothing at all.' For half-an-hour Hancock played with his hands and studied his feet. Finally Rounce got up to go. At the door she turned and saw Hancock looking at her with 'great wells of tears in his eyes'.

'Oh well,' said Rounce. 'Cheerio.' Hancock silently watched her leave.

Rounce's association with a 'wonderful, lovable, hideous, vile, hateful, glorious, idiotic genius' was over. She had never been in love with Hancock – 'not in a woman to man thing' – but for five years she had endured his tantrums like a mother and suffered his imperfections like a wife. 'You could kill him one minute for being an absolute pig and hug him the next for doing something hilarious. You needed an awful lot of patience and the ability to take an awful lot of stick.'

The following Saturday Hancock typed his own letter to Ronald Waldman. It informed the BBC producer that from Monday, 19 October, he would be represented by 'Messrs Archie Parnell & Co Ltd of 3 Golden Square, W1'.

Phyllis Rounce has repeatedly and publicly blamed the loss of her client on Hancock's future press agent – and later wife – Freddie Ross. Through years of interviews Rounce has said: 'She [Ross] hated the sight of me and if she could do something to get me out of the dressing room she would.' Rounce's memory is incorrect. Hancock would not meet Freddie Ross until a year after he had sacked his agent.

Hancock still could not understand why his sat-upon face and flummoxed silence on stage should produce so much amusement. Dennis Main Wilson had a name for it. He called it Hancock's 'frog face'. It was a reaction which increasingly worried the comedian whose concern was genuine and childlike in its naïvety. Far from recognising his hapless confusion as a talent to be developed and exploited, Hancock felt he was defrauding the audience by not working hard enough, as if his non-reaction – his bewilderment – was a sign of weakness or inexperience.

Just when Hancock realised the potential of silence is unsure. It was almost certainly an accident. Dennis Main Wilson believed he witnessed one of the first incidents during a Hancock pantomime appearance. Phyllis Rounce, as one of her final acts as Hancock's manager, had booked her client to play Buttons in a 1953 Christmas production of *Cinderella*. It was his third staging of the pantomime and his second as the ugly sisters' put-upon man-servant. Towards the end of its run, Main Wilson drove to Nottingham to watch Hancock at the Theatre Royal. One of the show's stars was George Bolton, a music-hall comic who had been a regular guest at Durlston Court and a drinking companion of Jack Hancock. Bolton relied heavily on traditional music-hall routines. During his first appearance on stage he would sum up an audience and then spit out a particular routine, much the same as game plays are spontaneously used to confuse the opposition in American football.

Hancock and Main Wilson were sitting in the wings as Bolton, dressed as the Dame, was about to make his entrance for a kitchen scene. 'Right,' he barked at Hancock, 'we'll do the teapots,' and promptly marched on stage.

'What?' Hancock asked.

'Something about teapots,' Main Wilson offered.

For twelve minutes Hancock stood motionless on stage as Bolton performed 'the teapots' – a double-handed routine – solo. Hancock stared 'frog faced' at Bolton. Waves of laughter rolled towards the stage. 'The less Tony understood Bolton's antics the more laughs he got,' recalled Main Wilson.

Phyllis Rounce had her own 'frog face' theory. People laughed at him, she claimed, because Hancock was a 'natural comedian' and that is very different to a comic. 'A comic is somebody who has a script of jokes, a comedian is a whole person. Tony was a whole person and the public instantly saw him as such. He could stand there with just his feet and they would fall about laughing. He didn't have to say anything, he would have that hopeless look on his face and shuffle about and the whole place would be in uproar.'

A few months later London audiences were treated to the same unscripted mayhem. Jimmy Edwards, like Hancock, had an exceptionally low boredom threshold. Unlike Hancock, whose instinct was to turn his back on the source of his suffering, Edwards would short-circuit the irritation and amuse himself by ad-libbing. Marooned in the middle of a sketch by an unscripted and unexpected line Hancock's mind would go blank. Dennis Main Wilson was frequently present when 'Jim would throw out some outrageous ad-lib and get a huge laugh . . . Tony would just stand there, in the middle of the stage, and shut up – the full frog face – and so the circle started. The more Tony shut up the more laughs he got, and the more laughs he got the more Jimmy would ad-lib.' The Adelphi has a long, narrow auditorium with a very direct sight line. 'From there you could see row upon row of shoulders rocking with laughter,' added Main Wilson. To Edwards it was a mischievous game. Hancock, however, found the audience's disloyalty as frustrating as his own inability to respond. 'Why are they laughing at me?' he would ask Main Wilson. 'Jim's the star, not me.'

Hancock had, by this time, developed his own theory about audiences. He found them conversely fascinating and frightening; invariably malevolent and always unanimous. 'Sometimes,' he explained, 'I think an audience assembles in Hyde Park and decides what sort of an audience they're going to be. When they've all decided they go to the theatre.' When it wasn't part of his job to confront them he would eagerly pay to hide among them. At least once a week

Hancock escaped alone to the cinema. In the darkness – and usually at the back – he would sit unrecognised and relaxed. It never occurred to him to invite Cicely.

It was while he was playing Buttons in Nottingham that Hancock decided to change agents a second time in less than three months. Once again he did not have the courage to end the albeit brief association face to face. Back in London, Phyllis Parnell began to hear rumours that her new client had agreed to join Kavanagh Associates, an agency originally founded for radio writers. Parnell telephoned Hancock in Nottingham. He confirmed he had spoken to Jack Adams at Kavanagh's and Parnell, a fierce but courteous businesswoman, wished him well.

Two days before the end of the year Hancock sat in his Theatre Royal dressing room and typed a letter to the BBC's television booking department. It 'officially' advised the corporation he had appointed 'Messrs Kavanagh Productions Ltd, of 201 Regent Street, London W1' as his agents for all television and radio work. All enquiries, contracts, correspondence and payment cheques should be sent direct to his new agents.

Kavanagh Associates was founded in 1945 by the scriptwriter and *ITMA* co-creator, Ted Kavanagh. Born in Auckland, New Zealand, Kavanagh had come to Britain after the First World War to study medicine at Edinburgh University, but soon discovered his real talent lay in comedy writing. One of his first successes was a joke column in *G. K.'s Weekly*, the magazine founded and edited by G. K. Chesterton. By the late 1930s he was an experienced and prolific BBC staff writer. He could devise and dictate an *It's That Man Again* script in three hours – 'Ted was the only person I've met who could write as quickly as I could type,' his secretary, Sybil Dickinson, admitted – and in the first ten weeks of the war Kavanagh wrote thirty-four radio shows. His long-held ambition was to launch a literary agency for the 'comfort and protection' of radio writers. In 1947 Kavanagh Associates was joined by Denis Norden and Frank Muir, then still in the RAF, and one of its earliest clients was Jimmy Edwards.

*

Hancock's radio appearances, although popular, left him frustratingly faceless and anonymous. Only a tiny percentage of the general public lived within travelling distance of the Adelphi and few of his wireless fans could afford the price of a theatre seat. The recognition Hancock sought among his peers, particularly established and experienced variety entertainers, was equally elusive. It was left to George Fairweather, his mentor from Bournemouth, to make the introductions.

Olivelli's was an Italian restaurant just off the Tottenham Court Road. The public ate in the ground-floor dining room, but down a short flight of stairs was a second room which had become an unofficial club for artistes and entertainers. All four walls were jigsawed with signed photographs and posters of pre-war variety stars. The flat above the restaurant was occupied by Jack Wilson, one-time member of the dance trio Wilson, Kepple and Betty. The 59-year-old soft-shoe dancer from Liverpool had made his first stage appearance in vaudeville in 1909 and was, in Hancock's eyes, a show-business legend. In exchange for free meals Wilson would play the piano.

Fairweather was a frequent visitor to the Hancocks' Queen's Gate Terrace flat. One night, as he and Cicely waited in her husband's Adelphi dressing room, Fairweather suggested they have supper at Olivelli's. To his surprise, Hancock admitted that, despite serving in Italy during the war, he had never eaten Italian food. As he consumed his first bowl of spaghetti, Fairweather introduced him to many of the veteran performers he had only seen across the footlights of Bournemouth theatres or in the bar of the Durlston Court Hotel. 'Hancock was thrilled,' recalled Fairweather. 'I introduced him to Jack Wilson and they got on famously. Tony was so excited to be in the presence of these people. He appreciated the theatrical tradition and this was like shaking hands with the Gods.'

Lesser mortals were equally fascinating to Hancock, even those with the thinnest show-business connections. Michael Tobin was a former Navy stoker and middleweight boxer who worked as a stagehand at the now closed Scala Theatre. When not working, Tobin was a regular at the majority of Soho public houses. The origins of his friendship with Hancock remain obscure: they first met at the Swiss, the York Minster, or the Wheatsheaf in Charlotte Street, Tobin could never remember exactly which.

Hancock was intrigued by the way Tobin sprinkled his conversation with 'whistles' (suits) and 'syrups' (wigs) and other more colourful rhyming slang. Tobin was also addicted to familiar saws, his favourite being 'the only sin is to be skint.' Hancock ensured it rarely happened and the stagehand repaid the occasional fiver by insisting on calling his friend 'Mr Hancock'. 'I wouldn't see him for weeks and then I would bump into Mr Hancock and his wife several times in one week,' recalled Tobin. 'No matter whose company he was in he would always shake you by the hand and make you feel an equal. Sometimes you felt he was embarrassed by his own wealth and popularity. He just wanted to have a night out with the lads and as long as nobody recognised him, Mr Hancock enjoyed himself.'

1954

IT WAS A bitterly cold February day. Hancock, Bill Kerr, Ray Galton and Alan Simpson were walking back to the BBC's Paris studio. Throughout lunch Kerr – who was now starring in his own weekly Radio Luxembourg show – had regaled his companions with tales of his antipodean childhood and, as the quartet crossed Berkeley Square, one of the writers suggested using an Australian character in Hancock's forthcoming series. 'That's not a bad idea,' he admitted.

A few days earlier Dennis Main Wilson had been recalled to oversee the final ten editions of *Star Bill*. The regular team included Hancock, Graham Stark and Moira Lister, who as a fifteen-year-old had launched a South African Broadcasting Corporation children's series with a part-time actor and full-time Johannesburg hairdresser called

Sid James. The producer, who was also busy formulating Hancock's planned situation comedy, announced his intention to 'find a few really new names to put into the show'. It was assumed – at least by Lister and Stark – that they would automatically be carried over to the new series. If, as Galton and Simpson now suggested, Bill Kerr was offered a part, then someone would have to be dropped.

By the time the group turned into Lower Regent Street Hancock had convinced himself Graham Stark should be the one to go – he also decided who should have the delicate task of telling his long-time friend.

Late the next month Stark was called in to see Main Wilson at his Æolian Hall office. The actor was informed there would be six more *Star Bills*, but after that 'there would be some policy changes'.

'You mean that I'm not going to be in the new series?' demanded Stark.

Main Wilson looked embarrassed. 'It's just that we . . .'

'We?' interrupted Stark. 'What do you mean we? Do you mean you personally or Ray or Alan?'

Main Wilson was blushing. 'No, Tony feels . . .'

'Tony isn't the BBC,' said Stark. 'We started *Star Bill* without Tony, he was brought in. It helped make him a star. And if I may say so, you and I and Ray and Alan contributed much more.'

'I know. I agree,' said the producer, attempting to reassure Stark. 'Don't worry, Graham, we'll do six more shows, the last six. There's no question of you not being in them.'

It was then, remembered Stark, that the penny dropped. 'How could Tony do this to me? I couldn't understand it. We got on great and I didn't compete with him. Suddenly it was going to be *Hancock's Half Hour* and I wasn't going to be in it.'

Years later Dennis Main Wilson would lay the decision to exclude Stark firmly on Hancock's ruthless ambition. 'He walked in one day and announced he had had this great idea,' remembered the producer. 'Tony wanted Bill Kerr in the cast and had convinced himself it would give the show more depth. I was not so sure. It was one of the few times we argued.' For his part, Hancock resolutely blamed Main

Wilson, claiming the producer refused to hire Graham Stark because their voices were too similar. 'It broke my heart because I thought we were great friends,' said Stark. 'I owed him a great debt, but the rift was there.'

Under Dennis Main Wilson's guidance and with a dedicated team, *Star Bill* was becoming a Sunday night must for Light Programme listeners. During the first February show – broadcast from the Garrick Theatre – the producer was informed that 'a strange man in evening dress and top hat' was trespassing backstage. Main Wilson found the offender watching the live broadcast from the wings and asked him to leave, but the stranger justified his presence: 'After all, it *is* my theatre.'

Main Wilson apologised to Jack Buchanan. As he turned to leave the veteran music-hall comedian added: 'I do walk-ons, you know.' The following week, Buchanan was the show's star guest.

Securing the services of another star was not so easy. Maurice Chevalier was appearing at the London Hippodrome where the French singer and actor was rumoured to be getting several thousand pounds a week. Undaunted, Dennis Main Wilson telephoned Chevalier at his hotel and asked him to appear on *Star Bill* for one hundred and fifty guineas. Chevalier seemed interested, despite the size of the fee, and asked what was involved. The producer explained he wanted a four-minute solo, a three- or four-minute exchange with Hancock and a second solo lasting about eight minutes. There was a pause. 'Chevalier cannot work in eight minutes,' said the star sniffily. 'Chevalier needs an hour.'

'But the whole show is only an hour long,' retorted Main Wilson.

'Zat is your problem,' said Chevalier.

The BBC was as eager as Main Wilson to accommodate the Frenchman. He was given permission to record Chevalier's hour-long act and extract two suitable solo spots. During the studio session an awe-struck Graham Stark found himself standing next to Chevalier who was continually popping boiled sweets into his mouth. 'I can't ask him why,' Stark told himself. 'He's God.' It was Chevalier who offered an explanation: 'I have just given up ze smocking.'

While Hancock was working at the microphone, Chevalier whispered: 'I laik ze way you work togazzer, you don't bozzer about ze leetle laughs, but wait for ze big one.' He then proceeded to give Stark a complete exposition on comedy. 'It was magnificent, a real privilege,' remembered Stark. 'And I've forgotten every bloody word of it.'

Jack Hylton decided to follow the successful run of *London Laughs* with a new show, to be called *The Talk of the Town*. His latest production would open for a summer season in Blackpool before moving to the capital, and would again star Jimmy Edwards and Tony Hancock. To replace Vera Lynn the impresario hired Joan Turner.

Hancock and Cicely rented a furnished flat overlooking the promenade and moved to Blackpool in time for the start of rehearsals during the second week in May. A week or so later Dennis Main Wilson arrived in the Lancashire resort to discuss Hancock's radio series, by now scheduled for an October launch, and to catch some time with a woman he was dating in the show's chorus line. As the producer walked along the promenade towards the Opera House, he recognised a slim, attractive young woman he had not seen for several months. 'I'm off to watch Hancock and Jimmy Edwards,' he told Freddie Ross. 'Why don't you come along?' It was an invitation that would change the course of Hancock's life.

Freddie – 'daunting, dynamic and driving' – had just launched her own public relations company and one of her first clients was the Ted Heath Band. She was in Blackpool to make press and publicity contacts for the orchestra's summer tour. Main Wilson and Freddie Ross walked to the theatre and, to keep out of sight, watched the final rehearsal from the back of the circle. Hancock was on stage. 'His hair was longer than it should have been and he looked as if he was carrying all the troubles of the world on his shoulders,' Freddie remembers thinking. The stage was chaotic and noisy and cluttered. Hancock was dressed in his favourite casual clothes: a sweater over an open-necked shirt and baggy trousers from which poked a pair of scuffed suede shoes.

Aware of Hancock's talent for mimicry, Galton and Simpson had created a sketch they dubbed the 'Crooner'; it was a sketch he would use – overuse – for the rest of his career. That night it would get its first airing. 'Here is another singing sensation,' the off-stage announcer would proclaim. 'You've heard of Johnnie Ray. Now here's Britain's answer to them all – Mr Rhythm himself – Tony Hancock.' Suitably clad in a square-cut, pale-blue velveteen frock coat, bootlace necktie and suede brothel-creepers, Hancock would slink his way to the centre of the stage. Chorus girls, planted in the audience, would scream and faint. Hancock would twitch his lip and strut for a few seconds before bringing on his pianist: 'Now, I'd like to introduce my pianist, arranger, composer and brother-in-law, Sam.' His stooge would appear dressed in an identical zoot suit and, for the next five minutes, Hancock would growl his way through *The Little White Cloud That Cried*, a weepy made famous by Johnnie Ray.

Watching Hancock rehearse was a painful, sometimes infuriating, experience. Once it was perfected, he would rapidly lose interest in a sketch or routine. When *The Talk of the Town* run-through was over he shuffled off-stage and Main Wilson offered to introduce Freddie. She remembers Hancock appearing like a bloodhound wearing an enormous thick sweater. Close up, the thirty-year-old comedian looked tired and sleep-worn. His voice was animated yet flat, like someone whose mind was elsewhere. Freddie had a reputation for straight talking and honest – sometimes painful – advice. She told him: 'If I had a talent like yours I'd be proud, not worried.' Hancock never forgot or forgave the comment.

Freda Ross – the Freddie would come later by deed poll – was born in 1930 within the sound of London's Bow bells. Her father, Harry Ross, was a religious quiet-spoken bookmaker, her mother a prototype Jewish woman dedicated to keeping the family's middle-class Hampstead home clean and tidy and a suitable place to raise her daughter and son, Leonard.

Always ambitious, Freddie was educated at South Hampstead High School, before completing a Regent Street Polytechnic commercial course. The world of show business fascinated her, and the Ross family had at first indulged and then supported her ambition to one day run her own public relations company. Her first job, with a shipping line, was followed in the early 1950s by one with a film company.

The *Talk of the Town* opening night went well. After the show Hancock and Cicely suggested Main Wilson and Freddie join them for a meal. When they arrived at the Hancocks' flat Freddie let slip she was a 'publicity agent'. It was as if a curtain had slammed shut in front of Hancock; he became belligerent and defensive, virtually accusing his guest of a parasitic existence, living off the talent of her clients.

'We argued,' Freddie remembers of their first meeting. 'We never really stopped arguing. He was an exciting personality. He did not smile all that often, but when he did it was worthwhile. His eyes smiled a lot. He had a lasting effect on me from that moment.' At twenty-four Freddie Ross had fallen in love with a married man six years her senior.

The Talk of the Town opened at Blackpool's Opera House on 5 June and would run for four months. Within a week Hancock was complaining to Cicely about the show; it was a mistake, he was bored, his performances were a disaster. By the second week he had telephoned Jack Adams, his agent at Kavanagh Associates, voicing his dissatisfaction. Before the end of June Hancock had decided – and announced – he wanted out. Hylton's grip on his performers was legendary and Adams attempted to persuade his client to stick it out. The only way to get himself 'honourably released' from the contract was to be certified medically unfit, an idea, Jimmy Edwards later admitted, he jokingly suggested one night at the Hancocks' flat.

Hancock promptly made an appointment with a psychiatrist fifty miles away in Bolton. After the consultation, Cicely drove him back to Blackpool with a letter claiming his part in the show was 'seriously affecting his state of mind'. Hylton – who was born in 'bloody Bolton' and therefore mistrusted every doctor practising in the town – blasted his way through the ploy.

Back in London, Adams and the other senior members of Kavanagh Associates found themselves with a tricky problem. The reasons for Hancock's decision to leave the show were not understood or appreciated. They were, however, Hancock's agents and friends and obliged to support him. Hylton had threatened to subject his unwilling star to a new psychiatric examination, but when Adams suggested Hancock return to London for a second opinion he refused.

Denis Norden takes up the story: 'In the end I rang up a Harley Street man, told him what the position was and asked if he could help in any way. He said he couldn't go to Blackpool, but if I came along and saw him we might be able to plot some kind of campaign. So I underwent a strange kind of once-removed analysis. I actually lay down on the couch and poured out someone else's problems. The most interesting thing we discovered was that Tony owned three cars but couldn't drive. This was right up the psychiatrist's alley. "Obviously there is some sort of problem there," he concluded.'

Hylton's friend and legal adviser was Oscar Beuselinck, a tough and ambitious 34-year-old solicitor who had grown up in a cramped one-bedroomed Holborn flat. The solicitor prided himself on – and even cultivated – his image as a vulgar-speaking East End boy, politically incorrect with women and mockingly respectful of class.* Beuselinck – who was to dominate show-business law and litigation for the next four decades – advised Hylton to sue 'and ruin Hancock'. The lawyer informed Hancock of his options and Hancock decided to stay with the show.

Each morning would find Cicely patiently suffering her husband's attempts at learning to drive as he negotiated the roads to Fleetwood or Lytham St Anne's or crawled through the Lancashire countryside. When Hancock eventually took his driving test it was his enmity towards the car – and mechanical objects in general – which contributed to his first-time failure. Cicely remained content to chauffeur her husband, while Hancock was glad to leave such complicated devices as gearboxes and windscreen wipers to his wife.

Throughout the spring and summer Ray Galton and Alan Simpson were busy weaving the first tentative strands of a radio fable. Although

---

* In later life Oscar Beuselinck was equally proud of the achievement of his son, the actor Paul Nicholas.

Hancock's imaginary home would not be fixed in the public's imagination for at least another year, the writers had already decided he should live in the dowdier end – the east end – of Cheam, the middle-class dormitory suburb which housed Phyllis Rounce's mother.

Within his shambling East Cheam residence Hancock would hold court. Galton and Simpson now needed a coterie of friends to play against their hero's pomposity. Bill Kerr had already been recruited, but the embryonic Hancock would also need a forceful girlfriend, someone to 'take him in hand'. The ideal choice was Moira Lister. To complete the trio Galton and Simpson had a character, but no actor. By early March they had an actor – but no name. 'We had already decided we wanted a shady, crooked character,' explains Ray Galton. 'And we knew who we wanted for the part. What we did not know was his name.' The pair had seen the actor in the 1951 Ealing comedy, *The Lavender Hill Mob*. The film was now on its second release and Galton and Simpson tracked it down to a flea-pit cinema in Putney. When they took their seats the film had already started. The man they wanted was playing Lackery. 'We knew that this wonderful face had always played crooks in films,' said Galton. 'But we had to sit through the entire film until the credits came up and we could find out his name.' The man they wanted was Sid James.

Dennis Main Wilson arranged a Sunday meeting for them at the Garrick Theatre between the rehearsal and the live evening broadcast of *Star Bill*. When James arrived he was met by Galton and Simpson and taken to Hancock's dressing room behind the stage, where the writers outlined the new series. Then Hancock, who had only recently signed his contract for his new series, invited Sid James to join the cast. To everyone's surprise, James appeared hesitant. The meeting was friendly enough, but at first he refused to commit himself. Less than eight years after his arrival in Britain he was an established stage and screen actor, having appeared in nearly fifty films, and a month earlier, in February, he had taken over the part of Nathan Detroit in the musical *Guys and Dolls*.

In desperation James admitted, 'I'm not really a radio actor.' As ever it was a half-truth. James already had considerable radio acting experience. Only weeks before he had appeared in *Another Part of the Forest*, part of the BBC's highly acclaimed Twentieth Century Theatre. Dennis Main Wilson kept up the pressure and Hancock naïvely assured him, 'There's nothing to it … it's easy.' James ultimately agreed, with the proviso that if either of them felt the show was suffering because of his acting, he should be allowed to drop out.

Many years later, Sid James claimed he agreed to do 'one show at a time' because he didn't want to get too involved with *Hancock's Half Hour*. 'At first I said no,' he admitted. 'I think I am a very bad radio actor. I like to work with my hands and my face, and I said, "No, I don't fancy it." Then Dennis Main Wilson said, "Well, just try one." So I tried one, and then I tried two, and I'm very glad I did.'

There were two reasons for James's reluctance, but neither would become apparent for another seven months.

For many years type-cast as a 'heavy', Sid James was now fast earning his life-long reputation as a comic actor – 'Above all I am an actor who plays comic parts.' James had never worked with a comedian before. The prospect of being forced into ad-libbing appalled him as much as it did Hancock. Attempting to keep pace in front of an audience while recording a show terrified James even more.

The cast of *Hancock's Half Hour* assembled for the first time at 10am on Saturday, 30 October. Main Wilson's initial choice for a studio had been the Paris Cinema but in the end he had to settle for the Camden Theatre. The morning rehearsal and early-afternoon recording would allow Sid James to appear in the matinée performance of his West End musical, *Guys and Dolls*. The initial read-through went well and Main Wilson called a technical run-through to check equipment and sound effects. He discovered Sid James's hands were shaking so much he could not turn the pages of the script without the rustle being picked up by the microphones. They tried placing the sheets of paper on music stands. This time James caused chaos by flourishing his hands, sending the stands crashing down and the pages fluttering across the stage.

Hancock went out to warm up the audience. When he was joined by the rest of the cast, James shuffled on stage with his trilby pulled down over his eyes and the script held up to hide the rest of his face. 'He was shaking with fear,' remembers Alan Simpson. 'He was petrified of the audience.' The recording had to be stopped several times – Sid James was holding the script so close to his face that all the microphones could pick up was a series of mumbles.

That summer a young composer called Wally Stott* had been asked to attend a meeting in Dennis Main Wilson's office. The producer invited the musician to write the music for his autumn comedy series after attempting to describe the *Hancock's Half Hour* format and acting out parts of the script. Stott thought that 'the whole thing was very unfunny and even quite boring'.

Wally Stott was one of the BBC's most prolific composers. In the early 1950s Stanley Black – who Main Wilson had originally asked to write the *Half Hour* music – was so successful he could not handle all the assignments offered him and Stott took over several of Black's commissions, including a Jerome Kern album, two films – *Hindle Wakes* and *Top Secret* – and the BBC's innovative *Goon Show*.

Main Wilson had estimated he would need opening and closing signature tunes and playout music. To cover the demands of future, and so far unwritten, scripts, he also commissioned nineteen link pieces ranging in length from one minute fifteen seconds down to a snappy seven seconds. The incidental and cue music was recorded one evening at the BBC studios in Piccadilly and a short time later the main *Half Hour* theme was laid down during a session at the Æolian Hall. 'There was never any special meaning behind the signature tune,' Stott admitted many years later. 'I had been playing with the tune, or something very like it, for some time. I was simply given a chance to use it.'

Popular legend has it that the signature tune was written as a pompous musical representation of the comedian himself. Hancock is

---

* After moving to the United States Wally Stott underwent a sex-change operation and is now known as Angela Morley.

In seventeen years Hancock sank from a confident up-and-coming star to a neurotic drunk. Between 1950...

1958   ... and 1967.

One of the few surviving pictures of Jack Hancock (left). Taken in the entrance of the Railway Hotel, Hancock's father is talking to Bournemouth band leader Percy Pearce (right) and Charles Coburn, one of the few men who literally broke the bank of Monte Carlo.

The Railway Hotel, Holdenhurst Road, Bournemouth. Hancock was three years old when the family moved into the attic apartment. © *The Daily Echo, Bournemouth.*

Lily Hancock: she became an enthusiastic spiritualist after the death of her eldest son.

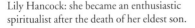

ABOVE RIGHT A rare picture of the three Hancock brothers – Colin (left), Tony (centre) and Roger – with their mother and family friends at the rear of Durlston Court. Colin would disappear while flying with the RAF in the Second World War. © *The Daily Echo, Bournemouth.*

The *Wings* tour opened at the New Opera House, Blackpool, on 28th April and ended twenty-one weeks later at Morecambe. During the run Hancock celebrated his twenty-third birthday.

Durlston Court Hotel, Bournemouth. During the war it was requisitioned by the Army Pay Corps. © *The Daily Echo.*

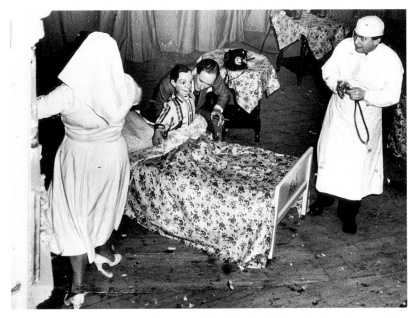

On tour with Archie Andrews and Peter Brough. In this sketch Hancock plays a doctor and Hattie Jacques (left) a nurse.

In the early 1950s Hancock's voice was more familiar than his face. For those who recognised him he was happy to pose for a holiday snapshot.

Hancock rides pillion to his mentor George Fairweather. Behind him is Slim Miller, his fellow RAF Regiment recruit and first comedy partner. © *George Fairweather*.

Hancock – who had a thing about hats – and his wife, Cicely. Despite owning three cars Hancock rarely drove – 'It's my feet, I tell them to apply the brake and they hit the accelerator'. © *George Fairweather*.

Hancock and Cicely and George Fairweather outside a Bournemouth public house in the early 1950s. An apparently happy marriage and his wife's Cordon Bleu cooking soon took their toll on Hancock's waistline.
© *George Fairweather*.

GROUP 3 presents

BRIAN REECE · MARGOT GRAHAME

RAYMOND HUNTLEY · SIDNEY JAMES

in

ORDERS ARE ORDERS

DISTRIBUTED BY BRITISH LION

CLIVE MORTON with PETER SELLERS AND INTRODUCING TONY HANCOCK

CAMPAIGN SHEET

Hancock's abiding obsession was his 'anarchist' feet – 'They've been put on wrong. They don't join at the ankle. I can feel them flapping about like penguins'.

In 1953 Hancock made his first film *Orders are Orders*. During shooting at Beaconsfield Studios he was introduced to Sid James – 'The only good thing about the film'.
© *Tony Hillman Collection*.

It's never me, but I'll admit to it

RETAIN FOR ARCHIVES

TONY HANCOCK
with
MOIRA LISTER, BILL KERR AND SIDNEY JAMES
in
"HANCOCK'S HALF HOUR"
(First of series)

Dramatis Personae

Tony Hancock (a cad)................ Mr. Anthony Aloysius St.
John Hancock II

Moira Lister (Tony's girl friend), Miss Moira Lister

Bill Kerr (Tony's best friend).... Mr. Bill Kerr

Sidney James (a friend)........... Mr. Sidney James

Coatsleeve Charlie................ Mr. Gerald Campion

Lord Dockyard..................... Mr. Kenneth Williams

INCIDENTAL MUSIC COMPOSED BY STANLEY BLACK
and recorded by the BBC REVUE ORCHESTRA,
conducted by HARRY RABINOWITZ

SCRIPT BY RAY GALTON & ALAN
SIMPSON

ANNOUNCER: LESLIE MALLER

PRODUCED BY   DENNIS MAIN WILSON

REHEARSALS: SATURDAY 30th OCTOBER 1954:   10.00-12.00p.m. CAMDEN

RECORDING: SATURDAY 30th OCTOBER 1954:   12.30-1.15pm. CAMDEN

TRANSMISSION: TUESDAY 2nd NOVEMBER 1954:   9.30-10.00pm. LIGHT & G.O.S.

                SATURDAY 6th NOVEMBER 1954:   10.30-11.00am. G.O.S.

REPEAT:

B.R.REF.NO: TLO 65477

Hancock with *Half Hour* writers Alan Simpson (left) and Ray Galton (right) – the trio would dominate British comedy for the next seven years. © *BBC*.

LEFT The first page of the first ever *Hancock's Half Hour*. The incidental music – written by Wally Stott – has been incorrectly credited to Stanley Black. © *BBC*.

For twelve years, from 1956 until he died, Hancock used a tape recorder to help him learn his television and film scripts.

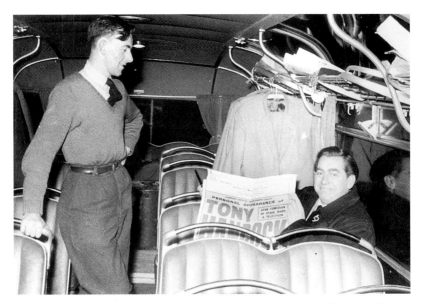

In March 1957 – while taking part in a Combined Services Entertainment Show at RAF Wunstorf, West Germany – Hancock allowed an airman to take his picture. The photographs have remained unpublished for more than forty years. © *J Harker*.

Stars of the RAF Wunstorf show (left to right): Ben Lyon, Vera Lynn, Max Geldray, Hancock and Tommy Godfrey. © *J Harker*.

portrayed by a tuba, a fortuitous choice of instrument in the light of his East Cheam nickname of 'Tubs'. In reality Stott had never seen Hancock. The pair did not meet until several months later when, after Stott had sat through a *Half Hour* recording, Hancock shook hands with the composer and briefly thanked him for his 'nice tune'.

The British public heard Stott's 'nice tune' for the first time on Tuesday, 2 November, 1954. It was a damp miserable day across most of Britain, with London shrouded in thick fog. The BBC planners had given *Hancock's Half Hour* a Light Programme slot between 9.30 and 10.00pm. The theme – described as 'Hancock opening' on every subsequent script – is now part of radio and comedy history. So, too, is Hancock's 'signature' title line: *'H-H-H-Hancock's ... Half Hour'*. The suggestion to open the programme with this was Dennis Main Wilson's. Hancock thought the idea too much of a gimmick and said so. For several weeks before the first recording he attempted to persuade the producer to drop the breathless stammer. 'I asked him to trust me,' said Main Wilson.

The plot, although not one of their best, demonstrates Galton and Simpson's ability to reproduce the scripted equivalent of a hall of mirrors, a feat they repeated several times during the next seven years. As the theme fades the announcer sets the scene:

> Yes – this is the first night of the lad's new radio series. Such occasions are usually marked by a small celebration of some sort, but Tony Hancock is really doing it in style – he is going to throw a cocktail and dinner party ...

To the sound of someone slowly and deliberately pecking at a typewriter Hancock delivers his first *Half Hour* line:

> Hancock: Hurry up, Kerr. Haven't you finished typing out those invitations yet?
>
> Bill:　　 Don't rush me, don't rush me.
>
> Effects:　TYPEWRITER CONTINUES SLOW CLACKING.

Hancock: It might help if you took the boxing gloves off.

Dennis Main Wilson's instinct that Kerr's accent would contrast well with Hancock's still rather high-pitched voice proved instantly justified. It soon became apparent there were other benefits. The inclusion of an Australian allowed the writers to develop not only a different accent, but a different attitude, and to show listeners, sometimes for the first time, how people lived outside the United Kingdom. More importantly, Kerr feels with hindsight, it allowed someone from the far side of the world to show how they would react to England and the English.

Two other actors appeared in the first broadcast. One would never work with Hancock again. The second would first become a friend – and then a threat.

Galton and Simpson had written a small part for a character they called 'Coatsleeve (sniff, sniff) Charlie'. The writers suggested Gerald Campion, an actor friend who ran a West End theatrical club called the Buxton. A generous man, Campion – already a television star in his own right – allowed out-of-work pros to run up slate accounts and pay when they could. Despite being a grown man he had, two years earlier, proved instantly successful as *Billy Bunter of Greyfriars School*. The television adaptations of Frank Richards's misadventures of William George Bunter would run for ten years, but Campion's association with Hancock lasted a single episode.

By the middle of October – and with less than three weeks before the first recording – Dennis Main Wilson still needed an actor versatile enough to cope with the numerous odd-ball characters Galton and Simpson were writing into the scripts, sometimes as many as five or six in each episode. Main Wilson telephoned various agents without success. Finally, one suggested he could do worse than sit through a performance of Shaw's *Saint Joan* at the Arts Theatre. Playing the part of the Dauphin was a tall, elegant young actor the producer had never heard of, but, borrowing a copy of *Theatre World* magazine, which featured a review of *St Joan*, Main Wilson thought he might, at last, have found the actor he was looking for. 'Here is a young actor who likes to play unusual comedy roles that have more depth and scope than the juvenile parts in most plays.'

The BBC producer would never forget his first meeting with Kenneth Williams. Arriving at the stage door Main Wilson asked to see the actor. He was, he later admitted, about to do Kenneth Williams the 'biggest favour of his life'. To his surprise Main Wilson was informed: 'He's very busy ... you'll have to wait.'

Main Wilson adjourned to a nearby public house where Williams eventually swept majestically into the bar and boomed: 'Well, what do you want?'

'I'm a BBC producer ...'

'Mmm ...' interrupted Williams. 'I don't like the wireless.' He accepted the offer of a light ale and then demanded: 'Well, what's it all about then?'

For half-an-hour Main Wilson enlarged upon his 'great idea for a show'. The gauche and still pimply 28-year-old Williams listened contemptuously. Suddenly he crumpled in a fit of giggles. 'I don't care,' said Williams. 'I'll do it. I'll do it.'

Main Wilson arranged a formal interview at the BBC for Tuesday, 19 October. 'I am to play some old lord in a minute spot,' Williams noted that night in his diary. In reality he would perform in twelve of the sixteen first-series episodes and go on to appear in eighty-eight radio and six television shows. He would record *Hancock's Half Hour* in the mornings and then return to his role as the Dauphin each evening. In the first episode Williams plays the part of an elderly duke who unknowingly lends Hancock his flat for the weekend and returns to discover 'there's jelly on my Rembrandt'.

Main Wilson admitted Williams's duke was 'every bit as good' as Shaw's ageing king. But it was the actor's manipulation of dialogue – of individual words – which first impressed and then annoyed the gimmick-hating Hancock. From the second *Half Hour*, Williams would play the postman or the policeman or the irate neighbour. While still performing in *St Joan* he would deliver Shaw's line, 'I am not such a fool as I look. I have my eyes open' and, in what seemed the same breath, deliver the classic nasal *Half Hour* plea, 'No, no, stop messing about.'

As Main Wilson had promised, joining the *Half Hour* stable would prove to be the biggest break of Williams's career. His appearance also put a chink in the writers' vision of an honest and truthful situation comedy. 'After the first week with Ken in the show, bang went our idea of no funny voices and no catch phrases,' says Ray Galton.

It would be another three years before Williams admitted to Hancock his habit of keeping a diary, a grinding routine which both horrified and fascinated the comedian. Williams's daily records – only published after his 1988 death – are spiky and arrogant. 'During the day Ken would be happy and helpful and quite a nice guy,' remembers Alan Simpson. 'What we didn't know was that each night he went home, dipped his pen in the vitriol, and tore us all to pieces.'

The November show would be the first of more than one hundred radio *Hancock's Half Hours*. Under a three-year contract, signed in 1952, Ray Galton and Alan Simpson were still writing variety scripts for *Star Bill*, and the addition of up to twenty situation comedy episodes week after week proved challenging. Alan Simpson remembers deciding 'to do something completely different out of sheer desperation because we couldn't think of anything else'. Moments of lost inspiration produced *The Moon and Tuppence Halfpenny*, a three-sketch parody on Somerset Maugham's rubber-plantation stories, or, more frequently, yet another fall-back encounter with the East Cheam Repertory Company.

Within a month of the first *Half Hour* episode, Dennis Main Wilson's policy that the question of any supporting cast would be left open for as long as possible was under financial and executive threat. The weekly budget for each show had been set at £260, to include writing off one-twentieth of the cost of the incidental music recording. This, bemoaned Main Wilson, left him only £20 for extra voices for each show.

Far more restrictive was an edict from the BBC's head of variety putting a 'flat-out ban' on guest stars. The producer fired back a memo:

> Obviously, having spent three years suffering the normal run of guest stars in the conventional hackneyed manner, I am not going to be so foolish as to go back to an 'old hat' production style, especially having received a certain amount of kudos on the first Listener Research report for having no guest stars.
>
> However, as the co-deviser/producer of this show, it was agreed long before the series started that the show should be as near to true life as possible, and that if Tony Hancock buys a race horse, it could only strengthen the show if he were rude to Gordon Richards about Richards' horsemanship – with motor-cars to Mike Hawthorn about his driving – Hancock the great actor being rude to Jack Hawkins about the latter's acting – Hancock the footballer to Stanley Matthews, etc.
>
> This was a point which we agreed a long time ago and which we have in our advanced plans for plots in the weeks to come – and which I think it would be wrong to have to abandon when H.V. [head of variety] is asking us to build new presentation style for pure radio idiom.

The ban effectively remained in force for fifteen months and three further series of *Hancock's Half Hour*. Main Wilson 'bent the rules' during the first series by prerecording extracts from Brian Johnston and Raymond Baxter. Although non-actors, both men were BBC commentators and, reasoned the producer, not subject to the 'guest star' veto. It was not until the final episode of the third series that he was officially allowed to use sporting celebrities. In *The Test Match*, Sid James is now chairman of the MCC and makes Hancock captain of the England cricket team. The cast list includes Colin Cowdrey, Godfrey Evans and Frank Tyson and the BBC's 'voice of cricket' John Arlott.

It took three weeks for the BBC Audience Research Report on the first

Hancock's Half Hour to land on Dennis Main Wilson's desk. The programme had replaced a slot previously occupied by *The Al Read Show* which had attracted 25 per cent of the adult population of the United Kingdom. Hancock held on to just 12 per cent.

> Tony Hancock was given a great welcome by the vast majority of this sample audience who were delighted that he should have his own programme. Although the low appreciation index (52 as opposed to the average variety 'Gang' show of 62) suggests an unenthusiastic response to the show as a whole, there appears no doubt that its star enjoys widespread popularity.

Dennis Main Wilson's new format – no 'moaning crooners' or 'shrieking choirs' – appeared to have been appreciated. The listeners were not so appreciative of Galton and Simpson's script. 'There are a few amusing moments,' said an anonymous clerk, 'but the script was generally pretty weak.' Another research volunteer 'failed to see the funny side' of Hancock wrecking Lord Dockyard's home – 'very poor stuff'.

The response was good enough for the BBC. Within a week – and before the arrival of the second audience report – it was decided to retain Hancock, while delaying any commitment to a second *Half Hour* series. Hancock was summoned to a meeting with Pat Hillyard, the BBC's head of variety, and that afternoon, 6 December, Hillyard circulated a 'confidential' memo, headed 'Long-term exclusive contract'.

> I have now discussed the above subject with Hancock. He is not, however, interested in any form of long-term contract, and explained that he is very keen on making a name for himself in films, which would preclude any sort of tie-up with the BBC.

With hindsight, Hancock's decision to remain employed by – but not bound to – the BBC was the correct one. His single excursion into films was hardly the stuff on which careers were built, yet he realised the 'only way to become famous – internationally famous – was in films'.

Hancock and Cicely had returned to their Queen's Gate Terrace flat in early October, with just enough time for Hancock to throw himself into the final preparations for the radio series. His concentration was broken only by an 'irritating' week in Oxford. Jack Hylton had booked *The Talk of the Town* into the New Theatre for a single week prior to the show's London season. Just when Hancock needed to focus his energies on the Galton and Simpson scripts he was forced to return to the 'excruciating boredom' of variety.

Freddie Ross had visited Blackpool twice during the summer; on both occasions she visited Hancock's dressing room. He would tease her about her 'middle-class bourgeois Jewish background' and the fact she was still living at home and, more pointedly, about her career as a press agent. He believed most entertainers were ultimately responsible for their own publicity. It could not, he felt, be manipulated or manufactured. The only kind of publicity, Hancock pronounced, was a good notice.

The Talk of the Town opened at the Adelphi Theatre on 17 November. One review, in *The Times*, particularly pleased him:

> The buffoonery is clean and gay Mr Hancock comes into his own as a transatlantic music hall star passing to and fro between the portentous and the ridiculous.

The next day Hancock received a handwritten note of congratulation from Freddie Ross – 'When I read that review I thought how right he was.'

Freddie continued her visits to his dressing room. One day, while Hancock was making up, she noticed a suitcase on top of a cupboard. 'What's in the case?' she asked.

'Letters,' said Hancock, not bothering to look up.

'What's inside the letters?' Freddie persisted.

Hancock turned to face the armchair in which his visitor was sitting. 'I don't know, I've never opened most of them.'

Ignoring your fans was a 'no no', Freddie informed Hancock. 'It's like leaving home without making your bed, your mother will find out.'

Hancock reluctantly agreed to allow Freddie and an agency secretary to sort the letters and draft any replies. Every day the two women would arrive at the Adelphi dressing room to open, sort and reply to his growing number of fans. Hancock left them respectfully alone and would go to the cinema, play golf or waste the afternoon mooching around the West End pubs; he never went back to his Queen's Gate Terrace flat to spend time with Cicely.

Jimmy Edwards, like most of the band and stagehands, would spend the last quarter-of-an-hour before curtain-up smoking outside the stage door. Each evening, and with just ten minutes to go, a 'sad and dejected' Hancock would turn into Maiden Lane. As he passed his co-star Hancock would nod and sigh and disappear into the theatre. 'It was like watching a man walk to the gallows,' said Edwards. 'But it was every night.'

One friend, Rex Jameson, was working the nearby Astor Club while Hancock was appearing at the Adelphi. 'I once caught his act from the side of the stage and he went down a bomb,' recalled Jameson. 'The audience adored him. But he came off stage shaking. He looked at me and said, "I've been a failure Rex – it's all a disaster."'

1955

HANCOCK HAD BEEN married to Cicely for little more than fifty months when he proposed to Freddie Ross.

Their relationship had progressed rapidly from a working partnership to a physically passionate, yet unconsummated, affair. 'I found him the most exciting person I had ever met,' Freddie admits. 'There was a closeness between us. I can't explain why because he was a very difficult and unpredictable man, yet I found him very easy to be with.'

For Hancock their intimacy was unplanned, almost accidental. One morning Freddie arrived at his Adelphi dressing room as the part-time secretary was getting down to work. A few minutes later Hancock arrived. He thumbed through half-a-dozen letters, drank two cups of tea and a cup of coffee and informed his newly-acquired press agent: 'That's enough, I think we had better have a staff outing.' Freddie, imagining a thank you restaurant lunch, dutifully followed as Hancock led her down the Strand and across Trafalgar Square. They eventually arrived at a greasy spoon café in Whitcomb Street.

Stuffing two hot lamb sandwiches into his duffel-coat pocket, Hancock crossed the road to a nearby cinema and bought two tickets. At the foyer kiosk he paid for two bars of chocolate. 'Pudding,' he announced.

'We hardly said a word through the entire programme,' recalled Freddie. 'I sat with a hot lamb sandwich in one hand and a bar of milk chocolate in the other and wondered what on earth I had got myself into.'

When they emerged into the sunshine Hancock blinked and looked around like some animal that had just emerged from its winter sleep. 'That was nice,' he said, before ambling back to the Adelphi alone.

As the weeks progressed Hancock came to enjoy his afternoon outings with Freddie. They would spend hours in seedy drinking clubs and backstreet pubs. During the summer he took her to watch the Test cricket at Lord's. Cicely, aware of her husband's growing attachment, chose to ignore the possibility their marriage might well be breaking up. An old school friend remembers pleading with Cicely to confront Hancock. 'There was a part of her nature,' she recalls, 'which found it easier to follow, to obey Tony rather than attempt to lead him. She was deeply in love with him and in many ways he could do no wrong.'

Cicely, however, was seeing less and less of her husband. Hancock would sleep late before leaving for the theatre or a BBC engagement, and after his Adelphi performance he rarely arrived home before midnight. When they were alone they invariably fought; over money, over Hancock's slovenliness and his all-consuming preoccupation with his career. During one noisy row, a dress which Cicely had spent all day making was torn to shreds and hurled from their fifth-floor window. Bruises were also beginning to appear on Cicely's arms and shoulders.

'Tony was pushing her to the edge,' adds the friend. 'Cicely had great fortitude and bearing, that is why she would never allow Freddie to see what her relationship with Tony was doing to the marriage. One day we were having tea in a West End hotel. They had been fighting the night before. Her voice was quite calm, but tears were streaming down her cheeks. She refused to let herself go.'

A naïve truce developed between Cicely and her husband's factotum. 'Cicely and I got on fine together,' Freddie has continued to maintain. To others the situation was obvious and untenable. 'Freddie was around a lot and was clearly in love with Tony,' Dennis Main Wilson has said. 'I knew it would never last.'

Freddie Ross had effectively taken over from Phyllis Rounce as Hancock's Adelphi chaperone. Her professional association allowed her to call at the theatre unannounced; wives, as Cicely – and later Freddie – quickly discovered, were effectively banned whenever and wherever Hancock was appearing. Most nights Hancock would insist on seeing Freddie home from the theatre. They would talk about the future and hold hands and kiss. Freddie never let it go further. 'Nice girls didn't behave that way with married men,' she said, 'and I was a very nice girl from Hampstead. He was married and of a different religion and at first I just thought it was one of those things.' There was, she admits, a mental attraction between them, but 'Tony was far more physical about it than I was.'

When Freddie refused to give in to Hancock's fumbled and drunken attempts at seduction he announced his marriage was over and that he was about to leave Cicely. 'I was very frightened of the whole situation,' Freddie said in her *Hancock* biography. 'I was worried about what people might say and that it might affect his career. I was frightened of the total personal commitment he demanded.' In an attempt to prove Hancock's obsession was one-sided, Freddie cut her visits to the Adelphi, and when she and Hancock did meet, she deliberately asked his advice about the men she was dating.

However, whenever Freddie thought she had broken free, Hancock would arrive unannounced at her office. When his pleading failed – 'I can't stay away from you' – his tone would turn to childish hurt – 'You can't pick me up and put me down whenever you feel like it' – and then to unreasonable and contrived demands. After a holiday in Antibes, Hancock telephoned Freddie from France and asked her to fly to Paris with some extra cash. Once back in London, Hancock rebuked his press agent. 'It was terrible to be in Paris with you and Cicely,' he told her. 'I can't take that sort of stuff. You must never do it again.'

Part of Hancock's genius was his ability to control – and increasingly extend – radio pauses. With no formal theatrical training, it was an instinctive and formidable gift. The BBC and its listeners had experienced nothing like it before; deliberate and precious seconds of total silence which forced an audience to hold its breath in case it missed something. In Tony Hancock's hands silence was one of the greatest comedy tools ever invented.

For Dennis Main Wilson, as producer, it was a highly dangerous experiment. In the early 1950s a pause on radio 'was like bringing the curtain down in a theatre half-way through the act'. Intentionally waiting for three, four, or even five seconds took nerve and confidence – 'Make 'em laugh, make 'em cry, but, above all, make 'em wait.' When a laugh came it was twice as big. It is still an awesome feat for any radio performer. Richard Briers, who starred in the 1970s hit television comedy *The Good Life* and later took the part of the dead comedian in *Hancock's Last Half Hour*, has attempted to analyse Hancock's talent. 'He obviously had a wonderful ear, a musical ear to a certain extent,' explains Briers. 'He was also a great phraser of lines. Hancock was like Bing Crosby in many ways, he had great phraseology. Their interpretation and delivery are very similar.'

As Briers, and every other comic actor discovers, timing is a gift. 'You can improve your timing, you can make it better, but it takes a lot of years,' adds Briers. 'You have to learn to be authoritative. To take command and hold a pause with total confidence. In the end it is all a matter of absolute confidence in what you are doing.'

In a radio interview, long after Hancock's death, Sid James praised his late colleague's timing as one of his greatest gifts. 'A lot of actors say this is a bad word to use. I don't think so, there isn't a better expression for it,' said James. 'It's like timing in golf; timing in boxing; your weight is in the right place when you throw the punch or when you are hitting the ball. It's exactly the same with comedy. Tony had instinctive timing for radio, and stage, and television. It was split-second perfect.'

The contrast between the floundering, mediocre, unimpressive Anthony Hancock, the 1941 confidential comic, and the East Cheam Hancock is so great as to suggest that until the BBC tapped his enormous reserve of invention and energy and will power, his true professional personality lay dormant. It soon became obvious to other members of the cast, as it had to Main Wilson several years earlier, that Hancock possessed an intuitive sense of line delivery that originated deep within his psyche. He rarely, if ever, mistimed a laugh. Reading the script in front of the microphones, most of the cast looked up occasionally to see how a line or a specific gag would be received. 'You needed to see the other person's face to gauge the timing,' explains Bill Kerr. With Hancock they didn't bother. They knew, they felt – and so did the audience – exactly what he would do. And Hancock never let them down.

*

Week by week the shows improved and the cast matured. Hancock was descending from the high of music hall and bash-bash laughs – the genesis of all previous radio comedy – to the 'super truth' the *Half Hour*'s four creators had envisaged.

Hancock's Half Hour was energetic in a landscape where so many other radio comedies appeared tired. Its humour was new where others' was old; rich and aggressive in areas where others' seemed poor. The scriptwriter Barry Took – who, with Marty Feldman, later wrote *Beyond Our Ken* and *Take It From Here* – claims Hancock's interpretation of the Galton and Simpson scripts produced some of the 'most thrilling comedy' ever heard on radio or seen on television.

Tony Hancock did not invent situation comedy; he discovered it. What Hancock – and his writers – did was to redefine the principles and practices of comedy. For Hancock, at least, it was a winning formula riddled with imperfections. No matter how far Hancock went, comedy, he admitted, had to begin with the individual, 'at home'.

One day, Sid James was throwing a party at 35 Gunnersbury Avenue, his Ealing home. The *Half Hour* trio were discussing the direction of comedy when Bill Kerr admitted he would like to do just one perfect show – 'where the script is brilliant, where you know every word and every line is delivered right on the button, the band is great, and the audience love you … the perfect show'.

Hancock was horrified. 'I'd never want to do a perfect show,' he protested. 'There should always be something slightly wrong with it, probably me, so that I could go out next time and try to put it right and just keep on getting better.'

In a perverse way Hancock's law of perfection inspired those around him. It forced everyone to run faster and keep pace, believed Dennis Main Wilson: 'He would never have admitted it, but Tony had the brilliance to inspire people.' For Hancock, situation comedy was far more than simple theory or technique or even a way of life – it had become life itself. Each Galton and Simpson script, whether for television or radio, achieved its potential only in performance, only by Hancock living it.

'The early *Hancock's Half Hour*s were a revelation of economy and insight, a mixture of fantasy and the mundane that put the programme right at the top of the heap,' Barry Took explains in his book, *Laughter in the Air*. 'Galton and Simpson's greatest contribution to radio comedy was their knack of reproducing mundane conversation and lifting it to the level of high art. Whereas Muir and Norden's skill lay in the elegant contrivances of their parody, Galton and Simpson's trump card was the seemingly spontaneous stream of consciousness decorated by their extraordinary inventiveness. They wrote the character – Hancock interpreted it. It was chamber music of the mind.'

For the first *Hancock's Half Hour* of the New Year, the tenth of the series, Dennis Main Wilson wanted to record the show at the Paris Theatre. As ever, the show was scheduled for its regular Tuesday night slot, but the only vacant date in the Lower Regent Street studio long enough that week for rehearsals and recording was the day before, the Monday. There would be little room for error, and, if things went wrong, no time to rerecord. To avoid the prospect of a 'flat' or unresponsive audience Main Wilson issued instructions that tickets were only to be given to 'professional entertainers or those in the business'.

The recording was set for 11.30pm, late enough to allow anyone performing in the West End or taking part in other BBC broadcasts to attend. More importantly, it allowed Hancock to deliver his *Talk of the Town* performance before returning to record the *Half Hour*. After spending all day rehearsing at the Paris, Hancock left for his evening performance at the Adelphi. During the interval Kenneth Williams called at Hancock's dressing room where the comic advised Williams, a man only two years younger and with vastly more theatrical experience, that he was 'wasting his time in legit' and that Williams should concentrate on variety. 'But, of course it's the entrée that one needs,' Williams dutifully commented in his diary. When the show was over Hancock and Jimmy Edwards raced back to the Paris in a taxi to allow the recording to start on time.

The irony of the late-night recording did not escape Hancock. By some quirk of fate Galton and Simpson had produced a script they unofficially called, *Cinderella Hancock*. Forced to do the housework by Bill, and forbidden to go to the National Film Ball, Hancock manages to go in disguise as Sheik Aly Aga Khancock. Time is running out. Hancock's costume is rented only until midnight – the very second the real recording was due to end.

There was a power-house within Hancock which Moira Lister never truly understood. 'I never discovered what drove him,' she admits with hindsight, 'but whatever it was took a tremendous toll on his nerves, his persona, in fact his whole life.' Hancock's myopic vision was blinkered by perfection and focused no further than the next show. 'It was obsessive dedication that pushed him to the heights he achieved and also, in the end, destroyed him.'

It soon became apparent to Lister that Hancock's own neurosis would smother any attempts by the rest of the team to make it a 'relaxed and happy show'. He refused to socialise with other cast members. To Lister all that interested Hancock was 'perfecting his art'. She recalled that 'when he came to rehearsals he was extremely worried about what he was doing, he was at the writers all the time'.

Even on radio, Hancock never found the self-confidence that would allow him to relax. Before a show he was wound up like a taut piece of string. Afterwards, the string curled and twisted itself into a ball of introspection and critical appraisal. Each performance had to be – needed to be – better than the last. It never was. While the audience were still shuffling out of the Paris Cinema a cloak of depression would descend on the *Half Hour* star and envelop him for days.

Hancock became more paranoid as the first series progressed. By early 1955 Lister discovered she was pregnant and announced she would not be able to return for an already talked-about, but not yet contracted, second series. To add to Hancock's annoyance, Lister asked to be written out of one of the final episodes. She had been invited to a South American film festival and felt her absence for a single week would hardly be noticed. Hancock disagreed. 'Absolutely out of the question,' he erupted during a rehearsal. 'We have just established your character, and if the character disappears then the whole thing is out of the window. There is no way you can go.'

Lister never forgave Hancock. She felt he had crossed not only the bounds of professional decency, but also common courtesy with his public outburst. 'I regretted that deeply,' she confessed many years later. The pair never worked together again.

The first radio series of *Hancock's Half Hour* ended on 15 February while its star continued to appear in *The Talk of the Town* at the Adelphi Theatre. Not for the first time Hancock found himself, and his humour, under analysis. He was, according to J. B. Priestley writing in the *New Statesman*, a 'very clever performer, owing more to art than nature'. Tony Hancock, the piece continued, '... comes on all smiles and confidence, to recite, to sing, to dance, but is quickly reduced by the malice of the circumstances ... to a gasping, pitiable wreck, his gleaming rolling eye pleading for tolerance, for just another chance'.

Priestley – lamenting the demise of the old-style music halls as training grounds for comics and the 'whizzing stardom of the new drolls' – went on to pin down Hancock's own personality far more accurately than he would have imagined. 'Good clowns never try to be funny,' Priestley concluded. 'They are very serious, but eager and hopeful creatures lost in a hostile world; and with great clowns ... the very furniture is menacing, never to be trusted.'

The ratings were climbing steadily and the Broadcasting House management decided to sanction a second series of *Hancock's Half Hour*. It gave Dennis Main Wilson just eight weeks to find Hancock a new 'girlfriend'. The producer approached a 22-year-old actress called Andrée Melly, whose brother was the jazz musician and writer George Melly. Examining a sample script Melly immediately had doubts about accepting the offer. 'I'd never heard of the show, nor heard of Tony Hancock,' she admits. 'At the top of the script was the first line of dialogue. It said, "Tony: H ... H ... H ... Hancock's Half Hour" and I thought, "What's funny about that?"' Dennis Main Wilson eventually persuaded Melly not only to join the cast but to stay for a total of thirty-two episodes.

It was now up to Galton and Simpson to invent an entrance for the Liverpool-born actress. The opening show has Hancock and Bill leaving for a holiday in Southend. Not surprisingly they end up in Paris and meet a heavily-accented Andrée. She is subsequently smuggled back to England where, as Dennis Main Wilson confessed, her French accent thankfully faded as the series progressed. Having accepted the part, Melly now found herself in the unusual position of working on a hit radio show – minus its star.

Hancock had been plotting his disappearance for several days. The signs, unnoticed and unread by his friends, were becoming increasingly obvious. He was missing Freddie Ross, by now attempting to force an end to their affair with an enforced separation, and felt aggrieved and neglected. As the start of the second *Half Hour* series approached his depressive moods swung from morose silences to a talkative and nervous agitation.

On Tuesday, 12 April, he purchased a ticket for a late-night flight to Rome. It was dated the coming Friday. Hancock knew that to check in at the British European Airways' west London terminal with enough time to catch the connecting coach to London Airport, he would need to escape from the Adelphi before the end of the first of Friday's two *Talk of the Town* evening performances.

Hancock spent most of Thursday in a deep, but not unusual, silence. Cicely had no inkling of what was to come. Dennis Main Wilson telephoned the Queen's Gate Terrace flat to say Galton and Simpson had delivered the first script of the new radio series, due to be recorded that coming Sunday, and at Hancock's suggestion Main Wilson agreed to deliver the script to the Adelphi the following evening.

When the producer arrived at the theatre he was greeted by 'toothless Fred' the stage door keeper. 'If you're looking for the boy,' Fred announced, 'he's gone.'

Main Wilson checked his watch. 'He couldn't have,' he said. 'He hasn't done the finale for the first house yet.'

Hancock had been on stage in the middle of his solo act; his co-star Jimmy Edwards, all the stagehands and most of the band were in nearby public houses. Only two musicians had stayed behind in the orchestra pit to play cards. When they looked up, they discovered the stage was empty, panicked, grabbed their instruments and started playing different tunes. Within minutes the word had spread through the Maiden Lane pubs: 'Tony's off ... Tony's off.'

Hancock had stopped in mid-sentence, stared for a few seconds into the auditorium and then shuffled from the stage. A few minutes later he reappeared from his dressing room wearing his top coat and clutching a small overnight bag. Challenged by the stage manager he mumbled something about the stage being 'too steep'. By the time Jimmy Edwards reached the stage door Hancock was waiting for a taxi. 'His head was going up and down with shock and his whole body was shaking,' recalled Edwards. 'It was the first time I had seen anyone in deep shock and it was a frightening sight.'

Hancock stared through his co-star. 'I'm sorry,' he repeated. 'I'm sorry.'

By the time Main Wilson had arrived at the theatre the management had already arranged for Dickie Henderson Jnr to replace Hancock in the second house. The BBC producer found Jimmy Edwards in his dressing room, but he had no explanation for Hancock's walk-out. He went upstairs to see Joan Turner, again without success. During the second house Main Wilson toured the local pubs and clubs, hoping to find Hancock skulking in a corner. Back at the Adelphi he telephoned Hancock's flat. Cicely was alone and knew nothing about her husband's disappearance. Jack Adams, his agent, was equally baffled. By now it was almost midnight and Main Wilson and Jimmy Edwards widened the search to include every legal – and illegal – drinking establishment they could think of. Still no Hancock.

Main Wilson had just arrived home. It was early Saturday morning and still just dark. The telephone rang. The voice was familiar, but faintly ominous. 'Ginger' Rose was a Scotland Yard detective who, two years earlier, had earned his reputation as a 'tough cookie' after being seconded to Kenya to help suppress the Mau Mau uprising. He was now a chief superintendent with Special Branch. Earlier that week Main Wilson had literally bumped into Rose, a long-time friend, in Bond Street and offered him two tickets for Sunday's *Half Hour* recording. Rose's manner was brusque and direct. 'What's the bloke we're going to see tomorrow evening doing getting on the last plane to Rome?' he asked the bemused producer. 'Do you want him followed?'

Main Wilson thought for a moment. 'Yes,' he said.

'Ginger' Rose momentarily replaced the telephone receiver, then he listened for the Scotland Yard operator – 'Get me Interpol headquarters in Paris.' Hancock, the Italian police later reported, had spent the night in a Rome hotel before hiring a car to take him south to Positano on the Neapolitan Riviera. There, late on Saturday, he checked in to a cheap pensione and was apparently enjoying his role as an anonymous English tourist.

Saturday in London was proving far less relaxing. George Black Ltd – the producers of *The Talk of the Town* – which had 'licensed' Hancock to appear on BBC radio immediately withdrew permission for its star to broadcast. By midday, any Broadcasting House optimism that Hancock might make a last-minute appearance had evaporated. The other members of the *Half Hour* cast – Sid James, Bill Kerr, Andrée Melly and Kenneth Williams – were summoned to the producer's office in the Æolian Hall and informed of the crisis. Dennis Main Wilson was ordered to find a replacement.

Somewhere, deep inside, the producer refused to believe Hancock would not – could not – return for the recording. He left it until Sunday morning before telephoning Peter Eton, a fellow BBC producer currently overseeing *The Goon Show*. Eton confirmed he had no objection to Harry Secombe standing in for the absent Hancock and helpfully agreed to rearrange the rehearsal times to allow Secombe to record both shows. Main Wilson then rang Jimmy Grafton, an old friend and Harry Secombe's agent. Grafton was, at first, reluctant to allow his client to take over the lead in a show so obviously written for an individual comic. There was no time for Galton and Simpson to rework the script. The giggling, raspberry blowing, ad-libbing, *Goon Show* Secombe would have to become Hancock in all but name.

Main Wilson's third, and final, call was to Secombe himself, by now at the Paris studio about to record that week's *Goon Show*. 'I knew Tony well,' admits Secombe, 'but I also knew his timing and delivery were different from mine, and before I read the Galton and Simpson script I was afraid it might not work as well with me in a role that had been tailor-made for Tony. As it turned out, the script was so beautifully written and the supporting cast so strong in performance that anyone could have done it.'

The show was rehearsed and recorded at the Camden Theatre. That night Kenneth Williams recorded his verdict on Secombe's performance:

> Harry is a comic in the true 'lunatic grotesque' tradition. His antics are fantastic and very funny. He takes the lifelike ingredient of a character and then proceeds to blow it up to enormously fantastic proportions, the slightest nuance is blown up to embarrassingly revealing proportions and the act is a riot. He played Tony's lines without any attempt to impersonate, just taking them as he came to them, like a thoroughbred horse taking jumps – confidently and with great style. He kept the pace of the show bubbling with laughs and the success of the evening was largely due to him.

Two days later, on Tuesday evening, eager listeners tuned in, only to hear Robin Boyle announce: 'We present *Hancock's Half Hour* starring Harry Secombe, Bill Kerr, Sidney James . . .' There had still been no contact from Italy.

Hancock's vanishing act was almost certainly suggested by an incident he discussed four years earlier with his agent Phyllis Rounce. For several days in November, 1951, the newspapers had speculated on the disappearance of the actor Valentine Dyall.

A suave, soft-spoken Englishman, Dyall found fame in the late 1940s as *The Man in Black*. Sid James, now working with Hancock, had played his first joint lead with Dyall in the film of the same name. The circumstances of the actor's 'lost weekend' were startlingly similar to Hancock's disappearance. Dyall, like Hancock, always doubted his ability to live up to his rapid elevation to star status. He was also becoming increasingly unhappy and agitated about his performances in a London play, and, again like Hancock, he was days away from recording a new radio series, *Bumblethorpe*.*

One Friday morning and 'badly off balance', Dyall had caught the boat train to Calais. He was finally traced to a friend's apartment in Paris. On his return he attempted to explain his escape in an exclusive *Sunday Dispatch* interview: 'The real answer to my walk-out is that I had been overworking and over-worry. I felt ill, tired, and depressed, the sort of feeling when one is keyed up. Elastic can be stretched too far . . . I felt I had to get away from it all before I went round the bend . . . When you have a nervous breakdown you do not have to climb the curtains, have trembling hands or make funny faces. I didn't.'

Phyllis Rounce remembered Hancock arriving at her Irving Street office the following morning with the newspaper. 'He kept saying how much he sympathised with Dyall,' she said. 'Disappearing made absolute sense to him. As far as I was concerned it was just a matter of time.'

With no communication from Hancock, and little prospect of his returning, Secombe's agent was even more reluctant to allow his client to become a 'permanent' stand-in. For the second show Galton and Simpson had time to alter the script: Andrée has been smuggled across the channel and Bill is lodging as Secombe's unwelcome guest. Together they show Andrée around London – and get involved in Sid's plot to steal the Crown Jewels.

The twelve *Half Hours* of the new series had been commissioned and paid for. At least half the scripts had been written and the BBC

---

* *Bumblethorpe* was written by Spike Milligan, Larry Stephens and Peter Ling. Hancock made one appearance on the show – as 'this week's Bumblethorpe' – on 31 December, 1951.

was determined to salvage something from the wreckage of Hancock's vanishing act. After the second show, Dennis Main Wilson took Secombe aside. It was quite obvious, he said, the corporation would not suffer Hancock's absence for much longer. Would he be willing to take over the series? 'I admit I was tempted,' says Secombe.

By the following Sunday – and the third *Half Hour* episode – it looked certain that Tony Hancock's career with the BBC was over and Harry Secombe had found a new comedy vehicle. There was even a suggestion the programme's name might be changed halfway through the series. Dennis Main Wilson's verdict on the three shows was: 'The first one was a *Goon Show*. The second one, Harry got the hang of it. And in the third he showed what a fabulous comedy actor he was.'

Then, without warning, Hancock arrived at the Camden Theatre. The recording had just started. He found a seat in the back row and watched the show, unrecognised and in silence. Backstage Hancock approached Main Wilson 'like a dog with its ears down and its tail between its legs'.

After the two Sunday recordings – *The Goon Show* and *Hancock's Half Hour* – Secombe had travelled to Shrewsbury where he was appearing all week. On the Monday evening there was a knock on his dressing-room door. In walked Hancock. He was unrepentant, but apologised for his absence. 'I didn't think it was right to ask him where he'd been and he didn't offer any explanation,' recalls Secombe. 'After he thanked me for holding the fort he drove off in his green Jaguar.'

As ever, a final and vitriolic verdict on Hancock's absence is left to Kenneth Williams. He had appeared in all three programmes. Twenty years later his diary noted: 'I've liked Harry [Secombe] without reservation since I worked with him at the Camden when he took over from Hancock and was so brilliant! What a lift he gave to that series! And how much better he was than the absentee.'

Meanwhile, Dennis Main Wilson found himself under orders to 'lose' one of the *Half Hour* programmes. On June 16, an explosion had ripped through the British submarine HMS *Sidon* while on exercise in Portland Harbour. The rescue operation continued for several days until all hope of saving the sixteen-man crew was abandoned. By pure bad luck the next *Half Hour* episode to be recorded after the disaster included a naval storyline. *The Three Sons* told the story of old Ebadiah Hancock and the respective careers of his three offspring, Anthony, a doctor; Gideon, a gangster and Rodney, who joins the Royal Navy.

The programme, with Hancock playing all four parts, was broadcast as usual the Tuesday evening following the tragedy. By mid-morning the next day, Broadcasting House was bombarded with letters and telephone calls denouncing the plot as bad taste. On Saturday the BBC issued a statement: 'Because many people throughout the British Isles are deeply concerned about the disaster of the submarine *Sidon*, the Light Programme will not, on Sunday, 26th June, repeat the *Hancock's Half Hour* programme broadcast on 21st June. This is because the programme contains a sketch which, though wholly inoffensive in itself, could at this time be considered to be in questionable taste.' In its place Dennis Main Wilson decided to rebroadcast the seventh programme of the series in which Hancock stands for Parliament – and dreams of becoming Prime Minister.

For Hancock the monotony of the twice-nightly Adelphi perform-ances ground on. Five weeks after he turned his back on the second *Half Hour* series, Hancock collapsed on stage at the Adelphi. When a doctor arrived he found the comedian's temperature was 103°F and ordered him out of the show. In August, Hancock left the show again, this time with Hylton's permission and ostensibly for a three-day clinic diet. Unofficially he was resting to head off what Cicely told a friend 'looked like another of Tony's nervous breakdowns'. It was while Hancock was in a Hampstead nursing home that he received a script from the Rank office at Pinewood Studios.

'I've really made the grade,' Hancock recalled. 'At thirty-one you're the tops – they want you to play a fifty-year-old bishop.'

The film was called *The Big Money* and the director, John Paddy Carstairs, had specifically asked for Hancock to fill the role of the portly bishop. The comedian was not impressed by the John Baines script, nor the plot which he considered more a high-spirited lark than a true comedy. The film – which revolves around a family of petty crooks ashamed of its incompetent eldest son – was eventually made starring Ian Carmichael, Kathleen Harrison and Leslie Phillips. The part of the bishop went to a suitably rotund Robert Helpmann.

Then came Hancock's second film offer of the year. Rank, arguably the most productive if not the most innovative British film corporation of the 1950s, was determined to capitalise on his ever-growing reputation. However, the film maker had failed to appreciate its potential star's already fine-tuned sense of comedy. 'I took one look at the script,' recalled Hancock. 'It said something about a race track attendant following the dogs round with a dust pan. Sorry, that type of humour just isn't me.' The part earmarked for Hancock was offered to Frankie Howerd and the film was eventually released as *Jumping for Joy*.

Hancock was talking more and more of making a second film. 'The trouble with British films and scriptwriters,' he explained, 'is they can think of humour in only two ways – broad comedy, or something stuffed with actors, like *Whisky Galore*.' He was, he admitted, spoiled with writers of Galton and Simpson's calibre who not only understood what he was trying to achieve, but also understood his personality. 'If I am offered a film it should be written around me,' he said. Despite several more approaches, Hancock remained adamant. He explored the possibilities of making a film in France where 'they know what to do with their comics'. When, in 1960, Associated British finally gave him the chance, Hancock turned to Ray Galton and Alan Simpson for the script.

From October, 1955 – and the start of the third radio series – the BBC felt confident enough to commission twenty episodes from Galton and Simpson. It was a tight schedule. Each script was conceived, written and delivered within a week and the production process settled into a creative and highly effective routine. It also allowed the writers, for the first time, to fix Hancock in his legendary home at 23 Railway Cuttings, East Cheam.

Dennis Main Wilson was also looking for a more permanent home for his increasingly popular production. The Paris studio was once again booked for *Take It From Here*, and, although the late-night New Year's Eve recording had proved a success, Main Wilson felt the exclusively show-business audience had laughed on cue rather than spontaneously with the script. Lunchtime matinée recordings at the Camden Theatre had attracted an equally unsuitable audience – 'too many housewives'. For the third series the producer settled on the Fortune Theatre in Russell Street, only yards from where Hancock had once shared a flat with Larry Stephens.

Each Monday morning Galton and Simpson would start work on a new script. When it was completed, usually by Thursday, it would be delivered to Dennis Main Wilson at his Æolian Hall office. Copies of the script were rarely circulated prior to the first read-through at 10.30 on Sunday morning. Hancock was, by now, confident of his craft. 'He could go through a script on the first read-through, the first time he'd seen it, and every line would be right on the nail, the timing, the delivery, the rhythm,' adds Ray Galton. 'He was a great interpreter of lines.' Spontaneous, first-sight laughter from Hancock and the other cast members was a useful indication of a script's worth. A second read-through for timing was followed by lunch. When rehearsals resumed it was the turn of the technical staff to perfect any sound effects. As listeners across Britain were settling down to catch the five o'clock repeat of the previous week's episode, the cast were starting a final rehearsal of the new programme. By 8pm the audience had started to arrive for the recording.

For Sid James – whose ambition was every bit as hungry as Hancock's – the working relationship soon developed into a personal friendship: 'I really think Tony was the greatest friend I ever had.' More and more Sid James became the *Half Hour* team's 'father figure'. Several younger actors and actresses, hired for one-off roles, regarded James as the mainstay of the radio – and later the television –

programmes. 'He was a yardstick for both performance and temperament,' recalled one actor who got his first break on a Hancock radio series, 'if Sid thought something was wrong, you knew it was wrong.'

Hancock, forever worried about his performance, also came to rely on Sid's judgment. 'He used to lean on me quite a bit,' admitted James. 'Which suited me because I felt I put him at ease a lot. He would come to me and ask, "How do you think that was?" And I'd always say he was marvellous – but make one or two suggestions, especially later when we were working in television. Perhaps it would be better if the camera went back to him for his reactions, which really were Tony's prime thing.'

James found himself in the uncomfortable position of walking the tightrope between Hancock's professional concerns and his private ego. The greatest single difference between the two performers was in confidence and self-worth. Increasingly during rehearsals Hancock was overcome by self-doubt. As the performance approached his confidence would turn sour in his stomach and he would disappear to vomit into a sink or bucket. In front of a live microphone and engrossed in his character, he began to relax, and when things went wrong he enjoyed himself even more.

Occasionally during rehearsals a line – the image of a line – would metamorphose Hancock into Phyllis Rounce's 'big white rabbit' and he would collapse, in full view of the studio audience, rolling helplessly around the floor, clutching his sides and gasping for breath. The tension of recording before an audience reduced Hancock's control still further, although many of the funniest mishaps were never heard by the majority of the show's fans.

The first *Hancock* series included an episode entitled *A Trip To France*. Sid persuades Hancock to finance a spot of smuggling and Hancock agrees to pay for the hire of a boat – but only as long as he can do all the steering and wear the cap with the 'egg and custard' around the peak. The pair put to sea and rendezvous with a French trawler. Sid shouts: "Allo Jacques, ici Sid 'ere.' The next line in the script read: 'Bring the boat along side and get the stuff aboard.' It came out as: 'Bring the boat along side and stuff the broad . . . I'll read that again.'

The recording had to be halted for ten minutes as Hancock unsuccessfully attempted to compose himself.

By the mid-1950s Hancock's paranoia over his professional association with Sid James was still buried among his other neuroses. James was not yet a threat. His screen work, as many as ten films a year, was so dissimilar to Hancock's vision of his own screen career that there was little friction between them. 'Tony wasn't jealous of Sid,' Ray Galton recalls. 'The sort of parts Sid was doing Tony wouldn't have wanted.' Hancock and James drank and skylarked and talked like grown-up brothers who relished their weekly reunion. The completion of another show was always an excuse to hit the town. Cicely and Val James watched each show from the back of the auditorium, but a day in the studio was inevitably followed by a night in the clubs. Ray Galton and Alan Simpson – referred to as 'the boys' – were never invited.

To his friends Hancock's increasingly idiosyncratic view of money could be highly annoying or deeply touching. He would wear a suit until it was threadbare, yet arrive home clutching a rare expensive bottle of wine. His shoes – forever painful – were worn until the stitching parted, and frequently to the most expensive restaurants in London. Money, to Hancock, possessed the magic quality of happiness. He took no pleasure in settling an anonymous and faceless account, which he delayed for as long as possible, but he regularly over-tipped a waiter or crossed the street to drop a pound note into a busker's cap.

Billy Cotton Jnr was introduced to Hancock during his first Adelphi run. As a BBC executive, Cotton would often look in on *Half Hour* rehearsals. Hancock would be wearing his oldest clothes. 'He would look like a tramp who had just walked in off the street,' Cotton remembered. 'After cadging cigarettes from everyone else he'd shuffle up to me and ask, "Have you got five shillings for my lunch?" Cotton never refused. By the end of a series he realised he had parted with £2 10s and subsidised most of Hancock's meals. 'I don't think he was mean in the traditional sense,' added Cotton. 'I just think he was forgetful. There were other more important things on his mind.'

If there was a single year in which *Hancock's Half Hour* found its place in the heart of the nation it was 1955. Of the forty-eight episodes in the first three *Half Hour* series no less than thirty were broadcast during 1955. The year even began and ended with the same *Cinderella Hancock* episode; the first broadcast proved so popular, Main Wilson persuaded his star to record a second version.

Tony Hancock, the nation was learning, was producing a very singular brand of radio comedy. The problems caused by his complicated personality were still very much a trade secret. Nobody saw the business of comedy quite as Hancock perceived it. He was rarely funny off stage and his introspection frequently surfaced as apparent belligerence. Yet it was this hostility, combined with every comic's great vulnerability, that made Hancock unique.

Unlike Chaplin – who he was later to meet and idolise – Hancock added a second dimension to the latent sensitivity of his character – that of aggression. He was the first comic to fight back and the public loved him for it. Buffeted by fate and bruised by the scams of his East Cheam cohorts, Hancock's flashes of clipped and sardonic anger have become classic comedy. 'At a time when the citizens of Britain were being assured they had never had it so good,' explained Freddie Hancock and David Nathan in their book *Hancock*, 'he was the inadequate one who was missing out and wanted to know why. He was the puritan who always suspected that someone somewhere was having a good time. He was the man doomed to be forever out and who desperately wanted to be in.'

Hancock's Half Hour owed much of its success to social timing. Britons were experiencing the weightless, passing freedom at the summit of a political roller-coaster. The long, grinding, ten-year haul away from the Second World War was finally over. Shortages and rationing were, for the moment, a thing of the past. It was an exhilarating prospect. Hancock's arrival at the apex of post-war comedy was, for the first time, a truly shared experience. The anarchic screams of the *Goons* had been new and funny, yet always isolated from everyday life. Hancock – like everybody's brother or husband or uncle – had come of age with a generation. He, too, was looking down on a different world and sharing a sense of freedom.

1956

HANCOCK'S PHYSICAL APPEARANCE baffled and frustrated him but to his fans he possessed the lugubrious charm of a dog that had strayed from its kennel and couldn't find his way back. One newspaper described him as having 'a face like an overloaded hammock and the figure of a melting snowman ... with all the poise of a barge in a typhoon'. 'Let's face it,' Hancock admitted. 'I look odd.' In his youth he imagined himself as some kind of grotesque. 'I was an odd-looking, ugly-looking feller,' he confessed. 'Photographs taken at the time show me looking like an Italian waiter or a single, disembodied eye. People laughed at me.'

A legacy of Hancock's childhood rickets was that his shoulders appeared rounded and shapeless. One attempt to straighten them involved hanging from a bar, with his feet off the ground, until his arms gave way. It lasted until he caught sight of his own shadow: 'I looked like a bloody great bat.' Another phobia was the length of his arms. He joked that during the war he had been rejected for pilot training because his arms were too short to reach the controls.

However, Hancock's abiding obsession was with his 'anarchist' feet. 'When I walk into the Dorchester they know I'm trying to impress somebody and they bloody well go off on their own,' he would rant.

'They flap about. I feel as if my shoes are on the wrong feet . . . they've been put on wrong. They don't join at the ankle. I can feel them flapping like a penguin's. It is almost as though they were separate, not part of me at all.' When a friend offered Hancock and Cicely a basset hound, he studied the animal and politely refused. He later confided he thought the dog's feet were too similar to his own: 'I'd look a right bloody fool taking it out for a walk.'

Hancock's new preoccupation was his weight. On New Year's Day, 1956, he checked himself into the London Clinic, ostensibly to lose two stone. It was a Sunday. He was let out to record a *Half Hour* episode and returned late that evening after a drinking session with Kenneth Williams. A few days later Williams called at the clinic to visit him. On the bed was Wells's *Outline of History* and on a table beside an easy chair Bertrand Russell's *History of Western Philosophy*. Stacked on the floor of the private room was the set of encyclopaedias he insisted on taking everywhere. Hancock, as Williams had come to realise, was fascinated by the universe and mankind and his place within it. He devoured philosophy with the innocence of a child and the confusion of an adult. He would arrive at rehearsals carrying a copy of Kant's *Critique of Pure Reason* or Spinoza's *Ethics* and read passages aloud to anyone who would listen.

If walking through Knightsbridge, Hancock would drag Sid James into Harrods' book department. 'He would browse for hours and hours and hours,' James complained. 'Tony would pull out the biggest, thickest books you ever saw and announce, "I've got to have that one" – it would be about twenty-four quid – and order a copy. He would then see something on acting and decide he would have to read that. And then he'd grab a book on make-up, which he never used.' When Hancock attempted to 'improve' James's mind the South African rebelled.

'For God sake, learn a little,' Hancock persisted.

'I know enough for what I need, Tony. I'm not going to be a professor,' James replied. 'Is this going to improve my performance?'

Hancock, obviously irritated by his fellow actor's indifference, snapped back: 'It might, you never can tell. You might make a gesture this way instead of that.' James walked off to buy a copy of *Sporting Life*.

In Kenneth Williams he found – and to a lesser extent Williams found in Hancock – a fellow human being at least willing to consider the possibilities of 'no one being up there . . . and all of this being a joke'. Hancock suggested he read Nietzsche's *Zarathustra* and Williams found it 'incredibly illuminating – a truly brilliant, flashing, poetic mind'.

Williams's autobiography, *Just Williams*, describes their all-night discussions. 'Tony always returned to the same themes – "What is the purpose of human existence?" and "Is there a discernible pattern in human progress?" Again and again he held that such imponderables were unanswerable and when I ventured to suggest that only faith would explain apparent meaninglessness he rejected that on the grounds that it was unprovable. "Our reasoning must be answered by reason," he would say. "Men want a rational answer, not mystery and magic." He was married to Cicely then and I remember the nights at their flat in Hyde Park Gate where she would wearily announce that she was going to bed, leaving the two of us arguing into the early hours with wreckage of empty wine bottles and overflowing ash trays all around us.'

Yet beneath it all was pure Hancock, raw nuggets of golden philosophy, melted and poured into comic ingots. 'When I think of bicycle clips I die with laughter,' he would suddenly announce, or, more personally, 'Underneath the hand-made crocodile shoes there are still toes.'

Privately, Williams decided it was time to 'state my worth as an artist'. Writing in his meticulously kept diary, he took time off from recording his barbed show-business observations to declare his 'professional truth'. The passage is so resonant of Hancock's own 'philosophy of comedy' it is safe to assume the rationale is a distillation of both their views. Substitute 'comedy' for 'art' and the words are undoubtedly Hancock's:

Because now I see that in Art is man's striving for the truth – for the order – for the sense, which has evaded him in the stupidity of existence. Only in the recognition of this Truth in Art can my respect be commanded. Here is where my duty as an Actor lies. I must be the perceptive eye. With what fundamental truths I possess, I must judge and work from there. There is not one dramatic organisation in this country which is worthy of my talents.

Early in 1956 Hancock and Kenneth Williams were outwardly, at least, still friends. However, within a few months Hancock's obsessive pursuit of 'truth in comedy' would shatter their fragile relationship. Williams, in turn, would brand Hancock 'tasteless and inept'. He had already turned his critical scalpel on Ray Galton and Alan Simpson. In one *Half Hour* episode – *The Newspaper* – Hancock steps in to edit *The Sentinel*. Sid is the crime correspondent, with the knack of reporting the crimes before they happen. 'The script was appalling,' slammed Williams. 'The whole thing was just unfunny and incredibly verbose ... I have never felt so acutely embarrassed.'

Any dissatisfaction Hancock showed for the scripts usually surfaced only fleetingly, but after a three-week diet of raw apple and pear and slices of dry toast he was becoming scratchy. He telephoned Dennis Main Wilson at the BBC and demanded the producer leave immediately for the London Clinic. When he arrived Hancock was stretched out on his bed and quite obviously suffering under the strict regime.

'Tony trying to get angry was quite a giggle,' recalled Main Wilson. 'He just couldn't do it very well.' While the producer attempted to keep a straight face, Hancock complained his radio character was sliding too far down market. Galton and Simpson, he protested, were getting too fond of sleazy settings: 'You'd better tell the boys that if they don't get me out of the doss-house, I know other writers.' Main Wilson left the room choking with laughter.

Hancock was, at last, free of what he described as the 'crushing monotony' of *The Talk of the Town*: 'Let's face it, I wasn't cut out for variety.' He was replaced for the show's last two months by another comedian, Dave King.

The previous year, while Hancock was preparing for one of his last Adelphi performances, television owners in London and the home counties were retuning their sets for the launch of Britain's first independent television channel. There were four-and-a-half million television licence holders by late 1955, but only twelve per cent could receive the new programmes. Winston Churchill dismissed ITV as a 'tuppenny Punch and Judy Show'. On 22 September, 1955, the new channel went on air and, at 8.12pm, Gibbs SR toothpaste made history by becoming the first product to be advertised on commercial television.

Throughout the winter Hancock had remained under exclusive contract to Jack Hylton and George and Arthur Black. The pugnacious impresario waited until the third radio series of *Hancock's Half Hour* ended on 29 February before snapping the trap on his troublesome, but hugely popular star. Hylton had formed his own television production company to make programmes for Associated-Rediffusion, the newly formed commercial station, and was already its light entertainment adviser. He wanted Hancock to make his first television series for ITV, and when the BBC objected, Hylton threatened to withdraw permission for Hancock to appear in any future radio shows.

Morale within the BBC was at an all-time low; entire television crews were defecting to the new and livelier rival. BBC radio, although unaffected, was reluctant to allow staff confidence to slide still further by the loss of one of its biggest stars. 'It really was a bad time for the corporation,' recalled Dennis Main Wilson. 'Tony had been groomed for television; to lose him now – and possibly forever – would have been a disaster.'

Forced to relent, the BBC released Hancock for two Independent Television series of six programmes each. Hancock – and Hylton – demanded the corporation also allow Galton and Simpson to script the shows. Once again the BBC refused – not as the writers believed, because they were being held rigidly to their three-year BBC contract signed in 1954, but because it was feared the pair could not write for both the BBC and ITV and maintain their high standard. If the independent deal went ahead, Galton and Simpson would be expected to deliver twenty-eight *Half Hour* radio scripts plus twelve television shows: a total of twenty hours of comedy. It was a risk the BBC was not prepared to take. Concluding an internal memo the head of copyright posed the question:

> On the face of it the suggested deal whereby Hancock is to be allowed to give 20 sound programmes and 6 television programmes for us provided Simpson and Galton write material for 6 commercial television programmes for Hancock is a good one, but I cannot see how two writers can do thirty 30-minute sound variety programmes (I understand that during the current contract year they will be doing 23 for certain and probably more) plus 6 BBC television shows at fortnightly intervals plus 6 commercial television shows. It does not seem to me possible to get this amount of work out of two writers in the course of a year.

For Galton and Simpson, and certainly for Hancock, the main benefit of working on the commercial television series would be money. Under the writers' current contract with the corporation – signed in July, 1954 – they received seventy-five guineas for each radio or television *Half Hour*, rising to eighty-five guineas per show in the final and third year. 'We were offered money to write for ITV which was twice what we'd ever been offered by the BBC,' said Alan Simpson. 'The money they were paying at that time was incredible.'

Hancock, by comparison, was set to earn considerably more. In January he had signed a BBC contract for his first television series of *Hancock's Half Hour*. The fee for each of the six fortnightly programmes was £500. His payment for each of the commercial television programmes was exactly double, making him the first television entertainer to receive £1,000 for a single show.

As part of the BBC contract, Hancock had agreed not to appear on Independent Television during the television run of *Hancock's Half*

Hour. The BBC series was initially scheduled to start on Tuesday, 22 May, and end on 31 July, a direct overlap with *The Tony Hancock Show*. Once again Hylton applied pressure, this time claiming his television contract with Hancock – signed in the summer of 1955 – predated the BBC's January deal and, therefore, gave him programming priority.

With Galton and Simpson effectively barred, Jack Hylton turned to two of Hancock's long-time friends and asked Eric Sykes to write all six ITV shows, with Larry Stephens collaborating on the first two programmes. The regular cast members had already been contracted and included June Whitfield, John Vere and another of the star's friends, Clive Dunn. The invitation for Dunn to join the series had come one evening the previous autumn while he and the Hancocks were drinking at a Montpelier Square pub, just around the corner from their Queen's Gate Terrace apartment. Dunn remembers Hancock announcing he was going to do some television work and 'wanted some support from friends'. The series also gave Dunn his first opportunity to play a forgetful, irascible old man, a character he would make his own, not least as Corporal Jones in *Dad's Army*. The inspiration was, indirectly, down to Hancock.

Four years earlier the pair had celebrated Hancock's invitation to appear at the Royal Command Performance, with two bottles of Champagne at Rules restaurant. Hancock departed and Dunn 'was left in a rapidly emptying dining room feeling full of fizz and vicariously triumphant'. He summoned a crotchety, ancient waiter and ordered some risotto. 'As the waiter ambled off I heard him mutter "fucking risotto",' recalled Dunn in his autobiography, *Permission to Speak*. 'One character that Eric [Sykes] wrote into the show was an old chap called Herbert Crutch and, remembering the waiter from Rules restaurant, I gave it the works. Another was in a sketch for Hattie Jacques playing Lady Chatterley, myself as her eighty-year-old lover. Tony played the detective Poirot who had to investigate the death of Lord Chatterley. Tony, in thick French accent, had to ask me if I had any references from His Lordship. My answer was: "No, but 'er Ladyship gave me a few."'

Dick Emery had also been signed to appear in all six live shows, but left after the second broadcast in early May. Clive Dunn, like most of the cast, sensed a growing antipathy between Hancock and Emery: 'I suspect because he was too much a comedian in his own right.' Emery, at Hancock's insistence, was removed from the series. Although he would appear in three future *Half Hours*, Hancock's insecurity would, once again, permanently fracture a long-standing friendship.

'We had a lot of script difficulties,' Hancock later confessed. 'Nobody's fault really. We didn't understand how much preparation has to be done before you start. A tremendous amount of work needs to be done before you get on air and we failed to do enough.' In *Tony Hancock 'Artiste'*, Roger Wilmut is more specific: 'The shows are very ambitious, with a fair amount of music and singing, but suffer from under-rehearsal – particularly the second show, which has one or two minor clangers, such as a stagehand appearing in shot. The later shows are rather better in this respect, although the whole series is marred by some very clumsy sound mixing.'

Part of the problem was Hancock's relationship with Eric Sykes. Still good friends, they frequently disagreed over the scripts. Sykes recalled: 'We were similar in temperament, but different in working methods. He had to have something down on paper, get hold of a line and rehearse it and rehearse it.' It was, Sykes told Hancock, as if he were wringing 'all the juice' out of a script before the public got to see it.

Hancock was equally fastidious about script changes. Sykes was a professional and accomplished writer. His scripts were always delivered to the producer by Monday morning. However, on Thursday, and with two full days of rehearsal, he would decide to rewrite an opening or change a punch line. Hancock objected, demanding to use the scripts as written. 'I'm not writing classics,' Sykes would reply. 'I'm writing comedy. It changes every day like we do.'

The disagreements rumbled on until Sykes could take no more and walked out. That weekend he and his wife escaped to Paris. They had barely unpacked and gone down to the bar when Tony and Cicely walked in. 'I know a place where we can get some mussels,' announced Hancock, apparently oblivious to the previous day's discord. They never found the restaurant, but ended the evening drunken friends.

There was a gap of just five weeks before viewers could switch channels and watch Hancock on BBC television. The man charged with 'breathing life' into *Hancock's Half Hour* was Duncan Wood[5], a former radio producer with whom Hancock had worked on a 1951 edition of *Western Music Hall*.

At thirty, the Bristol-born Wood was just two years younger than Hancock. He joined the BBC as an engineer after war service in the Royal Tank Corps, and in the late 1940s 'Hot Lips Wood' played trumpet in his own dance band. As a potential variety producer, his first chance came at the BBC's Lime Grove studios with the Terry Scott and Bill Maynard situation comedy, *Great Scott – it's Maynard*. During the next five years he would produce all sixty-three of Hancock's television *Half Hours*.

By their own admission Galton and Simpson were basically dialogue writers. Unlike Eric Sykes, who 'watched' a sketch in his head before describing it on the page, they 'did not think too much about the visual requirements'. A radio *Half Hour* script averaged seven and a half thousand words – exactly the same length as a television show.

The writers decided the BBC television debut – on 6 July – deserved something special. Two years earlier Hancock had celebrated his first ever *Half Hour* with a 'radio' party. This time a broken leg threatens Hancock's first television appearance. Sid James insists the show must go on and masterminds the broadcast from Hancock's hospital bed.

The writers were also responsible for a more controversial decision. They decided Hancock needed only one television foil, and the obvious choice was Sid James. Both Bill Kerr – who had so far appeared in every radio *Half Hour* – and Andrée Melly were excluded from the television programmes.

Like Hancock's Independent Television series, his BBC debut was also plagued by problems. One major complaint, at least as far as

Duncan Wood was concerned, was the choice of studio. All six programmes in the first series were broadcast live from studio 'G' at Lime Grove. The floor of the pre-war Gaumont-British film complex was irritatingly uneven – 'Attempting to track the camera was like riding a switchback,' said Wood. His camera angles were also severely restricted. The studio was ninety feet long and very narrow, allowing just four rows of seats facing the side-by-side sets. There was so little space in front of the seats the cameras could not get far enough back for head-on shots. Much to Wood's relief the second series would move to the Riverside studios.

Reaction to the first BBC programme was cool, although viewing figures were respectable. More than 36 per cent of Britain's TV-owning public watched the first *Hancock's Half Hour*, the equivalent of 16 per cent of the adult population. By now addicted to Hancock's radio series, most viewers were disappointed at the transition. 'Adult mentality is surely above this sort of rubbish,' a viewer complained. 'Senseless bilge from beginning to end.'

Meanwhile, Hancock's material success was growing. By the end of 1956 he had passed his test and was running two cars. He owned two flats, one in London and one in Antibes, and a houseboat on the River Wey, south-west of London. His attempts to join the Surrey river set proved as disastrous as his driving – he gave up after a minor accident – and potentially just as lethal. The combination of Hancock, a body of unpredictable water and a craft built 'entirely of rusty metal and blotting paper' was a formula worthy of Galton and Simpson and doomed from the start.

Hancock had acquired the houseboat – an ex-Army pontoon – for £100. 'A converted pontoon, that's as low as you can go in the boat business.' What the previous owner had neglected to inform him was that the boat had a tendency to sink, usually while he and Cicely were on board. It did, however, stay afloat long enough to be renamed. Two of the most regular subjects for the gossip columns of the day were Sir Bernard and Lady Docker, with their luxury yacht, *Shemara*, an obvious attraction for newspaper and magazine picture editors.

Hancock grandiosely announced his new boat would be called *Shemara II*. To rechristen it – and cash in on the publicity – Freddie Ross arranged for Fleet Street columnist Noël Whitcomb to crack a bottle of Coca-Cola across its rusty bow.

By now the Hancocks were spending most weekends on the river. One week Cicely was invited to a social function at a nearby public house and a reluctant Hancock was persuaded to dress up for the occasion. Just as the couple were about to step ashore they heard shouting. Two men in an equally leaky canoe were paddling furiously towards the houseboat. In a premonition of *The Radio Ham*, Hancock sprang to the rescue. 'Leave it to me,' he shouted confidently. After dragging the two men aboard, Hancock, dressed in his midnight blue dinner jacket and playboy suede shoes, stepped into the canoe – which promptly sank.

'What did you want to do that for?' asked an irate Cicely as she watched her husband wade ashore.

'It wasn't for the sake of a cheap laugh,' Hancock replied.

The houseboat's days were numbered. Not long after, it was sold and the couple acquired a 35-foot converted Breton fishing boat called *Fredericka*. The under-powered and cramped vessel, complete with parrot, and permanently moored in the south of France, was renamed *Wokki*, Hancock's pet name for his wife.

The controller of the BBC's Light Programme had long ruled that episodes and storylines used for radio *Half Hours* should not be adapted for television, but he was forced to make an exception as the first television series was drawing to a close. Galton and Simpson had written a script called *The Diplomat* which Duncan Wood intended using as the final live broadcast on 14 September. With the Suez Crisis bubbling throughout the summer, however, it was ruled that a Hancock swipe at the Foreign Office – while its diplomats were apparently hard at work attempting to avert a war – was 'unpatriotic'. Wood was ordered to find a replacement script, so, with Galton and Simpson away on holiday, he hurriedly made his own adaptations to *The Chef That Died of Shame*, broadcast the previous year during the second radio series. Hancock is a pie-stall cook, 'Iggins, who rises to the heights of haute cuisine only to return to obscurity through drink.

As the weeks progressed Hancock's character – bulging-eyed, kipper-footed and always on the verge of hysteria – strutted and swaggered his way from disaster to disaster. Just as they had done for radio, Ray Galton and Alan Simpson fashioned a working-class and working man's comic paladin. They placed a Homburg on his head, which Hancock somehow turned into a head-dress as impressive as a crown; they hung an astrakhan-collared coat about his shoulders, which he wore with the dignity of a coronation cape, and, nose-to-nose with his inevitable destiny, Hancock became possibly the most 'real' fantasy character in the history of popular entertainment – Anthony Aloysius St John Hancock; actor (at rest); twice candidate in council elections (twice defeated); self-appointed squire of Railway Cuttings, East Cheam.

The television series, as a whole, won critical acclaim. In a letter responding to a *Guardian* critic one Sussex viewer commented:

Like most television reviewers, while justly applauding Tony Hancock, Mary Crozier unaccountably ignores his partner in misadventure, Sidney James. Yet, clever comedy team that they are, it is difficult to divide the honours: both should share star billings.

Perhaps James is overlooked because so many of us have something of Hancock in us that, having been frequently 'nobbled' by the less scrupulous, and only reaching success in empty dreams, we have a vicarious aching sympathy towards him. Whereas with James we see just too faithful a portrayal of the spivvish mercenary who, with 'his eye on the main chance', is undeterred by moral considerations; in fact, a deserving realist.

The *Half Hour* is, for all its bubbling humour, a deeply satiric reflection on life and this acquisitive society, which, uncompromisingly, gives us the choice of being a hammer or anvil, a James or Hancock.

*

The decision to adapt *Hancock's Half Hour* for television had been the BBC's; it could not have done otherwise. Yet much of the innovation – the sheer energy and arrogance – which secured its ultimate success came from Hancock. The idea of tight television shots so that his face all but filled the screen was as frightening to a television producer as silences had been to Dennis Main Wilson. It was, Hancock claimed, the 'biggest battle I ever won – to do comedy in close-up'.

For Duncan Wood, already an experienced producer, Hancock was rapidly becoming 'one of the great television revolutions'. By the mid-1950s – and with shows still broadcast live – it could be assumed that a half-hour light entertainment programme would require around one hundred and fifty camera shots. Each *Half Hour*, however, doubled the camera rate. 'Suddenly you were having to work at twice the capacity on camera routines, and this put pressure on the crews, and on everyone,' explained Wood.

Sid James, who by now had completed fifty films, as opposed to Hancock's one, felt the most comfortable in front of the cameras and lights. From the start his performances were, and remained, less self-conscious and more relaxed than Hancock's. Of those early days Duncan Wood admitted, 'Sid was a very good technician, very experienced in films; he knew what a reaction shot was all about, and so Tony quickly twigged the reaction shot business. I was having to break sentences down into half, so that Tony would say a line in a close-up, half the sentence, then cut to Sid for a reaction, and then back to Tony for the remainder of the sentence, and then back to Sid for the reaction.'

The result was that viewers would often respond to a line – sense its coming – before Hancock opened his mouth. It was unique Hancock. No other television comic had so keenly developed the ability to materialise a thought in close-up and millions would mouth Hancock's about-to-be-delivered reactions – 'This man's a bloody idiot and I'm going to tell him so.'

Although excited by what he could achieve – what he was achieving – with television, Hancock never allowed it to dominate his performance. Television, he promised himself, would always be the tool, never the tyrant. 'People technicalise too much,' he moaned. 'I am a practising comedian. A working comedian.'

For J. B. Priestley the 'character Hancock built on television was a development in depth of his stage figure, and much more effective because we were so much closer to him, so that every little gesture, every look, came home to us'. A self-confessed *Half Hour* addict, Priestley remembered how Hancock came 'out of the dark, the faceless mask, for twenty-five minutes, hopeful, almost glorious, and then goes shrugging back into the dark again'. Each television episode, the writer felt, told us more of the human condition, more about the failure of 1950s society, than a hundred student demonstrations.

As a friend, Harry Secombe could see – could sense – the difference television made to Hancock. 'He was never completely happy in variety theatre,' Secombe said in *Strawberries and Cheam*. 'The strain of repeating the same performance night after night and trying to invest it with apparent spontaneity was more than he could bear. His timing and delivery were never better than when he was doing something fresh – creating and not recreating. That was why he took to television so well . . . it gave him new situations in which to work his magic.'

Comedy had undergone a major sea-change in the ten years from 1946. In that decade Hancock's role changed from a passive participant to an innovative force, but it was only in the last two or three years that he was finally able to find a direction. The far-sighted Phyllis Rounce had predicted her client's fame lay in television comedy.

Reflecting on his ten-year progression from stage to radio to television, Hancock explained:

There is a strange difference between pre-war and post-war comics. We were put in the position of doing fresh material every week on radio, or whatever it was, and now it becomes necessary. There is no excitement in repetition. Admittedly when you are in the theatre and have the audience really going it is a wonderful snowball reaction, and very exciting, and it takes you out of yourself.

But there was a change in comedy fashions which began to help me, a reaction to the patter style of people like Max Miller and Tommy Trinder. It was a return to a more subtle and more visual humour. I'd never been very hot on the patter and my act was really completely visual.

When I tried radio I found it very difficult. I still feel a visual comic. The first broadcast got a laugh, but it was a series of noises and silences as far as the audience at home was concerned. When I finally got into radio properly I really had to work harder than in any other medium. When I changed to television it was with a sigh of relief.

*

However far Hancock's comedy had come, there was always Sunday afternoon on the Light Programme; radio remained his most natural and fertile environment. The fourth series of *Hancock's Half Hour* began on 14 October and would run, with a Tuesday night repeat, until the end of February, 1957.

Inspiration came from many sources. During a break in rehearsals Freddie Ross amused the cast and writers with the story of her 'rubber' income tax return. Answering her annual tax form with 'no', it was promptly returned with a letter asking her to complete it correctly. At the second attempt she used the word 'none'. The tax statement was sent back a third time asking her to use the word 'nil'. A little over a month from the telling, Hancock is faced with a similar dilemma in *The Income Tax Demand*. Refusing to pay a tax bill for £14 12s 3d, he hires Sid as his accountant. The result is even more expensive.

Hancock was, by now, receiving as many as a thousand letters a week. For many fans his two-up-two-down terraced home was as real as the news or the sports reports. Convinced that the Railway Cuttings chaos was real, several hundred wrote suggesting Hancock needed a secretary. Within weeks she made her appearance as the outsized, aggressive and incompetent Grizelda Pugh.

Hattie Jacques, already a close friend, had first worked with

Hancock five years earlier in *Educating Archie*. She would appear in forty of the next fifty-four radio *Half Hours*. An experienced and versatile actress, Jacques found herself mesmerised by Hancock's performance: his technique, she remembered, was 'so brilliant that several times I was late on my entrances because I was so enthralled watching Tony work'.

Hancock, always the gossip, relied on Jacques for a constant stream of jokes and humorous anecdotes. 'He laughed himself silly at something someone did or said and which I didn't think was all that funny,' she recalled. 'Whenever we stopped for a break he would almost demand a new story from me.' A year later, when Jacques made her first television *Half Hour* appearance, she realised Hancock had been fermenting the idiosyncrasy in every story. He was a man with incredible insight into human behaviour, she discovered. 'Tony would suddenly do something that you'd recognise, that I'd told him months before. Something you never recognised had a comic capacity – but he had.'

One departure for Hancock was his first appearance in a straight acting role. Dennis Main Wilson had adapted H. G. Wells's *The Man Who Could Work Miracles* from the author's own screenplay. He persuaded Hancock to play the title role of George McWhirter Fotheringay and recruited a number of *Half Hour* regulars, among them Kenneth Williams, Hattie Jacques and Warren Mitchell. Other members of the eighteen-strong cast included Deryck Guyler, Miriam Karlin, Alfie Bass, Harry Fowler and Dennis Price.

Rehearsals started the week before Christmas at the Piccadilly Studio and Main Wilson soon discovered Hancock was far from happy as a straight actor. In one scene Fotheringay, endowed with the power to summon anyone to appear before him, orders the world's monarchs and heads of state into his presence. Unable to use modern stereo techniques, Main Wilson produced a distancing effect by placing Hancock on one side of the microphone and the entire cast facing him on the other. There was obviously something putting Hancock off. During a break he sidled up to the producer who asked what was wrong. 'I find it terribly embarrassing,' Hancock admitted. 'All these marvellous actors facing me and there's me, rubbish, looking at them and making an ass of myself.' When Hancock arrived at the studio to record the ninety-minute play on 20 December, he discovered the ever-resourceful Main Wilson had moved the microphone to allow Hancock to act with his back to the rest of the cast.

Hancock was unimpressed with the final product, transmitted on the last day of the year. As ever Kenneth Williams, who played the aptly named Silas Maydig, recorded his own unforgiving verdict: 'He [Hancock] failed to come up at the end, and I know it was because he didn't believe in what he was saying. If he is philosophically opposed to a script idea, he doesn't seem to be able to perform it.' Hancock, believed Williams, 'has got sincerity for life and sincerity for work hopelessly intermingled and merged'.

While his radio shows were running almost continually – twenty-one in 1956 – Hancock spent the greater part of the year alternating between BBC and Independent television. The first ITV series of six shows was followed almost immediately by *Hancock's Half Hour* and, in November, a second fortnightly run of Jack Hylton's *The Tony Hancock Show*.

However, things were not going well at Associated-Rediffusion, and the BBC was getting worried. Ratings for the *Hancock Show* were dropping off dramatically and Hylton once again asked the BBC to allow Galton and Simpson to replace Eric Sykes as scriptwriter. Fearing a bad showing by its top-rated comedy star might well damage the spring return of *Hancock's Half Hour*, the corporation agreed, provided the writers went uncredited. Galton and Simpson, already hard at work on the new television *Half Hour* scripts, took time off to write six sketches, effectively writing the last two shows of the ITV series.

Hancock had one more pre-Christmas task for Galton and Simpson. He had been invited to appear in a January edition of Alan Melville's BBC series, *A–Z: The ABC of Show Business*. With the inspiration of a teenage promise – 'Look at that stupid budgie. One day I'll do an act about that' – the writers produced one of Hancock's most successful television and stage routines.

Beaked and befeathered, Hancock's belligerent budgie struts around its cage waiting to be fed by Irene Handl:

> Handl: Beauty – look what Mummy's got here – has she got Beauty's din-din . . . lovely din-din – look . . .
>
> Hancock: Well come on, then, poke it through – stop playing about.
>
> Handl: Look, Beauty, nicey-nicey . . . all gone!
>
> Hancock: I know how to eat it, just poke it through. She does carry on so – if she ever leaves that door open I'm off. Sparrows or no sparrows, I'll take me chance.

1957

THE HANCOCKS WERE still living in their fifth-floor Knightsbridge apartment. What had once been a tastefully and expensively decorated flat had now degenerated into a seedy but expensive slum. At home – and there were few visitors – Hancock was a slovenly indolent. In the 1950s Philip Oakes, who would one day collaborate on a film with the comedian, was a freelance writer and poet. To interview Hancock for a magazine he climbed the stairs to the Queen's Gate Terrace flat, unsure and unaware of what he would find. He was introduced to Cicely and then to two enormous poodles called Charlie and Mr Brown: the older dog was an extrovert and Mr Brown was a nervous wreck. Hancock claimed the animal saw ghosts.

The beautiful and charming Cicely was attempting to keep order in the shambling and crowded flat. 'What I remember about it most was the lavatory,' said Oakes. 'The floor was piled high with letters, stack upon stack of fan mail.' Returning from the toilet the writer asked Hancock why they were there. 'It's the only place I have time to read,' he was told. Despite the help of a secretary, Hancock still treated the ever-increasing tide of letters as an intrusion.

Dennis Main Wilson recalled another visit to the flat: 'There was an old leather club armchair with the stuffing coming out, a few other odd chairs and a Put-U-Up settee. There was an underfelt on the floor but no carpet. There was a mark where someone had been sick. There were piles of fan letters behind the lavatory pan. I looked into the bedroom one Sunday and there was a *Sunday Pictorial* from the previous week still sticking out of the bedclothes.' Hancock was both fascinated and repelled by seediness. He enjoyed the physical process of making money, yet rarely spent it to improve his quality of life. It was a contradiction of his character which, particularly in later years, allowed him to live in unnoticed and unconcerned squalor while at the same time drinking Chablis and eating the most expensive salmon from the tin.

The more he studied philosophy and world religions, the more he ceased to care about possessions. Hancock would buy clothes from the most expensive stores in London and still look a wreck. He had no interest in art or pictures. He loved brass bands and male voice choirs and – in later years – piano jazz. One of his favourite composers was Rimsky-Korsakov. His heroes were Bertrand Russell and the science fiction writer, H. G. Wells, but he rarely read for pleasure; when he did it was Stephen Leacock and A. A. Milne. His idea of the perfect tragic hero was still Christopher Robin's donkey Eeyore, forever robbed of his special thistles.

Faced with someone else's tardiness Hancock could become sarcastic and cruel. Given a dirty glass in a restaurant he would demand to see the waiter or manager. Holding the glass aloft and pointing to the offending mark he would say: 'Do you think you could go away and put some grease, some lipstick and a few more fingerprints round the edge and make a proper job of it?'

Generosity, from whatever source, fared little better. Hancock and Sid James were in a bar when a group of fans came over and offered them a drink.

'I'll have a large vodka and tonic,' said Hancock.

James was clearly uneasy. 'Look,' he protested, 'it's not fair to ask those poor people for a large one when they've been good enough to offer you a drink.'

'If people want to buy me a drink,' Hancock snapped back, 'then they can damn well buy me what I want.'

On 21 February, 1957, Dennis Main Wilson produced the last of his sixty-eight *Hancock's Half Hours*. The episode was prophetically titled, *The Last of the McHancocks*. The producer would never see Tony Hancock again.

With the fourth radio series over, the BBC had scheduled the start of its second television *Half Hour* run for April. The prospect terrified Hancock. Unlike the ITV shows, which were little more than televised stage sketches and therefore carried a momentum of their own, the Galton and Simpson scripts were comedy dramas in their own right. For the first time Hancock was forced to memorise every line of the sixty-page foolscap scripts. It was a fraught and torturous experience.

Even more daunting was the fact that Hancock would once again be surrounded by professional actors; in one programme, *The Tycoon*, by as many as forty-one. The majority were theatre actors who had learned their trade the hard way in repertory: performance followed performance; lines were either being delivered or rehearsed. Hancock had no such discipline and, in effect, was attempting to memorise the equivalent of a third of a feature film each week. 'The responsibility of broadcasting live worried him a great deal,' recalls George Fairweather. 'He was a comic working with actors. They left him standing where the words were concerned.' The more Hancock worried the more he found it hard to concentrate.

If he couldn't learn the lines by sight, Hancock reasoned, he would learn them by ear, and he bought himself a Grundig reel-to-reel tape recorder. His plan was to read the script on to the tape, leaving sufficient gaps to deliver his own lines. First however, he had to get the tape recorder to work. Hancock would have been happier 'in a world free of machines and the people who keep inventing them'. When his electric razor stopped working, for no apparent reason, he asked a friend to try and mend it. As the shaving head was removed it disintegrated in an explosion of millions of compressed hairs. Hancock never realised it needed cleaning. His latest encounter with something mechanical left the floor of his sitting room ankle-deep in tape and Cicely near collapse with laughter. Hancock turned to Sid James for help.

Only two short recordings of his early practice sessions have survived, the first on the day Hancock acquired the tape recorder. Having set up the machine, James checks the microphone: 'One, two, three, four, five ... six ... say something else, say something else, something else, something else [turning to Hancock] now, let's see if it's working all right.'

The second recording is a rare example of Hancock rehearsing. He is reading lines from *The Servants* in which Hancock and Sid attempt to find work. They dress up as an elderly couple to get jobs as servants, but when they take it in turns to be the woman their employers smell a rat. The lines – to be spoken by John le Mesurier and Mary Hinton – are delivered in Hancock's ordinary, rather toneless voice. Taken alone they make little sense. 'They're buttercups ... (*long pause*) ... That is the tennis court ... Oranges in this country ... Well now my dear, perhaps you'd like to ask Mrs Gabriel a few questions about her duties while I have a little eh, no dear, now tell me, Martha isn't it? ...' No tele-recording of the actual show has survived. The five minute and forty-five second tape is the only surviving extract.

Hancock had conceived a system of line-learning which, for the moment, appeared to be working. With his wife asleep in the flat's main bedroom he would tuck himself up in a spare bed next door. On a nearby table would be the tape recorder and a bottle of whisky.

Hancock would repeat and fine-tune his own lines until he eventually fell asleep with exhaustion and drink. Sometimes Cicely would find the machine still running, flaying the end of the tape.

George Fairweather has always claimed the all-night sessions with the tape recorder marked the start of Hancock's serious drinking. For the first time he began to look pale and drawn and Cicely complained of his raw, angry temper. When Fairweather tackled his friend about the effect the long hours and alcohol were having on him, Hancock replied he was 'following in Sid Field's footsteps – he was a drinker and it didn't do him any harm'.

By comparison, Dennis Main Wilson was convinced his star showed no signs of alcoholism throughout the producer's time on *Hancock's Half Hour*. His heavy drinking did not surface until his move to television, claimed Main Wilson. Until then he was 'strictly a half-pint of beer man and a tight-fisted bugger at that. Tony was not a boozer – in fact he was a bloody mean person to drink with.' After greeting his friend for a lunchtime drink, Hancock would always suggest they 'go Dutch'.

One reason was that until 1957 Hancock was on a very short financial leash. Although by the end of his second Adelphi run he was receiving at least £600 a week for his stage appearance, and each *Hancock's Half Hour* earned him another £600 with repeat and overseas fees, from this he was allowed just £20 a week pocket money. The weekly hand-out was partly an attempt – with Hancock's consent – to curb his growing social extravagances which, if left unchecked, included large quantities of Champagne and brandy. Each week his agent, Jack Adams, first deducted his commission and then his client's pocket money; the rest he banked on Hancock's behalf. Only Cicely was allowed to write cheques or draw on the account.

Hancock's face – and not just his voice – was now instantly recognisable. Those who worked with him noticed a growing aloofness and professional solitude, itself a recognised milestone towards alcoholism. Only a few years down the road Hancock would confess: 'A star, a real star, is someone who is out of reach.'

Unlike Sid James, who enjoyed the company of fellow actors and technicians alike, Hancock kept his after-hours contact with the studio and production staff to a minimum. At the end of each series it was a BBC tradition to celebrate with a last-night party. Hancock always attended but refused to contribute. Halfway through the third series the cast and crew were recording a Christmas special – *The Trial of Father Christmas* – at the Playhouse Theatre on the Embankment. Main Wilson suggested to Hancock he thank everyone who had made the series a success by funding a Christmas party, and a room in a nearby pub was booked. Hancock stood the first round and insisted someone else buy the remaining drinks.

The second fortnightly television series of *Hancock's Half Hour* began on April Fool's Day. Sid James, who would miss the first two shows, was invited by the *Radio Times* – through the imagination of Galton and Simpson – to expound on *My Boy Hancock*:

I have been asked to contribute four hundred words on my impressions of Tony Hancock. This is going to be very difficult on account of I don't know four hundred words. But I shall have a go and try not to repeat too many times the ones I do know.

I first met Tony Hancock on the railway line that runs past Wandsworth prison. I'd just finished the long climb down the wall, and he was trying to thumb a lift to Brighton. From that day we have been inseparable. Not because I like him, but with what he knows about me I daren't let him out of my sight.

What were my first impressions of him as we stood facing each other across the sleepers? He appeared to be a podgy, seedy little man, in a shabby suit, going a bit green across the shoulders, his shirt collar slightly frayed, a faded Royal Air Force tie, and grubby spats only partly hiding a pair of elastic-sided boots, right down at the heel. There, I thought to myself, is a man who's seen better days. Afterwards I found out I was wrong. He hadn't seen better days; he'd always been that way. However, he took a liking to me and pledging our everlasting trust in each other, we shook hands and two days later I sold him his wrist watch back.

Hancock is now one of the highest paid comedians in Britain. He doesn't know this, of course, because I am also his agent. I am not frightened about him reading this, as I also happen to be his publicity agent, and advise him on what, and what not, to read. And on top of that there's what I cop from being in his radio and television shows, his personal manager, financial adviser, income-tax consultant and landlord, so you can see why I'm not particularly worried about the increase in the Bank Rate.

Finally I would like to thank the BBC and members of the public for the continued interest in my boy, and I hope they will enjoy this new series on television as much as I'm going to enjoy banking my nineteen and six out of every pound he makes.

Kenneth Williams – who had been performing with Alec Guinness in *Hotel Paradiso*, and had not been available for the transitional series the previous summer – returned as a regular contributor to the second television series. It would be his last.

The antipathy between Sid James and Kenneth Williams was now rubbing bare. Although both actors worked well together – producing some of the funniest *Half Hour* encounters – their backgrounds and personal self-image kept them fixedly apart. Williams's habit of flaunting his homosexuality was a problem for James, not so much for his sexual preferences, more his flouncy effeminacy. Also, James, who had effectively dropped out of school before his teens, found Williams's spiky intelligence unnerving. The biggest difference, however, concerned their attitude towards acting.

James's philosophy for success centred on a tight, professional performance no matter what the style of production or type of medium. Williams, on the other hand, made a public spectacle of himself and chose to live as many of his waking hours as possible in front of his public. His pointed nose and flaring nostrils were as immediately recognisable as James's furrowed forehead and tangerine-skinned nose, or Hancock's round and hunched shoulders. Yet

Williams only needed the promise of an audience – any audience – for the fluting of his voice to go into overdrive.

From the start of the series it was obvious Hancock was developing his own antipathy towards Williams. In the rehearsal room and studio he attempted to hide his displeasure through a smoke-screen of nit-picking. In one scene the pair innocently hold hands. Hancock thought the routine looked 'too poofy'. After each show he would protest because Williams's entrance – like his own first line of a radio script – invariably produced a cheer of approval. 'It's my show,' Hancock would complain. 'I don't want this to be a double act' – the same line he would use to justify his eventual break-up with Sid James.

Perhaps the greatest irritant was a squeaky, elastic, whingeing tone Williams adopted early on and the writers dubbed 'snide'. When Williams used his 'snide' voice during rehearsals for the last show in the series Hancock exploded: 'I don't want that in my show. I don't want stereotypes.'

Rounding on Galton and Simpson he said: 'Look, I've asked you to cut this out.'

'But it's funny,' defended Simpson. 'It gives the show a lift.'

'I don't care about that,' slammed Hancock. 'I don't want it. It's a gimmick and I will not rely on gimmicks. I want real characters, not funny voices.'

Williams was out of the television *Half Hour*s. That night he wrote in his diary:

It was all rather bad. I have been poorly treated throughout the six episodes and had a chat with Tony. I don't think he wants me in the set-up in the future. He thinks that 'set' characters make a rut in story routine – the only one he wants back in October is Sidney James. He is mad about him, and nowadays they go everywhere together. Obviously I won't be asked for the October series, so that's that: so much for the obligations of loyalty. Tonight's show was rather dull, I thought. I didn't have a drink with them after – just got the bus and came home, feeling rather sad about it all.

The antagonism was far from one-sided. Williams, who regularly met Hancock and Cicely socially, thought the couple's behaviour 'appalling'. They would frequently arrive late for parties and always depart drunk and boisterous. At other times they would decide to go to a nightclub or restaurant, rather than keep a long-standing invitation.

Part of Hancock's comic genius lay in his sarcastic slant on life and his visceral – almost compulsive – need to have the last word in any situation. 'Tony didn't worry about the shows as a whole. He had complete faith in the scriptwriters and other actors,' explained Duncan Wood. 'He was worried about his own contribution. His biggest worry was drying up or fluffing.' Just as Hancock's 'frog face' curled pantomime or Adelphi audiences, so his fumblings to regain the script would ignite a *Half Hour* studio. Wood claimed that in twenty-five shows, Hancock dried up no more than four times. 'The way he got out of it every time was the funniest thing in the show.'

In one episode he was supposed to round off a scene with Sid James by saying, 'Our conversation is at an end.' Both got tangled up, but somehow fluffed and fumbled through. Hancock finally announced: 'Our conversation, such as it was, is at an end.' On another occasion the script demanded he take dancing lessons from Hermione Baddeley. The sequence showed them dancing the waltz, the lancers and tango. At rehearsals the pair executed their ballroom moves perfectly, but during the live show a studio technician played the wrong side of a record – and Hancock was forced to improvise a square dance.

Arguably his longest, and most famous, ad-lib came during a third-series television *Half Hour* called, *There's An Airfield at the Bottom of My Garden*. Sid has sold Hancock a house adjacent to an air base, and when he refuses to hand the money back Hancock is forced to sell the house and shows round a surveyor. The set was rigged so that each item collapsed as Hancock touched it. Again, the final rehearsal was faultless but on air, and in front of a packed studio a table first wobbled and then started to fall apart prematurely. Hancock was forced to play the entire scene holding up the table so that he could let it fall on cue.

John Findlay McWatt was a BBC cartographer whose speciality was making up maps for television documentaries and current affairs programmes, but one diverting assignment was writing the cue cards for Hancock. Towards the end of the week, McWatt would leave his Lime Grove office-cum-studio and attend the *Half Hour* rehearsals. 'Tony would not use "idiot boards" to a great extent,' recalls McWatt. 'When it was necessary they would contain only basic phrases.' Hancock and Duncan Wood would select out-of-shot places – inside a wardrobe door or on the seat of a chair – to paste McWatt's prompt cards, but one long exchange between Hancock and Sid James proved particularly trying. In the end it was decided both men should sit with their feet up on the kitchen table – so that Hancock could read the cues stuck to the soles of James's shoes.

The cartographer always found Hancock an 'insular and morose' character. A few years later when production had moved to the partly-built Television Centre in Wood Lane, McWatt met Hancock again. A large room had been divided by doors, one side of which was used as an art studio, the other for rehearsals, and during breaks Hancock would slip in to the cartographer's room to listen to the cricket commentary on the radio.

For the BBC, audiences had become part of the science of broadcasting. For Hancock they remained an unpredictable and necessary evil. He was not, however, beyond weighting the odds in his favour. During the early summer, Kavanagh Associates was asked if its client would agree to a short stage tour. Hancock, who had played variety for two years, was reticent. Before he agreed, he spent an entire Sunday sticking hundreds of coloured pins into a map of the British Isles. Each pin represented a fan letter. The density of the pins around certain cities and towns gave him an indication of where he could expect the best and worst houses. The heaviest clusters surrounded Manchester,

Bristol, north London, Liverpool, Hanley and Birmingham. He agreed to the tour – on condition he only played the most favourable venues.

Hancock still regarded Birmingham as his home town. It was also, he told one interviewer, his 'Waterloo', explaining: 'There [Birmingham] I am the prophet, unaccepted in his own country. They are a hard and tough audience and because I am one of them, they expect a great deal of me, but I am not complaining; I don't want any favours. This is a challenge which I respect and welcome. When I get on stage in Birmingham and put on my most belligerent glare, they just glare right back as if to say "All right then, show us what you can do – and it had better be good."'

Hancock's 'belligerent glare' was not restricted to the audience. To save on the payroll, the management recruited and trained the six dancers it needed from each of the four cities it visited. They were usually amateurs and always inexperienced. In Birmingham a local dance troupe, the Betty Fox Dancing Teenagers, provided the high-kicking chorus line. Hancock arrived at the Hippodrome for the Sunday afternoon rehearsals, hung-over and quite obviously wishing he was somewhere else. For one routine the comedian was on stage with the six dancers. Frustrated by Hancock's apparent lack of concentration, someone whispered a sarcastic comment. Rightly or wrongly Hancock picked on a teenager who looked most guilty and ordered her off the stage and out of the show. 'We were all terrified in case we were chosen to replace her,' admitted one Betty Fox understudy. 'Some of the girls in the wings even fled in tears and refused to have anything to do with him. None of us liked him.'

At the BBC Hancock was, by now, attempting to surround himself with an informal repertory of support actors. In October, John le Mesurier[6] was performing at a tiny south-London theatre. Hancock sat through the play and then called at le Mesurier's dressing room. The pair had first met when Hancock was appearing in *Educating Archie* with le Mesurier's future wife, Hattie Jacques. During a drink at the bar, Hancock told the actor he liked his work and wanted him to join the *Half Hour* team.

John le Mesurier – who later went on to become the inimitable Sergeant Wilson in *Dad's Army* – was born John Elton Halliley in 1912. After a six-year career in a solicitor's office, he came to London and signed on for the Fay Compton Studio of Dramatic Art, adopting his mother's maiden name of le Mesurier. Among his fellow students, and enrolling on the same day, was Alec Guinness. In 1940, le Mesurier turned his back on repertory and enlisted in the Royal Armoured Corps. He was demobbed in 1945 at the rank of captain.

Le Mesurier made his first appearance in a December *Half Hour* as a bemused judge, as Hancock, a defence lawyer, talks himself into jail. 'Tony was a joy to work with,' le Mesurier states in his autobiography, *A Jobbing Actor*. However, 'Like Peter Sellers, Tony was very much the introvert, capable of deep moods of depression and uncertainty.'

Hancock's boundless faith in a small circle of fellow performers frequently blinded him to their faults, yet it was the sort of blindness which blocks out obstacles and leads to bold ventures. Hancock's commitment to comedy was total. For several years he had nurtured a plan to buy a large country house where friends and writers could gather and strike sparks off one another in a kind of informal comedy workshop. As ever, he had outlined and described his dream so often he had doomed it to failure. Cicely, however, was determined they should move out of the Knightsbridge flat and, once again, set about finding them a new home.

Val Fleury was an intimidating stone and brick-built house, standing in one-and-a-half acres of garden, just off the main road which ran through the centre of the Surrey village of Blindley Heath. At first Hancock was unimpressed. The house, which smelt musty and unaired, had been empty for more than a year, blighted by the construction of a council estate in an adjoining field. Its only redeeming feature, Hancock felt, was the Red Barn restaurant and country club a short walk away at the end of Tandridge Lane.

High on the roof was a stone unicorn and for some untraceable reason the builder had incorporated a relief portrait of the Marquis of Worcester over the large front door. Hancock would claim it bore a closer resemblance to Spike Milligan. When the deeds arrived, he discovered the house had been commissioned and built by a merchant called MacConkey. The house, Hancock insisted, should be rechristened MacConkeys after its original owner.

By late November the Hancocks and their two poodles, Mr Brown and Charlie, were rattling and scratching around the empty rooms of their new country home. The main hall was dominated by a huge fireplace; upstairs there were five bedrooms. 'The main bedroom was furnished,' recalled Freddie Ross, 'the others were not. One served as a clutter room for Cicely and another as a study for Tony. In it he had a desk, a couple of chairs, a telephone, a portable typewriter, a tape machine and books including the *Kinsey Report*, dictionaries, and a glossy magazine about how the BBC Television Centre would look when it was finished.' The walls of the study were painted white and on them Hancock used a black crayon to scribble down the sayings of Descartes and Russell, Kant and Ayer – what he described as 'gems from the philosophers' and what, he hoped, would one day metamorphose into a complete understanding of life.

The move had left Hancock tired and depressed. A bout of Asian flu – which had forced the cancellation of a live November *Half Hour* – left him morose and badly in need of a rest. In addition to the four remaining television shows, he had also been contracted to appear in a BBC Christmas Day extravaganza. Even the Guild of Television Producers and Directors' announcement that its members had voted Hancock Comedian of the Year failed to lift his spirits.

Faced with an extra thirteen minutes for the final show of the series, Galton and Simpson opted to change the format. The programme – renamed *Hancock's Forty-Three Minutes: The East Cheam Repertory Company* – was little more than a thinly-disguised variety show, with Hancock as an unconvincing compère. The actor, John Gregson, was the star guest and the cast list included genuine variety artistes such as the harmonica-playing Max Geldray, Alf Silvestri the juggler and Dido the Chimp.

The show was broadcast live on Monday, 23 December, and

Duncan Wood thought it 'quite the worst' of the series. He later admitted in a BBC memo that he had feared Hancock was 'running out of steam' and might not be able to complete his third television series. However, like Main Wilson two years earlier, Wood did not appreciate how black Hancock's mood had become.

In the final episode Hancock played two parts, Aladdin and Robin Hood; as did Sid James, with Friar Tuck and the Genie. Another member of the cast was the diminutive Charlie Drake. After the day's shooting Drake found himself chatting to Hancock at the bar of a nearby club. The pair were eating cold chicken and drinking gin.

'What do you feel about committing suicide?' Hancock asked his companion.

Drake thought for a minute. 'What do you mean – together?'

'Yes,' said Hancock dryly. 'We've done it all, haven't we? Let's commit suicide.'

Drake downed the remains of his gin. He could see by the expression on Hancock's face he was deadly serious and desperately lonely.

'Well,' said Drake, 'I'm not sure my wife will understand.'

1958

RAY GALTON AND Alan Simpson were so fine-tuned to the agonies and frustrations of everyday life, they could create classic comedy from the most obscure subjects.

On crumpets:

The butter keeps disappearing down the holes ... you

think there's none on it, take a bite, and whoosh, all over
your tie.

On excitement:

Will you stop jumping up and down ... my boiled egg's
running over the side of the shell.

On teeth:

Is that tooth loose ... or is my finger just going in and
out?

On parks:

Sunday morning isn't the same without a couple of goes
on the roundabout and a slide down the chute when the
keeper's not looking.

Galton and Simpson were determined to steer clear of pretension
and parish-pump humour. Life, they reasoned, was reflected in
popular newspapers and double-feature film programmes.

By the late 1950s, the writing team were spending their days
ensconced in a Knightsbridge office, distilling and condensing the
world outside. In less than eight years they had become a comedy
institution, successfully turning a passion first into a hobby, then a
business, and finally an industry. Like their creation, the pair had also
earned themselves establishment respectability. Interviewed for a
Times arts feature, 'Mr. Alan Simpson and Mr. Ray Galton' were first
inspected and then quizzed on their craft:

Mr. Galton was the first to arrive at their office opposite
Kensington Gardens: tall, slim, with dark hair and an
extensive dark beard, he looked in his slightly Edwardian
suit rather like a du Maurier illustration of artist life, an
illusion completed by a Sherlock Holmes-style meerschaum

pipe. While Mr. Simpson disentangled himself from the
intricacies of moving house we talked of British second
features, for which both partners, and Mr. Hancock himself,
have a passion – as many regular viewers of the show will no
doubt have guessed. Mr. Galton's enthusiasm at the thought
of double-bills at Kensal Rise or Fulham Green was soon
interrupted by the arrival of Mr. Simpson, finally free of
electricians (will they, one wondered, turn up in a future
Half Hour with Hancock?). Mr. Simpson is also tall, though
shorter than Mr. Galton, broader, and with a certain elusive
resemblance to the star of their shows.

Writing for television was not that different from writing for radio,
they told *The Times:*

Admittedly we are exceptions: most writers find they write
about half the amount of dialogue for television that they do
for radio, but we write almost exactly the same amount. Of
course, there are things which you would have to underline in dialogue for the radio which on television can be
immediately conveyed by facial expression. The basis of
television is the close-up, which allows the audience to see
facial expression in detail, and in this sense television is a
visual medium, but it is a dialogue medium as well; that is
why some of the most exciting television consists of
interviews with people who have something interesting to
say and are interesting to watch while they say it. To capture
a television audience you don't have to move the camera
about and give them a great variety of sets; you just have to
put something interesting to look at in front of the camera,
even if it's only a single person who reacts interestingly to
what he says and to what people say to him.

Hancock's *Half Hour* character developed naturally over the years,
and transferred almost seamlessly from radio to television as a

conglomeration of all three of its creators. Freddie Ross explains it as a kind of two-way, cross-fertilisation of words and interpretation. 'Words don't mean anything without a performer and a performer isn't anything without words. All three, Tony and Ray and Alan, were very fortunate they refined their artistry together and grew together and matured together.'

Yet Galton and Simpson's image – perception – of 'their' Hancock remained constant and separate from the situations demanded by the weekly format. Since their first *Half Hour* script, they had developed and dusted and re-focused the character to the people's mood, never allowing him to lie down or admit defeat. He goes on blustering and fighting even when circumstances are completely beyond his control. When Hancock appeared ineffectual, half the nation shared his inadequacy. Even his supposed insight is the sort of tatty intellectualism picked up by the ignorant. His quotations are always recherché but wrong, his allusions deliberately obscure. He is a misfit in the world, incapable of fulfilling his grandiose dreams. 'As far as the character is concerned, I always think of Tony Hancock as Tony Hancock, and the *Hancock's Half Hour* character as something that we created, developed and invented,' claims Galton.

J. B. Priestley, who followed Tony Hancock's career from his Adelphi days, disagreed. 'They understood him, gave him what he could do best, were partners and not mere line-providers,' asserted the novelist. 'They gave him magnificent scripts, often worked out to the tiniest detail of "business", but it was his unique personality as a performer that added the magic.'

Quite often Hancock was himself the catalyst: 'There were phrases and idiosyncrasies of his we used,' said Simpson, 'but on occasions we gave the character completely opposing attitudes to Tony's. Take his attitude towards food and France, for instance. One week, we'd give him "bloody French food, don't stick that foreign muck in front of me", when Tony himself loved both food and France. We'd make the character very chauvinistic, and if there was one thing Tony really hated it was patriotism in the nationalistic sense of the word. At other times we'd go the other way. He'd have an argument with Sid about culture and he'd praise French culture and literature and French food. It worked because on the radio Hancock was a man whose attitudes would change depending upon the kind of person he was talking to. If he met an intellectual he would either try to keep up with him or he would say: "What a load of old rubbish!" If he was talking to a clod like Sid or Bill he would go the other way.'

Just as Hancock had established silence as 'one of the greatest comedy tools ever invented', Galton and Simpson now applied the same principles to movement.

At first, like everyone else, we were obsessed with making everything visual: we had characters rushing round all the time to give it movement and wrote in purely visual gags. But gradually we came to see that a lot of movement only muffled the effect and confused the audience, while the specifically visual jokes were the least funny sections of the show. We were finally confirmed in our opinion when we wrote a scene which consisted entirely of Tony Hancock and Sidney James sitting in chairs talking to each other, very simply presented in cross-cut close-ups. This ran nine full minutes by the watch, and no one noticed except to remark that it was the funniest part of the show.

Early in the first radio series Hancock had been amused to find that the writers – or at least one of them – had written in a part for himself. It was a clever device which allowed Galton and Simpson to punctuate Hancock's long rambling monologues with placid agreement, and save Dennis Main Wilson or Duncan Wood the trouble of hiring and paying another actor.

> Hancock: . . . Well, as I was saying, I've been here before.
> I was nicked for collecting betting slips in
> Hyde Park. Of course, I denied it. I told 'em I
> was the keeper and I lost me stick with the
> spike on the end. Anyway, they brought me in.
> There was the judge sitting in the box with the

crest on. Like a Command Performance. I was
second bookie, on after the drunks. Anyway,
the judge started.

Simpson: Who was he?

Hancock: You know him. Little bloke. Looks like a
cocker spaniel with a wooden hammer.

Simpson: Oh, him.

Hancock: Yes, that's right. Easter Humphreys.

Simpson: Christmas.

Hancock: Eh?

Simpson: Christmas.

Hancock: Oh. Happy New Year.

Simpson: Thank you.

Hancock: Good health. Anyway, he was in a bad mood
that morning.

Simpson: Was he?

Hancock: Can you imagine Gilbert Harding with an
ulcer?

Simpson: Yes.

Hancock: That was him. Well, he heard the evidence and
he glowered. I thought, Hello, he's going to
make an example of me. He said, 'Were you or
were you not' – 'cos they talk like that you
know – he said, 'Were you or were you not
collecting bets for next Saturday's Derby?' I
said, 'Yes I was.' Well, that settled it. A mean
look came over his face, sort of enjoying it

> he was, triumphant. He picked up his pen,
> dipped it in the ink ... and do you know what
> he gave me?

Simpson: What?

Hancock: Three tanner up-and-down cross doubles any
to come one and six on the Lincoln.

Alan Simpson enjoyed these brief moments of performance far more than his less gregarious partner and he appeared in no fewer than sixty radio shows and ten television *Half Hours*, making him the fourth most regular performer after Sid James, Bill Kerr and Kenneth Williams.

The Rank Organisation which, two years earlier, had failed to entice Hancock into a contract, was once again pressuring him to make his second film – this time employing a deft form of flattery. Rank wanted him to play the part of Sid Field, his brief but lasting comic hero. Hancock admitted he was tempted – 'until they wanted to cut the money and put in a love interest'. Another proposal came from Eric Maschwitz, suggesting Hancock take the title role in *The Gent*, a reworked version of Molière's *Le Bourgeois Gentilhomme*.

Both approaches followed Hancock's portrayal of Hlestakov, the penniless but plausible loafer in a live BBC adaptation of Nikolai Gogol's *The Government Inspector*. The *Birmingham Post* echoed the qualified praise for the comedian's performance:

> Tony Hancock made an amusing impostor in Gogol's classic
> comedy *The Government Inspector*.
> There could have been more of the smart-aleck about the
> minor clerk who is mistaken for a major official visiting a
> small Russian town.
> But Mr. Hancock, approaching this assignment as if it
> were 'Ancock's 'Our and a Quarter, took his good luck and
> his bribes without changing his dry, almost expressionless

style. He is the natural clown who can afford to let the world go mad around him.

The old comedy trimmed for modern requirements went reasonably well and probably made more friends for World Theatre than any previous production in the perversely difficult BBC series.

*

The fifth radio series of *Hancock's Half Hour* began transmission on the BBC's Light Programme on Tuesday, 21 January, with a different producer for the first time in almost seventy episodes. Dennis Main Wilson had been replaced by Pat Dixon, but the new partnership between the regular cast and the producer failed to gel. After the planned twenty episodes, his place for the 1958 Christmas Day *Half Hour* special and the subsequent sixth and final radio series was taken by Tom Ronald.

The situation was not helped by Kenneth Williams, having been dropped from the television series, progressively distancing himself from the *Half Hour* cast – 'I don't care for any of them at all ... This team is so dreary to me now – how different to the jolly warmth of "B[eyond] O[ur] K[en]" – this crowd, especially James and Hancock, are so listless and disinterested and their conversation is real pleb stuff.'

Williams's scribbled pot-shots were not restricted to his fellow performers. After recording one May episode – *The Junk Man* – he fumed: 'The scripts seem to get worse and worse. There was a time when Tony would have complained. He seems quite happy with them. They are terrible. This one was a load of inconsequential rubbish about rubbish. Hardly a joke anywhere.'

Another problem facing Pat Dixon was his star's insistence that he take part in a Mediterranean tour of Malta, Tripoli and Cyprus to entertain British troops. The BBC compromised by rearranging schedules and recording two programmes on the same day late in February. The situation was not ideal, but Hancock agreed to allow the Royal Air Force to fly him back to England. His first London day trip produced one of the funniest and most endearing of all the radio recordings. In *Hancock's Car*, his vehicle has been parked outside 23

Railway Cuttings for ten years, to the annoyance of the local authority which wants to re-surface the road. Kenneth Williams, as a policeman, orders him to 'move it' and Hancock – as in real life – admits he is the world's worst driver.

When Hancock arrived in London for his second Sunday session he was presented with a classic Galton and Simpson script. It is noteworthy, not so much for its content, as the writers' ability, once again, to transform the true – and current – events of their star's life into a work of comic fiction. Hancock has been booked to entertain the troops in Malta. Instead he is diverted by Sid and unwittingly joins the Foreign Legion.

Another actor who joined the Mediterranean tour was Hugh Lloyd, a former journalist who made his stage debut with ENSA during the war, and shared the suffering of rising through the ranks of stand-up comedy. Lloyd had first worked with Hancock four months earlier when he was offered several small television parts. It surprised him to see that, despite topping the bill, Hancock became increasingly nervous before making his appearance: 'He was still very, very frightened.' In one comedy sketch Hancock was a great, but inept, juggler. In another he delivered readings from Charles Dickens, with Lloyd as his footman. By the time they returned from the tour of British bases they were firm friends.

Hancock – never a respecter of rank – preferred the down-to-earth rowdiness of the sergeants' mess to the formal company of officers. Amidst the bonhomie of the officers' mess he was confronted by men eager to ingratiate themselves and most nights ended in a sullen and abrupt departure. One young officer remembers Hancock 'switching off' when he became the centre of attention. 'You could see it in his face and hear it in his voice, as if someone had suddenly turned on a cold shower.' Most put it down to the comedian's considerable intake of alcohol. Hugh Lloyd witnessed the same scene night after night. 'If people started telling funny stories and expected him to reply with jokes Hancock would get very short. He couldn't bear that. He hated people expecting him to be funny off stage as well as on.' Hancock had long since developed a means of escape. Actress Annabelle Lee remembers: 'Whenever anyone told Tony a joke he didn't want to hear, he used to hobble away complaining of pains in his legs.'

Only rarely did Hancock find someone who shared his growing interest in philosophy. At one base he sat through the night, long after the mess had closed, with a twenty-year-old subaltern, dissecting the merits of various obscure religions. The discussion eventually ended at four in the morning, recalls former Lieutenant David Hooper. Later that day, as the troupe was about to depart, Hancock sought out the young officer. 'I expected him to say goodbye,' says Hooper. 'Instead he picked up exactly where we had left off. No niceties. No handshake. He just wanted to talk.'

On 5 July, an advertisement appeared in *Film Fun* magazine announcing 'here is the man who makes millions laugh' and inviting readers to 'follow the screamingly funny adventures of Tony Hancock'. With his last radio *Half Hour* series just ended and a new television series more than six months away, Hancock was about to break into a new medium – as a comic strip character.

Hancock 'appeared' in *Film Fun* from 12 July, 1958, to 8 September, 1962. The initial art work was old-fashioned and in the same pre-war style as the magazine's other cartoon stories. For the first year Hancock – for some reason wearing a Billy Bunter-style school blazer and striped tie – was pursued and conned by wide-boy Sid Sharkey. The early stories appeared on a single page. By May the following year, Hancock's misadventures were *Film Fun*'s most popular story and the Hancock strip was promoted to the front and back covers.

Pressure from both the BBC and Sid James's agent forced Hancock's cartoon antagonist, Sid Sharkey, to be replaced by Sid James, and the strip's previously unspecified location now became East Cheam. As in real life, James made his last appearance on 20 May, 1961, coinciding with the start of Hancock's new 'solo' television series. The following week, Hancock returns from holiday to find a goodbye note from James. When *Film Fun* merged with *Buster* in September, 1962, the Hancock strip was dropped.

Hancock's drinking was, by now, well beyond the apocryphal. One night at the end of a long and determined day's drinking with journalist Jeffrey Barnard, both men could barely stand. Hancock had urinated in his trousers, already scuffed and torn from several tumbles, and the newspaper man, only slightly more aware of his situation, realised his famous companion was in no state to find his own way home, so hailed a taxi. A succession of cabs ignored what the drivers considered a pair of wealthy, but out-of-control drunks. Eventually, however, a taxi pulled over and Hancock was manhandled into the back where he collapsed on the floor. The journalist, himself only managing to stay upright by clinging to the door, noticed that the crumpled Hancock was searching his pockets, where he finally located a visiting card and offered it to his companion with the words: 'If ever you need my help just call me.'

After a puzzled silence, as he attempted to focus on the card, the journalist asked: 'Why on earth should I want help from you?'

Hancock waved him closer. 'Because,' he whispered, 'I think you might have a drink problem.'

Early in 1958, Hancock invited some of his closest friends to examine his new Surrey home. Among the guests were John le Mesurier and his wife, Hattie Jacques. The house itself was still sparsely furnished, even though it was several months after the Hancocks had moved out of London; most of the rooms were bare, one had a couple of armchairs, another an old and rickety table. Only the main bedroom and Hancock's study appeared lived in. The duty tour was completed, the group reassembled in the large living-room. 'It's okay,' Hancock announced, 'the drinks will be arriving any minute.' At that exact moment, as if by magic, a three-wheeled van turned into the drive and pulled up at the front door. It was loaded to the roof with cases of vodka. As the driver carried the boxes into the house, Cicely issued each guest with a beer mug. Hancock then filled each glass with the newly arrived vodka: no ice; no tonic; no lemon; just a pint of straight vodka.

Other visitors to MacConkeys were made less welcome. On one occasion Bill Kerr and Eric Sykes drove down from London, to arrive unannounced, around five o'clock in the afternoon. Hancock appeared at the front door in his dressing gown. 'I'm sorry I can't invite you in,' he said, 'I'm not entertaining today.'

'You bugger,' Sykes snapped back. 'We've driven thirty-five miles to see you.'

Hancock thought for a moment before asking: 'Can you come back later?'

Cyril Fletcher, who eight years earlier had magnanimously praised Hancock at a *Workers' Playtime* audition, only had resentful memories of his visit to MacConkeys. Hancock's Blindley Heath home was less than ten miles north of East Grinstead, where, during the war, Sir Archibald McIndoe, the consulting plastic surgeon to the RAF, had based his special unit at the town's Queen Victoria Hospital. It was here that badly burned and injured airmen, their faces and limbs rebuilt by pioneering surgery, became the founding members of the Guinea Pig Club. Throughout the 1950s, Lady McIndoe and Cyril Fletcher's wife organised all-star fundraising concerts to support the Guinea Pig charity. Among those who volunteered to perform were Bebe Daniels and Ben Lyon, Bob Monkhouse, Vera Lynn and Elsie and Doris Waters. The charity had booked Arthur Askey for the 1958 event, but when Askey fell ill, Cyril Fletcher suggested Hancock as a near neighbour of the hospital.

Fletcher, remembering his previous meeting with the then unknown Hancock, telephoned several times to invite the now famous comic and television star. Hancock flatly refused. The prospect of meeting badly scarred and disfigured patients horrified him. In desperation, Fletcher went in person to beg Hancock to attend: 'He said he planned a Sunday evening at home that night.'

Duncan Wood had spent most of the spring telephoning agents. He was, the BBC producer told them, looking for experienced character actors to fill walk-on and minor speaking roles in *Hancock's Half Hour*. Among those who survived the reading audition were Leslie Smith, Richard Statman, Bruce Wightman and Alec Bregonzi, and they appeared as the 'crimson alligator', the 'green lizard' and two Arabs in the opening episode of the third television series.

During the summer, Bregonzi – who would eventually appear in twenty-two *Half Hours* – walked into the bar at the Prince of Wales Theatre to find Hancock in the middle of an impromptu rehearsal. 'What are you doing here?' the comedian asked, before informing Bregonzi he was about to embark on a short tour prior to his appearance at that year's Royal Variety Performance. Before he left the theatre Bregonzi had been invited to join the tour.

Hancock shared the billing with Diana Dors and the run opened at Gloucester late in July. He makes his first appearance of each show wearing his Homburg hat and trademark overcoat. The accompanying music, played at double tempo, is conducted from the orchestra pit by Bregonzi. The two men argue. Hancock demands his entrance be played again. This time Bregonzi conducts at funereal pace. After yet another alteration Hancock is joined on the stage by two associates. He removes his overcoat to reveal a frilly shirt and all three attempt a juggling act. Bregonzi, still in the orchestra pit, continues to heckle during an open-air theatre sketch in which Hancock attempts various Shakespeare speeches from *Hamlet* and *Richard III*. The first half ends with Hancock dressed in his by now familiar 'Crooner' zoot suit and suede shoes. It was tried and tested and safe material.

The day after the tour opened, Ray Galton and Alan Simpson arrived at the theatre. Hancock wanted them to adapt the budgerigar sketch, which he had first performed the previous year on BBC television, for the November Royal Variety Performance. As a try-out, it would replace one of the tour sketches, but after a week of discussions and script changes, and with the show moving on to Liverpool, the idea was dropped.

Hancock was at the height of his popularity and – on stage at least – of his confidence. When the twice-nightly tour opened at the Liverpool Empire early in August every seat was pre-sold. The *Liverpool Echo* was equally impressed:

If Tony Hancock could split himself into 50 Tony Hancocks

of equal wit and bubbling folly, there would be no moaning to the bars of our theatres. Mr Hancock must have sent so many people home determined to buy a television set just to see him again.

As it is he tries to give us some kind of inkling why the stage sees him so rarely.

They could use him at The Regent Park Open Air Theatre despite his offish yellow wig, if only he could remember the tune of Hamlet's Soliloquy.

They could use him at music halls if he could juggle with more than one hoop.

They could make records of his crooning, if he would stand still for a moment somewhere near the microphone.

They could almost certainly make a comedian of him, if his confidence wasn't permanently shattered by the awful half pitying, half loathing stares of his sinister and unwilling assistant, Johnny Vyvyan. On his own admission, Mr Vyvyan's stare gives Hancock a cold feeling in his spine, and our sympathy expresses itself by the tears in our eyes, even if the sound we are making is suspiciously like laughter.

The tour had been planned more to suit Diana Dors' film commitments than Hancock's demanding public. Having played through August, it broke up early in September when the actress left to begin shooting at Elstree. Dors, however, agreed to play one last date at the Hanley Empire late in October.

With less than a week before the Command Performance, Hancock decided to give the now reworked budgerigar sketch an airing. By Thursday, however, he was becoming increasingly nervous and announced he was dropping the sketch from the remaining tour performances and intended using the 'Crooner' routine at the following Monday's royal performance. On Saturday, and less than an hour before the first of the evening's shows, he decided to substitute the budgie sketch. It was, according to one critic, the 'funniest and most original comedy I have seen in years'. Hancock remained unconvinced.

The 1958 Royal Variety Performance was the first of the long-running series of collaborations with Bernard Delfont as producer and Robert Nesbitt as stage director. With Hancock as the nation's top radio and television comedian it was natural he should be included. The date was the same as his previous Command Performance six years earlier, 3 November, a fact Hancock saw as an omen. Sharing the London Coliseum bill were several of his 1952 co-stars including Norman Wisdom and Jerry Desmonde, by now a film comedy partnership in their own right. Also appearing was Eve Boswell, the drowsy, confidential singer, born the day before Hancock in Budapest, and whose early career had frequently collided with the comedian's; both had appeared on the same *Henry Hall's Guest Night* and Boswell had replaced Vera Lynn for a night in *London Laughs*.

The one and only rehearsal for the Monday night gala was called for the Sunday afternoon. That morning Hancock telephoned Hattie Jacques, who was already on the royal cast list, to ask if she would perform the budgerigar sketch with him. Irene Handl, his original television 'owner', was unavailable at such short notice.

The Coliseum was packed with journalists, press agents, impresarios and friends of the cast. Overseeing the rehearsal was the show's stage director Robert Nesbitt, a man who kept a tight rein on audience reaction and demanded absolute concentration from his performers.

The curtain rose to reveal a caged Hancock dressed as a giant budgerigar, complaining because his mistress has spent too much time at the pub and neglected to feed him – 'It's not right. It's not good enough. How can I stop me feathers dropping out without me nourishment?' As he swaggered about, admiring himself in the mirror and pecking at a bell, the audience dissolved in howls of laughter. Even Nesbitt could not resist an appreciative smile.

The next night, little more than twenty-four hours later, the same sketch was a disaster. Of Hancock's irascible budgie one newspaper reported: 'It was the brightest new idea in humour, but the cold audience froze it off the stage.' The problem, however, lay not with the audience, but with Hancock. His performance had lost the previous day's spontaneity; his words were mumbled and off-hand; Hancock was – and looked – bored. Having delivered one hilarious performance he had, overnight, convinced himself the sketch was old hat. The rapturous reaction, albeit from the wrong audience, had justified his comedy instincts. For Hancock's blind perfectionism it was time to move on.

The sketch included a brief appearance, and the off-stage voice, of a vicar, played by Alec Bregonzi. Not wanting to 'upset' the Queen or the Church of England, Delfont insisted the character be changed to a scout master. Despite Bregonzi protesting his part was an 'honour', Hancock insisted he would pay his expenses. Nothing was forthcoming, however. Whenever they met to film a subsequent *Half Hour*, Hancock would take the actor aside and say: 'Alec, I'll give you your expenses.' Three years later, at the end of a second tour, Hancock called Bregonzi to his dressing room and finally gave him a cheque for £10.

Within a month Hancock had donned the budgie suit again, this time for a prerecorded BBC *Christmas Night with the Stars*, and it would get its final airing in 1966 when Jimmy Grafton adapted the original sketch for ITV's *Secombe and Friends*. Galton and Simpson would make use of the same idea – this time with Hancock dressed as a canary – for a short sequence in his first solo film, *The Rebel*. In the intervening years Hancock would transform the budgie sketch, with its roots in his teenage imagination, first into a symbol of his success and then, as both his confidence and popularity deserted him, into a crutch.

Hancock was, by now, a regular Christmas attraction. *Hancock's Half Hour* had been off British television screens for exactly a year and the BBC planners had scheduled the fourth series to begin on Boxing Day. The previous series had ended on Christmas Eve, 1957, with the tired and disastrous *East Cheam Repertory Company*, and Duncan Wood did not intend to make the same mistake twice.

The producer had devised a plan to take the pressure off his star. The new series would intersperse nine live broadcasts with four prerec-orded programmes. The taped shows would take the place of each fourth live transmission, ensuring Hancock would not be called upon to work more than three successive weeks. The first show – *The Set That Failed* – was recorded halfway through November, and the remaining three the following month. In the event, however, all four taped programmes were used at the start of the new series, allowing Hancock to concentrate on rerecording four radio shows for the BBC's Transcription Service.

Two new actors joined the cast early in the new series. Rolf Harris played an Australian barman and Andrew Faulds – the future Labour MP – made the first of two appearances as a 'radio' voice. He would later achieve minor comedy immortality as the 'mayday' voice of a stricken yachtsman in *The Radio Ham*.

It was only the second time the *Half Hour* team had used the Sulgrave Boys Club, in Sulgrave Road, for pre-studio rehearsals. Hancock was late, remembers Rolf Harris: 'He came rushing in asking for someone to lend him ten bob for the taxi. I rushed forward, here to please, with a ten shilling note. Tony took it and went out to pay the cab. Everyone else stayed where they had been waiting, quite un-interested. Sid James turned to me and said, "You'll never see that ten bob again." I couldn't believe him, but he was right. The subject was never raised again.'

Andrew Faulds was impressed at how 'ordinary' Hancock was, 'not the rumbustious character' he had expected. During a break in rehearsals Hancock would plunge into one of the prop armchairs and read the *Guardian* – 'expressing his pessimistic reaction to whatever crisis was uppermost at the time. He was not a happy man and seemed preoccupied with the dangerous international situation.'

Hancock's Half Hour was, the BBC quickly realised, a valuable entertainment commodity. Telerecordings were sent around the world to various networks and broadcasting organisations. Commonwealth countries with a high expatriate population – Australia, New Zealand, Canada and South Africa – took readily to Hancock's humour. The

Americans suffered a common problem – and offered a disastrous solution.

The BBC office in New York had successfully interested CBS Television executives in Hancock as a variety comic, but when they watched an episode of *Hancock's Half Hour* they encountered a 'really tricky problem'. Ronald Waldman, the BBC's television business manager, apologised to Hancock's agent:

> Everybody says they can't understand Tony! This matter of accent is an extremely difficult one because Tony's accent in the show is, in my opinion, an essential part of his characterisation and yet if people in New York are having difficulty in following him what on earth is going to happen in the Middle West?

Further negotiations followed and it was clear the Americans had devised an under-the-table solution. The BBC was reluctant and Hancock was horrified. CBS – and later NBC – intended to purchase the *Half Hour* series with no promise of a screening date; then, having bought the script rights, it would scrap the British recordings and remake the shows with American actors and Americanising the humour.

Hancock's dedication to his art was total. It transcended his marriage, possessions and the minutiae of personal life. One May, Sid James was about to leave his Ealing home for a studio session when Val James reminded her husband to give Hancock her best wishes.

'Many happy returns, mate,' James dutifully told Hancock.

Hancock looked blank. 'What are you talking about?'

'It's your birthday today, isn't it?'

Hancock searched his memory. 'Is it?' he said. 'I didn't know.'

Another colleague with experience of Hancock's narrow and oblique concentration was Liz Fraser. The pair had met for the first time in 1956 as the cast gathered for an early television *Half Hour*. The teenage Elizabeth Fraser – the Liz would come in the 1960s – had been hired to play a teddy girl whom Hancock attempts to entice on to the dance floor with a seductive kick. Fraser responds by delivering her first line on live television: 'Who are you kicking, you great lump?' for which she receives a fee of £2 10s.

In the last few days before Christmas, pre-recording rehearsals were being held in rooms just off Kingsway. This time Fraser had been hired to play a girl in a milk bar. As the read-through ended Hancock informed the young actress: 'I haven't bought a single present, let's go down Oxford Street.'

For more than two hours the pair jostled their way through the late-afternoon shoppers, lurching from one shop to the next. Hancock finally steered Fraser toward Berry's, an Oxford Street wine lodge, and insisted on treating her to a thank you drink. 'I never drank then,' she recalls, 'so I ordered a small sherry.' With each round the waiter delivered a complimentary miniature. 'By the time Tony took me home in a taxi I was virtually paralytic,' admitted Fraser. 'The only thing I can remember about that evening was me staggering up my front steps and dropping an armful of these tiny sherry bottles.'

1959

FREDDIE ROSS HAD finally given in. After five years of passionate, but unconsummated, love she was now Tony Hancock's mistress. The first time they slept together was in a hotel suite in Bond Street, borrowed from one of her clients; at twenty-nine Freddie was still a virgin and living with her parents. After their second act of adultery she attempted to escape from what she saw as a hopeless situation. 'I was scared of what I was getting into,' she confesses. 'I was trying to prove to myself that I wasn't going to get drawn into this web because I knew it was a scenario that every mother dreads for her daughter: a married man with a different religion, and a "theatrical" to boot.'

Confused by guilt and shame and an overpowering desire, she left home and went to work in America – 'All the time we were parted I knew I could lift the phone and get him back and he knew the same about me.' Freddie's sojourn lasted three months. When she returned, Hancock was overjoyed to see her and, not for the first time, informed her his marriage to Cicely was over. To persuade her, he even visited a solicitor to discuss the formalities of a divorce.

Freddie's brother Leonard, himself a solicitor, knew from experience any attempt to pressure his sister into ending the relationship would inevitably spark an argument. 'I couldn't believe, before she told me, she was capable of having an affair,' said Leonard Ross. 'Freddie had a very naïve approach to sex and men in general.'

Attempts to keep the affair secret were spectacularly unsuccessful. Cicely, who had long had her suspicions, found herself suddenly confronted by her husband and his press agent in a West End street. Stepping into a shop doorway, she watched the pair walk past arm in arm, Hancock 'looking happier and more at ease' than she had seen him for years. 'It was at that moment Cicely knew her marriage had ended,' said a friend, 'and her drinking started in earnest.'

Cicely arrived at her friend's apartment in tears. 'It was almost a monthly ritual for Tony to announce their marriage was over, and this time was no different,' recalled the former classmate. 'There was no confrontation, no screaming rages. Right to the end, through his marriage to Freddie and their divorce, Cicely was convinced Tony would come back to her.'

Hancock himself was confident he could keep both his marriage and his affair alive. Liberated by alcohol, he suffered few sexual taboos: 'Get your legs round a good man,' he would publicly advise his sexagenarian mother. 'That'll put you right.'

For Sid James, sex existed and he enjoyed it, usually with any consenting female, but in reality, James's Victorian sexual conscience was walking a tightrope. The one thing guaranteed to make it wobble was any form of lewd or suggestive behaviour – particularly in front of his third wife, Valerie. Hancock and Cicely were on holiday in France and had arranged for Sid and Valerie James to join them in Paris. On their first night together, Hancock insisted the quartet visit a certain restaurant. What he hadn't told James was that the establishment was more famous for its risqué menu than its culinary prowess.

The four chatted over an aperitif as the waiters fussed around the table. The bread arrived. Each roll had been fashioned and baked to resemble the male genitals. James munched his way through the crusty testicles and the oversized penis with obvious unease, while Hancock beamed like a mischievous schoolboy – but the joke wasn't over. Hancock, who claimed to visit the restaurant regularly, insisted on ordering the dessert for Cicely and Valerie James. When the ice cream came it, too, was shaped like a giant penis and dripping in thick, white cream. There was only one house rule, announced Hancock. The women were not allowed to use a spoon or fork – they had to lick it with their tongues.

Sid James erupted in anger and embarrassment. He stood up and informed his wife – who was quite willing to join Cicely in entertaining the waiters and other guests – that they were leaving. When she protested, James stormed out of the restaurant.

Because Hancock and Sid James saw so much of each other, they agreed that family holidays should be taken separately: a social bargain which lasted less than a single summer.

One bright sunny morning, Sid and Valerie James were lying on the beach at Juan-les-Pins in the south of France when they noticed two people waving frantically and walking towards them. The man, who was accompanied by a beautiful woman in a bikini, was wearing a large straw hat and ludicrously long shorts. 'Lie still and pretend we're asleep,' whispered James out of the corner of his mouth.

The pair heard someone pad to a halt in front of them. 'You're pretending to be asleep aren't you,' announced Hancock.

When the couples did agree to holiday together, Hancock – generally unshaven, in a loud Hawaiian shirt, blue trousers and dark glasses – found it impossible to relax. 'It made me so mad,' complained James. 'He always wanted to get on with his great career.' Lying side by side on a crowded Riviera beach, and turning a deep shade of lobster red, Hancock would start to fidget. James knew what was coming and closed his eyes even tighter. After half-an-hour of squirming, Hancock would finally stand up and glare down through his huge sunglasses at the still peaceful figure of his companion.

'Come on,' he'd announce. 'We're going home.'

Hancock's attempts to holiday with the Milligans proved equally disastrous. He had persuaded Spike Milligan and his first wife to join them for a holiday in Antibes. On the first night they went out for dinner and Hancock, who had obviously recovered from his childhood encounter with French seafood, recommended the fish. When it arrived the fish was complete and its eyes were white and staring.

Mrs Milligan shuddered and announced: 'Oh, I couldn't eat that.'

'That's that, then,' announced a disgruntled Hancock. 'Garçon! Some beans on toast and four cups of tea.'

Weeks after the end of a series and miles from home, Hancock would go to elaborate lengths to produce a comic effect. Working with Patrick Cargill, he discovered they had both booked a holiday in the south of France within days of each other. Hancock agreed to meet for a drink in a particularly smart bar. When Cargill arrived – four months after the appointment was made – he discovered Cicely waiting for him. 'Tony will be along in a minute,' she said offering him a drink. When a ruffle of disapproval spread through the bar, Cargill turned to be confronted by Hancock, sockless in sandals and wearing grey flannel trousers rolled up to the knee, an open white shirt and a knotted handkerchief on his head.

On yet another occasion, Hancock invited Ray Galton and Alan Simpson, Beryl Vertue – his secretary at Associated London Scripts – and his own mother to join them on a holiday in Antibes. 'I remember one evening we had a super French dinner at a very ordinary place,' said Vertue. 'It was very casual and Tony was very relaxed there. It was a second home to him. We had a lot of wine and then we played poker for matchsticks. The matchsticks were worth a fortune and the card game went on for hours. It was one of those rare occasions I remember being hysterical with laughter, he was so funny. Ray was doing particularly well and had a lot of matches. Tony didn't have any. He would look at Ray and in a very posh voice say, "Mr Galton, I wonder if you could see your way clear to financing a little project." It was a happy time.'

Vertue had never before met the 69-year-old Lily Walker and found her a 'quite extraordinary woman'. Each morning, Lily would strut across the Mediterranean beach to where the party was encamped. 'She was something of a little actress, full of funny anecdotes and with a kind of feigned vagueness about how to tackle any particular problem,' added Vertue.

Those working with Hancock, particularly on his television programmes, began to sense a growing unease; almost an irritation. Plots and script lines which he would once have laughed over were now, suddenly and aggressively, objected to. 'Anyone close to Tony knew he was becoming bored. Dissatisfied. He wanted a change,' recalled his television producer Duncan Wood.

Within the BBC a different kind of doubt was being expressed. One fear was that the frustration being felt by its prime comedy star would prompt a defection to Independent Television. Others feared the continued pressure of both TV and radio *Half Hours* was causing Hancock to 'burn out', a phenomenon already experienced by Duncan Wood at the end of 1957. More unjustly, Galton and Simpson's capacity as writers was also under scrutiny.

Stanley 'Scruffy' Dale, as Hancock's agent and Galton and Simpson's partner at Associated London Scripts, was called to a meeting at Broadcasting House. Its purpose was 'to explore how much radio and television Hancock and the writers could undertake in any one year'. Summarising the discussion, Tom Sloan, BBC television's assistant head of light entertainment, noted:

It was agreed that Hancock should be pressed to make up his mind once and for all as far as radio is concerned, and that he and the writers should be invited to attend a second meeting as soon as possible to discuss the amount and type of output they wish to undertake for the BBC. In principle, if Hancock accepts a series of 13 radio programmes to be done in the April/July period this year, then I have some reservations about the writers being able to maintain 20 television scripts in the balance of the year without severe dilution. Dale also raised certain points about the time and placing of any repeats on television – in principle he would like the Autumn series to be repeated within seven days as we did with the first series of 'Whack-o!' – but I really think we must wait for Hancock's decision regarding radio before taking this matter any further.

Dale also convinced Sloan that Hancock's loyalties lay firmly with the BBC, but within the corporation the niggles rumbled on. Seven weeks later, the previously untouchable comedy triumvirate of Tony Hancock and Galton and Simpson was once again under attack, this time from Cecil McGivern, the deputy director of television broadcasting.

On Wednesday, 1 April – six years almost to the month since Dennis Main Wilson had submitted his memo for *Hancock's Half Hour* – McGivern invited the controller of programmes and head of light entertainment to discuss the future of the corporation's flagship comedy. Neither Hancock nor his writers were invited.

In an aide-memoire after the meeting McGivern recorded:

Following our discussion this morning on the Hancock and Galton and Simpson contracts, I would like to restate the main points I made at the meeting.

1. This is now a very expensive contract and a very expensive programme. If knowledge of this price got abroad, it could considerably affect the prices we are at present paying for American telefilms.

2. For the amount we are now paying, we must extract the maximum, in content, in placing and in size of audience figures.

3. In my opinion, the production (as opposed to the content) is

far too slow. I know the producer Duncan Wood would retort with the inevitable slowness of television as opposed to film, the changing of clothes and set, the necessity to hang on to the captions, bridging shots and all the rest of it. Nevertheless, despite that, this production must be quickened up and the writers should be told this. Live television need not be so far behind the speed of *Bilko*.

4. As regards placing, our Sunday evenings need a considerable strengthening in popular appeal in the early part of the evening. Two comedy shows running would be a useful advance and one of them could be Hancock.

McGivern could so far not see the possibility – and advantages – of using filmed sequences to speed up the autumn *Half Hour* series.

Hancock, aware of the meeting, but unaware of McGivern's comment, mounted his own defence in a newspaper feature. It is, perhaps, one of the first newspaper interviews to advocate and explain the benefits of 'pre-filmed' comedy shows:

> When a comedian takes on a television series booked for a thirteen week run, he comes right up against the real problem of TV comedy work – to keep the fun moving. I don't mean by this that the screen has got to be kept as full of action as a race track. I mean keeping things moving over a number of fields of comedy invention.
>
> Television drives us comedians to seek pastures new. We each have our special style of comedy. On the variety stage it can be put over successfully with a few gags, one or two sketches and routines, and these can remain almost the same from performance to performance. On a weekly show inside viewers' homes it is a very different matter. Repeat anything and they will tell you that you are slipping – and rightly so. Yet your particular style must remain the same, or they won't know you as they have come to like knowing you.

So your style must be exploited in as many different forms of comedy situation as you can find in thirteen weeks.

If you have some success one week, the fun you caused will be remembered and talked about. They will look forward to your next show and expect you to amuse them as much. But if you play it more or less the same way, the fact is they won't think you as funny as the last time. To some degree you have got to develop the fun. This can be done by concocting situations in widely different places, and even different ages historically. But I think there's a sharp limit to what can be done in this way. I believe that somewhere along the line of thirteen weeks I have to make a quite considerable change.

When I do this, I risk putting some viewers off, simply because the new set-up is so different. But because it is so fresh, I think it will register some degree of original fun. That will count in the end; for the next week, I can extend that new approach in a different situation. All the time, one is really winning the viewing audience over and over again in order to hold them. I think the viewer, whether he knows it or not, wants to be kept guessing all the time so that he is always discovering new facets of the comic's style.

This calls for team work in the preparation of television programmes. It is little use the comedian thinking he is developing the exploitation of his style, if his scriptwriters, supporting cast and producer cannot see what he is after: the way forward must be found together. In this situation frankness is essential.

My scriptwriters tell me if I am not playing their stuff as they intended it to be played; and I tell them if I think their stuff cannot be played the way I want to take the programme. And the producer makes no bones about telling both sides what he wants. Out of this grinding democratic mill there issues in the end something which is, I hope, better than 'corn'.

This pressing need for development during a series means that one is always anxious about rehearsing adequately to achieve the right effects. We normally rehearse first for nearly a week then take a weekend right away from the job to forget it, and hope to come back to the final rehearsals fresh. Even so, performing a live TV show, just once, puts all the preparation to risk. If the programme does not click on the night, though it may have been effective at rehearsal, well – the opportunity to go back and make it click has gone forever.

For this reason I favour the pre-filming of comedy shows. Immediately one says this one raises that criticism of television using 'canned' shows, as though these are somehow second-hand. Given that filmed vision and film-recorded sound are technically as good as live vision and sound, I think only one element is lost in a pre-filmed show. This is the sense the viewer feels that the thing is actually happening, there and then at that moment.

I don't think that we have really found out if this is so valuable an element as to outweigh the advantages of pre-filming. The main advantage to the comedy show is that the players are not dependent on the single moment of perform-ance on the night. If a strived-for effect does not come off properly in filming, you can re-shoot. You can also revise by editing – taking bits out and putting second thoughts in.

The BBC's deputy director of television was ultimately overtaken by technical and scheduling pressures and the corporation consented to Hancock and Wood's argument that all future *Half Hours* should be pre-recorded. Nor was the programme moved to Sunday night to bolster ratings; the fifth series would begin with *The Economy Drive* on Friday 25 September.

For the next ten weeks Duncan Wood presided over the *Half Hour* rehearsals at the Sulgrave Road Boys Club. It was here, among the ping-pong and snooker tables and with the air smelling of sawdust and damp coconut matting, that Hancock subconsciously worked some of his most precious magic. When the club was occupied the read-throughs were moved to the Student Movement House in Gower Street, just off the Euston Road.

Late in September Patricia Hayes was invited to make her second *Half Hour* appearance. Hayes started her broadcasting career in 1922 and, for five and a half years, had worked with Ted Ray on *Ray's a Laugh*. A versatile character actress, she had first worked with Hancock on radio. A little over a year earlier, producer Tom Ronald had invited Hayes to join the cast for a single live *Half Hour*. Hancock was so impressed he insisted she return for another four.

Hancock made an equally long-lasting impression on the 'awe-struck' actress. 'I used to look at him and think "aren't you lucky?" He had everything. He was a very attractive person, he was brilliantly gifted, he had two of the best writers of comedy, and he had Sid James working with him so selflessly.' To Hayes the winning formula was as obvious as it was elusive to Hancock. 'He was unfailingly hilarious,' adds Hayes, 'and yet he seemed to have no faith in himself.'

Duncan Wood took the actress to one side in the Gower Street rehearsal room, and in a voice of mock gravity he announced: 'A great honour is going to be bestowed upon you Miss Hayes, you are going to play Mrs Cravatte.' To regular *Half Hour* viewers Mrs Cravatte was a spectral figure, often referred to but never seen. 'Nobody has ever set eyes on her before so you will create this person.'

The character hovered, through numerous episodes, somewhere between Galton and Simpson's imagination and Hancock's on-screen pomposity. The writers decided it was time to give form to this rude and disrespectful 2s 6d-an-hour charwoman who cleaned Hancock's Railway Cuttings abode and hurled his breakfast at him with equal distaste. The 'outrageous, discontented and moody' Mrs Cravatte makes her first physical appearance in *The Two Murderers*, the second programme of the fifth television series.

'The thing we always found difficult to reconcile with Pat,' ponders Ray Galton, 'was that she was always so well spoken when she was off screen and difficult to imagine as this terrible Cockney cleaner.' Hancock and Hayes did share one amazing quality, adds Galton, they were both instant and brilliant sight readers. 'When Pat and Hancock used to rehearse together at the first read-through it was as if they already knew the script by heart. Immaculate. Every inflection would be perfect, all the timing would be right.'

A little time later, and with Hayes making her third appearance as Mrs Cravatte, the actress thought it was about time for a pay rise. Her agent's request was turned down and the irascible cleaner was dropped for eight shows. When Hayes was invited back, Hancock approached her and announced: 'The trouble with you is that you are too expensive.'

'Well, Tony,' said Hayes, 'I think I am worth about half of what you get.'

'No, you're not,' said Hancock. 'When you're as well known as I am, you'll be worth about half what I get.'

'No,' Hayes snapped back. 'When I'm as well known as you are, I'll be worth the same as you are.' Hancock turned away in silence.

For a less experienced and assured actress Hancock's reputation and introspection could be daunting. Annabelle Lee was given the part of a 'girl' in five *Half Hour* episodes. On several occasions she found herself sharing a taxi with Hancock as they were ferried between the rehearsals and the television studio. Each journey, she remembers, was 'sheer murder'. 'I was in total awe of Tony,' she explains. 'He was one of my heroes. I just couldn't think of a thing to say to him.' Hancock made no attempt to open the conversation. Most journeys were completed in total silence.

It was at the Sulgrave Road Boys Club that some of the gnawing doubts over Hancock's comic ability began to nibble away at his confidence. More and more, he used the unhurried and informal atmosphere of the rehearsals as a delaying tactic; something to cloud the spectre of his own lack of conviction. 'We would arrive around 10.30 and have a cup of coffee and a game of snooker,' Sid James recalled. 'After a brief run-through we would play snooker or table tennis for a couple of hours and then go to lunch.' Two hours later the cast and crew would reassemble. 'We would have another game of table tennis and do another couple of hours' rehearsal. By this time it would be about six o'clock and the boys would start to gather for the opening of the club.' As James and the rest of the cast prepared to leave, Hancock would announce: 'Can we go over this line once more? I don't think we have got it right yet.'

Duncan Wood never forgot the 'hard work and torture' of working with Hancock. 'He never knew when he was at his peak,' recalled the producer. 'He always thought there was one step more to be taken and this is where you had to step in as a director, and say, "No, that is as far as we can go with this. There isn't anything more to be got out of this page of script."'

The alcohol was taking its toll on both Hancock and Cicely although, in the late 1950s, they still appeared to be in control. It affected them in different ways. In the relaxed atmosphere of a nightclub or restaurant Cicely seemed to be enjoying herself and genuinely pleased to meet people, but after just a few drinks Hancock withdrew – not from the world, which, through the haze of gin or vodka, spun affectionately around him, but from reality. In the small hours he wanted to talk of philosophy and injustice; the booze had made him a social bore.

Val James recalls: 'Tony seemed always to be searching for something. And yet, in some strange way, I felt he didn't know what it was he was searching for. Frankly, I was always a little scared of him. He was such an introvert. He never seemed to have much conversation. Try as we did over the years, it was impossible to get close to Hancock.' It did not, however, stop the quartet having fun. One episode could have been scripted by Galton and Simpson. Hancock and Sid James had been invited to the London première of a cowboy film. The invitation stipulated that guests would not be admitted unless wearing western costume. For days Hancock and James ribbed each other about who would be the best-dressed cowboy. All four swaggered into the foyer of the Leicester Square cinema with their spurs clinking and looking as though they had tethered their horses to the front steps, only to be greeted by a wall of soberly dressed cinemagoers. Hancock had got the date wrong – the fancy dress was next week.

Hancock had decided his sixth radio series would be his last. The medium which had made him a household name had been superseded – at least in Hancock's vision of success – by television. Because both Sid James and Kenneth Williams were committed to filming *Carry On Constable* from early November, and the series would start at the end of September, it was decided all but one episode should be recorded during a three-week period the previous June, frequently two in one day.

For the first time Galton and Simpson found themselves creating two scripts a week, and Hancock – who later claimed he only undertook the series because the writers 'needed the money' – expressed doubts about the standard of the finished programmes. In reality the fourteen-week radio series contained some of Galton and Simpson's funniest and most sardonic scripts.

On Monday, 8 June, Kenneth Williams telephoned his agent. He wanted out of *Hancock's Half Hour*. 'There is no point in my working in this set-up any more,' he confided to his diary after the first day's recording. Of the two *Half Hours* recorded that day – *The Smugglers* and *The Childhood Sweetheart* – Williams complained he was 'given an innocuous part in one, and a "spot" in the other . . . neither of them worth anything artistically'. He also sniped at the cosy *Half Hour* cadre. 'The atmosphere of Kerr, Sid James, etc, is utterly stultifying for me – there is simply no point of contact – their world is totally alien to mine, and they and me are better apart.' It would be the last time Williams, already out of the television shows, would appear in a radio *Half Hour*.

His final verdict on the programmes came eight years later, when Williams recorded:

They now seem so slow and pretentious. Sid James and Bill Kerr and Hattie Jacques were just awful. Reading lines like they had scripts in their hands. Recitative. Hancock doing his pompous bit in too slow a tempo. I think this was the great defect with Hancock: the absence of real professional expertise and technical cleverness. The sort of rough ability he did have was sufficient for a duo of the Morecambe and Wise type of act, but not for the more advanced kind of comedy which he really admired (Benny, Tati etc.). It's really the difference between a comic and a comedian. Hancock never properly decided on either.

Rehearsals were pruned to an absolute minimum. For Hancock and the two-man *Half Hour* company of Sid James and Bill Kerr, the recordings at the Playhouse Theatre in Northumberland Avenue, near Charing Cross, were treated almost as a 'live' performance. For Fraser Kerr, who, with Warren Mitchell and Fenella Fielding, supplemented the regular cast for *The Poetry Society* episode, it was an enlightening experience.

All three were told to report to the Playhouse by 6.30pm. They had not been told which parts they would be playing, nor issued with copies of the script, and the recording, in front of the studio audience, was scheduled for 8.00pm – ninety minutes away. Tom Ronald, the producer, arrived to hand out the scripts and assign the roles. It was, by now, almost a quarter-to-seven. Kerr – no relation to Bill Kerr – was growing increasingly concerned. The first read-through was accomplished in record time and with 'little feeling for the script'. The final lines were drowned by Sid James leaping up to announce: 'Come on lads, we're wasting drinking time.' The cast and producer then crossed the road to the Sherlock Holmes pub. After a brief chat Ronald returned to check on the sound effects, and a few minutes later the call boy popped his head round the pub door: 'Are you ready gentlemen? The mics are up.'

A second rehearsal followed, again, to Kerr's dismay, 'without any feeling', and James and Hancock then led a second charge across Northumberland Avenue. This time the drinks were already lined up on the bar. It was 7.45pm. 'With seven or eight minutes to go we slipped backstage through a secret door,' adds Kerr.

Hancock endured – even enjoyed – slip-ups during the show; it was all part of the fun and, in its way, produced a kind of spontaneous comedy. Breaching the show's warm-up etiquette inevitably unsettled Hancock and provided him with an excuse for an imagined lapse in performance. Fraser Kerr explains: 'I came on stage with Fenella, followed by Warren Mitchell, who did the unthinkable thing of introducing Tony to the studio audience. Tony should have been introduced last by Sid James. Tony was now in the ignoble position of having to introduce Sid and Bill Kerr – he was not amused.'

Working with Hancock, however, provided its own brand of kudos, particularly among other actors and BBC staff. *The Poetry Society* was not broadcast until six months later. In it Fraser Kerr plays 'Rupert', a member of an élite and pompous poetry circle which meets at Hancock's house. Rupert's offering is an obscure and pretentious poem called 'Blank Detail'. The day after the show's December broadcast, Kerr had just finished a live morning story and made his way down to the BBC canteen for lunch. As he walked in, the entire restaurant rose to its feet and recited:

> Straw in the wind . . .
> Straw in the wind . . .
> Straw in the wind . . .
> Straw in the wind . . .
> Straw in the wind . . .
> Fly . . .
> Fly . . .
> Fly . . .*

*

Since the mid-1950s Lily and Robert Walker had managed the Harbour Heights public house and lived at 51 Lansdowne House, an apartment block in nearby Christchurch Road.

---

* Galton and Simpson's scripts also inspired other radio writers. On 10 June, 1960 – six months after the broadcast of Hancock's *Poetry Society* – Eric Merriman wrote his own 'poetry society' for *Beyond Our Ken*, in which Kenneth Horne recites a spur-of-the-moment verse and is elected the group's new leader.

Robert Walker was still a handsome man. At fifty-five years old he had kept his youthful good looks and his footballer's energy. Through twenty-three years of marriage, Lily Walker had endured his constant womanising and affairs, and their relationship had always been a stormy one. In recent months, however, Walker had, uncharacteristically, become moody and sullen. He refused to argue. At times he appeared distracted and fretful.

Early in 1959, a young man walked into the Harbour Heights and demanded to speak to Robert Walker. The two men spoke quietly at one end of the bar, then, in the next few weeks Walker received several telephone calls. Each month thereafter, the man would call at the pub and receive an envelope of notes. Throughout the summer the amounts had progressively risen, from £25 to £30 to £35, and finally, to £40 a month. The last cash withdrawal from their joint bank account was made on 16 November. Lily Walker had no idea her husband was being blackmailed.

On Tuesday, 17 November, Walker attended a regular brewery sales meeting, and his 69-year-old wife remained at the Harbour Heights. The morning meeting went well. The board was satisfied with the pub's summer sales figures and discussed arrangements for Christmas promotions and deliveries. Just before lunch, Robert Walker walked the mile or so from the brewery offices to the couple's Christchurch Road apartment. He collected some cushions from the living-room and carried them into the flat's small kitchen. Opening the cooker door he arranged the cushions, switched on the gas, and lay down with his head in the oven.

Two days later the inquest into the publican's death was brief and formal. Lily Walker officially identified her husband's body. He had died, it was stated, from 'asphyxia from coal gas poisoning' while the balance of his mind was disturbed. The reason for his temporary insanity was left unexplained. There was no mention of the blackmail, or a new threat to expose him to his employers unless he agreed to another monthly increase in payments.

Hancock, although aware of his step-father's philanderings, was equally ignorant of the extortion. It was not until he arrived in

Bournemouth for the funeral and agreed to sort the family papers and oversee the legal formalities that he discovered the mysterious monthly cash payments. For the first time his mother also admitted that she and her husband had been forced repeatedly to end the tenancy of a succession of pubs and hotels because of his adultery. When they secured the Harbour Heights, Walker had promised it would never happen again.

Ray Galton and Alan Simpson had joined forces with Spike Milligan and Eric Sykes to form Associated London Scripts. Each member agreed to contribute his entire earnings and draw ten per cent of the group takings as salary. The four had planned to name their co-operative Associated British Scripts, but were warned by Companies House that they were not big enough. Hancock refused to join. He claimed the benefits, by the group's very name, would go primarily to the writers. The quartet hired rooms five floors above a Shepherd's Bush greengrocer's shop – to get there friends and producers had to push their way through boxes of rotten fruit and vegetables – and quickly discovered they needed a secretary.

Ray Galton approached an old school friend. Like the writer, Beryl Vertue had grown up in Brixton. As a teenager she had also contracted tuberculosis, before training as a typist and secretary. Vertue already had a job near her home and didn't relish the thought of travelling across London; the rush-hour journey would have taken at least an hour-and-a-half. To let her friend down gently, she decided to overprice herself and ask for £10 a week. To her surprise Galton agreed – £10 split four ways meant they were each contributing just £2 10s.

Hancock was not the only one who had second thoughts about joining ALS. Ray Galton remembered: 'Sellers was going to come in originally, but his financial adviser said Peter would only come if we all contributed the same amount of money – whereas we'd planned to work on a ten percentage basis and take our chance. No, said the financial adviser, that means Peter will be parting with more actual money than anybody else, because he's already making more.

'Around about 1955, Peter came into the office and announced, "I need £400 or I'll be thrown out of my flat." He was married to Anne, had children, and hadn't paid the rent. Ray, Spike, Eric and I gave him £100 each in cash. Off he went. Spike said, "You won't see that again – he'll spend it." Three weeks later, Peter Sellers comes into the office again in a new suit, with £400 which he dealt out note by note, like playing cards. He'd just got the job in *The Ladykillers*, was flush, and came to pay us back.'

One comedian who thought differently was Frankie Howerd. He had previously formed his own company – Frankie Howerd Scripts Ltd – which, in turn, paid his manager Stanley 'Scruffy' Dale. Not long after ALS's launch it merged with Frankie Howerd Scripts to form one of the strongest and most powerful co-operative agencies in London.

When his five-year contract with Kavanagh Associates expired, Hancock decided it was, at last, time to transfer to Associated London Scripts. Scruffy Dale, whom he had known since the early fifties, suggested Hancock should form several limited companies as a hedge against taxation, so his television and radio fees were credited to Tony Hancock (Television) Ltd and Tony Hancock (Radio) Ltd.

By the late 1950s, Beryl Vertue had relinquished her secretarial duties to take over as agent: 'Not because I was brilliant, but because I was the only one in the building who wasn't a writer.' It gave her a unique opportunity to witness some of Britain's most ingenious and inventive comedy writers at work. Vertue, who is now a leading television producer, recalled that Eric Sykes would spend most days on the golf course, apparently ignoring script deadlines. 'He'd then suddenly appear and type like a maniac until the script was complete and delivered on time. That's what he'd been doing on the golf course – thinking it all out.

'Spike used to write the first thing that came into his head and then he would rewrite and edit endlessly until it was just as he wanted. Ray and Alan would sit in their office and stare . . . and stare . . . and then when they had it firmly in their minds they would write it – and that was it. Scarcely a word had to be changed.'

Always on hand, Vertue became the first audience for some

outstanding television and radio material: 'Spike would read a script aloud, flinging his arms around and doing all the voices. Eric would act it out, playing the various parts. Ray and Alan would just hand me the script without a word and go home.'

The Football Pools – the last of twenty television *Hancock's Half Hour* episodes broadcast during 1959 – was transmitted on 27 November. Three days later Kenneth Adam, controller of programmes for BBC television, wrote to Hancock:

> Despite your own ill-health and your domestic tragedy, in both of which I greatly sympathise, you have just triumphantly concluded another series. We all think that this was without any doubt the finest you have yet done, and though we know the standard you are setting is very high indeed, we are confident that the next one will be even better. I hope you will now have a good rest yourself and a quieter time around you. Thank you for all the personal enjoyment I have had on Fridays this autumn.

The BBC was already putting together yet another financial package to entice its top-rated comedian to sign a long-term contract. The proposal would tie Hancock to BBC Television for one year from September, 1960. During that period the corporation wanted to make another twenty *Half Hours*, of which ten would be guaranteed a repeat screening sometime in the future. Hancock's fee for each programme would remain the same, but the corporation had cleverly side-stepped restrictions on its production budget and, for the first time in its history, offered payment on a fixed number of repeats. In return Hancock would receive £25,000.

The proposal was linked to a parallel contract offered to Galton and Simpson. During 1959 alone, the pair had produced no less than thirty-four radio and television scripts. If their star agreed to the new deal, the writers would receive £600 for each script and £300 for each of the ten repeats. Again the only improvement was the guaranteed repeat screenings.

Hancock did not even consider the new contract. His endurance of East Cheam and everyone associated with it was running down and running out. 'I've done everything in that bloody room except be indecent in it,' he confessed to Freddie Ross. 'I've stood all over it. I've touched all parts of it. I can tell you where every knot in the wood is. Where I burped. It's like a bloody death cell with an execution once a week.' Instead, he called a meeting at home at MacConkeys. Among those present were Ray Galton and Alan Simpson and his television producer, Duncan Wood. Sid James was not invited.

Everyone knew what was coming. Hancock told them he was bored and frustrated with the pompous character in the Homburg hat, and the confined world he inhabited at 23 Railway Cuttings; the set was too dowdy and parochial; Sid's cockney accent had become irritating – 'I am tired of being common, it's about time I got a bit of class.' At the end of one heavy silence he announced the end of *Hancock's Half Hour*, and then, like a quick-tempered schoolboy realising he had gone too far, he quickly backed down. He would do one more television series, but only if he was allowed to move out of East Cheam – and away from Sid James.

'We went along with him,' the scriptwriters recall, 'because we realised that Tony's success – or the show's success – could be maintained without Sid. He was a marvellous foil, but Sid James could work separately.'

Duncan Wood believed Hancock also hoped his writers shared his desire to expand. 'He sincerely thought Ray and Alan would like a new dimension in which to write,' explained the producer. At the time, Galton and Simpson claimed they could have gone on writing for Hancock and James indefinitely, but, with hindsight, both admit they benefited from the enforced change in direction.

Like his 1955 disappearance, it is possible Hancock's petulant decision was rooted in an incident ten years earlier. Throughout his West End career Sid Field, Hancock's comic hero, had worked with Jerry Desmonde. Soon after the pair opened in the 1949 production of *Harvey*, Field dropped out through ill-health. During his absence, a newspaper remarked that he and Desmonde, who later became Norman Wisdom's film straight man, had effectively become a double act – 'would Sid Field be as great without Jerry Desmonde?' Field refused to return to the Prince of Wales show until Desmonde had been sacked.

A few days after the MacConkeys meeting, Duncan Wood telephoned Sid James to arrange a meeting. James left his west London home in high spirits. When he returned he was close to tears and more upset than Valerie James had ever seen him. 'Tony doesn't want me in the show any more,' he finally explained. 'He wants to go alone.'

Hancock's cowardice once again stopped him short of confronting his own actions. This 'out-of-the-blue betrayal', as James once described it to a close friend, left James shattered. 'What hurt most,' Val adds, 'was that it was the BBC who broke the news and not Tony himself.'

Hancock, it seemed, had discussed his decision with almost everyone but his co-star. Years later Liz Fraser admitted: 'Sid didn't know about this, but Tony told me he was worried that "Hancock and James" were becoming a fixed double act in the eyes of the public. Tony never had the courage to talk it over with Sid.' The way in which Sid James was eventually given the news left the actor 'devastated', claims Fraser. 'There had never been any deterioration in the relationship between Sid and Tony. Suddenly it just stopped. Sid was distraught, he just couldn't believe it.'

1960

EARLY IN JANUARY Hancock arrived at a television rehearsal, obviously excited. 'You just won't believe it,' he kept repeating, 'you just won't believe it.' At last he confided he had been invited to take part in one of the BBC's notorious *Face to Face* interviews.

Launched the year before – and conducted by *Panorama* journalist

John Freeman – *Face to Face* was the first television programme to attempt to peel away the mask of public figures and reveal their true character. Freeman, a junior minister in the first post-war Labour Government, was a gentle yet remorseless interrogator. He would, the following year, become editor of the *New Statesman*, and later British Ambassador to Washington from 1969 to 1970. *Face to Face*, however, was universally disliked by the critics who dubbed it 'torture by television'. *The Times* said the programme's only attraction 'was seeing how the next man stood up to the rack'.

Part of the programme's 'terror' came from its sparse setting and clinical execution. Freeman sat within a few feet of his guest; only the back of his head was visible. The lighting was harsh and unflattering and there were no comforting pot-plants or other domestic props. The cameras closed in on the subject as fearlessly as Freeman, who said: 'The subject had the whole screen, the whole of the time. The camera was used almost as a secondary interrogator, capturing every flicker of an eyelid, every bead of sweat.'

Sid James, like the rest of the cast working on the final *Half Hour* series, had reservations. 'That's marvellous,' he told Hancock. 'But you won't do it?'

'I know I won't do it,' Hancock replied. 'But it's bloody marvellous he's asked me. You know he's done Prime Ministers. Fancy asking me.'

During the day's rehearsal, Hancock changed his mind, and in an afternoon tea break he took James aside: 'What happens if he asks me about religion? You know how I feel about religion.'

'Well I wouldn't say you were an atheist because that might lose you a lot of customers,' said James.

'Well that's unlucky,' Hancock snapped back. 'I am an atheist and that's the way it is. I've got to tell him because, after all, it's *Face to Face* isn't it and I've got to tell the truth.'

James was shocked by Hancock's awestruck naïvety. 'For God's sake don't answer everything truthfully, you'd be right in it.'

The programme was recorded on 28 January, 1960. In the days before the interview, Hancock began compiling a list of questions he wanted to be asked. 'You know,' he told Sid a day or so later, 'he didn't ask me one bloody question of the ones I'd put down.'

Here, for the first time, is a complete BBC transcript of the *Face to Face* interview:

Freeman: Tony Hancock, the whole of Britain knows you in your professional comic mask, and tonight we want to try and find out what lies behind the mask. Now, are you in the mood to come clean?

Hancock: Yes, indeed.

Freeman: You know you're on your own, you're without your scriptwriters, and you'll tell us the truth?

Hancock: I'll try to, yes.

Hancock: Do you like talking about yourself or not?

Hancock: Yes, up to a point, particularly in relation to what I do, in relation to comedy, yes.

Freeman: All right then, I'll ask you first of all – Why are you a comic?

Hancock: Well, I think I always certainly wanted to be from the first time I can remember, and perhaps looking like this it was perhaps the only thing I could do! So I turned this sort of deficiency into a workable thing, if you understand what I mean.

Freeman: Yes, but let's go a bit deeper than that. Do you think the world is a comic place or is it a tragic place?

Hancock: Well, I think it consists of two things, both

funny and sad, which seem to me to be the two basic ingredients of good comedy.

Freeman: Basic ingredients. What is being funny? Is it mixing them together? How do you tell what is funny?

Hancock: Well, I think they exist together anyway, by the way we live. When we attempt to be affected or pompous or – what can I say? – we are sort of all unsure of ourselves and what we live in. We try to live in a certain way, we try to – we are, I suppose to a certain extent, all affected and that is both funny and sad, I think.

Freeman: So that being funny is showing how people are affected? Is that what you're trying to say?

Hancock: I think so. I think you express your own pomposity and other people's and get probably to the real truth of the way you live.

Freeman: And so that being funny is part of the business of finding out the truth about life?

Hancock: Entirely. Yes. You can't think of it in any other way.

Freeman: Now, your own comedy character, the one we know in *Hancock's Half Hour* – swagger, bluster, and then not being very effectual in the end – is that right?

Hancock: I don't think you can sort of really theorise entirely about these things. As I say, this is all sort of part of what you are and part of what everybody else is. It's a comment on yourself and a comment on everybody else, I think.

Freeman: Well, how much is it a comment on yourself?

Hancock: Oh, to a great extent, to a great extent. I mean, shall we say the character that I – it isn't the characters I play that I put on and off like a coat. It is greatly a part of me and part of everybody else that I see.

Freeman: Are you trying to say it's something which is serious? Is there a message or are you simply trying to make people laugh?

Hancock: Not exactly a message, I think, if you go to that extent I think perhaps you lose the intuitive thing, which is bad. No, I think it's just a true observation of the way things are as far as you can see it yourself.

Freeman: Looking at yourself as a comic – after all, in the television and film era you've seen yourself as a comic very often, which many of the great comics didn't. What is there about you, you think, that makes people laugh?

Hancock: Well, it's difficult to say. I don't think I can be very objective about that. I think I know where my mistakes are as I make them. I don't think I gain anything by seeing myself.

Freeman: Is it facial expression? Is it good scriptwriters? Is it a sense of timing? Is it a knowledge of what constitutes comedy? You must have some idea?

Hancock: It's a knowledge of what constitutes living in general, I think. As I say, you take the weaknesses of your own character and of other people's characters and you exploit them. You show yourself and you show them up.

Freeman: Now it's often been said about you – I don't know whether you think this is true or not – that one thing that you do in your comedy is to ridicule the things that you dislike in life. Is that true?

Hancock: Yes. That also applies to the things you dislike in yourself.

Freeman: All right. Well now, what are they?

Hancock: Oh I think a certain affectation. I mean I know – for instance I often find in a script things that I've said in all seriousness which they later write up in detail and absolutely which later turn out to be funny. If I've been angry or something like that. I look at this and I think 'yes, that's very funny, unfortunately.' It's something that I've said at the time and been rather pompous about, and they've noticed this and written it down, and there it is.

Freeman: This is an example of debunking yourself. Now how much do you try and debunk other people as well?

Hancock: Oh well, you do that shall we say generously. Yes, you debunk pomposity and affectation.

Freeman: What are the things – can you tell me that? There are particular things in the world that you know you dislike – personal characteristics first of all. Is it pomposity that you're after?

Hancock: No, you don't dislike them. You accept them. I mean, you're tolerant towards them . . .

Freeman: But these are what you'd like to pillory if you could?

Hancock: Yes. As I say, by fitting yourself in everything that you see.

Freeman: Pomposity is the first one. Anything else? Bad temper, greed?

Hancock: All those things, yes.

Freeman: And in the world apart from people, in the world outside, what would you most like to reform about the world if you had the chance?

Hancock: I'm not capable of doing that.

Freeman: Well, don't you have dreams about it?

Hancock: No, no, no, no, no. You just observe and practise within the limitations of your own talent what you see around you.

Freeman: You've never dreamed of playing Hamlet?

Hancock: No, no, no, no, no. I'd hardly ... for me ...

Freeman: You must have – Oh, and indeed I believe you have in fact got quite a lot of personal opinions all the same. Let's just take some of them. Have you got any religious views?

Hancock: No, I have no religion now.

Freeman: That means that you're not interested or that you're not religious?

Hancock: I'm deeply interested and shall we say I'm trying to find a faith, but I've had to throw away the initial faith that I was brought up in, and therefore am now starting again from scratch.

Freeman: Well now, what were you brought up in?

Hancock: The Church of England.

Freeman: I see. And you've thrown that away. Does that mean you don't believe in God any longer or might you adopt some other Christian religion?

Hancock: I'm completely, as I say, this has been eliminated now. This I no longer believe in, so therefore I have to have an open mind and look for something else.

Freeman: Can you recall any moment in your life when this particular God failed you?

Hancock: I think not, no – it is a thing I think that you – I began to see first when I was about fifteen or sixteen. I think I was fairly deeply Christian before that and it just failed. It was no longer believable.

Freeman: Do you find yourself answerable in your moral judgment to anybody except yourself?

Hancock: No, I think actually it's as strong – you are more moral because it is true to say of morality, surely, that it is without a reward, or should be without a reward. It must be purely and simply moral and for no reason.

Freeman: Yes, but you must have some standard of judgment. Do you judge by anything except your own built-in conscience?

Hancock: No. Your own experience, I suppose.

Freeman: What about politics? Any political beliefs?

Hancock: Then again, unformed I would say at the
moment. No, not really. Not to a sort of a –
any sort of particular affiliation.

Freeman: Are you interested in the sort of lives that
ordinary people have? Do you try and ...

Hancock: Indeed, I think any actor – that is the raw
material – that is where you draw from. That's
the whole of it.

Freeman: Do you find that as great successes come to
you you've become separated from ordinary
people?

Hancock: No, no, no. Even more – I'm completely in
love with my own profession, if you can call it
that, and the people are as I say, the people
that you observe, they – you find more
tolerance towards them and they are what you
get your – inspiration is too big a word, but
what you get your – as I say, your work from.

Freeman: Most actors you know I think are in love with
their own profession, but you now have
reached a level – it's said of you and I suppose
it's true – that you earn something like thirty-
five thousand a year –

Hancock: I don't!

Freeman: Well, you can deny that if you like, but I bet
you earn not far short of that.

Hancock: Well, I don't actually, because I don't work
very much. I work for a short time, very hard,
and then I don't work at all, because I need to
think, and I'm also trying to educate myself, so
I spend – I don't make a lot of money, not all

that much money, because I take a long time off to think and prepare for what I want to do in the future, you see.

Freeman: Well, I don't want to stay on this too long, but while we are on it, do you deny the story which has often been published, and which I don't think you've denied before, that you're getting about thirty thousand a year from the BBC?

Hancock: Yes, I deny it. (LAUGHTER) Just about.

Freeman: Just about. Yes, all right. Well, we'll leave it at that. Now, tell me then a bit – you say that you still have contacts with ordinary people and I want to ask you a bit how you do live. Do you live, for instance – town or country?

Hancock: In the country. I have a house in the country.

Freeman: And some kind of flat in London or not?

Hancock: I usually take a flat for the time that the series is on, because of travel and that sort of thing, and when the pressure is on I find that I need to.

Freeman: But your normal home is in England, in the country?

Hancock: Yes.

Freeman: Now, you do go abroad a lot, don't you?

Hancock: Yes. Well, I find that shall we say that the only use I have for money really is to travel and to have the luxury of independence to choose what work I do and to read and to learn, and therefore to put back into my own profession a

little more, shall we say. I mean the two things
go together. You must – the more you expand
as an individual, the more you see, the more
you read, the more you learn, the more you
have to offer.

Freeman: Well, let's talk for a moment about travel.
What sort of travel? Do you travel rough, in
unexplored countries?

Hancock: Oh no, not so much that. I love France. I find
it very relaxing and I relax there better than
anywhere, I think . . . Well, partly because of
the licensing laws, I think, but halfway really,
you can, shall we say, you go to Paris – people
say you go to Paris – why do you go to Paris
to rest? But I do rest there, because you can go
to sleep six hours in the afternoon, you can get
up and go out all night if you want to.

Freeman: And of course you're not known?

Hancock: No, not at all.

Freeman: Have you ever in fact performed in Paris?

Hancock: Never, no.

Freeman: Would you like to?

Hancock: Very much.

Freeman: How good is your French?

Hancock: Pretty bad.

Freeman: Could you do a show in French?

Hancock: No, not really. One could a sort of a – you
know – the lido things, something like that

where you talk half in French, little bits and pieces and – but not truly, no. But I hope to learn French enough to be able to do that.

Freeman: Well, let's go on about your life. What sort of relaxation and hobbies – now, for instance, you spoke a moment ago about reading. Do you read a lot?

Hancock: Yes, I do now.

Freeman: What sort of stuff?

Hancock: I read history, philosophy, and all the things that come off it, naturally.

Freeman: Now, I wonder, is this a recognition that perhaps earlier in your life you didn't do all this reading? Are you trying to catch up?

Hancock: Oh yes, indeed. It seems as if, for the first thirty years, my eyes were closed and then I became interested and found a real thirst for knowledge, and now I fortunately have the opportunity to put right this lack of education.

Freeman: Can you give me – is there any memory in your mind of a turning point about this? Do you remember something which happened, which suddenly opened your eyes? Or a person?

Hancock: I think, as a very simple example, I suppose, I read the Wells *Outline of History* – simple, maybe, but it put the thing into perspective, it put you into an entirely different position, if you understand? Viewing your own sort of ego and personality in terms of this vast time, and that really started me reading many other things.

Freeman: And you've gone much more deeply into it since then. Is Wells still a hero?

Hancock: Oh, indeed! I think it was a tremendous attempt to cover such an enormous thing in one volume which ... doing very, very well.

Freeman: Do you read the psychologists at all?

Hancock: Yes, I do, but only sort of outlines at the moment because I need to read introductions. I can't – start like that.

Freeman: But this is a real notion in your life, that you'd like to read more and you'd like to go further into these things?

Hancock: Oh, I must. As I say, I'm entirely interested in – comedy, this is so much part of it, and it is the sort of raw material. It began it. It is absolutely necessary.

Freeman: Well now, turning to the rather lighter side of reading, just tell me by name, what daily newspapers do you read?

Hancock: Practically all, I'd say. I think that's absolutely necessary. I also think it's necessary to watch nearly all television, for instance.

Freeman: Good lord.

Hancock: Yes, I know, it's hard to bear, isn't it? No, I think – otherwise, shall we say, if you want to see something that needs burlesquing or something you want to have a go at maybe, then you have to see it all.

Freeman: Do you read the criticisms about yourself?

Hancock: Reluctantly, yes.

Freeman: Do they hurt?

Hancock: Yes, they do actually. I try to eliminate that but it's not possible.

Freeman: Do you find that the newspaper critics are to be taken seriously? Do you really think about the points they make?

Hancock: Well, as a matter of fact, I think you think about the point anybody makes. I mean, it would be nice to say you were beyond that, maybe, but you never are.

Freeman: You've got an awful lot of money now. We won't argue about how much. What do you spend it on? Motor cars?

Hancock: Yes, up to a point. My wife actually drives. She's the enthusiastic driver. I gave it up some time ago. I wasn't very good.

Freeman: Was that proved to you physically, or ... ?

Hancock: It was physically, yes.

Freeman: In circumstances which brought you to court, or not?

Hancock: No, actually. There was an accident and that was the end. But actually I never had any idea of it really.

Freeman: Do you spend money – I know it's difficult to answer this question, but try – do you spend money extravagantly or not?

Hancock: I suppose so. Sometimes, yes. It depends what
sort of relaxation you need to find, but always
with an end in view.

Freeman: What are your extravagances?

Hancock: Well, I like staying at big hotels in a suite
occasionally for a couple of days. That sort of
thing. Or to travel, to travel in considerable
luxury, maybe. That's about all.

Freeman: Do you have – for instance, you live in the
country. Where abouts in the country?

Hancock: Lingfield.

Freeman: Do you have a lot of friends in that
neighbourhood?

Hancock: Not really. We haven't been there very long,
but we bring friends down to the house. One
of the most interesting things – the best things
– the house is a valuable thing to me because it
means that we can talk down there. I can have
people down there, and I find that the biggest
relaxation I can have is to talk with people that
I like, probably about this business maybe, all
the things that come off it, and we talk and
talk, you know, long into the morning, and it's
a relaxation. Also ideas spring from that.

Freeman: Are these show-biz friends, or friends who've
been with you all your life?

Hancock: Well yes, they are to a certain extent. You can
say they're show-business people but most of
the show-business people I know are not solely
interested in that. They are particularly
interested in – well, there are so many things

that come off it. Perhaps we talk about the show for about ten per cent of the time.

Freeman: Now – very intimately – you say talking far into the night – do you, as a matter of fact, sleep well when you go to bed?

Hancock: No.

Freeman: Do you take sleeping pills?

Hancock: M'm.

Freeman: Why don't you sleep, do you think?

Hancock: Well, I think that you – in these days of the challenge of this particular medium anyway, your mind works high, quick – you are permanently on an edge, and a good one, I think, and therefore it is difficult to relax while a thing is on – while a show is on – but no, generally not particularly well.

Freeman: It's said about you that you worry a lot about your weight – is that true?

Hancock: M'm. Well I don't – no, I've got it more or less sorted out now – well, within reason. If I can – you know – I was about two-and-a-half stone heavier than this at one time.

Freeman: Do you follow stringent diets and all the rest of it to keep your weight down?

Hancock: Shall we say for a time I do and then after a show is over – after a series is over I do anything, whatever I want, and then pull right down.

Freeman: Why do you worry so much? A funny man can be fat perfectly well without...

Hancock: I think it makes you sluggish generally. Your mind is sluggish and I think it's a bad thing, really.

Freeman: You haven't got any children, have you?

Hancock: No.

Freeman: Would you like to have?

Hancock: No.

Freeman: Why no, I wonder?

Hancock: I don't know. I think ... I don't know, really.

Freeman: Do you have anything against children – 'flipping kids'?

Hancock: No, nothing at all! No, no.

Freeman: 'Flipping kids' doesn't represent any antipathy to children?

Hancock: No, no. None at all. No, I love other people's children.

Freeman: Did you have, on the whole, a happy childhood yourself? Do you look back on it with pleasure?

Hancock: I think perhaps the earliest part, yes.

Freeman: Your father – one reads about you – was a pub keeper. Now, I don't know what that means. Was it a little working-class pub, or was it a posh hotel, or what?

Hancock: Well, actually he was rather like me in a way. He had a lot of moods, he did all sorts of things. He was a laundry owner, a pub keeper, a hotel keeper, a boxing referee – all sorts – also a semi-pro comedian.

Freeman: But pretty well off, I should think from what you've just said.

Hancock: Oh no, he fluctuated a great deal.

Freeman: Ah! I see. You were – do you reckon that – you were in Birmingham ... were you?

Hancock: No, no. They left Birmingham ... when I was three years old we left Birmingham. For his health. He went to live in Bournemouth.

Freeman: In Bournemouth. Now, were you – would you say you were middle class or working class?

Hancock: I should say sort of lower middle, I should say.

Freeman: Lower middle, yes. Do you remember that with pleasure? Did you like the life – in a hotel, for instance?

Hancock: No, it's a bit impersonal, really. They were much too busy to really spend a great deal of time with us. And actually, anyway he died when I was about eleven years old, so I didn't see all that much of him.

Freeman: You say 'with us'. You're not an only child?

Hancock: No, no, no. There were three. My elder brother was killed during the war. I have another brother, younger brother.

Freeman: You were given – perhaps I can say this? – slightly unexpected names – Anthony, Aloysius, and St John. Any special family reason for this?

Hancock: They're not true. Those are created by the scriptwriters.

Freeman: Those are entirely created. And what is your real name, then?

Hancock: Anthony John Hancock.

Freeman: Did you in extreme childhood think well of yourself – were you sort of independent and brash, or were you an introverted little boy?

Hancock: No, I was pretty much of an extrovert till the age of about fourteen I think and then it sort of packed up.

Freeman: Well now, why?

Hancock: I've no idea.

Freeman: What clear memories do you have of your mother? At that age. I know she is still alive. But in your childhood.

Hancock: Oh, one of deep affection. Do you mean ... what?

Freeman: Yes, I wonder if you've got any early and vivid memory that stuck in your mind through the years?

Hancock: Not really. The memory I have best of her really is the encouragement she gave me to do what I wanted to do, though I showed no sign at all of being able to do it initially.

Freeman: And yet this was really following your father?

Hancock: Yes, I think in many ways it was a deep thing with me to try and justify it. Because I believe he was pretty good.

Freeman: You went to a public school. Now, was this a natural thing to do? Were you among people of your own sort of type and class there, or were you...

Hancock: I should say not. No, they considered it was – they tried to give me the best education that they possibly could which I think was a fine thing for them to do, because neither of them had an education really, you know, and I didn't want it. I felt it was making the thing too much in a mould...

Freeman: No, wait a minute, wait a minute! At the age of fourteen you can't have thought it was making you too much in a...

Hancock: Yes I did – most definitely – and I left there. I left there myself and it was one of the best decisions I made, I think.

Freeman: I was going to ask you. You left at sixteen, didn't you?

Hancock: Fifteen.

Freeman: Fifteen. Well now, what did you – you didn't do very much immediately you left, did you?

Hancock: No!

Freeman: Well, why did you leave then, exactly?

Hancock: I wanted to get into the theatre. As I say, I'd shown no particular sign of ability at that time, but I felt that I could do it somehow – I don't know why, really – and well, it more or less – I went to a technical college and learnt

shorthand and typing, did a few sort of odd
jobs for a short time and then when the war
started I went into troop entertainment.

Freeman: You in fact went into the RAF presumably as
an ordinary oik, and then drifted into
entertainment. Is that correct?

Hancock: No, I was doing it before, when I was about
seventeen.

Freeman: But your first professional experience was with
– what – ENSA or – ?

Hancock: First professional experience wasn't really till
after the war – 1947.

Freeman: But you had a good deal of experience of
entertaining on a fairly large scale, even if not
professionally, while you were in the RAF?

Hancock: Oh yes, because I went into the Gang Show –
Ralph Reader's Gang Show, and that was a
great experience for all of us really because we
played in all sorts of circumstances – in ships,
in caves, in the backs of lorries and everything,
and we did a lot of things that we weren't able
to do. I mean there were only eleven men in
the company and everybody had to do things,
you made about fourteen appearances in a
show, you see, and although you did a lot of
things that you weren't really suited to do it
somehow opened us up a little more and you
saw possibilities of expanding in a way that
you hadn't thought of before.

Freeman: Now, when you were demobbed did you go
pretty quickly into professional show-biz?

Hancock: No, not really. There were quite long periods of nothing, and ...

Freeman: Well, what happened? Tell us what nothing means.

Hancock: Well, I came out of the Air Force in November, 1946, and there was the gratuity of course – that lasted about three weeks – then there was sort of – certain loans and bits and pieces, then I got the first job I think about May, 1947.

Freeman: And what was that job?

Hancock: That was in a thing called *Wings*. That was the first professional show that I did. That was again with Ralph Reader. Well, it didn't – it was on tour for several weeks but then again there was another nasty gap and I was living in a room in Baron's Court and eating a particularly horrible brand of sausage, which at least was filling and sort of kept me going, that sort of thing. There was quite a long time before it really began to take any shape or that you could say that you were earning a living out of it.

Freeman: Well now, when did you earn a living?

Hancock: I should say from about 1948 onwards.

Freeman: And how did it start?

Hancock: At the Windmill, really.

Freeman: At the Windmill in London? A rather specialised form of entertainment. You didn't strip, presumably?

Hancock: No! Fortunately not. No, it's a marvellous

place, really, to run in an act. We did six shows a day, six days a week, and you learnt to die like a swan, you know gracefully. I mean I used to go on, the show used to start at 12.15, I used to go on at 12.19 to three rows of gentlemen reading newspapers, and nothing, you see, absolutely nothing, but you'd learnt to die with a smile on your face you see, and walk off. Then you came back again at two o'clock to the same people, and you died again you see. But it was a great experience. I didn't enjoy it at the time, but it's been a great benefit afterwards.

Freeman: Did you ever succeed in making them put their newspapers down before you finished?

Hancock: No, but I'll tell you what was the best thing, was the drunks used to come in about twenty past three, when the pubs were closed, and they were quite lively – you know – sort of made the day go.

Freeman: And then after the Windmill, then radio came. And you pretty rapidly became a national figure?

Hancock: No. Then again there were quite long gaps between. There were a lot of summer seasons and things that were valuable experience to me during this time, and only a few broadcasts.

Freeman: I noticed looking through what's been published about your career that there's a bit of obscurity about this, but it seems as if, three times in recent years, you've had some sort of a

breakdown in health. Is this true? Is your
health a bit ropy?

Hancock: Oh no, I don't think so. This is mainly from
the Adelphi. This stems from one occasion at
the Adelphi. I was there for ... I went in as a
replacement, and I went in too quickly and the
act that I had wasn't particularly good and we
were doing it twice a night and the show ran
for two years and the act was a little dodgy,
shall we say, and if I didn't work absolutely to
pitch every performance it didn't go very well,
so I had to force myself into this position, and
eventually it did just sort of wear me out and I
went off for a month. That's all.

Freeman: You never had any experience of this kind at
the Windmill? It was the particular
circumstances of this show?

Hancock: The Windmill was too quick. You know – you
were sort of on and off and on and off – it
was different – and it wasn't doing the same
thing, you see, over and over again for two
years. Is a long time, twice a night.

Freeman: Ah, now you like to change all the time?

Hancock: I love it, yes.

Freeman: This is perhaps why you've specialised in radio
and TV?

Hancock: It is entirely, because now I think I would hate
to do a show like that any more. I like the
challenge of new material every week.

Freeman: Now, did you in fact have a health breakdown
earlier – well, last autumn – or not?

Hancock: That is purely and simply – there is a thing
sometimes happens in this business – I have a
lot of dialogue to learn every week and
sometimes, if you get on to the sort of vicious
circle of getting too tired to learn and then not
sleeping because you're worried that you're not
learning you go to – you know – you
eventually come down to this, and I had a
week off and a sleep and it was all right again.

Freeman: It's often said of you – and I think my own
observations, for what they're worth, bear this
out – that you don't find it very easy to
incorporate women in your act. There've been
some exceptions – Hattie Jacques, for instance –
but on the whole you have had difficulty.
Now, why? Is it something to do with your
own brand of comedy?

Hancock: No, I don't think so. I think you can only –
Hattie is fine because she plays a sort of comic
character anyway, but a sort of straight love
interest with the character I play is virtually
impossible.

Freeman: Why?

Hancock: Well, it would seem so to me. You know, I
mean you can't really get romantic about the
sort of gentleman in the Homburg hat and the
fur collar, surely? It just doesn't apply.

Freeman: Are you absolutely stuck in this character now?
Do you see it modifying and developing at all?

Hancock: Oh yes, I think so. Definitely. There are certain
things I'd like to get away from now, really.
They're difficult to talk about – impossible to

talk about really – but gradually you do pull away from – you try and throw away the rubbish – I mean it accumulates all the time. You try and throw it away and come down to what is really your own personality. In other words you spend most of the time discarding, not gathering.

Freeman: And this is a job that you've not finished doing yet?

Hancock: Oh, by no means.

Freeman: Facing an individual performance, do you actually enjoy it, or is it hell while you're doing it?

Hancock: No, it's a bit of hell just before it starts. There's a lot of – you know – champing around and trying to get the right edge so that you are relaxed but also have a kick, so that you're going to be alive and also relaxed. It means a great deal of concentration and hold upon yourself to do this. It's a little too quick to really enjoy, I think, but there you are, it's very challenging. It is enjoyable as a whole. There's too much immediate concentration to really – you can't really completely say oh well, we can have a bit of a ball, you know.

Freeman: Looking back on your first thirty-five years – a jolly straight question – are you happy, or not?

Hancock: I've been very fortunate, I think. I have everything that anybody could want to make them happy but ...

Freeman: Ah now ...

Hancock: ... Wait a minute. I haven't finished yet. I was going to say that the only happiness I can achieve would be to perfect the talent that I have, whatever it may be, however small it may be. That is the whole purpose of it, and that is the whole purpose of what I do.

Freeman: Some of the newspaper writers who've tried to puzzle out what makes you tick have said that you're the Angstman, the Anxiety Man. Now have you any notion of what your anxiety is? Do you in fact get a kick out of your anxiety?

Hancock: Anxiety. Would you explain that a bit more?

Freeman: Well, something appears to me, even at the end of this conversation, to be eating you. You say that your happiness is just ahead of you still. There's something troubling you about the world. I'd like to know what it is.

Hancock: I wouldn't expect happiness. I don't. I don't think it's possible. But I'm very fortunate to be able to work in something that I like. I think to work in something that is pleasure is all anybody can ask.

Freeman: You wouldn't then change your way of life at all?

Hancock: I'd try and improve it, yes.

Freeman: Well, improve it, but you'd go on in the same way, getting better at what you're doing?

Hancock: Yes, and if such a time came that I found that I'd come to the end of what I could develop out of my own ability, limited however it may be, then I wouldn't want to do it any more.

Freeman: Tony Hancock, I wonder if you really get very much out of your triumphs? You've got cars that you don't drive, you've got health which you tell me is a bit ropy because you find . . .

Hancock: I didn't tell you that!

Freeman: . . . find it so difficult to learn your lines, you've got money that you can't really spend, you worry about your weight . . .

Hancock: I spend the money. I do. I enjoy it!

Freeman: Well, what I want to put to you as a final question is this. You could stop all this tomorrow if you wanted to. You're rich enough to coast along for the rest of your days. Now why . . .

Hancock: Money is of no account in this.

Freeman: Well, tell me why you go on, as a late answer.

Hancock: Because it absolutely fascinates me, because I love it and because it is my entire life.

Watching the interview almost forty years later, it becomes clear that Hancock was quickly aware of his failings, yet stubbornly insisted on having his own way. He is self-critical and self-confident, intellectually sure yet temperamentally shy.

The public were, for the first time, confronted not only by Hancock's honesty but his sense of truth. He felt himself honour-bound to listen to the questions as well as answer them. As he listened – both to himself and to Freeman – his thoughts showed on his face and the radio and television buffoonery was exposed as no more than a brilliant suit of armour. Hancock the comic was a highly competent and contemporary joker. Hancock the man was seen to be an anxious, fragmentary, endearing individual.

Hundreds of fans wrote to empathise with him for having endured Freeman's surgical questions, yet Hancock refused to hear a word against Freeman. It had been a 'great experience', he claimed. The encounter, and its backlash, produced an instant and lasting friendship between the two men. Hancock even went to Freeman's home the following week to view a recording of the programme and 'felt no embarrassment' whatsoever.

The questions Freeman asked – and the answers they produced – caused a ripple of concern at the BBC. It was even suggested the 7 February transmission should be shelved, not because of Freeman's persistence, but because the corporation's lovable clown appeared less of a buffoon and certainly far less lovable. Hancock was more concerned that the controversy would reflect badly on Freeman. 'They were tough but good questions,' he said. 'I was very surprised at the reaction.'

The public – and by now the critics – continued to attack the programme and its interviewer. Freeman consulted Hancock and then wrote to the *Telegraph*: 'I judged, I believe correctly, that more of Hancock's complex and fascinating personality would appear on the screen if he was kept at pretty full stretch. I hope viewers generally did not equate that with hostility. I am sure Hancock didn't.'

Several years after the *Face to Face* interview Freeman gave his own verdict on Hancock's confessional. The reason Hancock wanted to become a comic, Freeman concluded, was that he needed to expose what he thought was the idiocy of the world. It was a mission ill-befitting a 'very sad and serious man'. 'He really was a man who wanted to make the world very public and understand the stupid and horrible place the world was. People nowadays say that he destroyed himself because he sought applause to a degree which wasn't appropriate. I disagree, I don't think it was applause he sought. He wanted the public to share the joke with him. He wanted them to understand what it was he was talking about. He wasn't successful at that and he became sadder and sadder.'

For Hancock – and many of his close colleagues – the interview became a watershed. Hancock had never truly understood his own popularity. He was baffled by his own success. The *Face to Face* interrogation changed his focus, not of himself, but of his own self-importance. For the first time, Hancock felt it was not only his art – his comedy – which attracted people to him, but that people wanted to talk to him as a person; that, for the first time, Tony Hancock the man was equally important.

Hancock persuaded himself he could do no wrong and, for the first time, consciously and ruthlessly closed the gap between acting and reality; between comedy and real life. 'You have got to get rid of everything inessential,' he argued. 'I want to stand there as I am. No props. No pretence. No defence. And say "there it is – here I am".' It was a self-inflicted myopia which was to leave him 'blind' for the rest of his life.

During the aftermath of the Freeman interview, Freddie Ross decided that at thirty it was time she left her parents' Hampstead home and found a flat of her own. So far her love-making with Hancock had been confined to borrowed apartments and overnight hotel rooms. Her solicitor brother, Leonard, already had an office in Dorset Square, across the road from Marylebone railway station and just around the corner from Regent's Park. When the apartment above became vacant, Freddie moved in her possessions and her business.

It was here that Hancock sought refuge from Cicely's increasingly heavy drinking and the rapidly solidifying atmosphere at MacConkeys. Over the next three years, as Hancock's marriage disintegrated, Freddie would bury her fears and attempt to turn the Dorset Square apartment into a new and safe home for her lover. 'She tried to give Tony the kind of home she felt he had never had with Cicely,' remembers Sally Mordant, one of Freddie's assistants in the rapidly expanding agency. 'For Tony it was like living in *Emergency Ward 10*, as he flicked ash into an ashtray she would remove it and clean it. Freddie thought that if she gave him the security of a well-run home, that if she organised him like an office, it would give him an anchorage.'

*

Any sympathy Hancock earned over the *Face to Face* interview was swiftly turned against him when details of his break with Sid James leaked from the BBC. News of the split between Hancock and the nation's 'number one feed' broke as James was on location at Chatham Dockyard, filming *Watch Your Stern* with Kenneth Connor and Hattie Jacques.

James, quite rightly, denied there had been any form of confrontation with Hancock. Years later he admitted he had 'argued with Tony for days – argued like hell' to prevent the break-up and, as a compromise, to complete at least one more series together – 'but only one'. Hancock, somewhat dismayed by the publicity so many months after the decision was made, felt himself backed into a corner.

For public consumption, Sid James went along with Hancock's reasoning of needing to try something new and adventurous – 'You can't go on doing the same thing. I don't care who you are or how good you are, the public gets sick of the sight of you' – but the way in which Hancock had planned and executed the parting, as an open secret with James in the dark, rankled deeply and James admitted he never got over the feeling of hurt. 'We could have made a fortune if we'd stuck together,' he said, 'but Tony had a thing about repetition. It sent him crazy.'

If Hancock was openly frustrated by James as a foil, he showed no sign of wanting to end their friendship. In six years the pair had just one stand-up row. They were playing pontoon during a break in rehearsals, and James stuck on twelve. The move infuriated Hancock who claimed it was illegal. James defended himself by saying Hancock had invented the rule because he was losing. What impressed the onlookers was not that the pair were blazing away at each other – itself unique – but the fact that James and Hancock had subconsciously slipped into their TV personas and appeared to be acting out yet another Galton and Simpson sketch.

The writers themselves agreed the time was right for a change. They have differing views, though, on how prepared Sid James was for the inevitable. Alan Simpson still agrees with Hancock's claim that his association with James had turned into a Laurel and Hardy partnership: 'Wherever Tony went people would shout out, "Where's Sid?"'

'Tony's gripe was that he didn't seem able to appear without Sid James,' adds Ray Galton, 'and James seemed to be appearing in every film that was being made in Britain. So Tony thought it was time he reasserted his own personality.'

Ever since Hancock's MacConkeys announcement, Duncan Wood had been attempting to dissuade his star from breaking up what was, after all, a winning formula. Wood's argument, sometimes over a quiet beer, was always the same. 'Jack Benny has done thirty years on the main facets of meanness, vanity, age and violin playing,' he would tell Hancock. 'Are you sure you have exhausted the vein of what you are about?' No one connected with *Hancock's Half Hour* was quite sure the nuggets had come to an end.

Kenneth Williams, for once, sided with Hancock. He was convinced there was no jealousy or malice or professional malevolence behind Hancock's split with James: 'I think that if you have a vision in your head – as Tony did – of the way comedy should be played, then invariably you move towards being a solo performer. It is too simple and too glib to reduce a man like that to being jealous of someone else getting laughs.'

Some years later, Hancock would admit he had made a mistake. 'I had to do something new,' he told one of his last scriptwriters. 'I had to progress. Looking back it was a case of throwing the baby away with the bath water. Maybe I should have kept the props. After all, Chaplin never really abandoned his cane.'

The working partnership between Tony Hancock and Sid James came to an end on 29 April, 1960, with the conclusion of the sixth television series. The fifty-seventh and last programme – at least how the original quartet of Hancock, Main Wilson, Galton and Simpson had envisaged it – concluded with a suitably schizophrenic plot. Hancock receives a succession of poison-pen letters. The police are unable to trace the author and it is left to Sid to solve the mystery. Hancock is writing them to himself – in his sleep.

The press and the public were already aware of Hancock's decision to go it alone, but, despite the publicity, he felt he should make an 'official' announcement at the end-of-series party. Eric Sykes and Bill Kerr – who had appeared in his last radio *Half Hour* ten months earlier – decided to gate-crash the gathering; armed with flamenco guitars the pair intended to provide an impromptu cabaret. They arrived just as Hancock was attempting to tell everyone what they already knew. Kerr remembers it as 'one of Hancock's saddest and most dramatic moments'.

In a brief interview for the BBC's *Newsreel* programme, Hancock was naïvely frank. Asked why he was leaving Railway Cuttings and the old format, he admitted, 'It was so comfortable. It was time we changed and got away from that surrounding. Six years on radio and four years on television begins to limit itself.' Any future series, he confessed, would have a 'negative background'.

The public – admittedly not party to Hancock's reasoning – remained unconvinced. So, too, were his most loyal critics. Robert Ottaway would lament:

By destroying all the paraphernalia of quirks and tantrums that he acquired as the East Cheam also-ran, Hancock is mutilating his own superb gifts too. For the warmth and sympathy he unearthed in that character could only be translated to other situations, other suburbs where the ambitious sadly or funnily fail to make reality of their aspirations. We can, I think, respect Hancock for his uneasy search, whilst remaining sceptical of his reasons for it. For surely his real dilemma is that he has mistaken width for depth. Even if we find this winter, or next, that Hancock can stand on his head or do a Lancashire monologue, there'll be a little disappointment in our applause. The response to Anthony Aloysius Hancock was so overwhelming because we recognised bits of him in our neighbour, in our husband, in ourselves. How sad that the only man who cannot see that affinity is – Tony Hancock.

One prop from the final series has, over the years, developed its own intriguing mythology. Late in February, 1960, Ray Galton and Alan Simpson were working on a television script for the new *Half Hour* series. They already had a storyline. Hancock borrows a book from his local library. He takes the murder mystery home and reads it in one sitting – only to find someone has torn out the last page. Hancock, accompanied by an equally perplexed Sid James, sets out to track down the author. Their search leads them to the British Museum where they discover another copy of the book. It, too, has the last page missing.

The book Galton and Simpson invented to frustrate Hancock was *Lady Don't Fall Backwards*, by Darcy Sarto – 'this is the little beauty I'm after'. After its initial appearance in the March screening of *The Missing Page*, the book reappears a year later during Hancock's final series for the BBC. Alone in his Earl's Court bedsitter, Hancock is again seen reading *Lady Don't Fall Backwards*. This time the dust jacket gives the author as Darcy Clinto.

Darcy Glinto – not Clinto – was one of four pseudonyms used in the 1930s and forties by Harold Ernest Kelly. In July, 1942, Kelly and his publisher were each fined fifty guineas, with an equal amount in costs, after pleading guilty to publishing two obscene books. One was called *Lady Don't Turn Over*. Ray Galton and Alan Simpson had both read Glinto's shilling thriller in 1947, while recovering in the TB sanatorium. To avoid copyright complications they changed the name to *Lady Don't Fall Backwards*.*

With his sixth television series behind him, Hancock refocused his attention on his second film. It was a project he had been discussing with his writers for several months. Hancock and Galton and Simpson fleshed out the story and the trio pitched the idea to Associated British which agreed to finance the venture.

The writers and the star saw the film – and what it could achieve – in different ways. Although the screenplay was largely the work of Galton and Simpson, the power of veto remained with Hancock. For

---

* More than thirty years later, Joan le Mesurier adopted the same title for her memoirs in which she describes her brief affair with Hancock.

Galton and Simpson, who were given an office at Elstree Studios and time to produce a script, it was the big screen debut of the familiar 'Hancock' persona:

'That's a self-portrait.'

'Who of?'

'Laurel and Hardy. Who of? Buffoon!'

It also contained a line which, over the next eight years, would increasingly crystallise Hancock's frustration and, prophetically, offer a solution:

'Why kill time when you can kill yourself.'

For Tony Hancock, *The Rebel* was more than a simple career progression. It was, as far as Hancock was concerned, a flight of fancy, a magic carpet capable of flying the Atlantic; when it landed in America he would be hailed an international star. Hancock had met and talked to the ageing Stan Laurel, the legendary Hollywood comedy actor. He explained the plot of his first film and asked Laurel's advice. 'Cut out the slang,' he was told. Hancock returned to Britain, determined to excise the very gems which had made his radio and television comedies sparkle. *The Rebel*, he demanded, would be written in an international and homogenised language. The comedy would speak for itself. 'I am aiming at a universal comedy that will transcend class and state barriers,' he pronounced.

Each scene – each line – was vetted by Hancock for its international appeal. If he couldn't lose the bizarre British 'Ancock he would set him down amid the artistic community of Paris, a place which had attracted the American imagination for almost a century. Prime sections of Galton and Simpson dialogue were cut because 'they won't understand that in America'.

Another suggestion was rapidly axed. The writers wanted a *Rebel* cameo role for Sid James, in the same way Bing Crosby continued to make brief appearances in Bob Hope's solo films after their *Road-*movie partnership ended. There were various suggestions: one had James surfacing from a swimming pool, winking, and then disappearing; another had him playing the part of a customs officer towards the end of the film. Hancock rejected both ideas as 'old-fashioned', fearing any suggestion the old partnership might be revived.

Years later – when Hancock had turned his back on everyone who had helped make him famous – his old friend Spike Milligan suggested his own scenario for reconciliation. Explaining it to Galton and Simpson, the former *Goon* said: 'It starts with Tony in the Labour Exchange and behind him is Sid and all the other people he put out of work. Then you see him get off a bus a few doors from the Galton and Simpson office. He takes a taxi so that he can draw up in style and shouts up at the window, "Hello lads, I want to give you another chance," and then he starts telling you where you went wrong. "It was when you decided not to write for me any more," he says. "All this *Steptoe and Son* stuff – there is nothing in it." '

From their first-floor office at Elstree Studios, Galton and Simpson set about keeping their promise to continue writing for Sid James. The pair would intermittently work on Hancock's *The Rebel* and Sid James's first solo television series, *Citizen James*. If *The Rebel* was a feature-length *Hancock's Half Hour*, then *Citizen James* was Sid without Tony. The background consisted of a drinking club, back-streets and a racing stadium. The dialogue revolved around booze, dogs and, above all, dodges for making easy money. James, as a weather-beaten layabout, is pursued by Liz Fraser, who runs the drinking club and is determined to marry him. 'It was exactly the way we had been writing up Sid for the Hancock shows,' admits Simpson. 'We took Sid away from Hancock so he could carry on working on his get-rich-quick schemes.'

Hancock was less afraid of using other *Half Hour* regulars such as John le Mesurier, Hugh Lloyd, Mario Fabrizi and, on his former co-star's urging, Liz Fraser. The part of the shy genius, whose work is mistakenly credited to Hancock, went to Canadian Paul Massie.

Associated British and Warner-Pathé, the film's joint backers, insisted on an established American favourite to boost the film's transatlantic attraction. Robert Day, *The Rebel*'s director, suggested

George Sanders and a meeting was arranged at Claridges. 'I was dreading it,' admitted Hancock. 'Everything about him was suave and sophisticated.'

George Sanders was best known for his portrayal of *The Saint*, Leslie Charteris's reformed British gentleman-crook who becomes a Robin Hood of crime. Hancock soon discovered he was 'barking mad'.

The two men shook hands. 'Hello, Tony,' said Sanders.

'Hello, how are you?' replied Hancock.

'Not too good, old boy,' confided Sanders. 'I've got to the age where a good shit is better than a good fuck.'

Sanders, who was to play the art critic and dealer Sir Charles Bruard, was a dedicated drinker and a frustrated carpenter. Whenever he was filming away from his American home his luggage invariably included a carpenter's hold-all, complete with saws, drills, hammers and chisels. Sitting in his hotel bedroom after an evening in the bar, Sanders would suddenly decide a chair was lop-sided or a door too tight and that he was compelled to 'mend' them. It didn't matter how old the door or precious the piece of furniture. 'I always do that when I've had a drink,' he told Hancock. 'It relaxes me.'

The film received its international première at the Beirut Film Festival. With its UK release still a month away, Associated British 'ordered' Hancock to attend the 1960 Cannes Film Festival as a star guest. 'Cicely and I went along from a small hotel we were staying at further along the coast,' he recalled. 'I was told to keep on shaking hands with foreign journalists who had never heard of me. "What films have you been in?" they asked. Well, the only film that had ever been shown was *Orders are Orders*, in which I had a spit-and-a-cough. So I told them the title and the conversation flagged. I couldn't stand it, so we fled back to where we had come from.'

Before his departure, David Nathan – a Fleet Street journalist who nine years later would collaborate with Freddie Ross on the biography *Hancock* – arranged a joint interview with Hancock and Trevor Howard. Both 'expressed boundless admiration' for each other's work and, publicly at least, promised to discuss the possibility of a future television comedy.

A few weeks later, *The Rebel* was given a London trade screening. In the audience was BBC researcher David Whitaker. His précis of the plot is as good as any:

> The plot concerns Anthony Hancock City worker whose future expectations are retirement in twenty-five years, speech of gratitude and a silver cigarette box. At heart Hancock is an artist. When his landlady objects to an enormous stone figure he is carving in his rooms and his boss objects to his sketch work during office hours, he decides to throw everything up and live on the Left Bank in Paris, sinking himself in art. Here his paintings are so childlike and his approach to art so juvenile, that his philosophies are taken to be genius and he leads a new Renaissance. He becomes the darling of artistic society sharing a studio with another painter who has no confidence in his own work (played by Paul Massie). Hancock attempts to encourage him but Massie decides to give it all up and return to England, leaving his paintings behind as a gift to Hancock. An art critic (George Sanders), hearing of the new idol of Paris, visits Hancock and becomes ecstatic about Paul Massie's paintings, not about Hancock's work at all; so our hero is forced to pretend he painted them himself. All these paintings are sold and the art critic decides to have a London showing with the new collection of paintings. Hancock urgently contacts Paul Massie, who has been painting in his spare time, although he now works in an office. Hancock and Massie rush the new pictures to the gallery only to discover there that Massie has altered his style. The art critic is not dismayed. These new paintings are even better than the others. Hancock then reveals who the real artist is and goes back to his old rooms and starts carving another enormous stone figure.

Whitaker's subsequent comments are even more revealing. Part of the film's failure, he reports, is not so much down to Hancock as to lost opportunities by the director, Robert Day.

> Parts of this film are extraordinarily good. I think Tony Hancock has a lot to learn yet about filming. His continuity of expression, for example, is not yet adapted to the short-take, but this will obviously amend itself in time. I would not have said that his screen writers, Galton and Simpson, rose to the occasion in any particularly brilliant way, although they have provided the proof Hancock will, in time, make extremely good films. Basically, I think the film fails because of an undisciplined imagination by the director. It is all very well to plunge Hancock into a party of French beatniks, artistic curiosities and Left Bank oddities, and Technicolor can always be relied upon to provide bizarre images, but when you expect comedy from Tony Hancock he cannot stop because the film wants to provide splashes of colour or touches of weirdly imagined life. Thus, all too frequently, Hancock is left floundering and the action of the picture rises and falls into a series of perhaps comic, perhaps unfunny sequences. Strong support is given by George Sanders who was far better than the written part, George Aslan as a patron of arts and the husband of a beautiful wife who discovers a passion for the new artist, Paul Massie as the shy, retiring genius and John le Mesurier as the general manager of the city firm. Dennis Price makes a brief appearance as a Salvador Dali character and Liz Fraser has second billing for five lines.

The conclusion of the piece would have pleased Hancock. It compares him to some established comedy stars, including his hero Sid Field:

> This is a much more promising start than Sid Field's first film, but shall we say, has not the insurance of Norman Wisdom's. Hancock, of course, has never been noted for particular sketches or particular routines as was Sid Field. One feels a Chaplinesque

touch here and there and with the right imaginative director he will obviously go on to much better things.

The Rebel was a major success in Britain. It became one of the most popular 'star comic' films of the post-war era, out-grossing the established high earners of British cinema such as the year's two *Carry On* films – *Constable* and *Regardless* – and the latest additions to the *Doctor* and *St Trinian's* series. To Hancock's dismay, however, *The Rebel* failed to set the international film world alight.

Hancock was convinced – and rightly – of the benefits of laughter. 'I do believe comedy is terribly important in the world today, and can really help,' he said. 'When people say you have really made them laugh, and they can say it honestly, it is not a thing to throw away or say it doesn't matter. It is the real thing.'

His own comedy standards were equally exacting. His inspirational hero, apart from Sid Field, was Chaplin:

Chaplin's *City Lights*, which I think is the finest full-length comedy I have seen, has wonderful moments of comedy which come naturally out of the action. Among present-day comics I am most influenced by Jacques Tati. *Monsieur Hulot's Holiday* had some of the most inventive business comedy I have ever seen since Chaplin. *Mon Oncle* was an advance in a way but not as hilarious by any means.

People coming out with things, and doing things, that everyday life would restrain is a great source of comedy, of course. Natural antagonism. Like the Marx Brothers, all doing things that would be unacceptable. One realises why Groucho is so great.

The idea of the little man in comedy is mostly mistaken. Chaplin is always referred to as a little man. Sometimes he is extremely aggressive. Remember the scene in *City Lights* when he is in a Rolls-Royce and he gets out of the car, kicks a tramp in the stomach, picks up a cigar butt and drives off? Nowadays you would probably be advised not to do it. Only the great could get away with it.

*

Lily Walker's faith in her second son was as relentless and supportive as ever. 'My Mum is absolutely wonderful,' Hancock would say. 'She follows every move of mine and keeps every cutting she can get about me. She kept me on my toes when I got going in my career, and now she expects me to keep her on her toes.' Lily had travelled to Paris during the filming of *The Rebel*. Whenever Hancock telephoned with news of a new booking or contract she would ask: 'How much? Enough for me to go to . . . Greece?'

In many ways Lily refused to allow her son to grow up. He would, forever, remain the chubby-cheeked boy in short trousers. One day Cicely was driving Hancock and his mother around the English countryside. 'Look at the choo-choo puff-puff,' Lily told her son.

'I'm thirty-two for Christ sake,' protested Hancock.

In other ways they were no longer mother and son, they had evolved into a Laurel and Hardy double act: the frail innocent and the dumpy extrovert. Since the war, Hancock had called his mother by her Christian name. For anyone who overheard their conversations and arguments – about cricket and golf and sex – they were the original odd couple, fretful yet faithful friends.

Hancock, as his mother well knew, could be irrationally stubborn. Not long after her second husband's suicide, Lily Walker became friends with a retired civil servant, and Hancock disapproved of his mother's deepening relationship, and her intention of moving into Henry Sennett's home at Ferndown, north of Bournemouth. On 7 September – three days after her seventieth birthday – Lily Walker married Sennett, formerly a senior executive officer with the Ministry of National Insurance, at Poole register office. Cicely unsuccessfully attempted to persuade Hancock he should attend his mother's wedding. Instead he sent a present and a telegram and stuck by his excuse – 'I don't want to involve her in possible publicity.'

There was another reason. In recent years Hancock had defined within himself the frightening ability to perceive warmth or cold in a person, energy or inertia. On the rare occasions he met his future step-father, Hancock was struck with an almost overpowering sense of death.

1961

HANCOCK HAD SPENT all day in the studio, recording an episode of his new television series. Soon after six o'clock Cicely arrived to drive him back to Blindley Heath. They had just crossed the Surrey border when Cicely, a fast but careful driver, was forced to brake violently to avoid some road works and Hancock's head shattered the windscreen. As he was being helped into an ambulance, a young policeman at the scene spotted a sheaf of paper in the passenger foot-well of the car. It was covered in broken glass and spots of blood. Shaking off the debris, the officer was about to return the script to Hancock when he read the title page – it was called *The Blood Donor*.

Hancock was taken to a nearby hospital where cuts to his head and hands were treated. He was obviously suffering from concussion, but when it was suggested he spend the night in a private room for observation he refused. The next morning, Saturday, waking up in his own bed at MacConkeys, he found it impossible to focus his eyes, and his head was splitting. By Sunday evening Hancock was irascible and frustrated; he was also drinking heavily. Cicely told a friend the bruising across the bridge of his nose and around his eyes made him look like a 'grumpy raccoon'.

The double vision was still with him when he woke on Monday morning. A few hours later, Cicely dropped her husband in Sulgrave Road and watched him trudge painfully into the club. From the first read-through, it was obvious to Duncan Wood, who had assumed his star would take a week off to recover, that Hancock was having difficulty reading the forty-three-page script. The concussion had reduced his concentration span to a few minutes and his memory to almost nil.

By lunchtime Hancock could recall just four pages. It was, said Wood, as if the rest had been 'swallowed by the emptiness behind Tony's eyes'. As a compromise, the producer suggested the coming Friday's programme should be recorded using teleprompters and idiot boards; this would at least save Hancock from learning the lines and give him a few days off rehearsals.

The next morning, Wood hastily rearranged the week's schedule. Assuming Hancock was well enough, three days of rehearsals would start on Thursday, with all day Sunday for the actual recording. He also arranged with Autocue Ltd for the hire of the teleprompters and was told the BBC would be charged twenty guineas a day for rehearsals and forty-five guineas for a complete day's recording. Wood reassured his superiors that the £110 Autocue bill was still within the programme's budget.

There was still one 'technical' problem. For some reason the BBC Ticket Unit had admitted parties containing dozens of young children. During the recording of *The Bowmans* – the day of the accident – the erratic audience reaction had forced numerous delays and retakes. The same thing had happened, Wood was informed by a colleague, on a recent recording of Michael Bentine's *It's a Square World*. Coaxing a credible performance from his concussed star would be bad enough; expecting Hancock to deal with distractions like those of the previous Friday's recording was expecting too much.

Roger Hancock, Tony's younger brother – now working for Associated London Scripts – had also complained about the disruption. So, in a memo to various heads of department, Wood attempted to forestall future problems:

On all counts the efforts of all concerned with this show were decimated by the competition of the studio audience. Included in our audience were approximately seventy infants of an average age of eight years. They came principally in two organised groups complete with chaperones etc, and understood not one word of the show from start to finish. Naturally, they reacted accordingly with resounding silence and since they occupied large sections of the best seats one can imagine the results.

This is just not good enough.

I presume Ticket Unit do not send an adult audience to see Lenny the Lion and I would have equally presumed that their professional judgment would preclude an infant audience for Tony Hancock. If we had done a three-act version of Little Bo Peep they would probably still be cheering. However, the Hancock script is aimed at a slightly higher age group than this.

Can we once and for all make the point that for Hancock we ask only for an intelligent adult audience – or even an adult audience who lack the adjective. Anything would be preferable to last Friday's orphans' picnic.

In conclusion, I'm sorry to have to inform you that major retakes were necessary due primarily to the artists being completely thrown by the audience reaction, or lack of it, and as a result the show is not as good as it could have been.

On Sunday Hancock arrived at the studio happy to go ahead with the recording; the rehearsals had gone well. He was still groggy and was relieved at not having to learn every line of *The Blood Donor* script. Arriving at Television Centre he received the heartening news that his decision to go it alone had been vindicated. *The Bedsitter*, his first show deliberately without Sid James, had entered the television top ten at number five. It was the highest-placed BBC programme and shared the slot with an Independent Television drama, *Boyd QC*.

In his dressing room Hancock was 'buoyant'. His part-time secretary, Lyn Leonard remembers him signing letters and cheques and being 'very happy and very cheerful'.

Beneath each of the five studio cameras was placed an Autocue machine. For the short-sighted June Whitfield – who had never seen an Autocue before – the prompters were of little benefit. 'It was a very odd sensation,' recalled Whitfield, who plays a nurse in *The Blood*

Donor. 'Your eyeline is all wrong. I was looking at Tony and he was looking just behind me.'

It was a line written for *The Blood Donor* that earned Galton and Simpson their place in *The Oxford Dictionary of Modern Quotations*: '. . . a pint – why that's very nearly an armful! I'm sorry. I'm not walking around with an empty arm for anybody.'*

Ray Galton and Alan Simpson watched the tele-recording from the control room. 'For the first time in his television career Tony read his entire part,' remembers Simpson. 'From then on he thought he was released from having to learn seven and a half thousand words a week. Tony never learnt another line from that day on.'

For the writers the series marked another shift in their professional association with Hancock. 'Tony was always a heavy drinker but he never drank before a show,' explains Alan Simpson. 'His drinking was confined to after work. He never went on drunk, never worked drunk.' With one programme left to record, Hancock made no attempt to study or memorise the script. 'And that was when he started drinking,' adds Simpson. 'Now he could drink and not worry about anything.'

Faced with a new comedy challenge, Hancock had started the year on a high. 'This could be the beginning of a greatness in comedy that TV has never known,' reported Kenneth Baily in the *People*, 'or the end of a big hope.' Hancock was sure it would be the former and, making an effort to curb his drinking, had regained some of his infectious confidence. However, rumours began to circulate – inaccurate as it turned out – of a 'nervous and moody' Hancock who, living a 'monk-like existence', had ordered a complete news black-out on his forthcoming television series.

*

* In January, 1994, *The Blood Donor* plot was used in a *Look In* magazine *Scooby Doo* cartoon strip. Scooby Doo, a pompous and cowardly dog, offers to give blood. When he is asked for a pint of blood he replies: 'A pint? But that's nearly a pawful.' Informed he possesses rare rhesus negative blood he changes his mind, 'We rhesus negatives have to stick together.' Later, Scooby Doo is rushed back to the hospital to be given a transfusion with is own pint of blood.

Hancock's last performance before a live audience had been at the 1958 Royal Variety Performance. It took Bernard Delfont – the impresario Hancock had impressed with his carpet sliding act – another three years to persuade the comedian to return to his variety roots.

The Hancock Show opened at the Granada, Shrewsbury, on 6 March, 1961, and ended, six weeks later, at the New Theatre, Oxford; the format and sketches were a copy-cat of the 1958 summer tour, and to supplement the traditional variety acts – 'unusual foot jugglers' Leo, Bassi and June and 'international eccentrics' the Ghezzi Brothers – Hancock had, once again, recruited several of his former *Half Hour* repertory, including Johnny Vyvyan and Alec Bregonzi. Also on the bill was a singing trio called the Springfields whose lead singer, Dusty Springfield, was famous for her back-combed hair and heavy, black eyelashes; during the final week at Oxford, the group returned to London to make their first hit record, *Breakaway*.

In the sixpenny programme, Granada patrons were informed of a special offer by Wildings of Shrewsbury: *This is Hancock* and *Pieces of Hancock*, both issued on long-play records the year before, could be bought for '£1 14s 1d each, including tax, post free'. It also offered a potted, and outstandingly inaccurate, biography of the show's star:

The great T.V. comedian Tony Hancock, just back from entertaining troops in Cyprus, appears this week at Granada Shrewsbury in his first stage production for two years on the first leg of his provincial tour.

Hancock made his theatre name overnight in his first West End appearance with Jimmy Edwards in *London Laughs* at the Adelphi Theatre. He originally began his show business career by entertaining the troops in the Bournemouth area where his parents ran a hotel.

After leaving the RAF he appeared in plays, cabaret and pantomime, before going on radio in the Archie Andrews series. It was then that people began to hear of Hancock in a big way, and the Jimmy Edwards theatre show made him a national name.

Hancock is married to tall, auburn-haired, ex-model Cicely,

who shares his enthusiasm for squash, golf, cricket, motoring and good food. Hancock gave up motoring some time ago. 'I wasn't very good at it', he says sadly. He is a perfectionist and polishes every move he intends to make in his shows until it shines. He worries about his work and all his performances are preceded by hours of mental agony. 'Simply can't stop worrying' admits Hancock.

Hancock is that extremely rare thing – a comic who can act. In this he is greatly helped by having a face that seems as pliable as rubber. Over 11 million viewers will look eagerly in May – when the new series of *Hancock's Half Hour* begins – for that special sad-glad Hancock face, like a shaggy dog mourning for a lost bone. He doesn't have to fall flat on his face to be funny, nor does he have to say a word either. Very few comics have this Chaplinesque gift – which perhaps makes it less surprising that he has risen to the summit of the entertainment world and seems sure to stay there.

*

Before Hancock's departure for Shrewsbury and the start of the six-week tour, he had one final meeting with Galton and Simpson. The writers, like their star, had become annoyed by repeated press comments on the viability of a future series without Sid James. More irritating was the implication that no one involved in the production – Hancock or the writers – could 'make it work' without James as foil. Galton and Simpson suggested they attempt to create a script for a solo Hancock, 'without any support whatsoever'. Hancock told them to go ahead.

The script the pair delivered to Hancock's Granada dressing room was unlike anything they had previously produced. Written with the working title *Hancock Alone* it was renamed and broadcast as *The Bedsitter*. Hancock began reading the script; suddenly a grin spread across his face. 'Marvellous,' he said without looking up. 'Brilliant.'

It was, recalls Alan Simpson: 'Pages and pages of instructions, which we'd never really done before, as opposed to dialogue. We were worried about it because it was a complete break from anything we had written for Hancock.'

The diminutive Johnny Vyvyan had appeared more than thirty-five times as a member of Hancock's *Half Hour* repertory, and during the late 1950s and early sixties he had himself become a household name for his appearances on a television game show called *Laugh Line*, in which actors posed cartoon-like in front of a celebrity panel, who then rearranged them and thought up suitable punch lines. The week at Shrewsbury ended and Hancock, Vyvyan and the company manager agreed to travel together by train to Newcastle. A couple, walking through the carriages, passed the trio and then returned for a second look. The man pointed at Vyvyan. '*Laugh Line,*' he announced loudly before roaring with laughter.

'I might as well go home,' grumbled the unrecognised Hancock. He 'immediately plunged into a silent and accusing mood', recalled Vyvyan.

During May and June, Hancock recorded his seventh, and final, television series for the BBC. Because three minutes had been trimmed from each episode – now twenty-five instead of the long-established twenty-eight minutes – the BBC decided to lose the *Half Hour*. The new series would simply be called *Hancock*.

The six-week series began its run with *The Bedsitter* on 26 May and three shows still had to be recorded. On the day of his accident Hancock had been recording *The Bowmans*, a skit on the long-running BBC radio series *The Archers*. His part was itself a parody of Walter Gabriel, a 'yer-tiz' yokel and one of the show's oldest characters. To Hancock's amusement, Wally Stott created *The Bowmans* signature tune by rewriting and playing *The Archers* theme – 'Barwick Green' – backwards.

From the philosophical isolation of *The Bedsitter*, through the mayhem and confusion of *The Radio Ham,* and the misguided and self-centred *Blood Donor*, Hancock was finally fretting over his *Succession*:

What have you achieved? What have you achieved? You lost your chance, me old son. You contributed absolutely nothing to this life. A waste of time you being here at all. No plaque for you in Westminster Abbey. The best you can expect is a few daffodils in a jam-jar, a rough-hewn stone bearing the legend 'he came and he went', and between – nothing!

It was Hancock at his melancholy best. Ray Galton and Alan Simpson had created a Walter Mitty soliloquy and, in some perverse foretelling of Hancock's ultimate fate, the writers had composed the comic's self-mocking obituary.

Nobody will notice you're not here. After about a year somebody might say down the pub, 'Where's old Hancock? I haven't seen him around lately ... Oh, he's dead, you know ... Oh, is he?' A right raison d'être that is. Nobody will ever know I existed. Nothing to leave behind me. Nothing to pass on. Nobody to mourn me. That's the bitterest blow.

In seven years to the month, *The Times* would deliver its own verdict on Hancock's life and career. Like Galton and Simpson's foresight, the newspaper's hindsight is equally relevant to his departure from the BBC and his self-imposed eviction from 1950s East Cheam.

In Tony Hancock, much that is sadly typical of his age was crystallised and found expression. He was the chronicler of social disorientation, of submission to undigested or indigestible little ideas dressed pompously in big words, of a craving for intellectual and social eminence on the cheap. Whether by instinct or design, these things found in him a mercilessly derisive commentator.

*

By the time the series ended on Friday, 30 June, Hancock had rekindled his capacity for clearing public houses and leaving chip shops and bingo halls deserted: one in three television-owning adults had tuned in to watch the close of a comedy era. For six weeks, Hancock had proved the newspaper critics and pundits wrong and had produced some of his, and Britain's, most memorable and classic comedy. More importantly he had proved to himself that he was capable of working – and winning – without Sid James.

'When Tony said he didn't want me on television with him any more, the most fantastic offers were made to get us to stay together,' Sid James complained many years later. 'I lost a certain £55,000 in contracts covering two years because Tony insisted on the split. Tony himself turned down a certain £80,000.' Forever a victim of his own imagination and desperate need for money, James's memory is incorrect. The 'fabulous' deals repeatedly laid before Hancock throughout 1960 and early 1961 were remarkable, not so much for the sums involved, but more for the sea-change of policy and programming needed within the BBC to put them together.

Beryl Vertue, who, by now, had taken over as agent at Associated London Scripts, received the latest proposal from the head of BBC television light entertainment. This time Tom Sloan was offering Hancock a contract for six shows – without James – during May and June. The fee would be £1,750 per show, to include one repeat and possible overseas sales. To sound out his reluctant star, Sloan took Hancock to lunch. Hancock was buoyant and 'most interested to return to the BBC', Sloan reported in an internal memo. To underline just how far the corporation had shifted the goal-posts to accommodate Hancock and his agent, Sloan wrote to Vertue:

I think it is only fair to say straight away that much as we appreciate the particular value of any artist, there must come a time when an increase in fees can possibly prejudice repeat rights, and most certainly transcription sales. It is with this in mind that we have made our proposal a composite guarantee which produces immediately an increase over previous fees but at the same time in our view makes both repeats and transcriptions a reasonable possibility.

For the first time in my experience the BBC Television service is in fact prepared to underwrite repeats and transcription fees in order to achieve a guaranteed minimum financial return for all concerned.

Hancock reiterated his MacConkeys promise of completing just 'one more' contract with the BBC. Throughout the meal, Hancock had repeated his interest in film rather than electronic methods of image recording, as currently used by the BBC. 'The film world was his sole interest,' recalled Sloan, who also came away with the impression he was to be given 'first option' should Hancock decide to return to regular television work.

Hancock, however, had already been approached by Independent Television. Beryl Vertue, and her London Scripts associate Roger Hancock, discussed their client's future plans with another BBC executive, Ronald Waldman. He was 'pretty stunned' by Hancock's by now public decision to defect to Associated Television. Hancock, without realising it, had thus lost an ally at the BBC equally dedicated to conquering the American market; like the star, Waldman was also convinced the corporation would eventually be forced to use 'pure film', if it wanted to exploit overseas markets.

In the early 1960s, the majority of BBC programmes were electronically tele-recorded, but overseas sales were up – 130 per cent in 1961 – despite this technical handicap. 'It was a market full of potential,' said Waldman, and the corporation had counted on Hancock being a leading player in this sales drive. Part of the campaign was a full-page advertisement in the American entertainment magazine, *Variety*, offering US networks the chance to buy hit BBC programmes, including *Hancock's Half Hour*. Just when Hancock needed all the American exposure he could get the advert was scrapped and replaced by one in which he no longer featured.

Graham Stark had remained friends with Ray Galton since the demise of *Star Bill* and the pair frequently met for tea at The Buxton, a small actors' club off the Haymarket. Stark arrived one day to find the writer gloomy and upset, reading a copy of the *Evening Standard* containing an interview with Hancock in which he claimed he had gone as far as he could with the BBC and was moving to Independent Television. 'Christ,' said Galton. 'Why didn't he tell me?'

Hancock's twenty-one-year association with BBC radio and television was over. To its surprise the corporation was about to discover it had not only let its biggest comedy star slip through its fingers, but it had also lost control of the 'programme' which made him famous.

With Hancock's adventures on the front and back covers of the best-selling *Film Fun* magazine, it was inevitable a toy manufacturer should want to cash in on his popularity with younger readers by bringing out a *Hancock's Half Hour* board game. Chad Valley, the toy and game maker, had designed one the year before and approached Beryl Vertue at Associated London Scripts. The playing area of the game was a map of East Cheam, showing Hancock's regular haunts. Each player would choose a Tony Hancock token as his marker and the object of the game was to start at Hancock's House and return to Railway Cuttings via the pawnbroker's, barber's, laundry, Labour Exchange and town hall, losing as little money as possible to Sid James and his theatrical agency on the way. It was only when the game was launched on the 1960 Christmas market, and long after a deal had been struck, that the BBC became aware of its existence.

Leslie Page, as television establishment officer, found himself bombarded by internal memos demanding immediate legal action against Chad Valley, to recover what his superiors euphemistically described as the corporation's 'lost standing'. His replies were not hopeful:

> . . . I imagine that the title *Hancock's Half Hour* certainly belongs to Associated London Scripts, but the fact that it is the title of a B.B.C. programme (both on Sound Broadcasting and on Television) clearly gives the Corporation some rights in the matter and some entitlement to a publicity mention on the game itself, the ability to say whether the particular form of the game is or is not

likely to reflect adversely on the B.B.C. programme, and some royalty income from sales.

However, I suppose that this is yet another example of the Corporation learning about a game being manufactured after the event, and therefore we cannot hope for very much in the way of acknowledgement from Chad Valley ... I would have thought that it would be in Chad Valley's own interests to come to an amicable arrangement with the Corporation in this matter, in so far as they would no doubt wish to manufacture games in the future based on B.B.C. programmes.

In the five years since the first television *Half Hour*, Hancock had set and shattered records on both sides of the camera. He was the first person to be paid £1,000 for a single programme, initially with ITV and then the BBC. With overseas sales his earnings from a show never fell below £2,000. His ratings were even more staggering. At a time when BBC executives were happy if a light entertainment or comedy broadcast attracted twelve per cent of the nation's viewers, Hancock was regularly watched by 23 per cent of the adult population; at the end of 1959 this had risen to 27 per cent.

The corporation, however, was not finished with Hancock. There was, as far as the BBC was concerned, one piece of unfinished business – Hancock's drinking debt. During the recording of *Hancock*, its star had persuaded his BBC dressers to keep him supplied with alcohol. When the final show was recorded on 9 June, Hancock departed owing ten shillings on a bottle of brandy and thirty-seven-and-six for gin. An assistant at Television Centre wrote to Roger Hancock at Associated London Scripts asking for payment. The account was settled, plus a £6 tip for the dressing-room staff.

Alan Freeman had just finished watching *The Blood Donor* when the telephone rang. It was Les Cox, a producer with the Pye record company. 'What did you think of Hancock?' Cox asked.

'I thought it was one of the funniest things I've ever seen,' Freeman admitted. 'Let me talk to Tony.'

An hour later Freeman had tracked Hancock down to his Surrey home. When he explained he wanted to issue *The Blood Donor* on disc Hancock was dismissive. 'I'm not recording that,' he told Freeman. 'That's gone. Finished.'

'But Tony,' Freeman persisted, 'that was a classic piece of British comedy. It's got to go down for posterity.'

Hancock promised he would think about it, but Freeman knew he wouldn't. 'Tony just wasn't commercially minded,' Freeman recalled. 'I knew that if I left it up to him nothing would come together. I contacted Galton and Simpson and they agreed *The Blood Donor* would make a great record. Between us we finally got Tony to agree.'

Freeman had founded his own record label, Polygon, in the early 1950s where his first two signings were Petula Clark and Jimmy Young. In 1954, Polygon merged with Pye Records and Freeman was appointed an executive producer. With Pye's financial clout and reputation, it was easy for him to build a catalogue of comedy records. For copyright reasons, however, Pye's first two Hancock releases – *This is Hancock* and *Pieces of Hancock* – were little more than edited versions of radio *Half Hours*. This time, after three months of cajoling, Freeman had at last persuaded Hancock to rerecord two television scripts. To complement *The Blood Donor*, he chose *The Radio Ham*.

The Pye executive planned the recording session with equal care. Although he was in overall charge of the project, Freeman admitted he did not have enough studio production experience to do justice to either Hancock or the scripts. So, when he was asked who he wanted to take charge of the recordings, Hancock suggested the veteran BBC producer Leslie Bridgmont. It was Bridgmont who had given Hancock his first radio spot on the *Forces Programme* twenty years earlier.

Freeman, as executive producer, announced he wanted the entire production treated – and the finished product to sound – as if it were a radio or television show. The venue booked for the all-day Sunday session was the Star Sound Studio, just off Baker Street. 'It was a diabolical studio for music,' Freeman recalled several years later. 'For speech it was great, partly because it was built with the acoustics of a theatre and I wanted an audience. I would not record comedy without

an audience.' To complete the illusion, Freeman insisted that only BBC
sound engineers and technicians were hired, and that everyone should
have previously worked with Hancock on a *Half Hour* broadcast.

Hancock still saw his professional future very much as a partnership
with Galton and Simpson and could see no reason why their six-year
collaboration should not last at least a decade more. It was a view
shared by the writers. In an interview with the *Sunday Telegraph*
Hancock outlined his comedy vision:

> Alan Simpson and Ray Galton and myself, after six-years
> together are very close, both professionally and in every
> other way. We think the same about humour, we think the
> same about things we want to achieve. It does not absolutely
> bind us for ever, but we think in the same terms.
>
> We are going to do another four or five films with ABC,
> with whom we did *The Rebel*. That will be over four years.
> Then we hope to be able to put our own money into *Half
> Hour* TV films, or, eventually, bigger films of which we can
> own the negative. We feel that so much stuff we've done has
> gone into thin air. We still have the scripts but not the
> finished products.
>
> We haven't got the story for the next film yet, but as with
> the television series, we're moving away from plot – at least
> from plots that bind you down too much. We intend to have
> a story out of which emerge high spots of comedy, maybe
> for four or five minutes, to get them really rocking in the
> cinemas.

To Galton and Simpson the discussions on Hancock's next film
appeared to be long and, so far, fruitless. Within weeks of the
completion of *The Rebel*, the writers had moved into Hancock's
Blindley Heath home. Various ideas were discussed and rejected. One
involved the day-to-day domestic survival of a seaside Punch and Judy
man. It, too, was abandoned. Eventually, all three agreed on a plot.

Hancock would be the slothful and work-shy son of a supportive father; his three brothers all successful businessmen. When the patriarch dies, Hancock is forced to return to England and work for each of his brothers in turn, with disastrous results.

Galton and Simpson returned to their office and started work. They were about a third of the way into the script when Hancock telephoned. He feared the finished film would not be 'international enough'. The writers agreed to try again, and returned for another brain-storming session at MacConkeys.

This time Hancock would become a passenger on a cruise liner, and the locations would be as 'international' as the production money allowed. There was no fixed plot; Hancock would simply react to incidents and situations as they arose. Galton and Simpson had almost completed the script when Hancock rejected the idea. It was, he claimed, too similar to *Monsieur Hulot's Holiday*. 'We were terribly annoyed and upset,' Ray Galton admits. 'We put in a hell of a lot of work, and then he just turned round, without even reading the scripts, and said, "It's just not right. We can do better. We can get something to really knock their eyes out."'

A third weekend at Blindley Heath produced a working title and a storyline so simplified – so basic – Hancock 'really went overboard for the idea'. It would be called *The Day Off*. The plot involved nothing more than one man's mishaps away from work. Two months passed. Once again, Galton and Simpson had almost completed the first draft of the script when Hancock crustily informed them he had gone cold on the idea.

At the inevitable confrontation, Hancock appeared unconcerned the writers had spent six months writing without earning a penny. It was obvious he had not bothered to read a word of what they had written. More annoying was his apparent determination to press ahead with the idea they had initially rejected as unprofitable: Hancock was deter-mined to make *The Punch and Judy Man*, the story of a jaded seaside puppet artist who accepts life and marriage with the same submissive inevitability.

To Beryl Vertue, responsible as much to Galton and Simpson as

Hancock, it seemed he was constantly looking for excuses to reject the latest film script. 'He kept saying things to me like, "I'm sure I'm not going to like it." He seemed to have conditioned himself to rejecting it,' remembers Vertue.

Rightly or wrongly, Hancock had talked himself into believing Galton and Simpson were to blame for limiting his comedy horizons. The real confrontation, although Hancock never admitted it publicly, was that he felt the writers had failed to 'grow' with him, and showed every possibility of remaining confined by the breed of comedy they had created and dominated for so many years. 'Their language is colloquial and a lot of their situations are parochial,' Hancock told a close friend.

Beryl Vertue had also failed to appreciate the extent of Hancock's self-delusion over his next film, and the depths to which he would sink to bring it about. Unknown to anyone at Associated London Scripts, Hancock had approached, and agreed to work on the script with, another writer. They had, in fact, already started.

Late in October, Hancock telephoned Vertue asking her to arrange a meeting with Ray Galton and Alan Simpson. It would take place, he unilaterally informed her, this coming Sunday. When Vertue and the two writers arrived it was obvious Hancock wanted the meeting over as quickly as possible. He was blunt to the point of rudeness. 'I've decided I don't want to do any more programmes with you,' he informed Galton and Simpson.

Before anyone could speak he rounded on the agent: 'And because of your involvement with Ray and Alan, it would be too embarrassing for you to look after me. I don't want you to do that either.'

'We were all staggered,' recalls Vertue. 'It was the first time I personally had seen his ruthless quality. He had given no warning and made no apology. The boys had gone up there expecting him to criticise the film. I'd gone simply because he asked me. I felt desperately near to tears and the terrible shock of it made me feel ill for a week afterwards. He had already abandoned Sid James, and the way he did that was unhappy, but to abandon Alan and Ray . . . He could afford to abandon me because there are other good agents in London who could have looked after him, but I couldn't understand about Alan and Ray.

'They wrote for him so marvellously that when you heard the three of them talking together it was like a script in itself. They were him and he was them. They created this character between them. They observed him so closely, and he gave so much, that something marvellous came out of it. But it was much more than that. We were devoted to him and he dismissed the friendship of years in an effort to attain a height in his career which we could all have helped him achieve out of friendship and regard.'

Tony Hancock's seven-year partnership with Ray Galton and Alan Simpson was over. Even Sid James – still a friend, despite suffering the cutting edge of Hancock's ambition – failed to persuade him to reconsider. The BBC, sensing the destruction of a unique and prize-winning team, reopened negotiations with Roger Hancock, but it was soon obvious their one-time star was already out of reach; Roger Hancock would also be leaving Associated London Scripts, to manage his older brother's affairs.

Tom Sloan, head of light entertainment, reluctantly closed the door on the corporation's dealings with Hancock with an internal memo:

> His loss is to be greatly regretted, but one must remember he will be without his producer [Duncan Wood] and his scriptwriters [Galton and Simpson] – and Sidney James. The result could well be unfortunate.
>
> Hancock is a moody perfectionist with a great interest in money and no sense of loyalty to the Corporation.
>
> I am satisfied that we did everything possible to keep him within the fold but unless we were prepared to resign our production control and underwrite the project with something like £150,000 for 13 programmes and film them rather than telescreen them we could do no business.

The BBC still had one valuable asset it was determined 'to do business' with – the writing talent of Ray Galton and Alan Simpson. Both had wanted to write for Frankie Howerd, but Sloan suggested a series of ten separate television programmes under the umbrella title of *Comedy Playhouse*. The characters, situations and plots for the thirty-minute shows would be left entirely up to the writers. The fifth programme was called *The Offer* and featured father and son rag-and-bone men, Albert and Harold Steptoe. The follow-up series, *Steptoe and Son*, would run to fifty-seven editions and prove one of the biggest comedy hits of the 1960s and seventies.

The man Hancock elected to replace Galton and Simpson was poet, novelist and critic Philip Oakes. Hancock telephoned Oakes, who lived a few miles from MacConkeys, to explain he was no longer working with Galton and Simpson, and to ask if the writer would like to collaborate on a 'Chaplin-style' film. 'I've even got the title,' said Hancock. 'We'll call it *The Punch and Judy Man*.'

Oakes was one of the few film critics and modern writers Hancock respected. They had first met in 1957 when Oakes interviewed Hancock for *Books and Art* magazine. 'He is a highly disciplined, professional writer,' Hancock said of Oakes, whose recent novel, *The God Botherers*, the comedian never ceased to recommend. There was, according to Barry Took, an element of intellectual snobbery in his choice: 'Hancock felt the need to be near a man of such obviously distinguished intellectual and artistic qualifications, forgetting incidentally, that anyone writing for Hancock would think, if only unconsciously, in the style and manner of the Galton and Simpson radio and television scripts.'

For Hancock, at least, there was another advantage to collaborating with Oakes. As they lived only a few miles apart, Hancock could telephone or call on his partner whenever he felt the urge to work. It was, as Oakes would soon discover, a short-lived obsession.

The pair met and Hancock outlined his idea. The basic storyline, he told Oakes, was of a failing marriage, sinking into dangerous apathy. Hancock would play a *Punch and Judy man* in a suitably run-down seaside resort, where the town's progressive councillors were attempting to kill off the traditional forms of seafront entertainment. While Hancock conducts a lonely rearguard action against the snobbery of the town's mayor and sycophantic entertainment committee, his souvenir-shop-owning wife yearns for social acceptance. Although she is willing to sacrifice her husband's self-respect, the ever practical Hancock sees through his wife's gullibility and the film ends in hope for them both.

Hancock was adamant his next film should be shot in black and white. Justifying his decision he claimed: 'Colour slows down comedy. It is too peaceful. *The Rebel* had to be made in colour because of the paintings. Some films simply have to be in black and white.' He was gambling heavily on the public's perception of humour and, still more, on its acceptance of a 'new and honest Hancock'. We are trying to be accurate, explained Hancock, 'to make a film that is true, that is real, as against fiddling around with cartoon comedies. So that if an audience doesn't think life funny, it will not find the film funny and appreciate it.'

Although he never openly admitted it, much of the project's dry irony was inspired by the increasingly volatile and increasingly estranged state of his own marriage. Preliminary work on the script went well. Hancock had a clear vision of what the film – and his future comedy – should be. '*The Punch and Judy Man* is a cold, close look at the situation of marriage, which is pretty ghastly anyway,' Hancock admitted. 'There is no happy ending, only a faint hope. When marriage gets scratchy and when, after some years, you know the other's weaknesses, you also know how to go for them. This works for both sides. The experienced destroyer of individuals who happen to live together, that's really the theme. People keep up the illusion and know how hard to hit each other (in the subtlest possible way) and become expert in tearing each other apart.'

During the year Hancock attended film festivals in Karlovy Vary in Czechoslovakia and Beirut, yet his sights were focused on America and the October première of *The Rebel*. A trip to America would effectively put the emotional distance he needed between himself and his former writers, the very men whose work he was counting on to establish him as an international star.

There was another reason for Hancock's visit to the States. For some months he had been talking about using his name to raise the necessary funds to finance a London entertainment complex. It would, Hancock promised, provide 'popular entertainment at popular prices'. The development, the first of its kind in Britain, was to include a theatre, a cinema and an assortment of restaurants and bars. To experience his idea first-hand, Hancock flew direct to Las Vegas where he got drunk with Laurence Harvey and Ken Tynan.

Back in New York, the première was a disaster. Unknown to Hancock, the television networks were screening an American Civil War series, called *The Rebel*. Without consulting its star or producer, the film's US distributors renamed it *Call Me Genius*. Hancock arrived in New York to face the full fury of American hypocrisy; not only did the majority of east coast critics dislike the film, branding it 'too predictable, too slap-stick ... and too English', they also took exception to the 'pomposity of the title'. The fact that Hancock's fame was founded on the pretensions of a bombastic fool went unnoticed.

Blinkered by his conviction that the only true light of fame had its source in Hollywood, and that any cloud in New York was sure to cast its shadow over England, Hancock refused to return to London. Convinced he was about to face a mob of rabid British reporters, only too eager to resume the mauling he had received after ditching Sid James, Hancock sought refuge in a Paris hotel, not far from the Champs-Elysées. Here he took over three rooms – two as bedrooms and the third as an office complete with desk, typewriter and a stock of Pastis – and invited Oakes to join him and restart work on *The Punch and Judy Man*. 'There we were,' recalled Hancock, 'me and this suave, sophisticated journalist, and we wrote the title on a sheet of paper. Then, over a fortnight, we got down about twelve pages of script. They were awful, unusable.' By the end of the second week, both men were struck by an aching malaise. Hancock insisted it was food poisoning. Oakes knew full well it was alcohol poisoning.

Between Hancock's bouts of drinking and self-remorse, Oakes attempted to persuade him to concentrate on the script. 'It was a great experience, working with Tony,' Oakes recalls. 'Like surgery.' He soon gave up, however, and returned to his Surrey home. Hancock followed a few days later, bolstered by news of his first film's success in the far less influential cinemas of Canada. The Canadian Broadcasting Corporation had bought in a short run of *Half Hours* as a summer replacement for a television series which had failed to materialise, but when the CBC announced it would not be screening any more Hancock, it was bombarded with protests until it relented. So, a few months later, the renamed *Call Me Genius* was released north of the forty-ninth parallel and echoed its British success. A reviewer for the *Winnipeg Free Press* confidently announced: 'If you sit down and analyse this film you'll probably decide it's horrible rubbish. As pure, golden foolishness, however, it ranks as a sort of miracle. A Hancock tour de force.'

In 1961 André Deutsch published *Anthony Aloysius St John Hancock*. It was the first time any Galton and Simpson scripts had been available to the general public. The book, reissued a year later as a paperback, contained four complete television *Half Hour* scripts: *The Economy Drive* (first broadcast on 25 September, 1959); *The Train Journey* (23 October, 1959); *Mayday*, more popularly known as *The Radio Ham* (9 June, 1961), and *Going Down, or The Lift* (16 June, 1961).

The introduction to the paperback is worth reproducing in full, not only for its entertainment value, but also as yet another example of how Galton and Simpson were able to weave Hancock's real-life posturing into a piece of apparent fiction.

> The following dialogue took place three weeks before the publication of this book in the public bar of a hostelry favoured by rubber-backed carpet manufacturers, second-hand car dealers, bingo operators and other representatives of the nouvelle vague of Britain's impending economic recovery.

The time is ten minutes to three. Enter Tony Hancock, Ray Galton and Alan Simpson. They make their way across the floor, each showing great courtesy in allowing the other two to reach the bar first. Mr Hancock, being outmanoeuvred in a brilliant piece of positional play by the others, finds himself with his foot on the rail under the frosty eye of the barmaid.

Tony: (*pleasantly*) Good afternoon, madam.

Barmaid: (*unpleasantly*) Hurry up.

Tony: (*less pleasantly*) What are you going to have?

Ray: (*triumphantly*) A large Pernod.

Alan: (*rubbing it in*) Twice.

Tony: (*totting it up*) And a half of bitter.

Barmaid: (*unpleasantly*) Ten and six.

Tony feels in his pocket. A smile spreads across his face.

Tony: That's strange, I could have sworn ...

Alan: (*to barmaid, resignedly*) How much?

Barmaid: (*unpleasantly*) Ten and six.

Tony: No, no please, I insist. (*to Ray*) Lend me a quid.

Ray: All right then ... here you are.

Tony: Thanks. I'll buy the next round then. Oh ... just a minute.

Barmaid: (*unpleasantly*) What?

Tony: I don't think I'll have the half of bitter ... um ... a large brandy.

Alan: She's already poured the bitter.

Tony: Oh. Well, never mind. I'll use that as a chaser.
          You don't mind?

Alan: (*beaten*) No, no, of course not.

Barmaid: (*unpleasantly*) Another six shillings please.

Tony: Well ... good health.

Ray: Cheers.

Tony: (*placing an ill-fitting cashmered elbow into a
          puddle of lager and lime*) Well now, about this
          book.

Alan: Yes?

Tony: Well ... I'm not getting anything out of it, am
          I?

Ray: (*quickly*) Have another drink.

Tony: No, it's just that, well, I thought as I was in
          the shows originally, and well, you know
          they're using my pictures, and well, I just
          thought that perhaps ...

Alan: Ah well, yes, that's quite true, but they're only
          buying the copyright you see, the written
          word.

Tony: Oh quite, quite, I do see that. It's just that I
          will have another drink.

Ray: A large brandy and two halves of bitter, please,
          miss.

Tony: You do realise, it's not the money, it's just that
          ... well, I naturally thought that taking into

consideration my connection with the shows,
and all things being equal, by and large ...
well, it was my agent really, he thought that as
you were using my name and my photographs,
that taking things all round, in the final
analysis, so to speak ... he felt that I would be
entitled to at least ...

Alan: Have a cigar?

Tony: Oh, thank you. The ones in the metal tubes,
miss, yes one of those ...

Barmaid: (*unpleasantly*) Three?

Alan: One. And ten Barons, please.

Ray: Well, the fact is, Tone, old man, none of us are
likely to make a fortune out of it. I expect
we'll be lucky to get back what we've paid out
in drinks here ... (*laughs gaily*).

Tony: Well, exactly. That's just what I told my agent,
but he thought that if I was to share in the
loot, I would feel more sort of ... connected
with it.

Ray: Well, I don't know, I mean you can't really
assess just exactly how much it will be worth
to you ... I mean money isn't everything.
There's all that free publicity, pictures all over
the bookshops ... newspapers ...

Tony: Quite, quite. (*pause*) But how much money do
you think you're going to get out of it?

Alan: Money? Oh, nothing much ... chicken-feed, a
few bob here and there, cigarette money. It

341

> wouldn't even be worth bothering your
> accountant with.

Ray: It's just nice to see the scripts in print. Prestige
... up on the bookshelf at home, you know.
Makes you feel more literary.

Tony: Hmmm. How much is it selling for?

Alan: Two and six, I think... It's a paperback.

Tony: Two and six. How much are they paying you
in advance royalties?

Ray: Have another drink?

Tony: Oh, thanks. Two and six a copy. Let's see, say
fifty thousand ... and you'll be on a percentage
... at two and six, that's ... two fifties are a
hundred, six fifties are ... no, wait a minute,
five sixes are ... no, hang on...

Ray and Alan move off left and converse animatedly in whispers.
They return to the bar.

Ray: Look, I'll tell you what we'll do. We've had a
chat, and while we do not agree with your
agent –

Alan: We are prepared, under the special
circumstances –

Ray: Though admitting no liability... Taking into
consideration the effect your enormous personal
popularity will have on sales of the book –

Alan: And bearing in mind the value of your name
and how closely – no, inextricably – you are
connected with the manuscripts concerned –

Ray: (*furtively*) We are prepared to offer you, in
         your back pocket, in ones, a lump sum, no
         questions asked, no income tax, it won't go
         through your accounts ... in cash, a settlement
         in lieu of your interests.

Tony: How much?

Ray: Thirty bob.

Tony: Two quid.

Ray: It's a deal.

Tony: There you are, I knew we wouldn't fall out
         over money. The best of luck with the books
         then, lads.

Alan: Thank you very much.

Tony: Have you got the old, er ... you know ...
         have you got it on you?

Alan: Oh, I'm sorry. A quid each. Do you mind
         silver?

Tony: No, no.

Money changes hands.

Tony: (*enthusiastically*) Well then, I think it's my turn
         to buy the drinks. Drink up.

Barmaid: (*pleasantly*) Time, gentlemen, please. No more
         orders.

Tony: Oh, what a shame. Never mind, next time.
         Cheerio then.

Galton
and
Simpson: Cheerio.

*

The script of Hancock's second film was slowly – very slowly – taking shape. He and Oakes would meet and work and drink. 'Sometimes it's very exciting, other times it's as dull as hell. When I'm not working I fret. I read – anything,' Hancock observed. 'The tiring bit is doing nothing. Observation and resilience are most important. The boring bit is hanging around, scripting, throwing away and throwing away all the time until the actual performance.'

When inspiration evaporated, the pair would escape to London Zoo or the theatre. For ten minutes at a time Hancock would stand in front of the heavy, black-painted bars incarcerating a huge ape, called Guy the Gorilla. Staring in silence at the creature, he saw its existence as a reflection of his own life: an animal – its intellect and potential untested – caged behind bars of his own making.

One evening Freddie and Philip Oakes suggested they all go to the Queen's Theatre to see the ground-breaking musical *Stop The World – I Want To Get Off*. Anthony Newley, who co-wrote the production with Leslie Bricusse, played the clown-philosopher Littlechap. Hancock eventually sat through the show five times; each time Newley sang *What Kind of Fool Am I?* Hancock wept.

1962

HANCOCK LED THE young woman away from the cameras and sound equipment and paraphernalia of the Elstree film set. As they sat on boxes in a dark corner, he settled into a long and uncomfortable silence.

'It's doomed,' Hancock eventually said, wringing his hands. 'It's Punch, he won't let it happen.'

Filming for *The Punch and Judy Man* had started on 2 April after three weeks of rehearsals the previous month. In the intervening weeks, Hancock was introduced to Pat Williams, an author who specialised in the occult and the supernatural. It was a subject which intrigued and intimidated him, and Williams – no relation to Kenneth Williams – was invited back to MacConkeys. Hancock and Cicely were drinking heavily, as was everyone else. The writer took Hancock's hand and started to read his palm. 'No you don't,' he said, snatching his hand away.

'Why?' asked Williams.

'I don't want to know,' said Hancock, obviously uneasy. 'All this is much closer to me than you realise and I'm scared – I hate it.'

Hancock was, Williams soon discovered, a 'deeply superstitious man who was not only afraid of almost everything he could not under-stand, but a man who deliberately sought out and blamed his worst nightmares': a phasmophobic mesmerised by his own fear. 'He knew he was destroying himself,' she said. 'He knew he was being stupid about his friends. He knew that all this information about himself was just behind a thin partition in his mind and didn't want to know.'

Hancock saw in Williams someone with the ability to translate his own intuition, his own sensitivities: 'and he wanted none of it. He was desperate to keep the future at arm's length.'

To Hancock, disaster was a physical entity: something which could be seen and identified but, in his own mind at least, never avoided. He would look into the sky and recognise malevolence in the shape of clouds, the way a child might imagine it sees a horse or a flower. Hancock's fear – a real fear – extended to colours. He once bought Cicely, who was part Irish, an emerald ring. After one or two minor mishaps he saw the ring as a gem of ill-fortune and threw it away. Events contrived to support his theory. On tour he was doing his Quasimodo impression, when someone had the idea of spotting him with a green light. The laughter instantly died. 'Hello,' said Hancock, ad-libbing, 'they must have put a mouldy penny in the meter.' The white light returned, but not the laughter.

Since Lily Sennett's conversion to spiritualism, mother and son would talk – and frequently argue – about reincarnation and the afterlife. Lily was convinced she had made 'contact' with Colin, her long-dead eldest son, and Hancock never contradicted her. He, too, had developed a nagging belief in ghosts; and if not ghosts, then the power of the dead to inhabit and manipulate physical objects.

While filming *The Punch and Judy Man*, Hancock was given a 'slinky', a child's toy made from coiled steel which, by the pull of gravity, flip-flopped its way down stairs or slopes. To Hancock the innocuous steel spiral was possessed. In a frenzy of fear and hatred he hurled it against walls and jumped up and down on the innocent toy in an attempt to bend it out of shape. Nothing would destroy it. Late one night, Hancock took a shovel to the beach, waited until the tide was out, and buried the 'evil thing' six foot under the sand.

Hancock frequently claimed he could 'sense' a person's attitude towards him simply by shaking hands. He could, in some circumstances he told Williams, intuit a person's wellbeing. 'Tony was,' Williams later admitted, 'almost mediumistic – and he didn't like it. It frightened him.'

During the pre-filming rehearsals, Hancock was also introduced to Joe Hastings, a professional Punch and Judy man. It was Hastings' job to teach Hancock how to operate the puppets and to use a 'swozzle', the small metal gadget held in the roof of the mouth to produce the Punch voice. Hastings was a small, slick-haired, chain-smoking man whose appearance and growling cough horrified the film's star and co-writer. He had heard a cough like that once before; it was the cough of a man dying of lung cancer.

Punch – the evil genius of Hancock's childhood nightmares – was already destroying his film and those associated with it.

Publicly at least, the film had an auspicious launch. Late in January, 1962, Associated British Elstree Studios issued a press release headed: 'Hancock Forms Production Company'.

Tony Hancock today announced the formation of his own production company, which will be responsible for producing a minimum of four films in association with Associated British Picture Corporation. The deal that was signed over the weekend by Hancock and J. R. Wallis, on behalf of A.B.P.C., supersedes his previous contract with the corporation, under which he was committed to make several films for the studios on a starring-only basis.

The upbeat statement – which claimed Hancock's previous film, *The Rebel*, had set a release record for Associated British cinemas in London – also announced that negotiations had opened with a 'well-known' actress to play the female lead. The actress in question was a young star called Billie Whitelaw, but when executives at Associated British discovered Whitelaw was already booked for another film, they suggested Sylvia Syms.

Hancock's eight-month absence from the country's television screens was taking its toll. His status as Britain's highest-paid television comedian had been lost to his friend Eric Sykes, who was also named Light Entertainment Artist of the Year, and, after so many years putting Hancock at the top, readers of the *Daily Mirror* now voted Charlie Drake their favourite comedian.

Hancock was uncharacteristically resigned to his slip in popularity. The BBC, like its former star, had set its sights on America and persuaded a coast-to-coast network to schedule an hour-long showcase for three British comedians, including Hancock, called *International Show Time*. To be broadcast during peak viewing hours, the programme would include extracts from Hancock's *The Blood Donor*, *Sykes and a Bath* and a sequence from Benny Hill in which he conducts an inquiry into television.

One night in February, Hancock took his lover to see *The Private Ear and The Public Eye* at London's Globe Theatre. Its stars were Maggie Smith and Kenneth Williams. After the performance Hancock went back stage to the actress's dressing room and, while all three were chatting, Kenneth Williams walked in.

Hancock, who had quite obviously been drinking, for some reason seemed preoccupied with the 'power of evil' in the world. Turning to Williams, he suggested they should once again work together. 'Not all that old trick stuff we were doing, but something good,' Hancock told him. 'I don't know what you thought about all those things we used to do on sound, but to me they were cardboard, the characters were cardboard. I want to get to grips with the real thing, just keep a camera on a man's face for ten minutes if necessary, because that's what life is.'

It was, for Kenneth Williams, quite literally the termination of his relationship with Hancock. 'This is the dead end for him and me. There were not any tricks in it for me. All the tricks were by him. This is what he will never see. This is the tragedy of the actor *manqué* every single time.'

The Punch and Judy Man script was finished early in 1962, and Hancock wrote to Sir Arthur Bliss[7], the 71-year-old Master of the Queen's Musik, inviting the composer to write the film score. Bliss replied with a flattering letter, but regretted he was too old. The comedian kept the folded letter in his wallet until the day he died.

Hancock's second choice was Derek Scott. Fourteen years after their 'Derek Scott and Hank' appearances at the Windmill, the pair were still friends who met occasionally or talked on the telephone about cricket. Scott agreed to compose *The Punch and Judy Man* music and arrived at MacConkeys one Friday to discuss the project and make notes. Having consumed the best part of a bottle of vodka into the small hours, the pair went to bed. Scott, who was due to rehearse at the London Palladium that morning at nine, asked to be woken in time to catch the London train. Shortly after seven Hancock shook him awake – and placed a pint glass of beer on the bedside table.

Associated British began to express doubts over the script. Hancock and Oakes defended its dry, pessimistic view of marriage, but conceded the final scenes were 'too narrow'. Numerous alterations were drafted and rejected, some not far removed from silent-movie slapstick. Oakes was experiencing first hand Hancock's subconscious single-shot philosophy of performance. 'We overhauled the script again and again,' Oakes says in his book, *The Entertainers – Tony Hancock*. 'The fault, as far as we could tell, was not in the lines. The situations, especially those worked out by Hancock, had great potential. When he described them, when he acted them out, his audience would fall about with laughter. But in front of the camera the comedy died.' In the end it was decided to shoot the script as originally written.

The script contains several Chaplinesque mime scenes, most invented and developed by Hancock, which presented unique problems for the props department. In the opening sequence – played with sparse dialogue – Wally Pinner (Hancock) and his wife Delia (Sylvia Syms) demonstrate the silent bitterness of a foundering marriage. Wally descends from the couple's flat above his wife's souvenir shop. He picks up a bunch of flowers and a china pig. The first draft sees Pinner ram the flowers into the pig's snout. 'It's not strong enough,' protested Hancock. 'They have to go up its arse.' Despite a month-long search, no china pig could be found with a suitably large orifice. In the end a made-to-measure pig was ordered by the studio.

Hancock's ego and self-confidence demanded he be surrounded by friendly and suitably respectful faces, including Hugh Lloyd and Mario Fabrizi. Another was John le Mesurier, recovering from a stomach operation and coming to terms with the end of his marriage to Hattie Jacques.

Few actors enjoyed working at Elstree. Associated British Pictures kept a tight rein on its production staff and, more seriously, on its actors. The studio managers were instructed to keep a 'black book' and record details of set arrival times and the number of takes each actor or actress required to complete a scene. Staff on the gate contributed by noting exactly who went across the road to the Red Lion public house for a lunchtime drink and what time they returned. It was a 'big brother' intrusion which made the cast suspicious and stifled their performances. 'I loathed the place,' commented le Mesurier. 'This really was the last sort of place for Tony to work in.'

To give Hancock behind-the-camera veto, it was agreed Jeremy Summers should direct, with his star doubling as 'associate director'. Rising from studio tea-boy, Summers had worked extensively in television and made several second-feature films. The pair discussed the project at a pre-rehearsal meeting and Hancock found the 30-year-old a 'man of extreme sensitivity'. Summers saw the film as his 'big chance – if anyone thinks *The Punch and Judy Man* is an extension of *Hancock's Half Hour*, he is in for a shock. This film adds a new dimension to Hancock's versatility which, I think, his public will be quick to appreciate.'

To John le Mesurier, who had worked with Hancock under the strong directorship of Duncan Wood, the film's director was 'charming, inventive, technically sound, but had no idea how to deal' with his star. Summers' main problem, however, was once again the Elstree front office. 'He was constantly being pestered and badgered as to what was going on and never left to get on with his job,' adds le Mesurier.

Each night Hancock, Summers and Philip Oakes would sit in the studio screening room and watch the rushes with growing despair. During the day the French photographer, Henri Cartier-Bresson, followed Hancock's antics through his viewfinder with a similar feeling of desperation. 'Each day was an agony, for me as a photographer and for Hancock as a comedy actor,' said Cartier-Bresson. 'What I was seeing was not the Hancock the world loved.' His plan to record the making of the entire film was abandoned.

Even with his attention focused on *The Punch and Judy Man*, Hancock could not summon enough discipline to curb his drinking. His befuddled arrival on set held up shooting and drove the film off schedule and over budget from the start. Angry clashes with the producer, Gordon L. T. Scott, wasted more time, and the film's publicity man resigned after Hancock rounded on one television interviewer – 'Look at the length of your fingernails, you've got to be homosexual.'

Once or twice a week, Cicely would arrive at the Hertfordshire studios intent, it seemed to the cast and crew, on continuing the quarrel she and Hancock had started the previous night. At best the noisy and bitter rows were confined to Hancock's dressing room. At worst they spilled over on to the studio floor and, on more than one occasion, ended in physical violence.

Hancock felt isolated and lonely and under siege. To make matters worse he had also quarrelled with Freddie Ross. Late one afternoon, he made a fumbled pass at his co-star when the pair were sitting in Sylvia Syms's dressing room. 'Do you fancy me, Sylv?' Hancock asked.

'I love you, you're gorgeous,' Syms naïvely replied, 'a lovely feller.' Hancock gave a quizzical smile and then said: 'I don't half fancy you – what about it?'

It suddenly struck Syms that Hancock was deadly serious. 'No thanks,' she said. 'I like you very dearly, but I am very happily married and I'm also pregnant and I do so hate complications.'

'You're awfully square you know,' said Hancock, giggling nervously. 'You really are a dreary bitch, but lovely.'

'I suddenly realised that he wanted more than a motherly cuddle,' she recalls. 'But I would have been no use to him at all because he frightened me. He was never violent when I was there, but I'm afraid of people when they're drunk.'

One feature writer visiting Hancock's Elstree dressing room commented on his tape recorder. Hancock fudged an explanation. He used the machine, he said, for 'experimenting and working out comedy routines . . . a lot of what goes on the tape is the most awful bosh, but a few good ideas emerge which make it worth while'.

In reality, Hancock was still using the machine he had bought in 1956 as a mechanical prompt, laboriously reading everyone else's words on to the tape and leaving gaps long enough for him to deliver his own lines. The long after-hours sessions inevitably became a haze of frustration; as always, Hancock turned to alcohol. The more he drank, the harder it became to concentrate. By the first studio call the next morning, his memory was as empty as his dressing-room brandy bottle. 'Champagne is safe, sherry is the halfway house and brandy is the end of the road – a touch of the infuriator,' he would jokingly inform Syms.

One problem still remained. With the three weeks of interior shooting at Elstree almost over, Hancock had still not cast the part of Peter, a small boy destined to become *The Punch and Judy Man*'s tormentor.

Hancock, as ever, knew exactly the kind of child he wanted for the part; his vision of the character demanded a true Hancock alter ego, a mirror image, not only of the man, but a reflection of Hancock the confused and lonely child.

Sylvia Syms suggested her nephew Nicholas Webb. When the seven-year-old arrived at Elstree, he politely shook hands with Hancock and remained blankly unimpressed. 'Nick had never been in a film studio and didn't know anything at all about famous people,' explains Syms.

As Hancock walked away to brief the crew for the film test, Webb – who bore a striking resemblance to the young Hancock – turned and said: 'Well, I don't know Aunty Sylv, he didn't make me laugh.'

'That's the child I want,' Hancock announced, abandoning the audition.

There was an immediate affinity between the boy and the man thirty years his senior. When they were not needed on the studio floor, the pair would play endless rounds of Flounder in Hancock's dressing room. One member of the crew, sent to quell the noise, found Hancock and his youngest cast member on the floor in near-hysterics, kicking their legs in the air. When the filming was over, Hancock presented Webb with an expensive and elaborate chess set.

The schoolboy took it upon himself not only to learn his own part, but Hancock's as well. Whenever the comedian hesitated during filming, no matter how intentionally, Webb would whisper a prompt. 'Do you mind, Nick,' Hancock would gently chastise. 'I am allowed to pause, you know.'

In one scene, Wally Pinner and Peter are trapped by a torrential rain storm and together take refuge in an ice-cream parlour. Wally offers to buy an ice cream and the boy promptly chooses a cream- and cherry-topped Piltdown Glory. When it arrives, Wally orders one for himself. In total silence he matches the boy spoon for spoon until, in final triumph, he flips the cherry into the air and catches it in his mouth.

The scene was originally written to last no more than ninety seconds. Hancock, aware of its silent potential, developed it until it extended for more than eight minutes. Ultimately it is one of the film's funniest sequences, but not for Hancock, who had a lifelong loathing for ice cream. After each take he washed his mouth out – with vodka.

At the end of April the cast and crew transferred to Bognor Regis, where Hancock had spent the 1949 summer season in *Flotsam's Follies*. The script demanded a pier and Hancock had wanted to use Bournemouth but, when civic permission was refused, it was decided to use the Sussex resort.

The film's underlying gloom went with them. Bognor, recalled le Mesurier, was pretty much a disaster area: 'The trippers had stayed away in swarms that year and the few brave regulars, who could not quite bear to break the habit of a lifetime, sat about in sad, usually damp, little groups reflecting on the irony of paying for a holiday that was best calculated to bring on a fit of depression.'

For Hancock and John le Mesurier there was a brief comic interlude when the pair were 'arrested' by Butlin's security guards. The holiday compound, on the outskirts of the town, was surrounded by high wire fences and run 'like a better class of concentration camp'. Hancock had agreed to present the prizes for a fancy dress competition and, even more reluctantly, temporarily to leave the bar and the free drinks. The contest was won by a giggly young woman dressed as a duck. Hancock kissed her on the beak and fled. As he and le Mesurier were approaching the main gate, they were pounced on by a uniformed patrol and marched to the guard house. No one recognised them. After several ungracious telephone calls the pair were informed: 'Okay, you can go.'

The final sequence of the film starts with a celebrity guest, played by Barbara Murray, switching on the seaside illuminations from the town hall balcony, as the mayor and his party are barracked by the impatient crowd. The night before the scene was due to be shot, Hancock decided he wanted to offer the part of a front-row heckler to his friend George Fairweather.

The next day, and with less than twelve hours' notice, Fairweather set off on his motorcycle to ride the seventy miles to Bognor. When he arrived at Hancock's hotel, he was informed the cast and crew were filming on the seafront. Fairweather's four-line scene was scheduled for eight o'clock that evening. It was midnight before the pair settled down for a chat in Hancock's room.

Fairweather, who had not eaten since breakfast, asked if he should order some food. 'I'm not hungry,' said Hancock, pouring the remains of one vodka bottle into a glass and opening a new one. Picking up the telephone, Fairweather informed room service: 'Mr Hancock would like a large pot of coffee and some sandwiches.'

'Tony,' he recalls, 'had been drinking all day. When the food arrived I took the bottle away from him and hid it in my bedside cabinet. It was a lot harder to get him to eat something.'

Fairweather awoke the next morning to see Hancock's hand emerge from under his bedclothes, open the cabinet and lift out the near-full vodka bottle. 'Put that back,' ordered Fairweather. A string of muffled obscenities punctuated Hancock's claim that he could not 'stomach the day' without a drink. When breakfast arrived at seven o'clock, he reluctantly took some toast and black coffee.

'How do you feel?' asked his friend.

'Funnily enough,' admitted Hancock, 'I feel great.'

'That's what it's all about,' added Fairweather.

'What I really need,' admitted Hancock, 'is someone like you to keep me off the bottle.'

Fairweather was getting dressed. 'If you pay me fifty quid a week and give me a couple of lines each week I'll look after you,' he said. 'I'd keep you off the drink all right.'

By now Hancock was getting enthusiastic and insisted on shaking hands on the deal. It was, he kept telling his friend, 'a new start . . . a good start'. A week later, and back in Bournemouth, Fairweather had still not heard from Hancock.

It soon became obvious, even to its creator and star, that *The Punch and Judy Man* was plummeting to disaster. 'I would have liked to quit the film in the middle,' Hancock later confessed to Sid James, 'but by then we'd gone too far and I had to finish it.' When it was completed he said: 'I just wanted to go away and dig ditches or something; anything; go to France; be a beachcomber; anything to get away from it.'

Channel storms battered the south coast and the final days of filming were dogged by bad weather. Hancock stood on the seafront at Bognor as lightning hissed and crackled overhead. The rain dribbled down his face and soaked his clothes. Turning his face skyward he shouted: 'Go on, make it worse.' To the end, Hancock blamed the film's misfortune on the brooding spitefulness of Mr Punch.

For Philip Oakes – as for everyone concerned – it was a gruesome experience. He admitted, 'The real reasons for the disaster were manifold: a script, mine, which needed more jokes; an inexperienced director who allowed Tony to bully him, and serious treachery on the part of ABC who screwed up the distribution and withdrew moral support at a crucial time. Worst of all was Tony's own state of mind. His marriage was falling violently apart and his drinking was out of control. As a reaction comic he absorbed so much vodka and brandy that his wonderfully mobile face turned to wood.'

Sylvia Syms blames Hancock's irrational perfectionism. 'One of the saddest things I can remember of the film is that he would tell me the lovely things he was going to do in a scene and make me hysterical with laughter. The way he described it was so funny. When we moved to the set we would get it exactly right for the first take and then Tony would insist on going on and on until he hammered the idea into the ground.' Hancock's true talent, she maintains, would have been as a director: 'His way of explaining an idea was brilliant, if only he could leave the actors and actresses to work the magic.'

Charlie Chaplin had, by now, been elevated far beyond Hancock's transatlantic mentor. Chaplin the perfectionist film maker – unlike Chaplin the comic character – had become an obsession. It was an obsession which blinded Hancock's far-sight of reality and blunted his instinctive grasp of comedy and how he could best deliver it. 'Chaplin's scenes were shot over and over and over again until they were perfect,' explained Roger Wilmut, in his book *Tony Hancock 'Artiste'*. 'Hours and hours of rehearsal would go into getting the timing perfect to the split second before shooting even started. Chaplin and his actors raised their performances to an incredible pitch of perfection by this technique. Hancock always gave his best performance on the first try, and subsequent repetition only resulted in deterioration ... the result was that the takes which he finally accepted were usually nowhere near as good as the first takes.'

Attempting to explain Hancock's behaviour is an occupation fraught with its own hazards. As Freddie Ross and David Nathan say in their book, *Hancock*: 'From the moment the perfection of the creation was achieved the clown struggled to free himself from it. It was like watching a man trying to lose his own shadow.'

Hancock had won his 'biggest battle to do comedy in close-up' on television, but the lingering silences and facial torture did not transfer so easily to the cinema screen. In his book, *The Life and Death of Peter Sellers*, Roger Lewis comes closest to the truth when he says: 'Hancock's moroseness was the very content of his humour – a humour based on the boredom and exasperation of a man who hated being ordinary ... Hancock's success lay in his television self having absolutely no sense of humour. He blusters too much. His Homburg-hatted grouch was funny to the viewer because he was so literal. He had no idea how to be creative, though he thinks he has.'

Lewis continues: 'Where the television camera could linger on his Eeyore-looks for 30 minutes and it could still be tolerable, Hancock's dyspepsia and dismay, prolonged to feature-film length, were a torment. What made him a star on the box denied him popularity in the movies – just as the moodiness and ennui which was comic in his work was tragic when it seeped into his private life.' Hancock did not possess a television talent, it possessed him. 'He was made for TV. The black and white gloom and blurry tuning were apt, too, for the mood – Hancock's old programmes appear made in the midst of foul weather, which emanated (like the fireballs and storms in Romantic literature) from somewhere toxic inside him.'

It was not as simple as that, however. Once Hancock had discovered the winning formula – and he despised formula comedy – he sought to change it. It was as if by some mysterious alchemy he had chanced upon his own success, and then obsessively attempted to break it down into its base elements; to dissect and examine every move and its motive until he could no longer reassemble or even recognise his own individual talent.

'It's a problem for every artist,' explains Sean Kenny, the stage designer who became a close friend. 'Once you are accepted you are finished really because it is very difficult to explore any more. Tony wanted to take a chance but the more he took a chance the more they laughed and the funnier he became. He was stuck, caught in the net of the clown. The sadder his face, the more people laughed. He couldn't get out of it. He wanted to become a serious artist. He was very talented. He could sketch very well, draw cartoons – fantastic cartoons – of people. His hands were good, he could dance well and he had a musical ear. He was an all-round artist in a sense, but he had this bloody clown face and they kept laughing at him. All he had to do was put his coat on and everyone would break out laughing. He was caught as a clown and he couldn't get out of it and this was what was frustrating him.'

Arguably, Hancock owed his popular success to the genius of his writers. The gullible, pompous, ever-hopeful character Galton and Simpson created was the public face of Hancock, the face on which – as far as his fans were concerned – Hancock's success was founded. When he turned his face away; when he sought to improve his comedy in another direction; when the wind changed; he discovered he was stuck with a monster of his own making.

Hancock reasoned that what the public saw on its television and cinema screens should be the real Hancock – the naked Hancock. He believed the public, having adopted the comic Hancock, would readily accept the angst-ridden human Hancock with all his frailties and failings. He was wrong. Over the next five years, as the alcoholism and depression took hold and the press took an interest, the public was at first fascinated and then disgusted by what it saw.

Hancock's private life would grow so grotesque and threatening it would ultimately push him over the edge. For many years the tenderness – the fond memory – remained, until Hancock's ruthless-ness had first hacked away his personal friends and then laid waste his baffled public. 'Occasionally comedians become so personally obnox-ious that no one will employ them, and deprived of the oxygen of exposure their comic flair dies and they become forgotten,' Barry Took once wrote of his friend. 'The awful truth about comedians is that the public only want them to be funny. They don't want philosophers or pundits or politicians they just want a man to tell them something that will make them laugh.'

Under Freddie Ross's guidance, Hancock attempted to use the press as a buffer between his increasingly turbulent private life and the wreckage of his marriage. In the summer of 1962, with *The Punch and Judy Man* about to be released, he agreed to a second *Face to Face* type of interview, this time for *Woman's Mirror* magazine.

It was a poor reflection of John Freeman's original confrontation two years earlier. Ray Nunn met Hancock, who was wearing 'a rust-brown jacket, baggy slacks and suede shoes', at Freddie's Dorset Square flat. 'He paces the carpet twice, then sits down nervously and removes his shoes without untying the laces,' noted Nunn.

Much of the interview repeats the Hancock myth. One or two questions probe – occasionally prick – Hancock's private life and thoughts:

Nunn: Why are you sitting there with your shoes off?

Hancock: Because it relaxes me. I always do it.

Nunn: Some people say you are careful about money. True or false?

Hancock: I have been careful, but now I'm not particularly interested in money – except that it enables me to do what I want.

Nunn: We have now reached the point where we will turn off the smiles, get serious, and show how

very different the real Tony Hancock is from
the comic everyone knows.

Hancock: I'm a difficult person to get to know.

Nunn: Is there another side to you that most people
don't know?

Hancock: How do you manage to light your pipe
without burning your fingers? You keep
burning the matches right down. I've been
watching you closely. How do you do it?

Nunn: You're very observant. This is the kind of
incident you'll remember and put into one of
your comedies: you usually do. But don't
change the subject.

   The Hancock of films and TV enjoys talking
about his imaginary conquests, and how well he
thinks he gets along with the ladies. Do you
think you have sex appeal?

Hancock: How the hell should I know? I get plenty of
letters from women, but I have never got
around to finding out how old they are – they
never tell you.

Nunn: Shall I now start probing a bit deeper?

Hancock: You know I never talk about my private life.
What goes on behind my front door is my
secret.

Nunn: Yes, and you've stuck to it all through your
career. Why?

Hancock: Because it would embarrass me to talk about it.
It's too intimate. And I don't like being
photographed in an apron at the kitchen sink,
helping to wash up. I feel it's private.

Nunn: If your career is the most important thing in your life, how much time do you spend at home?

Hancock: Quite a lot really – I go for concentrated lumps of work and then long rests at home.

Nunn: Do you know whether you believe in the perfect marriage?

Hancock: Yes, I think it exists. I think a marriage can go on getting better and better. I think that one woman can be everything to a man. And when marriages fail, the blame is about fifty-fifty. I'm sure that's true of the majority of broken marriages.

Nunn: I think we have the real Hancock in focus now. He seems to be quite different from his film and TV image. Tell me, your father died when you were 12. Do you think this had a lasting effect on your personality?

Hancock: I prefer not to answer that.

Nunn: What do you hate most of all?

Hancock: Any form of cruelty.

Nunn: Well, you are famous and rich, too. Have you ever wanted to be a father?

Hancock: That's a very personal question. I'd rather not answer.

Nunn: All right, but I've noticed that many men seem to want to leave something behind them when they die. Do you follow me?

Hancock: To look for immortality? Yes, I suppose almost
everybody does, and the average person leaves
children. But I see myself as a small speck on
this spinning world.
   Who cares what I leave behind? Life for me
never gets anything less than more interesting
as every day passes. That is all I care about.

*

The BBC was still receiving a stream of letters from angry and
frustrated *Half Hour* fans. 'They clamoured for Tony and Sid to get
back together,' said Valerie James. 'What they had was something
unique and the public loved them.'

Sid James was missing Hancock more than he would have imagined
or admitted. 'Sid never wanted to be a star on his own,' recalled Val
James. 'He was content to share the limelight.' Although his new
television series *Citizen James* was a hit with the public, James had so
far failed to find the 'spark of magic' he had relished in *Hancock's Half
Hour*. Around his west London home he talked of little else.

Val James wanted the matter resolved as quickly as possible and
persuaded her husband to confront the *Half Hour* star head on. With
Hancock and Cicely on holiday in Antibes that meant an evening
flight to France.

When they arrived, Hancock was tanned and relaxed and eager to
talk about new projects, so, late one night, after Cicely and Valerie had
gone to bed, James suggested it was time the two men should once
again work together. To the South African's surprise Hancock readily
agreed. Knowing how much Hancock's consumption of alcohol
affected his judgment – and memory – James waited for the morning.
This time Hancock brought the subject up; what about a new series or
possibly a show? 'We came away very happy,' said Val James. 'Tony,
for all he had said in the past, was equally keen on them starting again.'

Two weeks later a short, hand-written note arrived. It was from
Hancock. He had changed his mind. He did not want to restart the
partnership – and that, he cruelly told James, 'is my final word on the
subject'.

The BBC fared little better. One project involved a play by N. F. Simpson entitled *The Form*, and Hancock was offered the lead. His refusal was 'polite but pompous', recalls one corporation executive. 'He did not even want to discuss it.' Another internal memo suggested asking Hancock to play Jack Point in a television adaptation of *The Yeoman of the Guard*. Scribbled across the bottom of an archive copy of the memo is the comment: 'Hancock has made it clear he never again wishes to work for the BBC.'

The head of MacConkey Productions attempted to escape the partly-imagined problems of his latest film – and the all too real disaster of his marriage – by immersing himself in a new television series. After years of attempting to lure Hancock away from the BBC, and back to the independent network, the bosses at Associated Television now found themselves with an enthusiastic and eager star. Hancock had approached Bernard Delfont with the idea, who then sold the series as a package to Lew Grade at ATV. Hancock's demand for full 'producer' control was a small concession for a prestige comedy.

The thirteen-show series, with its *Hancock* title poached from the BBC, was tentatively scheduled for the first week of the New Year, with filming under way by November. Although he had retained Philip Oakes as script editor, by the conclusion of *The Punch and Judy Man* Hancock had still not commissioned any scripts. His instinct was to approach Ray Galton and Alan Simpson, who were still smarting at the treatment of their film script.

The writers were, by now, committed to *Steptoe and Son*. 'For the first time in our career, we had become identified as ourselves,' they said. 'Before that we had been known as Hancock's scriptwriters. The success of *Steptoe* convinced us that we didn't want to write for comics as such any more; that it was much better to write for straight actors. So we probably wouldn't have done it even if we could.'

Hancock's next choice was Godfrey Harrison, the writer of his *Kaleidoscope 'Fools Rush In'* sketches. Harrison's reputation for well-crafted scripts was almost outweighed by his eccentric and erratic production methods. In 1953 he had created *A Life of Bliss* for David Tomlinson. The actor was replaced, less than two months later, by George Cole who kept the role on and off for the next sixteen years. In January, 1960, the show had moved to television, where Harrison was both writer and co-producer. Hancock not only admired Harrison's work, but was fascinated by the hair-raising and hilarious stories which trailed in his wake. On more than one occasion during the *Life of Bliss* radio run, Cole and the rest of the cast arrived for the Sunday afternoon recording to find Harrison had completed just five pages of the script – and was still typing.

Philip Oakes had agreed to act as script adviser for the new Independent Television series, but, to his frustration, Hancock began unilaterally commissioning scripts. When Oakes protested he was abrasively informed: 'What the bloody hell do you know about it? I'm the one paying the money.'

By August, Oakes could take no more and resigned. Time was running out and Hancock found himself with no scripts and no script consultant. Someone suggested the ventriloquist Ray Alan who, under the pen name 'Ray Whyberd', had written several scripts for *Bootsie and Snudge*, a spin-off from the 1950s national service comedy *The Army Game*.

Roger Hancock approached Alan who agreed to spend a weekend at MacConkeys. He arrived at Redhill station the next Saturday morning to be met by Cicely. On the eight-mile drive across country to Blindley Heath she warned him that Hancock had started drinking early and that he should not be surprised if her husband was a little under the weather. 'Sadly, Tony was very much "under the weather",' recalls Alan, 'and despite my efforts to interest him in two ideas I had been working on, it was not until after lunch and a long sleep that he was at all responsive.'

Before his Sunday night departure, Alan agreed to produce a sample script of a plot which, on first hearing, had received Hancock's approval. In it the normally belligerent Hancock becomes a department store assistant and is challenged to work for a week without offending anyone. When the completed script arrived at MacConkeys, Hancock became even more convinced he had discovered the person to write the entire series and invited Alan back for a second weekend meeting.

'By the time I arrived at the house a few days later Tony had decided to change his image,' said Alan. 'Rather than talk over storylines, he wanted me to do a re-write on the first script and cut out all the old Hancockisms that had made him the character we loved. He wanted to change his appearance, too, and become smart and more "with it".'

When the ventriloquist-cum-writer suggested Laurel and Hardy had only remained popular because they had retained their established image, Hancock turned thoughtful and reached for another bottle of wine. 'I knew then that I could never work with Tony,' said Alan. 'I simply did not want to be involved with what I believed to be a disaster.'

Cicely was, by now, drinking as heavily as Hancock. What had started as an altruistic delusion – she repeatedly justified the downing of her husband's neglected vodkas by saying 'the more I drink the less there is for him' – was rapidly becoming a painful and jealousy-fuelled addiction. According to one life-long friend, Cicely 'only started drinking in earnest when she knew she had lost Tony'. For Hancock, his wife's 'undignified' drinking was not so much to do with her unhappiness, but yet another attempt to blackmail him into ending his affair. They quarrelled and fought and only Cicely's teenage judo classes saved her from several vicious beatings. When he realised what he had done, Hancock would slink away to drown his guilt in more alcohol and to make love to Freddie.

To give himself an alibi, Hancock was 'officially' staying at a Hampstead flat owned by his record-producer friend, Alan Freeman, but everyone, including Cicely, knew he was sleeping with Freddie in Dorset Square.

Late one afternoon, Hancock's part-time secretary, Lyn Leonard, telephoned to say that Cicely had been admitted to a Redhill hospital after breaking her leg while playing with the dogs in MacConkeys' one-and-a-half acre garden. Hancock resolutely refused to visit or telephone his wife. 'She's done it on purpose,' he told Freddie angrily. 'She's trying to get me back.'

When Leonard eventually persuaded her employer into returning to Surrey, he marched into his wife's private ward and, after a cursory greeting, began reading aloud extracts from a book by Bertrand Russell. Cicely broke down in tears and Hancock left to sign autographs for other patients. Back at Blindley Heath he admitted to Leonard – who later married the writer and comedy historian Barry Took – that he 'no longer loved his wife and hadn't loved her for some time'.

During his days in London, and while Freddie used her Dorset Square apartment as an office, Hancock turned to John le Mesurier. 'The best I could do to help was to listen and occasionally try to snap him out of his self-preoccupation with some happy diversion,' the actor recalled. One afternoon le Mesurier suggested Hancock should borrow some of his jazz records. He never saw them again. Hancock's verdict: 'You have got to have suffered to appreciate jazz.'

Hancock's immediate problem was the quality of the scripts he was being offered for his new series. The slow, but talented, Godfrey Harrison had by now been joined by Dennis Spooner and Richard Harris. When the series began its November recording, it was soon apparent the comedy was fatally out of balance. Working from the written page, the mistakes were masked by Hancock's repeated demands for rewrites. To Alan Simpson – watching the shows on television the following year – the fault-line was obvious: 'You have to have a reason for Tony being pompous and nasty, and we always provided that as a matter of course, but that was thrown away and Tony was unnecessarily nasty. You can't be nasty without a reason and be funny. To be nasty after you have been rejected is reasonable. To be nasty before you have been rejected is gratuitous.'

To bring the scripts together, Hancock recruited a 32-year-old former furniture designer. Terry Nation[8] was a cheerful and amiable

Welshman who made friends easily. He joined Associated London Scripts in 1955 and was soon co-writing scripts for *The Frankie Howerd Show* with Dick Barrie, Johnny Speight and John Antrobus. His other 1950s credits included *Floggets, Idiot's Weekly* and *A Show Called Fred*.

When Nation arrived for the obligatory MacConkeys meeting, Hancock insisted they walk around the garden. 'To my amazement all he wanted to do was talk about the universe and what part we played in the cosmic scheme of things,' Nation recalled. 'I had always been interested in science fiction, but Tony's thinking was far more involved, far more philosophical.' Hancock's immediate problem was scripts for his forthcoming tour. Nation agreed to help and they arranged to meet at Freeman's flat the next weekend.

The writer arrived at midnight on Friday after attending a dinner party. The pair talked and drank and swallowed stay-awake pills for the next forty-eight hours. On Monday morning, Nation went home to his wife, Kate, dishevelled and exhausted. Over the next ten days they created and wrote numerous sketches, only to discard them the closer Hancock's tour became. Nation – like Philip Oakes before him – was suffering Hancock's insecurity. 'When Tony first acted out an idea we would collapse in fits of giggles,' said Nation. 'When it was on the page, in black and white, he went cold. It was as if the act of writing anything down sparked a huge and lingering doubt, first in the material and then in himself to deliver it.'

The autumn tour had been arranged by Bernard Delfont as a two-man show, with the singer Matt Monro filling the first half and Hancock's non-stop act completing the second. Hancock had driven down to Southsea in a huge, chauffeur-driven American car, with Terry Nation and Glyn Jones, the Delfont agency's road manager. As ever Hancock insisted on going direct to the venue.

'He stood on the stage and smelt the place,' Freddie Ross relates. It was a ritual he practised whenever he arrived at a new auditorium or theatre. 'He looked at the rows of empty seats and saw where the nearest and furthest members of the audience would be sitting. He touched the walls and paced the stage. He stretched himself and flexed his muscles like a boxer about to enter a ring.'

The next morning Hancock woke his writer early. 'He was visibly shaking and covered in sweat,' said Nation. When they arrived at Southsea's King's Theatre, Hancock sat through the day's rehearsals, mumbling his lines and hurling pages of his script into a waste bin. More and more of the new sketches were abandoned and replaced by old and worn and safe material. On opening night, the local critics felt cheated. One, writing in the *Portsmouth News*, complained: 'We have seen it all before – a dozen times.'

There were enough laughs, however, to bolster Hancock's ego and the show moved to Liverpool. Nation had intended to return to London, but Hancock insisted he stay with the tour. 'I had finished the writing and he could have got rid of me at any time,' said Nation. 'He was paying me £100 a week to virtually baby-sit him.' The first night on Merseyside, Hancock looked into the wings and saw Matt Monro helpless with laughter. The next day he informed Nation it was time to try some of the new scripts.

After each show the pair would lie on their beds and drink and chat until early next morning. One idea they talked through was for a film in which the earth's human population had been destroyed and the planet was governed by robots. Neither could remember whether it was science fiction or comedy. As they began to 'design' the androids, Hancock's imagination ran riot; his favourite was an inverted cone, covered in ping-pong balls and with a sink plunger sticking out of its head. The film came to nothing.

When the three-week tour was over, Nation returned to his television scripts, including episodes for *The Saint*. He was also invited to write for *Dr Who*, the BBC's long-running Saturday afternoon adventure of a time traveller, and his first episode heralded the arrival of the Daleks. When Hancock watched the mechanised aliens he pointed at his television screen and shouted: 'That bloody Nation, he's stolen my robots.'

*

Filming for the new *Hancock* series started on 4 November with a
Godfrey Harrison script entitled *The Eye Witness*. Each of the thirteen
programmes would be recorded at weekly intervals, overlapping with
the first transmission three days into the New Year. The director, Alan
Tarrant, had persuaded Hancock to allow him to balance out the series
by shuffling the good and bad shows. The first to be broadcast – *The
Assistant* – was based on Ray Alan's original storyline and was the
seventh to be shot.

To his surprise Tarrant was faced with a director's nightmare – his
star was more relaxed and funnier off screen than on. 'He would talk a
great deal about philosophy and deliver a Cockney version of various
philosophies,' he recalls. 'It was spontaneous and superbly hilarious.'

On 25 November, the team gathered for a recording of *The Memory
Test*. Not only had Tarrant to contend with his star's daily intake of
alcohol, but the cast also included two other 'championship drinkers' –
Wilfrid Lawson and Edward Chapman. With the prospect of all three
spending the lunch break in the studio bar, the director could virtually
write off the afternoon's shooting schedule. To divert the trio, Tarrant
devised a plan and recruited another member of the cast.

Shaw Taylor had launched *Police Five* in the Midlands television
area that summer, but he was still better known as a compère of such
quizzes as *Pencil and Paper*, *Dotto* and *Tell the Truth*. During the
morning Tarrant took Taylor aside. 'What I'm going to do,' the
director explained, 'is tell them I know a smashing little pub a short
drive away. We'll shove all three in the back of my car and I'll drive
around for most of the lunch break and just give them a quick one in a
nearby local before we start recording again.'

Hancock readily accepted the suggestion of a few drinks in a rural
pub and happily wedged himself between Chapman and the bewhiskered Wilfrid Lawson. After thirty minutes of bouncing through the
country lanes, the rumblings started. 'Where's this bloody pub?'
Hancock demanded. 'You said it was only five minutes' drive away.'

When it was evident a riot was about to break out in the rear of his
car, Tarrant whispered to Taylor: 'Ask them what they're drinking. As

soon as I stop, nip in and order the drinks – and make sure they're singles.'

'Almost there fellers,' said Taylor, turning to meet three glaring faces. 'What's your poison?'

Hancock ordered a double gin and tonic and Chapman a double scotch. Lawson said: 'I'll take a triple brandy, dear boy, and I'll pay for it myself.'

'That's all right,' Taylor replied. 'I'll get it.'

'Certainly not,' Lawson said in his deep, already gravelly voice. 'I never allow a fellow thespian to be out of pocket because of my dedication to the grape.'

Taylor was first out of the car, explained the situation to the barman and had 'small' singles lined up on the counter as Tarrant and the trio walked in. All three sat down and gazed at their glasses. 'Tony looked puzzled as only he could,' recalls Taylor, 'and Chapman vaguely inspected his glass like a urinologist with an interesting specimen. But Lawson simply stared at the glass on the table and began to rumble and shake like a volcano about to erupt. He was an impressive sight with his great shaggy beard and long hair.'

A frightened hush descended on the bar. 'What?' cried Lawson in a booming crescendo. 'What do I see before me?'

The barman grabbed the brandy bottle and was frantically filling Lawson's glass to the brim.

Throughout the summer Hancock had been trying unsuccessfully to shake himself free of Mr Punch's evil influence. *The Punch and Judy Man* was shunned by the distributors and slated by the critics, and Hancock made no attempt to hide his mounting despair. Initial plans for a West End première were discreetly dropped, as was Associated British Pictures' option on the three remaining projects, and Hancock admitted to George Fairweather he had lost more than £5,000 on the film.

In September, Hancock received news that Walter Hudd, an extra from *The Punch and Judy Man*, had suddenly died, then, halfway through the first week of the tour, he learned of the death of Joe Hastings, the man who had taught him the art of Punch and Judy performance; Hancock ordered a large floral tribute in the shape of Punch. Less than two months later Mario Fabrizi, who had played the film's 'seafront photographer', was also dead.

Hancock sent the occult writer Pat Williams a note – 'I told you it was doomed.'

1963

THE FRONT DOOR at MacConkeys was wide open. It was one o'clock in the morning and the house was as dark as the moonless January sky. From one of the mansion's five bedrooms drifted the scratchy sound of a Carmen McRae record. Hancock was lying naked across one of the beds.

After yet another holiday brawl Hancock had left Cicely nursing a black eye in the South of France and flown home alone. For some reason he decided to return to MacConkeys instead of spending the night with his lover in London. He knew that Freddie Ross would be attending the opening of a new restaurant and, a little after seven, Hancock had telephoned and asked to speak to her. His voice was hoarse and he sounded 'very ill'. Throughout the evening the calls became increasingly frantic and Freddie had decided to drive down to Blindley Heath. Unsure exactly what she might find, and fearing the worst, she asked Sally, her secretary, and Sally's husband John Knight, to accompany her.

While Freddie and Sally waited in the car, Knight explored the freezing house. What little furniture there was had either been upturned or pushed aside; empty vodka and brandy bottles were everywhere; pieces of a broken glass had been trodden into the carpet.

In the mechanical silence between the record ending and starting again Knight could hear what sounded like someone snoring beneath a pillow. Upstairs he found Hancock.

'Eventually, he woke up, and we persuaded him to put on some underpants,' recalls Knight. As the sound of the continuously playing record penetrated his subconscious Hancock raised a tired hand and announced: 'Listen to that, innit great?'

While Freddie ransacked the kitchen for food, Sally and John Knight supported the 37-year-old Hancock down the stairs. 'Somehow, Tony managed to set light to Freddie's dress,' adds John Knight. All she could find were some eggs, a tin of kidney beans and an open jar of anchovies. Propped in his chair and still very drunk, Hancock refused to eat the red bean omelette Freddie had made until she promised to spoon-feed him like a child.

'I think that was the night I decided for good or ill that I was going to look after him,' admits Freddie. Within days, and while Cicely was still in France, Hancock had moved into a small Marylebone hotel not far from Dorset Square. A few weeks later he had unloaded the encyclopaedias and his typewriter from the boot of his car and moved in permanently with Freddie. 'I was,' she confesses, 'a funny sort of mistress. I paid the rent and for all the food and Tony paid the drinks bill.'

Ray Alan had been proved right. By the end of January – and with five of the thirteen Associated Television programmes broadcast – more than three million television owners had switched over to the BBC. By early February the series had dropped out of the top twenty viewing figures, and Hancock was faced with the disheartening task of recording the remaining weekly shows aware the downward slide was already unstoppable.

To those associated with the series the rot had set in two months earlier. 'Tony wouldn't rehearse and for the first time he was boozing while he was working,' recalled Terry Nation. For the actor Derek Nimmo, the fault lay not so much with Hancock as the series director, Alan Tarrant. 'The situation was made worse by those working with

Tony, and who should have known better,' explains Nimmo. 'When Tony failed to learn his lines, it wasn't "Why haven't you?" but always, "Don't worry about it, we'll put them on idiot boards." ' It got so bad that one studio joke advised the next producer wanting to work with Hancock to book twice as many Autocue machines as cameras.

Hancock maintained it took him time to deliver the perfect line; to find the artlessness in his new comic art. 'Everyone must know that you are only pretending to be uncertain,' he explained. 'I would work at an inflection as if I were writing a sonnet. I worried about every word. And if the anxiety shows, if the entertainer is flustered, the unease communicates itself.'

There were other reasons for the series' failure and not all of Hancock's making. By some quirk of television planning, the BBC had scheduled the second series of Galton and Simpson's *Steptoe and Son* for earlier the same evening as Hancock's ITV series. Also, for the second year running, bad weather was affecting the nation's electricity supply, cutting reception to entire regions. Defending the series to the *Daily Express*, he said: 'There are 365 reasons why people don't watch you, but in this case I really believe the viewers hadn't the chance. All they could see was a postage-sized Hancock and so they switched off. There is nothing, absolutely nothing wrong with my new series.'

Roger Wilmut saw the thirteen shows as a series of two halves:

It is a little more alarming to watch the whole series. The early shows, if not in the Simpson and Galton class, are still well performed and highly enjoyable. The second half of the series, once the strain had begun to have its effect, is startlingly different – so much so that it is almost difficult to believe that it is the same series. One wonders how things would have gone if more time could have been allowed for recording the series, and if the original script difficulties could have been overcome.

*

Late the previous year, Hancock had agreed to be the guest of honour at an Australian television award ceremony. However, by the time shooting for the final ITV show was completed on 15 February – and with less than a week before he was due to fly to Sydney – the show's star was depressed and drinking heavily. Hancock cancelled the trip, claiming 'exhaustion', and caught the first Saturday morning flight to Paris. When he was involved in a drunken and obscene confrontation with some other hotel guests, it was only the swift intervention of the hotel manager that saved him from a night in a French police cell and the inevitable bad publicity. By the end of February, Hancock had returned to England and checked himself into a nursing home. He was, Freddie Ross maintained, suffering from 'pneumonia'.

The only lifeline of 1963 came in June when Bernard Delfont persuaded Hancock to accept a booking at a 'steak-and-one-frozen-veg' theatre-restaurant converted from the former Leicester Square Hippodrome. This six-week Talk of the Town date would start in August with one condition – that he agree to complete a short warm-up tour.

On Monday, 15 July, Hancock opened a six-day run at Nottingham's Theatre Royal. Ten years earlier he had appeared at the same venue as Buttons in the pantomime *Cinderella*, earning little more than the £2.10s which the management was now charging for a box to watch *Tony Hancock Entertains!*

The twice-nightly performances – 6.15 and 8.30 – did not go well. Bernard Delfont, who had teamed up with MacConkey Productions to finance the tour, was unhappy at the public criticism of Hancock's performance and the backstage gossip about his drinking. There were also too many empty seats for the impresario's liking. Sadly, the public would return its own verdict: the following week, when Hancock had departed for Manchester, the Royal staged a sell-out performance of the Agatha Christie thriller, *Murder at the Vicarage.*

The illogical potent chemistry of show business had finally let Hancock down. Shaken by the failure of his television series, he saw the tour and his six-week cabaret booking as some kind of reaffirmation of his original faith; as if he could shrug off the criticism as easily as he delivered his loose-jointed stage send-up of himself. By the time Hancock returned to London, however, his ever vulnerable confidence had evaporated and he waited 'drunken and frightened for the final crack of doom'. The next day he telephoned the impresario and pulled out of the Talk of the Town booking.

Bernard Delfont replaced him with Joan Turner. One night, during her six-week run, the comedienne was told Hancock had sat through her act and wanted to see her. They talked backstage for more than an hour until Hancock rose and, mumbling an excuse, announced: 'At least you've got some new impressions in your act, my lot are all dead.'

Climbing the stairs from Turner's basement dressing room, Hancock walked to the edge of the unlit stage and, like someone testing the ice on a frozen pond, tapped the wooden floor with his foot. 'What are you doing?' asked Turner.

'I'm just getting the feel of the place,' he said gaining confidence to walk further on to the stage. 'Yes. Yes.' He sniffed the air. 'I think it's going to be all right.'

Billy Marsh was working late in his London office on Monday, 5 August, when he received a telephone call from an agitated stage manager. Arthur Haynes, one of the agency's biggest-earning clients, had collapsed shortly before his nightly appearance at the Palladium. A few minutes later, Marsh was discussing possible replacements with his employer. The comedian's illness, Bernard Delfont told him, had already made the nine o'clock BBC news.

The phone rang again. This time it was Tony Hancock, calling from Freddie Ross's Dorset Square flat. Marsh, who had masterminded Hancock's provincial tours since the 1950s, admitted he had a problem.

'All right,' said Hancock, 'if you want me, I'll take over.' The agent thought for a minute and then agreed. The stand-in engagement was to last nearly eight weeks.

As ever, Hancock had created the opportunity without considering the consequences. Haynes would be a hard act to replace. The majority of critics were already proclaiming the 49-year-old comic as Hancock's independent television heir apparent, and Haynes – who for years had been a Gunnersbury Avenue neighbour of Sid James – had already broken Hancock's record of being the highest-paid comedian on television. The nerves mounted. By the time Hancock arrived at the Argyll Street theatre the next evening, he was twitching with fear.

Alan Freeman, who had overseen the production of Pye's record issue of *The Blood Donor* two years earlier, heard the news of Haynes's illness only hours before Hancock was due to go on stage: 'I thought, my God, Tony will be panic stricken.' Freeman hurried to the Palladium. When he arrived, Hancock was alone in his dressing room with his two poodles. 'He was white as a sheet and terrified,' recalled Freeman.

'Thank God for a friendly face,' said a relieved Hancock. He then asked Freeman to sit through the show in the stalls. 'I want at least one person in the audience laughing.'

Richard Beeching, the chairman of the British Railways Board, had just unveiled his controversial plan to reshape Britain's rail system. From a 1930s high of 19,000 miles of track, the Beeching Report – dubbed the 'Beeching Axe' by the press – wanted a slimmed-down network of just 10,000 miles. Hundreds of branch lines and stations were closed. Protesters saw Beeching as a balding, lofty bureaucrat, out of touch with the everyday traveller. To soften the report's image, public relations experts at British Rail decided they needed a 'common man' to sell the cuts. 'It became obvious that a need existed to show that our railway system is run by people. That despite its enormous size and complexity, British Rail is a human organisation, with human faults – and virtues,' spouted one BR publication. They chose Tony Hancock.

A young copywriter, David Gillies, spent several hours listening to Hancock records before creating a series of newspaper advertisements parodying Galton and Simpson. British Rail claimed the response to the campaign 'was good – extraordinarily good'. The public were not so easily fooled. Objectors giving evidence at inquiries up and down the country claimed that Hancock – still the public's favourite buffoon – undermined the seriousness of the issue. Cardiff City Council even went as far as saying that because Hancock was seen as approving the Beeching cuts, the average traveller assumed they must be acceptable.

In the first advertisement, 'the latest and greatest of all "reports" on the railways – *The Hancock Report*', a cigar-smoking Hancock expounds as he relaxes in a first-class compartment.

So this feller Beeching says to me, 'Hancock, we've called you in because we want a really top brain on this job.' Seems his report on the railways didn't exactly send people wild with joy, so he wants me to follow it up and tell 'em what to do. Well, I'm a busy man already. But he talked me round in the end. 'The nation needs you Hancock,' he says, '£100,000 a year and free luncheon vouchers.' So here I am on this diesel thing. Ninety miles an hour and no nonsense about seat belts. The VIP treatment! There must be a catch somewhere though. They can't fool me that all their trains are like this . . .

The campaign was not without its own humour. Asked about the style, Galton and Simpson quipped: 'We have hereby been done out of a job.' Filmed in crush-hour chaos, Hancock was back on *Half Hour* form:

Whew! Each man for himself, women and children to the wall. I'm beginning to wish I hadn't taken on this railway job, I can tell you. 'Investigate the suburban services, Hancock,' this Beeching feller says to me. 'The railways didn't create the rush. Look into the question of staggering office hours.' Staggering hours – I ask you! The only thing this merry mob think about is staggering into their seats and devil take the hindmost. Make one continuous train from London to Brighton so people can walk along a corridor, that's my answer!

Although the British Rail campaign ran throughout the summer, the photographs had been taken over a four-day period in February, during the coldest winter for a decade. While shooting a 'summer' bank-holiday scene the photographer's cameras froze solid. At Waterloo station the arrivals board suddenly showed every train was running forty-five minutes late. Hancock giggled himself senseless as he watched passengers and staff panic – unaware the board was being used as a backdrop.

Throughout the spring and summer, Hancock and Freddie's affair became an increasingly open and bizarre secret. Weeks of apparent harmony would be shattered by savage and peremptory fights, usually sparked by Freddie's attempts to hide or pour away her lover's alcohol. Summoned after one quarrel, Leonard Ross describes how he arrived to find a panic-stricken Hancock waiting outside in his carpet slippers. 'Freddie was lying on the couch upstairs. The rooms looked as if a typhoon had hit them. God knows what had been going on. I thought she was shamming. She had obviously been crying. I said, "Come on, Freddie, I'm here; it's going to be all right." I gave her a little push and she fell off the couch, striking her head on an enamel-topped table. She was a dead weight. I called the doctor and he ordered her to hospital. Tony and I followed in a taxi. He was in a terrible state, very upset.'

After each beating, Hancock would retreat to Blindley Heath and Cicely and, for the time being at least, slip unconsciously back into the role of burdensome but dutiful husband. Writers and journalists – after interviews dutifully arranged by Freddie – would return to London satisfied that life at MacConkeys was content and peaceful and rippled only by the occasional domestic dispute. Few were sensitive enough to detect the counterpoint of sarcasm played out on their behalf. When Cicely, invariably dressed in sweater and smart slacks, called in to say 'goodbye' before driving to nearby Redhill or Crawley, Hancock played the concerned husband. 'Be careful, darling,' he would warn. 'It's been raining. The roads are tricky.' In private, the house was a physical and emotional battleground.

Hancock was at home one October Saturday when John le Mesurier arrived at MacConkeys. With the actor was an attractive, dark-haired woman in her mid-thirties. Her name was Joan Malin.

It was a crisp, late-autumn morning. As the car came to a halt outside the house, Joan felt a twinge of apprehension. She had met le

Mesurier a few months earlier at the Establishment Club in London's Greek Street and, as their affair developed, she knew that one day she would have to meet the man who dominated her lover's concerns and fears. Each time le Mesurier returned from visiting Hancock in a clinic or hospital, his voice would quiver with frustration. Tears would well in his eyes. 'Tony was sitting dejectedly in the garden,' le Mesurier had said once. 'He was trying to make a fucking coffee table in order to please his therapist.'

Joan was torn between the pompous, bumbling Hancock she had watched on television and the images of le Mesurier's description – 'an intense, self-involved hypochondriac, lacking the humour in real life he so brilliantly displayed on the screen'.

The front door opened. 'Welcome to MacConkeys,' Hancock announced as he threw his arms around the couple's shoulders. 'Come and meet Cis.'

Joan shook hands with Cicely and sensed an air of coolness. In contrast, Hancock was bubbling with energy. 'I was bowled over by him,' Joan confesses in her book, *Lady Don't Fall Backwards*. 'Here was this laughing expansive man with bright blue eyes. I knew instantly why John was so fond of him.'

Before coming to London, Joan – whose showman father ran the Merry England funfair beneath the cliffs on Ramsgate's seafront – had met and married the future *Coronation Street* star Mark Eden. After five years and one son, David, the couple had separated.

John le Mesurier and Joan Malin had known each other for barely a year. Le Mesurier was still married to Hattie Jacques, herself in the middle of an equally open affair with a smart, good-looking, fast-talking East End car salesman called John Schofield. When her husband had confessed his own romance, Jacques 'took charge'. Within days she had located and rented a London flat for her husband and his lover. With his wife's blessing, le Mesurier ended their marriage with £200, an assortment of furniture and the family car.

Joan finally agreed to give up her job as a clerk at Marylebone labour exchange, but she had had little experience of running a home or managing an actor's business affairs. Once again, Jacques came to the rescue, opening several charge accounts and teaching her husband's lover how to balance the books. In return, the pair agreed to do everything they could to speed the divorce.

After lunch, Hancock took Joan's hand and steered her around the house and gardens. He was charming and attentive and desperate to know more about the woman with whom his friend was clearly infatuated. Watching his two giant poodles, Charlie and Mr Brown, chase each other around the lawn, Hancock launched a stream of questions. What book was Joan reading? What did she think of this film? What about that piece of music?

Cicely drove the party to several nearby village pubs where the four played shove ha'penny. Characteristically Hancock had left his wallet at MacConkeys, but he refused to allow le Mesurier to pay for any drinks, insisting the drinks were always put on the pub tab.

On their way back Hancock persuaded le Mesurier and Joan to remain for dinner and stay the night. During the meal he nodded conspiratorially at Joan and said: 'You've got to keep this one, Johnny.'

'I've asked her to marry me,' le Mesurier replied. 'But she doesn't want me.'

'Then you're a fool,' Hancock told Joan.

In less than three years it would be Hancock who would plead with Joan to marry him.

1964

HANCOCK AND FREDDIE glared at each other. 'If you take another drink, I'll take a pill,' Ross threatened her lover. Hancock raised his glass and emptied it of vodka.

Freddie grabbed the only bottle of tablets she could find in the flat. Storming back into the lounge, she unscrewed the cap and popped a pill into her mouth. Hancock downed another glass of spirit. Freddie swallowed another pill.

At eight drinks, Hancock collapsed in giggles. It was then that Freddie realised her life was in less danger than Hancock's – she had been trying to kill herself with vegetable laxatives. The next day Hancock felt great and Freddie was confined to the bathroom.

Her other attempts at suicide were far more serious. 'I thought in my twisted mind that I could bring him to his senses.' It was, she admits, pure blackmail. 'I thought my death, which wouldn't harm a lot of people, would make him realise what a wonderful talent he had and was wasting.'

Despite the bruises, a broken nose and a pierced eardrum, Freddie always maintained Hancock was never a 'fighting drunk'. On several occasions he knocked her out cold. The violence was always Hancock's reaction to his lover's attempt to stop him drinking. 'He was a very strong man and simply struck out,' Freddie claimed in his defence. 'He had this ability to just chop you down with the side of his hand whenever you reached for his bottle. It wasn't as if we had punch-ups. I was too scared to fight back, he would have beaten me senseless.'

The harder Freddie defended herself, the more jealous and violent Hancock became. For much of their relationship and later marriage, she was forced to wear long-sleeved blouses or pullovers, in case someone spotted the purple bruises and red weals on her arms. Her personal loyalty as Hancock's press agent added to the physical pain. 'Most of the stress came from trying to keep it out of the papers and protecting his fantastic talent and career.'

Some of Freddie's friends found it harder than others to forgive the violence. 'I know he treated my sister very badly, but I felt this was an enormous clash of temperament rather than cruelty on his side or misunderstanding on hers,' said Freddie's solicitor brother, Leonard Ross. 'Overall, the balance of his character was in his favour.'

Sally Mordant, one of Freddie's assistants, claims her employer 'guarded her love for Tony ... even after the beatings she had from him you would never hear her criticise him'.

Freddie's suicide attempts – five in two years – were still acts of bravado; blackmail ventures whose success or failure still needed to be witnessed. Arriving for work at the Dorset Square flat-cum-office became a testing experience. 'Freddie's suicide bids made me sick because there could be a time when she might do it and no one would be around to pick up the pieces,' said Mordant. 'Freddie could not do anything less than the big gesture. Everything was for an Oscar.'

Hancock's last radio recording had been the previous October with a thirty-minute programme for the Midland Home Service called *That Reminds Me*, and there were no plans for any stage or television appearances, but he now announced he wanted to concentrate on his film career. However, the first offer, when it came, proved too close for comfort.

In 1949, Hancock's hero Sid Field had played Elwood Dowd, the middle-aged drunk with an imaginary white rabbit as his friend, when *Harvey* opened in London. The following year James Stewart turned the part into a classic with Mary Chase's adaptation of her own play for the screen. The suggestion of a British remake of *Harvey* had been bubbling for years. By 1964 there was only one comedian whose experience and reputation qualified him for the role.

In one scene the alcoholic Elwood describes a fiction which, in a few short years, would become Hancock's reality.

Harvey and I have things to do . . . we sit in the bars . . . have a drink or two . . . and play the juke box. Very soon the faces of the other people turn towards me and they smile. They say, 'We don't know your name, mister, but you're all right.' Harvey and I warm ourselves in these golden moments . . . They come over. They sit with us. They drink with us. They talk to us. They tell us about the great big terrible things they've done and the great big wonderful things they're going to do . . . All very large, because nobody ever brings anything small into a bar.

Hancock, who had seen the film several times, read the script with mounting unease. When he got to the part where Elwood, under threat of certification, announces, 'I've wrestled with reality for thirty-five years, and I'm happy, doctor, I finally won out over it', Hancock decided the part was not for him.

It was two years since *The Punch and Judy Man*. Among his closest friends and associates, Hancock still talked of conquering America, the only country, he believed, capable of granting him artistic recognition. Ironically, one project on which he lavished first his enthusiasm and then his scorn was the single film most likely to have attracted critical acclaim.

Four years earlier, in 1960, Hancock had sat among the audience at London's Royal Court Theatre to watch *Rhinoceros*, a play by the king of absurdist theatre, Eugène Ionesco. The Orson Welles production involved a man who suddenly discovers his neighbours are changing into animals. 'It was ridiculous,' Hancock commented at the time, but, presented with the Clive Exton screenplay and an invitation to play Berenger, who refuses to accept his transformation into a rhino, he was less sceptical.

The Woodfall Films adaptation was as far removed from formula humour as Hancock could have wished. As a screen project it was also riddled with eccentricities and human coincidences. Ionesco's first theatrical experiences were eerily similar to Hancock's. As a child he had visited the Luxembourg Gardens in Paris to watch a Punch and Judy show. Recalling how he stood in silence, surrounded by the laughter of other children, Ionesco later wrote: 'It was the spectacle of the world itself in an infinitely simplified and caricatured form, as if to underline its grotesque and brutal truth.'

Woodfall contracted Alexander 'Sandy' Mackendrick to direct *Rhinoceros*. To British cinemagoers he was responsible for several Ealing classics including *Whisky Galore, The Man in the White Suit* and *The Ladykillers*. It was an odd pairing of director and actor. Where Mackendrick was meticulous, Hancock was haphazard; when a critical situation demanded calm and reason from Mackendrick, it would elicit only panic from Hancock. One talent unknown to Hancock – but almost certainly welcomed by his agent and brother

Roger – was Mackendrick's ability to 'help actors reach emotional depths of which some would not have believed themselves capable'.

Problems over Hancock's involvement surfaced almost from the beginning. Oscar Lewenstein, the producer, found himself battling with insurance companies over cover for his star. It was only granted after the insertion of a clause stating that:

> In the event of any insurance claims arising through the artiste having met with an accident or suffering from an illness attributable directly or indirectly to alcoholism, such claims will be subject to a deduction in excess of $10,000.

The weeks dragged on. Hancock fretted. Lewenstein remembers: 'Tony was enthusiastic about *Rhinoceros*, but impatient. He did not seem able to grasp that it takes a long time to get the script right and to build a dummy rhino that would really work.'

One casualty along the way was Hancock's professional relationship with his brother. Both Mackendrick and Roger Hancock were anxious the film should have a top-name cast. They flew to New York in a vain bid to recruit the comedy actor Zero Mostel. By the time they returned, Hancock was still hesitating over signing the Woodfall contract. The brothers agreed to part and Hancock moved to the Bernard Delfont Agency and the amiable and fatherly care of Billy Marsh.

To bring the matter to a head – and to offer himself an escape route – Lewenstein set a deadline. He advised Hancock by letter that:

> . . . I think I ought to say that I don't feel that you should sign the contract for any other reason than that you want to do the film because if you do it for any other reason I don't see how the film can be a pleasure for any of us.
>
> May I suggest, therefore, that you should think carefully about the matter and if you feel happy to work on the film with Sandy Mackendrick directing it and with our company [Woodfall] producing it, then I would like to exchange contracts with you. If

you don't want to do this then please let us know through Billy Marsh. If we have not exchanged contracts within the next three days then we will take it that the whole thing is off.

Both Sandy and I feel it would be a tremendous pity if you were not to do the film in which we feel you are absolutely ideally cast, but if you do it we want you to do it of your own free will and not for any reasons of obligations.

Forever the compromiser, Hancock telephoned the producer. During the conversation, which lasted for almost half-an-hour, he expertly – and characteristically – backed away from nearly all his concerns. The contract was signed the next day. The negotiations rumbled on for almost a year, but *Rhinoceros* was never made.

Sometime in the early summer, Hancock suffered a painful and mysterious injury which he seldom spoke about and which has never been fully explained, even by Freddie Ross.

A date had already been set for the filming of *Those Magnificent Men in Their Flying Machines,* or *How I Flew from London to Paris in 25 Hours and 11 Minutes*, a knockabout comedy with the dubious distinction of featuring as many top-name stars as words in its title. Hancock had been hired to play Harry Popperwell, an eccentric inventor who not only designs some of the aircraft but takes part in the 1910 air race. However, with less than a month before shooting, Hancock apparently tripped and snapped his ankle. Waiting in agony for his foot and leg to be set, he was informed by a doctor he had both broken and dislocated his ankle, a classic Pott's fracture. The name, once the pain killers took effect, tickled Hancock's sense of whimsy. 'This is a Pott's fracture...' he bragged sniffily, as if the break was as rare as his blood group in *The Blood Donor*, '...named after Sir Percival Pott, 1780.'

No one was quite sure how the accident had happened. John le Mesurier always maintained his friend fell during an argument with Freddie. His one-time writer, Terry Nation, understood Hancock had lost his footing on some stairs. Whatever the circumstances, Cicely was convinced her estranged husband had been drunk at the time.

Walking with his foot encased in plaster to the knee was awkward and excruciatingly painful, but Hancock refused to pull out of the film contract and shuffled through his brief part in *Those Magnificent Men*, fortified with equal measures of pain killers and alcohol.

It was a mishap too good for the film's publicity machine to ignore. When Twentieth Century-Fox issued its campaign book to cinema managers, the colour brochure boasted:

> The plaster cast on Tony Hancock's foot in *Those Magnificent Men in Their Flying Machines* was not put on by the studio make-up department but by an M.D. The popular comedian broke his foot just before he was due to start his role of Popperwell, the eccentric plane inventor, and figured he would have to bow out of the part. However, producer Stan Margulies had a new scene written which provides an alibi for the plaster cast. Through the picture Hancock hobbles around with cane and cast and while these may have added to his discomfort they added to the humour in some of the comedy action.

The film's English and 'French' coastal sequences were shot overlooking the Channel in Kent. In one scene, John le Mesurier plays a French painter whose sand dune studio and nude model are overflown by the racing aircraft, so Hancock took the opportunity of driving down to Folkestone to meet up with his old friend. Both men were depressed – Hancock about his health and le Mesurier about his impending divorce – and drank their way through several bottles of vodka.

The film would not be issued for another eight months. Hancock's cameo, no matter how entertaining, was lost among the blur of other international actors and actresses – all of whom were overshadowed by the film's real stars. The British Film Institute's review noted:

> As pretty playthings, old aeroplanes have rather more to offer

than old cars like *Genevieve* or old trains like the *Titfield Thunderbolt*, and yet one hardly expected an international cast to be so totally eclipsed by authentic reproductions of early flying machines. The main reason for this is the script, which goes back further than 1910 for most of its humour, and which tends towards the assumption that wogs begin in Calais ... Still it's all good fun if you like that sort of thing.

*

Hancock was now forty. Billy Marsh was barely eight years older, but his experience as an agent had somehow preserved his faith in human nature. Verbal bookings were always honoured and a handshake was law. Hancock found in him the detached affection he imagined existed between a father and son. Whatever chaos Hancock sowed in the studio, theatre or on the film set, Marsh never reprimanded or preached; like a father's his disapproval was silent and weighty and Hancock realised he had at last found someone he could respect. As with Phyllis Rounce more than a decade earlier, he took to dropping in on his agent unannounced, soaking in the silence and the security of his office and leaving without a word.

Marsh was unprepared for – and unaccustomed to – a client with such a wilful attack of nerves.

The agent had accepted a £1,000 booking for Hancock to appear on Independent Television's prestige variety programme, *Sunday Night at the London Palladium*. It was natural, Marsh knew, for a top-of-the-bill entertainer to be concerned about his performance, but Hancock appeared to be 'petrified by the responsibility'. As part of the Delfont empire, which also owned the Talk of the Town, its agency arranged a series of early morning rehearsals at the cabaret-restaurant, and it was only Freddie's nagging persistence that got Hancock to the theatre and through his routine. 'He hated me for it,' she admits. 'We rowed and Tony grumbled and sulked, but the only way he was going to be any good was to know his act inside out.'

When John le Mesurier and Joan Malin visited Hancock's Palladium dressing room during the interval, they found him wrapped in his favourite white towelling robe. His face was grey and puffy and his hands were shaking uncontrollably. 'If this is what show business does,' commented Joan, 'I'd rather be a lavatory attendant.' Hancock laughed dolefully.

Although his Sunday night performance had attracted the week's highest viewing figures, Hancock once more found himself without a contract and began a frenzied round of friends and one-time colleagues – anyone who might listen to his film or comedy ideas.

Denis Norden, who had been one of Hancock's joint agents at Kavanagh Associates, found himself the recipient of one of his former client's lunchtime fantasies. 'It was impossible right from the outset. He started with three triple brandies and through lunch talked nonsense,' says Norden. 'But suddenly he got to reminiscing about forgotten acts in the variety theatres and we remembered a conjuror who did the egg in a black bag trick, which anyone can buy in a magic shop. You pull the black bag inside out, show there is nothing inside, and then produce an egg. The conjuror turns to the audience and says, "The man must be in league with the devil." Tony identified with and delighted in that kind of humour.'

The people who surrounded Hancock – his lover, his estranged wife, his agent, his friends – were coming to terms with his drinking. His alcoholism, his bottled cancer as John le Mesurier called it, was a disease which rarely killed its victim; those left in its wake were less fortunate. For anyone who did not know Hancock, or how to handle him, his drunkenness could be a vengeful and destructive force.

For Freddie Ross it was a love affair of extremes. 'But Tony wasn't just an alcoholic, he was a chronic alcoholic,' she now admits. 'To live with an alcoholic is bad enough, it's a terrifying disease, but to live with it and not be able to tell anyone, not even my parents – who had pleaded with me not to marry Tony – was an extra burden.'

By November, Hancock's eccentric and endearing cosiness – he would watch television with a slipper balanced on his head because it made him feel 'secure' – had given way to alternating bouts of manic indecision and energy. In one surprising burst of confidence, he demanded Freddie publicly and officially announce the end of his marriage to Cicely and their own engagement. With the newspapers sniffing a scandal, and to take the pressure off both Cicely and Freddie, he moved into the Maharajah Suite of the Mayfair Hotel.

Freddie's parents were, by now, so disgusted by Hancock's brutality and their daughter's blind devotion that the only communication between them was by letter, but Leonard Ross agreed to attend a small Champagne celebration at the Mayfair. When Freddie and her assistant, Sally Mordant, arrived, however, Hancock's mood visibly changed.

'Darling, what is it?' asked Freddie. 'Have you got the blues?'

'Yes,' snapped Hancock. 'I'm going back to Cicely.' After an hour of tears and hysterics, through which he sat 'quietly ignoring the whole situation', Hancock admitted his mind had been changed by Mordant's sequin-covered hat.

From the Mayfair, Freddie took a black cab to the Savoy Hotel and checked in. At the desk she told the receptionist she had a migraine and didn't want to be disturbed. Once inside her single bedroom, she filled her hand with sleeping pills and swallowed them before telephoning her brother. 'I asked Leonard to keep Tony's name out of it,' recalls Freddie. 'He would only walk away from it anyway.' When Leonard Ross asked his sister where she was, Freddie refused to tell him. Cryptically she admitted it was 'somewhere where Tony and I had been very happy'. By a process of elimination – and with very little help from Hancock – Ross reached the Savoy in time to save his sister's life.

From his Mayfair suite Hancock moved to a service flat in Grosvenor Street, a fifteen-minute walk from Dorset Square. By the middle of December, the arguments had started again. One vicious fight left Freddie with a punctured eardrum and a broken nose. When, a week before Christmas, she was dragged out of the flat and into the street in the early hours of the morning, wearing just a coat, Freddie decided she could take no more.

Hancock had only one other booking in 1964. On 21 December he recorded a Christmas Day show for the BBC called *'Ancock's Anthology*. It involved the comedian introducing records and readings and interviewing another of Freddie Ross's clients, the retired racing driver Stirling Moss.

Moss's career had ended after a near-fatal crash, and while he was recovering in the Atkinson Morely Hospital, his press agent had arrived with Hancock in tow. The trio set off around the grounds with Moss in a wheelchair and Freddie pushing. Her steering terrified the seasoned racing driver. 'What are you doing you stupid bitch,' Moss bellowed. 'You're too close to the fucking wall.' The trail of expletives followed them in a blue wake around the hospital corridors, and Freddie protested. 'He's only shouting at you because he cares about you,' reprimanded Hancock. 'You don't understand that man at all.'

The studio session went well and Hancock left Broadcasting House in good humour. By the time he returned to Grosvenor Street, however, he was barely able to stand. Stumbling around the flat Hancock tripped and cracked his forehead on the edge of a dressing table.

After his injury was treated at a local hospital, Hancock was transferred by ambulance to the Holloway Clinic, a rambling Victorian mansion at Virgina Water, near Windsor. His head had been shaved to stitch the wound and Hancock looked as frightening as the rambling, bar-windowed institution in which he found himself.

Despite everything Hancock had inflicted on her, Freddie booked into a nearby hotel and went straight to the clinic. She was shocked by his appearance; dazed by the combination of pain killers and alcohol aversion drugs, he was physically shaking; he drooled his words; behind his eyes he struggled to make sense of what was happening. Holding Freddie tight with one hand, he gently stroked her hair. 'He was just like a baby,' Freddie remembers. 'That's why you never had the hardness to turn your back on him.'

1965

THE PERSPIRATION WAS running down Hancock's forehead and stinging his eyes. Urged on by his mother, he stretched out his thick, shaking hands and placed them on his step-father's bare chest. 'It was a dramatic and traumatic experience,' recalls Freddie Ross. 'Tony's mother desperately wanted to believe he had the gift of healing.'

Soon after their marriage in September, 1960, Lily and Henry Sennett had bought a flat in Crescent Court, a modern development overlooking Durley Chine, on Bournemouth's west cliff. Before their third anniversary, the retired civil servant had been diagnosed as suffering from diabetes mellitus. Sennett continued to lose weight and his skin took on a bronzed, almost suntanned appearance. His doctor, already certain of the outcome, ordered more tests early in 1964, and it was confirmed the 74-year-old was suffering from haemochromatosis, a fatal disease in which excessive iron accumulates in the liver, pancreas and skin.

Throughout the previous October and November, and with his mind focused on his forthcoming *Sunday Night at the London Palladium* performance, Hancock would catch the train or be driven down to Bournemouth to comfort his mother and sit with his dying step-father.

Lily, by now a committed and open spiritualist, had enlisted the help of a medium she introduced to her son as 'Bill'. Hancock – who would later mention 'Bill' in one of his suicide notes – enjoyed talking to the psychic, but was never convinced of his healing powers or his promises of a bright, forgiving afterlife. Death, Hancock knew from his own childhood, was a slow and painful and desperate business. It was also a condition he had long since convinced himself he could 'sense' in a person. When his mother suggested he take part in a laying-on of hands, Hancock reluctantly agreed. The experience left him physically and mentally exhausted.

By late December, Lily could no longer cope and her husband was moved from their Crescent Court flat to a private nursing home at Boscombe. On 15 January, she telephoned her son at his Grosvenor Street flat to break the news that his second step-father had died. Lily, by now in her mid-seventies, had been widowed for the third time.

January was a bad month for Hancock. Within a few days of Henry Sennett's death, Freddie would be in hospital undergoing surgery, and Hancock would fly to New York to suffer the indignity of hearing the Americans reject his television series. He had already parted company with his old friend Philip Oakes.

The *Punch and Judy Man* co-writer had been hired by the BBC to script a series of 35-minute radio programmes inspired by the *'Ancock's Anthology* broadcast Hancock had made the previous Christmas Day. One problem its producer, Richard Dingley, found hard to resolve was Hancock's inexperience at 'being himself'. With no character to project, Hancock's voice sounded flat, 'almost disinterested'. Dingley admitted: 'The programme was pleasing enough to listen to, and attracted a decent audience, but was nothing special.' He was surprised then that his superiors at Broadcasting House thought it worth hanging a series on it. Unknown to Hancock, the BBC had approached Oakes, and then a meeting was arranged with the star and his producer. In a post-meeting memo, Dingley voiced his concern and expected it to be 'even more difficult to get Hancock to concentrate on a series of six programmes than it was for the original recording'.

At first Hancock liked the idea. It would be his first make-or-break involvement with any series since the final radio *Half Hour*s in 1959, and with a script and prepared interview questions there would be no lines to learn. Within days, the accumulated stress of his Christmas head injury, his step-father's death and Freddie's impending operation had ground his confidence so thin that he began looking for excuses. He settled on boredom and persuaded himself a new series – any series – would be 'returning to the bad old days'. Disagreements, mostly deliberate and petty, arose between Hancock and Philip Oakes, and

Dingley arrived one morning to discover Hancock had 'fired' the writer and was refusing to work with him. The project was dropped.

Freddie had been scheduled for a New Year operation for several weeks. To Hancock, any form of physical illness was a weakness which demanded a certain amount of pity and understanding, emotions he found embarrassing and distasteful. He had only just survived the harrowing visits to Bournemouth and the Crescent Court flat which, he told a friend, 'smelt exactly as the hotel before my father's death'. The thought of visiting his lover in hospital terrified him and the day after Freddie was admitted to hospital he flew to New York.

The American networks were awaiting the arrival of eight 'pilot' recordings of Hancock shows, but they had not expected the star to deliver them in person. Neither the tapes nor Hancock impressed the executives, who dutifully watched the tapes in the cinema of a New York studio. One recalls: 'Hancock, like his material, was too British. He was charming and curious and gentlemanly. That was the problem – no one took him seriously.' There was also trouble in understanding his 'too British' sense of humour. For the second time in his career, 'It was suggested we buy the rights and rewrite and remake the shows for a US audience. We certainly didn't want Hancock.'

Undeterred, Hancock flew to Los Angeles with his American agent, Bernie Lang, for a meeting with the Walt Disney organisation. Disney were about to start casting a new children's western and needed a British actor to play an itinerant thespian. No deals were struck, but Hancock still considered his only chance of transatlantic – and international – success lay in breaking into Hollywood. As he repeatedly informed Freddie in a constant stream of letters and telephone calls, if that meant moving to America, so be it.

Back in England, Freddie had booked them into a Sussex health farm as a brief respite from what looked as though it might be a grim twelve months. After a leisurely drive from London, they arrived at the Bexhill establishment, only to be told Disney had been trying to contact him all day. Hancock rang his agent and then Los Angeles. It was raining and giant waves, whipped by a force seven gale, were crashing over the shingle beach. Hancock and Freddie had arrived at

Bexhill prepared for seven days of lettuce leaves and carrot juice. Instead they were huddled together in the darkness of his car, eating fish and chips and pickled onions – and dreaming of his first Hollywood film.

Although not a star-studded movie, *The Adventures of Bullwhip Griffin* would at least allow Hancock to work with some of the most popular Hollywood actors and actresses of the decade: Roddy McDowall, Suzanne Pleshette, Karl Malden and Cecil Kellaway. Another cast member was Hermione Baddeley, who had been given the unenviable task of teaching Hancock to dance in an early television *Half Hour*. Adapted from the Sid Fleischman novel, *By the Great Horn Spoon*, the story follows two Eastern aristocrats tempted by the 1849 Californian gold rush and accompanied on their cross-country trek by their butler.

Hollywood was everything Hancock had hoped it would be. He was met at Los Angeles International Airport by a barrel-chested black driver who had the intriguing habit of walking three or four paces ahead of his passenger, sweeping a path through the crowded terminal like a snow plough. The star – and stardom – had arrived. Beguiled and bamboozled by his own importance, Hancock became the self-inflated and pompous *Rebel* of his own creation.

Disney had checked Hancock into the plush Beverly Wiltshire Hotel in downtown Beverly Hills. There were still almost three weeks before Hancock's scenes were due to be shot and the loneliness and fragility of his situation soon marked him as an oddity among a society which survived on brash confidence.

Surrounded by bikini-clad women and bare-chested men, Hancock insisted on remaining suited and tied as he sat under a poolside umbrella, attempting to learn his lines. Each day he telephoned Freddie, and each day, as the expectation and isolation took hold, he consumed more expense-account Champagne. By the time the read-throughs started, he was scratchy and opinionated. One rehearsal was almost abandoned, recalls one studio insider, because Hancock didn't think his lines were 'good enough'.

'Hollywood is a place of many insecurities and the cardinal sin is to show them,' explain Freddie Ross and David Nathan in their biography of the comedian. 'Hancock's air of desperation was too savage a reminder to other actors in the vicinity of the impermanence of fame and fortune.'

After two weeks Bernie Lang, his representative from the William Morris Agency, who had flown to the West Coast to keep Hancock company, had to return to New York. The calls to Freddie became more despondent and more desperate. 'Fly out tomorrow,' he pleaded. 'I need you here.' When rumours of Hancock's drunken behaviour began to filter the 5,500 miles back to London, Freddie decided it was time to fly to Los Angeles.

'Great,' Hancock exploded into the telephone. 'I'll have a surprise for you at the airport.' Forty-five minutes after Freddie's plane landed, Hancock shuffled towards her through the crowded terminal, 'red-eyed and unshaven and alone'.

'I'm sorry I'm late,' he said. It was at that moment Freddie realised she was in for a bumpy ride.

Her first decision was to move Hancock out of the Beverly Wiltshire and into adjoining suites at a Burbank motel called the Sportsman's Lodge. Here she could chaperone her lover and attempt to dry him out in time for the first day's shooting.

Each morning Hancock would rise at 5.30am and spend an hour practising his lines. 'He was having tremendous difficulty remembering them after years and years of reading from an Autocue,' said Freddie. After a light breakfast she would drive him 'rigid and white faced' to the Disney studios in time for his 7.30 call. While he was on the set, Freddie would wait in his windowless dressing room or go shopping for a picnic lunch. To avoid the midday temptation of the commissariat they would eat alone.

Most days the temperature outside was in the nineties; under the studio lights it was well over 100°F. On 27 May – fifteen days after his forty-first birthday – the set temperature was so high it began to melt the scenery glue. Hancock was the only member of the cast wearing a heavy tweed suit and trilby hat. As he was about to return to the *Bullwhip Griffin* set after lunch, he suggested Freddie go back to their Burbank Motel for a swim. She had just settled herself by the pool when she was summoned to the telephone. Her 'husband', an executive at the Disney studio informed her, had suffered what appeared to be a fit and collapsed. It was the opportunity the film company had been waiting for.

Unknown to Hancock or his American agent, a Disney casting manager had approached actor Harry Guardino about taking over the British comedian's part less than a week after his Los Angeles arrival. 'As soon as they realised what state he was in the rumours started to fly,' recalled Hermione Baddeley. 'From what I gathered, Disney was quite openly waiting for Tony to make a mistake – the only person on the film who didn't know was Tony.' This was confirmed by the film's star, the British-born actor Roddy McDowall, who thought Hancock was a man 'weighted by some obscure responsibility'. He was on set, although out of camera shot, when Hancock's knees gave way and he fell to the floor. As the comedian was carried to his dressing room McDowall recalled he 'felt an undercurrent of relief' from almost every production manager and executive. A few days later, he claims, he was told of two telephone calls made by the studio front office on the afternoon of Hancock's collapse. The first was to Hancock's 'wife' informing her of the incident. The second – even while Freddie was making the fifteen-minute journey to the studio – was to Harry Guardino's agent, offering her client Hancock's still contracted part. The method of ditching *Bullwhip Griffin*'s English star had already been worked out.

Despite Hancock's protests – and Freddie's evidence – that he had not been drinking, Disney claimed his insurance cover would be withdrawn unless Hancock allowed himself to be admitted to a Burbank hospital to be given a clean bill of health. He had already passed a pre-contract medical back in England. 'It was then that we started to feel something was rumbling,' admits Freddie. The tests were prolonged and painful and proved heat exhaustion had triggered Hancock's collapse, but even before the medical report was written, Hancock was informed he had been fired from *Bullwhip Griffin*.

From Los Angeles the pair flew first to New York for talks with Hancock's East Coast agent, and to discuss the possibility of suing Walt Disney for breach of contract. The prospect of months – possibly years – of litigation, with both sides attacking and defending his drinking, terrified him. Freddie, supported by the hospital report, urged her lover to stand and fight, but Hancock, as always, decided to catch the next plane for France.

Telephoning to arrange a further meeting, Hancock's agent was informed by the hotel reception that his client had already checked out. When he was put through to the couple's fifth-floor suite Freddie protested: 'That's impossible, I've got his suitcase and his coat.'

Out in the street, Freddie hailed a yellow cab. 'Get me to Kennedy in thirty minutes and I'll give you $25,' she told the driver. It was all the cash she had in her purse. Hancock had left an airline ticket for her at reception, but no money.

He was queuing at the Air France check-in desk when Freddie tapped him on the shoulder. 'Haven't you forgotten something?' she asked.

'Like what,' Hancock replied, apparently unconcerned.

'Like me for instance.'

They crossed the Atlantic in silence. 'We made lots of journeys that way,' recalls Freddie.

The situation was to become even more bizarre. When they finally reached Cannes, Hancock perversely telephoned Cicely who promptly flew to France to comfort her estranged husband. The legal wrangling over his divorce from Cicely had rumbled on for months, and a July date had already been set for the decree nisi hearing. All three drank and argued and sulked and drank some more. Despite sharing an apartment with his lover, Hancock would wander off with Cicely for hours on end, oblivious of Freddie's jealousy or concern. 'It was like living with a volcano that was about to erupt,' she later recalled. 'Tony was burning himself up from the inside.'

Emerging from a leatherwear shop, Hancock and Freddie literally bumped into Bernard Delfont. The impresario, whose agency had brokered the Disney deal, demanded to know why his client wasn't at work on the other side of the world. 'He was very angry about the way Disney treated him,' Delfont remembers.

As they spoke Hancock appeared determined to put the *Bullwhip Griffin* fiasco behind him and re-establish his stage career. He confidently suggested that Delfont should book him for a short run at the Talk of the Town, despite having withdrawn two years earlier when his nerve gave out. Delfont shook hands, 'and off he went and I thought I'd hear nothing more about it. I duly got back to London and he rang me and said, "I'm rehearsing and I feel great." ' They agreed Hancock should take over a Talk of the Town midnight cabaret slot starting on 28 June – just ten days away.

Hancock needed some new material quickly. He telephoned Ray Galton and Alan Simpson, only to be told they were too busy writing *Steptoe and Son*. Whenever he came close to calling the show off Freddie would cajole or bully him into carrying on. It was, Delfont rightly concedes, 'too much responsibility for him'.

The six-week show was billed as *Fatal Fascination* and Hancock agreed to take a percentage of the seats sold rather than a flat fee. Attendances were above average and good enough to make him around £500 a week.

His off-stage psyching had by now progressed from the mumbled rehearsals in the Adelphi wings to a nightly ritual of brutal and vicious self-effacement. Hancock, head bowed and oblivious to his surroundings, ranted aloud: 'Professional idiot. That's what I am, a professional idiot.'

'I give myself a bit of a coating before I go on,' Hancock reluctantly explained. 'Sort of helps make my shoulders drop when I start. Takes about half-an-hour of abuse. Self-abuse. Some people think it's intended for them, which is a pity. Occasionally the odd right-hander, also helps.'

One actor who had taken several small parts in the television *Half Hours* went along to watch his 'hero' at work. He recalls: 'Hancock's performance was terribly disappointing. His material was old, very old, and taken from his 1950s stage shows.' He also remembers Hancock being 'very nervous, almost too preoccupied to perform'.

Another problem was Hancock's imminent divorce from Cicely. He felt himself responsible for his wife's ill-health and unhappiness yet, surprisingly, refused to accept any kind of blame for her alcoholism. On 6 July, Cicely was granted a decree nisi. As grounds she cited Hancock's adultery with Freddie Ross. That night, Hancock arrived at the Talk of the Town early. Although he had obviously been drinking, he appeared more agitated than usual. After their star had vomited several times in his dressing-room sink, the management considered calling a doctor, but instead someone had the idea of asking Dennis Main Wilson, who was working just around the corner, to call and reassure his former associate. The pair had not met since February, 1957. When Hancock was told the BBC producer was waiting to see him, he refused to come out of his dressing room or to let Main Wilson in.

John le Mesurier and his fiancée had finally set a date for their wedding. When they called at the Talk of the Town one evening to give Hancock the good news, they found Freddie Ross and Hancock's mother in attendance. 'Tony looked tired and tense,' Joan recalled, and after just a few minutes the pair were brusquely ushered out.

Even while they were still working together Hancock was always embarrassed at the idea of Sid James watching him perform on stage, and the pair had decided a pact was needed. James would never tell Hancock if he was going to be in the audience at one of his stage shows, and Hancock would never warn James if the situation were reversed. 'I think he was right,' James said. 'For him to see me in his audience would have thrown him. I reckon if I had spotted him in my audience I would have felt it, too.' Coming off stage early one Sunday morning a few days later, Hancock was told James, who had sat through the show unannounced, wanted to see him. The South African explained the reason for his visit. An American producer had sent James what the actor claimed was 'the best film script he had ever seen'. It had been written specifically for Tony Hancock and Sid James. 'It would have set the world alight, that bloody film,' James explained.

The star's dressing room at the Talk of the Town was a suite of rooms with a bar always kept well stocked with Dom Perignon. The more he drank, the more Hancock became animated about the possibility of a new film. Several hours later, and with the summer sun streaming through the dressing-room windows, the pair emerged from the stage door. Describing their dawn departure, Sid James recalled: 'I saw him away through the empty West End streets with a promise he'd join me that afternoon and that we'd go and talk turkey with the film producer. I felt that early Sunday morning was like a new birth.

'We had the meeting with the producer. Tony was still all for doing the film. Then, the next morning, Monday, came the letter.

'It said, simply, he had had second thoughts through the night and that he was now quite sure again that it would be a backward step for him to work with me. It was unbelievable. Tony just didn't want to know when the real chances for us to get back together came up.'

Hancock, as his friends and colleagues were coming to realise, had perfected the art of walking backwards. He blindly turned away from the possibility of survival and ultimate success.

The BBC unwittingly nurtured Hancock's ever-deepening neurosis when it announced plans to repeat the entire last three television series of *Hancock's Half Hour*. To cash in on the publicity, it was suggested he should record two television *Half Hours* for release on disc. The producer would again be Alan Freeman, who had been instrumental in signing Tony Hancock for the Pye label in the 1950s. This time he had persuaded Decca to issue the long-play record.

Unaware of Hancock's recent decision to back out of his film promise, Freeman contacted Sid James to ask if the actor was once again willing to work together. James, about to leave for a week's holiday in Majorca, was confused but enthusiastic: 'To work with Hancock again, I'll even give up the holiday.' He later admitted he was given the impression the idea for the studio remakes had come from Hancock himself.

To add a twist of irony to the situation, one of the episodes chosen was *The Reunion Party*, and not only was Hancock working with Sid

James for the first time in years, he also asked that Graham Stark be offered a part as one of his wartime cronies.

Hancock arrived at the studio at 10am and Freeman sensed impending disaster. As the day ground inevitably and painfully on, not even Freeman had the nerve to inform Hancock what a shambles he was making of his performance. 'It was not a happy experience,' Freeman later admitted. 'Tony had had too much to drink and I couldn't stop him or we would have lost everything. We just kept the tape rolling and edited afterwards.' Each television script had been written to run for exactly twenty-eight minutes, perfect for one side of a 33rpm disc, but in the event *The Reunion Party* took forty-two minutes and *The Missing Page* over-ran by ten minutes.

To recreate the atmosphere of the original shows, Freeman had decided to record the remakes in front of a live audience. Among the onlookers were Ray Galton and Alan Simpson. 'Tony's performance was remarkably bad,' recalls Simpson. 'His timing was bad. He was slow. He had no emotion. It was dreadful.' To salvage the project, the producer asked the two writers to help with editing out the pauses and the fluffed lines, and to attempt to disguise Hancock's poor timing. Listening to the play-back in the control room, Freeman was dismayed to discover a problem he had failed to notice during the recording. The gales of laughter from the audience did not correspond to the actual script; Hancock's off-mic antics and facial expressions had generated a bigger response than his lines.

For Sid James it was the end. Not only had his old friend repeatedly broken his promises, Hancock had now betrayed James artistically. Sid James – the consummate professional – swore he would never work with Tony Hancock again.

After Hancock's attempt to sell the nation a slimmer, healthier railway network under Lord Beeching, he was offered the chance to push a different kind of propaganda. Each year the Egg Marketing Board based its sales campaign around a new slogan. For 1965 it decided on: 'Happiness is egg shaped.'

Hancock was shown the story-boards for each of the television commercials and liked the concept. 'I didn't know whether it was right for me to lend myself to advertising,' he said. 'I wouldn't have done corsets, or that toothpaste that gives you a ring of confidence, or a smelly mouth, or whatever it is. But eggs, they're different. Nourishing. Wholesome. So I took the plunge.'

The adverts, destined to become classics in their own right, used miniplots which blatantly exploited Hancock's East Cheam persona. The public was being offered – or at least the Egg Marketing Board hoped it would recognise – a glimpse of the old Railway Cuttings resident.

The studio and film crew had been booked, and Ken Carter, given the task of producing the commercials, met the comedian to discuss details. It was the first time Hancock had seen the actual scripts. To Carter's amazement Hancock refused to say 'Happiness is egg shaped', the basis of the entire campaign. The phrase, he claimed, was 'trite and silly – an excuse'. As ever, Hancock was gripped with self-doubt.

Carter reported the deadlock to the board which, not surprisingly, insisted on Hancock honouring his contract. In desperation, the producer suggested someone else should say the slogan, Hancock would merely have to react to it.

The scripts were hurriedly rewritten, this time to include the Galton and Simpson creation of Mrs Cravatte, played in the television *Half Hours* by Patricia Hayes. Carter contacted Hayes and found she was available but, when she returned to the BBC wardrobe to retrieve Mrs Crevatte's fruit-and-flowers hat, she found it had disappeared. Hayes eventually made a replacement from her family's dressing-up box.

In one commercial Mrs Crevatte leans into the camera to deliver the line: 'Happiness is egg shaped.' Hancock reacts by commenting: 'Oh dear, oh dear, oh dear. You ask them for a bit of glamour . . . and this is what they send.'

To Carter, and the Egg Marketing Board, Hancock was merely living up to his everlasting reputation as a 'troublesome performer'. For Hancock, the scripts simply did not feel right; a view supported by Hayes: 'Of course Hancock was right. His instinct as a comedian was always right.'

*

Thirteen years after Tony Hancock and Peter Sellers first appeared on screen together – in *Orders are Orders* – the demons which ruled and ruined their lives brought them together one final time. Bryan Forbes, hired by Columbia to direct *The Wrong Box*, had long felt that in private Hancock and Sellers 'were both searching for an elusive bluebird of happiness'. By 1965, Hancock and Sellers were embarking upon the final and saddest phases of their lives. John Mortimer, the barrister and author, once admitted: 'The two saddest men I ever met were Peter Sellers and Tony Hancock, and I give thanks daily to God, or destiny, that I never took up life as a comic.'

Hancock had less than three years to live and Sellers had already strayed into the wasteland which bordered his paranoid schizophrenia. Spike Milligan, who was to deliver perhaps the ultimate verdict on Hancock's life, was already detecting the destruction to both men: 'Hancock kept looking for something to do when he thought his star was waning; like Peter, he got rid of people systematically. They both destroyed themselves over and over.'

The beguiling helplessness which stemmed from their insanity also produced more subtle similarities of character. They were both superstitious about the colour green, particularly in theatres or on film sets, and they both did little to conceal their frustration of long theatre runs. Both revelled in any form of 'off duty' fancy dress, and, although Hancock rarely drove, both had developed a fascination for fast and flamboyant cars.

The Wrong Box was an ill-conceived and incoherent adaptation of Robert Louis Stevenson and Lloyd Osbourne's light-hearted novel, and its only motive was as a big-screen vehicle for Peter Cook and Dudley Moore. Two elderly Victorian brothers find themselves the only survivors of a tontine and attempt to murder each other. Hancock – whose appearance is restricted to the final fifteen minutes of the film – is the detective who attempts to unravel the convoluted plot. 'He attacks his part with gusto,' Roger Wilmut claims, 'but tends to be warped by the inclination of the writers to "improve" the original by the addition of a wide variety of intrusive comic devices.'

The result is best summed up by Harry Thompson in his biography, *Peter Cook:*

The Wrong Box, sadly, turned out to be a thoroughly incoherent and mediocre piece of work, a classic example of the British film industry's traditional custom of applying famous comedians en masse to a feeble script in the hope of papering over any cracks. Besides Peter, Dudley, Hancock and Sellers, the cast included Irene Handl, John le Mesurier, John Junkin, Norman Rossington, Leonard Rossiter, Nicholas Parsons and Jeremy Lloyd, not to mention the Temperance Seven as a group of undertakers. All concerned overacted strenuously. The result was what might be called a 'romp' (in the worst sense of the word), full of reaction shots to jokes: when one of the cast fell over, for instance, Forbes cut away to a bunch of cute children laughing. Supplying one's own on-screen approval for a joke is an insecure device that rarely works. The direction was generally turgid, the incidental music too heavy, and the film's interpretation of Victorian England strictly Carnaby Street. Insofar as it was meant to be a parody of a leaden Victorian melodrama, *The Wrong Box* failed utterly, by wholeheartedly resorting to the trappings of a leaden Victorian melodrama.

Of the twenty or so credited stars, no less than eight had previously worked with Hancock, either in his radio or television *Half Hour*s or films. One was Norman Bird. He had spent five weeks filming *The Punch and Judy Man,* never having passed more than a 'hello' with the film's co-writer and star. His impression of Hancock was of a 'rather quiet, slightly sad man'. Hancock and Bird appear in a graveyard scene in *The Wrong Box.* The tombstones had been erected in Bulstrode Park, not far from Pinewood Studios, and the filming had momentarily stopped. To Bird's surprise, Hancock turned to him and said: 'Well, our last film together was a big success wasn't it, Norman?' Bird was not sure how to take the remark. He mumbled something ambiguous and Hancock was called away, 'still looking rather sad'.

Nanette Newman – whose husband, Bryan Forbes, was directing *The Wrong Box* – had appeared in *The Rebel* as a green-lipped hippy. Hancock and Newman were sitting in a caravan waiting for the rain to stop. 'He was very depressed and felt his career was going nowhere,' she said. 'It was such a contrast from the energy and genius of *The Rebel*.' Her abiding memory is of his generosity: 'During location shooting in Paris, Tony would take the cast to his favourite bars and restaurants. He would always pick up the bill.'

Relieved of the burden of responsibility Hancock could still deliver a stunning performance, but pressured by new demands or fretful of new expectations he withdrew. Allowed to interpret and express a script in his own way, unharried by the need to justify his comic creativity, he remained a genius. After the false start of *The Rebel* and the isolation of *The Punch and Judy Man*, his cameo performances as the absent-minded eccentric Henry Popperwell in *Those Magnificent Men in Their Flying Machines* and the detective in *The Wrong Box* were at last earning him the international attention and overseas royalties he deserved.

Clive Dunn, the comedy actor, tells the story of an encounter with Hancock in the toilet of a Marylebone recording studio. 'Don't you get nervous, Clive?' Hancock asked.

'Always,' replied Dunn.

Hancock thought for a moment. 'You've got it made,' he said. 'I often wish I just played character parts like you.'

At the time, Dunn did not fully understand. 'What he really meant was that he envied my lack of responsibility for the success of the show,' Dunn later concluded. 'A character support actor goes on and tries to steal a few laughs, but takes no blame if the show is a flop.'

However brittle Hancock's self-regard, he was still regularly fired with flashes of ambition. He would talk enthusiastically about persuading the London County Council to rebuild the bombed-out Avenue Theatre in Shaftesbury Avenue. Then, once it was open, he would complete an unlikely triumvirate with Wilfred Lawson and Richard Burton to play a fascinating round robin of Shakespear's *King Lear*;

Dinner-suited with Sid James and
Peter Sellers...

... but Hancock was more relaxed in his
favourite duffel coat. © *J Harker*.

At the height of his career a BBC
survey showed 23 per cent of the British
population watched *Hancock's Half Hour* –
a record which won Hancock a clutch of
comedy awards. © *BBC*.

Hancock shunned public attention but enjoyed his popularity among fellow stars. With Liz Fraser...

... and two of the Beverley Sisters.

Hancock and his *Rebel* co-star Paul Massie and their wives at Elstree Studios.

Hancock and Cicely share a break on the *Rebel* set with his mother, seventy-year-old Lily Walker – only days away from her third marriage.

Hancock with his two poodles Charlie and Mr Brown. He claimed one was an extrovert and the other a 'psychic wreck'.

For Hancock each stage was a cold and frightening and lonely place. Walking from the wings he looked like a 'small, brown bull going into the arena to meet his end'. © *J Harker.*

Rehearsing for a one-week variety show at Nottingham's Theatre Royal. © *Evening Post, Nottingham.*

Cinema managers were issued with a campaign book for each new film. In 1965 Hancock was one of more than twenty stars appearing in *Those Magnificent Men in Their Flying Machines*. © *Tony Hillman Collection.*

Hancock, Gerald Sim (centre) and Nanette Newman chat in Bath's Royal Crescent before the start of location shooting for *The Wrong Box*. © *The Bath Chronicle.*

2 December, 1965: Tony Hancock and Freddie Ross marry at Marylebone Register Office – he had spent the previous night spying on his fiancee.

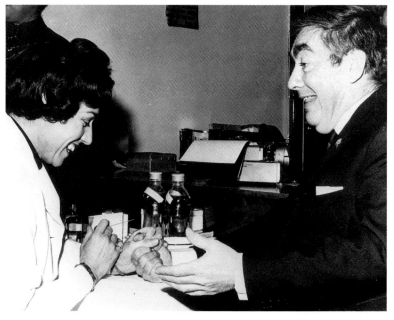

'That's almost an armful' – Hancock was persuaded to give blood as a publicity stunt for his disastrous 1966 tour. © *D C Thomson & Co.*

Hancock rehearsing for his 1966 one-night show at the Royal Festival Hall – the next day he disappeared with his best friend's wife.

1989: Joan le Mesurier

Hancock with quiz-master and talent-spotter Hughie Green entertaining the troops in Aden.
© *M Garrett.*

One of the last pictures of Tony Hancock before his suicide – Things seem to go wrong too many times.

one evening Burton's Lear to Lawson's Fool, the next Lawson's Lear to Hancock's Fool.

Another project – for which his enthusiasm increased the more remote the possibility of production became – was for a musical adaptation of André Obey's play *Noah*. Bernard Delfont had hired Ray Galton and Alan Simpson to write the script. The music and songs would be composed by Leslie Bricusse who, with Anthony Newley, had co-written *Stop the World, I Want to Get Off* and whose song, *What Kind of Fool Am I?*, had reduced Hancock to tears. However, it wasn't until the set designer Sean Kenny was given a copy of the script that it was suggested Hancock should be cast as the unwilling and peppery biblical patriarch. 'It was never conceived with Tony in mind,' the writers admitted. 'It was only because Sean said that every line sounded like Hancock that we even started thinking about him.' Kenny quickly converted Leslie Bricusse and together they approached the producer. Delfont, who never wavered in his faith in Hancock, thought the role could well be the turning point in Hancock's career.

Galton and Simpson were not so sure. No doubt chastened by the recording fiasco earlier in the year, and as the only people with direct experience of Hancock's latent antipathy to long theatre runs – the £100,000 production would need at least a year to break even – they doubted if he would even be interested.

'Everyone took the view that Tony's main trouble was that he had not done anything good for a long time,' Galton recalls. 'Remedy that and he'd be right back at the top. If we could have done it with Tony, say ten years before, it would have been fantastic because he was dead right for it then.'

In Sean Kenny the 41-year-old comedian found a friend who squinted at the world in the same visionary way. As Noah, Hancock would look skyward and ask: 'But where am I going to get the wood from?' Kenny's answer was to shower the stage with timber. The Irishman once sent Hancock a copy of Chairman Mao's little red book inscribed: 'What about this for a musical?'

Surrounded by apparent goodwill, Hancock's passion quickly

turned to obsession. He talked of little else, telephoning Delfont's office to demand how the pre-production discussions were going or calling at Kenny's London home unannounced. By the late autumn, however, the project had been shelved and the rights sold to an American company. Only Hancock refused to allow the idea to die.

Glyn Jones had entered show business at the age of fourteen, working in shows like *Casey's Court* and taking bit parts in Will Hay films. In his late teens, he progressed to variety, singing and dancing in double acts. His post-war move into management coincided with the boom in nude revues, and Jones frequently found himself at odds with local authorities who banned his touring revues as unsavoury. Rescued by Lew and Leslie Grade, he quickly earned himself a unique place as tour manager to the international stars of light entertainment. His duties involved total care – business, leisure and spiritual – for such artists as Frank Sinatra, Sammy Davis Jnr, Nat 'King' Cole and Betty Hutton when they arrived for summer seasons at the London Palladium. As a meticulous organiser and respecter of deadlines and rehearsal calls he was, reasoned Billy Marsh, the ideal person to chaperon Hancock on an Australian tour. For Jones, ten years the comic's senior, it was a turbulent assignment.

Hancock was booked for three weeks' cabaret at Sydney's Chevron Hilton Hotel opening on 2 November, and on the way he intended to stop over in Fiji. Early one morning the telephone rang at Freddie's Dorset Square flat. It was Hancock calling from the Pacific. He sounded happy and admitted he had had 'a couple of beers'. Freddie exploded. One of the last promises he made Freddie – who would be flying out later – was that he would not drink. For several weeks before his departure Hancock had managed to remain sober. 'I went hysterical,' she recalls, 'because one beer was the same as a bottle of vodka to Tony. Once the alcohol had got into his system it was just a matter of time before he was back on it properly.'

Freddie first telephoned Hancock's London doctor and then his mother in Bournemouth. Both, in turn, called Hancock, 10,000 miles away in Fiji, urging him to lay off the drink. He swore to all three that the beers were a one-off and that he was back on the wagon. Freddie was not convinced. She would fly out to Australia early.

Cicely Hancock's decree absolute would become effective while Hancock was in Australia. The original plan had been for Freddie to join Hancock towards the end of the Hilton booking and for the couple to fly to Honolulu where they would marry, miles from England and with the minimum of publicity. The flight to Sydney took more than twenty-four hours. Freddie, racked by doubt yet still determined to marry Hancock, was still haunted by the vision of her dishevelled lover weaving through the travellers at Los Angeles International Airport. This time Freddie was greeted by a clean-shaven and bright-eyed Hancock. They drove to the hotel in a large limousine that smelled of warm leather and polished wood. It was evident the combined long-distance badgering and Glyn Jones's fatherly shepherding had worked. Hancock had not touched a drop for days.

Rehearsals for the act were going well, although Hancock was still jittery about having anyone he knew in the audience. He allowed Freddie to sit through the first night and then demanded she remain in their suite for future performances. The days – and nights – dragged on. For someone as nervously energetic as Freddie the 'enforced confinement was torture'. Hancock would sleep until mid-morning and eat a late breakfast. He would then read the papers while Freddie watched the television and drank interminable pots of tea. After a week she could stand it no longer and insisted he take her shopping.

Hancock's act meant disillusionment for many people. In the audience for one of the Chevron Hilton cabarets was Ed Dolan, a radio disc jockey. He had 'adored Tony Hancock for as long as Tony Hancock existed'. Watching his hero on stage, Dolan was willing to forgive almost anything. 'I begged him to be brilliant and he wasn't,' said the presenter. 'I came away so disappointed, it was as if the man had personally let me down.'

Hancock's aversion to television adverts continued with a disastrous attempt to launch a new biscuit. He had been contracted to record a series of commercials, each advertisement ending with him reminding the Australian public of the brand. The problem was Hancock could not, or pretended he could not, remember the name. Take after take he fumbled the lines. Eventually a name – any name – would pop into his head and Hancock would triumphantly announce: 'Don't forget . . . Silvikrin Shampoo.' After a day's shooting the commercial was abandoned. One of the studio crew is convinced Hancock's memory problem was more temperament than temporal. 'We had all been warned how difficult Hancock could be,' she said. 'Hancock was bored from the moment he walked into the studio. It was obvious he did not want the job and he did his utmost to wreck the whole thing as "innocently" as possible. It was a classic piece of acting.'

Hancock's marriage to Cicely Romanis had lasted fifteen years and two months. Confirmation of his divorce arrived in a telegram and to celebrate he and Freddie reserved rooms at the Honolulu Hilton. On the second day of what the couple hoped was to become their honeymoon they attempted, for the first time, to get married. However, anyone applying for a marriage licence in Hawaii is required to undergo a blood test. The queue in the medical examiner's office was endless and they were told to wait. 'Blood,' Hancock erupted, 'you can have it if it's really necessary. Plenty to spare of the stuff. Oh dear, yes, gallons of it.' The line of Hawaiian, Puerto Rican, Mexican and Philippine couples watched Hancock's outburst in bemused silence. After twenty minutes his patience gave out. He stormed to the head of the queue and announced: 'I came here in good faith to give 'em a spoonful of the best British blood. If they don't want it – the best of luck. I'm off.'

Hancock and Freddie arrived back in England during the last full week in November. Just before lunch the following Monday morning, Freddie was at her desk when a reporter from the London *Evening Standard* telephoned. He wanted to confirm she was marrying Tony Hancock at St Marylebone Register Office at 11.30 the coming

Thursday morning, 2 December. Freddie pleaded ignorance. A few minutes later Hancock burst in to 'give her the news'.

Hancock had effectively moved into Freddie's Dorset Square flat, but the night before the wedding he agreed to return to his own apartment. Within hours he was back, this time skulking in the shadows and doorways of nearby Balcombe Street and Gloucester Place, convinced his wife-to-be was planning one last night of passion with a younger and less demanding lover. Sometime after midnight, and long after the lights had gone out in Freddie's flat, Hancock gave up and went home.

His suspicion and bad humour were barely submerged the next morning. One of the bride's friends, Kati Hannan, remembers: 'Freddie was nervous and Tony was quite high.' Things did not get any better.

Inside the wedding suite, the ceremony lasted barely two minutes. When it came to completing the certificate, Hancock gave his profession as 'actor' and confirmed his previous marriage had been dissolved. Freddie recorded her occupation as a public relations officer. Both gave their address as 17 Dorset Square. When Hancock attempted to pay the 8s 6d fee with a pound note, the register office staff did not have any change and Freddie settled the bill. It was a 'debt' her husband owed until the day he died.

As the party attempted to adjourn to a nearby hotel they were surrounded by a gaggle of demanding journalists. Tony Bissett was one of more than a dozen photographers who regularly covered Marylebone register office's usual round of celebrity weddings. Waiting for Freddie to arrive, Hancock chatted and posed for pictures. 'When he emerged down the front steps his mood had thickened and he was really quite nasty,' recalls the award-winning photographer. 'It was a real Jekyll and Hyde transformation, in fifteen minutes he had become aggressive and violent and it was clear he just wanted to escape.'

The reception was little better. 'Tony's family were sitting against one wall of the hotel suite and hers against the other and they were all watching Tony drink,' says Kati Hannan. When she suggested the newlyweds cut the cake, Hancock complained she was acting 'like a bloody Butlin's redcoat' and Freddie fled to a bedroom in tears.

After the reception Leonard Ross drove the Hancocks to his nearby home so that his sister could change before he drove them on to catch their flight to Ireland. When they arrived at the house, Ross had somehow misplaced the keys and they had to smash a window to get in. At Heathrow Airport the car boot would not open and they had to force the lock to retrieve Hancock and Freddie's cases.

As they boarded the Aer Lingus flight Hancock slumped into his first-class seat and into a monosyllabic silence. Freddie had been married just four hours and had somehow already offended her new husband. 'For God sake,' she demanded. 'What have I done wrong?' To Hancock's misguided sensibility the fact that Freddie, with just three days to prepare for her wedding, had not changed the name on her passport became a question of pride; if she did not want to be Mrs Hancock she should have said so.

When they arrived at Dublin's Gresham Hotel for the honeymoon, Hancock slipped the barman a £10 note. Every time he was served a large orange juice it was laced with an equal measure of vodka. To keep up the pretence, Hancock made a point of showing his wife the 'untouched' vodka bottle in their bedroom mini-bar. What Freddie did not know was that Hancock was topping it up with water after each illicit drink.

Hancock agreed they should share a furnished flat overlooking the Edgware Road and within walking distance of Hyde Park. The move failed to occupy Hancock, and his boredom invariably slid into quarrels and threats of separation. The Friday before Christmas – after a noisy and violent row – Hancock walked out. 'It's all over,' he screamed at Freddie. That night, less than three weeks into his second marriage, Hancock returned to his first wife.

The next morning, while it was still dark, Hancock telephoned Len Costa. He informed the scriptwriter he had left Freddie and had spent the night at MacConkeys, where Cicely still lived. 'Pack a bag,' Hancock said enthusiastically. 'We are going to write.' When Hancock and Cicely arrived to drive him to the house the atmosphere in the car was brittle. It was obvious, recalls Costa, they had rowed on the way up to London.

Back at MacConkeys, and on what Cicely now considered her property, the tension eased. Hancock and Costa discussed ideas for a television series in the upstairs study. Cicely was drinking heavily, however, and, as the weekend progressed, Hancock became fretful. Costa explains: 'It was clear that he was fond of Cicely, but I am convinced that he never considered going back to her. Tony and Cicely were friendly, nothing more. It was a reasonable relationship.'

Cicely, however, was being far from reasonable about her claim for maintenance. The legal wrangle over exactly how much allowance Hancock should pay his ex-wife, and how the property should be split, had dragged on for more than two years. On the Sunday morning, while Costa was working, Hancock announced he was taking the car. The incident, which started as 'half-joking, half-fighting' banter, soon turned violent.

Costa takes up the story: 'Tony and Cicely started to spar and then it became a wrestling match. It was a test of strength. And then Cicely threw Tony. He landed on a small side table which collapsed just like something in a film scene. Then it developed more seriously, probably because he had been thrown and it was an affront. I started clearing things up in the study; it was obvious we weren't going to stay.'

Cicely appeared in the study doorway and announced she had called the police. Asked why, she told Costa: 'Oh, it all got too much.'

By the time the police arrived, Hancock had consumed still more vodka and was still insisting he take the car. The officers were willing to write off the argument as a domestic incident, but warned Hancock against driving. Costa, too, was unwilling to let Hancock drive him back to his Enfield home. 'There was a big argument. Eventually, Tony agreed that he wouldn't drive and hired a car to take us.'

On Christmas Day Freddie finally persuaded her husband to face up to his alcoholism. 'You're right,' he told her. 'I've got to get dry. We've got to give this marriage a really good chance.' For Hancock, by now almost a veteran of drying-out clinics, it was the first time he accepted the cause and effect of his disease.

The day after Boxing Day – and exactly a year after the horrors of the Holloway Clinic – Hancock allowed himself to be admitted to a Hampstead nursing home for a two-week course of aversion therapy. Freddie spent New Year's Eve sleeping on the floor beside her husband's bed: 'We entered 1966 with heads held high and looking forward to a dry and successful marriage.'

1966

THE GUESTS IN the studio 'green room' turned towards the commotion. Hancock was shouting into a telephone and waving his free arm in the air. 'It's going to be a bloody disaster.'

This Is Your Life had been produced by Malcolm Morris for more than ten years, and when he invited Hancock to appear in a brief guest spot, he had had little expectation of an acceptance. The live broadcast was scheduled for a 10.30pm slot after the main evening news and Morris met Hancock at the studio entrance a little after nine. His first impression was of a 'charming, funny and warm' man, but as the pair walked to the 'green room' and talked about the programme the producer noticed Hancock was becoming more and more nervous.

After five bitter lemons and three or four trips to the lavatory, Hancock announced he wanted to ring Freddie. Using a telephone in the corner of the hospitality suite, he berated his wife for almost forty-five minutes: 'Why the hell did you let me agree to come on this damn show?'

The show was presented by Eamonn Andrews, a relaxed and professional Irishman. 'By this stage I was very nervous and told Eamonn to be very careful with Tony on the programme,' said

Morris. '"What do you mean very careful?" Eamonn asked. I explained that Tony was almost hyperventilating and that we should be prepared for anything that might happen.'

As Hancock left the stage at the end of the half-hour show, Morris greeted him with congratulations; his brief appearance had been 'funny and confident and quite brilliant' and the audience reaction enthusiastic and loyal. Hancock, straight-faced and disinterested, insisted on telephoning Freddie a second time. After an hour's analysis of his performance, he began phoning his friends 'pleading for their honest opinion'. He was, adds Morris, 'one brilliant and tormented man ... Tony and I were both wrecks by the time he left the studio. It was a show that had gone extremely well. I dreaded to think what happened to him when things went badly.'

Shortly after his November return from Australia, the Bernard Delfont Agency informed its client it had booked him for a New Year tour of provincial theatres. Hancock was dismayed. He would be sharing the bill with the Billy Cotton Band and, as far as he could see, the majority of venues were in outlying areas of Britain. Considering the winter weather, it was not a combination likely to relaunch his stage career.

Hancock opened at the Palace Theatre, Dundee, on St Valentine's Day. It snowed the entire week – 'Cold! We had to run from the dressing room to the stage to get some heat from the footlights.' What little remained of Hancock's self-confidence was also frozen solid. As ever he would massage the circulation back into his courage with a litany of self-abuse: 'Get out there, you wanker, Hancock. Get out there and give them your best performance. Get out there, you fucker.'

By the time the company had moved to the Aberdeen Tivoli the following week, the snow had turned to non-stop rain. Hancock sat in his dressing room, listening to the Billy Cotton Band playing a selection of Sunday lunchtime favourites and wartime melodies and receiving so little applause he could not hear it on the Tannoy. When he walked on to the stage after the interval, it seemed as though the auditorium was empty.

The only seat William Watt could afford was in the Tivoli upper circle. When he reached his seat, Watt found he had the 'gods' to himself. Hancock appeared a 'lonely and pathetic star' performing in front of the Cotton Band. 'I just could not resist shouting down to him, "Carry on Tony, you're doing fine." He looked up, gave a little wave and smiled,' remembered Watt.

It was a humiliating experience. Hancock telephoned his agent, Billy Marsh, to warn him he was about to walk out of the tour. Marsh allowed his client to let off steam and then quietly and firmly warned Hancock that if he 'abandoned the show he would be abandoning his career'. Hancock stayed and the show moved to Glasgow. As part of a publicity stunt for the Blood Transfusion Service he agreed to give blood and re-enacted his 'that's almost an armful' routine from *The Blood Donor*.*

Hancock was in love – or convinced himself he was in love – with Freddie. Throughout his adult life, she was the only woman to whom he wrote love letters; even Cicely had not warranted a single letter of affection. Back in London he basked in the company of his second wife and relished the trivialities of marriage.

His attempts at housekeeping invariably ended in disaster. Whenever Freddie was ill, Hancock insisted on making the tea. She finally found enough courage to ask her husband why each brew was taking at least thirty minutes. Convinced you could only make a good cup of tea by warming the pot, Hancock reasoned it would be that much better if he heated the entire tea service. On another occasion, Freddie returned to their Edgware Road apartment to be informed her husband had dusted and polished with that 'nice smelly stuff' – it took them months to remove Freddie's hair lacquer from the furniture. Hancock was magnanimous about his wife's failures: when her cheesecake mixture refused to set, he poured the yellow liquid into a drinking glass and announced: 'You know Fred, it's got a wonderful flavour.'

When the laughter ran out, any close contact between Hancock and Freddie could produce a static charge powerful enough to knock them

---

* In *The Blood Donor* Hancock was given the rare blood group AB Negative. He was actually A Positive, a common group.

both senseless. Both were obsessives: Hancock intent on reforming and reshaping comedy and Freddie intent on rehabilitating her husband. 'I was a neurotic-hysteric doing my best to preserve this wonderful talent,' Freddie recalls. 'When you love, you can love too much. I'm not the perfect person and maybe my biggest mistake was trying to save Tony from drink.'

Hancock would counter Freddie's relentless attempts to curb his drinking with accusations of infidelity and betrayal. In a lava flow of recriminations he would accuse her of being unfaithful with the most unlikely and unsuitable men. Freddie's devotion – and her ability to lie for her husband – eventually ran out and she finally realised she was unable to make a significant difference to his way of life. Eight years of inventing different illnesses to protect Hancock each time he retreated to a nursing home to dry out had begun to wear down her own health.

Late in May Freddie visited her doctor and, after tests, was told she needed an immediate operation to remove a possible cancerous growth. Preparations for *The Blackpool Show*, a Sunday-night variety series to be hosted by Hancock from the Lancashire resort, were well under way. Much to Freddie's annoyance, her husband had arranged to meet the show's young writers, John Muir and Eric Geen, on his forty-second birthday. Characteristically, Freddie delayed her hospital admission until after Hancock's Blackpool run, fearing the disruption and guilt would throw his performance off balance.

A day or so after rehearsals for the show had started, Hancock telephoned George Fairweather in Bournemouth and asked him to come to Blackpool for the weekend. There was, the hairdresser noticed, an 'edge of despair' in his friend's voice. Despite the rain, Hancock insisted they walk around the tower zoo. 'Come on,' he told Fairweather, 'I must take you to see my mate.' Fairweather assumed he was about to be introduced to a keeper or one of the attendants, until Hancock stopped in front of a cage containing a huge long-haired sloth.

'This is my friend,' he announced. 'He's the only one who knows exactly how I feel – hanging on for grim death and trying not to fall off.'

As ever, Hancock's best performance was witnessed by the smallest of audiences. ABC-TV executives decided they wanted a pilot episode of the show recorded at the ABC Theatre on 12 June. 'It was really fantastically successful,' remembers one of the writers. 'It was a big theatre, but Tony paralysed them; he was quite as funny as he had ever been.' After Mike and Bernie Winters' machine-gun humour of the previous year, Hancock did what he knew best and with a few irreverent and well-aimed stabs deflated the sycophancy of television compèring.

Despite the relatively modest fee of £1,000 – the same as he had received for each of his 1956 ITV shows – Hancock was enjoying himself. For the first time in years, he felt exhausted but exuberant; there was nothing else to give. The pilot was so impressive, it was decided to use the same script, but with different artistes, for the first show of the eight-week series. Unsurprisingly, Hancock was appalled at the thought of repeating what he now considered 'old material'. He was even more uneasy when the director, Mark Stuart, announced Matt Monro had been engaged at the last minute to top the bill. Hancock and the singer had shared the tour together four years earlier and fallen out after a drunken incident on a train returning to London. 'We got away with it,' recalled John Muir of the first show, 'it was all right, but it wasn't anything like it had been the week before.'

Hancock was on his way back to Blackpool the following weekend when the ratings were published. *The Blackpool Show* was an immediate top-ten hit. One critic described Hancock's performance as 'titanic' and one sketch as 'near perfect'.

Peter Black, in the *Daily Mail*, remained convinced of Hancock's greatness:

> It's not what he says or does but the interaction of the whole personality with a theatre audience that makes him irresist-ibly watchable ... he seems to be living out a badgered and baffled section of his life in public ... the watchful distrust and sense of looming catastrophe are projected with great

technical skills out of his performance ... It is also very funny.

*

Each weekend settled into a well-planned, yet risky routine. Hancock had arranged to be driven from his Knightsbridge flat to Blackpool each Saturday morning. After rehearsals all day Sunday, each show was recorded in front of a live audience starting at 8.30pm. The director and crew had just thirty-five minutes to edit and clean up the tape before the 10.05pm broadcast.

At home, things were going from bad to worse. Hancock came back each morning to face a round of vicious noisy rows, suicide threats from Freddie and yet more brief drunken reconciliations and promises.

The week after the third show in the series was particularly violent. Things in Blackpool were not going well. The later Muir and Geen scripts had turned Hancock from a fresh belligerent compère – 'Well, we've got a right load of rubbish here tonight' – into little more than a stand-up comic. Muir admitted: 'It didn't really work.'

By 10am on the Saturday morning he had already consumed a bottle and a half of Champagne; Freddie unscrewed the top of one of his pill bottles and began swallowing the contents. 'I want to die,' she informed him.

Hancock calmly sat on the edge of the bed from where he could see to brush his hair in the mirror. 'Make a good job of it,' he said, straightening his tie. 'Take enough this time, because I shan't be calling an ambulance.' As he left the room, Freddie downed another handful of tablets.

Hancock had been booked to make a personal appearance in Liverpool and decided to travel up by train. When his driver went into the bedroom to collect the bags, Freddie appeared confused and unwell. 'Just a migraine,' she said reassuringly.

Outside the flat the concerned chauffeur said he thought Freddie was ill. 'Fuck her,' snapped Hancock.

The couple's cleaner arrived a few hours later, to find Freddie unconscious, and called an ambulance. Hancock, by now at his Liverpool hotel, was contacted by a doctor at the Middlesex Hospital and informed that his wife's condition was 'serious'. Swearing into the telephone, he refused to return to London. When he was asked if he knew what pills Freddie had swallowed, Hancock pleaded ignorance, even though the barbiturates had been prescribed for him.

He then emerged from the hotel lift to be confronted by a posse of journalists and photographers – 'She has tried this kind of thing before. It doesn't work any more.' By the time he reached the ABC Theatre, he had convinced himself the marriage was over and that somehow Freddie had maliciously tipped off the press to blacken his career. Hancock's marriage – his eleven-year relationship with Freddie Ross – had physically and metaphorically ended where it started – in Blackpool.

Hancock delayed his return to London until Tuesday. In hospital Freddie was still groggy and disorientated. When he began to shout and swear, Freddie burst into tears and Hancock stormed out of the room and out of his wife's life. His marriage to Freddie Ross had lasted just 229 days.

As ever when under stress, Hancock retreated into illness. That week's show – the fifth in the series – was hurriedly rewritten to allow idiot boards to be placed in the wings and orchestra pit. His performance was stiff and unresponsive. The next day, 25 July, he was admitted to a nursing home with 'nervous exhaustion'. The following week, the comedian Dave Allen stepped in as compère, and Hancock's place in the final show was taken by Bruce Forsyth.

By the mid-1960s, Hancock's alcoholism was merely a symptom of a longer and deeper-rooted disorder. It seemed to Hancock, as a man in his early forties, that he had spent the greater part of his life in a state of blame. Heaped upon his irrational childhood shame – the remorse at losing his father and the endless quest to 'please' him – and his two failed marriages was his professional guilt: the crippling stage fright, the lost and misremembered lines; the cruel and cowardly dumping of his friends and associates; his unbending perfectionism; the broken promises and lost opportunities; the inability to deliver his own film ambitions; his American rejection; and, above all – because of all – his increasing fear of any new or untested material.

Long before the implosion of *The Blackpool Show*, Hancock had conceived the idea of a 'make or break' one-man show. With Freddie effectively out of his life, the production took on a kinetic urgency, a final push to prove himself and break the taboo of his dwindling popularity. With Bernard Delfont's help, he booked the Royal Festival Hall on London's South Bank. Sandwiched between the London Mozart Players and a screen version of *La Bohème*, Hancock set himself the ultimate challenge. Within a few days the booking notices began to appear:

Thursday, 22nd September: The Lad Himself will Entertain You.

*

John le Mesurier and his wife Joan were about to leave after a visit to the Bexley home of singer Dorothy Squires[9]. Summer was all but over and, even though the sun was shining, there was a chill rippling breeze. Joan turned to Squires and said: 'I suddenly feel so sad. It seems like the end of something good.' It was Sunday, the 28th of August.

The le Mesuriers returned to their Baron's Court flat and decided to have an early night. They had been asleep for less than an hour when the telephone rang. The voice was slurred and hesitant. It was Tony Hancock. He needed to talk.

'Don't worry,' John le Mesurier assured him. 'You can stay here the night. I'll be over in a few minutes.'

Hancock was living in an expensive but unfurnished apartment in Lowndes Square, just off Knightsbridge. When le Mesurier arrived the front door was open and there was no response from Hancock. The flat was all but empty and a 'pitiful sight'; every trace of Freddie had been removed from his life and his surroundings. For days Hancock had lived in self-imposed exile, uncombed and unshaven, wrapped in his favourite 'Manchester Mauler' dressing gown and refusing to answer the telephone or the door. The large bedroom contained only a single unmade bed, there was one upright chair placed in the middle of the living-room, and Hancock was sitting on the floor, surrounded by empty vodka bottles and downing the remains of another.

Back at le Mesurier's own flat, Joan was shocked at both Hancock's physical appearance and mental state. Despite his thin, sickly appearance he was grinning inanely and appeared responsive and happy. 'I had prepared some food, but he wasn't hungry,' she recalls. 'He just wanted to drink, and talk, but not about himself. He evaded that subject. He just wanted companionship.' Wearing a borrowed dressing gown, Hancock fell asleep on the sofa. Twice during the night, John le Mesurier was woken by a muffled thud as his guest rolled on to the floor.

After breakfast, a contrite Hancock returned to his own flat, Joan took her son back to school in Ramsgate, and John le Mesurier fell asleep. The telephone rang once again. This time it was the actor's agent, telling him there was a seat reserved on a flight to Paris early the following morning and his services had been booked for the Anthony Quinn film, *The 25th Hour*.

On Tuesday, Joan returned from driving her husband to Heathrow Airport to find Hancock sitting on the doorstep of her flat. Over a cup of tea he confessed he was an alcoholic – something he had only recently learnt to do – and that the Delfont agency had booked him into the London Clinic for yet another detoxification regime. He begged Joan to escort him through the painful drying-out treatment. When she agreed, Hancock telephoned for his car, an over-sized, silver-blue Cadillac complete with uniformed chauffeur. 'My God,' said Joan, 'that's modest.'

They sat in the back of the car with the hood down and Hancock held Joan's hand in silence. It was, she felt, like taking a small frightened boy to the dentist. 'Joan was selfless and impressionable,' recalled her husband. 'A dangerous combination when she had to respond to a cry for help from one of the saddest, but best-loved, characters in British entertainment.'

Despite being sedated, Hancock was allowed out of the Highgate clinic for late-night rehearsals. Each evening at exactly 10.30pm a taxi would collect Joan and deliver her to the Prince of Wales Theatre. There she would watch Hancock attempt to rehearse, his dull listless voice echoing around the empty stage. After fifteen minutes his energy would flag and he would shuffle silently around, flapping his arms like a dejected penguin. 'The light had gone out of Tony during those meetings,' said Joan. 'The sedatives had dulled him and he was vague and slightly dreamy, without his confidence-restoring alcohol.'

There was another bizarre reason for his apparent lethargy. Through the haze of the drugs and the fatigue of his treatment, Hancock convinced himself the fabric of the Coventry Street theatre possessed some kind of spiteful presence which vilified his material and sapped his self-confidence. This he credited to the spirit of his comic hero Sid Field, who had collapsed and died at the theatre sixteen years earlier. Hancock once described the sensation to a friend: 'I never saw him, but he was there, I could feel he was there, mocking every word I said and everything I did.'

Despite the ill-feeling which had soured the final weeks of the ABC-TV series, Hancock insisted John Muir and Eric Geen should write the script for his Festival Hall performance. After his personal friendship with Eric Sykes and his long-term association with Galton and Simpson, he was convinced good – honest – comedy writing had more to do with empathy than entertainment. 'The important thing is that writers should get to know as much as they possibly can about me,' Hancock would explain. 'Burrow into my psyche. Sort out the inner man.' Both Muir and Geen confessed they had got 'awfully sick' of Hancock, whose helplessness nurtured its own kind of perverse devotion, but they reluctantly agreed.

'It was at this time that Tony Hancock came back into my life,' recalls Phyllis Rounce, the agent he had deserted in October, 1953. By chance, Muir and Geen were being represented by International Artistes. However arrogant his own behaviour, Hancock expected – even assumed – a certain loyalty from those he had offended. Rounce did not disappoint him. 'It was obvious Tony was in a very bad way,' she says. 'His confidence was in tatters and he was staking everything on this one performance. Whatever I said to him, however much I tried to get him to relax, nothing worked. He would telephone me in the small hours of the morning and describe a comedy routine or sketch he wanted the writers to incorporate into his act.' Hancock had obviously been drinking and Rounce refused his demands to 'call the boys and get them round now'.

One major problem still worried Muir and Geen. Was Hancock capable of learning their new material? 'We did write a new act,' explains John Muir. 'He got it, read it, and was delighted with it. He literally did not put the script down for three weeks. He always had it clenched, rolled up, in his hand – but he never got past the first page.'

Hancock's agent, Billy Marsh, was also concerned that Hancock might be frightened by the new material and suggested a trial run. The management of the Winter Gardens in Bournemouth jumped at the chance of filling a late-season slot with such a prestigious local star and Hancock was booked for a week, opening on 5 September. It was, Marsh later admitted, an error of judgment.

The agent had chosen the south-coast resort because he assumed the public would readily forgive Hancock if the new script flopped. It was a brave decision which ran contrary to his client's state of mind. Before each Bournemouth performance Hancock diligently rehearsed the new act, yet within minutes of stepping on to the stage, and without the script to prompt him, he reverted to his act of a decade or more ago. Muir and Geen, watching from the wings, found it 'bloody frustrating'.

A day or two before he arrived in Hampshire, Hancock telephoned George Fairweather. He sounded cheerful and confident. 'You must take the week off,' he urged his old friend. 'We'll have a golfing week.' Unfortunately, Fairweather was too busy to leave his salon at such short notice. When he tried to explain, Hancock slammed down the receiver.

The following Monday, the hairdresser called at the Winter Gardens' stage door to explain in person. A few minutes later he was curtly informed by a stagehand: 'He's too busy to see you.' Not for the first time Fairweather lost his temper. 'Tell him if it wasn't for me he wouldn't be in the top position he is now.'

When the week's run was over, Hancock had still made no attempt to contact his old friend, and Fairweather told himself the 'Lad' had let him down for the last time.

The following spring, Hancock arrived at Fairweather's Westover Road salon and was brusquely told to go away. 'You can't turn me out now,' he said, settling himself in one of the hairdresser's chairs. 'I'm a customer and I want a shampoo and my hair cut.'

Fairweather had never trimmed Hancock's hair before. When he had finished, Hancock made a twenty-five-minute trunk call, shook hands and walked out without paying a penny. George Fairweather would never see or talk to the comedian again.

It was during the Winter Gardens booking that Cicely made one last desperate attempt at reconciliation. In the fourteen months since their divorce, Hancock had emerged from a second doomed and disintegrating marriage and had already convinced himself he was about to fall in love a third time. Cicely – like most of the women in his life – still believed Hancock would one day return, repentant and reliant and with his devotion magically restored.

Late one night, Hancock arrived at the Royal Bar Hotel to find his ex-wife waiting for him. She was sober and smartly dressed, and had obviously made an effort to impress him. Hancock, tired and badly in need of a drink, listened to Cicely's pleading until he could stand it no longer and told her he was already involved with another woman and, as far as he was concerned, their marriage was 'dead and buried'.

Hancock's infatuation was already gathering speed. Each day he pestered Joan le Mesurier by telephone, frequently ringing before breakfast or after midnight. 'He never flirted with me – the idea of Tony flirting with anyone would have seemed ridiculous,' says Joan. 'I didn't realise it at the time, but the feeling growing between us was much more serious.'

The Bournemouth show ended on Saturday night and Hancock telephoned Joan from the station as he waited for the last train back to

London. With her husband still filming in France, Joan asked Hancock round for Sunday lunch and, as a precaution, invited several other friends. 'The lunch was a disaster,' she recalls. 'Tony made it quite obvious he wanted to be alone with me. The sooner everyone left, the happier he would be.'

While Joan was in the kitchen making coffee, Hancock slipped in and put his arms around her. 'I've missed you,' he said.

'Please don't go on with this,' she told him, shaking uncontrollably. 'I can't fight you.' It was the moment, Joan confesses, when she should have used all her self-will to say no.

'I'm John's best friend and I'm in love with his wife,' Hancock confessed. 'I'm sorry, I didn't intend this to happen.'

Hancock and Joan waved goodbye to the last guest from the window of the flat – and went to bed.

John le Mesurier's Air France flight landed at Heathrow soon after eleven the next morning and his wife was at the airport to meet him. Driving back along the M4 motorway, she announced she had fallen in love with another man and wanted to move in with him. By early afternoon Joan had packed her clothes and a few personal belongings and started her new life with Tony Hancock.

There had been no warning. In his autobiography, *A Jobbing Actor*, John le Mesurier attempts to rationalise his wife's love: 'I think she felt, rightly or wrongly, that Tony needed her more than I did, that she could be a steadying influence on him – even that she might eventually stop him drinking. She also felt that if he could regain his professional confidence, then all would be well. But like all alcoholics Tony was really two people. He was the life and soul of the party, the funny man who inspired love and affection, the generous friend who sought approval and desperately wanted to be liked. And he was a drunken braggart whose black moods of self-loathing always ended in violence and abuse at those who loved him most.'

During the day Hancock and Joan talked and made love and allowed nothing to interrupt their new-found passion. 'Our lovemaking, as close and fulfilling as our companionship, had stripped away the last vestige of control. We were in the grip of what can only be described as a grand passion. Tony had become the centre of my life and his happiness my first priority,' Joan confesses in her book, *Lady Don't Fall Backwards.*

Each evening, Hancock would call a taxi and they would eat in some quiet out-of-the-way restaurant. Remaining unrecognised somehow excited Hancock and, night after night, he would progressively be more blatant about his identity; taunting the other diners to recognise him.

The Lowndes Square flat, only weeks before stripped of Freddie's presence, now echoed to plans of divorce and marriage. When he was alone, watching the Knightsbridge traffic, or when he was listening to Joan in the kitchen, Hancock continued to worry about hurting his long-time friend. Le Mesurier was convinced his wife would be back by Christmas.

On one occasion Freddie telephoned Hancock, probing, like Cicely a few weeks earlier, for a possible reconciliation. It was impossible, Hancock informed his wife, 'I've found someone younger and prettier than you.'

Both Hancock and Joan admitted that people would have to be told about their affair, but when he telephoned his mother in Bourne-mouth, Lily Sennett seemed unperturbed at the news of her son's latest relationship. Joan then rang her parents in Kent and, passing the receiver to Hancock, left him to explain and arrange a meeting.

It was bright and sunny the day the couple set off for Ramsgate, a Kentish seaside town where the Malins had raised and educated their two children, and Hancock insisted the hood of the Cadillac be left down. On the way, a group of dismounted motorcyclists were lounging on a roadside verge. The jeers and cat-calls which greeted the approaching silver-blue convertible changed to whistles and applause the moment Hancock was recognised. As the car passed he stood to face the gang of admirers, bowing gently and rolling a royal wave.

As ammunition, Hancock had filled the car boot with several cases of Dom Perignon Champagne. For Joan's son David, who lived with his grandparents, he armed himself with a football. Even more than women, children troubled Hancock. You could never lie to children, he once admitted, because they would always find you out. That afternoon the couple waited outside David's school for the boy to emerge. The football delivered, Hancock suggested they visit a local ice-cream parlour. It was a scene strangely reminiscent of *The Punch and Judy Man*: Hancock, the life-long ice-cream hater, devouring giant Knickerbocker Glories to please his young friend.

Back in London, and with just twelve days before the Festival Hall event, Hancock found it even harder to concentrate. By now the performance had become his personal apocalypse: a revelation, impressive but final. He took to informing people he intended 'going out with a bang and not a whimper'. When one journalist, scenting a Hancock retirement, enquired about his future plans, the performer told him he was going to live in Ramsgate for the fishing.

'Why Ramsgate?' The reporter asked.

'None of your fucking business,' Hancock snapped back.

Hancock even deluded Joan le Mesurier into thinking this might be the end. At one point she even feared he might break off his act and deliver his farewell speech from the Festival Hall stage. In her book she admits: 'He became so obsessed with the idea of burning all his bridges I began to believe he would really go through with it.'

The sticking point in his act was a long speech from *King Lear* which began: 'Blow winds and crack your cheeks . . .' Hancock would get halfway and stumble. 'Ladies and gentlemen,' he would improvise for Joan. 'As I'm obviously dying a death up here I'm not going to bore you any longer with this load of old rubbish, all of which you have heard before, so I'm off to Ramsgate to fuck my brains loose.'

Another version would end: 'Ladies and gentlemen and Lily [he knew his mother would be in the audience], owing to the fact I have been fucked from arsehole to breakfast time of late, I have come to the conclusion that there's more to life than standing on a stage making a prick of myself.'

Hancock began a frantic and drunken round of attempts to salvage what he described as a 'night on the *Titanic*'. Without consulting his writers or their agent, he contacted Ray Galton and Alan Simpson to ask if they could write a new sketch. They refused. On Monday, 19 September – only three days before the performance – Hancock decided he wanted to include the *Aeroplane* sketch from the *Half Hour* series. For that he would need Kenneth Williams. They had not met since their encounter at the Globe Theatre four years earlier, after which, the actor had declared, 'This is the end for him and me.'

Williams was filming *Carry On – Don't Lose Your Head* at Pinewood Studios and ignored Hancock's repeated telephone calls. That night Williams wrote in his diary:

The sheer impertinence of this man is phenomenal! First he makes my position in the radio show embarrassing and cuts down the parts to nothing – actual one-liners – and ends up by insulting me in front of everyone about the 'snide' characterisation so I leave the show . . . When I did meet him, accidentally, he said he was doing the *Punch and Judy Man* film (which he'd written himself and it was the flop of all time) and said 'I'm really excited about this – I'm doing the sort of comedy I've always wanted to do – I'd like you to do something with me – not those funny voice "cardboard" characters of yours – but comedy based on truth.' One stood there being patronised and denigrated and one smiled and said thank you. Now he wants me to work with him again! He must be either very stupid or mad. I'd rather leave the business than work with such a Philistine nit.

After one call, Williams told Sid James of Hancock's idea for the last-minute Festival Hall sketch. 'You're joking,' James said. 'You'd be mad to work with him again – the man is a megalomaniac.'

Hancock had returned to demanding out-of-hours script conferences with Muir and Geen. Most proved unproductive. Hancock would suggest outlandish sketches – frequently elaborations of *Half Hour* plots – and most 'pathetically inadequate'. When the writers refused to attend further late-night meetings, Hancock turned on their agent. 'I wasn't annoyed,' admits Rounce, 'that was the way Tony was.

He came alive at night. Talking the night through, inventing plots and sketches, was far more satisfying to him than writing them all down the next day. By then he was bored. The real work had already been done.'

On 16 September, Hancock was interviewed live on BBC2's *Late Night Line-Up* about his forthcoming Royal Festival Hall performance. His questioner was Joan Bakewell. The forty-minute programme went out after the 11pm news and Hancock arrived at the studio late, razzled with drink, barely able to stand.

Dennis Main Wilson was working on a camera script in his office in Television Centre. A little after eleven, his phone rang.

'Is that Mr Wilson?'

'Yes, who is that?'

The man introduced himself as one of the BBC doormen Main Wilson knew: 'The Boy's on, sir, and he's making a right arse of himself. Can you come down?'

The producer dropped his script and hurried to the *Late Night Line-Up* studio where Hancock had just finished his interview. 'I didn't barge in,' recalled Main Wilson. 'I just let him know I was there.' Hancock ignored his old friend, but made no attempt to leave. After waiting for almost half-an-hour, Main Wilson was approached by two uniformed studio attendants. 'I'm sorry, sir,' they politely, but forcefully, informed him, 'Mr Hancock wants you to leave.'

'He had me ejected,' said Main Wilson bitterly. 'He would not even talk to me. He'd been drinking and had lost his way and I am sure he did not want me to see him in the state he was.' It was the last time Main Wilson would set eyes on Hancock.

Press photographs taken during the Festival Hall rehearsals show a drawn and emaciated Hancock. He was consuming large quantities of alcohol and burning equal amounts of nervous energy. Forty-eight hours before the performance he developed an attack of diarrhoea. The following night he awoke shaking violently and soaked in sweat. When

Joan switched on the light she feared he might be having a heart attack: his lips and hands were blue.

At times of particular stress Hancock was prone to extravagant and outlandish gestures. He would buy the most expensive case of wine he could find, or insist an embarrassed waiter pocket a £50 tip. This time, he and Joan moved out of their Kensington flat and into the Maharajah Suite at the Mayfair Hotel, the same apartment in which Hancock had celebrated his engagement to Freddie Ross.

Lily Sennett arrived unannounced at the Mayfair and was shown to their suite by a bell boy. The lounge and bedrooms were empty. 'Are you in there, Tony?' she said knocking on the bathroom door. Hancock and Joan were making love on the bathroom floor.

It was the kind of situation which tickled Hancock. The more Joan struggled, the more her lover giggled. 'All right, Lily,' he shouted through the closed door. 'We're just coming.' Still more horrified at what Hancock's mother would think, Joan began to kick out in panic.

'You can be so vulgar sometimes,' she hissed at him. 'That's your mother out there.'

Hancock and Joan eventually emerged wearing the hotel's 'his' and 'hers' bathrobes. Lily, who had already ordered tea and sandwiches, benevolently shook hands with Joan.

Hancock's was a perverse sense of embarrassment; he would gleefully watch others squirm, while going to great lengths to hide his own personal discomposure. Toilet noises – anyone's – caused him acute unease. Each visit to the bathroom was accompanied by a transistor radio tuned to the loudest station. 'Are you really sure you want to carry on with this?' he would ask Joan.

'Yes,' she replied. 'Farts and all.'

The couple drove to the Festival Hall in silence. At the stage door Hancock said: 'Ring your dad and find out if there's a vacancy for a crane driver in Ramsgate. I'm going to be out of a job by tomorrow.'

As he turned, Joan recalls he looked like a 'small, brown bull going into the arena to meet his end'. In a later interview with the *Observer* Hancock confessed: 'I decided that if I'd got fifteen minutes in and hadn't got anywhere, I'd make this terrible speech and that would be the finish.'

Every Festival Hall seat had been sold and Lily Sennett and Joan le Mesurier were watching from the back of the theatre; Hancock had insisted their seats should be far enough and high enough from the stage to avoid possible eye contact. The audience arrived, to find they were expected to sit through a ninety-minute first half without Hancock. On his dressing-room loudspeaker he could hear waves of restless shuffling as the singer Marian Montgomery was plagued by a series of technical problems. Hancock vomited into the sink and drank his way through a bottle of brandy.

As he walked on stage the orchestra played 'Mr Wonderful' and the audience erupted in applause. 'I've never seen such an ornate garage,' he said, looking around. 'Tonight, for the price of a packet of fags, I'll be going through the card.' The banter continued. 'This show is going out to all nations, and by Early Bird to my mother in Bournemouth.'

When his confidence ran out – as it had done in Bournemouth – Hancock ditched the Muir and Geen script and relied on his fifteen-year-old variety material of long-dead actors. 'Here's one for the teenagers, George Arliss.' To work his way through part of *The Blood Donor* he needed idiot boards in the wings.

The next morning – and with Lily on her way back home – Hancock and Joan made their escape. He was even more convinced his career was over. The previous night's performance had been so appalling – 'so amateurish' – nobody would want him back; this time there would be no comeback; no return. Typically, Hancock needed to seal his fate with a gesture.

As they were packing, a maid was clearing away the breakfast tray. From somewhere Joan found a pair of Hancock's cufflinks; it was the pair Freddie had given him more than ten years ago, engraved with the words: 'If I had a talent like yours . . . I'd be proud not scared.' Hancock snatched the cufflinks and asked the maid if she was married. 'Then give these to your husband,' he said. 'They might give him a bit more confidence.'

By the mid-1960s Ramsgate was grubby with neglect. Its harbour was better known for its winter collection of celebrity-owned yachts than for the seafront's cramped and tacky summer amusements. It was 23 September and the summer season was already over. Hancock and his lover cruised the town in their Cadillac until they finally spotted a 'to let' sign taped to the window of a flaking Victorian house overlooking the harbour from the East Cliff.

The landlady recognised Hancock but said nothing. 'He looked so shabby,' she recalled many years later. 'At first I thought I must be wrong, and then he opened his mouth and I knew by the voice it was Tony Hancock.' She will always remember how ill Hancock looked: 'Almost weak, as if he were just getting over a long illness, and this was his first time out of hospital for a long time.' When the landlady agreed to show them the flat, Hancock became excited, almost pushing past the woman.

Four hours earlier, Hancock and Joan had been sharing the pampering of the Mayfair Hotel. Now, they were contemplating a first home of such 'transcendental horror' they froze with shock. Hancock, forever amused by the lunacy of life, began to giggle as the landlady led them from room to room.

'The kitchen floor was covered with curling red lino and contained (along with the obligatory cooker) one of those hideous green and cream enamel kitchen dressers with a pull-down work top,' recalls Joan le Mesurier in her autobiography. 'There was a blue Formica table under the window, flanked by two red plastic and chrome chairs. And there was a hook-on draining board attached to the sink. It was made of aluminium and was bent and crooked so that things were always sliding off. The floorboards were loose so that the whole kitchen jingled musically when we walked across it. The living room contained a brown plastic three-piece suite with red upholstered seats, a hideous sideboard, a worn, threadbare rug over more peeling linoleum, a hissing old gas fire with a coin meter alongside, and two cheap prints of sailing boats at peril on stormy seas.'

The rent was £6 a week. Hancock paid two weeks in advance. His driver helped carry the suitcases up the stairs and was sent back to London with instructions to sell the Cadillac and buy a Mercedes.

There was no telephone, no television, and, to Hancock's delight, no callers. Only a handful of people knew where they were. Each afternoon they would collect Joan's son from school and all three would kick a football along Ramsgate's pebble beach. At night Hancock and Joan would lie in bed and listen to the world on a small transistor radio.

By early October, Billy Marsh had been informed of his client's whereabouts. So, too, had the press. Reality, like winter, was closing in. For nearly two weeks Hancock had restricted his consumption of alcohol to an all-time low, but he was now drinking heavily. On one occasion he tripped and slid down the stairs, landing unhurt on his bottom at the landlady's feet.

'Mr Hancock,' the woman said, slightly embarrassed, as if they had passed each other on the way to the bathroom.

'Lovely carpet,' Hancock remarked, patting the faded Wilton. 'And soft, too.'

Despite Hancock's ill-conceived Blackpool excursion for ABC, he had remained very much a corporation star. For six months the previous winter, the BBC had repeated twenty-six *Half Hour* episodes, the complete fifth, sixth and seventh series. Hancock was once again a household name. He was also hugely popular with a new and younger generation of television viewers. By the late summer, he had already agreed to appear with *Secombe and Friends* on network television, and the show was scheduled for mid-November. Hancock, once again, insisted on his budgerigar sketch, this time rewritten to include Harry Secombe. It would be the last time he would wear his bird costume.

The BBC was anxious to salvage something from the hour-long Festival Hall performance which had been recorded for BBC2, the corporation's recently launched second channel. However, lingering doubts about Hancock's ability to deliver had prompted BBC2 controller, David Attenborough, to sanction the recording without setting a transmission date. Watching the live show, and later the edited videotape, opinions differed within the BBC hierarchy. Attenborough thought the show was good, as did his assistant the veteran comedy writer Frank Muir. Tom Sloan felt it had been a 'disaster'. From the outset Hancock had demanded the right to veto any transmission. By early October, and left to reflect unpressured, he convinced himself it was one of his better performances. The show was eventually broadcast on 15 October.

The Ramsgate flat was becoming too well known. Even the local newspaper had carried a story debunking Hancock's intention to retire. Joan knew the only chance of saving her lover's career lay in the illusion of a safe and secure home, a belief remarkably similar to Freddie Ross's six years earlier. Within a month the dream would become a nightmare.

Discreet enquiries, always in Joan's name, were made with local estate agents. The only place which sounded remotely suitable was a ten-year-old bungalow in nearby Broadstairs. Hancock was sceptical: the property was called Coq d'Or, the golden chicken, and the ever-suspicious Hancock mistrusted birds. When the taxi pulled up outside he was horrified to find chicken motifs on the gates and a cockerel weather vane bolted to the chimney.

The bungalow itself was modern and airy and built with vast French windows overlooking the clifftop garden and the sea beyond. One feature did fascinate Hancock: in a corner of the living-room the owners had installed a bar. Joan was horrified as Hancock fingered the empty wine racks and optic stands. At £13 a week, with an option to buy, the bungalow was, Hancock admitted, too good to miss. As with so many addicts, the physical act of drinking was as important as the effect of the alcohol consumed. Hancock was drinking vast quantities of tea and coffee, but mostly he was drinking wine and neat vodka and within days of moving in, he was obsessively maintaining the stock of the built-in bar.

Not long after they took possession of the bungalow, Joan invited her parents and son to dinner. It was her first chance to entertain and show off their new home. Hancock was not enamoured with the idea and refused to help with the preparations. He drank heavily and pompously throughout the meal, enthusing about this or that wine.

When he produced a bottle of brandy, Joan's heart sank. Cicely had warned Joan to keep Hancock away from brandy – 'He turns into a killer on the stuff.'

Hancock downed three large brandies in quick succession. As he was pouring a fourth his face and mouth tightened: 'You Mancunian cunt.' The unprovoked obscenity was spat at Mrs Malin.

The silence was broken by Jack Malin. 'I think it's time to leave,' he said, pushing his chair from the table. 'Come on, mother, get your coat.' As Joan saw her son and parents to the door, Hancock slumped into a chair and began chain-drinking the brandy.

'How dare you talk to my mother like that?' Joan demanded as soon as they were alone. Before Hancock could answer she had grabbed the bottle and emptied the remaining spirit down the kitchen sink, hurling the empty bottle against the kitchen wall.

'You stupid bitch,' Hancock growled, shaking with anger. 'That cost a lot of money.'

Joan stood her ground. 'You are never going to bring that stuff into this house again,' she said. 'If you do, I leave.'

The frustration had turned Hancock's face purple: 'You parochial cunt. Don't give me orders.'

Turning back into the lounge, he pounced on a large, cast-iron coffee table. Lifting it over his head he began staggering toward the French windows. Fearing he might hurl himself, as well as the table, through the expanse of glass, Joan managed to make fingertip contact with a table leg before Hancock tottered, swore, and collapsed backwards.

The pair lay on the floor surrounded by debris. The shattered table had missed Joan, but landed on Hancock's forearm. Sobered by the shot of pain and the sight of blood, he nonchalantly commented: 'I do love these quiet after-dinner chats, don't you?'

The next morning, Joan telephoned Lily Sennett in Bournemouth. When his mother arrived late that afternoon Hancock was barely able to stand. He was morose and justified the day's drinking by complaining about the pain in his hand. Lily, fearing more violence, asked Hancock's chauffeur to stay. Nearing midnight Hancock – who had consumed a bottle of wine and two bottles of vodka – was drifting in and out of consciousness. A local doctor was called and announced Hancock needed immediate and long-term help. Joan telephoned the London Clinic. They would accept him that night.

Joan helped the driver carry Hancock to the new Mercedes. Semi-comatose, he stank of alcohol and wine and as they lifted him he vomited. Lily sat in the front passenger seat while Joan cradled Hancock in the back. No one spoke. Both feared Hancock had at last gone too far. The driver covered the seventy miles to London in record time.

For the third time in less than ten months, Hancock was back in hospital. This time the treatment – what he could remember of it – was both painful and humiliating.

Before his psychiatrist could tackle the underlying cause of his patient's alcoholism, it was vital to halt any further liver damage. Hancock was sedated, and while he slept he was given regular and massive injections of the multi-vitamin Plurentavite. The doses were so high that even Hancock's sweat and urine had the musty smell of Vitamin B.

The first phase of his treatment was complete. After forty-eight hours of sedation, allowing Hancock's system to expel its stored alcohol, it was now time to subdue his addiction. The treatment involved electric shock therapy. For three successive days Hancock was left stunned and zombic. He would lie in his bed with vacant, staring blue eyes, 'helpless and bovine'.

In his moments of blurred and scrambled consciousness, the 42-year-old Hancock begged Joan to forgive him. He had no recollection of what exactly had occurred. 'We reiterated our vows to each other, and I swore that I would stay with him through thick and thin, as long as he kept off the alcohol,' said Joan. His craving smothered by the fear of loneliness, Hancock agreed.

Gradually his health improved. Joan, who had visited him daily, was allowed to take her lover back to their Knightsbridge flat. Before she collected Hancock, she was issued with strict instructions and an assortment of vitamins, sleeping pills and tranquillisers. It was vital that

Hancock should take his morning Antabuse tablet – even the smell of alcohol would make him violently sick.

There had been happier times. During the early months of the relationship, Hancock and Joan flew to Paris. Hancock strutted up and down the cabin aisle, pretending to be the pilot who seemed to know nothing about flying and even less about aeroplanes. The passengers and crew were in hysterics.

While they were living near Broadstairs, Hancock heard a local hospital had started a fund to buy a film projector for its children's ward. He immediately went out to purchase a 16mm projector, a screen and several feature films. He left them at the porter's lodge, with no indication who the gift was from.

However, by late November, 1966, his separation from Freddie had become 'official' and once again – and not unnaturally – Hancock blamed the newspaper attention on his wife's connections with the press. This time he did not need to plan his escape, he was already booked to go to Hong Kong.

Hotel cabaret is an unforgiving environment and the organiser, Maggie Christensen, who had never actually met Hancock, was under no illusions about the pressure a two-week pre-Christmas booking at the Mandarin Hotel would place on the comedy star: 'Anyone associated with the hotel industry will know it is a tough territory in which to operate. Behind the suave smiles the law of the jungle operates.'

Each artist in the show had demanded his own facilities. Tommy Cooper required a small room immediately adjacent to the stage, in which to store his props, and Edmund Hockridge insisted on a piano in his suite for rehearsals and vocal limbering. After discussions with Billy Marsh in London, it was decided Hancock's prime requirement would be a chaperon. Christensen recalls: 'Dear old Tony needed a "minder", who travelled out with him from London in order to ensure he appeared on stage on time and sober each night – not to mention someone to sit in his room after each performance to keep him company and feed his ego until he had talked himself to sleep.'

Hancock had his own theory and fears about flying. He would never fly without a drink in his hand, frequently ordering his first from the stewardess at the door. He also believed there was no such thing as a sober pilot. The steel-jawed, blue-eyed pilot who chatted to the passengers as he made his way to the flight deck was a BOAC diversion, Hancock claimed – as a five-foot-three-inch, unshaven, punch-drunk pilot with bifocals boarded secretly from the front.

Hancock once again agreed to be accompanied by his road manager, Glyn Jones. The marathon flight was made bearable for Hancock only by the continuous supply of complimentary Champagne. One in-flight incident illustrates his reserve of kindness. Seven-year-old Peter Clarkson was travelling with his mother to spend Christmas in the crown colony with his Army officer father. The comedian was on his way to the toilet when he was approached by the youngster.

'My mum says you're Tony Hancock.'

'She's right,' Hancock replied.

The pair chatted for a few minutes. As the boy was about to return to his seat he informed Hancock: 'My teddy bear's called Tony.'

'In that case,' Hancock replied, 'we better make it official.' He then wrote a signed message on the bear's cotton vest.

The flight landed at Hong Kong. As the passengers were queuing to leave the aircraft, Hancock found himself standing in front of Clarkson and his mother. He turned and asked the boy, proudly clutching his teddy: 'Is your bear really called Tony?'

'No,' the boy admitted. 'But he is now.' Clarkson, now a serving officer himself, still has the toy and its Hancock autograph.

Teddy bears – large or small – had a special significance for Hancock. As a child, one of his favourite toys, long into his adolescence, had been a small bear with black stitching for its nose and eyes. Long before their marriage, Freddie Ross's nickname for her lover had been 'my living teddy bear'. Once, as they arrived at Heathrow after a holiday abroad, Freddie remembered they had failed to buy her four-year-old niece a present, so they had scoured the terminal shops until they found a teddy bear big enough to salve Hancock's conscience.

Maggie Christensen was waiting at Kai Tak International Airport to greet the Mandarin's latest star guest, and had arranged a press conference. From a distance she could be mistaken for Freddie Ross. Hancock, who had never met Christensen, spotted her across the tarmac and wrongly assumed Freddie had flown out to watch his performance and discuss a reconciliation. 'When he found it wasn't me, he was desperately disappointed,' his estranged wife recalls. Hancock refused to talk to the press, or even pose for pictures, and demanded he be driven straight to his hotel. To distract him, Christensen suggested the star and his 'minder' take a drive through the cramped and bustling streets of Hong Kong.

From the car Hancock spotted an enormous teddy bear and insisted they stop and buy it. The bear spent the rest of Hancock's stay propped up in the corner of his hotel suite. When it was time to fly back to England, he refused to allow the six-foot toy to be stowed in the hold as baggage and insisted it travel in the cabin as hand luggage. The teddy was so large it needed a seat to itself, for which Hancock happily parted with £25 for a child's fare.

To justify the extravagance Hancock would explain: 'It said on the menu, "flown in by BOAC", so I thought I might as well fly something out.'

1967

IT WAS NEW YEAR'S EVE. Joan le Mesurier opened her eyes to find Hancock standing at the foot of the bed, supported by two uniformed security guards. He was naked, except for a jockstrap which he was wearing back to front.

As the guards helped put the giggling Hancock back to bed, Joan was treated to the details of his escapade.

When the lease on his Lowndes Square flat expired in December, 1966, the pair had found a smaller, two-bedroomed apartment just around the corner in William Mews, but it needed redecorating. To bridge the gap, Hancock rented an 'ugly' service flat overlooking the Thames at Pimlico. The Dolphin Square complex included a ground-floor bar and restaurant. While Joan slept, Hancock had tip-toed naked out of their apartment, descended in the lift and followed the music to a New Year party. As he began to circulate, unclothed and unconcerned, a woman let out a moral howl. Hancock marched to her table, pointed to his exposed penis and said: 'Madam, I don't suppose you've seen one of these before?'

The woman's husband took an indignant swing at Hancock, who ducked with the agility of a drunken schoolboy, before he was dragged backwards out of the restaurant waving benignly at the open-mouthed revellers.

Hancock had emerged from the oblivion of Christmas with the crumpled, painful body of an alcoholic and the sleepless mind of a five-year-old child. Unaware of the chaos he had caused, he thanked the men for escorting him home from the 'shops'. Inside his head he was convinced he had been to Harrods to buy a present for his mother.

Somehow he had persuaded his psychiatrist that he was capable of continuing his drying-out treatment at home. What Hancock hadn't told him was that Joan would be in Ramsgate for Christmas, and unable to supervise his regime of Largactil and barbiturates. When she returned the day after Boxing Day, she discovered Hancock had befriended an alcoholic married couple on the floor below and had spent the entire holiday mixing his tablets with vast quantities of wine and spirits. For some reason the mixture of alcohol and Largactil had reversed the effect of the barbiturates and made him hyperactive and sleepless. Hancock now needed to overdose on sleeping pills to combat his insomnia. The three-way combination had also reduced his inhibitions to nil and his memory to a few minutes.

For Joan, 'it was like having a large sleepless child on my hands, who couldn't be left alone for a moment'. Hancock's condition swung from dementia to delusion. One minute she would have to tease him to swallow each spoonful of food by pretending it was an aeroplane. The next he would be in Paris demanding Champagne.

His favourite 'game' was pretending to sit in the first-class cabin of an airliner. 'Bring me a bottle of Dom Perignon,' he would demand. In the kitchen Joan would fill a champagne glass with tonic water, add a dash of ginger and serve it to him on a tray. Hancock – looking like 'a large playful St Bernard dog' – would take a sip and proclaim: 'Ah yes, you can't beat this Dom Perignon.'

Then, as the alcohol drained from his body and the final effects of the tablets wore off, Hancock woke one morning to find 'his brains back in place'. He was ravenously hungry. While Joan made scrambled eggs her lover shaved and showered.

From the kitchen Joan heard a half-sob, half-choke. When she got to the bathroom, Hancock was thrashing around on the floor and foaming at the mouth. His face was contorted and blue. The same security guards who had returned the naked Hancock now held down his convulsing body until a doctor arrived.

Giving him a Plurentavite injection, the physician warned Hancock that he could have a second fit at any time: the alcohol had severely damaged his liver, which was triggering epileptic attacks. Hancock's psychiatrist arrived soon after. His diagnosis was even more severe. 'If you don't stop drinking,' he warned Hancock, 'you'll be dead within three months.'

The possibility that his death might not come at his own hand, that he might be cheated of his own depression, shocked Hancock. On 18 January, 1967, he visited his solicitor to sign his will. With the breakdown of his second marriage, he decided to leave his entire estate to his 76-year-old mother. Lily Sennett[10] was, by now, living at Redroofs Hotel, a residential home in Bournemouth's Bath Hill. The will named Hancock's surviving brother, Roger, and accountant Sidney Goldwater as executors.

For Hancock it was the start of a nostalgic week. Alan Whicker had first met the comedian five or six years earlier in the Lime Grove BBC

Club. Whicker was a member of the current affairs programme *Tonight*. Tired of the inevitable post-broadcast analysis from his fellow presenters, Whicker would join a 'tubby, mournful little chap who looked as though he had dressed in the dark'. Hancock was always alone, 'lonely, defeated and morose'.

By 1967, Whicker had established his own brand of self-mocking, awe-struck commentary in *Whicker's World*. He decided he wanted to devote a programme to stand-up comics. It would be called: *If they don't like you, you're Dead*.

The interview – one of the last in-depth interviews Hancock gave – discussed the 'craft' of comedy. Whicker also spoke to Mike and Bernie Winters, Charlie Chester, Ted Ray, Alfred Marks and the *Till Death Us Do Part* writer Johnny Speight. The only refusal came from Charlie Drake.

For several hours one afternoon, Whicker filmed a long conversation with Tony Hancock. 'It was a rambling stream-of-thought,' Whicker says in his book *Turn Over, Camera!*. 'But it contained some of the essence of a comic genius who had just come off the boil and was living through a new situation.' Hancock, he remembers, was thoughtful and troubled. 'I found the interview sad, honest and revealing.'

A few weeks later, Whicker returned from a filming trip to the Far East to be informed by his director, David Rea, that the entire Hancock interview had been dropped from the laughter-makers programme. Rea felt Hancock was 'too deep and too slow'.

'I could imagine his rueful, gloomy acceptance of that last failure,' wrote Whicker. 'The shrug of those overburdened shoulders at his final dismissal . . . I can see him now, scrunched up despairingly in that hospitality room at Lime Grove like an untidy heap of old clothes that was slowly absorbing white wine – and talking his own epitaph.'

Although Hancock's contribution, for which he received twenty guineas, was never screened, Whicker kept his question-and-answer notes. Hancock was forty-three and, after twenty years as a professional comedian, his responses appear philosophical and introspective.

Whicker: Your Lad from East Cheam was one of
television's richest creations, yet since you
shrugged him off you've never stopped giving
yourself these convulsive remoulds . . . ?

Hancock: I'm not remoulding myself, I've just got older.
The British public is extremely loyal, but very
against change. I mean, some of those serials
that have been drearing on for years and years
and years, you know – the dog gets killed and
the nation goes into mourning. The loyalty is
immense.

I didn't change because I can't – this is all I
can do. But the background should be changed.
Railway Cuttings as an example, Dick Van
Dyke for another, you make it like a cake: take
one comedian, one pretty wife, and two funny
people in the office. The scriptwriter's churning
these things out endlessly – it would drive me
up the wall. It's formula comedy – but where
did Laurel and Hardy live? Nowhere. Chaplin
didn't live anywhere.

Whicker: Just as there are Cary Grant parts and Margaret
Rutherford parts, so presumably there are
Anthony 'ancock parts?

Hancock: With the East Cheam thing we found a serious
identity which is very potent and it became
very identifiable, which was good. It also
became more difficult to write and perform.
And eventually we got a bit bored with it – at
least I did.

Whicker: So what sort of comedian do you want to be?

Hancock: A funny one. We used to have a convention in
England that if a bloke didn't get a quick

laugh, he'd gone. You know, he'd come on
with long boots and a revolving bow tie and a
movable feather and all this business. Then
these gentlemen started wandering on in
beautifully cut silk suits and just sort of said,
'It's very lovely to be here . . .' for the first ten
minutes. I'd think, he's going to die a terrible
death, I'll have to go because I can't even
watch my worst enemy die – it's a most painful
experience. I remember seeing Danny Thomas,
and for ten minutes nothing happened at all. I
thought, how can I get out without looking
rude, because it's an unprofessional thing to do
and I wouldn't do it. And gradually he got it,
and he got it, you know? And when he went
off, there was stamping, clapping and
everything. It was a different approach, just a
gentle, seductive approach, as against the
gimmicks.

Whicker: What do you find goes best?

Hancock: True comedy. Honest comedy. Things that are
recognisable. Situations that are recognisable. It
is interesting to watch repeats of my own show
because we tried to get things that wouldn't
date. The one-line gag does date, in my
opinion. But we were happy to see that most
of it didn't date at all. It was still a man in a
particular situation.

Whicker: You've had a sort of mish-mash of emotion in
public: your divorce and remarriage and
separation and psychiatric help was all
published, along with your weight problem and
your drink problem . . . How has your career

been affected?

Hancock: I don't think it's affected at all. In any case, very few people go through life without something of this sort.

Whicker: With all this, you've been called 'the master of the self-inflicted wound'. That's not a bad phrase . . .

Hancock: No, it's not a bad phrase; whether it's accurate or not is another thing. I think if you're trying to achieve as much perfection as you can, within whatever limits comedy should have, then you're going to go through certain experiences – not always particularly pleasant – or I don't think you'd be able to give whatever is necessary.

Whicker: But you've had a fairly tortured time of it?

Hancock: Who hasn't? There's a certain sensitivity demand if you're going to make anything in this business, which is an awful word anyway. But it makes one a little more vulnerable, possibly. That's something you have to accept.

Whicker: I'm wondering how this kind of torment, such as it is, has affected your work?

Hancock: It's helped. For one thing, you have a deeper understanding of other people's problems – and that's all comedy is really about. I don't regret it, but I wouldn't want to go through it again. I have done the very best I can – nothing is worse than to come off and disappoint 'em. That's awful, because you can't blame anybody but yourself.

Whicker: I'm sure I'm typical of all the people who watch you, and if you're not doing well, I'm broken up ...

Hancock: May I ask you a question? Don't you think sometimes perhaps you ask for a little more than there is to offer?

Whicker: Of course – we always want more ...

Hancock: Yes, and I'm trying to give more, you know, so we're mutually dissatisfied ... *City Lights*, which I think is the most exquisite full-length comedy I've ever seen, was panned you know. It was Chaplin's statement. I thought it was absolutely magnificent and I went to see it five times. Maybe sometimes the audience ask a little too much. We just try to give as much as possible.

For the second time in his career, Hancock had allowed his personality to cloud his professionalism and seemed incapable of distilling his fixation with comedy into a cohesive and successive argument. As ever, it was left to print journalists to sift the rubble of a one- or two-hour interview and fashion what remained into a reasoned – and sometimes highly persuasive – argument.

Hancock was naturally, gently obsessed with comedy. Throughout the 1960s he had become increasingly irritated by what he saw as American comedy, delivered 'in a plastic bag'; Jack Benny and *I Love Lucy* had given way to an homogenised *Dick Van Dyke Show*. Comedy, Hancock liked to repeat, is not an instrument of fashion – 'It's about people, and they don't change.'

'Comedy should be placeless and timeless,' he told one *Observer* writer. 'It doesn't have to follow gimmicks. I love comedy. I'm attached to a principle of comedy. I want to experiment. It's all much more difficult now, deeper, more interesting. I'm not working so much for myself – to be discovered, watched, laughed at. Now I want to get at the art of the thing and that's endless.'

A few hours after recording the Whicker interview, Hancock appeared on *The Frost Programme*. During an interview with David Frost he recalled his father's semi-professional career as an entertainer and mentioned a sentimental ballad Jack Hancock sang as part of his repertoire. Hancock could not remember its name or the words. Early next morning, a viewer supplied the programme with a copy of the sheet music and Hancock was invited back to give his own rendition of his father's song.

By early February, work on 9 Whaddon House, William Mews, was finished and the move was completed. Hancock urgently needed a distraction to bolster his new-found resolution to end his addiction and announced he was going to write his first book. One of the flat's two bedrooms had been converted to a study. On a shelf above his desk stood his Personality of the Year award. His book, he told guests, would be 'large and spiritual'. For days he would sit and stare at the title page. When he got bored he would scrunch the sheet up and tap out the title afresh: *The Link, or Anyone for Tennis?* He never wrote another word.

There were other, more enjoyable distractions. When Joan's son David stayed for weekends, Hancock insisted they all visit an old friend at London Zoo. He had not seen Guy the Gorilla since 1961, when he had introduced Philip Oakes to the ape. Surprisingly a keeper remembered Hancock's visits and offered to take him to a special feeding enclosure. Guy eagerly accepted peanuts, but when Joan offered it ordinary animal food the anthropoid turned its back in moody disgust. 'Poor sod,' said Hancock. 'I know what he feels like.'

Negotiations were already under way for a new ABC-TV series. Unlike *The Blackpool Show*, the new series would return to a traditional format, devised as a safety net for ABC, if not for its star. All six shows would have a similar theme, with Hancock as the owner-manager of a nightclub. Alternating with his own comedy routine – as the hat-check man, croupier, gypsy fiddler and wine waiter – he would introduce a series of variety acts. ABC management reasoned that, should Hancock prove difficult, it would be a simple matter to edit him out and insert more acts.

Discussion about the new series forced Hancock to cut short a stay at the Broadstairs bungalow and return to their Knightsbridge flat, just ten minutes' walk away from the le Mesuriers' Baron's Court home. Joan took the opportunity to talk to her husband and found him as understanding as ever. The week-long visit, and Joan's frequent meetings with her estranged husband, kindled in Hancock a new insecurity and a malice aimed primarily at Joan's son David, which would ultimately destroy their relationship.

Dorothy Squires was in concert at Swansea. Hancock reluctantly accepted the singer's invitation to accompany Joan and David for a weekend in Wales and they set off early one Saturday morning. Less than thirty miles into the journey, Hancock told his driver to find somewhere for breakfast. While the others drank tea, Hancock downed Champagne perry. 'It's a bit early for that, isn't it?' said Joan.

Hancock drained another glass and tried to reassure her: 'It's okay, it's like drinking lemonade.' Half an hour later the Mercedes stopped at another restaurant and Hancock ordered another bottle of perry.

They made five more stops that morning, by which time Hancock had moved on to brandy. When they eventually pulled in for lunch he was by now abusive and noisy and ordered escargots. David took one look at the dish. 'Yuk,' he announced.

'What do you mean, "yuk"?' shouted Hancock. 'You ungrateful little bastard. These are delicious. Go on, eat one.'

The restaurant had fallen silent as the diners and staff watched Hancock's drunken display of anger. He grabbed the boy's chin and attempted to stuff a snail into his mouth.

Joan pushed Hancock away. 'Leave him alone,' she said, comforting her crying son.

Hancock made a second grab at the boy. 'Look at him, Mother's little darling. There is not a tear in the little bastard's eye.'

It was all Joan could stand. Grabbing her son, she ordered their driver to take her to the nearest railway station. Hancock staggered after them, bumping into tables and slurring apologies and trying to drag the boy back into the restaurant. 'Leave him alone,' said a near-hysterical Joan. 'You're a monster.'

Back in Broadstairs, Hancock drank himself unconscious. Joan had an emergency number for his London psychiatrist, and when she explained the morning's events the doctor admonished her. 'You should have left him as soon as he took that first drink. He has got to believe that you mean what you say,' he said. In the lounge, Hancock had vomited and defecated in his trousers. Unaware of his surroundings or what was happening to him, he was delivered, once again, to the London Clinic.

For Hancock – both personally and professionally – the second ABC-TV series was a disaster, but it was not all Hancock's fault.

John Muir and Eric Geen, who provided the ill-used Festival Hall script, agreed to continue with Hancock, as did the *Blackpool Show* director, Mark Stuart. The only other regular performer would be June Whitfield.

For some unexplained reason, the show's senior production staff agreed to let the writers sort out studio problems, instead of dealing directly with its star. Also, Hancock found the rigid, minute-by-minute production schedule increasingly frustrating. He missed the relaxed, yet inventive, atmosphere of the Sulgrave Boys Club and the benign authority of Duncan Wood, his BBC producer. Hancock likened it to his military service:

> They call a script conference for 11 o'clock. But you mightn't be feeling like it. Then they sit you down in the board room, with carafes of water and pencils and pads with ABC stamped on them. It's all so unreal. Like saying from 1900 hours to 2000 hours would be for dinner. Who eats then? Comedy isn't running a destroyer.

Recording for the *Hancock's* series began early in April, with the weekly transmissions scheduled to start on 16 June. It was decided to shuffle the programmes into a more balanced order, another ruling Hancock learnt second-hand from the scriptwriters, not the senior staff.

For the first two weeks, Hancock made a considerable effort to remain sober and concentrate on the scripts, despite some irritating distractions. The production executives attempted to impose one storyline in which the *Hancock's* nightclub is taken over by an American film company. The subsequent script gave most of the lines to other actors, with Hancock relegated to the role of 'yes' man. He refused to co-operate and the idea was dropped.

So far, Hancock had kept to his promise of telephoning Joan as soon as the rehearsals were over. She remembers: 'Tony stayed sober and worked to a strict timetable for the first few weeks, I could have set my clock by him. I would be standing by the phone, waiting for him to call and say he was on his way home.' Then, for the first time in more than three weeks, the telephone did not ring.

At eight-thirty Hancock arrived, clutching a giant bunch of yellow roses and with his eyes full of tears. 'I've let you down,' he said as he knelt and rested his head on Joan's lap. They were both crying.

'Don't be upset,' Joan said, stroking his hair. 'It's all right, we'll start again tomorrow.'

She suddenly realised Hancock was attempting to smother his giggles in her dress. 'I'm a bloody genius though,' he said looking up, 'I really got them at it today.'

The third programme had included a sketch with Hancock as a croupier. He was apparently enjoying the first read-through and, turning to the writers, said: 'This is as good a script as has ever been written for me.' However, before the studio rehearsal, he cornered the director, Mark Stuart, and complained he was not getting enough close-up shots. Stuart conferred with Muir and Geen and all three agreed Hancock should have his way. Watching the playback, Hancock was dismayed. 'I look like a fucking frog,' he said and stomped off to get drunk for the first time in almost a month.

By the end of April, Hancock was becoming fractious and claimed he needed a break. By objecting to a second script, he hoped to force a week's adjournment in the filming, but Muir and Geen worked continuously for three days to rewrite the dialogue and maintain the production timetable. A few days later, ABC announced that the sixth and final episode would involve a police raid, with the club closing for good. Hancock took the idea as a thinly-veiled criticism of his performance and – rightly as it turned out – believed a planned second series had been axed, even before the first had gone to air.

Like every other director and writer in Hancock's career, John Muir had soon discovered his star's aversion to rehearsals. 'All the way along you got your best performance from Tony at the first read-through,' recalls Muir. 'After that it was just a steady decline. On the first read-through it would be funny – and you'd wonder how it could be, it was the first time he'd ever seen it.' For Eric Geen, the golden Hancock years were on radio. 'I think he could have gone on working in radio, if you rehearsed the rest of the cast, and then suddenly stuck him in front of the microphone with a script. He probably could have gone on forever, and really that's what he should have done.'

Fuelled by drink, Hancock began a relentless round of arguments and nit-picking. Told he was working too slowly and his pauses were too long, he demanded Autocues and idiot boards. When ABC refused, Hancock insisted, 'they've got to see these bleeding eyes'. To everyone's relief, the eight-week recording session came to an end, but Hancock's torment was not yet over.

The critics were unanimous in their dislike of the series. The *Daily Mirror*, succinct as ever, thought it was 'just not Hancock'. The *Observer* claimed to echo the majority of viewers by branding the first two episodes a 'disappointing puzzle ... His unique gifts of fantasy, timing and imitation seem buried under a cumbersome pseudo-night-club setting.' *The Times*, a little more kindly, said Hancock had been let down by the script, and the *Guardian* complained:

> All we get is some tired clowning: the well-known turns of the recent poor years of Hancock, the mock-Churchillian and pseudo-Shakespearian ...

Compère and stand-up comic is his least effective role. I suppose it is some personal ambition that he is determined to fulfil. Remembering his team work with Sid James, with those scripts by Ray Galton and Alan Simpson (and even thinking of his very funny egg commercials with Mrs Cravatte), it is extremely hard to see why he should continue in this particular form of suicide.

*

On Saturday, 14 May, Hancock had been drinking at his flat and attempting to forget how much he hated the *Hancock's* series.

The telephone had been ringing on and off for most of the afternoon. When he finally picked it up, a woman's voice said: 'Tony Hancock, please.' He thought about not answering and hanging up, but something inside made him reply, 'Yes. This is Tony Hancock.'

The woman introduced herself as a reporter for a Sunday newspaper. Hancock did not recognise the name, but there was something faintly familiar about the sound of the journalist's voice. 'I'm sorry to bother you at a time like this.' Hancock was confused. He sensed something terrible had happened during the afternoon and that he had missed it, that he had slept through some shocking public tragedy.

'It's okay,' Hancock replied. The words hissed into each other.

'I wondered if you might want to say a few words about Sid James?' The woman paused, and then went on: 'All the Royal Free Hospital are saying is that Sid has been admitted for a "rest". We know it's a heart attack and he isn't expected to live.'

There was a long silence. The reporter could hear Hancock rasping into the mouthpiece. 'Sid?'

'Yes, Sid James.' Hancock's confusion, she felt, was far shallower than shock – as if he were first trying to remember who 'Sid' was.

Hancock replaced the receiver.

The previous day, Sid James had been working at Thames Television's Boreham Wood studios, filming the latest series of *George and the Dragon*. The cast, which included Joan's husband John le Mesurier, had been pushing hard for weeks, with seven programmes rehearsed and recorded in quick succession.

At lunch, James complained to his wife, Valerie, about a pain in his chest, but he refused to see a doctor. When the day's shooting was over, he drove himself back to his Buckinghamshire home. At two on Saturday morning, James suffered a massive heart attack. He was driven the twenty-seven miles to a London hospital where specialists admitted his chances of survival were slim.

Hancock waited until the Monday. When the telephone rang at Delavel Park, Iver, Valerie James instantly recognised the slow, deep, familiar voice: 'How is he then?' There was no conventional greeting. No 'hello'. No preamble.

'Oh, Tony.' Valerie was almost crying with delight. It was years since she had heard from Hancock. 'Sid will be so pleased to know you phoned.'

The call was short. Hancock listened and then wished his old friend well. The conversation ended as abruptly as it had begun. He would not make contact again.

In July, the day before the final *Hancock's* was broadcast, he had escaped to Aden to entertain the troops. His co-star on the five-day tour was the Canadian ex-pilot Hughie Green, whose ITV quiz *Double Your Money* had been running continually since 1955. One night the pair were woken by rattling walls and falling plaster as their hotel was shelled. The next day, Hancock told the story on stage and, to his surprise, the Army responded by giving him a twenty-four-hour armed guard.

The closeness of the fighting and the danger of being blown up or shot had little effect on Hancock. 'Tony was drunk when we boarded the RAF plane taking us to Aden and drunk when he landed back in England,' recalled Green. The next day, Hancock again checked himself into the London Clinic, this time the excuse was 'nervous exhaustion'.

For weeks during the summer, Hancock quite literally staggered between his triple curses of alcoholism, depression and guilt; one feeding off the others. Worse still was his inability to feel. In his more rational moments, Hancock hated himself deeply for having come so low, seeing it as some macabre and hideous inversion of childhood. He could not speak. He could not read. He had lost all sense of time and future. He could not think of anything but his own suicide, but death was an equally frightening prospect and Hancock turned to the only obliterating force he knew. He wandered the streets, drunk, in stained and dirty clothes, his mouth hanging open and dribbling like a cretin. Few people recognised him. His dishevelled appearance shocked many of his old friends.

Sid James was driving down London's Piccadilly. It was one of his first outings since his near-fatal heart attack the previous May. The taxis and buses slowed to a crawl as a ragged figure lurched across the road and finally took refuge on a traffic island. As James passed, the unshaven face and sleepless, sunken eyes turned to examine him. There was no flicker of recognition. It was Tony Hancock.

'He looked dreadful, quite dreadful,' Sid James recalled. 'He really looked miserable. I tried to pull up and get over to him. I got the car parked, but by then he had disappeared. He was so full of liquor he didn't see me. I wish to God I had been able to reach him, because little things like that can change people's lives.' James would never see Hancock again.

Within a week or two, Bill Kerr had also caught his last glimpse of Hancock. It was just after seven in the evening and the Australian, appearing in a West End show, was on his way to the theatre. Hancock was wearing a frayed old coat, the collar turned up and his hands plunged deep into the pockets. The two men greeted each other. 'Come in and have a Turkish bath,' said Hancock, nodding toward the imposing entrance of a nearby health club. 'We can have a yarn.'

Kerr apologised, sensing his old friend was genuinely pleased to see him. Hancock explained he was staying the night at the club. 'When you close, at eleven, come down,' said Hancock. 'I'll be here. We can talk.' Kerr watched as the hunched figure climbed the stone steps and disappeared inside. 'Tony looked as though he didn't have two bob in the world.'

When Joan wasn't there to look after him, Hancock found their apartment cold and oppressive. He would abandon the flat and move into the poshest and most respectable London hotels. Dragging a large suitcase rattling with vodka bottles, a heavy book bag and his giant yellow teddy bear, he would demand a room. When the complaints of his obscene language and drunken behaviour became too much, the management would evict him. By the end of 1967, he was effectively banned from every top hotel in the capital.

Joan remembers: 'Tony was drinking heavily and was in and out of nursing homes, where he was dried out, relieved of vast amounts of money, filled with tranquillisers and sent home none the better. Alcohol was his cloak of comfort, his retreat from reality, and he couldn't or wouldn't give it up.'

Each treatment was followed by an even shorter period of resolution. What had once lasted weeks could now be measured in days. It was, for Hancock, an ever-decreasing and ever-accelerating circle. In the morning his hands would shake with delirium tremens; he could not even hold a cup or open a door. Joan diluted two ounces of alcohol with water and let him sip the mixture from a spoon until the symptoms slowly subsided. Even in the security of their flat, Hancock would be seized by a panic attack that only a drink would absolve. At other times, hours slipped from his memory in waking black-outs. When the longing became too much, he would slip out of the apartment, too possessed and too ashamed to ask Joan for help.

His disappearances grew longer, his returns more pathetic and apologetic. On one occasion, Hancock arrived back unwashed and unshaved, his eyes sore and bloodshot. The buttons on his shirt were in the wrong holes and his tie was hanging down his back. His baggy trousers were so low on his hips, his underpants were showing. Full of remorse and begging forgiveness he stayed dry for four days, progressively becoming scratchy and frustrated. On the Saturday morning he disappeared once again.

Late the next Thursday afternoon, the doorbell rang at the Whaddon House flat. Hancock – looking 'dreadful, haggard, drawn, unwashed, crumpled and forlorn' – was holding a large bunch of red roses. For Joan the months of anguish and the days of worry were finally exhausted. She shouted and ranted and told him the affair was over.

Barely able to stand, he followed her around the flat, demanding sex and mouthing crude suggestions.

Joan escaped into the bedroom and shut the door. She unscrewed a tablet bottle, filled the palm of her hand with Valium capsules and swallowed a week's dose in one go. As she fell asleep she remembers hiding the bottle under the mattress. In the next room Hancock drank a bottle of vodka and then most of a bottle of brandy. He staggered into the bedroom, grabbed Joan by the hair and dragged her on to the floor. Through eyes too drugged to make sense of what was happening, Joan watched Hancock attempt to make love to her. When it was over, and she was once again alone, she retrieved the pill bottle and took the remaining Valium.

Early the next morning, their cleaning lady first discovered the still senseless Hancock and then the comatose Joan. They were taken to hospital in separate ambulances. When she was allowed home, Joan fled to a friend's house, vowing never to see Hancock again. It was a lost promise.

Throughout their affair, Hancock's appetite and sexual demands had both frightened and fascinated Joan. His need for sex – the more spontaneous the better – was intense. One night, the pair had just started dinner at a Kensington restaurant when Joan flashed a white lace garter she had bought in Harrods. Hancock called the waiter, paid the bill and dragged her back to their flat.

Sometimes he would at least make an effort to curb his lust. 'I'm going to draw an imaginary line down the middle of this bed,' Hancock informed Joan, 'over which no tits, arses or willies must stray.'

There were other times when nothing would satisfy him. Hancock would sit surrounded by a blue haze of depression, his longing for a drink competing with a deeper and more secret yearning.

Hancock's latent homosexuality – more inquisitive than focused – increasingly began to surface after his thirty-fifth birthday. Throughout his life, Hancock's bisexual appetite appears to have been blessed with more than its share of good luck and a desire for anonymity by everyone concerned.

Although never officially reported, Hancock was involved in at least one homosexual incident while serving in the RAF. Rather surprisingly, the 23-year-old Hancock found himself the object of a 'crush' by a fellow Gang Show performer at least ten years his senior. Hancock did his best to ignore the airman's growing affection and only gave in, according to his brief lover, 'more out of curiosity than desire'.

Three or four times, and usually after consuming a considerable amount of alcohol, the two men 'made clumsy love' in some dark and out-of-the-way corner of the camp. 'Here I was, attempting to seduce this very beautiful young man, and all he could do was giggle,' recalls the airman involved. 'The more Tony fumbled the more he giggled. It was more sexual farce than sexual fantasy.'

The late-night encounters abruptly ended when the pair were discovered by a flight sergeant. The NCO turned and walked away without saying a word, and Hancock sweated out the next day awaiting the inevitable summons from his section commander. That evening, after the show, the flight sergeant cornered Hancock. 'He was a man who had served in the RAF considerably longer than most of us,' added the fellow Gang Show member. 'I suppose being assigned to look after an entertainment unit, he came to accept all kinds of behaviour the RAF would not normally have put up with. He gave Tony a friendly talking-to and that was the end of the matter. Tony never spoke to me again.'

Twelve years later, when the former airman was suggested for a small part in a television *Half Hour*, Hancock vetoed the choice.

In his diary Kenneth Williams records – third hand – an incident involving Hancock and the singer Matt Monro. Williams and Sid James and the other members of the *Carry On* team were sitting in a coach in Slough High Street during the filming of *Carry On Abroad*:

He [Sid James] talked at length about Hancock and said that he used to go about the flat naked and with excreta and vomit about and that his sexual appetites were depraved and that Matt Monro told him he'd woken up one night to find Hancock going down on him for the fellatio, and that Matt had 'given him a right hander'. This is certainly a new twist. I'd never heard that Hancock was interested in homosexuality. Sid said 'It got so that he'd try anything . . .'

With a note of caution, Williams added: 'Of course one wonders how much of this is factual and how much gossip put together from disjointed accounts.'

The truth behind the 'gossip' is even more bizarre. In October, 1962, Hancock was starring in his own three-week tour. The run opened at the King's Theatre, Southsea, before moving north to Liverpool and then back to Brighton on the Sussex coast. It was basically a two-man show, shared equally between the singer Matt Monro and Hancock. The second week ended on a high. Travelling with the comedian and Monro were Glyn Jones, the show's road manager, and Terry Nation, whom Hancock had hired as a scriptwriter but who, by his own admission, had assumed the role of '£100-a-week baby sitter'. The group decided to catch the overnight sleeper from Liverpool to London for a brief stop-over before the Monday night opening in Brighton.

The drinking had started early. Crowded into one of the first-class compartments, the quartet downed still more wine packed in a hotel hamper before staggering off to bed. When they awoke, the train had long since arrived at Euston. Nation went to wake Hancock, only to find the road manager was already in the compartment. The still-stupefied Hancock was naked and lying on his bunk in full view of the carriage window and other passengers walking along the platform. Jones hurriedly pulled down the blind. 'We decided to get Tony dressed and out of there as quickly and discreetly as possible,' Nation said. Hancock awoke as Jones was attempting to pull on his socks. He raised his head, focused on Nation, and pronounced: 'Glyn is trying to give me a fitting for a sock.'

They managed to get the comic dressed and off the train. Matt Monro had already departed and Hancock could remember nothing of the previous night's celebrations. 'Did I offend anybody?' he kept asking. 'I sometimes wander out into the corridors stark naked. Are you sure I didn't offend anyone?' Nation assured Hancock the journey had been uneventful.

'What happened was more shocking than it was surprising,' confessed Nation for the first time more than twenty-five years later. 'Sometime in the early hours, I woke up to an argument. When I got to Matt's compartment Hancock was naked and cowering in the corner.' It was obvious from Monro's distaste that Hancock had attempted to sexually molest the singer while he was asleep. Nation eventually calmed Monro and led the drunken Hancock back to his berth. When he returned, Monro was threatening to abandon the tour and start legal action. 'I had to work very hard to get him to change his mind,' said Nation. 'In the end we agreed never to mention the incident again.' As far as Hancock was concerned, it had never happened.

Not long after, Nation gave Hancock a script in which he wakes up in a hotel room after a drunken night of revelry and repeatedly demands: 'Did I offend anyone last night?'

Hancock read the script in silence, grinned and handed it back to Nation. 'You bastard,' he said.

During what his lover, Joan le Mesurier, described as his 'guilty benders' – some of which lasted for as long as a week – Hancock would apparently disappear from the face of the earth. Attempts to track his progress through the seedy pubs and backstreet drinking clubs of London invariably failed. The Metropolitan Police, if they had been asked, would have told her exactly where to start looking.

The maze of courts and narrow streets that make up London's Soho never sleep. In the late 1960s, it seemed that almost every building had been converted to a strip joint, nightclub or sex shop, with a back-alley bar for every sexual fetish and persuasion. Most establishments were part of a few well-ordered and viciously disciplined underworld empires. To keep the doors open and the profits rolling in, the Soho bosses knew they not only had to keep their customers satisfied, but also keep the police at arm's length. This they did by making 'insurance' payments to a protection syndicate operating from within

Scotland Yard. Few premises escaped payment. The smaller, one-man establishments were forced to join the umbrella of immunity by the larger sex empires. Anyone who refused could expect a police raid and inevitable closure. Each week two junior detectives were rostered to collect the brown paper bags stuffed with grubby, used notes. When they returned to their Scotland Yard squad room the cash was divided proportionately by rank and distributed.

One detective sergeant – later imprisoned for his part in the corruption scandal – recalls making a cash collection from a plush mirror-lined office just off Broadwick Street. To get to the office, the policemen had to walk through a basement bar, one of several used by London's homosexual community as a meeting place and pick-up joint.

As the officers descended the stairway they were forced to wait while two doormen attempted to eject a middle-aged customer. 'He was very drunk and very abusive,' the sergeant still remembers. 'They were trying to keep things as quiet as possible, but he was shouting and waving his arms about. Somehow he wedged himself in the doorway and they couldn't shift him.'

Irritated by the delay, and the thought of attracting unnecessary attention, the detectives grabbed the drunk and dragged him up the stone steps and on to the pavement. 'He was in an appalling state,' adds the ex-sergeant. 'He had obviously not changed his clothes for several days and they stank of alcohol and urine. He could hardly stand.'

The officer was about to walk away when something about the man's unshaven face and puffed, watery blue eyes seemed familiar.

'Is your name Hancock?' he asked.

The drunk stiffened and began to sway in slow, controlled circles. 'Yes,' he admitted.

Asked if he knew where he was, Hancock once again replied: 'Yes.'

The policemen then formally identified themselves and Hancock's attitude changed. The fear of being arrested – never a real threat – seemed to steady his body and his voice. 'I must go now,' he said flatly. 'I must go home.' When the detectives returned to the street after making their cash collection Hancock had gone.

Two weeks later the detective sergeant, this time with a different partner, saw Hancock again. He was sitting in the far corner of the same gay bar and, although he was drinking, appeared sober. He was talking to two young men. 'The room was packed with fags and transvestites and no one was paying him any undue attention,' recalls the officer. 'Hancock was wearing a jacket with a sweater underneath and with his shirt collar only half tucked in. Somehow he looked too respectable and too old for Soho at that time of the morning. He looked up and saw me watching him. He didn't recognise me, and he didn't want me to recognise him.'

Over the next two months Soho sightings of Hancock – both sober and drunk – were regularly reported to the vice squad offices. There was even an unofficial suggestion that he should be given a friendly warning about his behaviour. Although his apparent homosexual leanings attracted the usual lurid jokes from the all-male officers, Hancock was 'well respected' as a comedian – 'most of us had grown up with him'. Someone, it was agreed, should warn Hancock before he was recognised and the press tipped off.

Joan knew none of this. Throughout the summer, she continued to endure Hancock's alternating bouts of drinking and contrition. They fought and made love. Whenever it became too much, she would flee to her parents in Ramsgate or to Dorothy Squires.

Squires, born in a van parked in a Carmarthenshire field and christened Edna May Squires, was still smarting over the demise of her nine-year marriage to the future James Bond star, Roger Moore. Always a heavy social drinker, the singer was by now like Hancock, a fiery and bitter alcoholic.

When a drunken Hancock tracked his lover to Squires' Bexley mansion, threatening to drag her back to their London flat, the 52-year-old singer suggested she and Joan should make a midnight dash to a friend's Brighton seafront house. During a weekend dinner party there, Joan found herself sitting next to a recently bereaved widow. The woman listened as Joan related the horrors of the previous year and attempted to justify her irrational love. Suddenly the woman asked: 'If your man had an incurable illness would you give him up?'

'Of course not,' Joan replied.

'Isn't alcoholism an incurable illness, and often fatal?'

Joan realised the truth of her neighbour's statement. She excused herself and telephoned Hancock in London. He arrived, two hours later, with no money to pay the taxi. The next morning, the pair attempted to persuade Squires everything would be all right. The singer, who possessed a hard-headed reputation, broke down and sobbed: she was convinced the relationship was doomed and Hancock's life would end in tragedy.

What Hancock needed more than anything else was work. Several approaches were made to individual BBC producers without success. There was, Hancock's agent Billy Marsh informed him, nothing on the horizon.

In the early hours of a late-summer morning, the telephone rang in Phyllis Rounce's Earls Court flat. It was already getting light outside. The agent struggled to answer the phone. 'It's me,' Hancock announced as if he had been away for the weekend. 'I'm in the West End and I need to talk to you.'

'It's four in the morning,' protested Rounce, still remembering his demanding earlier morning calls of the previous year.

'You've got to come and see me. Please come, please come, please come...' Hancock had quite obviously been drinking.

When Rounce asked where he was Hancock arranged to meet her at Leicester Square. She got on her bicycle and pedalled through the deserted London streets. Hancock was, she remembered, in a dreadful state – 'He had been sick down the front of his jacket and he was wearing odd shoes.'

For the next two hours, Rounce propped up Hancock as they walked round and round the square, occasionally diverting to a nearby cabby's café to collect more black coffee and sandwiches. As the sky lightened and the roads became busier, Hancock announced he had to go. He refused to let Rounce take him home. 'He just turned his back and walked away,' she said. 'No thank you for getting out of bed. No thank you for walking miles. No thank you for the food and drink – he didn't even wave goodbye.'

Over the next few weeks, the dawn meetings continued. Rounce, like all the other women in Hancock's life, persuaded herself he was 'coming back' to her, that if she worked hard enough to rebuild his self-confidence, he might give up the drink. Early in September, the pair were sitting on the steps in the centre of Piccadilly Circus when the agent noticed that although Hancock's clothes were still casual, they somehow seemed less scruffy, as if someone had attempted to press them without cleaning them first.

Without warning, Hancock announced he was off to Australia. The Bernard Delfont Agency had been contacted by the Melbourne-based entrepreneur, John Collins. He wanted to book Hancock. For more than a year, Australian television had been screening *Hancock's Half Hour*, and Collins, through Willard King Productions, intended to cash in on the comedian's new-found popularity. With equal determination, Hancock informed Rounce he intended to stay dry throughout the Australian booking.

This time the strict London Clinic diet and regime of vitamin supplements and psychological support appeared to solidify Hancock's resolve. In little under a month he lost thirty-two pounds and looked slimmer and fitter than he had done for a decade. When he flew into Melbourne's Essendon Airport on 3 October, he was sober and in control. The weather, by contrast, was stormy and wet.

The following day, Hancock opened at the Dendy Cinema, in the Melbourne suburb of Brighton. It was a hybrid evening, common to Australian audiences, but which had not been fully explained to the comedian. He would play the first half of the show and would be followed, after the break, by a feature film. Hancock was, in effect, a celebrity warm-up man. His determination, so far untested, won through and he told the first-night audience:

Tonight you are getting the lot – I shall not be hanging around – I shall not be rushing on here shouting 'stone me' and 'he's gone bonkers' and 'fetch him a punch up the bracket' – there will be no

mention of an armful of blood. Tonight you are getting the lot –
you'll be getting Terpsichore ... dancing ... sword-swallowing
... (painful, but lucrative) ... impressions, Shakespeare – I shall
be going through the card, because you are looking at Mr Show
Business himself.

Unlike British theatre and television audiences, the Australians had
not yet been satiated by 'The Crooner' and *The Hunchback of Notre
Dame* and 'George Arliss'. Hancock was getting the kind of response
he had not felt since the early 1950s. The reviews were good, and by
the end of the first week most houses had sold out.

On Tuesday, 10 October, Hancock was driven across the city to
tape a television interview with Nancye Hayes, one of Channel
HSV7's prime-time chat-show hosts. His ten-minute guest spot, for
Something Special – Nancye, was held for eight months before it was
eventually screened. After the recording, the company executives
staged an impromptu green-room party in his honour. At first
Hancock resolutely insisted on being served only tomato juice, but it
was not long before he had downed several beers and had moved on to
vodka. By the time Hancock arrived at the cinema, he was unable to
stand.

His performance lasted just twenty minutes. When he appeared
incapable of remaining upright, the audience began to boo and hiss.
During one over-enthusiastic impression, he disappeared into the
wings and got lost: the only way back on to the stage was by crawling
up some steps. His reappearance was greeted by still more jeers and
catcalls. Hancock ordered a spotlight to be shone on one obscene
heckler and a fight broke out. Whispered attempts from the wings to
lure him off failed and it was only when the cinema manager rem-
onstrated with him in the centre of the stage, and in full view of the
audience, that Hancock agreed to call it a night.

A variety of excuses were concocted for his 'collapse'. At the end of
the premature interval, the Dendy's manager, Robert Ward, apologised
for Hancock's performance and blamed the combined effect of a series
of cholera injections he had received in preparation for an equally

fictitious stop-over in Hong Kong on his way back to England. The press were surprisingly tolerant. 'I thought I was dying,' he lied. 'I've never felt so terrible in my life. I should have cancelled the performance. Everyone thought I was drunk. I wasn't. I was just so ill. First the blasted cholera shots, and then the high protein diet I have been on. Two beers added to that knocked me down like a bomb.'

The next night he bounced back, sober and word perfect. 'As I was saying when I fell off the stage . . .' he began. The following Sunday, Hancock gave a free performance for everyone who sat through his night of disaster.

While Hancock was in Australia, Joan le Mesurier returned to her husband. Hancock had left during one of their long separations and had made no attempt to contact her. In many ways, Hancock saw it as a test. If he could make some kind of stage come-back and stay off the drink, he would, once again, be able to face his lover. He had, however, omitted to inform Joan.

After three weeks at the Dendy Cinema, Hancock flew to Hobart in Tasmania for a series of hotel cabaret bookings. Collins, meanwhile, flew the six hundred miles to Sydney to open discussions on an Australian television series. Executives at ATN7 were enthusiastic, yet surprisingly no one bothered to raise the subject with Hancock or watch his act. With the *Half Hours* high in the television ratings, it was assumed they would be getting the 'genuine' Hancock.

Reports began to filter through from Hobart that Hancock had once again started drinking, so Collins dispatched the scriptwriter Hugh Stuckey to Tasmania, to keep Hancock out of trouble while talking him into signing a television contract. Stuckey – who found Hancock 'very unsophisticated' – arrived with the intention of keeping his charge fully occupied. He soon discovered the more he kept Hancock amused, the less he drank. On one occasion, the writer suggested they visit a farming show. Concerned he might be recognised, Hancock bought a cap and a scarf and a pair of dark glasses. The disguise failed. As he walked through the crowd people would turn to him and say: 'Hello Tony.'

*

During the autumn of 1967 – and while Hancock was in Melbourne – the novelist and playwright J. B. Priestley was completing the final revision of his latest book. It was a rolling monster of a novel, and at 300,000 words the longest of his career. Called *The Image Men*, it would be published in two parts, *Out of Town* and *London End*.

Working in the study of Kissing Tree House, his Alveston, Warwickshire, country home, the 73-year-old Priestley drew heavily on the men and women he had met and written about as an essayist for the *New Statesman*. One was Tony Hancock.

Priestley first saw Hancock on the Adelphi stage in the early 1950s. 'What caught my fancy was the psychological distance he put between himself and his act,' he recalled. Writing in the *New Statesman* about the new breed of 1950s comics, he described how Hancock 'comes on all smiles and confidence' only to be 'reduced by the malice of circumstances'. Priestley and Hancock had met for a brief drink and then quickly lost touch.

In *London End*, the writer describes a 'difficult' comedian he calls Lon Bracton – 'indecisive, moody, probably quite neurotic'. Although he denied it at the time, Priestley later admitted his inspiration was Hancock, and the personality Priestley portrays is instantly recognisable.

Bracton has an American agent, Wilf Orange. Describing his client, Orange says:

Tried nearly everything, Lon has. Been analysed twice – the lot. Look – half the time – no, say a third – he's a wonderful hardworking comic. For two years they worshipped him on the box – television I mean. They rolled over soon as they heard his name. Then suddenly he couldn't do it – broke his contract – doctor's orders of course. Same with pictures. Same with live shows.

The money's been enormous, but even so I've had more trouble with him than any other three clients put together. 'Cos the other two-thirds of the time Lon's beany, foofoo, nutty as a fruit-cake. It's not the sauce, the hard stuff, though he can lap it up. It isn't even the women though there's always one around, sometimes married to him, sometimes not. It's Lon himself. He's several people. He goes to the can a good sweet guy and comes back a lousy bastard. You help yourself to a drink, turn round, and it isn't the same fella. He'll keep you up and you'll be falling about laughing, and the very next day he'll tell you he can't work. For weeks on end he can be more dippy-batty than half the people put away in mental homes. Yet when he's really working and it's all coming through, I tell you, this is a great comic – the best we've got.

The agent consults Dr Owen Tuby, deputy director of the Institute of Social Imagistics, and one of *The Image Men*. Before analysing his new subject, Tuby goes to watch one of Bracton's films. He shares the circle with three other people, an experience Hancock himself endured when he slipped into a London cinema to watch *Orders are Orders*.

He had his funny moments, but all too often he just missed the mark ... Unequal as Lon Bracton might be, when he was absent from the screen the film was trifling and tedious.

Professor Tuby – who thinks Bracton 'would have been happier if he'd stayed at the end of a pier pulling faces' – completes his diagnosis and delivers his cure. He informs Bracton:

You're a neurotic man who plays an even more neurotic man. Instead of trying to fight it, you go right along with it. Any audience you have will always have its share of neurotic people but you, Lon Bracton, will never fail to seem a damn sight worse than they are.

And they'll tell one another – not just the neurotic types but the whole of them – that Lon Bracton's just as barmy off stage as he is on it – crackers – bonkers! And as long as you watch your timing – and you know all about that, Lon – you can go on and do almost anything you like – and they'll love it. You could eat your supper and read the evening paper on the stage – and they'd still love it.

Hancock did not live long enough to read Priestley's judgment. *London End*, the second part of his novel, would not be published until 1969.

Hancock flew home early in November with a contract for an Australian television series in his jacket pocket. Backed into a corner by threats that ATN7 might pull out of the project unless he signed before he left Australia, he had committed himself without taking advice from anyone in England. 'My best is yet to come,' he informed the usual gaggle of Heathrow reporters and photographers.

Over the next few days, his confidence disappeared as quickly as his duty-free and Hancock found himself increasingly answerable and alone. As part of the deal, it was up to him to enlist both a director and scriptwriter. Billy Marsh refused to get involved because his client had agreed to the contract without prior consultation. Duncan Wood, Hancock's television producer, was unwilling and unable to commit himself to any non-BBC work, and John Muir and Eric Geen, who had written much of Hancock's recent material, took the opportunity of finally ending what had become a frustrating collaboration. Only Phyllis Rounce, his erstwhile agent, shared his enthusiasm and promised to look out for a suitable director.

John le Mesurier had accepted his wife's return 'lovingly and warmly, as if I had been on some heroic mission or had just come home from hospital after a long illness'. The affair, if that was what remained, would be conducted in secret and on Joan's terms. Alone in the flat they had shared – and with Joan's clothes taunting him from the wardrobes – Hancock attempted to rebuild his life with the rubble of his past.

Cicely, by now an alcoholic herself, had sold MacConkeys and was living in a nearby cottage. When Hancock telephoned to suggest lunch, she readily agreed. They talked of their mistakes and how much they had hurt each other, and by the time they had finished eating Hancock had agreed to try again. 'Cicely really was convinced he still loved her and wanted to start over,' a friend remembers.

The next day, Hancock telephoned Freddie. 'Please come back,' he pleaded, 'I need you. I miss everything. I can't go on without you.'

'I thought you didn't like the *Emergency Ward 10* atmosphere,' she said.

'I know now it was just organising.'

The conversation would be repeated several times over the next few weeks, and only ended when Hancock's solicitor informed him Freddie had initiated divorce proceedings.

About this time, Hancock's 78-year-old mother arrived in London with her new millionaire boyfriend. The couple booked into the Savoy to do some Christmas shopping, after driving up to London in the man's Rolls-Royce Silver Cloud. Hancock and Joan joined them at the theatre.

Whatever her sexual weaknesses, Lily Sennett was strong enough to stand up to her oldest surviving son when he was drunk or being wildly erratic, but when Hancock was in danger, she would defend him like a tigress defending her young. Lily was exuberant, earthy, irreverent, improbable, but her loyalty to her two surviving sons – and in particular to Hancock – was unqualified and unquestioning. When he returned from Bournemouth a little while later, he confessed to Joan that he had spent the weekend with an actress he had met while filming the *Hancock's* series. Lily had apparently accepted the change of partner without question.

Hancock continued to telephone his mother almost daily. Sometimes, he was so drunk she could barely understand what he was saying and Lily, sensing another crisis, suggested her son come down to Hampshire to recuperate.

The Saturday before Christmas, he checked into a Boscombe nursing home, ostensibly 'to recover from a bout of pneumonia'. It was obvious Hancock was in an advanced and critical stage of alcoholism: the destruction of his liver had yellowed his eyes and given his skin a jaundiced pallor, and the strain on his heart made his feet swell grotesquely. Days, sometimes weeks, had been wiped from his memory.

That Christmas – the last of Hancock's life – slipped painfully into an oblivion of sedatives and Plurentavite injections and fearsome bottomless depressions.

1968

LILY SENNETT's bedroom door inched open. It was two in the morning and Hancock was standing in the doorway gently rocking from side to side. 'I've drunk a bottle of brandy in five minutes,' he announced and fell flat on his face.

Lily was staying at the William Mews flat. She telephoned for a doctor and then rang Joan at the le Mesuriers' Baron's Court apartment. Hancock's local GP was on holiday, and by the time his locum arrived Lily had dragged her overweight and lifeless son on to the bed. His face and hands were turning blue and his eyelids and lips were bloated. Joan arrived as the doctor, a Scotsman, was attempting to revive her lover.

Hancock opened his eyes. 'Fuck off.'

'Do you want to die?' The doctor asked him.

'Yes,' mumbled Hancock.

It was the end of February and Hancock was becoming increasingly jittery about his new Australian series. The only way he would get through his Australian contract was to remain dry and this time, he told Joan, it would be for good. To give him added motivation she promised that if he could stay off the drink for exactly a year she would, once again, leave her husband – and marry Hancock.

The telephone rang at Michael Wale's London flat. It was a Saturday morning late in March. Wale looked at his watch – nine o'clock – and picked up the phone. 'This is Tony Hancock. I hear you'd like to write for me.' The voice was too perfect; at first Wale thought it was one of his friends playing a practical joke.

Trained as a journalist, Michael Wale was now an equally energetic scriptwriter and had met Hancock at numerous press receptions during the 1960s. He had also sat among the audience to watch Hancock take over from Arthur Haynes at the Palladium in 1963 and, two years later, his *Talk of the Town* cabaret.

When the writer arrived at William Mews, Hancock 'appeared well, if a trifle flustered'. While the comedian was making coffee, Wale took the opportunity of examining the apartment; it had an unlived-in, lonely feel about it, almost as if Hancock had just moved in and shunted the packing cases out of sight. The coffee, when it arrived, was lukewarm and instant and had not been mixed properly.

Hancock explained he was about to return to Australia to record a new series and wanted an English writer – 'someone who had grown up with the old Hancock' – to accompany him. Hancock failed to inform Wale that he was not his first choice, and that several other more experienced writers had turned him down flat.

The basic concept of the new series had already been agreed with Hugh Stuckey, the scriptwriter hired by the Australian network. Hancock would play the part of a British immigrant arriving on a £10 assisted passage. It was Michael Wale who persuaded him to revert to the East Cheam Hancock, created by Galton and Simpson. He even agreed to wear the black Homburg hat and the astrakhan-collared coat. 'He admitted he had been wrong in totally abandoning the character,' recalls Wale. As the writer was about to leave, Hancock showed him the Comedian of the Year trophy awarded him by the Guild of Television Producers and Directors in 1957. 'It's about time I won another of those,' Hancock told his new scriptwriter.

Hancock had promised to return to Sydney and start work by late March, so Michael Wale flew on ahead. The flight was broken at Teheran for a refuelling stop. In the airport lounge Wale met Paul McCartney and explained to the Beatle that he was on his way to Australia to write for Tony Hancock. 'I hope he does well,' commented McCartney. 'He must succeed again. We all want him to.'

Hancock was still unaware of his former agent's involvement in his revived career. When both John Collins and ATN7 failed to hire a director willing to take on the series, they had turned once again to Phyllis Rounce. She telephoned Eddie Joffe, a South African-born director who was then working for Grampian Television in Aberdeen, and whose credits included *The Golden Shot* and the children's magazine programme *Magpie*.

Joffe, a pragmatic and experienced television professional, was aware of Hancock's reputation 'but not how bad it had become'. He admitted to having misgivings about the series from the start, but when he questioned Rounce about the viability of the project, she persuaded the director he would be doing something 'fabulous' for Hancock.

Joffe flew down from Scotland to discuss the series with him. 'Tony had some pretty good ideas and luckily we got on quite well,' he said. What surprised him most was the bleakness of Hancock's mews flat: the only flash of colour came from the giant teddy bear propped in a corner. 'There was no furniture, not even a chair or bed,' recalled Joffe, 'just a few books and some empty bottles.'

Joan had tried, since January, to talk Hancock out of going to Australia. 'The thought of him being alone in a strange country for three months with no one to care for him or understand him filled me with dread,' she recalls. 'But he was firm, determined, and once Tony made up his mind about something nothing could move him.'

In the final days before his departure a melancholy settled over Hancock – not so much a depression as an acceptance of circumstance and realisation that his future, what future there was, would be determined solely by his own actions. It had an amazing effect on him. At the age of forty-three, he became a mature and thoughtful self-reliant adult. Joan le Mesurier remembers him as 'strong, sexy, considerate towards me and very determined'.

Joan was by now living a double life. Since her November reconciliation, John le Mesurier had been unaware of his wife's continuing adultery. At weekends, or whenever le Mesurier was not away filming, she had returned to the role of dutiful wife and mother. In the secret moments – in her secret thoughts – she remained Hancock's tangled and conspiratorial lover: determined never to hurt her husband again, yet promising herself that one day she and Hancock would marry. 'I am not proud of deceiving my husband,' she confessed years later. 'But that's what I did – every available minute God gave me.'

When they met in secret, Hancock never drank. He was making a conscious effort to cut back his consumption of alcohol. They talked in coffee bars and restaurants, only for the moment, never about what might be in the year to come. No hopes. No fears. No promises to break.

Joan agreed to spend Hancock's last weekend in England at the William Mews flat. Le Mesurier was away filming and assumed his wife was in Ramsgate with her parents.

On Sunday night, Joan ironed Hancock's shirts and pressed his trousers. When his two suitcases were packed, the couple went to bed. Hancock was, by now, addicted to sleeping pills, and tired and apprehensive he began to fall asleep before they could make love. 'He fell asleep with his head on my shoulder and one leg across me,' said Joan. 'It was the most uncomfortable night I have ever spent, but I was afraid to move and lose one inch of his closeness.'

Hancock was standing at the window. His head was low and his shoulders rounded in the familiar television pose. He was ostensibly watching for the taxi. When he turned Joan could see his eyes were brimming with tears. In the taxi they held hands. No one spoke. For Joan, the journey across London was a distorted reflection of the time she had accompanied Hancock to the London Clinic.

The taxi would drop Joan at Victoria Station and take Hancock on to Heathrow. The Ramsgate train was already standing at the platform. Rushing across the concourse Hancock suddenly stopped and looked resolutely at Joan. 'I'm leaving you here,' he said. When he walked away he did not look back.

Hancock flew out of a rain-swept Heathrow, preferring to break his 10,500-mile journey in New Delhi rather than Hong Kong. 'I can't stand the poverty there [Hong Kong],' he told an associate. 'Oh, it was all right for me, sitting in one of those clubs, with a boy to pick up your cigarette if you dropped it. The poverty there is appalling. There's all these people living in little more than rabbit hutches, all on top of each other. And there, slap in the middle of the place, is a neatly manicured cricket pitch.'

A more realistic reason for the New Delhi stop-over was an invitation from Hancock's *Face to Face* interrogator, John Freeman. The former BBC man was now British ambassador to India. Both men had become friends in the weeks following the television interview and had remained in touch throughout the 1960s, but Freeman had not seen Hancock for some time. 'He was very unhappy, but that was nothing new,' recalled the journalist-turned-diplomat. 'He seemed jittery and suspicious of everyone and everything – particularly the curries.'

One Indian he encountered fascinated Hancock. During his stay with the Freemans, he was introduced to a surgeon whose speciality was depression. The doctor had allegedly experimented by drilling holes in the tops of his patients' heads. 'When he'd bored the hole he would put a cork in it,' Hancock claimed. 'Then whenever the person was feeling depressed and wanted a bit of a lift all he had to do was pull the cork out for a few moments and he'd feel fantastic.' No one knew whether the story was true or simply a flash of Hancock mischief. He would alternately deliver it in stone-faced solemnity, asking his listener's opinion, or crumple into a heap of laughter from where he would deliver the punch line – 'the only snag is that you always have to wear a hat'.

Hancock had promised to write to Joan every day. To maintain the secrecy – both from John le Mesurier and Freddie Hancock's private investigators gathering divorce evidence – Joan had opened a post-office box in Ramsgate. The first letter to arrive had been written and posted in New Delhi. In it Hancock claimed that every Indian he had met sounded like a blacked-up Peter Sellers with a Welsh accent.

From India, Hancock flew first to Melbourne where Hugh Stuckey, the series' senior scriptwriter, lived. To Stuckey's surprise, Hancock was relaxed and readily accepted script suggestions. After work, Hancock would remain at the writer's home, enjoying a domestic evening chatting with Stuckey and his wife and playing with the couple's two young daughters. When the writer needed to take a half-day off to attend the girls' school sports day, Hancock said he would like to come along. 'I warned him it would be the dreariest event in Australia, but he insisted on joining us,' he said. Hancock was recognised immediately. For once he suffered the handshakes and autograph hunters with good humour: 'He genuinely seemed happy and kept thanking us for taking him.'

As a nation Australia really wanted Hancock to succeed, and he never truly appreciated the vast reservoir of good will surrounding him. In restaurants, people would quietly and charmingly approach him: 'I would just like to say how much we enjoy your work, Mr Hancock.' Each one was willing him to make his come-back a triumph.

Cricket had remained a passion for Hancock. The previous year he had asked to meet several of the Australian test team. This time he was made an honorary member of Melbourne's exclusive Fitzwilliam Cricket Club. Hancock returned from the club with another bizarre theory – he was convinced Harold Larwood, who had emigrated to Australia, had shrunk in size.

Hancock wrote every day and Joan collected the letters in batches of two and three. They were not love letters. They contained none of the sexual passion he had included in his notes to Freddie. Some were shy, almost apologetic. Others gushed with enthusiasm for the people he had met. All contained some hint of loneliness and his desire to return to England. 'If I had said "yes, okay, come home" Tony would have been on the next flight,' admits Joan.

In England, the separation grew too much, so Joan let herself into Hancock's William Mews apartment and telephoned his Melbourne hotel. Hancock would ring her back at prearranged times, continually promising he was 'not drinking and working hard'. It left him with a £1,000 phone bill.

By the middle of his second week in Melbourne, pressure cracks began to appear. At first, Hancock had kept his alcohol intake to a social level, even refusing drinks on several occasions, but he was now drinking heavily. At one of the final script meetings, he even appeared drunk.

Stuckey had arranged to accompany Hancock to Sydney, where the pair would be met at Sydney's Mascot Airport by network executives. The flight was called and Hancock waited until the last minute before entering the departure lounge. His eyes looked as though they were full of tears. He was shaking. At the barrier Stuckey heard him say: 'Oh God, I can't face it. I just can't go through with it.' He turned. 'Please . . . please,' said Hancock, 'take me back to my motel.' Stuckey put his arm around him and propelled him through the lounge and on to the plane.

The comedian's transfer to Sydney caused a variety of problems. Within hours of Hancock's arrival at the Travelodge Motel, John Collins – the Australian who had sold the Hancock project to ATN7 – demanded a meeting with Michael Wale. 'There's a bit of a problem,' he told the writer. 'Hancock's been on the booze.'

Hugh Stuckey was more concerned with keeping his star alive long enough to record the series.

Hancock's fingers were stained yellow with nicotine and his clothes smelt oppressively of cigarettes. He was smoking two, and sometimes three, packs a day, something he normally only did while drying out. Now he was drinking and smoking. Most days he would fall asleep with a lit cigarette still in his hand. On Hancock's departure from his Melbourne hotel, the management had complained about burns on the sheets and bedroom carpet. His suitcase was full of scorched shirts and underwear. In Sydney, Stuckey insisted on adjoining rooms and a spare key to Hancock's room; he was convinced his charge would one day set the bed alight.

Each night, Stuckey searched Hancock's room for concealed spirits and stayed to talk, sometimes not returning to his own room until well into the next morning. Hancock seemed to enjoy the company. As they talked, the writer realised: 'Whatever that magic quality is that gets to audiences, was in the man. He was so vulnerable, you had to do something.'

It was vital that news of Hancock's condition – like the comedian himself – be kept away from the press. For Wale the strategy was flawed from the start. 'Tony had been brought out far too early,' he said. 'Performers are usually bad travellers. They get bored easily. What else is there to do except drink away the boredom in their hotel?'

A series of outings was arranged to keep Hancock occupied, and with schoolboy obedience he accepted the role of part-time tourist and full-time Englishman. For those who witnessed his attempts to enjoy himself, it was East Cheam Hancock come to life.

His favourite diversions were sight-seeing tours of Sydney and trips to the city zoo. Dusty Nelson, an ATN7 stage manager with whom he had worked in England, would drive while Hancock sat in the back eating steak and kidney pies. One day he was taken to Chinaman's, a popular beach not far from the city centre. The temperature was in the high eighties, but Hancock strode through the ranks of semi-naked bodies still wearing his socks, suede shoes and grey flannels, and with a cardigan over his shirt. When it was suggested he go for a paddle to cool off, he looked horror-struck – 'You must be stark, raving mad. For God's sake don't go in the water, it's shark-infested.' As a concession to the heat, he undid the top button of his cardigan.

At the zoo Hancock would make straight for the koala enclosure and, as with the sloths at Blackpool, found it easier to identify with the world's animal inhabitants than his human counterparts. Someone had told him that koalas became intoxicated when they ate eucalyptus leaves. 'No wonder the poor little blighters hang on so tight,' he commented.

Once back at the Travelodge, Hancock would pour himself a large vodka and throw off his clothes, padding around his room in just his underpants. When the vodka ran out, he would shamble through the corridors, searching for what he euphemistically described as his 'medicine'. Janet Trewyn-Smith, celebrating her twenty-first birthday with a visit to Australia, recalls arriving back at the hotel after a day out and being confronted by a 'fat, half-naked man, rocking back and forth down the hall, totally unaware he was exposing himself'. The situation was more comic than frightening. 'He was obviously very drunk, but for some reason he was carefully carrying a glass ashtray overflowing with cigarette ends,' said Trewyn-Smith. 'As I stepped aside he stopped, mumbled an apology, concentrated on holding the ashtray level and then set off again.'

It was only when Trewyn-Smith reached her room that she realised who the man was. 'It was one of the saddest moments of my life,' she admits. 'At school listening to *Hancock's Half Hour* was a weekly ritual. At home we never missed one television programme. And here was this man I revered as some kind of god, reduced to a pathetic, semi-conscious drunk. I cried. It was as if someone had died. As if my childhood no longer existed.'

Hancock needed rescuing so frequently, staff at the hotel had their own alarm call – 'the Pom's out'. Guided by a pageboy, and occasionally the duty manager, Hancock would be led, quiet and uncomplaining, back to his room, where he would awake to find a new bottle of vodka on the table.

By now, Eddie Joffe had arrived in Sydney. Reading the Stuckey and Wale scripts, he felt the writers and star had scratched the surface to reveal a promising honesty – 'not Galton and Simpson, but not that far off'. Spontaneous script conferences were frequently held in Hancock's hotel room. 'It was a lovely chemistry because the four of us got on so well together,' recalls Joffe. 'Tony liked the writers. The writers liked him. The whole idea was right. This lad from East Cheam didn't go to Australia to start a new life – he dragged East Cheam with him. It had so much potential. I thought, "All I've got to do is stick some cameras on him and away we go. We've got a world-class winner here." '

Each thirty-minute episode would be a self-contained situation comedy. In one – and in true East Cheam style – Hancock boasts about his sporting prowess. A flash-back pictures him as a jockey. When the horses are released he is left high and dry in the starting stalls. Another has Hancock arriving at the studio for an audition. He gets lost in the maze of corridors and finds himself locked in the wardrobe overnight. Rummaging through the costumes, he goes through all his old stage routines and impressions. 'Tony loved the idea,' said Eddie Joffe. 'It meant he didn't have any lines to learn.'

By the middle of April, the series was being cast and the script was all but complete. As a practical joke during one of the numerous press interviews, one of the production team solemnly announced the series was to be called *Marie*. Years later the false name was still being quoted.

Hancock Down Under – a titled deemed inappropriate after his death – was to be the most expensive venture yet undertaken by any Australian television company. It would be shot entirely in 35mm colour, a format more attractive to American and other international networks.

Each day Hancock would telephone his mother in Bournemouth. The conversations regularly deteriorated into a catalogue of complaints from the son and a series of berating lessons from his mother. Hancock was less frank, but equally truthful, to Michael Wale. 'Do you know,' he told his writer, 'if this doesn't go right – and even if it does – I'd rather just be a bloody postman.'

Hancock's nerves were beginning to unravel. He had not worked in a television studio for almost twelve months, and the prospect of a repeat of the ABC *Hancock's* fiasco terrified him. However, he found he could cope with – almost enjoyed – live interviews, and when John Collins informed him he had been booked to appear on *The Mavis Bramston Show* he assumed the format would be informal and chatty. Watching the rehearsals, Hancock suddenly realised the programme was quick-fire and satirical and that he would be expected to perform. He walked out of the studios, claiming he had been insulted and mistreated by the production staff.

*

Everyone – including the studio executives – was getting nervous. As an opt-out clause, they demanded Hancock record a pilot episode. If the show was not good enough, ATN7 would be justified in cancelling the series and flying its star back to England. Stuckey and Wale were allowed to nominate a script and hastily rewrote one, placing the emphasis on Hancock's comic reaction and giving him fewer lines to learn. They called it *Sleepless Night.* Hancock liked the idea and claimed it reminded him of Galton and Simpson's final BBC series opener, *The Bedsitter*, but Eddie Joffe's sense of unease heightened. He had scheduled the pilot recording for a weekend, with the first day's shooting on Friday, 19 April, but during the week, several rehearsals had been either delayed or abandoned because Hancock was too drunk even to read his lines from the script.

On Friday, Hancock, who knew the studio would be full of extras and technicians, made the effort to arrive sober. The prospect of performing in front of an 'audience', as Joffe had gambled, helped rekindle the comedian's confidence. Behind the watery eyes there were flashes of Railway Cuttings. However, something was missing. For anyone who knew him, Hancock seemed incapable of allowing his talent to lead from the front; sometimes he even found it difficult to keep up.

The next day – scheduled for Hancock's solo and close-up shots – was a disaster. The previous evening, his driver had deposited him at his hotel and left him to drown his day's work. After an ugly and off-colour incident in the hotel restaurant, he had staggered off to bed, to wake up face down in a vicious circle of tranquillisers, vodka, amphetamines, and still more vodka.

The heat under the studio lights, even at nine in the morning, was oppressive, and Hancock, fearing another *Bullwhip Griffin* disaster, began chain-drinking cans of beer. When filming was halted by a bird, which had flown into the studio and perched on a lighting gantry forty feet above the set, he fell asleep. By the time the recording resumed after lunch, he could not even deliver his lines on cue.

In one sequence, Hancock is kept awake by a dripping tap. He dials the Australian equivalent of 999 and the operator asks: 'Which service, police, fire or ambulance?' By take thirteen it was obvious to everyone on the set that Hancock was incapable of delivering the scene; he would either forget to dial or forget to pick up the receiver or forget his line – 'Send all three.'

As Eddie Joffe recalls in his book, *Hancock's Last Stand*: 'He was physically present when we restarted, but he had no idea where he was or even who he was for that matter. Despite the safety net of his cue cards, the opiates and alcohol had disconnected his batteries and blitzed his brain. He could barely stand, let alone deliver, with those pills sloshing around in the alcohol in his belly.'

At teatime on Saturday, the shooting schedule was more than four hours adrift and it was decided to complete the recording on Monday morning. This time Hancock arrived not only incapable of remembering his lines, but oblivious of the scene, in which the pyjama-clad Hancock walks off the bedroom set and into the off-screen shower. When he returns he is dripping wet. Joffe's production assistant recalls: 'By this time, Tony didn't have the slightest understanding of what was going on; he was exhausted, defeated, bewildered. He didn't remember that bit of the script; he was just led through the moves with the director yelling, "Now make him wet. I want him really soaked, dripping. Soak him, now bring him through the door again." And poor Tony was pushed back into shot. The expression of utter bewilderment as he stood there, in the relentless eye of the camera, with water dripping off his hair and down his face, I shall never forget.'

Attempting to shoot the pilot had demoralised an enthusiastic and loyal crew and wasted a lot of expensive 35mm colour film. For Hancock it was the beginning of the end. Jim Oswin, ATN7's managing director, was 'incandescent with rage' and agreed with Joffe that it was not even worth processing the film.

Deep inside, Hancock knew how bad his performance had been, yet somehow he clung to the loyalty that obviously surrounded him, and to the belief that it would all come together in the end. Jim Oswin was more concerned with salvaging Australia's most expensive television series before the full horror of the situation leaked to the press. There was still one loose end to tie up: John Collins, the Melbourne entrepreneur, was 'ordered' to sell the series to the station, effectively giving Channel 7 the power to sack Hancock.

The final decision lay with the chairman of the ATN7 board. Ten days after shooting the disastrous pilot, Eddie Joffe was summoned to Rupert Henderson's office. Joffe was immediately struck by the irony of the millionaire's appearance: Henderson was a skeletally thin man who appeared to be wearing a shirt and suit two sizes too large. By the law of chance, which always adds a twist of humour to the most desperate situations, the director was suddenly aware of Henderson's startling resemblance to Wilfred Brambell, the British actor who played the cantankerous rag-and-bone man in Galton and Simpson's hit television series, *Steptoe and Son*. For days, Channel 7 had been unsuccessfully attempting to persuade Harry H. Corbett, the other *Steptoe* star, to fly out to Australia and take over the Hancock series. Another suggestion – Hancock's – was that the series should be shot in England.

Henderson was a hard-headed pithy Australian. 'Well,' he demanded from across his massive desk, 'what are we going to do?'

'There is only one thing we can do,' admitted Joffe. 'Abandon the series and cut your losses.'

'Do you think we could dry him out?' When Joffe explained that the treatment, no matter how harsh, appeared to have little lasting effect on Hancock, the chairman did not hesitate. 'Okay, fire him.'

Joffe, who by now had become extremely fond of his star, gently pointed out that both he and Hancock were employees of ATN7, and any sackings should be made by management.

'All right,' Henderson conceded. 'I'll do it. Have him here at noon tomorrow.'

Hancock knew what was coming; his first thought was to pack his bags and make straight for the airport. When Eddie Joffe informed him there was only one way of saving the project and that was for the comedian to confront Henderson and volunteer to take the cure, Hancock admitted: 'I couldn't do it. I've tried all sorts of clinic before and I've only managed to quit for a couple of days.'

The meeting with Rupert Henderson lasted exactly an hour. When he left, Hancock was driven first to the Travelodge Motel to collect his things and then on up the coast to the Cavell House Private Hospital at Rose Bay. For Hancock it was a major coup. Not only had he bartered the survival of the project for a stay at one of Australia's most respected detoxification clinics, he had also charmed the television executive into paying all the expenses.

Like most alcoholics, Hancock would cling to an odd scrap of kindness or trust and use it to keep himself afloat for a few more days or weeks. It was a false, but determined, hope and no matter how many people he had let down, Hancock was now obstinate enough to view his recovery as a personal debt to Rupert Henderson. The regime would be familiar and painful. To hasten the drying-out process, Hancock announced he would skip the pretreatment period of reducing and controlling alcohol intake; each day he allowed himself to be sedated and dosed with vitamins and nausea-inducing drugs.

Eddie Joffe witnessed one bout of delirium tremens: 'It was pitiful watching him willing his trembling hands to stir his coffee or struggling to lift to his lips a cup rattling against its saucer, scorning help from me or the duty nurse. The drugs and the withdrawal symptoms took a great deal out of him physically, and he grew weaker and more listless day by day.'

It was during his stay at Cavell House – when his determination remained high, but his reasoning was at its lowest – that Hancock resolved to kill himself. There were no longer any grey areas, he confided to a fellow patient, only black and white; right and wrong. 'He was a highly intelligent person who, in a moment of supreme clarity, had come to realise this was his last chance,' the Australian recalls. From somewhere Hancock had picked up an old Chinese proverb which he insisted on repeating to anyone who would listen: 'A strong man knows when to hang on. A wise man knows when to let go.'

In long, middle-of-the-night telephone calls to his mother and his solicitor, Hancock attempted to tidy his life and set the future. For so long sceptical of Lily Sennett's spiritualism, he made the startling confession that he had 'spoken' to his father, Jack Hancock. Lily gently dismissed the experience as a side-effect of the drugs and drying-out process, but on 12 May – his forty-fourth birthday – Hancock ended a call to his mother, by saying: 'Dad sends his love.'

By the end of May, Hancock was bored and fidgety and pestering his psychiatrist to allow him back to work. Psychologically he had responded well and it was agreed he could leave the Rose Bay clinic, but only under the protection of a trusted friend. Hugh Stuckey was reluctant to resume his role as chaperon. Hancock's appearance shocked the writer. In little over four weeks he seemed to have aged at least fifteen years; his skin was pallid and waxy and his eyes, always striking blue, now looked disinterested and grey. Hancock was a frail, tired individual wearing a bigger and fitter man's clothes.

Eddie Joffe – who noticed that for the first time he could beat Hancock at chess – had, by now, been joined in Australia by his wife and family, and the director agreed that Hancock could share a house with them all, if a suitable property could be found. After inspecting several houses, none of which offered Hancock enough privacy, they settled on an attractive double-storeyed house on Birriga Road in Sydney's Bellevue Hill district.

It was a select and expensive suburb. The family occupied the two main floors of the house, with its entrance on to the street, while Hancock moved into the garden flat at the rear. Built below the main part of the house, the apartment was private and self-contained. Beneath the main window flamed a poinsettia and beyond the sloping garden Hancock could look out across the Royal Sydney Golf Course and the red-tiled roofs to the blue water of the harbour. The only distraction was the whine of saws and the chatter of hammers from an adjoining building site.

Hancock appeared to be maintaining a fragile but firm grip on his day-to-day life. Each morning, Eddie Joffe would bang on the floor of the Birriga Road house with a shoe, and Hancock would reply with a broomstick to prove he was awake. He would then shuffle around his apartment until Dusty Nelson arrived to drive him and his director to the studio. On the way home, he would buy a cooked chicken or ready-meal and go straight to his apartment. He was still using a tape recorder to learn his lines and the Joffes could hear his muffled but distinctive voice below their feet.

The first of the thirteen planned episodes was shot during the last week in May. It opens with Hancock the emigrant on board ship and bound for Australia. When he lands he is directed first to an over-priced hotel and then to a flat owned by an amorous and man-hungry landlady.

For the first time in years, Hancock had made the effort to learn his lines. To everyone's surprise he knew the entire first episode by heart. The idiot boards, which Hancock had once insisted on, were now kept ready but out of sight, at once an invisible prop and threat.

As each show progressed from read-through to rehearsal to recording, Hancock generated a new, genuine and unique loyalty among the cast and crew. Carpenters and technicians volunteered to work all night to have sets ready, something unheard of under the tight union constraints of Australian television and film studios. 'For Hancock,' admitted Michael Wale, 'anyone would do anything. He was working better than I had seen him perform for years. Each Friday and Saturday, on the days we filmed, the studio would fill with staff just to see him work.'

The filming continued through June with a growing air of confidence, not least from Hancock. 'Everyone concerned with the shooting seems to have been over-optimistic about the quality of the series,' comments Roger Wilmut, 'partly because Hancock was showing up fairly well in comparison with the supporting cast, who were professionals but not in his class.'

Jim Oswin also appeared pleased with the first three episodes. He commissioned Stuckey to start work on outlining a second series of six programmes but, in a grave miscalculation, failed to inform his star. It was an approving and supportive decision which could very well have saved Hancock's life.

On the last Sunday in June, Hancock accepted an invitation from

Dusty Nelson to spend the day at his father's flat overlooking Sydney Harbour. It was a chatty gathering of television staff and actors, and Hancock was 'impeccably polite and cheerful'. He refused all alcoholic drinks and insisted on tomato juice. His host, Robert Nelson, retains the impression of an 'inexpressibly sad man'.

Hancock would frequently detach himself from a knot of people and make his way to the balcony. Standing alone, as if on a great sun-drenched open stage, he would throw out questions. Once he was overheard asking: 'What's ahead for me but work, work, work?'

When he was drawn back into the room Hancock would enthuse selflessly about great nights in the theatre, when great stars would win over their audiences by 'talent and guts'. Then, the conversations would tail off. Hancock was homesick and it showed. He admitted he missed 'the wet streets outside the London Palladium and the packed stands at Lord's cricket ground'. He quipped about spartan discipline and having to go where the work was.

Around eight that evening, Hancock once again returned to the balcony and was joined by Robert Nelson. It was a beautiful, blue-crystal evening with a slight breeze coming off the harbour. 'Do Australian newspapers print summaries of divorce court evidence?' he asked.

Hancock was aware of the time difference between London and Australia. He also knew that in just a few hours, possibly while he was sleeping in his Sydney apartment, his marriage to Freddie would, in London, be ending. For Hancock, who showed little interest in the mechanism of divorce, it was a supremely ironic moment: for the final hours of his violent and drunken second marriage he was frighteningly sober. He clung to the balcony rail until Nelson asked if he was all right. Hancock smiled. The moment – and his marriage – had passed.

Much to Hancock's annoyance, all the Australian newspapers carried brief details of the divorce: Freddie had been granted a decree nisi; the customary three-year separation period had been waived because of Freddie's claim of 'extreme hardship'. Details of the affair with Joan le Mesurier were left unsaid. Hancock, it was stated, had committed adultery with an unknown woman.

The British newspapers, when they arrived, were less kind. Joan le Mesurier had been cornered by two *Sunday Express* reporters and decided to deny everything: her affair with Hancock was over; she had no contact with him; she did not love him. After a week of no letters – the Australian postal service was on strike – he felt deserted and alone.

In desperation Hancock telephoned Cicely, ringing from the television studio, and had forgotten the nine-hour time difference. It was early morning in England and his ex-wife was hung over and coming round from a deep sleep. The realisation that she was being confronted by a doleful and apparently repentant Hancock turned to anger. When Cicely was asked to take back the husband she had divorced three years earlier, and who had spurned her own attempts at reconciliation, she slammed down the receiver.

There was only one person to whom Hancock could turn – and for the first time in their personal and professional relationship Phyllis Rounce would let Hancock down.

Filming at the ATN7 studio had finished for the day when Hancock was told there was a telephone call for him. Phyllis Rounce had flown in that morning from London with Rolf Harris and was about to catch a connecting flight to New Zealand for the first leg of the singer's tour. As a young actor, Harris had appeared in two 1959 television *Half Hours*.

Hancock was overjoyed and insisted the agent meet him for dinner. When she said it was impossible, he began shouting: 'No, no, you have got to come now.' Rounce tried to explain she was committed to her client's tour. 'I've got to get to New Zealand by tomorrow morning,' she said. 'I've got to set up all the scenery and organise the show. I promise I'll come the moment I get back from New Zealand. I'll get Rolf away on his tour and I'll fly back to Sydney and spend a few days with you.'

'You promise, you promise, you promise,' Hancock repeated.

Rounce could sense the melancholy in Hancock's voice. 'I'm coming back,' she tried to reassure him. 'You just carry on and I'll be back, I promise.'

*

Since his arrival in Sydney, Hancock had used one of the production secretaries to type up his letters to Joan, but doing this he could not share his emotions, so he wrote two private letters by hand. The tone had changed from optimism to resignation – 'What else is there to say? All will be well, just hold on to the fact that we will be together in time.'

The second was a letter to Mr and Mrs Malin, apologising for his behaviour and the pain he had caused, and promising never again to contact their daughter. To Joan he wrote: 'I loved you more than I thought possible, but now realise that you never shared this feeling. I now relinquish you to your life and will forget you in time. You admonished me many times about wasting my life. Now I say the same to you. I shall not brood over you. In a few weeks our relationship will be dead, cold and unremembered.'

One evening, on his way back from the ATN7 studio, Hancock asked his driver to take him to an address in the suburbs of Sydney. It was a flat above a shop selling hippie robes and accessories. Madame Sacha was a middle-aged clairvoyant and medium whose reputation had spread among Australia's show-business clique. When he telephoned to make an appointment Hancock had given his name as 'Bill', the same as Lily Sennett's medium friend.

For Madame Sacha – who instantly recognised her latest client – it was a frightening and disturbing meeting. For a woman who claimed to have experienced extra-sensory 'messages' from childhood, 'I had never encountered a human being so shrouded in death.'

She asked Hancock what kind of reading he required. He sat for several minutes in silence, his face puffy and his eyes lined and heavy. Without saying a word, he held out his hand. Almost thirty years after his death, and for the first time, Madame Sacha described her encounter with Hancock: 'He wanted me to read his palm, to tell him something about his future. I didn't need to. I only had to look at him.'

Madame Sacha spoke for half-an-hour while Hancock's car waited outside. As she mentioned names and places and events that only he would have known, Hancock nodded or grunted confirmation. 'We did not talk about his future,' she added. 'I knew – I sensed – he would be dead within a matter of days. What shocked me more was that *he* knew. It was almost as if he were using me as confirmation. It wasn't as simple as him already having made up his mind. It was as if, like me, he too could sense the inevitable, the predestined.'

Hancock paid for the reading and left. What Madame Sacha had not told him was that a second 'person' had arrived with her client. Sitting in a chair, behind and a little to Hancock's left, was a tall, handsome, elegantly dressed man in his mid-forties – an exact description of Jack Hancock.

John le Mesurier had been filming in Rome. He flew back to London early on Thursday morning. That night, his first in England for several weeks, Joan agreed to go out to dinner with him, and then on to an early-hours jazz club.

For the first time since his arrival in Australia, Hancock telephoned the le Mesuriers' Baron's Court flat. He was ringing from the ATN7 studio during a break in rehearsals. There was no answer. Hancock replaced the receiver and dialled his mother's Bournemouth home, something he was doing three or four times a day. Lily asked how he was getting on. He said he needed to talk to Joan. 'She will come back to me, won't she?' Hancock asked his mother.

'Of course she will,' Lily said, trying to reassure him. She promised to telephone Joan and get her to call Hancock direct.

It was after ten o'clock in England when Lily rang Joan's London home. There was still no answer. She then called Mrs Malin in Ramsgate. As far as the Malins knew, their daughter was happily reunited with her husband. They were unaware of Joan's continued adultery with Hancock. 'Joan's in Rome with John,' she lied.

Thursday, 24 June, was a rehearsal day. Before the studio work started, Hancock telephoned Spike Milligan at his Finchley home. In north London it was eight o'clock in the evening. To the ex-Goon it sounded as though Hancock had already been drinking heavily. 'It's wonderful out here,' Hancock told him. 'I've got a great series coming up, you must make sure you see it.'

By four in the afternoon, Hancock looked exhausted and Eddie Joffe made one last attempt to persuade his star to accept a dinner invitation. Hancock declined, saying he wanted to stay at home and concentrate on learning his lines. It was the last time Joffe would see Hancock alive.

Around eight o'clock, Hancock left his basement flat and knocked on the front door of the main house. He insisted on returning a jar of coffee he had borrowed earlier in the week, and only reluctantly agreed to stay for a cup. A few minutes later, Myrtle Joffe and Hancock were joined by Trevor Peterson, the owner of the house. He thought the comedian 'was in a good mood and in top form'.

Sometime between eleven-thirty and midnight Hancock said good night. It was June and mid-winter in the southern hemisphere and the night air was already crisp. To reach his flat he had to leave by the front door and walk, first down fourteen steps to a mossy courtyard crowded with rubber plants and a discarded tricycle and then, down a shorter flight, to the door of his apartment. Hancock turned the electric convector heaters to full. By the time he had undressed it was comfortable enough for him to wear only his pyjama bottoms.

In his hotel, Michael Wale was lying on the bed listening to the radio Test match coverage. England were playing Australia at Lord's. He thought how delighted Hancock would be at the England victory. Tony will go in and tell all the technical crew how they've been whacked by England, Wale laughed to himself.

Phyllis Rounce was packing in her Auckland hotel for her return flight to Sydney and her promised meeting with Hancock. Her last words to her former client were still on her mind – 'I'll be with you tomorrow morning. I'll see you tomorrow.'

For two hours Hancock forced himself to work until his reserves of self-belief – his will to live – had run almost to empty. The depression which had trailed him half his life now settled about him like some black, breathless cloud. Hancock no longer made any attempt to escape it. He could not escape. He did not have the energy to escape.

Stupefied by his second bottle of vodka, and becoming increasingly drowsy as the cocktail of drugs he was swallowing took hold, Hancock searched for something to write on. The only thing to hand was the script for episode four he had been attempting to learn. He turned over a sheet of yellow typescript and began to write.

The note was addressed to 'Dear Eddie'. The handwriting was jagged and uncoordinated. Hancock asked his producer to send his love to his mother and, in the inevitable whirlwind of publicity following his death, to assure her his decision to end his life appeared the only way out. He had lost his capacity to suffer – to understand and endure – defeat.

Barely able to focus his eyes Hancock began a second message to Lily Sennett. In ten ragged and drifting lines he asked 'Ed' to beg his mother's forgiveness and reassure her of one final reality, that he was convinced his spirit would live forever and could never be destroyed.

In the dream world somewhere between consciousness and death – between comprehension and bewilderment – Hancock believed he had discovered the truth. The enormity of what he had done was eclipsed by a pin-prick of clarity. The only person he thought would understand was Bill, the medium friend of Lily Sennett.

It is possible Hancock intended to write one more note. He had already turned over another sheet of script. Before he could begin his mind slipped into oblivion; a pen was still clutched in his right hand and a cigarette still burning in his left.

The demands of his profession shaped him, ground him down and eventually killed him, but he served it well.

Anyone who does a job of work and at the end of the day has nothing tangible to show for it, apart from his salary, has every reason to feel insecure. This is perhaps particularly true of show business – you can't frame applause, you can't place cheers on your mantelpiece and you can't plant a chuckle in a pot and expect it to raise laughs. All the

average comic is left with at the end of his career are some yellowing
newspaper cuttings, perhaps an LP or two and a couple of lines in The
Stage *obituary column. But, if he is one of the few greats, he leaves*
behind a legacy of laughter when he has gone, especially, it seems, if
there was an element of tragedy in his life.

HARRY SECOMBE

Hancock had collapsed diagonally on to the single bed; his right leg
was bent and raised; his left leg hung over the edge of the bed, not
quite touching the floor. Beneath his outsize body were his crumpled
striped cotton pyjamas. At the foot of the bed were his discarded shoes
and, in a heap to the right, his dressing gown.

The colour had finally come back to his staring blue eyes . . .

That there was in him, as in so many gifted men, a self-destructive
element, bent on final ruin, seems to me fairly obvious. It explains so
many of his crazy decisions. He was like a man in a leaky lifeboat,
throwing away one pair of oars after another. Consciously he was
becoming more and more independent, more and more ambitious, but
unconsciously he made move after move towards disaster. Most of us
are divided men, but in him the lack of any possible integration was
appalling. He could be Tony Jekyll in the afternoon and Hyde Hancock
all night.

J. B. PRIESTLEY

. . . The filter cigarette Hancock had been smoking had burnt down to
his middle and index fingers, scorching the skin. Collected in the folds
of the bedclothes was a scattering of white pills and multi-coloured
amylo-barbitone capsules. Resting against his arm was an empty vodka
bottle. The tape recorder continued to turn for the next four hours,
spooling the tape on to the floor . . .

If you laughed at Dickens, you laughed at Hancock; if you laughed at
Falstaff, you laughed at Hancock; if you laughed at W. C. Fields, you
laughed at Hancock. What you are remembering is your own laughter,

and for a comedian to leave behind that echo of remembered laughter is a tragedy.

DENIS NORDEN

. . . The room was sad and sparse and looked as though it belonged to a man with nowhere else to go. The only pieces of furniture were a chair, a small wardrobe, a bed and a dark-wood bookcase. Hancock's suitcase, still with clothes unpacked, had been placed on the floor beside the bed. Between the wall and the bed and acting as a bedhead was the bookcase. There were no books, only a telephone . . .

To be Tony Hancock was sufficient for several people's lifetimes. That he couldn't allow his own lifetime to run its natural course is a tragedy. Mercifully there are ample records of his work with Alan and Ray and Denis and Kenneth and Sid and Hattie and Bill and the rest. While the acetate holds out Tony Hancock is going to be with us. Silly, flawed, and infinitely original.

BARRY TOOK

. . . In England Joan le Mesurier looked at her watch. It was the one Hancock had bought as a present in Hong Kong the year before. The watch had stopped and no matter how hard she shook it, she could not get it to work. It was the moment of Tony Hancock's death.

As usual Myrtle Joffe banged on the floor above Hancock's flat with a shoe. There was no response. Her husband, hung over from his previous night's dinner, suggested his eldest daughter Lynn should go down and wake Hancock. 'She's not ready,' protested Myrtle, 'she's still having breakfast.'

Myrtle hammered on the floor a second time before setting off down the two outside flights of steps to the garden flat. Seconds later she was breathless and back in the main house. 'Something's wrong,' she shouted at her husband. 'You better get downstairs. Quickly.'

Something in the back of Joffe's head told him to expect the worst. 'I touched him, intending to shake him, hoping, I suppose, against hope, that he was resting before getting up,' recalls Joffe. 'His body was ice cold despite the heaters still on full blast.'

Picking up the two sheets of yellow paper, he tried to read the scribbled suicide notes, but he could no longer focus or concentrate. He closed the flat door and went upstairs to call the police.

'There's been a death here, a suicide,' he told the emergency operator.

'Who is it?'

'You'll know when you get here,' he replied. By the time the police arrived, Joffe was in tears. It would not be long, he reasoned, before the press picked up on the news.

It was just after 10pm on Monday night when the telephone rang in Lily Sennett's Bournemouth home. There was a slight echo but the line was clear. 'Hello, Mrs Sennett,' the director said. 'It's Eddie in Sydney. There's been an accident.' There was a pause and then Lily announced: 'Tony's dead, isn't he?' It wasn't really a question, more a statement, Joffe remembers.

'I told her I hadn't wanted her to hear the news on the radio, television or from the newspapers. I related, as best and as calmly as I could, a brief outline of the events leading up to Tony's death,' adds Joffe. 'She listened silently, asking only a few questions.' He then read Hancock's mother the two scribbled suicide notes.

On Wednesday, 4 September, 1968, the Sydney coroner decided that Tony Hancock had 'died of a heavy tranquilliser dose while under the influence of alcohol'.

Before recording a verdict of suicide, the coroner, J. J. Loomes, commented:

Looking at the background to the worries that concerned him, one can only admire his fortitude in carrying out his work and giving pleasure and enjoyment to people when he, himself, was beset with problems in his own life.

It is true these problems finally overcame him. Suicide is not a disease, a crime, or a sin. It is a symptom of many different problems ranging from chronic mental illness, to a crisis in an individual's life, and finally to an impulsive solution.

EPILOGUE ONE

FOR SIXTEEN YEARS Tony Hancock and George Fairweather had shared a private joke.

On the day Hancock received his invitation to perform at the 1952 Royal Command Performance, he was appearing in *London Laughs*. Fairweather was in his Adelphi Theatre dressing room. Hancock embraced his old friend and said: 'If it hadn't been for you, I would never have had this honour, you taught me everything I know.'

Tears began to fill Hancock's eyes. He sat down. 'If only Dad could have been here to see me,' he said.

'Don't you think he will be?' Fairweather replied.

Hancock looked up and smiled. 'Don't give me that rubbish,' he said. 'Only spirits come out of bottles.' It was a private moment. The phrase stuck. Several times over the intervening years Hancock and Fairweather would laugh at their private joke – 'Only spirits come out of bottles.'

Fairweather has never previously related this story to anyone.

Twenty-two days after Tony Hancock was found dead, George Fairweather received a typed letter. The single sheet contained no name or address.

Dear Mr Fairweather,

I understand you knew Mr Tony Hancock. I therefore feel that I must pass on to you what I believe to be a message from him.

I was recently sitting for meditation and I seemed to hear his voice saying clearly and recognisably: 'Blimey, this is a turn up for the books, I always thought only spirits came out of bottles, but I find that I am one now. Tell my friends I am not blotted out and I will see them again one day. In the meantime can they spare a few thoughts for old Tony.'

It was so vivid I felt impelled to convey it to someone, but of course you must do as you think fit. But if it would be of comfort and reassurance to anyone who was dear to him, I would feel glad. It is, however, a private matter and I don't think there should be any publicity.

[signed] K. R.

EPILOGUE TWO

DURING 1969, Joan le Mesurier purchased a Victorian terraced house in Ramsgate and to help her renovate her new home she hired a middle-aged cleaner.

One day the woman excitedly announced she had seen 'a round, rather scruffily dressed' man, slumped in one of the living-room armchairs. He was smiling and appeared at ease, almost as if he was waiting for someone. The woman – 'a sensible soul' – instantly recognised the man as Tony Hancock.

Joan questioned the cleaner. She described the hunched way the stranger had been sitting, a habit peculiar to Hancock. More convincing were the clothes she claimed the man was wearing. The jacket was Hancock's favourite and one Joan had packed in his suitcase the night before he flew to Australia.

NOTES

1. Dennis Main Wilson died on Wednesday, 21 January, 1997. He left the BBC staff in 1983. Like most producers of his generation, he worked in an age when the basic responsibility had been left in the hands of the creative producers. By the 1980s, he believed a producer's freedom had become 'increasingly restricted'.
2. Dick Emery died on 2 January, 1983.
3. Larry Stephens died on 26 January, 1959, from a brain haemorrhage. Spike Milligan, with whom he was having dinner, claims Stephens died in his arms on the way to hospital.
4. Charlie Chester died on Thursday, 26 June, 1997.
5. Duncan Wood died on 11 January, 1997.
6. John le Mesurier died on 15 November, 1983.
7. Sir Arthur Bliss (1891–1975), London-born composer, from 1942 to 1944 the music director of the BBC.
8. Terry Nation died on 9 March, 1997.
9. Dorothy Squires died on 14 April, 1998.
10. Lucie Lilian Sennett died on 18 November, 1969.

The Tony Hancock Appreciation Society publishes a monthly magazine, *Missing Pages*, and holds two annual conventions. Details from:

The Tony Hancock Appreciation Society
(Incorporating The Tony Hancock Society)
46 Queens Road
Hazel Grove
Stockport
SK7 4HZ

CHRONOLOGICAL TABLE

THE FOLLOWING CHART summarises the events of Hancock's life that can be dated from documents and archives. Column one shows the events of his life and personal history, together with key historical events. Column two gives dates of performances on radio, television and film. Taken together, the two columns convey some impression of the extent of Hancock's day-to-day activities.

Biographical	Performances
1888 John (Jack) Hancock born.	
1889 *23 November:* Harry Samuel Thomas and Clara Hannah Williams (Hancock's grandparents) marry at Christ Church, Sparkbrook, Birmingham.	
1890 *4 September:* Lucie Lilian (Lily) Thomas born at 323 Cooksey Road, Aston.	

1900
Jack Hancock joins Houlder Brothers
shipping line as a messenger boy.

1914
4 August: Great Britain declares war on
Germany.
22 August: Jack Hancock marries Lily
Thomas at St Oswald's Church, Bordesley, Birmingham.
September: The Hancocks move to Tyneholme, Stratford Road, Hall Green, Birmingham.

1916
Summer: Jack volunteers for the Army.
He is deemed unfit for service.

1918
28 March: Colin William Hancock born
at Tyneholme, Stratford Road, Hall
Green. He is the first child of Jack and
Lily Hancock.
Autumn: The Hancock family move to 41
Southam Road, Hall Green.
11 November: First World War ends.

1922
14 November: British Broadcasting
Company transmits from London for the
first time.

1923
23 November: 'Jack Hancock (Humorist)'
makes his radio debut on station 5IT,
Birmingham.
19 December: Jack Hancock makes a
second broadcast on Station 5IT, Birmingham.

1924
12 May: Anthony John Hancock is born at 41 Southam Road, Hall Green, the second son of Jack and Lily Hancock.

1926
27 January: Logie Baird demonstrates television for the first time.
Summer: BBC radio broadcasts *That Child,* the world's first situation comedy.

1927
1 January: Inauguration of the British Broadcasting Corporation.
Easter: The Hancock family visit Bournemouth; Jack and Lily decide to buy the Mayo Hygienic Laundry at 37 Wynyard Road, Winton.
Summer: Jack and Lily Hancock, their two sons Colin and Tony, and the family's nanny move to Bournemouth.
Christmas: Hancock contracts rickets. It leaves him with permanent physical damage.

1928
Spring: Jack Hancock takes over as licensee of the Railway Hotel, Holdenhurst Road, Bournemouth. The Mayo Laundry is sold and the family move into the public house.
3 July: First television transmission in colour by John Logie Baird; the first TV set goes on sale in America at $75.

1930
3 April: Cicely Janet Elizabeth Romanis is born in Harley Street, London.

1931
9 June: Roger – Jack and Lily Hancock's third son – is born at the Railway Hotel, Bournemouth.

Summer: Hancock follows his older
brother and attends Durlston Court Preparatory School, Swanage.
October: George Fairweather performs
on the same semi-professional bill as Jack
Hancock; the next day he meets Jack's
son for the first time.

1932
Easter: The Hancock family holiday in
the south of France; the young Tony
Hancock meets the comedian Sydney
Howard.
Autumn: Jack and Lily Hancock buy the
Swanmore Hotel and Lodge, Gervis
Road East, Bournemouth.

1933
July: Hancock makes his first stage
appearance, as a walk-on in a school
production of *The Gondoliers.*
August: The nine-year-old Hancock fails
a film test arranged by his father.

1934

1934
July: Hancock appears in his school production of *The Pirates of Penzance.*

August: Jack Hancock resigns the tenancy
of the Railway Hotel and the family
move to the Swanmore Hotel and Lodge.
It is renamed Durlston Court Hotel after
the boys' preparatory school.

1935
11 August: Jack Hancock dies of cancer at
the age of forty-seven.

1936
1 January: Lily Hancock marries Robert
Walker at Bournemouth Register Office.
March: Hancock is enrolled at St
Andrew's College, Bradfield, near Read-
ing.

1 October: BBC begins regular television broadcasts.

1939
July: Hancock leaves St Andrew's College.
August: The fifteen-year-old Hancock unsuccessfully attempts to join Willie Cave's Rebels.
1 September: The threat of war blacks out Britain's 5,000 television screens during a Mickey Mouse cartoon.
3 September: Great Britain declares war on Germany.
4 September: Hancock attends a 'commercial skills' course at Bournemouth Municipal College. During an afternoon break he announces, 'I want to make people laugh.'
4 November: Colin Hancock marries Pauline Mansfield at St Peter's Church, Bournemouth. Two days later he joins the RAF.

1940
January: Hancock's career as a tailor's assistant lasts exactly four hours.
February: Hancock joins the Board of Trade as a 'temporary unestablished assistant clerk – grade three' for £2 10s a week.

1940

Spring: Hancock is booked as a supporting act at Bournemouth's Avon Road Labour Hall. He is announced as 'Anthony Hancock – the man who put the blue in blue pencil'.
Summer: He auditions for the Bournemouth War Services Organisation.
Summer: Hancock appears at the Church of The Sacred Heart, Richmond Hill, Bournemouth. The audience walks out when he tells dirty jokes.

1941

Spring: Hancock gets a job as pot man at the Pembroke Hotel, Bournemouth.

1941

May: Hancock attends his first audition for BBC producer Leslie Bridgmont.
6 June: A La Carte – A Mixed Menu of Light Fare. Hancock makes his first radio appearance on the BBC Forces Programme.
Summer: Joining George Fairweather's Black Dominoes concert party, Hancock performs at Boscombe Hippodrome and tours nearby army bases.

Winter: George Fairweather receives his call-up papers and Hancock takes over as head of Bournemouth War Services Organisation.

1942

1 September: Colin Hancock's aircraft disappears over the North Atlantic.
November: Hancock is called up and joins the Royal Air Force Regiment and completes his basic training at RAF Locking, near Weston-super-Mare.

1942

Winter: Hancock performs in camp concerts and local talent shows while stationed at RAF Locking, near Weston-super-Mare.

1943

January: Hancock's first posting is to a Royal Canadian Air Force unit in Bournemouth.
March: Hancock posted to Marine Craft Section of RAF Wig Bay, near Stranraer.
Spring: Lily and Robert Walker take over the tenancy of the Green Dragon public house, Sambourne, near Redditch.

1943

December: Hancock attends an audition for ENSA at the Drury Lane Theatre, London, and is rejected because of his nerves.

1944

1944
January: Hancock attends a second
ENSA audition, this time as 'Fred
Brown', and fails a second time.
Spring: Ralph Reader auditions Hancock
and accepts him as a member of the RAF
Gang Show and posted to No. 9 Gang
Show.

May: Hancock's 11-strong gang show
lands in North Africa.
August: After touring North Africa, the
No. 9 Gang Show is shipped to Italy.

1945
May: No. 9 Gang Show returns to Britain
after a twelve-month tour.
8 May: VE-Day. Hancock celebrates at
Lily and Robert Walker's Sambourne
public house.
July: Hancock joins merged No. 4 and
No. 9 Gang Shows and flies to Gibraltar
for a European tour.
14 August: VJ-Day.
Summer: The Gang Shows are disbanded
and Hancock is transferred to RAF Light
Entertainment at Uxbridge where he runs
the wardrobe stores with Peter Sellers.

1946
7 June: BBC relaunches its television
service with a Mickey Mouse cartoon.
Announcer Leslie Mitchell quips: 'As I
was saying before we were so rudely
interrupted . . .'
6 November: Demobbed from RAF,
Hancock takes a room at the British Lion
Club in Ebury Street, London. After two
weeks he moves to the Union Jack Club
opposite Waterloo Station.

1947

1947
February: Hancock attends his second
audition for Ralph Reader, this time for
an RAF fundraising tour.

*28 April: **Wings over Homeland.** The tour opens with a week at Blackpool Opera House.

*5 May: **Wings over Homeland** at Theatre Royal, Nottingham; one week.

*12 May: **Wings over Homeland** at New Theatre, Hull; one week.

*19 May: **Wings over Homeland** at Empire Theatre, Sheffield; one week.

*26 May: **Wings over Homeland** at Theatre Royal, Birmingham; one week.

*2 June: **Wings over Homeland** at Hippodrome, Coventry; one week.

*9 June: **Wings over Homeland** at Empire Theatre, Newcastle; one week.

*16 June: **Wings over Homeland** at Empire Theatre, Edinburgh; one week.

*23 June: **Wings over Homeland** at Empire Theatre, Liverpool; one week.

*30 June: **Wings over Homeland** at Palace Theatre, Manchester; two weeks.

*14 July: **Wings over Homeland** at Hippodrome, Brighton; one week.

*21 July: **Wings over Homeland** at King's Theatre, Southsea; two weeks.

*11 August: **Wings over Homeland** at Palace Theatre, Plymouth; one week.

*18 August: **Wings over Homeland** at New Theatre, Oxford; one week.

*25 August: **Wings over Homeland** at Hippodrome, Dudley; one week.

*1 September: **Wings over Homeland** at Winter Gardens, Morecambe; one week.

*14 September: **Royal Air Force Association Festival of Reunion,** at the Royal Albert Hall.

Winter: While watching *Piccadilly Hayride* at the Prince of Wales Theatre, Hancock adopts the show's star, Sid Field, as his comic hero. Derek Scott – Hancock's future partner – is a member of the cast.

*25 December: **Cinderella.** First pantomime appearance as an Ugly Sister at the Playhouse Theatre, Oxford. Run ends 24 January, 1948.

1948

May: Hancock teams up with pianist Derek Scott to form 'Derek Scott and Hank'. The duo is accepted by agent Vivienne Black.

August: Phyllis Rounce, co-founder of International Artistes, watches Hancock at the Windmill.
Autumn: Ray Galton and Alan Simpson are admitted to Milford Sanatorium, Surrey, suffering from tuberculosis.
18 October: Phyllis Rounce signs Tony Hancock on a five-year contract, to International Artistes.

1949

25 February: Dennis Main Wilson, the BBC's unofficial head of auditions, watches Hancock perform at the Nuffield Centre.

1948
*26 April: **Peace In Our Time**.* Hancock has three small parts in the Playhouse Theatre, Oxford, production. Run ends 1 June.

*12 July: **Revudeville No. 214**,* at the Windmill Theatre, London. 'Derek Scott and Hank' perform until 21 August.

14 September: Tony Hancock auditions for BBC Television at the Star Sound Studios, accompanied by Derek Scott.
September: Hancock attends a second audition, this time at Alexandra Palace 'under normal television studio conditions'.
*1 November: **New to You**.* Hancock makes his first television appearance with Derek Scott.
December: BBC radio audition for *Variety Bandbox*.
*December: **Cinderella*** at the Dolphin Theatre, Brighton: Hancock plays an Ugly Sister.

1949
*9 January: **Variety Bandbox**,* from the Cambridge Theatre, London. First of fourteen appearances on the BBC Light Programme show.

*27 March: **Variety Bandbox**,* from the Kilburn Empire.
*April: **Feldman's Theatre, Blackpool**.* One week variety.

Autumn: Hancock is introduced to and becomes friends with script writer Larry Stephens.

December: Hancock and Stephens share a flat at 17 St Martin's Court, London WC2.

1950
January: Hancock and Larry Stephens move to a flat in Craven Hill Gardens, near Paddington Station.

3 February: Sid Field collapses and dies at The Prince of Wales Theatre.

March: Hancock and Larry Stephens share a flat near Covent Garden.

3 April: Cicely Romanis celebrates her 20th birthday with an ice-skating party and is introduced to Hancock.

*13 June: **Flotsam's Follies,*** at the Esplanade Concert Hall, Bognor Regis. Hancock appears in four sketches. Run ends late September.
*25 September: **Variety Bandbox,*** from the Camberwell Palace.
*19 October: **Stars of Tomorrow,*** on the BBC Home Service.

19 November: **Victoria Hotel, Sidmouth.** Hancock performs one night cabaret.
*8 December: **First House – Look Who's Here,*** on the BBC Home Service.
*December: **Cinderella,*** at the Royal Artillery Theatre, Woolwich. Hancock plays Buttons. Season ends mid-February.

1950
*1 January: **Variety Bandbox,*** from the Camberwell Palace.
January: Audition for BBC radio's *Workers' Playtime.*
*27 January: **Workers' Playtime,*** from Messrs Sterling Metals Limited, Coventry.
*20 February: **Flotsam's Follies.*** Hancock appears in a six-minute 'conjuror' sketch on BBC television.
23 February: **Claridges Hotel, London.** Hancock appears as the election-night cabaret.
*19 March: **Variety Bandbox,*** for the Light Programme and the BBC General Overseas Service (now the World Service).
*15 April: **BBC Ballroom,*** on the Light Programme. Hancock is one of two cabaret turns.
*2 May: **First House – Look Who's Here,*** on the BBC Home Service.
*28 May: **Variety Bandbox,*** from the Camberwell Palace.
*17 June: **Ocean Revue,*** at the Pier, and

July: Hancock proposes to Cicely Romanis and together they move into a one-bedroom flat in Clacton.

18 September: Anthony John Hancock marries Cicely Janet Elizabeth Romanis at Christ Church, Kensington, London.
20 September: Larry Stephens marries Diana Forster; Hancock and Cicely act as witnesses.

1951

then the Ocean Theatre, Clacton. Run ends 16 September.

25 August: **Summer Showtime,** on the Light Programme.
27 August: **Variety Bandbox,** from the Camberwell Palace.

2 October: **Hippodrome,** Birmingham. One week variety.
9 October: **Empire Theatre,** Liverpool. One week variety.
16 October: **Empire Theatre,** Newcastle. One week variety.
30 October: **Empire Theatre,** Glasgow. One week variety.
12 November: **Variety Bandbox,** on the Light Programme.
23 December: **Little Red Riding Hood,** at the Theatre Royal, Nottingham. Hancock plays 'Jolly Jenkins'. Run ends 10 March, 1951.
30 December: **Radio Parade,** on the Home Service. Hancock is one of eleven acts introduced by Bebe Daniels and Ben Lyon.

1951
7 January: **Variety Bandbox,** on the Light Programme.
21 January: **Variety Bandbox,** on the Light Programme.
11 February: **Variety Bandbox,** on the Light Programme.

Spring: Ray Galton and Alan Simpson submit their first script to the BBC; they are paid five shillings for each one-liner.

11 March: **Variety Bandbox,** on the Light Programme.

24 March: **Variety Ahoy,** on board HMS *Woolwich,* off Harwich.

1 April: **Variety Bandbox,** on the Light Programme.

29 April: **Variety Bandbox,** on the Light Programme.

4 May: **Kaleidoscope,** Hancock acts in a series of situation comedy sketches for BBC television.

14 May: **Variety Ahoy,** on board HMS *Indefatigable,* off Portland. Produced by Duncan Wood, Hancock's future television producer.

18 May: **Kaleidoscope,** BBC television.

21 May: **Empire Theatre,** Shepherd's Bush. One week variety.

4 June: **County Theatre,** Reading. One week variety.

6 June: **Western Music Hall,** for west of England Home Service.

15 June: **Kaleidoscope,** for BBC television.

19 June: **Workers' Playtime,** from Gracey Brothers Canneries, Hillhall, County Antrim.

21 June: **Workers' Playtime,** from Heller Confectionery, Bangor, County Down.

22 June: **Workers' Playtime,** from Messrs Teady McErlear Limited, Clady, Portglenone.

29 June: **Kaleidoscope,** for BBC television.

July: Hancock persuades his BBC producer to give Graham Stark his first radio engagement.

6 July: **Ritz Cinema,** Nuneaton. Midnight matinée.

9 July: **Palace Theatre,** Chelsea. One week variety.

16 July: **Palace Theatre,** East Ham. One week variety.

21 July: Festival Parade, the last of six Home Service programmes to mark the Festival of Britain. Hancock was one of ten acts.

23 July: **Empire Theatre,** Finsbury Park. One week variety.

1 August: **Century Cinema,** Clacton. Midnight matinée.

1 August: The Lighter Side – a humorous slant on current affairs – Food. A BBC television programme in which Hancock plays the civil servant.

2 August: Happy-Go-Lucky, for the Light Programme. Hancock joins the weekly show starring Derek Roy.

3 August: Educating Archie, for the Light Programme. Hancock joins the second series as Archie Andrews' tutor. He would remain with the radio show until January 1952.

5 August: Calling All Forces, for the Light Programme.

8 August: Variety Ahoy, from the Royal Naval Hospital, Haslar, Gosport.

9 August: Western Music Hall, for the west of England Home Service.

20 August: **Empire Theatre,** Sunderland. One week variety.

26 August: **Spa Theatre,** Scarborough. Sunday variety.

17 September: **Winter Gardens,** Bournemouth. Three days variety.

20 September: **Winter Gardens,** Eastbourne. Three days variety.

24 September: **Ritz Cinema,** Weymouth. One week variety.

1 October: **Empire Theatre,** Nottingham. One week variety.

8 October: **Empire Theatre,** Edinburgh. One day variety.

12 October: **Odeon Theatre,** Southampton. One day variety.

14 October: **The Palace,** Walthamstow.

One day charity variety performance.

15 October: **Palace Theatre,** Blackpool. One week variety.

22 October: **Opera House,** Belfast. One week variety.

3 November: **Dome Theatre,** Brighton. One day variety.

12 November: **Gaumont,** Southampton. One week variety.

19 November: **Embassy Theatre,** Peterborough. One week variety.

3 December: **Hippodrome Theatre,** Dudley. One week variety.

9 December: Hancock meets scriptwriters Ray Galton and Alan Simpson for the first time and compliments them on the sketch.

16 December: Archie Andrews' Party at the NAAFI club, Colchester. Broadcast 26 December.

17 December: **Windsor Castle.** Special Christmas cabaret for the royal family.

21 December: Archie Andrews' Christmas Party (matinées) and *Peep Show* (evenings) at the Prince of Wales Theatre, London. Run ends 19 January, 1952.

31 December: Bumblethorpe, Home Service. Hancock is this week's Bumblethorpe.

1952

1952

6 January: Trocadero, Elephant and Castle, starring Archie Andrews and Peter Brough with Hattie Jacques.

13 January: **Gaumont,** Lewisham. Sunday variety with Archie Andrews and Peter Brough.

20 January: **Odeon,** Barking. Sunday variety with Archie Andrews and Peter Brough.

4 February: **Empire Theatre,** Sunderland. One week variety with Archie Andrews and Peter Brough.

11 February: **Empire,** Shepherd's Bush. One week variety with Archie Andrews and Peter Brough.

17 February: **Alexandra Theatre,**

Birmingham. Charity Sunday performance
for the News Vendors' Benevolent Fund.
18 February: **Empire Theatre,** Hackney.
One week variety with Archie Andrews
and Peter Brough.
25 February: **Palace Theatre,** Leicester.
One week variety with Archie Andrews
and Peter Brough.
25 February: Calling All Forces, for the
Home Service. Hancock appeared doing
his own act.
2 March: 1951 National Radio Awards,
from the London Coliseum. Hancock
appeared in a five-minute extract with the
Educating Archie cast.
3 March: **Empire Theatre,** Leeds. One
week variety with Archie Andrews and
Peter Brough.
10 March: **Granada,** Rugby. One week
variety with Archie Andrews and Peter
Brough.
17 March: **Hippodrome,** Birmingham.
One week variety with Archie Andrews
and Peter Brough.
24 March: **Empire Theatre,** Glasgow.
One week variety with Archie Andrews
and Peter Brough.
31 March: **Empire Theatre,** Liverpool.
One week variety with Archie Andrews
and Peter Brough.
3 April: Workers' Playtime, from Messrs
Maurice Lee-Unger Ltd, Boothstown,
Manchester. Hancock appeared with
Peter Brough and Archie Andrews.

12 April: Hancock breaks the £500-a-
week barrier with his appearance in *London Laughs.*

12 April: London Laughs, Adelphi Theatre. Hancock stars with Jimmy Edwards
and Vera Lynn. His engagement – after
several breaks – ends on 7 December,
1953.
14 April: Calling All Forces, for the
Home Service. First of sixteen programmes jointly hosted by Hancock and
Charlie Chester. Series ends 28 July.

1 June: **Villa Marina,** Douglas, Isle of Man. Sunday variety.

22 June: **Pavilion,** Sandown, and **The Theatre,** Shanklin, Isle of Wight. Sunday variety.

29 June: Hullo There – a weekly radio programme for young listeners. Hancock guests on a prerecorded quiz.

8 July: Peter Eton, a BBC drama producer, dictates a memo outlining a situation comedy to star Tony Hancock and to be written by Larry Stephens. Eton suggests a title: *Welcome to Whelkham. Summer:* Hancock and Cicely move from their Clacton flat to a fifth-floor apartment in Queen's Gate Terrace, Knightsbridge.

13 August: Henry Hall's Guest Night – Highlights of the Show World, for the Home Service.

31 August: **Butlins,** Filey. Sunday variety.

15 September: Forces All-Star Bill, for the Light Programme. Hancock appeared as compère.

27 September: Recording for Radio Luxembourg from the London Palladium.

1 October: Henry Hall's Guest Night, for the Home Service.

13 October: All-Star Bill, for the Light Programme. Hancock appeared as compere.

3 November: Royal Variety Performance, at the London Palladium.

5 November: The Guy Fawkes Show, for the Light Programme. 'A musical-comedy travesty of history' written by Jimmy Grafton and produced by Dennis Main Wilson.

3 December: Henry Hall's Guest Night, for the Home Service.

13 December: **Showtime,** for Radio Luxembourg. Recorded at the London Palladium.

1953

6 January: Start of professional relationship with Galton and Simpson. The writers explore Hancock's situation comedy potential with *Forces All-Star Bill* sketches.

1 May: The head of variety at BBC radio receives a memo from *Goon Show* producer Dennis Main Wilson suggesting the format for a new comedy series. It was to become *Hancock's Half Hour*.

29 December: After just two months Hancock leaves Archie Parnell & Co. His new agents are Messrs Kavanagh Productions Ltd.

1953

6 January: **Forces All-Star Bill,** for the Light Programme. First of eleven programmes – two without Hancock – written by Galton and Simpson and produced by Dennis Main Wilson. Series ends: 26 May.

6 May: **Henry Hall's Guest Night,** for the Home Service.

30 May: **Variety Cavalcade,** for the West of England Home Service. Hancock was one of nine acts introduced by Benny Hill.

7 June: **Star Bill – The Best in Britain's Showbusiness,** for the Light Programme. Hancock appeared in the first nine weekly programmes. Last appearance 28 August.

Summer: **Orders are Orders.** Hancock plays Lieutenant Cartroad, a despairing band master, in his first film. Shot at Beaconsfield Studios.

30 August: **Pavilion,** Sandown, and **The Theatre,** Shanklin, Isle of Wight. Sunday variety.

13 October: Hancock ends his five-year contract with Phyllis Rounce and International Artistes.

19 October: Hancock signs with Phyllis Parnell at Archie Parnell & Co. He was introduced to his new agent by Sid James.

1 November: Top of the Town, for the Light Programme. 'On *Top of the Town* this week – Tony Hancock, and his home town Birmingham.' Script by Jimmy Grafton and produced by Dennis Main Wilson.

23 November: **The Frankie Howerd Show,** for the Light Programme. Hancock is a guest.

23 December: **Cinderella,** Theatre Royal, Nottingham. Hancock plays Buttons. Run ends 27 February, 1954.

1954

March: Prompted by Galton and Simpson, Hancock persuades Sid James to join the *Half Hour* cast.

June: Hancock is introduced for the first time to a public relations executive called Freddie Ross: she would first become his lover and then his second wife.

August: Armed with a psychiatrist's letter claiming the show was 'seriously affecting his state of mind' Hancock unsuccessfully attempts to leave *The Talk of the Town.*

1954

29 January: What Goes On, for the Midland Home Service. Interview with Hancock.

28 February: Star Bill, for the Light Programme. Hancock continues to work with Galton and Simpson in developing the 'Hancock' character. Series ends 2 May.

15 May: A Welcome To Her Majesty The Queen, for the Home Service and Light Programme. Hancock was one of nineteen acts.

17 May: Hippodrome, Brighton. One week variety with Jimmy Edwards.

5 June: The Talk of the Town. Hancock opens in the revue with Jimmy Edwards and Joan Turner at Blackpool's Opera House prior to a London season. Run ends 9 October.

24 June: Variety Fanfare, from the Hulme Hippodrome, Manchester.

30 October: First recording of the first *Hancock's Half Hour* at the Camden Theatre.

2 November: Hancock's Half Hour (first series), for the Light Programme. First of sixteen weekly programmes. The cast: Tony Hancock, Bill Kerr, Moira Lister, Sid James, Kenneth Williams and Alan Simpson. Script by Galton and Simpson and produced by Dennis Main Wilson. Series ends 15 February, 1955.

12 November: Hancock appears with Moira Lister on the cover of the *Radio Times*.

8 November: The Talk of the Town, New Theatre, Oxford. Run ends 13 November.

17 November: The Talk of the Town, Adelphi Theatre, London. Hancock's engagement ends – after several absences – on 31 October, 1955.

1955

Spring: Freddie Ross persuades Hancock to allow her to take over his professional correspondence.

15 April: Hancock walks off the Adelphi stage in the middle of his solo act and flies to Italy two days before recording the first show of the second *Hancock's Half Hour* series. His place, in the first three shows, is taken by Harry Secombe.

1955

19 April: Hancock's Half Hour (second series), for the Light Programme. First of twelve weekly programmes. Hancock is replaced by Harry Secombe. Andrée Melly has replaced Moira Lister. Script by Galton and Simpson and produced by Dennis Main Wilson. Series ends 5 July.

10 May: Hancock rejoins *Half Hour* cast; Harry Secombe makes a guest appearance.

20 May: During a performance of *Talk of the Town* Hancock collapses on stage and is ordered out of the show.

22 August: Jack Hylton allows Hancock to leave his Adelphi show for a three-day clinic diet.

22 September: Commercial TV begins in Britain with Gibbs SR toothpaste as the first advertisement.

19 October: Hancock's Half Hour (third series), for the Light Programme. First of twenty weekly programmes. The cast; Tony Hancock, Bill Kerr, Andrée Melly, Sid James, Kenneth Williams and Alan Simpson. Script by Galton and Simpson

31 October: After a series of 'illnesses' Hancock finally leaves the long-running *Talk of the Town.*

1956
1 January: Hancock is admitted to the London Clinic, ostensibly to lose two stone in weight.

and produced by Dennis Main Wilson. Series ends 29 February, 1956.

1956

6 February: Jack Hylton Presents, for Associated-Rediffusion television. Recorded at the Adelphi.
27 April: The Tony Hancock Show, for Associated-Rediffusion television. First of six live weekly shows with June Whitfield, Clive Dunn and John Vere. Script by Eric Sykes and Larry Stephens. Series ends 1 June.
1 July: House Magazine, for BBC television. Thirty-minute trailer for Hancock's first TV series. Taking part were Hancock, Duncan Wood, Ray Galton and Alan Simpson.
6 July: Hancock's Half Hour begins on BBC television. Sid James is the only regular member of the radio series cast to make the transition to the six fortnightly television programmes. Produced by Duncan Wood. Series ends 14 September.
20 July: The Laughtermakers – Tony Hancock, for the Home Service.
14 October: Hancock's Half Hour (fourth series), for the Light Programme. First of twenty weekly programmes. The cast: Tony Hancock, Bill Kerr, Sid James, Kenneth Williams and Hattie Jacques. Script by Galton and Simpson and produced by Dennis Main Wilson. Series ends 24 February, 1957.
31 December: The Man Who Could Work Miracles, for the Home Service.

Hancock appears as a straight actor – as George McWhirter Fotheringay – in an adaptation of the H. G. Wells story. Script and production by Dennis Main Wilson.

1957

1957
18 January: A–Z – The ABC of Show Business, for BBC television. Hancock first performs his 'budgerigar' sketch, written by Galton and Simpson.

21 February: Dennis Main Wilson produces the last of his sixty-eight radio *Hancock's Half Hour*s.
March: Hancock attempts to improve his 'line-learning blindness' with the aid of a tape recorder, a practice he would continue for the rest of his life.

17 March: **RAF Wunstorf,** West Germany. Combined Services Entertainment show.

*1 April: **Hancock's Half Hour*** (second series) for BBC television. First of six fortnightly programmes. Produced by Duncan Wood. Series ends 10 June.
5 August: Desert Island Discs, for the Home Service. Hancock is Roy Plomley's castaway guest.
19 August: **Palace Theatre,** Manchester. One week variety.
26 August: **Hippodrome,** Bristol. One week variety.
2 September: **Hippodrome,** Birmingham. One week variety.
9 September: **Empire Theatre,** Finsbury Park. One week variety.
28 September: These Are The Shows, for BBC television. Hancock and Sid James appear for *Hancock's Half Hour.*
30 September: Hancock's Half Hour (third series) for BBC television. First of twelve weekly programmes. Produced by Duncan Wood. Series ends 23 December.

November: Hancock and Cicely buy and move into Val Fleury, Tandridge Lane, Blindley Heath, near Lingfield, Surrey.

Hancock renames the house MacConkeys after its original owner.

18 November: Suffering from depression and the flu Hancock is forced to cancel a live television *Half Hour*.

December: The Guild of Television Producers and Directors vote Hancock Comedian of the Year. A BBC survey shows 23 per cent of the British population is watching *Hancock's Half Hour*.

1958

February: Rank unsuccessfully attempts to persuade Hancock to play the part of his comic hero Sid Field.

30 March: The RAF fly Hancock back to Britain from his Mediterranean tour to record a radio *Half Hour*; he returns the same day.

6 April: Hancock is flown home a second time from his Mediterranean tour to record a radio *Half Hour*.

12 July: The Adventures of Tony Hancock appear as a cartoon strip in *Film Fun*. Hancock would feature in the magazine for the next four years.

7 December: In Town Tonight, for the Home Service. Hancock interviewed.

25 December: Pantomania – Babes in the Wood, for BBC television. Christmas Day panto. Cast includes Hancock, Charlie Drake, Benny Hill, Sid James, Bill Maynard, Kenneth Connor and Terry Hall and Lenny the Lion.

1958

18 January: Saturday Night on the Light, for the Light Programme. Hancock interviewed.

21 January: Hancock's Half Hour (fifth series), for the Light Programme. First of twenty weekly programmes. The cast: Tony Hancock, Bill Kerr, Sid James, Kenneth Williams and Hattie Jacques. Script by Galton and Simpson. Produced by Pat Dixon. Series ends 3 June.

9 February: The Government Inspector, for BBC television. Hancock stars as 'Hlestakov' in an adaptation by Barry Thomas.

24 March: The start of a 23-day Mediterranean tour entertaining British troops in Malta, Tripoli and Cyprus. Tour ends 15 April.

July: Gloucester. One week variety.

3 August: **Welcome to London,** for the Light Programme. Hancock, Sid James and Bill Kerr appear in a Galton and Simpson sketch. The show honours Commonwealth Games athletes.

4 August: **Empire Theatre,** Liverpool. One week variety.

28 September: **Educating Archie,** for the Light Programme. Hancock makes a guest appearance.

27 October: **Empire Theatre,** Hanley. One week variety.

3 November: **Royal Variety Performance,** at the London Coliseum. Hancock performs his 'budgerigar' sketch.

20 November: **This is Britain,** for the BBC Transcription Service. Hancock is interviewed.

25 December: **Hancock's Half Hour Christmas Special,** for the Light Programme. Cast is Hancock, Sid James, Bill Kerr, Hattie Jacques and Warren Mitchell.

25 December: **Christmas Night with the Stars,** for BBC television. Hancock appears in his 'budgerigar' sketch.

26 December: **Hancock's Half Hour** (fourth series) for BBC television. First of thirteen weekly programmes. Produced by Duncan Wood. Series ends 27 March.

1959

4 January: **Hancock's Half Hour,** for the BBC Transcription Service. First of four weekly remakes of radio *Hancock's Half Hours* for distribution around the world. Recordings end 25 January.

4 January: **What's My Line?** Hancock appears as the guest celebrity.

1959

Spring: Hancock and Freddie Ross become lovers.

4 September: The BBC finally agrees to

allow Hancock and his producer to record all future television *Half Hours*.

Autumn: Hancock announces he does not want to make any more *Half Hours* for the BBC; he agrees to make one more television series – as long as Sid James is dropped.

17 November: Robert Walker, Hancock's step-father, commits suicide at his Christchurch Road, Bournemouth, apartment.

27 November: Tony Hancock is voted Comedian of the Year for a second time.

1960

29 April: Tony Hancock and Sid James record their last television *Hancock's Half Hour* together.

25 September: Hancock's Half Hour (fifth series) for BBC television. First of ten weekly programmes. Produced by Duncan Wood. Series ends 27 November.

29 September: Hancock's Half Hour (sixth series), for the Light Programme. First of fourteen weekly programmes. The regular cast: Tony Hancock, Bill Kerr and Sid James. Script by Galton and Simpson. Produced by Tom Ronald. Series ends 29 December.

27 November: Hancock's Half Hour. The fifth television series ends with a record 13.5 million viewers.

29 December: Hancock's Half Hour. The final radio broadcast.

1960

7 February: Face to Face. Hancock is interviewed by John Freeman.

4 March: Hancock's Half Hour (sixth series) for BBC television. First of ten weekly programmes. Produced by Duncan Wood. Series ends 6 May.

Spring: This is Hancock. Pye Records issues the first LP of Hancock's comedy. The disc features *The Wildman of the Woods* and *Sunday Afternoon at Home.*

July: Shooting begins at Elstree Studios for *The Rebel*, Tony's first full-length feature film.

9 July: In Town Tonight, for the Home Service. Hancock is interviewed about *The Rebel.*

Summer: The Rebel receives its international première at the Beirut Film Festival. It is followed a few weeks later by a screening at the Cannes Festival.

Summer: Pieces of Hancock. Pye

Records' second Hancock LP. The disc features *The East Cheam Drama Festival* and *The Secret Life of Anthony Hancock*.

7 September: Seventy-year-old Lily Walker marries Henry Sennett, a retired civil servant. Hancock refuses to attend the wedding.

1961

1961

*27 January: **The Rebel*** receives its trade showing in London.

*4 March: **In Town Today,*** for the Home Service. Hancock interviewed.

*4 March: **London Mirror,*** for the BBC's General Overseas Service. Hancock interviewed.

*6 March: **The Hancock Show,*** at the Granada, Shrewsbury. Begins a six-week sell-out tour.

*7 March: **Picture Parade,*** for BBC television. Hancock interviewed.

*13 March: **The Hancock Show,*** at the Empire Theatre, Newcastle. One week.

*20 March: **The Hancock Show,*** at the Gaumont, Southampton. One week.

*27 March: **The Hancock Show,*** at the Hippodrome, Brighton. One week.

*3 April: **The Hancock Show,*** at the Hippodrome, Bristol. One week.

*10 April: **The Hancock Show,*** at the New Theatre, Oxford. One week.

*23 May: **Today,*** for the Home Service. Hancock interviewed.

26 May: Hancock is injured when Cicely drives their car into roadworks as they cross the Surrey border on their way home.

*26 May: **Hancock.*** The final television series for the BBC of six weekly shows opens with *The Bedsitter*. Produced by Duncan Wood. Script by Galton and Simpson. Series ends 30 June.

9 June: Hancock records his last show for the BBC, ending a twenty-one-year association.

*30 June: **Hancock.*** The final show in the series is broadcast. It ends Hancock's association with the BBC.

October: Hancock severs his professional association with Ray Galton and Alan Simpson. He also sacks his agent Beryl Vertue.

October: Hancock unveils plans to build an entertainment complex in London; he flies to Las Vegas to research the project.

October: Philip Oakes is hired to co-write Hancock's second film *The Punch and Judy Man.*

November: Chad Valley issue *Hancock's Half Hour* as a board game.

1 October: Hancock. Studio remake of the BBC Television programmes *The Blood Donor* and *The Radio Ham.* Issued on LP by Pye Records.

October: US première of *The Rebel,* renamed *Call Me Genius* for the American market. The film is panned by the critics.

Winter: Little Pieces of Hancock – Vol 1. Issued as a seven-inch extended-play disc by Pye Records; includes *The Secret Life of Anthony Hancock* and *The Threatening Letters.*

Winter: Little Pieces of Hancock – Vol 2. Issued as a seven-inch extended-play disc by Pye Records; includes *Jack's Return Home* and *Look Back in Hunger.*

Winter: The Publicity Photograph. Issued as a seven-inch extended-play disc by Pye Records; includes specially recorded linking material.

Winter: Highlights From 'The Blood Donor'. Issued as a seven-inch extended-play disc by Pye Records.

1962

5 January: First broadcast of Galton and Simpson's *Steptoe and Son.*

March: Charlie Drake is named *Daily Mirror* readers' favourite comedian, replacing Hancock who had had several years at the top.

March: Eric Sykes takes over as Britain's highest-paid television comedian.

Spring: Derek Scott, Hancock's former Windmill partner, agrees to write the score for *The Punch and Judy Man.*

2 April: Shooting starts at Elstree Studios for *The Punch and Judy Man.*

1962

March: US networks screen the BBC showcase *International Show Time* featuring Hancock, Eric Sykes and Benny Hill.

May: Location shooting for *The Punch and Judy Man* starts at Bognor Regis. *Summer:* Sid James fails to persuade Hancock to work together once again.

5 May: **In Town Today,** for the Home Service. Hancock is interviewed.

8 October: **King's Theatre,** Southsea. Tony co-stars with Matt Monro. One week.

15 October: **Empire Theatre,** Liverpool. Tony co-stars with Matt Monro. One week.

22 October: **Hippodrome,** Brighton. Tony co-stars with Matt Monro. One week.

4 November: Filming starts for the new ATV series, *Hancock.*

1963

January: Hancock moves out of Mac-Conkeys and starts living with his press agent Freddie Ross. He returns at various times to live with Cicely.

1963

3 January: Hancock, for Associated Television. First of thirteen weekly programmes. Series is a MacConkeys production in association with Bernard Delfont. Produced by Hancock. Series ends 28 March.

January: **Face to Face.** Edited version of Hancock's February, 1960, interview with John Freeman. The LP's reverse features Hancock interviewing Stirling Moss.

July: Hancock pulls out at the last minute from a six-week cabaret booking at The Talk of the Town theatre-restaurant, London.

15 July: **Theatre Royal,** Nottingham. One week variety.

22 July: Scene at 6.30, for Granada Television. Hancock interviewed.

23 July: **Palace Theatre,** Manchester. One week variety.

August: British Rail pays Hancock £10,000 as part of a public relations exercise to sweeten planned cuts in services.

6 August: **London Palladium.** Hancock steps in to replace the unwell Arthur Haynes. Booking ends 28 September.

12 August: Today, for the Home Service. Hancock interviewed.

17 August: In Town Today, for the Home Service. Hancock interviewed.

October: John le Mesurier introduces his future wife, Joan Malin, to Hancock.

19 October: That Reminds Me, for the Midlands Home Service. Hancock interviewed.

November: **Hancock's Tune.** Pye Records issues the signature tune for the Associated Television *Hancock* series as a single. The theme is written by Derek Scott.

1964

February: Hancock turns down an offer to play Elwood Dowd in a British remake of *Harvey.*
21 April: BBC2 begins transmission.
Spring: Woodfall Films persuades Hancock to play the part of Bérenger in *Rhinoceros.* After various problems the film is never made.
Spring: Hancock moves to the Bernard Delfont Agency where Billy Marsh takes over as his agent.
July: Hancock suffers a Pott's fracture of the ankle in a mystery accident.
Autumn: Hancock publicly admits his marriage to Cicely is over.

1964

January: Pye issues a seven-inch single including extracts from *Wing Commander Hancock, Test Pilot* and *The Threatening Letter.*
Summer: **Those Magnificent Men in Their Flying Machines.** Film directed by Ken Annakin; Hancock plays Harry Popperwell, an eccentric inventor and flyer.
Summer: **A Tribute to Tony Hancock.** A World Record Club LP including extracts from *The Blood Donor, The Radio Ham, The East Cheam Drama Festival* and *The Wild Man of the Woods.*

15 November: **Sunday Night at the London Palladium.** Hancock tops the bill.
5 December: **Open House,** for BBC2. Hancock interviewed.
25 December: '*Ancock's Anthology,* for the Home Service. Hancock introduces a collection of his favourite music and writing.

1965

15 January: Henry Sennett, Lily's third husband, dies.
January: Freddie Ross is admitted to hospital for surgery; the following day Hancock flies to New York and auditions for Walt Disney in Hollywood.

1965

January: The BBC drops plans for another '*Ancock's Anthology.*

27 May: Hancock collapses on the set of Walt Disney's *The Adventures of Bullwhip Griffin*. He is sacked from the film.
26 June: Late Night Saturday, for the Light Programme. Hancock interviewed.
28 June: Fatal Fascination, at the Talk of the Town, London. Hancock appears in a late-night cabaret. Run ends 7 August.
August: Hancock makes a series of television commercials for the Egg Marketing Board; the adverts are not screened until the following spring.
August: The Wrong Box. Film directed by Bryan Forbes; Hancock plays a detective.
Autumn: Tony Hancock and Sid James work together for the first time in five years. They re-record two radio *Half Hours* for issue on disc.

6 July: Cicely divorces Hancock, citing his adultery with Freddie Ross.
July: Sid James approaches Hancock about making a film together; at first Hancock agrees and then backs out.

Autumn: Hancock agrees to perform the title role in André Obey's play *Noah;* the musical is never staged.

5 October: Late Night Line-Up, for BBC2. Hancock interviewed.
16 October: The Best of Tony Hancock, BBC television repeats 26 episodes of *Hancock's Half Hour.*
2 November: **Chevron Hilton Hotel,** Sydney. Hancock opens in three-week cabaret.
November: It's Hancock. Decca issue *The Missing Page* and *The Reunion Party* on LP, recorded earlier in the year.

2 December: Hancock marries Freddie Ross at Marylebone register office. The couple honeymoon in Dublin.
27 December: Hancock – who for the first time admits he is an alcoholic – is admitted to a London nursing home. The press is told he is suffering from 'nervous exhaustion'.

1966

1966
January: Hancock appears as a guest on *This Is Your Life.*
14 February: **The Palace Theatre,** Dundee. On tour with The Billy Cotton Band.

June: Freddie Hancock is admitted to hospital following a suicide attempt. Hancock is in Blackpool and refuses to return to London, effectively ending their marriage after just 229 days.

25 July: Hancock admits himself to a nursing home suffering from 'nervous exhaustion'.

30 August: Hancock is booked into the London Clinic by his agent.

September: Cicely confronts her husband while in Bournemouth and pleads for a reconciliation.

11 September: Hancock begins his affair with Joan le Mesurier. Within forty-eight hours she has left her husband and moved into Hancock's Lowndes Square flat.

23 September: Hancock and Joan le Mesurier escape to a seafront flat in Ramsgate.

October: Hancock and Joan rent Coq d'Or, a clifftop bungalow at Broadstairs.

October: After drinking himself unconscious Hancock is rushed to the London Clinic.

21 February: **Tivoli**, Aberdeen. On tour with The Billy Cotton Band.

28 February: **Empire Theatre**, Glasgow. On tour with The Billy Cotton Band.

19 June: The Blackpool Show, for ABC-TV. Hancock hosts six of eight weekly shows. Series ends 7 August.

31 July: The Entertainers, for BBC World Service. Hancock interviewed.

5 September: **Winter Gardens**, Bournemouth. Hancock tries out his forthcoming Festival Hall material for one week.

16 September, Late Night Line-Up, for BBC2. Hancock interviewed.

22 September: The Royal Festival Hall. Hancock's one-night show is also recorded for television. Doubts within BBC2 delay transmission until 15 October.

December: When the lease on Hancock's Lowndes Square flat expires, he and Joan move to a service flat in Dolphin Square, Pimlico.

1967
January: After collapsing with a fit Hancock is warned that unless he stops drinking he will be 'dead within three months'.
18 January: Hancock signs his will leaving everything to his mother Lily Sennett.

February: Hancock and Joan move into a Baron's Court flat. He starts work on a book, *The Link, or Anyone for Tennis?*
April: After a drinking session at the Broadstairs cottage Hancock is admitted unconscious to the London Clinic.

1 July: BBC2 begins colour transmissions.

22 July: The day after he returns from Aden Hancock checks himself into the London Clinic with 'nervous exhaustion'.

13 November: **Secombe and Friends,** for Associated Television. Hancock appears as one of Secombe's guests.
December: **The Mandarin Hotel,** Hong Kong. Two weeks cabaret.

1967

19 January: Alan Whicker interviews Hancock for a *Whicker's World* on stand-up comedians. His contribution is dropped for being 'too deep and too slow'.
19 January: **The Frost Programme,** for Associated-Rediffusion Television. Hancock interviewed.
20 January: **The Frost Programme,** for Associated-Rediffusion Television. Hancock interviewed.

16 June: **Hancock's,** for ABC-TV. Hancock begins first of six weekly programmes. The show is savaged by the critics. Series ends 18 July.

2 July: **Villa Marina,** Douglas, Isle of Man. Sunday variety.
17 July: Hancock starts a five-day tour entertaining British troops in Aden.

August: Joan le Mesurier attempts suicide at their Baron's Court flat while Hancock is comatose with drink in the next room.
September: Hancock checks himself into the London Clinic determined to arrive in Australia sober and fitter; he loses thirty-two pounds.
4 October: Hancock returns to Australia to appear in cabaret at the Dendy Cinema, Melbourne, followed by a two-week run in Tasmania.

4 October: **Dendy Cinema,** Brighton, Melbourne. Hancock warms up the audience with his one-man show before a feature film.
10 October: Something Special – Nancye, for Channel HSV7, Melbourne. Hancock appears as a guest. The show was recorded but not transmitted until *12* June, 1968.
10 October: **Dendy Cinema,** Brighton, Melbourne. The show is abandoned after twenty minutes because Hancock is too drunk to stand.
15 October: **Dendy Cinema,** Brighton, Melbourne. Hancock gives a free performance for the audience of his abandoned show.
16 October: Hobart, Tasmania. One week hotel cabaret.

1968

1968
14 January: The Eamonn Andrews Show, for ABC-TV. Hancock interviewed.
21 January: The David Jacobs Show, for Radio 1 and Radio 2. Hancock interviewed.

March: Hancock flies to Australia for his new Channel 7 comedy series. During a stop-over in New Delhi he stays with his *Face to Face* interrogator John Freeman.
March: Staying in Melbourne he works on the script with senior writer Hugh Stuckey.
April: Hancock flies to Sydney to begin rehearsals.

April: The Mavis Bramston Show. Hancock storms out of the studio claiming he has been 'insulted and mistreated' by the production staff.

*19 April: **Hancock Down Under.*** The recording of pilot programme proves disastrous.

April–May: Hancock admitted to the Cavell House Private Hospital, Rose Bay. He spends his 44th birthday in the detoxification clinic.
May: Hancock shares a house with Eddie Joffe and family at 98 Birriga Road, Belvue Hill, Sydney.

*May–June: **Hancock Down Under.*** The first three episodes of the planned 13-show series are recorded.
*12 June: **Something Special – Nancye,*** for Channel HSV7, Melbourne. Hancock appears as a guest. Recorded the previous October.

21 June: Freddie Hancock obtains a decree nisi in London.
22 June: Giving his name as 'Bill' Hancock visits a Sydney medium. Throughout their meeting Hancock is 'watched over' by the spirit of Jack Hancock.
25 June: Hancock is found dead in the garden flat of 98 Birriga Road, Bellevue Hill, Sydney.

1969
January: Cicely Hancock dies after falling downstairs at her Surrey cottage.

1972
25 January: Channel HSV7, Melbourne, transmits the three Hancock episodes completed just before his death.
*Summer: **Fifty Years of Radio Comedy.*** A BBC Records issue containing a three-minute extract from *Sunday Afternoon at Home.*

1973
*June: **The Unique Hancock.*** BBC Records collection of Transcription

Service recordings. The LP contains *Christmas – East Cheam Style, PC Hancock – Have Feet, Will Travel, Michael Hancockelo, The Doctor's Dilemma, Like a Dog's Dinner, Is that your car outside? With my woggle I thee worship* and *The Hospital, or Hancock Revisited.*

1974
Autumn: The Golden Hour of Tony Hancock. LP in the Golden Hour series containing edited versions of *The Wild Man of the Woods* and *The Secret Life of Anthony Hancock.*

1975
Summer: The World of Tony Hancock. Decca reissue of *It's Hancock*, originally recorded and released in 1965.

1976
Autumn: Comedy Spectacular – 40 Years of Television. BBC LP record including extract from *The Radio Ham.*
October: Hancock. BBC Records LP issue of two television comedies: *The Lift* and *Twelve Angry Men.*

1977
April: A Silver Jubilee of Memories. Includes extract from *The Radio Ham*; published by Pageant.

1980
November: Hancock's Half Hour. BBC Records LP and cassette of *The Poetry Society* and *Sid's Mystery Tours.*

1981
October: Hancock's Half Hour. BBC Records LP and cassette of *The Americans Hit Town* and *The Unexploded Bomb.*

1982
October: Hancock's Half Hour. BBC Records LP and cassette of *The Scandal Magazine* and *The Last of the McHancocks.*

1983
Autumn: Hancock's Half Hour. BBC Records LP and cassette of *The Sleepless Night* and *Fred's Pie Stall.*

1984
Autumn: Hancock's Half Hour. BBC Records LP and cassette of *Hancock's War* and *The Christmas Club.*

Complete BBC and ITV Cast List

Between November, 1954, and June, 1961, Tony Hancock appeared in 104 BBC radio and 63 television comedies.

In many ways the *Hancock's Half Hour* series and, to a lesser extent, the single series of *Hancock* were perhaps the greatest devourers and developers of new talent of the 1950s. What follows is a complete record of the 537 actors and actresses and other personalities, three groups and one chimp who appeared with Hancock during his time at the BBC.

Also included are the 31 shows Hancock made for Independent Television.

	Hancock's Half Hour BBC radio	Hancock's Half Hour BBC television	Hancock BBC television	The Tony Hancock Show ITV	Hancock ITV	Hancock's ITV
Mary Abbot		1				
Louis Adam		4				
Barbara Adams		1				
John Adams					1	
Nancy Adams		2				
Frikki Alberti					1	
Michael Aldridge					1	

	Hancock's Half Hour BBC radio	Hancock's Half Hour BBC television	Hancock BBC television	The Tony Hancock Show ITV	Hancock ITV	Hancock's ITV
Terence Alexander		4		1		1
Jack Allen						1
Peter Allenby		3				
Bert Allisom		1				
Astrid Anderson		1				
Ian Anderson		1				
Michael Anderson	1					
Stuart Anderson			1			
Barbara Archer		1				
Laurence Archer		1				
Ruby Archer		1				
Robert Arden				1		
Edward Argent					1	
John Arlott	1					
Phil Arthurs					1	
Keith Ashley		1				
Michael Aspel			1			
Edouard Assaly		1				
Alistair Audsley		1				
James Avon		1				
Roger Avon		3				
Caroline Aylett			1			
Stanley Ayres	1					
Wilfred Babbage	6					
Hermione Baddeley		1				
Peter Badger		1				
Michael Balfour		2				
Barbara Ball		1				
Bruno Barnabe			1			
Janet Barrow		1				
Hilda Barry					1	
Sean Barry					1	
Roy Bartley				1		
Ann Bassett		1				
Raymond Baxter	1					
Basil Beale		3			1	
Reginald Beckwith		2			1	
David Bell		1				
Deirdre Bellar		1				
Joan Benham					1	
Arthur Bennett		2				
Mark Bennett		1			1	
Elizabeth Bergan		1				

	Hancock's Half Hour BBC radio	Hancock's Half Hour BBC television	Hancock BBC television	The Tony Hancock Show ITV	Hancock ITV	Hancock's ITV
Sheila Bernette					1	
Barbara Bernol					1	
Emil Bibobi				1		
John Bluthal			1		2	
Ernest Blyth					1	
John Blyth		1				
Dorothy Blythe				1		
Monty Bond					1	
Claude Bonser		13				
John Bosch		1				
Michael Boudot		1				
Helen Boult				1		
Dennis Bowen				1		
Ben Bowers		1				
John Bramley		3				
Alec Bregonzi		21	1			
Nicholas Brent						1
Carole Brett		1				
Ronnie Brody		1			1	
Ray Browne				1		
Peter Brownlee		1				
Harry Brunning		1			1	
Dora Bryan	2					
Robert Bryan		1				
Victor Bryant		1				
James Bulloch		21				
Peter Burden		1				
Jean Burgess					1	
Bill Burridge					1	
John Cabot		1				
John Caesar		3				
Richard Caldicot						1
Gerald Campion	1					
Carmen Capaldi		1				
Betty Cardno		1				
Patrick Cargill			2		1	
Karen Carina					1	
Paul Carpenter	2					
Richard Carpenter			1			
Philip Carr		9				
Vikki Carr						2
Beatrix Carter		2				
Wilfred Carter					1	

	Hancock's Half Hour BBC radio	Hancock's Half Hour BBC television	Hancock BBC television	The Tony Hancock Show ITV	Hancock ITV	Hancock's ITV
Doreen Casey		1				
Lizbeth Cassay				1		
Philip Casson		1				
John Cater					1	
Robert Cawdron						1
Constance Chapman			1			
Edward Chapman					1	
Robin Chapman					1	
Norman Chappell					1	
Howard Charlton		1				
Victor Carrington		1				
Peter Chault			1			
Mary Chigwin		1				
Dennis Chinnery		9	1			
Anna Churcher		2				
Dany Clare					1	
Diane Clare					1	
Tom Clegg		4				
John Clevedon		1				
Peggy Ann Clifford		7	1			
James Cliston		3				
Juleen Clow		1				
Anne Clunes		1				
Olwen Coates			1			
Norman Coburn		1				
Beverley Cohen					1	
Frances Cohen					1	
Lynne Cole		3				
Mary Collins		1				
Eric Cooke		1				
Pat Coombs		1				
Valerie Cooney					1	
Leslie Cooper		1				
Kim Corcoran		5				
Bill Cornelius					2	
George Coulouris		1				
Con Courtney		13				
Ralph Covey		1				
Kenneth Cowan		1	1			
Colin Cowdrey	1					
Susan Cox		1				
Gustav Craig					1	
Joan Crane						1

	Hancock's Half Hour BBC radio	Hancock's Half Hour BBC television	Hancock BBC television	The Tony Hancock Show ITV	Hancock ITV	Hancock's ITV
Frank Crawshaw						1
Cyril Cross					2	
Robert Croudace		1			1	
Angela Crow		1				
George Crowther		12				
Rufus Cruikshank		1				
Leigh Crutchley	1					
Carmel Cryan						1
George Curtis					2	
Allan Cuthbertson					1	
Joanne Dainton		1				
Amy Dalby						1
Glyn Dale					1	
Pat Dane					1	
Alan Darling		2				
Claire Davenport						1
Len David		1				
Bernard Davies					1	
Bill Davies					1	
Kevin Davies			1			
Harry Davis					1	3
Anthony Dawes					1	1
Denny Dayviss		1				
Philip Decker		1				
Pamela Deeming				1		
Eileen Delamere		4				
Paula Delaney		1				
Vi Delmer					1	
Jessica Dent		1				
Geoffrey Denton					1	
Mary Denton					1	
Jay Denyer						1
Lorrae Desmond		1				
Patrick Desmond		1				
John Devant					1	
H. V. Diamond					1	
Antonita Dias			1			
Carmen Dias			1			
Dido the Chimp		1				
Anton Diffring		1				
Violet Dix					1	
Grace Dolan					1	
Alex Donald					1	

	Hancock's Half Hour BBC radio	Hancock's Half Hour BBC television	Hancock BBC television	The Tony Hancock Show ITV	Hancock ITV	Hancock's ITV
Robert Dorning		18				
Joanna Douglas		5				
Dick Downes		2				
Chris Dreaper		2				
Harry Drew		7				
Edmund Dring		1			1	
Noël Dryden	1					
André Ducane			1		1	
Bernard Dudley		1				
Colin Dudley		1				
George Dudley		1				
Betty Duncan					2	
Brenda Duncan		1				
Clive Dunn		1		6		
Grant Duprez		1				
Valentine Dyall		1		1		
Christopher Dyer		1				
Rex Dyer					1	
Michael Earl		3	1			
Bill Earle					1	
Esme Easterbrook		4				
Jeanette Edwards		3				
Paddy Edwards		7				
Bernard Egan					1	
Denholm Elliott					1	
George Elliott		1				
Peter Elliott		1				
Roslyn Ellis		1				
Vera Elmore		1				
Michael Ely		1				
Dick Emery		3		2		
Peter Emms		2				
Joe Enrikie		1				
Barbara Evans		1				
Edward Evans						1
Godfrey Evans	1					
Tenniel Evans					1	
Iris Eve		1				
John Evitts					1	
Gwenda Ewan		4	2			
Tommy Eytle		1				
Mario Fabrizi		22			1	
Alex Farrell					1	

	Hancock's Half Hour BBC radio	Hancock's Half Hour BBC television	Hancock BBC television	The Tony Hancock Show ITV	Hancock ITV	Hancock's ITV
Andrew Faulds		2	1			
Stephen Fawcett		1				
Eleanor Fazan		3				
Ricky Felgate		1				
Len Felix		1				
Liz Ferguson					1	
Fenella Fielding	1					
Kenneth Firth		1				
James Fitzgerald			2			
Maggie Fitzgibbon					1	
Ian Flemming		1				
Mary Fletcher		1				
Margaret Flint		3				
Moira Flynn			1			
John Foster		1				
Joan Frank	1					
David Franks			1			
Don Fraser					1	
Bill Fraser		5		1		
Elizabeth Fraser		6				
Moyra Fraser					1	
Valerie Frazer				1		
Dave Freeman		1				
Ray Galton	9	2				
Albert Gant		1				
Vicki Gate					1	
Max Geldray		1				
Charles Gilbert		3	1			
Terry Gilbert		1				
Peter Glaze			1			
Raymond Glendenning	1					
Keith Goodman		2				
Harold Goodwin		1				
Peter Goodwright	1					
Colin Gorden			1			
Elizabeth Gott		3				
Anthony Gould		1				
David Graham		2				
Guy Graham		1				
Leonard Graham		1				
Raymond Graham		1				
David Grain		1				
Albert Grant		2	1			

	Hancock's Half Hour BBC radio	Hancock's Half Hour BBC television	Hancock BBC television	The Tony Hancock Show ITV	Hancock ITV	Hancock's ITV
Barbara Grant		1				
Douglas Grant					1	
Maisie Grant					1	
Nicky Grant		1				
Norman Grant		1				
Lillian Grasson	1					
Reginald Green					1	
Mickie Greene		1				
Pamela Greer					1	
Alice Greenwood					1	
Michael Greenwood		1				
John Gregson		1				
Wilfred Greves		1				
Kenneth Griffith					1	
Nelson Grostate		1				
Ray Grover		2				
Donald Groves					1	
Stuart Guidotti					1	
Patrick Hagan					1	
Peter Haigh		2				
Cameron Hall		7				
Doris Hall		1				
Gwertl Hamer		1				
May Hamilton		1				
Irene Handl		3				
Jane Hann						1
June Hansant					1	
Herbert Hare		1				
Ann Harper		1				
Gerald Harper					1	
Max Harris	1					
Rolf Harris		2				
Michael Harrison		1				
David Hartford					1	
Norman Hartley		1	1			
Astley Harvey					1	
Louis Haslar		2				
Jack Hawkins		1				
Nicholas Hay		1				
Patricia Hayes	5	7				
Damaris Hayman						2
Dick Haymes						1
Joan Heal		1				

	Hancock's Half Hour BBC radio	Hancock's Half Hour BBC television	Hancock BBC television	The Tony Hancock Show ITV	Hancock ITV	Hancock's ITV
Donald Heath			1			
Thomas Heathcote					1	
Joyce Hemson		2				
Laurence Hepworth			1		1	
John Herrington		1			1	
Charles Heslop				1		
Arthur Hewlett						1
Donald Hewlett					1	
Stuart Hiller		4				
Mary Hinton		1				
Alfred Hirst		1				
Julian Holdaway					1	
Paul Holdaway					1	
Richard Holden					1	
Jerry Homes						1
Pat Horder		1				
Yvonne Horner						1
Christina Horniman	1					
Walter Horsbrugh						1
Arthur Hosking		1				
Barbara Howard					1	
Louise Howard		1				
Philip Howard		5				
Sean Howard					1	
Terry Howard		1				
Jack Howlett					1	
Noël Howlett			1			
Rose Howlett		8				
Hazel Hughes					1	
Martita Hunt					1	
Nina Hunt		1				
Ronnie Hunt		1				
Bernard Hunter			2			
Robin Hunter					1	1
Susan Hunter		1				
Raymond Huntley		2				
Betty Huntley-Wright				1		
Helen Hurst					1	
David Hyme		1				
Diana Irvine					1	
Hattie Jacques	40	6		2		
Donald James					1	
Godfrey James					1	

	Hancock's Half Hour BBC radio	Hancock's Half Hour BBC television	Hancock BBC television	The Tony Hancock Show ITV	Hancock ITV	Hancock's ITV
Jerry James		1				
Sid James	107	55				
Anthony Jannett		1				
Ann Jay		3				
Ryan Jelfe		2				
Ernest Jennings					1	
Peter Jesson		1				
Daphne Johnson		1				
Brian Johnston	1					
Vi Johnstone					1	
Glyn Jones		1				
Jenny Jones		1				
Margaret Jordan		1				
Eve Joyner		1				
Charles Julian		7				
Charlton Julian					1	
John Junkin					1	
Murray Kash		2				
Harold Kasket		1				
Susan Kay		2				
Gertrude Kaye					1	
Norman Kaye		1				
Geoffrey Keen					1	
Stella Kemball		2				
Clive Kemp					1	
William Kendall		3				
Anne Kennedy			1			
Barry Kennington						1
Jack Keonard		1				
Bill Kerr	106					
Fraser Kerr	2					
Patricia Kerry					1	
John Kidd					1	
Robin Kildair		1				
Ivor Kimmel		1				2
Diana King			1			
Leonard Kingston		1				
Sheila Knight					1	
Kenneth Kove		2				
Burt Kwouk		1				
Sam Kydd		1		2		
Thomas Kyffin					1	
Carl Lacy			1			

	Hancock's Half Hour BBC radio	Hancock's Half Hour BBC television	Hancock BBC television	The Tony Hancock Show ITV	Hancock ITV	Hancock's ITV
Anne Lancaster	2	4			1	
David Lander		2				
Marla Landi		1				
Harry Lane		6				
Gordon Lang					1	
James Langley		2				
Andrea Lascelles					1	
Andrea Lawrence					1	
Wilfrid Lawson					2	
John le Mesurier		7	1	1		
Annie Leake			1		1	
Graham Leaman		6				
Bert Leane					1	
Annabelle Lee		5				
Johnnie Lee		1				
Joy Leggat		1				
Michael Lehrer		1				
Tutte Lemkow		1				
Biddy Lennon		1				
Francis Lennon		1				
Jack Leonard		1				
Peggy Ler					1	
Rosamund Lesley		1				
Joseph Levine		1				
Geoffrey Lewis			1			
Andrew Lieven		1				
Marie Lightfoot		1				
Moira Lister	16					
Dorris Littel		1				
Doris Littlewood					1	
Frank Littlewood		7	1		1	1
Bernard Livescy				1		
Hugh Lloyd		22	3			
Lala Lloyd		2				
Betty Lloyd-Davies		1				
Charles Lloyd-Pack			1			
Arnold Lock		1				
Harry Locke		1				
Anita Loghade		1				
Michael Lomax						1
Frank Lonergan		2				
Henry Longhurst		1				
Arthur Lovegrove					1	

	Hancock's Half Hour BBC radio	Hancock's Half Hour BBC television	Hancock BBC television ITV	The Tony Hancock Show ITV	Hancock ITV	Hancock's ITV
Arthur Lown			1			
Evelyn Lund		15				
Mary MacMillan					1	
Fred MacNaughton					1	
Iain MacNaughton		5				
Ester MacPherson		1				
Carmen McRae						1
Edward Malin		2			1	
Dennis Mallard		1				
Alf Mangan					10	
Robert Manning			1			
Samuel Manseray		1				
Pamela Manson		4				
Ray Marioni		1				
Stella Maris					2	
Dorothy Marks	1					
Jean Marlow			1			
Joyce Marlowe					1	
Anne Marryott		14	1			
Makki Marsailles					1	
Bob Marshall		1				
Cynthia Marshall		1				
Lizanne Marshall		1				
Dickie Martin						1
Eric Martin		1				
John Scott Martin		1			1	
Leonard Martin		1				
Marina Martin					1	
Patricia Martin		1				
Vivienne Martin		1				
Drummond Marvin		1				
Margerie Mason		1				
Bill Matthews		5			1	
Don Matthews		1				
Francis Matthews					1	
Geoffrey Matthews			1			
Patricia Matthews					1	
Margot Maxine						1
Ronald Mayer		1				
Tom McCall		1				
Donald McCallum					1	
James McCloughlin		1				
Rory McDermot					1	

	Hancock's Half Hour BBC radio	Hancock's Half Hour BBC television	Hancock BBC television	The Tony Hancock Show ITV	Hancock ITV	Hancock's ITV
Parnell McGarry						1
Sheila McGrath					1	
Gilbert McIntyre		1				
Margaret McKechnie					1	
Errol McKinnon	1					
Gibb McLoughlin		1				
Alison McMurdo		1				
John McRay		1				
Lane Meddick					1	
Andrée Melly	32					
William Mervyn		1				
Guy Middleton		1				
Michael Middleton		1				
Robert Mill					1	
Betty Miller		1				
Herman Miller		1				
Norman Miller		1				
Spike Milligan		1				
Guy Mills		1				
Patrick Milner		17			1	
Bernadette Milnes						1
Billy Milton					1	
Barbara Mitchell					1	
Warren Mitchell	6	6				
Jean Mockford		1				
Virginia Mollett		1				
Marian Montgomery						1
Veronica Moon		1				
John H. Moore					1	
Simon Moore			1			
Edwin Morton		1				
Hugh Morton	5					
Maitland Moss					1	
Betty Mowles		1				
Barbara Muir		1				
Arthur Mullard		14				1
Pete Murray					1	
Judy Nash		1				
Pedro Navarro					1	
Herbert Nelson		15				
Nancy Nevinson					1	
John Newbury					1	
Nora Nicholson		1			1	1

	Hancock's Half Hour BBC radio	Hancock's Half Hour BBC television	Hancock BBC television	The Tony Hancock Show ITV	Hancock ITV	Hancock's ITV
Derek Nimmo					1	
Melville Noelly		1				
Jacqui Noone					1	
Joy Norton					1	
Phyllis Norwood		1				
Ralph Nossek		3				
Ronan O'Casey				1		
Kathleen O'Hagan	1					
Pat O'Meara		3				
Collett O'Neill		1				
Michael Oaley		1				
Roger Oatime		4				
Beatrice Ormonde		2				
Sylvia Osborn		1				
James Ottoway			1			
Brian Oulton		4	1			
Clare Owen					1	
Kendrick Owen					1	
Michael Oxley					1	
Stanley Paige		1				
Penelope Parry		1				
Frank Partington	1					
Eve Patrick		1				
Roy Patrick		1				
Shirley Patterson		2				
Tom Payne		1				
Bernard Peake			1			
Judith Pearson		1				
Felicity Peel		1				
Frank Pemberton		3				
Toby Perkins					1	
Lesley Perrins		2				
Sonia Peters		1				
Edna Petrie					1	
Michael Phillips		1				
Gordon Phillott		8				
John Pike		1				
Robert Pitt		3			1	
Victor Platt			1			
Brian Pollitt		1				
Olaf Poole					1	
Adrienne Poster					1	
Dennis Powell					1	

	Hancock's Half Hour BBC radio	Hancock's Half Hour BBC television	Hancock BBC television	The Tony Hancock Show ITV	Hancock ITV	Hancock's ITV
Fred Powell					1	
Mary Power		1			1	
Dennis Price					1	
Sian Price			1			
John Priestman					1	
Henry Prina					1	
Maureen Pryor					1	
John Pugh					1	
Keith Pyott					1	
Robert Raglan						1
Frankie Randall						1
Jimmy Raphael		1				
Rex Rashley		2			1	
Michael Rathborne					1	
Anthony Ray		1				
Philip Ray		1				
Ivor Raymonde		15				
Desmond Rayner		5				
William E. Rayner		1				
Sheila Raynor					1	
Anne Reddin		1				
Gavin Reed		1				
Jose Reed			1			
Myrtle Reed			1			
Olga Regan		1				
Anne Reid		5				
Don Rendall		1				
Cyril Renison				1		
Mary Reynolds		1				
Darrell Richards					1	
Betty Richardson					1	
Lee Richardson		1				
Edwin Richfield			1		1	
Jane Rieger		2				
Sandra Robb		1				
Bob Robert		1				
Nancy Roberts		3				
Rene Roberts		1				
James Robertson Justice	1					
Harry Robins		4				
Cardew Robinson		2				
Douglas Robinson		1				
Gareth Robinson					2	

	Hancock's Half Hour BBC radio	Hancock's Half Hour BBC television	Hancock BBC television	The Tony Hancock Show ITV	Hancock ITV	Hancock's ITV
Joe Robinson		1				
Ronnie Robinson		1				
Dorothy Robson		2				
Irena Rodzianko					1	
Judy Roger		3				
Rex Roland		1			1	
Rayment Rollett		6				
John Ronane					1	
Kay Rose		1				
Frances Rowe					1	
Heather Russell		1				
John Rutland					1	
Leonard Sachs		1				
Anthony Sagar					1	
Michael Sammes					1	
Nicholas Sandys		1				
Stuart Saunders					1	
Frederick Schiller		1				
Terry Scott		1				
Harry Secombe	4					
Stanley Segal		1				
Peter Sellers	1					
Patricia Shakesby		2				
Geoff Shang					1	
Leonard Sharp		3				
Sally Ann Shaw					1	
Viera Shelly		2				
Honor Shepherd		1	1			
Geraldine Sherman					1	
William Sherwood		2				
Bill Shine				1		
Alan Shire					1	
Anthony Shirvell		7				
Alf Silvestri		1				
Stan Simmons		2				
Bert Simms		2				
Alan Simpson	60	10				
John Simpson					1	
Richard Simpson			1			
Campbell Singer		3				
Mark Singleton		2				
Eugenie Sivyer		1				
Astor Sklair		3				

	Hancock's Half Hour BBC radio	Hancock's Half Hour BBC television	Hancock BBC television	The Tony Hancock Show ITV	Hancock ITV	Hancock's ITV
Patsy Smart					2	
Ann Smith		1				
Leslie Smith		6				
Harry Smith-Hampshire		1				
John Snagge		1				
June Speight					1	
Roy Spence		1				
Frances St Barbe-West		1	1			
Louise Stafford		2				
Michael Stainton		1				
Graham Stark	1	1				
Tony Starr					2	
Richard Statman		11				
Gorden Sterne		1				
Cara Stevens					1	
Edna Stevens		3				
Vi Stevens		1				
Edith Stevenson		1				
Phillipa Steward		1				
Joy Stewart					1	
Peter Stockbridge					1	
Judith Stott					1	
Jerry Stovien	2					
Bud Strait					1	
Richard Sullivan		1				
Bernice Swanson		1				
Eric Sykes		1		1		
Thomas Symonds		2				
Pat Symons		1				
Donald Tandy					1	
Manville Tarrant		24				
Rosamond Tattersall		2				
Leslie Taussig					1	
Kenneth Alan Taylor		1				
Norman Taylor		1				
Shaw Taylor					1	
Tottie Truman Taylor		7				2
John Terry						1
Marylyn Thomas		1			1	
Peter Thompson					1	
Jennifer Thorne		1				
Frank Thornton			1			
Laura Thurlow		4				

	Hancock's Half Hour BBC radio	Hancock's Half Hour BBC television	Hancock BBC television	The Tony Hancock Show ITV	Hancock ITV	Hancock's ITV
Royston Tickner		1				
Jennifer Tippet					1	
Bob Todd						1
Harry Towb	1				1	
Joe Tregoningo		1				
Austin Trevor		1				
Una Trimming		3				
John Tucker		1				
Brian Tyler		1				
Frank Tyson	1					
James Ure			1			
Judi Vague		1				
Brian Vaughan		1				
Peter Vaughan					1	
Patricia Veasey		1				
John Vere	1	23		7		
Diana Vernon		1				
Tracey Vernon		2				
Alan Vicars		1			1	
Mavis Villers	1					
Wilfred Villiers					1	
Sidney Vivian		4				
John Vyvyan		37				
Constance Wake		1				
Aubrey Danvers Walker			1			
Diana Walker		2				
Donald Walker		1				
Pauline Walker		1				
Alec Wallace		1				
Pat Wallen		1				
Bert Waller		1				
Barry Wallman					1	
Michael Ward		1				
Richard Waring					1	
Hugh Warren		1				
Kenneth J. Warren					1	
Neale Warrington				1		
Jack Watling			1			
Dorothy Watson		2				
Jack Watson	2					
Malcolm Watson		1				
Richard Wattis		2				
Eileen Way		1				

	Hancock's Half Hour BBC radio	Hancock's Half Hour BBC television	Hancock BBC television ITV	The Tony Hancock Show ITV	Hancock ITV	Hancock's ITV
Janet Webb						1
Laurie Webb		10				
Robert Weedon		2				
Peter Welch					1	
Vivien Weldon		1				
John Welsh		1				
Robin Wentworth					1	
Charles Western		1				
Richard Wharton		1				
Lionel Wheeler		4				
Fraser White		6				
Jimmy White				1		
Joan White			1			
Martin White		2				
Meadows White			1			
William White		1				
June Whitfield		1	2	5		
Bruce Wightman		4	1			
Brian Wilde					1	
April Wilding					1	
Anthony Wiles		2				
Elaine Williams					1	
Kenneth Williams	88	6				
Roger Williams		1				
Edward Willis		1				
Wilfred Willis					1	
Dennis Wilson	1					
Ralph Wilson			2			
Ronald Wilson	1					
Pauline Winter					1	
Eva May Wong					1	
Sidney Woolf					1	
Brian Worth		1				
Alex Wright		1				
Harry Wright		1				
Leslie Wright		2				
Michael Wyatt		1				
Pauline Yates					1	
Charles Young			1			
Robert Young		1				

Group	Hancock's Half Hour BBC radio	Hancock's Half Hour BBC television	Hancock BBC television	The Tony Hancock Show ITV	Hancock ITV	Hancock's ITV
The Glamozons		1				
The Keynotes		1				
The George Mitchell Choir		1				

Sources and Acknowledgments

THIS BOOK WOULD not have been written without the help I received from a great many people. It is impossible to measure their contributions. While some contributed part or all of a chapter others confirmed a date or provided a sentence. Others, through their expertise, helped me understand the complexities of Hancock's life.

My special gratitude must go to Sarah Berry, my secretary-cum-assistant-cum-researcher – but most of all friend. Without her faith and bullying this book might never have been completed. Also my agent, Jane Judd, for her unceasing loyalty and support.

I must thank Richard Briers for agreeing to contribute an introduction to this book and his insight into Hancock's art and comedy.

For many years the prime source for Hancock researchers and fans was Freddie Hancock and David Nathan's excellent biography *Hancock*. Permission to use material from this book was generously granted by BBC Worldwide.

Permission to use copyrighted material and photographs was kindly granted by *The Times*; Macmillan; Hodder & Stoughton Ltd; Heinemann; Hamish Hamilton; HarperCollins; Robson Books; The Book Guild; J. Harker; the BBC; *The Age*, Melbourne; *The Bath Chronicle*; the *Evening Post*, Nottingham; *The Daily Echo*, Bournemouth; D. C. Thomson & Co Ltd. I must also thank Trevor Ermel, of Monochrome, Newcastle, who exercised care and enthusiasm when copying some very valuable material.

My deepest thanks must go to Ray Galton and Alan Simpson – and their agent Tessa Le Bars – who very kindly granted permission to use extracts from their books and collection of *Hancock's Half Hour* scripts.

Finally, I must show my indebtedness to the following authors, publishers, institutions, individuals and societies whose sources I have drawn upon and who gave their time and goodwill and helped in the creation of this book.

(a) Principal printed material cited and quoted:

i. Books

DUNN, Clive. *Permission to Speak* (Century, 1986).
GOODWIN, Cliff. *Sid James: A Biography* (Century, 1995).
JOFFE, Eddie. *Hancock's Last Stand* (The Book Guild, 1998).
Halliwell's Film Guide (HarperCollins, 1991).
HANCOCK, Freddie and David Nathan. *Hancock* (BBC Worldwide Ltd, 1969).
HAYES, Patricia and Teresa Jennings. *A Funny Old Life* (Robson, 1990).
Kelly's Directory: Berkshire, 1939.
Kelly's Directory: Birmingham, 1923.
Kelly's Directory: Birmingham, 1926.
Kelly's Directory: Bournemouth, Poole & Christchurch, 1927.
Kelly's Directory: Dorsetshire, 1939.
Kelly's Directory: Hampshire, 1931.
Kelly's Directory: Hampshire, 1939.
KINGSLEY, Hilary and Geoff Tibballs. *Box of Delights* (Macmillan, 1989).
Le MESURIER, Joan. *Lady Don't Fall Backwards* (Macmillan, 1988).
Le MESURIER, John. *A Jobbing Actor* (Elm Tree Books, 1984).
LEWIS, Roger. *The Life and Death of Peter Sellers* (Century, 1994).
MIDWINTER, Eric. *Make 'em Laugh* (Unwin, 1992).
PRIESTLEY, J. B. *The Image Men* (Heinemann, 1968).
Register of Electors, Birmingham, 1926.
Register of Electors, Birmingham, 1927.
SECOMBE, Harry. *Strawberries & Cheam* (Robson Books, 1990).
STARK, Graham. *Remembering Peter Sellers* (Robson Books, 1990).
TAYLOR, Rod. *The Guinness Book of Sitcoms* (Guinness Publishing, 1994).
THOMPSON, Harry. *Peter Cook* (Hodder & Stoughton, 1997).
TOOK, Barry. *Comedy Greats* (Equation, 1989).
TOOK, Barry. *Laughter in the Air* (Robson Books, 1976).
WHICKER, Alan. *Within Whicker's World* (Elm Tree Books, 1982).
WILLIAMS, Kenneth. *Just Williams* (J. M. Dent, 1985).
WILLIAMS, Kenneth. *The Diaries* (HarperCollins, 1993).
WILMUT, Roger. *Tony Hancock 'Artiste'* (Methuen, 1978).

ii. Periodicals and Newspapers

ANON:
''Ancock in the 'ot Seat', *Picture Show*, 1960.

''Ancock's 'our and a Quarter', *Evening Mail*, Birmingham, 1958.

'BBC Not to Repeat Comedy Sketch', *Manchester Guardian*, 1955.

'Behind the Scenes at the Windmill', *Sunday Dispatch*, 1957.

'Both Sides of the Microphone', *Radio Times*, 1954.

'Can Hancock Bring it off on his Own?', *Sunday Express*, 1961.

'Death of Mr Jack Hancock', *Bournemouth Times*, 1935.

'Drugs With Vodka Killed Hancock', *Bournemouth Echo*, 1968.

'English Comedians in Peak-Time American Show', *Television Today*, 1962.

Film Fun, 1958–1962.

'Focus on ... Dick Emery', *Railway Cuttings*, May, 1995.

'Focus on ... John le Mesurier', *Railway Cuttings*, February, 1995.

'Hancock', *TV Times*, 1962.

'Hancock at the Mill', *Sunday Dispatch*, 1957.

'Hancock Drove Me to Try Suicide Five Times', *Daily Mail*, 1996.

'Hancock in Top Ten', *Daily Telegraph*, 1961.

'Hancock leaves £32,559', *Bournemouth Echo*, 1968.

'Hancock Off-Duty', *The Observer Review*, 1967.

'Hancock Tells the Lot', *Weekend*, 1958.

'Hancock's Final Half Hour', *The Australian*, 1968.

'Hancock's First Leading Lady', *Piltdown Glory*, November, 1994.

'Hancock's Half-Page', *Reynolds News*, 1956.

'Hotel Manager's Death', *Bournemouth Echo*, 1935.

'Hotel Will Make Way for Big Office Block', *Bournemouth Echo*, 1973.

'James's Half Hour', *Manchester Guardian*, 1955.

'Lady Don't Fall Backwards', *The Hall Green Tribune*, 1987.

'Lanning at Large', *TV Times*, 1966.

'Late Mr J. Hancock', *Bournemouth Times*, 1935.

'Mr Jack Hancock', *The Bournemouth Weekly Post and Graphic*, 1935.

'My Life With Sid', [unknown], 1972.

'No More Gaiety Through Paris', *The Stage*, 1995.

'Odd Odes', *Piltdown Glory*, November, 1995.

'Performer', *Daily Graphic*, 1952.

'Punch and Judy Man', *Films and Filming*, 1962.

'Ray Leaving "*Calling All Forces*"', *Daily Herald*, 1952.

'Real Snow – Just for Mr Hancock', *Evening Mail*, Birmingham, 1958.

'Saturday Postbag', *Evening Express*, Aberdeen, 1986.

'Sound and Sight', *Performer*, 1955.

'Sykes and the Great Gamble', *Northern Echo*, 1962.

The Radio Times, 1923–1965.

'This is the RAF Show', *The Evening Chronicle*, Blackpool, 1947.

'Thoughts in the Wilderness', *New Statesman & Nation*, 1955.

'Tony Hancock', *The Observer*, 1960.

'Tony Hancock Team', *The Times*, 1959.

'Tony, Local Boy Who Made Good', *Bournemouth Times*, 1968.

'Tony's Ugly Sister', *Piltdown Glory*, November, 1995.

'Van Damme Wins', *The People*, 1951.

' "Wings" is Refreshing & Original', *The Coventry Daily Telegraph*, 1947.

BATLEY, Nigel. 'Tony Hancock', *This England*, 1975.

BOWLES, Chris. 'Comic Who Had Little To Laugh About', *Daily News*, 1988.

BRETTON, John. 'Seven Days' Rehearsal', *Television Weekly*, 1951.

CRAWLEY, Tony. 'Half Hour with Hancock', [unknown], 1961.

DYALL, Valentine. 'Lost Weekend', *Sunday Dispatch*, 1951.

EDWARDS, Elizabeth. 'Hancock: The Bournemouth Connection', *Dorset Life*, 1987.

EVANS, Andy. 'Medical Matters', *The Stage*, 1995.

FERGUSON, Merrill. 'It's the Lad Himself', [unknown].

FIRTH, Vincent. 'Scene 403, Take 4!' *Film Review*, 1962.

FIRTH, Vincent. 'Sidney James – Prince of the Wide Boys', *Film Review*, 1960.

GAIMAN, Neil. 'Comedy Playwrights', *Knave*, 1985.

GODDARD, Alan. ' 'Ancock's 'Ardest Hour', *Weekend & Today*, 1964.

HAMMONDS, Jeff. 'Cue Hancock', *Piltdown Glory*, February, 1997.

HARRISON, Denise. 'Mentor to the Lad Himself', *Dorset Evening Echo*, 1996.

HILL, Derek. 'The Doomed Look', *TV Times*, 1959.

HILL, Derek. 'The Thinnest Skin in Show Business', *Picturegoer*, 1958.

HOLMES, Robert. 'What is Funny?', *TV Mirror*, 1956.

HOPKIRK, Elizabeth. 'Plaque Honours the Lad Himself', *Bournemouth Echo*, 1993.

HUTCHINSON, Tom. 'A Man Films Must Use', *Picturegoer*, 1957.

LIGHT, John P. 'Houlders' History', *Sea Breezes*, 1976.

LLOYD, Shane. 'Hugh and I', *Piltdown Glory*, February, 1998.

LONG, H. W. Shirley. 'What it means to be a Producer', [unknown], 1951.

McKERRON, Ian. 'Comic Drake Remembers Sadness of his Tragic Friend', *Daily Express*, 1988.

NATHAN, David. 'An Event Without Pathos', *The Independent*, 1993.

NORRIS, Fred. 'Tony, The Cloth Cap Comic Genius', *Evening Mail*, Birmingham, 1979.

NUNN, Ray. 'Face to Face', *Woman's Mirror*, 1962.

OAKES, Philip. 'The Clown Who Slaps Back', *Books and Art*, 1957.

OTTAWAY, Robert. 'The Lad Himself – A Master of the Self-inflicted Wound', [unknown].

PREVOST, Lucille. 'My Son Tony', *Bournemouth Times*, 1959.

PRIESTLEY, J. B. 'Life Class', *Sunday Times*, 1969.

PUNT, Steve. 'Eric Morecambe', *Sunday Times*, 1994.

PURSER, Philip. Interview, *The Sunday Telegraph*, 1961.

RAINBIRD, Walter. 'Steptoe and Son Strike it Rich', *Weekend*, 1959.

ROSS, Robert. 'The Films of Tony Hancock', *Stop Messin' About*, 1991.

RYAN, Michael. 'Grrr! Where's Sunny Australia Then?', *The Age*, Melbourne, 1968.

SMITH, Trevor. 'The Big Gamble', [unknown], 1965.

THOMAS, James. 'When the Words Ran Out, The Laughter Died', *Daily Express*, 1968.

ULLYETT, Kenneth. 'I Lived in a Gypsy Caravan', *TV Mirror*, 1959.

WALE, Michael. 'Death of a Comedian', *Birmingham Post*, 1969.

WARREN, Max. 'This is the Festival Spirit!', *Television Weekly*, 1951.

Journal of The British Puppet & Model Theatre Guild:
   Newsletter No. 395, 1993.
Journal of The Punch & Judy Fellowship:
   Newsletter No. 45, 1993.
   Newsletter No. 51, 1994.
Journal of The Tony Hancock Appreciation Society:
   Railway Cuttings; February, 1994.
   Railway Cuttings; May, 1994.
   Railway Cuttings; August, 1994.
   Railway Cuttings; November, 1994.
   Railway Cuttings; February, 1995.
   Railway Cuttings; May, 1995.
   Railway Cuttings; August, 1995.
   Railway Cuttings; November, 1995.
   Railway Cuttings; November, 1996.
Journal of The Tony Hancock Society:
   The Hall Green Tribune; 1987.
   The Hall Green Tribune; 1989.
   The Hall Green Tribune; 1994.
   The Hall Green Tribune; 1995.
   The Piltdown Glory; November, 1992.
   The Piltdown Glory; February, 1994.
   The Piltdown Glory; May, 1994.
   The Piltdown Glory; August, 1994.
   The Piltdown Glory; November, 1994.
   The Piltdown Glory; February, 1995.
   The Piltdown Glory; May, 1995.
   The Piltdown Glory; August, 1995.
   The Piltdown Glory; November, 1995.
   The Piltdown Glory; February, 1996.
   The Piltdown Glory; May, 1996.
   The Piltdown Glory; August, 1996.
   The Piltdown Glory; November, 1996.
   The Piltdown Glory; February, 1997.

The Piltdown Glory; May, 1997.
The Piltdown Glory; August, 1997.
The Piltdown Glory; November, 1997.
The Piltdown Glory; February, 1998.
The Piltdown Glory; May, 1998.
The Piltdown Glory; August, 1998.
The Piltdown Glory; November, 1998.
Stop Messin' About; Christmas, 1991.
Stop Messin' About; Winter, 1994.
Stop Messin' About; Spring, 1995.

iii. Songs and Dialogue

A Hudson Song; anonymous. From *Airman's Song Book* (William Blackwood & Sons, 1967).
I'm A Hero To My Mum; words by John Pudney.
Harvey; script by Mary Chase and Oscar Brodney, 1950.

(b) Institutions:

I am grateful to the following curators, archivists and reference librarians who donated a great deal of time and enthusiasm.

    Alcoholics Anonymous.
    Anne Dickie at *The Daily Echo*, Bournemouth.
    BBC Worldwide.
    BBC Written Archive, Caversham.
    Bournemouth Central Library, local studies department.
    British Airways.
    Commonwealth War Graves Commission, Maidenhead.
    RAF Museum, Hendon.
    The Tony Hancock Appreciation Society.
    The Tony Hancock Society.
    The Tony Hillman Collection.

(c) Archive Material:

i. Interviews and convention notes held in the archives of The Tony Hancock Appreciation Society and The Tony Hancock Society.

BREGONZI, Alec. Hancock convention, 1991.
CARGILL, Patrick. Society interview.
DRAKE, Charlie. Society interview, 1991.

EMERY, Dick. Society interview.
FREEMAN, Alan. Hancock convention.
FREEMAN, Alan. Society interview.
GALTON, Ray. Hancock convention.
HANCOCK, Tony. Recording of Denby Cinema show, Melbourne, 1967.
HAYES, Patricia. Society interview.
JOFFE, Eddie. Hancock convention.
KERR, Bill. Society interview.
MILLIGAN, Spike. Society interview.
RACE, Steve. Society interview, 1992.
ROSS, Freddie. Hancock convention.
ROUNCE, Phyllis. Hancock convention, 1993.
SCOTT, Derek. Hancock convention, 1993.
SIMPSON, Alan. Hancock convention.
SPARKS, Elsie. Society interview.
STARK, Graham. Hancock convention, 1992.
TOOK, Barry. Hancock convention.
WHITFIELD, June. Society interview, 1993.
WILMUT, Roger. Society interview.

ii. Written material and documents held in the archives of The Tony Hancock Appreciation Society and The Tony Hancock Society.

CAMPION, Gerald. Letters.
CHESTER, Charlie. Letters.
CROCKER, Peter. Letters and historical material on *The Punch and Judy Man*.
MORLEY, Angela. Letters.
NATHAN, David. Letters.
ROSS, Freddie. Letters.

(d) Radio Interviews:

BOYLE, Robin. Radio Leicester.
CARGILL, Patrick. *Hancock The Classic Years*, 1993.
CARGILL, Patrick. London Radio.
EDWARDS, Jimmy. *Hancock The Classic Years*, 1993.
FREEMAN, John. *Hancock The Classic Years*, 1993.
FREEMAN, John. *Whatever Happened to Tony Hancock?* 1973.
GALTON, Ray. *Hancock The Classic Years*, 1993.
GALTON, Ray. *Whatever Happened to Tony Hancock?* 1973.
HANCOCK, Tony. *Hancock The Classic Years*, 1993.
HANCOCK, Tony. *That Reminds Me* interview, 1963.

HANCOCK, Tony. *Radio Newsreel* interview, 1961.
HAYES, Patricia. *Hancock The Classic Years*, 1993.
JACQUES, Hattie. *Hancock The Classic Years*, 1993.
JAMES, Sid. *Whatever Happened to Tony Hancock?*, 1973.
JOFFE, Eddie. BBC interview, 1981.
KERR, Bill. *Hancock The Classic Years*, 1993.
Le MESURIER, Joan. West Midlands Radio, 1989.
LLOYD, Hugh. *Hancock The Classic Years*, 1993.
LLOYD, Hugh. West Midlands Radio.
MAIN WILSON, Dennis. *Hancock The Classic Years*, 1993.
MOSS, Stirling, *Hancock's Anthology*, 1964.
NORDEN, Denis. *Hancock The Classic Years*, 1993.
OAKES, Philip. *Whatever Happened to Tony Hancock*, 1973.
READER, Ralph. *Hancock The Classic Years*, 1993.
READER, Ralph. *Whatever Happened to Tony Hancock?*, 1973.
ROSS, Freddie. West Midlands Radio, 1986.
ROSS, Freddie. *Woman's Hour*, 1979.
SIMPSON, Alan. *Hancock The Classic Years*, 1993.
SIMPSON, Alan. *Whatever Happened to Tony Hancock?*, 1973.
SYMS, Sylvia. *Whatever Happened to Tony Hancock?*, 1973.
STARK, Graham. *Hancock The Classic Years*, 1993.
VERTUE, Beryl. *Whatever Happened to Tony Hancock?*, 1973.
WALE, Michael. *Whatever Happened to Tony Hancock?*, 1973.
WILLIAMS, Kenneth. *Desert Island Discs*.
WILLIAMS, Kenneth. *Hancock The Classic Years*, 1993.
WILLIAMS, Kenneth. *Midweek with Libby Purves*.
WOOD, Duncan. *Hancock The Classic Years*, 1993.
WOOD, Duncan. *Whatever Happened to Tony Hancock?*, 1973.

(e) Advertising:

Associated British Elstree Studios. Press release, 1962.
Chad Valley Toys. Games instructions, 1961.
Television advertisement. Ilford Film, Australia, 1968.
Television commercials. Egg Marketing Board, 1965.
The Hancock Show, Granada, Shrewsbury, theatre programme, 1961.
The Truth About The Railways – The Hancock Report. British Rail, 1963.
Twentieth Century-Fox. *Those Magnificent Men in their Flying Machines*, 1965.

(f) Personal Interviews:

I wish to thank the following people, whom I had the pleasure of interviewing or corresponding with during my research for this book.

Agnes Fairweather.
Alan Makey.
Angela Morley.
Billy Marsh.
Charlie Chester.
Dennis Main Wilson.
Dilys Laye.
Duncan Wood.
Geoff Turner.
George Fairweather.
Glyn Jones.
Hughie Green.
Janet Trewyn-Smith.
Madame Sacha.
Margaret Nangle.
Mary Hobley.
Maureen Woodford.
Michael Tobin.
Moira Lister.
Mrs H. J. Parrott.
Patrick Cox.
Peter Clarkson.
Peter Crocker.
Peter Harding.
Phyllis Rounce.
Richard Briers.
Roddy McDowall.
Stan Rowland.
Terry Nation.
Willie Rushton.

For background and insight material on Hancock's life I am also indebted to:

Dan Peat.
Dave Sandall.
Dr Geoffrey Smith.
Dr M. A. Serfaty.
Jeff Hammond.
Malcolm Chapman.
Michael Brown.

Every effort was made to trace and seek permission from those holding the copyright to material used in this book. My deepest apologies to anyone I may have inadvertently omitted.

The author and publishers have made all reasonable efforts to contact copyright holders for permission, and any omissions or errors in the form of credit given will be corrected in future printings.

Cliff Goodwin, 1999.

Index

McGrath, Sheila 546
McIndoe, Sir Archibald 250
McIntyre, Gilbert 546
McKechnie, Margaret 546
McKinnon, Errol 546
McLoughlin, Gibb 546
McMurdo, Alison 546
McRae, Carmen 370
McRay, John 546
McWatt, John Findlay 235
Meddick, Lane 546
Mediterranean Merry Go Round 52
Melly, Andree 196–197, 199, 201, 217,
    518, 546
Melly, George 196
Melville, Alan 225
Merriman, Eric 271
Mervyn, William 546
Messrs Kavanagh Productions Ltd 516
    see also Kavanagh Associates
Metropole Hotel, Bournemouth 60–61,
    136
Metropolitan Police 458
Middleton, Guy 546
Middleton, Michael 546
Mickey Mouse 97, 504, 506
Mike and Bernie Winters 416, 441
Miles, Bernard 131
Milford Sanatorium 99, 123, 508
Mill, Robert 546
Mills, Nat and Bobbie 162
Miller, Herman 546
Miller, Max 45, 147, 223
Miller, Norman 546
Miller, Slim 56–57, 59, 71
Milligan, Spike 79, 92, 95, 106–108, 119,
    154, 201, 238, 260, 273–275, 312,
    402, 488, 546
Mills, Guy 546
Milne, A.A. 115, 227
Milner, Patrick 546
Milnes, Bernadette 546
Milton, Billy 546
Mitchell, Barbara 546

Mitchell, Leslie 97, 506
Mitchell, Warren 224, 270–271, 522, 546
Mockford, Jean 546
Moffatt, John 85–86
Moliere 245
Mollett, Virginia 546
Mon Oncle 316
Monelle, Ray 52
Monkhouse, Bob 92, 149–150, 250
Monro, Matt 366–367, 416, 456–458, 526
Monsieur Hulot's Holiday 316, 332
Montgomery, Marian 430, 546
Moon, Veronica 546
Moore, Dudley 402–403
Moore, John H 546
Moore, Roger 460
Moore, Simon 546
Mordant, Sally 306, 380–381, 388
Morecambe and Wise 91–92, 164, 270
Morecambe, Eric *see* Morecambe and
    Wise
Moreton, Robert 66, 68–69, 92, 129
Morley, Angela *see* Wally Stott
Morris, Malcolm 412–413
Morris, Richard William (1st Viscount
    Nuffield) 103
    see also Nuffield Forces Leave Centre
Mortimer, John 402
Morton, Edwin 546
Morton, Hugh 546
Moss, Maitland 546
Moss, Sterling 389, 526
Mostel, Zero 383
Mowles, Betty 546
Mr Wonderful 430
Much Binding in the Marsh 148
Muir, Barbara 546
Muir, Frank 100, 124, 169, 194, 433
Muir, John 415–416, 417, 421–422, 427,
    430, 448–450, 467
Mullard, Arthur 546
Murder at the Vicarage 373
Murdock, Richard 155
Murray, Barbara 353